ACKNOWLEDGMENTS

Special thanks to Nolo Publisher Jake Warner—the cheerful perfectionist whose ideas infuse every page of this book—and to Nolo Editor Mary Randolph, who deftly whipped the early manuscripts into final shape.

Thanks, too, to the rest of the remarkable Nolo family for their invaluable contributions—especially Steve Elias, Robin Leonard, Barbara Hodovan, Jackie Mancuso, Tony Mancuso, Barbara Kate Repa, Beth Laurence, and Ilona Bray.

In addition to the folks at Nolo, these other professionals generously shared their expertise to make this book possible:

- Attorneys Charles Borgsdorf, Larry Ferguson, Sandra Hazlett, Peter Long, Michael Malley, Robert Stevenson, Nancy Welber, and Warren Widmayer.

- Certified Public Accountants Mark Hartley and Lonnie Loy.

- Insurance Specialists James Libs, Mike Mansel, and Dave Tiedgen.

Finally, thanks to my small business clients, who are a constant source of knowledge and inspiration.

Eighth edition

Legal Guide
for Starting
& Running a
Small Business

by Attorney Fred S. Steingold

edited by Ilona Bray

EIGHTH EDITION	MARCH 2005
Editor	ILONA BRAY
Illustration	MARI STEIN
Book Design	TERRI HEARSH
Cover Design	SUSAN PUTNEY
Production	SARAH HINMAN
Proofreading	ROBERT WELLS
Index	MICHAEL FERREIRA
Printing	DELTA PRINTING SOLUTIONS, INC.

Steingold, Fred.
  Legal guide for starting & running a small business / by Fred S. Steingold ; edited by
Ilona Bray. -- 8th ed.
    p. cm.
  Includes index.
  ISBN 1-4133-0177-0
  1. Small business--Law and legislation--United States--Popular works. 2. Business
enterprises--Law and legislation--United States--Popular works. I. Title: Legal guide for
starting and running a small business II. Bray, Ilona M., 1962- III.Title

KF1659.Z9S76 2005
346.73'0652—dc22

                                             2004065486

For information on bulk purchases or corporate premium sales, please contact the Special Sales
Department. For academic sales or textbook adoptions, ask for Academic Sales. Call 800-955-4775
or write to Nolo, 950 Parker Street, Berkeley, CA 94710.

Table of Contents

CHAPTER 4

Creating a Limited Liability Company

CHAPTER 5

Preparing for Ownership Changes With a Buy-Sell Agreement

CHAPTER 6

Naming Your Business and Products

CHAPTER 7

Licenses and Permits

CHAPTER 8

Tax Basics for the Small Business

CHAPTER 9

Raising Money for Your Business

CHAPTER 10

Buying a Business

CHAPTER 11

Franchises: How Not to Get Burned

CHAPTER 12

Insuring Your Business

CHAPTER 13

Negotiating a Favorable Lease

CHAPTER 14

Home-Based Business

CHAPTER 15

Employees and Independent Contractors

CHAPTER 16

The Importance of Excellent Customer Relations

CHAPTER 17

Legal Requirements for Dealing With Customers

CHAPTER 18

Cash, Credit Cards, and Checks

Chapter 19

Extending Credit and Getting Paid

Chapter 20

Put It in Writing: Small Business Contracts

Chapter 21

The Financially Troubled Business

CHAPTER 22

Resolving Legal Disputes

CHAPTER 23

Representing Yourself in Small Claims Court

CHAPTER 24

Lawyers and Legal Research

Introduction: Using This Book to Start or Run a Business

Starting and running a small business—one that's both profitable and emotionally satisfying—is a dream that you share with millions of other Americans. Being an entrepreneur offers rewards of many sorts: the opportunity to spread your wings and use your natural talents, the freedom of being your own boss, the possibility of huge financial success, and more. And in an era when job security is a relic of a bygone era, owning a business means you never have to worry about being fired or outsourced.

Of course, nothing this exciting ever comes without risk. Demographic changes, recessions, changing tastes and styles, new technologies—any of these factors can challenge even the most astute and experienced businessperson. There's no guarantee that any venture will succeed. But the positive side of being self-employed often outweighs the potential risks. That's especially true if you have confidence in your own judgment and abilities. You stand to earn more money than you ever have before—and to achieve a high level of self-fulfillment. In a November 2004 *Wall Street Journal* survey, 86% of small business owners said they'd do it all over again, and 76% said they believe they're better off financially than if they'd worked for another company.

What's more, the existence of risk doesn't mean you're helpless in the hands of the fates. You can greatly increase the chances of success by working hard and planning carefully. In particular, knowing how the law affects your business can help you avoid many costly risks. More and more, the law affects every aspect of a small business operation, from relationships with landlords, customers, and suppliers to dealings with governmental agencies over taxes, licenses, and zoning. That's where this book comes in.

For starters, this book will help you take key preventive measures that will dramatically cut the number of expensive visits you'd otherwise make to a lawyer's office. You'll know exactly where you may be vulnerable to lawsuits so you can wisely take steps to reduce the risks. And you'll know when it makes sense to call in a lawyer or a tax pro for special assistance so that small problems don't turn into huge ones.

This book uses plain English to cover all the major legal issues that a business is likely to face, including:

- Will I be personally liable for business debts?
- How is business income taxed?
- Does it make sense for me to form a corporation? How about an LLC?
- How can I protect my business name?
- Do I need a license or permit?
- What forms do I need to file with the IRS?
- How do I raise money for my business?
- What are the steps in buying an existing business?
- Is buying a franchise a good idea?
- What kind of insurance should I carry?
- How do I negotiate a lease?
- Will zoning affect my home-based business?
- What's the best way to avoid being sued by employees—or former employees?

This book provides easy-to-follow answers to these and dozens of other legal questions so that you can spend your time on what really counts: running a sound and successful business.

A. Is This Book for You?

This book focuses on starting and running a *small* business. Though much of what you learn here will also apply to larger enterprises, this book definitely is not concerned with the sorts of businesses that make headlines in *The Wall Street Journal*. We're focused on readers who fit this profile:

- You're looking to start (or buy) a small retail, service, or manufacturing business—for example, a restaurant or bakery, a dry cleaning establishment, a crafts gallery, an electrical contracting firm, or a modest manufacturing operation.

- You anticipate owning the business yourself, or with one, two, or a handful of other people.
- You'd consider setting up a corporation or LLC if doing so would be legally advantageous.
- You plan to play an active role in running the business—and perhaps even expect that it will provide your main source of income.

Does this sound like you? If it does, then this book has exactly the information you need to take the right legal steps and guard against lawsuits and other unexpected consequences.

B. How This Book Will Help

This book guides you through the many legal concepts and procedures that affect a small business. Here's a preview of what lies ahead.

1. Choosing the Best Legal Entity (Chapters 1 Through 5)

We start with the pros and cons of the types of legal entities used by small businesses—the sole proprietorship, the partnership, the limited liability company (LLC), and the corporation. You'll learn how each type of entity treats your personal liability for business debts. For example, can business creditors or lawsuit plaintiffs seize your house and personal bank accounts if the business falls on hard times? And you'll learn just how each entity gets taxed. For tax reasons, you may decide you'd prefer to have an S corporation rather a C corporation. (If these terms seem like a foreign language to you, don't worry. We'll get to them soon.)

Once you understand the differences between the basic legal entities, and have chosen one for your business, you'll go to a chapter that tells you how to create the entity—the documents you need to prepare and sign and, in some cases, register with a government agency. And if you decide to

form a corporation or LLC, you'll find time-tested tips for using the entity to the maximum extent possible to shield your home and other personal assets from business creditors.

If you aren't the only owner of your business, be sure to spend time with Chapter 5, which explains how to lay the groundwork for ownership changes with what's called a "buy-sell agreement."

2. Choosing Your Business and Product Names Wisely (Chapter 6)

You may already have a clever name for your business or product in mind. But don't start using it until you're sure you won't step on the toes of existing businesses. This chapter will explain how to research whether other businesses are using the names you're considering, register and protect the names you choose, obtain an Internet address (URL), and more.

3. Obtaining License and Permits (Chapter 7)

Chances are good that your business needs some sort of license or operating permit, whether from your federal, state, regional, county, or city government. Chapter 7 will alert you to types of businesses or activities that normally need licenses or permits, and explain where to go for details.

4. Meeting the IRS Rules (Chapter 8)

If the only tax return you've ever filed is the familiar Form 1040, you're nowhere near prepared for the complexities of business taxes. But with the help of this book, the task should be easier than you'd expect. You'll learn how to apply for an Employer Identification Number (which your business may need even if it doesn't have employees at first).

You'll find out, too, whether your business must pay income tax to the IRS, or whether you and any other business owners will personally bear the tax burden. In either case, you'll discover which tax forms to file and why. And since business deductions are always a good thing—they reduce the bottom line on which taxes are computed—you'll appreciate learning the ins and outs of deductions and depreciation.

Maybe you've never been audited before—but your luck may run out if you own a small business. The IRS views small businesses as an attractive audit target. So you'll find it comforting to learn how to deal with the IRS if your business does get audited. Knowing what to expect can reduce your anxiety and help you successfully complete the audit process.

5. Raising Money for Your Business (Chapter 9)

We'll cover in detail the two main ways to get money for setting up or expanding your business: loans and equity financing. (Most entrepreneurs prefer, if possible, to take out loans, so they can keep the business ownership all to themselves; equity financing involves shared ownership.) You'll find out where to look for money and how to create legal safeguards so that your interests are adequately protected. And you'll also learn about the protections that lenders and investors might seek for themselves.

Finally, if you think a bank is the only place to get money, you'll be pleased to discover that a number of other excellent sources are available. This is especially important for first-time business owners, given that banks are understandably reluctant to lend money to would-be entrepreneurs with no track record.

6. Alternatives to Starting From Scratch (Chapters 10 and 11)

While this book discusses many aspects of starting a business from scratch, we haven't forgotten that it's not the only way to go. Other options include buying an existing business or buying a franchise.

Buying an existing business is often an attractive choice because someone else has done the hard startup work. And the business has a financial history—you can tell whether it's has been successful so far. If so, you can be reasonably sure that it will continue to be profitable. But you may have to pay more for an existing business, since the seller will want to be rewarded for taking the startup risks.

Buying a franchise can also be tempting—but, as Chapter 11 will explain, you'll need to be aware of many hidden problems. You'll probably be asked to sign a long-term contract with terms that heavily favor the franchisor. Of course, it's true that once in business, you'll get the benefit of the franchisor's advertising and brand name. But offsetting this advantage, you'll be locked into a more-or-less rigid format for running the business—something that a freedom-loving entrepreneur may balk at.

7. Buying Business Insurance (Chapter 12)

Avoiding risk is a major theme of this book—and when it comes to the biggest risks, such as fire, injured customers, or lawsuits stemming from your own negligence, having an insurance policy in place can save you a bundle. On the other hand, you don't need to go hog wild buying insurance policies. This chapter will help you evaluate what insurance you do and don't need, and how to go about getting it at a reasonable price.

8. Finding Space for Your Business (Chapters 13 and 14)

Unless you sit in a coffee shop and conduct a Web-based business from your laptop, you'll probably have to think about where to locate your business. Chapter 13 discusses renting business space. You'll learn how to read the landlord's lease form and negotiate for more favorable terms. You'll be better prepared to avoid hidden costs and arbitrary actions by a landlord.

Chapter 14 discusses the ins and outs of running a business out of your own home. You'll find out how to comply with zoning ordinances, and see how the tax laws let you deduct some repair, utility, and other expenses associated with your home.

9. Hiring and Managing Employees (Chapter 15)

Even if you start out running the business yourself, sooner or later you'll probably need to hire employees. This can be one of the most legally challenging tasks you'll face. Federal and state laws regulate almost every aspect of the employment relationship. You'll need to know about wages and overtime pay, workers compensation, immigration law requirements, and numerous antidiscrimination laws such the Americans with Disabilities Act.

Even if you do everything right, you may eventually have to fire an employee. Termination can be a very delicate matter if you wish to avoid being sued for wrongful discharge. The information in this book will introduce you to safe hiring and firing practices so that you'll sleep better at night.

10. Dealing With Customers (Chapters 16 Through 19)

There's nothing so joyful as watching your first customers walk in the door. And there's nothing so frustrating and frightening as having them fail to pay their bills, sue you out of disgruntlement with your products or services, or complain about you to all their friends. Fortunately, many of these issues can be avoided—or at least prepared for—by developing customer policies that are friendly as well as legally sound. Chapters 16 through 19 will help you do this, with explanations of such issues as advertising, warranties, accepting payment by different methods, and extending credit.

11. Entering Into Contracts (Chapter 20)

Whether you're making agreements with customers or other businesses, chances are you'll want to commit some of these to writing. In this chapter, you'll learn what makes a valid contract, how to write a contract that will hold up legally, and when you can sue someone for breaching your contract.

12. When Trouble Comes (Chapters 21 Through 24)

Despite your best efforts, your business may run into financial trouble. Chapter 21 will help you turn your financially troubled business around, and if that's impossible, sell or close your business. Chapter 22 will teach you how to use tools like mediation or the court system to resolve legal disputes. Because many business disputes involve only a few thousand dollars (not enough to hire a lawyer for) we devote all of Chapter 23 to representing yourself in small claims court. However, if you do need a lawyer, see Chapter 24 on how to find the right one and make the most of your relationship.

C. Nonlegal Matters to Attend To

Dealing effectively with legal matters—the focus of this book—is a key component of running a successful business. But before you start a business or buy one, there are also a number of important practical and financial matters that need your attention. Here, we'll briefly review the most important ones, and direct you to other relevant resources for help.

1. Choose the Right Business for You

Your business should have a solid chance at turning a profit—but it should also suit your particular skills and strengths. It helps to start or buy a business that you know intimately—one that matches your experience, training, talents, and, hopefully, your passions. To put it bluntly, don't open a garden-supply shop unless you have a green thumb and are up to date on the state of the art in gardening products.

Still Tempted to Sell Something You Know Nothing About?

You wouldn't be the first businessperson to attempt a stretch beyond your own knowledge base. Many people have been lured by watching others make quick profits at say, "the latest thing." And some folks have plunged ahead rashly after waking up with a "million-dollar" idea or just a yen to do something new and unusual. You'll see headlines about the people who make it—but these obscure the stories of the thousands of enthusiastic but unprepared dreamers whose businesses crashed and burned.

If you're still inclined to leap into largely unknown territory, at least take steps to expand your knowledge before you proceed. Your best bet is often to become an employee in a similar business—even for free, if no one will pay a novice like you. From that insider's position, you stand to learn about every aspect of the business. And you'll soon find out whether you enjoy that line of work. If not, move on to something else.

Assuming you're thinking of making a business out of something you know and love, the next step is to talk to others in the industry to learn what it takes to run that kind of business. Learn all you can about startup costs, overhead and expenses, and how much revenue you can expect to take in. Maybe you have several interests and are not sure which business would work out the best. You can research the marketplace to see which types of businesses are most needed in your community.

Judge your ability and desire to handle every aspect of the business. If you want to become the millionaire next door, you have to be willing and able to handle many diverse chores—such as dealing with customers, keeping the books, and even flipping the burgers when your employees are out sick. Although employees can ordinarily handle many of the day-to-day operations, you may have to personally pitch in more often than you might imagine. If this is a turnoff, another business may suit you better.

Some businesses require extra caution. For example, there are inherent risks in businesses that use hazardous materials, make edible goods, care for children, sell alcohol, or build or repair buildings or vehicles. But you can usually reduce the risks to manageable proportions by forming a corporation or LLC, and by carrying adequate liability insurance.

2. Do a Break-Even Analysis

No one can tell for sure whether a particular business idea will be profitable. You can, however, make an informed judgment by doing what's called a "break-even analysis." This shows you how much money you'll need to bring in to cover your expenses, even before you make a dime of profit. You don't want to start or buy a business unless you're reasonably sure that sales will far exceed your costs of doing business.

To perform a break-even analysis, you'll have to make educated guesses about your expenses and revenues. This requires some preliminary research. To make the job easier, take advantage of business planning books and software, as well as the free Web resources listed below.

Here are the most important facts and figures you'll need to assemble for your break-even analysis:

- **Fixed costs.** These costs—sometimes called "overhead"—stay pretty much the same from month to month. They include rent, insurance, utilities, and other expenses that must be paid regardless of how much you produce or sell. Be sure to add another 10% to cover unexpected fluctuations in these costs, such

as a boost in insurance premiums or the price of natural gas to heat your business premises.

- **Sales revenue.** This is the total amount the business brings in each month or year. Be realistic in figuring the volume of business you can expect. You'll need to specifically identify your customer base, then do some demographic research to find out how many people who fit that profile you can expect to reach and attract.

- **Average gross profit for each sale.** This is how much you earn from each sale after paying the direct costs of the sale. For example, if you pay an average of $200 for each bicycle that you sell at an average price tag of $300, your average gross profit per sale is $100.

- **Average gross profit percentage.** This tells you how much of each dollar of sales income is gross profit. You divide your average gross profit (from above) by the average selling price. In the bicycle example, the gross profit percentage is 66.7% ($200 divided by $300).

Now you're ready to figure out the break-even point. Divide your estimated fixed costs total by your gross profit percentage. This tells you the amount of sales revenue you'll need to bring in just to break even. For example, if your fixed costs are $6,000 a month and your expected profit margin is 66.7%, your break-even point is $9,000 in sales revenue per month ($6,000 divided by .667). This means you must make take in $9,000 each month just to pay your fixed costs and your direct (product) costs. At the break-even point, there's no salary or profit for you.

If your break-even point is higher than your expected revenues, you'll need to figure out whether you can change your plan to make the numbers work better. For example, can you: Find a less expensive source of supplies? Do without an employee? Save rent by doing business out of your home? Sell your product or service at a higher price?

If you can work out a realistic break-even point that gives you reasonable assurance of earning a decent profit, you can move ahead with a more detailed business plan. Otherwise, you'll need to come up with a different business idea.

Want more information on researching and developing your break-even analysis? Check the following Websites:

- *www.businessknowhow.com/startup/break-even.htm*
- *www.toolkit.cch.com/text/P06_7530.asp*
- *www.businesstown.com/accounting/projections-breakeven.asp.*

3. Consider Writing a Business Plan

You may find it useful to capture your thinking about your business in a written business plan. If you need to raise money to start your business, a written plan will make it easier to explain your vision to lenders or investors. And even if you already have enough seed money, a written business plan can be a good idea. Putting your thoughts down on paper can help you fine tune your concept and spot any trouble areas.

Many excellent books are available to guide you, including *How to Write a Business Plan*, by Mike McKeever (Nolo), and *The Successful Business Plan: Secrets and Strategies*, by Rhonda Abrams (The Planning Shop). For software, *Business Plan Pro*, by Palo Alto software, comes very highly rated. Also, several websites offer practical suggestions and provide sample plans. You might start with the U.S. Small Business Administration site at www.sba.gov/starting_business/planning/writingplan.html, where you'll find advice and, through a link, can review dozens of real business plans.

But whatever source you turn to for ideas for writing a business plan, keep in mind that a short, simple plan is usually better than a long, complex one—especially for a small business that's just starting out. Formality can get in the way. One good approach to the task is to imagine that you're sitting across a table from a friend and want to take a few minutes to explain your business idea. What are the key things you'd say? What kind of language would you use? Try to capture that clear, conversational tone in your written plan.

There are many ways to organize your business plan. But however you decide you do it, you'll probably want to cover four main areas.

a. A Description of Your Business

Start with the business name and your Internet domain name, if you already have one. Then specify the products and services you plan to sell, and tell how your business will meet the needs of customers and clients. You can also describe where your business will be physically located—in rented, downtown space, for example, or in your home. It's also important to analyze the competition you'll face and why you think your business will survive and thrive despite it. This part of the plan is also the place to describe any demographic, economic, and industry trends that you believe will help the business get off to a good start.

b. Your Marketing Program

Here, you can set down your thoughts on who your customers and clients will be, and how they'll learn about your new business and be motivated to give it a try. First, you'll need to develop a profile of your typical customer. For example, if you're planning to start a self-storage facility, your customers may be apartment dwellers from nearby apartment complexes who lack sufficient closet space. Or if you're starting a landscaping service, your target clients may be people who are buying homes in new, suburban subdivisions. Once you have a good notion of the kind of customers you'd like to reach, think about the methods you'll use.

It's said that word of mouth is the best way for a business to build a loyal following, but that takes time. With a brand-new business, you'll have to prime the pump. There are lots of ways you might do this. Traditional advertising in newspapers and on radio or television is just the tip of the iceberg.

Among other things, you might consider newsletters; direct mail; a website linked to high-traffic sites; trade show exhibits; billboards; the Yellow Pages; discount coupons; event sponsorship; free classes; telemarketing; and favorable press reports. Many businesses use the sides of their vans and trucks to capture people's attention. (For more on advertising and marketing, see Chapters 16 and 17.)

c. How You'll Operate the Business

A key concern here is the competence of those who will be running the business. Be sure to include your own qualifications and those of any co-owners and managers in any plan that you'll be showing to others. List past business experience and any employment or training that's relevant to your new business. If a small business is organized as a corporation, then most likely the owners will be the board of directors. But if you'll have some outsiders serving on the board, you can name them here and give their qualifications. And consider naming your professional team—a lawyer and accountant whom you may consult from time to time.

You might also mention the number of employees—full-time and part-time—you expect to hire at the beginning, and give some idea of what their jobs will consist of. If you'll rely on independent contractors for some work, you can spell out their duties.

In addition to describing the business's workforce, it's often worth describing other aspects of your business operations, such as any special equipment you'll be using and your arrangements with suppliers. You might also describe any improvements you'll be making to the premises the business will occupy—usually rented space for a new business. If you already have some contracts lined up with customers or clients, that's great because you have a running head start. It makes sense to mention these in your business plan.

For many businesses, order fulfillment and customer service play a major role. Your business plan can explain how your business intends to handle these functions—hopefully in a way that will keep customers happy and coming back for more.

d. The Financial Highlights

Here, you should list your fixed costs and your estimates for other costs, and how much you'll need in startup funds—that is, funds to buy needed equipment, supplies, and inventory, with enough cash left in the till to cover other bills until adequate money starts rolling in (which may take several months). Explain where the startup funds will come from: your own funds on hand, or loans or cash from investors. Be sure to include your break-even analysis, too (see Section 2, above).

Probably the most difficult part of the financial highlights portion of your business plan will be your projections for gross income for the first three years. When you start a business from scratch, this is a largely unknown number. At best you'll be making a rough approximation. It's better to estimate on the low side and be pleasantly surprised if the income exceeds your expectations. If you estimate too high and it turns out there's not enough income to meet expenses, the business will struggle to stay alive and may ultimately fail. To be as accurate as possible in projecting revenues, you'll need to rely on your business acumen, information from multiple industry sources, and perhaps input from an accountant or other business consultant. With careful preparation, you can significantly reduce the risk that your income forecast will be far too high.

ICONS

Throughout the book, these icons alert you to certain information.

Fast Track

We use this icon to let you know when you can skip information that may not be relevant to your situation.

Warning

This icon alerts you to potential problems.

Recommended Reading

When you see this icon, a list of additional resources that can assist you follows.

Cross-Reference

This icon refers you to a further discussion of the topic elsewhere in this book.

See an Expert

Lets you know when you need the advice of an attorney or other expert.

Tip

A legal or commonsense tip to help you understand or comply with legal requirements.

Recommended Forms

This icon refers you to a related chapter in Legal Forms for Starting & Running a Small Business, *by Fred S. Steingold (Nolo), which contains legal forms and checklists.* ■

Which Legal Form Is Best for Your Business?

When you start a business, you must decide on a legal structure for it. Usually you'll choose either a sole proprietorship, a partnership, a limited liability company (LLC), or a corporation. There's no right or wrong choice that fits everyone. Your job is to understand how each legal structure works and then pick the one that best meets your needs.

The best choice isn't always obvious. After reading this chapter, you may decide to seek some guidance from a lawyer or an accountant.

For many small businesses, the best initial choice is either a sole proprietorship or—if more than one owner is involved—a partnership. Either of these structures makes especially good sense in a business where personal liability isn't a big worry—for example, a small service business in which you are unlikely to be sued and for which you won't be borrowing much money. Sole proprietorships and partnerships are relatively simple and inexpensive to establish and maintain.

Forming an LLC or a corporation is more complicated and costly, but it's worth it for some small businesses. The main feature of LLCs and corporations that attracts small businesses is the limit they provide on their owners' personal liability for business debts and court judgments against the business. Another factor might be income taxes: You can set up an LLC or a corporation in a way that lets you enjoy more favorable tax rates. In certain circumstances, your business may be able to stash away earnings at a relatively low tax rate. In addition, an LLC or corporation may be able to provide a range of fringe benefits to employees (including the owners) and deduct the cost as a business expense.

Given the choice between creating an LLC or a corporation, many small business owners will be better off going the LLC route. For one thing, if your business will have several owners, the LLC can be more flexible than a corporation in the way you can parcel out profits and management duties. Also, setting up and maintaining an LLC can be a bit less complicated and expensive than a corporation. But there may be times a corporation will be more ben-

eficial. For example, because a corporation—unlike other types of business entities—issues stock certificates to its owners, a corporation can be an ideal vehicle if you want to bring in outside investors or reward loyal employees with stock options.

Keep in mind that your initial choice of a business form doesn't have to be permanent. You can start out as sole proprietorship or partnership and, later, if your business grows or the risks of personal liability increase, you can convert your business to an LLC or a corporation.

 For some small business owners, a less common type of business structure may be appropriate. *While most small businesses will find at least one good choice among the four basic business formats described above, a handful will have special situations in which a different format is required or at least is desirable. For example, a pair of dentists looking to limit their personal liability may need to set up a professional corporation (PC) or a professional limited liability company (PLLC). A group of real estate investors may find that a limited partnership is the best vehicle for them. These and other special types of business organizations are summarized in Section F at the end of this chapter.*

You may need professional advice in choosing the best entity for your business. *This chapter gives you a great deal of information to assist you in deciding how to best organize your business. Obviously, however, it's impossible to cover every relevant nuance of tax and business law—especially if your business has several owners with different and complex tax situations. And for businesses owned by several people who have different personal tax situations, sorting out the effects of "pass-through" taxation (where partners and most LLC members are taxed on their personal tax returns for their share of business profits and losses) is no picnic, even for seasoned tax pros. The bottom line is that unless your business will start small and have a very simple ownership structure, before you make*

WAYS TO ORGANIZE YOUR BUSINESS

TYPE OF ENTITY	MAIN ADVANTAGES	MAIN DRAWBACKS
Sole Proprietorship (Section A)	Simple and inexpensive to create and operate Owner reports profit or loss on his or her personal tax return	Owner personally liable for business debts
General Partnership (Section B)	Simple and inexpensive to create and operate Owners (partners) report their share of profit or loss on their personal tax returns	Owners (partners) personally liable for business debts
Limited Partnership (Section F)	Limited partners have limited personal liability for business debts as long as they don't participate in management General partners can raise cash without involving outside investors in management of business	General partners personally liable for business debts More expensive to create than general partnership Suitable mainly for companies that invest in real estate
Regular Corporation (Section C)	Owners have limited personal liability for business debts Fringe benefits can be deducted as business expense Owners can split corporate profit among owners and corporation, paying lower overall tax rate	More expensive to create than partnership or sole proprietorship Paperwork can seem burdensome to some owners Separate taxable entity
S Corporation (Section C)	Owners have limited personal liability for business debts Owners report their share of corporate profit or loss on their personal tax returns Owners can use corporate loss to offset income from other sources	More expensive to create than partnership or sole proprietorship More paperwork than for a limited liability company, which offers similar advantages Income must be allocated to owners according to their ownership interests Fringe benefits limited for owners who own more than 2% of shares
Professional Corporation (Section F)	Owners have no personal liability for malpractice of other owners	More expensive to create than partnership or sole proprietorship Paperwork can seem burdensome to some owners All owners must belong to the same profession
Nonprofit Corporation (Section F)	Corporation doesn't pay income taxes Contributions to charitable corporation are tax-deductible Fringe benefits can be deducted as business expense	Full tax advantages available only to groups organized for charitable, scientific, educational, literary, or religious purposes Property transferred to corporation stays there; if corporation ends, property must go to another nonprofit
Limited Liability Company (Section D)	Owners have limited personal liability for business debts even if they participate in management Profit and loss can be allocated differently than ownership interests IRS rules allow LLCs to choose between being taxed as partnership or corporation	More expensive to create than partnership or sole proprietorship State laws for creating LLCs may not reflect latest federal tax changes
Professional Limited Liability Company (Section F)	Same advantages as a regular limited liability company Gives state licensed professionals a way to enjoy those advantages	Same as for a regular limited liability company Members must all belong to the same profession
Limited Liability Partnership (Section F)	Mostly of interest to partners in old-line professions such as law, medicine, and accounting Owners (partners) aren't personally liable for the malpractice of other partners Owners report their share of profit or loss on their personal tax returns	Unlike a limited liability company or a professional limited liability company, owners (partners) remain personally liable for many types of obligations owed to business creditors, lenders, and landlords Not available in all states Often limited to a short list of professions

your final decision on a business entity, check with a tax advisor after learning about the basic attributes of each type of business structure (from this chapter and Chapters 2, 3, and 4).

A. Sole Proprietorships

The simplest form of business entity is the sole proprietorship. If you choose this legal structure, then legally speaking you and the business are the same. You can continue operating as a sole proprietor as long as you're the only owner of the business.

Establishing a sole proprietorship is cheap and relatively uncomplicated. While you do not have to file articles of incorporation or organization (as you would with a corporation or an LLC), you may have to obtain a business license to do business under state laws or local ordinances. States differ on the amount of licensing required. In California, for example, almost all businesses need a business license, which is available to anyone for a small fee. In other states, business licenses are the exception rather than the rule. But most states do require a sales tax license or permit for all retail businesses. Dealing with these routine licensing requirements generally involves little time or expense. However, many specialized businesses—such as an asbestos removal service or a restaurant that serves liquor—require additional licenses, which may be harder to qualify for. (See Chapter 7 for more on this subject.)

In addition, if you're going to conduct your business under a trade name such as Smith Furniture Store rather than John Smith, you'll have to file an assumed name or fictitious name certificate at a local or state public office. This is so people who deal with your business will know who the real owner is. (See Chapter 6 for more on business names.)

From an income tax standpoint, a sole proprietorship and its owner are treated as a single entity. Business income and business losses are reported on your own federal tax return (Form 1040, Sched-

ule C). If you have a business loss, you may be able to use it to offset income that you receive from other sources. (For more tax basics, see Chapter 8.)

Legal Forms for Starting & Running a Small Business *contains a checklist for starting a sole proprietorship.*

1. Personal Liability

A potential disadvantage of doing business as a sole proprietor is that you have unlimited personal liability on all business debts and court judgments related to your business.

EXAMPLE 1: Lester is the sole proprietor of a small manufacturing business. Believing that his business's prospects look good, he orders $50,000 worth of supplies and uses them up. Unfortunately, there's a sudden drop in demand for his products, and Lester can't sell the items he's produced. When the company that sold Lester the supplies demands payment, he can't pay the bill.

As sole proprietor, Lester is personally liable for this business obligation. This means that the creditor can sue him and go after not only Lester's business assets, but his other property as well. This can include his house, his car, and his personal bank account.

EXAMPLE 2: Shirley is the sole proprietor of a flower shop. One day Roger, one of Shirley's employees, is delivering flowers using a truck owned by the business. Roger strikes and seriously injures a pedestrian. The injured pedestrian sues Roger, claiming that he drove carelessly and caused the accident. The lawsuit names Shirley as a codefendant. After a trial, the jury returns a large verdict against Roger—and Shirley as owner of the business. Shirley is personally liable to the injured pedestrian. This means the pedestrian can go after all of Shirley's assets, business and personal.

One of the major reasons to form a corporation or a limited liability company (LLC) is that, in theory at least, you'll avoid most personal liability. (But see Chapter 12, Section C, for a discussion of how a good liability insurance policy may be enough protection against personal liability for a sole proprietor.)

2. Income Taxes

As a sole proprietor, you and your business are one entity for income tax purposes. The profits of your business are taxed to you in the year that the business makes them, whether or not you remove the money from the business (called "flow-through" taxation, because the profits "flow through" to the owner's income tax return). You report business profits on Schedule C of Form 1040.

By contrast, if you form an LLC or a corporation, you have a choice of two different types of tax treatment.

- *Flow-Through Taxation.* One choice is to have the IRS tax your LLC or corporation like a sole proprietorship or partnership (discussed above). The owners report their share of LLC or corporate profits on their own tax returns, whether or not the money has been distributed to them.
- *Entity Taxation.* The other choice is to make the business a separate entity for income tax purposes. If you form an LLC and make that choice, the LLC will pay its own taxes on the profits of the LLC. And as a member of the LLC, you won't pay tax on the money earned by the LLC until you receive payments as compensation for services or as dividends. Similarly, if you form a corporation and choose this option, you as a shareholder won't pay tax on the money earned by the corporation until you receive payments as

compensation for services or as dividends. The corporation will pay its own taxes on the corporate profits.

In Section E of this chapter, I'll explain the mechanics of choosing between these two methods. For now, just be aware that this tax flexibility of LLCs and corporations offers some tax advantages over a sole proprietorship if you're able to leave some income in the business as "retained earnings." For example, suppose you want to build up a reserve to buy new equipment or your small label-manufacturing company accumulates valuable inventory as it expands. In either case, you might want to leave $50,000 of profits or assets in the business at the end of the year. If you operated as a sole proprietor, those "retained" profits would be taxed on your personal income tax return at your marginal tax rate. But with an LLC or corporation that's taxed as a separate entity, the tax rate will almost certainly be lower.

You can share ownership of your business with your spouse and still maintain its status as a sole proprietorship. *If you choose to do this, in the eyes of the IRS you'll be co-sole proprietors. You can either split the profits from your business if you and your spouse file separate returns (and separate Schedule Cs), or you can put them on your joint Schedule C if you file a joint return. Only a spouse can be a co-sole proprietor. If any other family member shares ownership with you, the business must be organized as a partnership, corporation, or limited liability company.*

3. Fringe Benefits

If you operate your business as a sole proprietorship, tax-sheltered retirement programs are available. A Keogh plan, for example, allows a sole proprietor to salt away a substantial amount of income free of current taxes. So does a one-person 401(k). You can't really do any better by setting up an LLC or a corporation.

A "C" corporation or an LLC that chooses to be taxed as a separate entity does have an advantage when it comes to medical expenses for the owner and his or her spouse and dependents. As a sole proprietor, you are limited as to how much you can deduct for medical expenses on your personal tax return: You can deduct only the amount that exceeds 7.5% of your adjusted gross income for the year. If you form an LLC or a corporation, however, and choose to have it taxed as a separate entity, you can have your business pay *all* of your family's medical expenses (so long as they're not covered by insurance) and then take these amounts as a business deduction. You won't be personally taxed for the value of this employment benefit.

In the past, sole proprietors could deduct only a portion of health insurance premiums for themselves and family members, while LLCs and corporations (if separate taxable entities) could deduct 100%. That sometimes provided a reason to form an LLC or corporation, but no longer. A self-employed person can now deduct 100% of those premiums.

If you form an LLC or a corporation, however, and choose to have it taxed as a separate entity, you can have the business hire you as an employee. The business can pay 100% of your family's health insurance premiums and uncovered medical expenses and then take these amounts as a business deduction; you won't be personally taxed for the value of this employment benefit.

Hiring Your Spouse Can Have Tax Benefits

If you choose to do business as a sole proprietor, there's a way you can deduct more of your family's medical expenses. First, hire your spouse at a reasonable wage. Then, set up a written health benefit plan covering your employees and their families. A sample form is shown below. Your business can then deduct 100% of the medical expenses it pays.

But balance whether such a plan can save you enough money to justify the effort. There may be some expense for setting up the plan and handling the associated paperwork. And remember that your business will be obligated for payroll taxes on your spouse's earnings. (See Chapter 8, Section C, for information on payroll taxes.) But this isn't all bad, since your spouse will become eligible for Social Security benefits in his or her own right, which can be of some value—especially if he or she hasn't already worked long enough to qualify.

If you're audited, the IRS will look closely to make sure your spouse is really an employee and performing needed services for the business.

To learn about how a person qualifies for Social Security benefits, see Social Security, Medicare & Government Pensions, *by Joseph L. Matthews with Dorothy Matthews Berman (Nolo).*

Sample Reimbursement Plan

Sam Jones, a sole proprietor doing business as Jones Consulting Services (the Company), establishes this Health and Accident Plan for the benefit of the Company's employees.

1. *Coverage.* Beginning January 1, 20XX, the Company will reimburse each employee for expenses incurred by the employee for the medical care of the employee and the employee's spouse and dependents, and for premiums for medical, dental, and disability insurance. The medical care covered by this plan is defined in Section 213(d) of the Internal Revenue Code. Dependents are defined in Section 152.

2. *Direct Payment.* The Company may, in its discretion, pay any or all of the expenses directly instead of reimbursing the employee.

3. *Expense Documents.* Before reimbursing an employee or paying an expense directly, the Company may require the employee to submit bills and insurance premium notices.

4. *Other Insurance.* The Company will reimburse an employee or pay bills directly only if the reimbursement or payment is not provided for under any other health and accident or wage continuation plan.

5. *Ending or Changing the Plan.* Although the Company intends to maintain this plan indefinitely, the Company may end or change the plan at any time. This will not, however, affect an employee's right to claim reimbursement for expenses that arose before the plan was ended or changed.

Dated: December __, 20XX

_____

Sam Jones, doing business as Jones
Consulting Services

4. Routine Business Expenses

As a sole proprietor, you can deduct day-to-day business expenses the same way an LLC, corporation, or partnership can. Whether it's car expenses, meals, travel, or entertainment, the same rules apply to all of these types of business entities.

You'll need to keep accurate books for your business that are clearly separate from your records of personal expenditures. The IRS has strict rules for tax-deductible business expenses (covered in Chapter 8, Section D), and you need to be able to document those expenses if challenged. One good approach is to keep separate checkbooks for your business and personal expenses—and pay for all of your business expenses out of the business checking account.

But whatever your system, please pay attention to this basic advice: It's simple to keep track of business income and expenses if you keep them separate from the start—and murder if you don't.

B. Partnerships

If two or more people are going to own and operate your business, you must choose between establishing a partnership, a corporation, or a limited liability company (LLC). This section looks at the general partnership, which is the type of partnership that most small businesses will be considering. The limited partnership is described in Section F1, below.

LAW IN THE REAL WORLD
First Things First

Ellen, Mary, and Barbara Kate, librarians all, planned to open an electronic information searching business with an emphasis on information of special interest to women. They would hold on to their daytime jobs until they could determine whether their new business could support all three women.

At a planning meeting to discuss buying personal computers and modems, Ellen said she wanted the business to be run as professionally as possible, which to her meant promptly incorporating or forming an LLC. The discussion about equipment was put off while the three women tried to decide how to organize the legal structure of their business. After several frustrating hours, they agreed to continue the discussion later and to do some research about the organizational options in the meantime.

Before the next meeting, Ellen conferred with a small business advisor who suggested that the women refocus their energy on the computers and modems and getting their business operating, keeping its legal structure as simple as possible. One good way to do this, she suggested, was to form a partnership, using a written partnership agreement. Each partner would contribute $10,000 to buy equipment and contribute roughly equal amounts of labor. Profits would be divided equally.

Later, if the business succeeded and grew, it might make sense to incorporate or form an LLC and consider other issues, like a health plan, pensions, and other benefits. But for now, real professionalism meant getting on with the job—not consuming time and dollars forming an unneeded corporate or LLC entity.

The best way to form a partnership is to draw up and sign a partnership agreement (discussed fully in Chapter 2). Legally, you can have a partnership without a written agreement, in which case you'd be governed entirely by either the Uniform Partnership Act or the Revised Uniform Partnership Act (explained in Chapter 2).

Beyond a written agreement, the paperwork for setting up a partnership is minimal—about on a par with a sole proprietorship. You may have to file a partnership certificate with a public office to register your partnership name, and you may have to obtain a business license or two. The income tax paperwork for a partnership is marginally more complex than that for a sole proprietorship.

1. Personal Liability

As a partner in a general partnership, you face personal liability similar to that of the owner of a sole proprietorship. Your personal assets are at risk in addition to all assets of the partnership. In other words, you have unlimited personal liability on all business debts and court judgments related to your business.

In a partnership, any partner can take actions that legally bind the partnership entity. That means, for example, that if one partner signs a contract on behalf of the partnership, it will be fully enforceable against the partnership and each individual partner, even if the other partners weren't consulted in advance and didn't approve the contract. Also, the partnership is liable, as is each individual partner, for injuries caused by any partner while on partnership business.

> **EXAMPLE 1:** Ted, a partner in Argon Associates, signs a contract on behalf of the partnership that obligates the partnership to pay $50,000 for certain goods and services. Esther and Helen, the other partners, think Ted made a terrible deal. Nevertheless, Argon Associates is

bound by Ted's contract even though Esther and Helen didn't sign it.

EXAMPLE 2: Juan is a partner in Universal Contractors. Elroy, one of his partners, causes an accident while using a partnership vehicle. Juan and all the other partners will be financially liable to people injured in the accident if the car isn't covered by adequate insurance. The same would be true if Elroy used his own car while on partnership business.

In both of these situations, the personal assets (home, car, and bank accounts) of each partner will be at stake, in addition to partnership assets. But remember that a partnership can protect against many risks by carrying adequate liability insurance.

2. Partners' Rights and Responsibilities

Each partner is entitled to full information—financial and otherwise—about the affairs of the partnership. Also, the partners have a "fiduciary" relationship to one another. This means that each partner owes the others the highest legal duty of good faith, loyalty, and fairness in everything having to do with the partnership.

EXAMPLE: Wheels & Deals, a partnership, is in the business of selling used cars. No partner is free to open a competing used-car business without the consent of the other partners. This would be an obvious conflict of interest and, as such, would violate the fiduciary duty the partners legally owe to one another.

Unless agreed otherwise, a person can't become a new partner without the consent of all the other partners. However, in larger partnerships, it's common for partners to provide in the partnership agreement that new partners can be admitted with the consent of a certain percentage of the existing partners—75%, for example.

State laws regulating partnerships dictate what occurs if one partner leaves your partnership and you don't have a partnership agreement that provides for what happens. In about half the states, the partnership is automatically dissolved when a partner withdraws or dies; the business is then liquidated. In such a state, it's an excellent idea to put a provision in your partnership agreement that allows the business to continue without interruption, despite the technical dissolution of the partnership. A partnership agreement, for instance, may provide a "buy-sell" provision that calls for a buyout if one of the partners dies or wants to leave the partnership, avoiding a forced liquidation of the business.

EXAMPLE: Tom, Dick, and Mary are equal partners. They agree in writing that if one of them dies, the other two will buy the deceased partner's interest in the partnership for $50,000 so that the business will continue. (Be aware that often a partnership agreement doesn't fix a precise amount as the buyout price but uses a more complicated formula based on such data as yearly sales, profits, or book value.) To fund this arrangement, the partnership buys life insurance covering each partner in an amount large enough to cover the buyout. If Tom dies first, under the terms of the agreement, his wife and children will receive $50,000 from the partnership to compensate them for the value of Tom's ownership interest in the business. Technically, the remaining partners would operate as a new partnership, but the important point is that the business would keep functioning.

Other states—generally those that have adopted the revised version of the Uniform Partnership Act—follow a slightly different rule. In those states, if your partnership was created to last for a fixed length of time or was created for a specific project, and a partner leaves before the fixed time expires or the project is done, the partnership isn't automatically dissolved. Instead, the remaining partners have the opportunity to continue the existing partnership rather than having to form a new one. But even if your state follows this more flexible approach, you'll still want to use buy-sell provisions to specify how the departing partner—or the family of a partner who's died—gets compensated for his partnership interest.

 Chapter 5 discusses buy-sell provisions in greater detail.

3. Income Taxes

In terms of income and losses, the tax picture for a partnership is basically the same as that of a sole proprietorship. A partnership doesn't pay income taxes. It must, however, file an informational return that tells the government how much money the partnership earned or lost during the tax year and how much profit (or loss) belongs to each partner. Each partner uses Schedule E of Form 1040 to report the business profits (or losses) allocated to him or her and then pays income tax on this share, whether or not this income was actually distributed during the tax year. If the partnership loses money, each partner can deduct his or her share of losses for that year from income earned from other sources (subject to some fairly complicated tax basis rules—see "Investment Partnerships," below).

Investment Partnerships

The above analysis assumes that the partner who deducts losses from other income actively participates in the business. If, instead, a partner is a passive investor (as is often the case in partnerships designed to invest in real estate) or receives income from passive sources (such as royalties, rents, or dividends), any loss from the partnership business is treated as a passive loss for that partner. That means that for federal income tax purposes the loss can be deducted only from other passive income—not from ordinary income.

4. Fringe Benefits and Business Expenses

When it comes to retained earnings, tax-sheltered retirement plans, and fringe benefits, a partnership is like a sole proprietorship, and the discussion in Section A3, above, applies to partnerships as well.

Likewise, business expenses can be deducted in the same way for a partnership as for a sole proprietorship; the discussion in Section A4, above, applies here as well.

⚠ **Put it in writing.** *If you go the partnership route, I strongly recommend that the partners sign a written partnership agreement, even though an oral partnership agreement is legal. The human memory is far too fallible to rely on for the details of important business decisions. Chapter 2 contains basic information on how to write a partnership agreement.*

C. Corporations

If you're concerned about limiting your personal liability for business debts, you'll want to consider organizing your business as either a limited liability company (LLC) or a corporation. (Of course, you may have other reasons in addition to limited liability for considering these two business structures.) Since the corporation has a longer legal history, I'll deal with it first, but the LLC—which is covered in Section D—may well be preferable for your particular business, despite its relative newness.

This book deals primarily with the small, privately owned corporation. I'll assume that all of the corporate stock is owned by one person or a few people, and that all shareholders are actively involved in the management of the business—with the possible exception of friends and relatives who have provided seed money in exchange for stock. Because there are many complexities involved in selling stock to the public, I don't discuss public corporations.

The most important feature of a corporation is that, legally, it's a separate entity from the individuals who own or operate it. You may own all the stock of your corporation, and you may be its only employee, but—if you follow sensible organizational and operating procedures—you and your corporation are separate legal entities.

All states have adopted legislation that permits a corporation to be formed by a single incorporator. All states permit a corporate board that has a single director, although the ability to set up a one-person board may depend on the number of shareholders. (See Chapter 3 for more details.) In addition, many states have streamlined the procedures for operating a small corporation, to permit decisions to be made quickly and without needless formalities. For example, in most states, shareholders and directors can take action by unanimous written consent rather than by holding formal meetings, and directors' meetings can be held by telephone.

1. Limited Personal Liability

One of the main advantages of incorporating is that, in most circumstances, it limits your personal liability. If a court judgment is entered against the corporation, you stand to lose only the money that you've invested. Generally, as long as you've acted in your corporate capacity (as an employee, officer, or director) and without the intent to defraud creditors, your home and personal bank accounts and other valuable property can't be touched by a creditor who has won a lawsuit against the corporation.

EXAMPLE: Andrea is the sole shareholder, director, and officer of Market Basket Corporation, which runs a food store. Ronald, a Market Basket employee, drops a case of canned food on a customer's foot. The customer sues and wins a judgment against the business. Only corporate assets are available to pay the damages. Andrea is not personally liable.

⚠️ **Liability for your own acts.** *If Andrea herself had dropped the case of cans, the fact that she is a shareholder, officer, and director of the corporation wouldn't protect her from personal liability. She would still be personally liable for the wrongs (called torts, in legal lingo) that she personally commits. So much for theory. In practice, incorporating may not actually give you broad legal protection.*

In the real world, banks and some major corporate creditors often require the personal guarantee of individuals within the corporation. So the limited liability gained from incorporating isn't always as valuable a legal shield as it first seems.

EXAMPLE: Market Basket Corporation borrows $75,000 from a bank. Andrea signs the promissory note as president of the corporation, but the bank also requires her to guarantee the note personally. The corporation runs into financial difficulties and can't repay the debt. The bank sues and wins a judgment against the business for the unpaid principal plus interest. In collecting on the judgment, the bank can go after Andrea's assets as well as the corporation's property. Incorporation offers no advantage over a sole proprietorship when an owner personally guarantees a loan.

As mentioned in Sections A and B, above, liability insurance can protect against many of the risks of doing business. Because of this, many businesses can structure themselves as sole proprietorships or partnerships without worrying about unlimited personal liability. But if you operate a high-risk business—child care center, chemical supply house, asbestos removal service, or college town bar—and you can't get (or can't afford) liability insurance for some risks that you're concerned about, incorporation may be the wisest choice.

EXAMPLE: Loren is afraid that a clerk at his After Hours beverage store might inadvertently sell liquor to an underaged customer or one who has had too much to drink. If that customer got drunk and hurt someone in a car accident, there might be a lawsuit against the business.

Loren contacts his insurance agent to arrange for coverage, but learns that his liquor store can afford only $50,000 worth of liability insurance. Loren buys the $50,000 worth of insurance, but also forms a corporation—After Hours Inc.—to run the business. Now if an injured person wins a large verdict, at least Loren won't be personally liable for the portion not covered by his insurance.

The lesson of these examples is clear: Before you decide to incorporate your business primarily to limit your personal liability, analyze what your exposure will be if you simply do business as a sole proprietor (or a partner in a partnership).

The limited liability feature of corporations can be valuable, protecting you from personal liability for:

- Debts that you haven't personally guaranteed, including most routine bills for supplies and small items of equipment.
- Injuries suffered by people who are injured by business activities not covered adequately by insurance.

Also, for a business with more than one owner, incorporating can offer a great deal of protection from the misdeeds or bad judgment of your co-owners. In contrast, in a partnership, as noted above, each partner is personally liable for the business-related activities of the other partners.

EXAMPLE: Ted, Mona, and Maureen are partners in Mercury Enterprises. Mona writes a nasty letter about Harold, a former employee, which causes Harold to lose the chance of a good new job. Harold sues for defamation and wins a $60,000 judgment against the partnership. Ted and Maureen are each personally liable to pay the judgment even though Mona wrote the letter.

If Mercury Enterprises had been a corporation, Mona and the corporation would have been liable for the judgment, but Ted and Maureen would not. Ted and Maureen would lose money if the assets of the corporation were seized to pay the judgment, but their own personal assets would be safe.

**LAW IN THE REAL WORLD
Going With Your Gut**

Several years ago, John took over his dad's rug cleaning business as a sole proprietor. He didn't expect the business to ever grow beyond its status as a small local facility with six employees and $400,000 in annual sales. But grow it did—first to ten, then to 25 employees, operating in four suburban cities and taking in $3.5 million a year.

About this time, John and his wife bought a nice house, put a few dollars in the bank, and finished paying off the promissory note to his dad for the purchase of the business. Things were going so well that John began to worry about what would happen to his personal assets if the business was sued for big bucks. He reviewed his insurance coverage and sensibly increased some of it. He reviewed his operations and improved several systems, including the one for storing, handling, and disposing of toxics. Still, he felt vaguely disquieted.

Finally, even though he couldn't identify any other risks likely to result in a successful lawsuit against his company, John decided to incorporate, to limit his personal liability for the business's debts. He tried to explain his gut feelings of worry to his father, but felt he wasn't quite making sense. The older man interrupted and said, "I think you're trying to say that things have been going so well lately that something is bound to mess up soon. And if they do, you want as much of a legal shield between your personal assets and those of the business as possible."

"Precisely," John said. "But I've already protected myself against all obvious risks, so I can't logically justify a decision to incorporate."

His father replied, "C'mon, son, business decisions are like any other—if your gut tells you to be a little extra careful, go with it. Running a small business means being ready to trust your own intuition."

⚠️ **Payroll taxes.** *Limited liability doesn't protect you if you fail to deposit taxes withheld from employees' wages—especially if you have anything to do with making decisions about what bills the corporation pays first. Also, because unpaid withheld taxes aren't dischargeable in bankruptcy, you want to pay these before you pay other debts (most of which can be wiped out in bankruptcy) in case your business goes downhill.*

2. Income Taxes

Federal taxation of corporations is a very complicated topic. Here I deal only with basic concepts.

The federal tax laws distinguish between two types of corporations. A C corporation is treated as a tax-paying entity separate from its investors and it must pay corporate federal income tax. By contrast, a corporation that chooses "S corporation" status doesn't pay federal income tax; instead, income taxes are paid by the corporation's owners.

a. S Corporations

Electing to do business as an S corporation lets you have the limited liability of a corporate shareholder but pay income taxes on the same basis as a sole proprietor or a partner. Among other things, this means that as long as you actively participate in the business of the S corporation, business losses can be used as an offset against your other income—reducing, maybe even eliminating, your tax burden. The corporation itself doesn't pay taxes, but files an informational tax return telling what each shareholder's portion of the corporate income is.

EXAMPLE: Paul decides to start an environmental cleanup business. Because insurance isn't available to cover all of the risks of this business, he forms a corporation called Ecology Action Inc. This limits Paul's personal liability if there's a lawsuit against the corporation for an act not covered by insurance.

Paul is also concerned about taxes. He expects his company to lose money during its first few years; he'd like to claim those losses on his personal tax return to offset income he'll be receiving from consulting and teaching work. He registers with the IRS as an S corporation. Unless he changes that tax status later, his corporation won't pay any federal income tax. Paul will report the corporation's income loss on his own Form 1040 and will be able to use it as an offset against income from other sources.

For many years, if you wanted to limit the personal liability of all owners of your business and have the income and losses reported only on the owners' income tax returns, you would have no choice but to create an S corporation. Today, you can accomplish the same goal by creating a limited liability company (LLC), as explained in Section D, below. Because, in addition, an LLC offers its owners the significant advantage of greater flexibility in allocating profits and losses, it's generally better to structure your business as an LLC than as an S corporation. (But see Section E for a discussion of when it might be better to create an S corporation.)

Should Your Corporation Elect S Corporation Status?

For federal tax purposes, it's often best for a start-up company to elect to be an S corporation rather than a regular corporation. This is so even though recent changes in tax rates have made this decision a bit more complex. Still, to make sure an S corporation is best for you, speak to a knowledgeable accountant or other tax advisor. Also keep in mind that a limited liability company (LLC) may be an even better choice than either type of corporation. (See Sections D and E.)

Starting as an S corporation rather than a regular corporation may be wise for several reasons:

- Because income from an S corporation is taxed at only one level rather than two, your total tax bill will likely be less. (But be aware that the two-tier tax structure for regular corporations can sometimes be an advantage. See the discussion below on how a regular corporation can achieve tax savings through income-splitting.)

- Your business may have an operating loss the first year. With an S corporation, you generally can pass that loss through to your personal income tax return, using it to offset income that you (and your spouse, if you're married) may have from other sources. Of course, if you're expecting a profit rather than a loss—because, for example, you're converting a profitable sole proprietorship or partnership to a corporation—this pass-through for losses won't be an advantage to you.

- Interest you incur to buy S corporation stock is potentially deductible as an investment interest expense.

- When you sell the assets of your S corporation, you may be taxed less on your gain than if you operated the business as a regular corporation (because of the dual taxation structure of corporations).

- Your decision to elect to be an S corporation isn't permanent. If you later find there are tax advantages to being a regular corporation, you can easily drop your S corporation status, but timing is important.

Limits on deductions. *You can deduct S corporation losses on your personal return only to the extent of the money you put into the corporation (to buy stock) and any money you personally loaned to the corporation. Also, if you don't work actively in the S corporation, there are potential problems with claiming losses, because they might be considered losses from passive activities. For the most part, you can use losses from passive activities only to offset income from passive activities. See your tax advisor for technical details.*

Shareholders pay income tax on their share of the corporation's profits regardless of whether they actually received the money or not. If the corporation suffered a loss, shareholders can claim their share of that loss.

> **EXAMPLE:** Assume the same facts as above except that there are two other shareholders in Ecology Action Inc. Paul owns 50% of the stock, and Ellen and Ted each own 25%. Paul would report 50% of the corporation's profit or loss on his personal tax return, and Ellen and Ted would each report 25% on theirs.

Most states follow the federal pattern in taxing S corporations: they don't impose a corporate tax, choosing instead to tax the shareholders for corporate profits. About half a dozen states, however, do tax an S corporation the same as a regular corporation. The tax division of your state treasury department can tell you how S corporations are taxed in your state.

 To be treated as an S corporation, all shareholders must sign and file IRS Form 2553. *For more information on this and other requirements for electing S corporation status, see Chapter 8, Section B.*

b. C Corporations

Under federal income tax laws, a C corporation is a separate entity from its shareholders. This means that the corporation pays taxes on any income that's left after business expenses have been paid.

As you saw earlier in this chapter, a sole proprietorship doesn't pay federal income tax as a separate entity; the owner simply reports the business's income or loss on Schedule C of Form 1040 and adds it to (or, in the case of a loss, subtracts it from) the owner's other income. Similarly, a partnership doesn't pay federal income tax; rather, the partnership annually files a form with the IRS to report each partner's share of yearly profit or loss from the partnership business. Each partner then adds his or her share of partnership income to other income reported on his or her personal tax return (the familiar Form 1040) or deducts his or her share of loss. And an S corporation is treated as a sole proprietorship or partnership for federal income tax purposes, depending on the number of owners.

A C corporation is different. It reports its profits on Form 1120 and pays corporate tax on that income. In addition, if the profits are distributed to shareholders in the form of dividends, the shareholders pay tax on the dividends they receive (creating the much-feared "double taxation" scenario).

In practice, however, a C corporation may not have to pay any corporate income tax even though it is a separate taxable entity. Here's how: In most incorporated small businesses, the owners are also employees. They receive salaries and bonuses as compensation for the services they perform for the corporation. The corporation then deducts this "reasonable" compensation as a business expense. In many small corporations, compensation to owner-employees eats up all the potential corporate profits, so there's no taxable income left for the corporation to pay taxes on.

> **EXAMPLE:** Jody forms a one-person catering corporation, Jody Enterprises Ltd. She owns all the stock and is the main person running the

business. The corporation hires her as an employee, with the title of president. The corporation pays her a salary plus bonuses that consume all of the corporation's profits. Jody's salary and bonuses are tax-deductible to the corporation as a corporate business expense. There are no corporate profits to tax. Jody simply pays tax on the income that she receives from the corporation, the same as any other corporate employee.

(1) Tax Savings Through Income Splitting

As an alternative to paying out all the corporate profits in the form of salaries and bonuses, you may want to leave some corporate income in the corporation to finance the growth of your business. You can often save tax dollars this way because, for the first $50,000 of taxable corporate income, the tax rate and actual taxes paid will generally be lower than what you'd pay as an individual.

The federal government taxes the first $50,000 of taxable corporate income at 15%. The next $25,000 is taxed at 25%. Taxable income over $75,000 is taxed at 34% until taxable income reaches $10,000,000—at which point the rate becomes 35%. Additionally, to make larger corporations pay back the benefits of these lower graduated tax rates, corporate taxable incomes between $100,000 and $335,000 are subject to an extra 5% tax. (See the chart in Chapter 8, Section C1d.)

Here's an example of how, with proper planning, a small incorporated business can split income between the corporation and its owners, retaining money in the corporation for expenses and lowering the corporation's tax liability to an amount that's actually less than what would have to be paid by the principals of the same business if it were not incorporated.

EXAMPLE 1: Sally and Randolph run their own incorporated lumber supply company, S & R

Wood Inc. One year their sales increase to $1.2 million. After the close of the third quarter, Sally and Randolph learn that S & R Wood is likely to make $110,000 net profit (net taxable corporate income) for the year. They decide to reward themselves and other key employees with moderate raises in pay, give a small year-end bonus to other workers, and buy some needed equipment.

This reduces the company's net taxable income to $40,000—an amount that Sally and Randolph feel is prudent to retain in the corporation for expansion or in case next year's operations are less profitable. Taxes on these retained earnings are paid at the lowest corporate rate, 15%. If Sally and Randy had wanted to take home more money instead of leaving it in the business, they could have increased their salaries and paid taxes at a rate of at least 10% but more probably 25% or 28% or higher, depending on their tax brackets.

⚠ **Watch out for a double tax trap.**
C corporation shareholders (like Sally and Randy) can also decide to take some income in the form of a stock dividend. Doing so, however, will often increase their tax burden because both the corporation and the shareholders will have to pay income tax. Still, in some situations, taking some dividends in place of some salary may make sense—for example, if the corporation is in the 15% bracket and the shareholder is in the 28% (or higher) bracket. This gets complicated, so let a tax pro help you figure it out. Also, be aware that paying dividends won't make sense if you have a Personal Service Corporation (defined in Section F2, below). Such corporations pay a flat 35%.

EXAMPLE 2: Now assume S & R Wood is not incorporated but instead is operated as a partnership. Now the entire net profits of the business ($110,000 minus the bonuses to workers and deductible expenditures for equipment) are taxed to Sally and Randolph. The result is that the $40,000 (which was retained by the corporation in the above example) is taxed at their individual rate of 25% or 28% or higher rather than the 15% corporate rate.

For a more detailed explanation of how income-splitting can be an advantage to owners of small corporations, see *How to Form Your Own California Corporation*, or *Incorporate Your Business: A 50-State Legal Guide to Forming a Corporation*, both by Anthony Mancuso (Nolo).

The main point to remember is that once your business becomes profitable, doing business as a C corporation allows a degree of flexibility in planning and controlling your federal income taxes that is unavailable to partnerships and sole proprietorships. To determine whether or not favorable corporate tax rates are a compelling reason for your business to incorporate, you'll need to study IRS regulations or go through an analysis with your accountant or other tax advisor.

Tax savings may be a largely theoretical advantage for the person just starting out. If your business is like many start-ups, your main concern will be generating enough income from the business to pay yourself a reasonable wage. Retaining profits in the business will come later. In this situation, the tax advantages of incorporating are illusory.

> **EXAMPLE:** In its first year of operation, Maria's store, The Bookworm, has a profit of $25,000. As the sole proprietor, Maria withdraws the entire $25,000 as her personal salary, which places her in the 15% tax bracket after she subtracts her deductions and personal exemption. It doesn't make sense for Maria to incorporate to take advantage of income-splitting techniques—even if she could get by on say, $20,000 a year, if she left the remaining $5,000 in the corporation, it would be taxed at the 15% corporate tax rate, so her total tax bill would be the same.

Lower Tax Rates Not Available for S Corporations

The lower tax rates for retained earnings don't apply to S corporations, because, as discussed in Subsection a, above, an S corporation does not itself pay taxes on earnings. Individual shareholders in an S corporation pay taxes on their portion of corporate earnings at their personal income tax rates (as if they were partners in a partnership). This is true whether or not those earnings are distributed to them, meaning that even if the shareholders do leave some earnings in the corporation, the shareholders will be taxed on them at their regular tax rates.

(2) Fringe Benefits

The tax rules governing fringe benefits are complicated. Generally, however, if your business will be offering fringe benefits to employees, you can enjoy a tax advantage if you organize as a regular corporation. The business can pay for employee benefits and then take these amounts as business expense deductions. You and the other shareholders who work as employees of your corporation can have the corporation pay for such employee benefits as:

- deferred compensation plans
- group term life insurance
- reimbursement of employee medical expenses that are not covered by insurance
- health and disability insurance.

But the real advantage is how these fringe benefits are treated on your personal tax return. As a shareholder, you won't be personally taxed for the value of this employment benefit. That's because none of the employees of a regular corporation—even if they're owners—have to pay income tax on the value of the fringe benefits they receive. So, for example, your corporation may decide to provide medical insurance for employees and to reimburse employees for uninsured medical payments. The corporation can deduct these payments as a business expense—including the portion paid for the owner-employees of the corporation—and you and the other owner-employees are not taxed on these benefits.

Other types of business entities can also deduct the cost of many fringe benefits as business expenses, but owners who receive these benefits will ordinarily be taxed on their value. That's because the tax laws distinguish between an employee and a self-employed person. The tax laws say that you're a self-employed person—and therefore are taxed on your fringe benefits—if you're a sole proprietor, a partner in a partnership, a member of an LLC that's taxed as a partnership, or an owner of more than 2% of the shares of an S corporation. An owner-employee of a regular corporation, however, isn't classified as a self-employed person. So when it comes to the taxation of fringe benefits, owner-employees of a corporation enjoy a unique advantage.

This favorable tax treatment may seem like a powerful reason to organize your business as a regular corporation. Not so fast. Obviously, there's no benefit unless your business provides these benefits to employees in the first place. And that may be too expensive for some new businesses—especially because many types of employee benefits must be provided on a nondiscriminatory basis to a wide range of employees or to none, and must not be designed to primarily aid the business owner. If you put together a fringe benefit package that favors you and other owner-employees, the IRS will require owners to pay tax on their portion. Few new businesses can afford to carry expensive benefit programs—a cost that typically more than offsets any tax advantage to you as owner of a regular corporation.

Here are some of the IRS ground rules for fringe benefit plans:

- **Medical Reimbursement Plans.** If your business promises to pay those portions of your employees' medical expenses that are not covered by health insurance, your plan can also include the spouse and dependents of each employee. Usually you'll set a limit on the total amount that can be reimbursed during the year; this limit must be the same for all eligible employees. In the typical small business, if you include owner-

employees in the plan, your plan must benefit 70% of all employees or at least 80% of all employees who are eligible to participate. You can exclude employees who are under 25, work seasonally or less than 35 hours per week, or have been employed less than three years. As long as you meet these rules, employees—even owner-employees—won't be taxed on reimbursements they receive. If you violate these rules, however, an owner may have to pay tax on all or part of the reimbursements that he or she receives under the plan. (These technical rules apply only to reimbursement of medical expenses—not to employer payment of medical insurance premiums.)

- **Group Life Insurance.** Your business can provide up to $50,000 of group term life insurance tax-free to employees (including yourself) if you meet certain conditions. As an owner-employee of a small corporation, you'll probably be a "key employee" under the tax laws. (A key employee is an officer who is paid more than $130,000 a year, an owner of at least 5% of the company, or an owner of at least 1% of the company who is paid more than $150,000 a year.) If you are a key employee and want to deduct the cost of the insurance from your gross income, your plan must meet special rules: It must benefit at least 70% of all employees, limit the number of key employee participants to 15% of all group participants, or meet other IRS guidelines for "nondiscrimination." All benefits available to participating key employees must be available to all other participating members as well. You can provide different dollar amounts of life insurance to different employees without being "discriminatory" if the amount of coverage is uniformly related to compensation. Also, you can exclude employees who've worked for your company for less than three years.

Clearly, this is technical stuff. Let's say you open a video store and hire a bunch of students to work part time during peak periods, and contract out for bookkeeping services. In such a case, you can set up a medical reimbursement plan without having to worry about covering a whole slew of employees. You could exclude the students because they're under 25 and work less than 35 hours a week. Your bookkeeper, being an independent contractor, wouldn't be an employee and wouldn't have to be covered. So perhaps your plan would cover only yourself and a few full-time employees, plus the families of all covered employees.

(3) Retirement Plans

It used to be that by incorporating you could set up a better tax-sheltered retirement plan than you could get as a sole proprietor, a partner, or a shareholder-employee in an S corporation. There are no longer any significant differences.

3. Attracting Investors

To start and successfully run a small business, you may need more money than you can muster from your own savings or the cash generated by the enterprise. As explained in greater depth in Chapter 9, you have two basic options in raising money from outside sources: borrowing it or getting it from investors. If you expect to seek money from investors—even if they're family members, friends, or business associates—there's a substantial advantage in forming a corporation.

Unlike a lender who, in return for providing money, receives a promise that you'll repay it with interest, an investor becomes a part-owner of the business. While it's possible to form a partnership and make an investor a partner or to form an LLC and make an investor a member, it's often more practical to form a corporation and make the investor a shareholder. That little piece of paper that the corporation issues—the stock certificate—is tangible proof of the shareholder's ownership interest in the business and it's something that most investors have come to expect. Put another way, if you offer an investor a partnership interest or an LLC interest,

you're more likely to run into resistance than if you offer him or her stock in a corporation.

Keep in mind that shareholders don't necessarily have to have equal rights to elect the board of directors or to receive dividends. To distinguish between various types of shareholders, you can issue different classes of stock with different rights, for example:

- common, voting shares to the initial owners who will be working in the business
- nonvoting shares for key employees to keep them loyal to the business
- nonvoting preferred shares to outside investors, giving them a preference if dividends are declared or the corporation is sold.

To repeat this key point, the fact that the corporate structure makes it relatively easy to distinguish between different investors by issuing different classes of stock is a real advantage.

Stock options can motivate employees. *Especially for a business that sells stock to the public or plans to do so before long, which allows the market to establish a price for the stock, issuing stock options to employees at a favorable price can be a great way to motivate them. That's because employees who hold options know that if the business is profitable and its stock price goes up, they'll be able to cash in their options at a substantial profit. This can motivate them to help make the business successful. Also, employees who get stock options are often willing to work for a slightly lower salary, making investment capital go farther in the early days of business life.*

Structuring your business as a corporation is not only advantageous but actually essential if—like many small business owners—you dream of someday attracting investors through a public offering. And, fortunately, it's become far easier than it used to be for a small business to do just that without turning to a conventional stock underwriting company. Congress and state legislatures have liberalized laws that enable a small corporation to raise from $1 million to $10 million annually through a relatively easy-to-use procedure called a "limited public offering."

Consider using the Internet to sell shares. *You may decide to market your shares by placing your company's small offering prospectus on the Internet—something now allowed by the Securities and Exchange Commission (SEC), the federal agency that watches over securities laws. If your company creates a website to inform the public about your* products and services, you can also use that site to distribute your prospectus and market your shares. Of course, you'll first need to take care of the paperwork required by federal and state securities laws.

 Forming and running a corporation is discussed in more detail in Chapter 3.

Illusory Incorporation Advantages

What, in addition to limited liability and some marginal tax advantages, can you gain by incorporating? In drumming up enthusiasm for incorporating, lawyers and accountants often point to additional supposed benefits—but these advantages are rarely all they're cracked up to be.

Illusory Benefit: Easy Transfer of Corporate Stock If You Sell the Business. The sales pitch is that if you want to sell your interest in the corporation (which may be as much as 100% if you own all of the stock), you simply endorse your stock certificate on the back and turn over the certificate to the new owner. The corporation then issues a new stock certificate in the new owner's name to replace the one that you endorsed.

Reality: There's not much of a market for a small company's stock. And most small business owners go to great lengths to restrict the transferability of their stock. Moreover, in most sales of a corporate business, the corporate assets are transferred rather than the stock. (See Chapter 10.)

Illusory Benefit: Continuity of Business. A corporation continues even if an owner dies or withdraws. (Plus, there may be a buy-sell agreement—perhaps funded by insurance—in which co-owners of the corporation have the right to buy out your inheritors.) Either way, the corporation stays alive, in contrast to sole proprietorships or partnerships, which are automatically dissolved when the owner or a partner dies.

Reality: The death of a principal is traumatic whether you're a sole proprietorship, a partnership, or a corporation. Usually the factors that allow a business to survive are personal and have nothing to do with its formal legal structure. You don't need to incorporate to ensure that your business will continue after your death. A sole proprietor can use a living trust or will to transfer the business to his or her heirs, and partners frequently have insurance-funded buy-sell agreements that allow the remaining partners to continue the business. (See Chapter 5.)

Illusory Benefit: Centralized Management. In corporations with a number of shareholders, management is typically centralized under a board of directors. With a partnership consisting of many partners, management can become fragmented.

Reality: If you are a partner in a partnership, it doesn't take a board of directors to centralize the management; chances are you and the other owners will make all decisions over a cup of coffee.

Conclusion: In weighing pros and cons of incorporation, concentrate on whether you believe you have a real need to limit your personal liability and also on whether you can get substantial tax benefits by retaining some earnings in the corporation and setting up fringe benefit plans. If you conclude that it would be beneficial to form a business entity that offers limited liability, the LLC (discussed in Section D) is often your best choice. And for many new businesses—especially those that won't run up significant debt or expose their owners to the threat of lawsuits—a sole proprietorship or partnership may be a perfectly adequate way to go, keeping in mind that you can always incorporate the business or form an LLC later.

D. Limited Liability Companies

The limited liability company (LLC) is the newest form of business entity. It has enjoyed a meteoric rise in popularity among both entrepreneurs and lawyers—and for good reason. It's often a very attractive alternative to the traditional ways of doing business, which are described in Sections A, B, and C, above.

The state laws controlling how an LLC is created and the federal tax regulations controlling how an LLC is taxed are still evolving. Fortunately, the evolutionary trends are extremely favorable to small businesses. On the formation side, it's becoming simpler and simpler to set up an LLC. On the tax side, LLCs are benefitting from increased flexibility.

 For an in-depth discussion of LLCs and step-by-step guidance on creating one: *see* Form Your Own Limited Liability Company, *by Anthony Mancuso (Nolo).*

Once you've decided that your business should be organized as an entity that limits your personal liability for business debts, you'll have to weigh the pros and cons of forming an LLC against the pros and cons of forming a corporation. Sometimes, one or the other will clearly emerge as the better choice.

Other times, the differences are more subtle—which often means that either will suit your needs equally well. After you've absorbed the information on both legal formats, see Section E for help in choosing between the two.

1. Limited Personal Liability

As with a corporation, all owners of an LLC enjoy limited personal liability. This means that being a member of an LLC doesn't normally expose you personally to legal liability for business debts and court judgments against the business. Generally, if you become an LLC member, you risk only your share of capital paid into the business. You will, however, be responsible for any business debts that you personally guarantee (of course, you can reduce your risk to zero by not doing this) and for any wrongs (torts) that you personally commit (a good insurance policy should help here—see Chapter 12, *Insuring Your Business*).

By contrast, as discussed in Sections A and B above, owners of a sole proprietorship or general partnership have unlimited liability for business debts, as do the general partners in a limited partnership (and limited partners who take part in managing the business—discussed in Section F1, below).

Corporations and LLCs Use Different Language

Although there are many similarities between corporations and LLCs, there are many differences as well—especially when it comes to terminology, as shown in the following chart:

CONCEPT	CORPORATION WORD	LLC WORD
What an owner is called	Shareholder	Member
What an owner owns	Shares of stock	Membership interest
What document creates the entity	Articles of Incorporation (or, in some states, Certificate of Incorporation or Charter)	Articles of Organization
What document spells out internal operating procedures	Bylaws	Operating Agreement

2. Number of Owners

Every state allows an LLC to be formed by just one person. This means that if you plan to be the sole owner of a business and you wish to limit your personal liability, you have a choice of forming a corporation or an LLC.

3. Tax Flexibility

If you create a single-member LLC, it will not be taxed as a separate entity, like a C corporation (see Section C), unless you elect to have it taxed in this manner. Normally, you won't choose corporate-style taxation, preferring to have your single-member LLC report its profits (or losses) on Schedule C of your personal return, just as a sole proprietorship would.

Similarly, if you have an LLC with two or more members, it will be treated as a partnership for tax purposes, with each partner reporting and paying income tax on his or her share of LLC profits unless you elect to have the LLC taxed as a corporation. Again, you normally won't elect to do this, preferring to have your multimember LLC follow the partnership tax route. This means that the LLC will report its income (or loss) on Form 1065, an informational return that notifies the IRS of how much each member earned (or lost). Each member will then report his or her share of profits or losses on her personal Form 1040.

Occasionally, the members of an LLC will conclude that there's an advantage to being taxed like a corporation, with two levels of tax—one at the business entity level (for company profits) and another at the owners' personal income tax level (for salaries and dividends). LLCs that are taxed like corporations are able to split monies between business owners and the business itself, resulting in some

situations in a significant overall tax saving. (See Section C2b(1), above, for a discussion of income splitting in the corporate context.)

If, after reviewing all the financial implications—and perhaps seeking the advice of a tax pro—you decide to elect corporation-style taxation, you'll do this by filing IRS Form 8832, *Entity Classification Election*. Where the LLC has two or more members, they can all sign the form or authorize one member or manager to sign.

Electing to have your LLC taxed as a corporation can be advantageous if you want to receive tax-free fringe benefits from the business. *If you follow the usual practice of having pass-through taxation for your LLC—meaning that the business isn't taxed as a separate entity—then as a business owner you'll be taxed on the value of the fringe benefits you receive from the LLC (unlike other employees). A different rule applies if you elect to have your LLC taxed as a corporation. In that situation, as long as you meet the IRS guidelines, you can receive fringe benefits as an owner-employee of the LLC and not have to pay tax on the value of those benefits. (For more on the tax treatment of fringe benefits, see Section C2b(2), above.)*

4. Flexible Management Structure

An LLC member may be an individual or a separate legal entity such as a partnership or corporation that has invested in the LLC. You and the other members jointly run the LLC unless you choose to have it run by a single member, an outside manager, or a management group—which may consist of some members, some nonmembers, or both. If you decide to form an LLC, I recommend that all the members sign an operating agreement that spells out how the business will be managed. Again, the details of how to do this are well covered in *Form Your Own Limited Liability Company*, by Anthony Mancuso (Nolo).

5. Flexible Distribution of Profits and Losses

The members of an LLC can decide to split up the LLC profits and losses each will receive any way they want. Although it's common to divide LLC profits according to the percentage of the business's assets each member contributed, this isn't legally required.

> **EXAMPLE:** Jim, Janna, Jill, and Jerry—certified personal trainers—form Fit for Life LLC to operate a family fitness center. Each contributes $25,000 to the enterprise. Because Jim, who has a strong business background, has put together the LLC, set up a bookkeeping system, arranged for a bank loan to purchase necessary equipment, and negotiated a very favorable lease at a good location, the owners state in their operating agreement that for the first two years, Jim will receive 40% of the LLC's profits and that Janna, Jill, and Jerry will each receive 20%. After that, they'll share profits equally.

By contrast, rules governing corporate profits and losses are considerably more restrictive. A C corporation can't allocate profits and losses to shareholders; instead, shareholders must receive dividends according to the number of shares they own—if they receive dividends at all. (But it is possible, although more cumbersome, to establish two or more classes of stock, each with different dividend rights.) Similarly, in an S corporation, profits and losses are attributed to the shareholders based on their shares: a shareholder who owns 25% of the shares in an S corporation ordinarily must be allocated 25% of profits and losses—no more and no

less. Sometimes, however, corporations can get away from this strict formula by adjusting the salaries of shareholders who work in the business.

The easy flexibility allowed to LLCs in distributing profits and losses permits businesses to be creative and even make distributions to members who have contributed no cash.

> **EXAMPLE:** Howard and Saul run a home repair business organized as an LLC. Howard puts up all the money to needed to buy a van, tools, and supplies and to pay for advertising brochures and radio commercials. Saul, who has little cash but loads of experience in doing home repairs, will contribute future services to the LLC. Although the owners could agree to split profits and losses equally, they decide that Howard will get 60% for the first three years as a way of paying him back for taking the risk of putting up cash.

 Starting and operating an LLC is discussed in more detail in Chapter 4.

For forms to use in setting up an LLC: *See* Form Your Own Limited Liability Company, *by Anthony Mancuso (Nolo), and Nolo's* LLC Maker, *an easy-to-use software program that simplifies and automates much of the work of forming an LLC.*

E. Choosing Between a Corporation and an LLC

Let's assume that you've read all the earlier material in this chapter and that you now understand the chief legal, tax, and financial characteristics of the main types of business entities. Let's also assume that you've concluded it would be advantageous to operate your small business through an entity that limits the personal liability of all the owners—even if following this strategy involves a bit more paperwork, complexity, and possible expense.

For the reasons explained earlier in this chapter, you've probably narrowed your choice of entity to either the tried and true corporation or the new and streamlined LLC. Which is better? There's no answer to this question that applies to every business. Nevertheless, some general principles may be helpful.

For the majority of small businesses, the relative simplicity and flexibility of the LLC makes it the better choice. This is especially true if your business will hold property, such as real estate, that's likely to increase in value. That's because C corporations and their shareholders are subject to a double tax (both the corporation and the shareholders are taxed) on the increased value of the property when the property is sold or the corporation is liquidated. By contrast, LLC member-owners avoid this double taxation because the business's tax liabilities are passed through to them; the LLC itself does not pay a tax on its income.

But an LLC isn't always the best choice. Occasionally, other factors may tip the balance toward a corporation. Such factors include the following:

- **You'd like to provide extensive fringe benefits to owner-employees.** Often, when you form a corporation, you expect to be both a shareholder (owner) and an employee. The corporation can, for example, hire you to serve as its chief executive officer and pay you a tax-deductible salary, which, from a tax standpoint, is far better than paying you divi-

dends, which can't be deducted by the corporation as a business expense and therefore wind up being taxed twice (once at the corporate level and once at the personal level). But corporate employees (including employees of a C corporation who are also owners) don't just receive pay—most also receive fringe benefits. These benefits can include the payment of health insurance premiums and direct reimbursement of medical expenses. The corporation can deduct the cost of these benefits and they are not treated as taxable income to the employees. Having your own corporation pay for these fringe benefits and then deduct the cost as a business expense can be an attractive feature of doing business through a regular corporation. These opportunities for you to receive tax-favored fringe benefits are somewhat reduced if you do business as an LLC. Also, a regular corporation may be able to offer slightly better retirement benefits or options under a corporate retirement plan.

- **You want to entice or keep key employees by offering stock options and stock bonus incentives.** Simply put, LLCs don't have stock; corporations do. While it's possible to reward an employee by offering a membership interest in an LLC, the process is awkward and likely to be less attractive to employees. Therefore, if you plan to offer ownership in your business as an employee incentive, it makes sense to incorporate rather than form an LLC.

Choosing Between an LLC and an S Corporation: Self-Employment Taxes Can Tip the Balance

You know that taxes are withheld from employees' paychecks. In 2005, for example, employers must withhold 7.65% of the first $90,000 of an employee's pay for Social Security and Medicare taxes, and 1.45% of earnings above that amount for Medicare taxes. The employer adds an equal amount (to match the employee's share of Social Security and Medicare taxes) and sends these funds to the IRS. The total sent to the IRS is 15.3% on the first $90,000 of wages and 2.9% on earnings above that amount. (See Chapter 8, Section C3.)

You may not be aware that the IRS collects a similar 15.3% tax on the first $90,000 earned by a self-employed person and a 2.9% tax on earnings above that amount for Medicare alone. For this reason, the Social Security and Medicare tax is often referred to as the "self-employment" tax.

For an S corporation, the rules on the self-employment tax are well established: As an S corporation shareholder, you pay the self-employment tax on money you receive as compensation for services—but *not* on profits that automatically pass through to you as a shareholder. For example, if your total share of S corporation income is $100,000 in 2005 and you perform services for the corporation reasonably worth $65,000, you will be taxed 15.3% on the $65,000 but not on the remaining $35,000.

By contrast, the rules for members of an LLC are more complicated, and, for now, somewhat unsettled. Proposed IRS regulations (which Congress has placed on hold) would impose the self-employment tax on your entire share of LLC profits in any of the following situations:

- You participate in the business for more than 500 hours during the LLC's tax year.
- You work in an LLC that provides professional services in the fields of health, law, engineering, architecture, accounting, actuarial science, or consulting (no matter how many hours you work).
- You're empowered to sign contracts on behalf of your LLC.

Even though these proposed regulations do not have the force of law, the IRS says it won't challenge you if you use them in determining your liability for self-employment tax. This means that if you don't fall into one of the three categories listed above, you can use the same rules as apply to S corporation shareholders. But if you *do* fall into one of the above categories, you should assume that 100% of your income from the business will be subject to self-employment tax (although the amount that's over the current year's Social Security tax cut-off figure—$90,000 in 2005—will be subject only to Medicare tax).

The point is that, in some cases, an S corporation shareholder may pay less self-employment tax than some LLC members with similar income. You'll need to decide whether these potential tax savings are more important than gaining such LLC advantages as flexibility in management structure and in distributing profits and losses.

F. Special Structures for Special Situations

It's very likely that the best organizational structure for your small business is either a sole proprietorship, partnership, corporation, or LLC. (See Sections A, B, C, and D, above.) There are, however, some situations in which other, less common entities will either offer some tax or other advantage or will be legally required. For instance, you and your tax advisor may decide that selecting a less common structure may be desirable for your business. Your real estate investment group, for example, may find some benefit in creating a limited partnership (described in Section 1, below). Or, you may find that the law in your state *requires* you to select a less common structure for your business; for example, if you're a doctor or an accountant and you want to limit your personal liability, state law may require you to form a professional corporation, a professional LLC, or a limited liability partnership (all of which are described below in Section 2).

1. Limited Partnerships

The kind of partnership covered in Section B, above, is a *general* partnership. It's very different from another form of partnership known as a *limited* partnership, which, in certain circumstances, can combine the best attributes of a partnership and a corporation.

Most limited partnerships are formed to invest in real estate because of tax advantages for those who are passive investors; the passive investor is often able to personally write off depreciation and other real estate deductions. For the majority of other types of small businesses with more than one owner, chances are that forming either a general partnership, a corporation, or an LLC will be the best way to go.

A limited partnership works like this. There must be one or more "general partners" with the same basic rights and responsibilities as in any general partnership, and one or more "limited partners," who are usually passive investors. The big difference between a general partner and a limited partner is that the general partner *is* personally liable for the obligations of the partnership and the limited partner is *not* personally liable for them. The most a limited partner can lose by investing in a limited partnership is the amount that he or she:

- paid or agreed to pay into the partnership as a capital contribution; or
- received from the partnership after it became insolvent.

To maintain this limited liability, a limited partner may not participate in the management of the business, with a very few exceptions. A limited partner who does get actively involved in the management of the business risks losing immunity from personal liability, meaning he or she would have the same legal exposure as a general partner.

The advantage of a limited partnership as a business structure is that it provides a way for business owners to raise money from passive investors (the limited partners) without having either to take in new partners who will be active in the business or to engage in the intricacies of creating a corporation and issuing stock.

> **EXAMPLE:** Anthony and Janice's plan is to buy rundown houses, renovate them, and then sell them at a good profit. All they lack is the cash to make the initial purchases. To solve this problem, they first create a partnership consisting of the two of them. Then they establish a limited partnership, with their own partnership as the general partner, and seek others who are willing to invest for a defined interest in the venture. Anthony and Janice figure that they need $100,000 to get started. They sell ten limited partnership interests at $10,000 each. The limited partners are given the right to a percentage of the profits for a specified number of

years, but they are not liable for any obligations of the partnership.

A general partnership that's been operating for years can also create a limited partnership to finance expansion.

EXAMPLE: Judith and Aretha have been partners in a small picture frame shop for two years. They want to expand into a bigger store in a much better location, where they can stock a large selection of fine art prints as well as frames. To raise money, they create a limited partnership, offering each investor an 8% interest in the total net profits of the store for the next three years as well as the return of the invested capital at the end of that period, in exchange for a $20,000 investment. They sell four limited partnership interests, raising $80,000.

There is a downside to limited partnerships: Doing business as a limited partnership can be at least as costly and complicated as doing business as a corporation. Although limited partnerships don't have to issue stock, state laws typically require that a limited partnership file registration information about the general and limited partners.

⚠️ **Watch out for confusing labels.** *Despite the similarity in names, there are major differences between a limited partnership (discussed above) and a limited liability partnership (discussed below). To summarize:*

- *A limited partnership consists of at least one general partner and one or more limited partners. A general partner in a limited partnership is personally liable for all debts of and judgments against the business—regardless of who incurred the debt or other liability. A limited partner is generally not personally liable for any debts or judgments unless he or she actively participates in the business.*

- *A limited liability partnership (LLP) is a special form of general partnership and is usually reserved for professionals such as doctors, lawyers, and accountants. Normally, a partner in an LLP isn't personally liable for the negligent acts of other partners but is liable for his or her own negligence and for other partnership debts.*

2. Choices for Professionals

If you are a professional, such as a doctor, lawyer, or accountant, your choice of business structure may have to take into account certain additional factors. These include your need to avoid group liability, and state laws or rules of professional ethics governing your choices of business structure.

a. Professional Corporations

Laws in every state permit certain professionals to form corporations known as "professional corporations" or "professional service corporations." In many states, people in certain occupations (for example, doctors, lawyers, or accountants) who want to incorporate their practice can do so only through a professional corporation. In some states, some professionals have a choice of incorporating as either a professional corporation or a regular corporation (which can elect to be an S corporation).

The list of professionals eligible to incorporate is different in each state. Usually, though, professionals that must create a professional corporation include:

- accountants
- engineers
- health care professionals such as audiologists, dentists, nurses, opticians, optometrists, pharmacists, physical therapists, physicians, and speech pathologists
- lawyers
- psychologists
- social workers
- veterinarians.

Call your state's corporate filing office (usually the secretary of state or corporation commissioner) to see who is covered in your state.

Typically, a professional corporation must be organized for the sole purpose of rendering professional services and all shareholders must be licensed to render that service. For example, in a medical corporation, all of the shareholders must be licensed physicians.

Professional corporations aren't as popular as they used to be. The main reason for professionals to incorporate—favorable corporate taxation rules—has disappeared. Before 1986, professionals who incorporated could shelter more money from taxes than sole proprietors or partners could. This has all changed. Most professional corporations are now classified as "personal service corporations" by the IRS (see "Personal Service Corporations," below). Because the corporate income of personal service corporations is taxed at a flat rate of 35%, there's no longer any advantage to be gained by the two-tiered tax structure that allows ordinary corporations to save taxes on some retained earnings. Tax laws, however, still give favorable treatment to fringe benefits for corporate employees in professional corporations. (See Section C2b, above.)

Personal Service Corporations

Personal service corporations are defined under federal tax laws and have two basic characteristics:
- the professional employees of the corporation own the stock; and
- the corporation performs services in the fields of health, law, engineering, architecture, accounting, actuarial science, performing arts, or consulting.

The other reason for professionals to consider incorporation is the limitation on personal liability. It's no secret that malpractice verdicts against professionals continue to climb. While incorporating can't protect a professional against liability for his or her negligence, it can protect against liability for the negligence of an associate.

EXAMPLE 1: Dr. Anton and Dr. Bartolo are surgeons who practice as partners. Dr. Bartolo leaves a medical instrument inside a patient, who bleeds to death. The jury returns a $2 million verdict against Dr. Bartolo and the partnership. There is only $1 million in malpractice insurance to cover the judgment. Dr. Anton (along with Dr. Bartolo) would be personally liable for the $1 million not covered by insurance.

EXAMPLE 2: Drs. Anton and Bartolo create a professional corporation. Dr. Bartolo commits the malpractice described in Example 1. Dr. Anton, a corporate employee, would not be personally liable for the portion of the verdict not covered by insurance. Dr. Bartolo, however, would still be personally responsible for the $1 million excess, because he was the one guilty of malpractice. (In some states, Dr. Anton would be free from personal liability only if the professional corporation carried at least the minimum amount of insurance mandated by state law.)

Insurance is a better alternative for most professionals than is the limited liability offered by incorporation. But with malpractice rates soaring for many professionals, it's often hard to afford all the insurance you could possibly need, so forming a professional corporation can be a useful backup.

As an alternative to incorporating, professionals wishing to limit their personal liability should consider forming a professional limited liability company (PLLC) or limited liability partnership (LLP) as described below.

b. Professional Limited Liability Companies

As explained above, licensed professionals are permitted to incorporate but, in most states, they can do so only by forming a special type of corporation—a professional corporation (PC). Similarly, in many states, licensed professionals who wish to form an LLC are required to use a special type of LLC known as a "professional limited liability company" (PLLC).

Lawyers or doctors in a group practice, for example, may find it advantageous to form a PC or PLLC so that each member of the group is legally liable for only his or her malpractice—not the malpractice of other members of the group, as would be the case in a partnership. Members of a PLLC also won't be personally liable for other business debts such as obligations owed to business creditors, lenders, and the landlord.

Typically, state laws require that all members of a PLLC be licensed to practice the same profession—accounting, for example, or engineering.

Especially if the PLLC consists of lawyers, accountants, engineers, doctors, or other health care professionals, state law may require that each member at least carry a specified amount of malpractice insurance or be bonded.

Check the law in your state before setting up a PLLC. *If you're a professional and considering the creation of a PLLC, you need to check your state's statute to learn which professionals can and can't form such an entity. There's wide variation from state to state. (For example, in California, many professionals, such as health professionals, therapists of any type, and architects, cannot form any type of LLC.) If you're a member of a state professional society, its administrator may know the answer, or you can check the statute book at a nearby public library. (See Chapter 24 for information on doing legal research.)*

c. Limited Liability Partnerships

In a few states, laws or professional ethics rulings prevent accounting or law firms from doing business as corporations or LLCs. If you're an accountant or lawyer in such a state and would like some limitation on your personal liability for business obligations, look into forming a limited liability partnership (LLP). Unfortunately, the protection it offers is usually less than you'd get by forming a corporation or LLC—but it's better than nothing.

Available in some but not all states, a limited liability partnership is simply a general partnership whose partners enjoy some protection from personal liability. LLPs are authorized under state statutes and there's a bit of variation from state to state.

Typically a partner in an LLP is personally liable only for his or her own negligence (malpractice) or that of an employee working directly under the partner's supervision; the partner isn't personally liable for the negligence of anyone else in the firm. That's helpful but, as a partner in an LLP, you're still personally liable for a large variety of partnership debts not involving your own negligent acts, for example, obligations owed to business creditors, lenders, and the landlord—regardless of which partner incurred the obligation for the partnership.

EXAMPLE: Hillary, Edgar, and Paula—all certified public accountants—want to form a new firm, but determine that ethics rules in their state prevent them from forming a professional corporation or PLLC. Instead, they form an LLP. Hillary, during a period of disarray in her personal life, messes up big time on a tax return for a major client, who has to pay huge penalties to the IRS. The client sues for malpractice and is awarded a $25,000 judgment. The LLP and Hillary are liable for paying the judgment. Edgar and Paula are not.

During the same period, Hillary also orders $15,000 worth of fancy office furniture, which the LLP can't afford. All three partners are personally liable for the furniture debt. (By contrast, if local ethics rules had allowed the three accountants to organize their accounting firm as a professional corporation or professional limited liability company and they had done so, none of them would be personally liable for the cost of the furniture unless they personally guaranteed payment.)

⚠ Check the law in your state before setting up an LLP. *If you're a professional and considering the creation of an LLP, you need to check your state's statute to learn which professionals can and which can't form an LLP, because of the wide variation from state to state. (For example, only architects, accountants, and lawyers can form LLPs in California, where LLPs are referred to as "registered limited liability partnerships," or RLLPs.) If you're a member of a state professional society, its administrator may know the answer, or you can check the statute book at a nearby public library. (See Chapter 24 for information on doing legal research.)*

3. Nonprofit Corporations

Each state permits people to form nonprofit corporations, also known as not-for-profit corporations. The main reason people form these corporations is to get tax-exempt status under the Internal Revenue Code (Section 501(c)(3)). To get tax-exempt status, the corporation must have been formed for religious, charitable, literary, scientific, or educational purposes.

If a corporation is tax-exempt under Section 501(c)(3), not only is it free from paying taxes on its income, but people and organizations who contribute to the nonprofit corporation can take a tax deduction for their contributions. Because many nonprofit organizations rely heavily on grants from public agencies and private foundations to fund their operations, attaining 501(c)(3) status is critical to success.

Tax-exempt status isn't the only benefit available to a nonprofit corporation. The nonprofit label seems to create an altruistic aura around the organization and the people running it. The message is, "We're not in this for the money—we really do love kids (or music or animals)." Also, an organization that plans to do some heavy mailing may be attracted by the cheaper postal rates that nonprofits are charged.

What kinds of groups should consider becoming nonprofit corporations? Here's a partial list:

- child care centers
- shelters for the homeless
- community health care clinics
- museums
- hospitals
- churches, synagogues, mosques, and other places of worship
- schools
- performing arts groups
- conservation groups.

Most nonprofit corporations are run by a board of directors or trustees who are actively involved in the work of the corporation. Officers and employees (some of whom may also serve on the board) usually carry out the day-to-day business of the corporation and often receive salaries.

Keep in mind that if you put assets into a nonprofit corporation, you give up any ownership or proprietary interest in those assets. They must be irrevocably dedicated to the specified nonprofit purposes. If you want to get out of the business, you can't sell it and pocket the cash. If the nonprofit corporation does end, any remaining assets must go to another nonprofit.

📖 *This book is addressed primarily to people starting and running a business for profit, so you'll find little here on the peculiarities of nonprofit corporations. If you want to learn about such corporations in greater depth, see* How to Form Your Own Nonprofit Corporation, *by Anthony Mancuso (Nolo). That book provides step-by-step instructions for forming a nonprofit corporation in all states.*

4. Cooperatives and Cooperative-Type Organizations

Some people dream of forming a business of true equals—an organization owned and controlled democratically by its members.

These grassroots business organizers often refer to their businesses as a group, collective, or co-op—but these are usually informal rather than legal labels. Everyone who starts a business with others needs to select a legal structure. Generally, this means picking one of the traditional formats described in this chapter: a nonprofit corporation, a partnership, a C corporation, or an LLC. However, some states do have specific laws allowing the formation of a "cooperative corporation." For example, in some states, a consumer "co-op" could be created to manufacture and sell arts and crafts.

If a co-op law exists in your state, it can help make the process of democratic ownership go more smoothly. Otherwise, you'll need to make sure your partnership agreement, corporate bylaws, or LLC operating agreement contains the cooperative features that you and the other members feel are appropriate.

 To learn more about cooperative-type organizations and how to start one, visit the website of the National Cooperative Business Association at www.ncba.org. You can order many helpful publications there. Another fine resource is Co-op Incorporation Sourcebook *(Center for Cooperatives, University of California at Davis). It reviews business feasibility and legal requirements for starting a nonagricultural cooperative in California.* ■

Structuring a Partnership Agreement

There are two kinds of partnership: the general partnership and the limited partnership. This chapter discusses forming the more common kind, general partnerships. See Chapter 1, Section F1, for basic information about limited partnerships.

Features of the General Partnership

Main advantages. Simple and inexpensive to create and operate. Owners (partners) report their share of profit or loss on their personal tax returns.

Main disadvantage. Owners (partners) are personally liable for business debts.

A. Why You Need a Written Agreement

When you form a partnership to run a small business, your partners will probably be family members, close friends, or business associates. You may think it's unnecessary to sign a document with people you know quite well. Experience proves otherwise. No matter how rosy things are at the beginning, every partnership inevitably faces problems over the years. A well-thought-out written agreement will help you preserve the business, as well as your friendships.

You can, however, have a legally valid partnership even without a written partnership agreement. If you don't sign an agreement, the laws of your state will dictate how the partnership is run. That isn't all bad. Every state except Louisiana has adopted either the Uniform Partnership Act (UPA) or the Revised Uniform Partnership Act (RUPA). States have sometimes made slight variations in these laws but there is still a remarkable amount of consistency from state to state.

These state laws solve many common partnership problems in a sensible way. For example, the UPA says that if you don't have an agreement, each partner shares equally in the profits and has an equal voice in management of the business. The UPA goes on to say that partners are not entitled to receive compensation for services they provide to the partnership.

While it's conceivable that the provisions of the UPA are exactly what you and your partners want, partners usually prefer to modify at least some of them. For example, if one partner contributes far more assets than others, that partner may deserve a greater share of the profits. Or you may want to allow one or more partners to receive a salary for their services. Or you may not want each partner to have an equal voice in running the business. Similarly, you may want to include customized provisions on how to value a partner's interest in the business if a partner dies or leaves. In that situation, many partners want to assign some value to the goodwill of the business for tax purposes—something that does not happen automatically under the UPA. With a written partnership agreement, you can tailor your partnership to fit your needs.

There are other benefits to working out the details in a written partnership agreement. You'll focus on issues you might not have thought of—issues about which you and your partners may have different opinions. For example, what if one partner wants compensation beyond a share of the profits to recognize work he or she performs in the evening or on weekends for the partnership? By getting issues out into the open early, you can nip problems in the bud.

B. An Overview of Your Partnership Agreement

It's up to you and your partners to decide what shape the partnership will take. A lawyer can help you focus on issues and suggest possible solutions, but you and your partners—not the lawyer—must make the basic choices.

This section goes through the clauses that are usually included in a partnership agreement for a small business.

Chapter 2 of *Legal Forms for Starting & Running a Small Business* contains a *sample partnership agreement.*

1. Name and Term

Although many partnerships do business using the last names of the partners, it's both legal and common for a partnership to have one name and to do business under another name. For example, the partnership of Jones, Gold, and Sanchez could decide to do business as Seafood Express. The name Seafood Express would be an assumed name, or fictitious name, which you'd have to register with the appropriate state or county office.

 Chapter 6 contains a thorough discussion of business and product names.

Another issue is how long the partnership will last. If you want it to go on indefinitely, include a clause in your partnership agreement like this:

> The partnership shall last until it is dissolved by all the partners or a partner leaves, for any reason, including death.

On the other hand, if you plan to develop a particular piece of real estate or do some other finite task, you might want a clause with a definite date, such as one of the following:

> The partnership shall commence as of the date of this agreement and shall continue for a period of _____ years, at which time it shall be dissolved and its affairs wound up.

> or

> The partnership shall continue until _____ [*specify an event such as "the completion and sale of The Commercial Office Plaza"*], at which time the partnership shall be dissolved and its affairs wound up.

2. Purpose

The purpose of the partnership should be broadly stated in plain English. The advantage of a broad statement of partnership purposes is that you have flexibility if the business evolves. Here are two typical purpose clauses:

> The purpose of the partnership is to operate one or more stores for the sale of records, tapes, compact discs, or other related merchandise.

> or

> The purpose of the partnership is to operate a bookkeeping and tax preparation service for individual clients and small businesses.

On the other hand, if you're sure you're creating your partnership for a short-term, specific purpose, such as presenting one trade show, it would be appropriate to use a more limited purpose clause, such as this one:

> The purpose of the partnership is to organize and present this year's Builders and Home Improvement Show at the Municipal Convention Center.

3. Contributions

Your partnership agreement should describe the initial contributions that you and your partners will make. Often, each partner contributes cash only.

The amounts of contributions may be equal, but don't have to be. For example, one partner might contribute $5,000 while another contributes $1,000 and a third contributes a pickup truck. If a partner contributes property such as a vehicle, tools, a building, a patent, or a copyright, you need to agree on the value of that property. You can also provide that one of the partners will contribute personal services (perhaps painting the business headquarters) in return for a partnership interest. Keep in mind that a partner can sell, lend, lease, or rent property to the partnership too.

a. Cash Contributions

It's logically neat if each partner contributes an equal amount of cash to a new business. Otherwise, partners who invest more money than the others may feel entitled to a larger voice in making partnership decisions. But in the real world, not all partners are always able to make equal contributions of cash. One way to handle this is to have the partner who contributes more lend the extra amount to the business rather than contribute it outright.

EXAMPLE: Ricardo and Alberta are opening a martial arts training center. Ricardo has just left a job at a corporation and received a handsome severance package. He's willing to put $40,000 into the business. Alberta, on the other hand, is a single mother who wants to start a business precisely because she is short of money. She can raise $10,000. Alberta could contribute $10,000 and Ricardo $40,000, with Ricardo having more say in partnership decisions than Alberta. But an easier and more democratic approach would be for each to contribute $10,000 in cash, with Ricardo lending the partnership the additional $30,000, to be repaid over three years at 10% annual interest.

A basic clause for equal cash contributions reads as follows:

> The initial capital of the partnership shall be a total of $_____. Each partner shall contribute an equal share amounting to $_____ no later than _____, 20____. Each partner shall own an equal share of the business.

If a partner can't initially contribute the desired amount of cash, another way to handle this problem is to agree that he or she will make payments over time. Here's a sample clause.

> Arthur Feldman shall be a partner upon making an initial contribution of $1,000 to the capital of the partnership. He will subsequently contribute to the partnership capital, and his capital account shall be credited, in the amount of $100 per month beginning July 1, 20__, until he has contributed the sum of $5,000 (including the initial $1,000 payment).

Interest on Partnership Investment: Should partners receive interest on their contributions of capital? Generally, no—after all, the money is already at work building a jointly owned business. But either way you decide this issue, cover it with a specific clause in the partnership agreement.

b. Contributions of Services

Sometimes, a partner's contribution consists wholly or in part of services. In the above example concerning Alberta's contribution to the martial arts training center, another way to handle the disparity in available cash would be for Alberta to agree to work a certain number of hours more than Ricardo at a fixed rate (say $20 per hour) until the contributions were equalized. After that, the partners would work an equal amount of hours each week. If a partner is going to contribute services in return for an interest in the business, this should be spelled out in the partnership agreement.

> **EXAMPLE:** Margaret and Alice form a 50/50 partnership for catering parties. Each will spend equal time on preparing the food and delivering it. Margaret contributes $10,000 to get the business going. Alice agrees to contribute unpaid labor as a bookkeeper and business manager for one year over and above the amount of time she spends on food-related work. Their

intention is to equalize the contributions of the partners.

c. Contributions of Property

Some or all of the partners may contribute property as well as, or instead of, cash. A clause covering this possibility might look like this:

> _____ shall contribute property valued at $_____ consisting of _____ _____ by _____, 20____. [If the property is difficult to describe, describe it in detail on a separate sheet of paper marked "Exhibit A" and add here, "and more particularly described in Exhibit A, attached to this agreement."]

Getting expert help. _If you're transferring property to your partnership, you may need the assistance of a tax expert. Such contributions raise questions about what tax basis (value) will be assigned to the property being transferred. The IRS looks at tax basis in determining how much profit you've gained when the property is later transferred or sold as well as the amount of losses you can claim on your tax return if the business is not profitable. These tax details are beyond the scope of this book._

4. Profits, Losses, Draws, and Salaries

How will partners be compensated? The first issue is how you'll divide profits once a year or at the end of some other fixed period. You should also determine whether any partners can receive an early draw against their share of the profits—that is, be paid a portion of profits sooner than other partners. This might be appropriate if one partner is coming into the partnership with less savings than the others and is counting on partnership income for living expenses.

You'll also need to decide whether any partners will receive a salary for work done in the business in addition to draws on their share of profits. If equal partners will all work a roughly equal number of hours, there's no need to pay salaries; an equal division of profits with or without a draw should be adequate. But if one partner will work more hours than the others, paying that partner a salary may be sensible. Or you could give the harder-working partner a larger share of the profits. If salaries are paid, they're a normal business expense and don't come out of profits.

If profits are shared equally, the following clause would be appropriate:

> The partners will share all profits equally, and they will be distributed [*monthly, yearly, etc.*]. All losses of the partnership will also be shared equally.

On the other hand, if profits and losses will be shared unequally, here are some sample clauses to consider:

> Partnership profits and losses will be shared among the partners as follows:
>
> | Name | Percentage |
> |------|------------|
> | _____ | _____ |
> | _____ | _____ |
> | _____ | _____ |
> | _____ | _____ |
>
> or
>
> Partnership profits and losses shall be shared among the partners as follows:
>
> | Name | % of Profits | % of Losses |
> |------|--------------|-------------|
> | _____ | _____ | _____ |
> | _____ | _____ | _____ |
> | _____ | _____ | _____ |

or

> Partnership profits and losses shall be shared by the partners in the same proportion as their contributions of capital bear to each other.

A draw is an advance of anticipated profits paid to a partner or partners. It's easiest if draws are to be made by all partners. But if you want to authorize draws for only certain partners, a clause like the following is appropriate:

> Partners _____ and _____ are entitled to draws from expected partnership profits. The amount of each draw will be determined by a vote of the partners. The draws shall be [*monthly or on any other kind of schedule that you agree to*].

You may also want to provide for the partnership to retain some profits in the business for new equipment, expansion, or employee bonuses. Here's a sample clause:

> In determining the amount of profits available for distribution, allowance will be made for the fact that some money must remain undistributed and available as working capital as determined by [*for example, "all partners" or "a majority of partners"*].

Even though profits are reinvested, you and the other partners are taxed on your shares of them at your individual rates. (Chapter 1, Section C2b, discusses how a regular corporation may afford tax advantages over a partnership when a business has retained earnings.)

The Authority of Partners

Do you want each partner to be able to make decisions that bind the partnership in the normal operation of its business? Or do you want some limitations—for example, that large contracts or purchases must be approved in advance by a majority of the partners? You can address this issue in your partnership agreement. But remember that while a limitation on a partner's authority is binding among the partners themselves, it doesn't necessarily limit liability to outsiders who deal with the partner.

EXAMPLE: Peggy, Roger, and Lisa run a bookkeeping and billing service for several doctors, dentists, and clinics. Peggy, who is a computer whiz, believes that there's no such thing as too much electronic equipment. So in the partnership agreement, a clause provides that any purchase of equipment requires the approval of at least two of the partners. Peggy buys three notebook computers, two laser printers, and assorted modems and fax machines for the partnership, without approval. The partnership and each partner are liable for the $12,000 bill, even though the partners limited liability among themselves. When Peggy purchased the equipment, the computer store didn't know what was in the partnership agreement—the usual case. And Peggy appeared to have authority to bind the partnership. The other partners, however, will have a legal claim against Peggy because she exceeded her authority under the partnership agreement.

LAW IN THE REAL WORLD
A Profitable Experience

Jan and Mike discussed forming a partnership to open a desktop publishing service aimed at helping small businesses design brochures, flyers, and other promotional material. The idea of sharing the work and profits 50-50 appealed to both of them. There was only one major hang-up: The partnership agreement form they looked at provided for profits to be divided at the end of the year. This was okay with Mike, who had received a generous severance package from a former job, but not for Jan, who was trying to put her daughter through college and had no financial cushion.

Recognizing their different circumstances, Jan and Mike agreed Jan would be allowed to take a monthly draw against her share of anticipated partnership profits of $3,000. And because they realized a new business needs all the cash it can get its hands on, Mike would wait and take the same amount at the end of the year. Then Mike and Jan would split any additional profits.

To guard against the possibility that Jan's draw would use up more than half of the profits and shortchange Mike, the partners, after checking the tax consequences with their tax advisor, also agreed that any amount Jan received over her 50% share would be considered a personal loan from the partnership, to be repaid out of her share of future years' profits.

5. Management Responsibilities

It's wise to pin down the basic way you'll operate the business. Commonly, in small business partnerships, all partners are involved in management and supervision, justifying a clause like the following:

> All partners shall be actively involved and materially participate in the management of operation of the partnership business.

You can go further if you want every partner to have a veto power:

> All partnership decisions must be made by the unanimous agreement of all partners.

Some small business partnerships distinguish between major and minor decisions, allowing a single partner to make a minor decision but requiring unanimity for major ones. If you decide to go down this road, you have to figure out how to define a major decision. The distinction between major and minor decisions—especially purchases or the undertaking of obligations—is often based on a dollar amount. A clause like this one would be appropriate:

> All major decisions of the partnership business must be made by a unanimous decision of all partners. Minor business decisions may be made by an individual partner. Major decisions are defined as all purchases and contracts over $5,000 [or other definition of major decisions].

If you want to provide for unequal management powers, here are some clauses to consider:

> Each partner shall participate in the management of the business. In exercising the powers of management, each partner's vote shall be in proportion to his or her interest in the partnership's capital.

> or

> In the management, control, and direction of the business, the partners shall have the following percentages of voting power:
>
> | Name | Percentage |
> |------|------------|
> | _____ | _____ |
> | _____ | _____ |
> | _____ | _____ |
> | _____ | _____ |

If the partners are going to contribute different types of skills, you may also want to state that in your partnership agreement. And while it may seem unnecessary to list the hours to be worked, you may avoid possible problems through a clause such as the following:

> Except for vacations, holidays, and times of illness, each partner will work _____ hours per week on partnership business.

Consider a clause on leaves of absence or sabbaticals. How much time off is allowed? And what happens to a partner's right to receive pay or profits while on leave?

Other financial matters to be dealt with in the partnership agreement may include the following:

- May partners borrow money on behalf of the partnership? Is there a dollar limit on how much a partner can borrow on behalf of the partnership without the prior consent of all partners?
- Are expense accounts authorized? If so, is there a limit on the amount?
- How many signatures are required on partnership checks and to withdraw money from the partnership bank account?
- How many weeks of paid or unpaid vacation each year are partners entitled to?

6. Partners' Outside Business Activities

A key partnership question is whether or not any partner can engage in outside business. In some instances, they must, at least at first, because the partnership business income isn't enough to live on. If a partner can engage in outside business, what types are permitted? You wouldn't want a partner to directly compete with the partnership. That would be a conflict of interest. But how do you define direct competition? If the partners are running a restaurant, can one of the partners own a catering business? Or work in a delicatessen? There are at least four different approaches to this issue. You can:

- Allow partners to engage in one or more other businesses except for those that directly compete with the partnership business.
- Allow partners to engage in other businesses without any other restrictions.
- List permitted activities.
- Prohibit partners from participating in any other business.

Here's an example of the first approach:

> Any partner may engage in one or more other businesses as well as the business of the partnership, but only to the extent that this activity does not directly and materially interfere with the business of the partnership and does not conflict with the time commitments or other obligations of that partner to the partnership under this agreement. Neither the partnership nor any other partner shall have any right to any income or profit derived by a partner from any outside business activity permitted under this section.

LAW IN THE REAL WORLD
Outside Interests

When Ted M. and Ted Y. formed a partnership and opened a bookstore (yup, they called it Two Teds), they didn't expect to make much, if any, money right away. According to their business plan, it would take two to three years for the store to be solidly profitable. In the meantime, both men would have to hold down second jobs. This led to a serious problem. Both men already worked in the book business (Ted M. managed a secondhand book shop, and Ted Y. was a sales rep for a large publisher) and wanted to avoid any hint of a conflict of interest between their personal and partnership interests.

Ted Y. explained his store plans to the publisher he worked for, who agreed to reduce his sales territory and let him work three days per week. (Ted Y. also promised to work 30 hours at Two Teds.) Because selling books to stores and selling them to the public aren't competitive operations, it was easy for the Teds to agree in writing as part of their partnership agreement that Ted Y.'s job didn't amount to a conflict of interest with the partnership.

Ted M.'s situation was tougher. No matter how much they thought about it, managing one store while owning part of another in the same city reeked of possible conflicts of interest. To solve this, it was decided that Ted M. would quit managing the other store. Initially, at least, he would work 55 hours per week at Two Teds and be paid a reasonable salary for the 25 hours per week he worked more than Ted Y.

7. Departure of a Partner—Buyouts

Now we're getting into one of the most essential—but complicated—areas of a partnership agreement: what you'll do if one of the partners voluntarily leaves, becomes disabled, or dies. These things are not easy to think about when you're caught up in the excitement of starting a new business. Still, it's risky to postpone facing them. Sooner or later the partnership will change and fundamental issues will come up. A partner may want to leave for any number of reasons—such as to start another business or to move to another part of the country. Or maybe a partner will retire or die. Can the departing partner sell his or her interest? Do the remaining partners or partner have the right to buy it? How is the purchase price determined?

If one partner quits or dies, most partnership agreements very sensibly require a departing partner to give the remaining partners the chance to buy out his or her share and continue the business before selling or transferring it to outsiders. Here's a sample "right of first refusal" clause designed to accomplish this:

> If any partner leaves the partnership, for whatever reason, whether he or she quits, withdraws, is expelled, retires, or dies, or becomes mentally or physically incapacitated or unable to fully function as a partner, he or she, or (in the case of a deceased partner) his or her estate, shall be obligated to sell his or her interest in the partnership to the remaining partners, who may buy that interest under the terms and conditions set forth in this agreement.

This option protects the remaining partners. But what if the departing partner has found a buyer who is willing to pay a hefty price for that partnership interest? Some partnerships don't compel a departing partner to take a lower price (as predetermined in the partnership agreement) than he or she would get from a bona fide outside buyer; their partnership agreements provide that the existing partners must pay the market price for the departing partner's share. Either way you resolve this issue, you should spell out your solution in the partnership agreement.

Here's a different approach:

> If the remaining partners do not purchase the departing partner's share of the business under the terms provided in this agreement within _____ days after the departing partner leaves, the entire business of the partnership shall be put up for sale and listed with an appropriate sales agent or broker.

a. Valuing a Partner's Share

One major issue in a buy-out clause is how you'll set the worth of the business—and the value of a partner's share. Let's look at some specific valuation methods.

The *asset valuation method* is based on the current net worth of the business (assets minus liabilities). As of the date the departing partner leaves, the net worth of all partnership assets is calculated and all outstanding business debts are deducted to determine net worth. Because goodwill isn't a tangible asset, it's not counted. The departing partner receives his or her ownership percentage of this amount, under whatever payout terms you agreed on.

The *book valuation method* is a variation of the asset valuation method. You calculate the value of all partnership assets and liabilities as they're set forth in the partnership accounting books, which basically means the acquisition cost. Because book value doesn't cover goodwill, in a successful business it has little relation to what the business is really worth. Furthermore, the acquisition cost of property is unlikely to be its current worth.

The *set-dollar method* involves an agreement by the partners in advance that if one partner departs from the partnership, the others will buy out his or her share for a preestablished price. Before adopting this method, be aware that the price selected may be arbitrary. Even if accurate for the present time, the worth of the business may fluctuate, making a predetermined value out of date. You might consider having the partners unanimously establish a value in writing for the partnership each year.

A *post-departure appraisal* means that you agree to have an independent appraiser determine the worth of the partnership when a partner departs. It sounds good in principle, but because many small businesses aren't amenable to precise valuation, even in the hands of an expert appraiser, it can lead to bitter arguments later.

The *capitalization of earnings method* determines what the business is worth based on what it earns. Unless there's an open market to set a price, the best estimate of what a business is worth often depends on its earning capacity. This method works best with a business that's been around for several years. First you need to measure the earnings of the business for a year or more. Then you must agree on a multiplier (often two to five) which, in effect, takes into consideration the fact that a buyer hopes to reap profits in future years. Finally, you multiply the earnings by your multiplier to arrive at a value. But how do you establish the multiplier? Often one is already loosely established in a particular industry. A consultant or trade magazine may tell you that profitable dry cleaning businesses are often sold on the basis of multiplying profits by a certain number. Be aware that this sort of information is at best an estimate, which can change by industry, individual business, and year. If you decide to use this method of valuing your business, you'll need expert advice.

You may want to have a different buyout price depending on when or why a partner departs. For example, a partner who leaves during the initial stages of a business (say, the first one or two years) may be entitled only to the balance in his or her capital account. After that initial period, the departing partner's interest could be calculated by a method that more accurately reflects the actual operation and success of the business.

You could also have varying formulas depending on why the partner leaves. For example, there might be one formula if the partner becomes disabled, retires over age 65, or dies, and another formula if the partner leaves under other circumstances.

b. Payments to Departing Partners

Your partnership agreement should provide for a payment schedule if there's a buyout. Otherwise, the departing partner would have the right to collect for the full value of his or her interest promptly. This could become a serious problem if a partner dies, since the deceased partner's family would likely insist on exercising this right.

Your decision on payment terms has a close relationship to the method you use for determining the buyout price. If the remaining partners can pay the price over a number of years, they're usually willing to pay a higher buyout price than if they must pay all the cash the day a partner leaves.

One of the best ways to finance the buyout of a partner's interest is through insurance. If a partner dies, the proceeds from the partnership-financed insurance policy are used to pay off his or her share, and partnership operating income doesn't have to be used. Many profitable partnerships buy insurance against each partner's serious illness, incapacity, or death. This can be a sensible way of obtaining money to pay off a deceased partner's interest; a term policy, which is relatively cheap, is especially good.

8. Continuity of the Partnership

If a partnership has more than two members, the remaining partners usually want to continue the business as a partnership when a partner leaves. Here's a clause that you can use to assure the continuation of a partnership:

> In the case of a partner's death, permanent disability, retirement, voluntary withdrawal, or expulsion from a partnership, the partnership shall not dissolve or terminate, but its business shall continue without interruption and without any break in continuity. On the disability, retirement, withdrawal, expulsion, or death of any partner, the others shall not liquidate or wind up the affairs of the partnership, but shall continue to conduct the partnership under the terms of this agreement.

9. Noncompetition of Departing Partner

Another issue relating to a partner who leaves the partnership is future competition. You may want to prohibit the departing partner from competing against your firm. This may include the protection of your trade secrets and customer lists.

Legally, this is a touchy area. Forbidding a partner from engaging in his or her usual way of earning a living is a drastic act, and courts often refuse to enforce unfairly restrictive terms. To be legal, a noncompetition agreement normally must be reasonably limited in both time and geographical area and be otherwise fair. State laws vary in regard to noncompetition clauses, and it's not always possible to tell whether or not a judge will enforce one. If you're determined to include a noncompetition clause in your agreement, it makes sense to see a lawyer familiar with small business concerns.

This sample clause will give you an idea of how these clauses are often drafted:

> On the voluntary withdrawal, permanent disability, retirement, or expulsion of any partner, that partner shall not carry on a business the same as or similar to the business of the partnership within the [*describe area*] for a period of [*time period you've agreed on*].

10. Control of Partnership Name

A business name can be valuable. The partnership agreement should spell out what happens to it if a partner leaves. There are a number of ways to handle this, including a clause stating that the partnership continues to own the name, that one partner owns the name, that control of the name will be decided on at a later date, or, finally, that in the event of dissolution, the partnership business name will be owned by a majority of the former partners.

11. Resolving Partnership Disputes

Suppose there's a serious disagreement between the partners and you can't resolve it by personal discussions and negotiations. You may find yourself in court, which is a costly, time-consuming, and emotionally draining way to deal with the dispute. Fortunately, there's a way around litigation as a means of resolving disputes. You can provide in your partnership agreement for mediation or arbitration or both. These subjects are treated in more depth in Chapter 22. Please read that discussion if you're not fully familiar with these methods.

Here's an example of a mediation clause:

> Any dispute arising out of this agreement or the partnership business will be resolved by mediation, if possible. The partners pledge to cooperate fully and fairly with the mediator in an attempt to reach a mutually satisfactory compromise to a dispute. The mediator will be _____. If any partner to a dispute feels it cannot be resolved by the

partners themselves, he or she shall so notify the other partners and the mediator in writing. Mediation will commence within _____ days of the Notice of Request for Mediation. The cost of mediation will be shared equally by all partners to the dispute.

To protect yourselves should mediation fail, you can follow up with an arbitration clause that takes over if a dispute can't be mediated to the satisfaction of the parties. The partners are bound by the arbitrator's decision, which can be enforced in court.

 See Chapter 22, Sections B and C, for additional mediation and arbitration clauses.

If you include both mediation and arbitration clauses in your partnership agreement, you need to decide whether the mediator and arbitrator should be the same person. If you have the same person playing both roles, you don't run the risk of having to present the case twice—first to the mediator and then, if mediation fails, to the arbitrator. On the other hand, the person who has ultimate power to make a decision as an arbitrator may be less effective as a mediator.

C. Changes in Your Partnership

As your business changes, your partnership agreement will have to change, too. For example, the addition of a new partner requires revision of at least the clauses listing the partners' names and those covering contributions and distribution of profits.

Even if you admit no new partners, the growth of your business may require you to change your agreement. You and your partners may decide to run your expanded business differently than the original business. Or maybe more cash is required, and the partners decide that their contributions should be in proportions different from those originally agreed to.

Any time you make a significant change in the structure or operation of your business, you should change the partnership agreement to reflect it.

The owners of most small partnerships specify that the partnership agreement may be amended only by the written consent of all partners. But you can create any amendment clause you choose. For example, you could specify that the agreement can be amended by vote of 51% of the partners or by 51% of the capital accounts.

At some point, your partnership may well decide to add another partner. You may need a new partner's contribution of cash or skills, or you may want to retain a key employee by making him or her a partner. Because a partnership technically is dissolved when a new partner joins it, it's helpful to include a clause in your partnership agreement such as the following one:

> Admission of a new partner shall not cause dissolution of the underlying partnership business, which will be continued by the new partnership entity. ■

Creating a Corporation

Chapter 1 introduced the basic business entities—the sole proprietorship, the partnership, the limited liability company, and the corporation. This chapter tells you more about setting up a corporation. We'll start with the structure of a corporation, including the roles of the key players: the incorporators, shareholders, directors, officers, and employees. Then we'll look at corporate finance—how you get money into the corporation and how you take it out. Next we'll walk step by step through the procedures for setting up a corporation. Finally, we'll examine some sound corporate business practices.

The material in this chapter applies to most, but not all, new corporations. Generally, this material will apply to you if your proposed corporation fits the following profile:

- A relatively small number of people—about ten or fewer—will own the corporate stock.
- All or most of the owners will participate directly in managing and running the business; investors who don't directly participate will generally be limited to friends or family members.
- All of the owners will live in the state in which you form your corporation and conduct your business.

Lawyers often call a small corporation that fits this profile a "closely held corporation." We'll borrow this term in its most general, nontechnical sense.

Classifying your corporation at the outset is important because if you're a closely held corporation and sell stock to only a few friends or family members, normally you'll be exempt from all but the most routine requirements of federal and state securities laws.

But if you sell stock in your corporation to outside investors—people who won't help run the business or aren't closely tied to people who are—you must comply with those laws. So if you want to sell stock to a wider range of people, especially if any of them live in a different state, you'll need to learn more about the requirements of the securities laws. In many states, there are generous exemptions that allow sales of stock to as many as 35 investors without complicated paperwork. But because this is such a technical area and laws vary from state to state, you should seek legal advice from a lawyer knowledgeable about securities laws before you offer stock to outsiders.

A. The Structure of a Corporation

Corporations are controlled primarily by state, not federal, law. This means that 50 different sets of rules cover how corporations are created. Terminology differs from state to state. For example, most states use the term "articles of incorporation" to refer to the basic document creating the corporation, but some states (including Connecticut, Delaware, New Jersey, New York, and Oklahoma) use the term "certificate of incorporation." Tennessee calls it a "charter," and Massachusetts uses the term "articles of organization." Fortunately, the similarities in corporate procedure outweigh the differences, so most of what you find in this chapter will apply to your own situation. Nevertheless, watch out for the differences.

People involved in a corporation traditionally play different legal roles: incorporator, shareholder, director, officer, employee. We'll look at those roles here. But, in virtually every state, there's a way that you can set up a corporation in which one or two people play all roles.

1. Incorporators

The incorporators (called the promoters in some
states) do the preparatory work. This may include
bringing together the people and the money to create the corporation. It always includes preparing
and filing the articles of incorporation—the formal
incorporation document that is filed with a state office such as the secretary of state. Although several
people can serve as incorporators and sign the articles of incorporation, only one incorporator is required by law. Once the articles of incorporation
are filed, the incorporator's job is nearly done. The
only things that remain to be done are to select the
first board of directors and to adopt the corporate
bylaws (although, in some states, bylaws may be
adopted by the directors).

2. Shareholders

The shareholders own the stock of the corporation.
One person can own 100% of the stock. Among the
things that only shareholders can do are these:

- Elect directors (although the initial board of
  directors is usually selected by the incorpora-
  tor or promoter)
- Amend bylaws
- Approve the sale of all or substantially all of
  the corporate assets
- Approve mergers and reorganizations
- Amend the articles of incorporation
- Remove directors
- Dissolve the corporation.

State laws typically require that the shareholders
hold an annual meeting. However, in many states, a
"consent action" or "consent resolution"—a document signed by all of the shareholders—can be
used in place of a formal meeting.

For the corporation to elect S corporation status under federal tax laws, all shareholders must sign the election form that's filed with the IRS. (For more on this, see Section F, Step 12.)

3. Directors

The directors manage the corporation and make major policy decisions. Among other things, the directors authorize the issuance of stock; decide on whether to mortgage, sell, or lease real estate; and elect the corporate officers. Directors may hold regular or special meetings (or both). However, in many states, it's simpler and just as effective for the directors to take actions by signing a document called a "consent resolution" or "consent action."

The incorporators or shareholders decide how many directors the corporation will have. The number of directors is usually stated in the articles of incorporation or in the corporate bylaws. Most states specifically permit corporations to have just one director. In the remaining states, the requirement is that there be at least three directors, but there's an exception for corporations with fewer than three shareholders. If there are only two shareholders, the corporation can operate with two directors; if there's only one shareholder, the corporation needs only one director.

> **EXAMPLE 1:** Anita, Barry, and Clint create a corporation in Michigan. They choose Anita to be the sole director. They can do this because the law in Michigan—as in many other states—permits a corporation to function with a single director regardless of the number of shareholders.

> **EXAMPLE 2:** Dustin, Erwin, and Faye create a corporation in California. They would like Dustin to be the sole director, but California law requires them to have at least three directors if there are three or more shareholders; they can have a single director only if the corporation has a single shareholder. Therefore, Dustin, Erwin, and Faye create a three-person board of directors and appoint themselves to those positions.

4. Officers

The officers are normally responsible for the day-to-day operation of the corporation. State laws usually require that the corporation have at least a president, a secretary, and a treasurer. The president is usually the chief operating officer of the corporation. The secretary is responsible for the corporate records. The treasurer, of course, is responsible for the corporate finances, although it's common to hand day-to-day duties to a bookkeeper. The corporation can have other officers—such as a vice president—as well. In most states, one person can hold all of the required offices.

> **EXAMPLE:** Abdul forms a Texas corporation. He provides for the two corporate offices—president and secretary—that are required by Texas law. He appoints himself to both offices. This is legal in Texas and in most other states.

5. Employees

Employees work for the corporation in return for compensation. In the small corporations we're considering in this chapter, the owners (shareholders) are usually also employees of the corporation.

It's through your salary and other compensation as a corporate employee that you'll receive most of your financial benefits from the business. Often the person who runs the business day-to-day gets the most compensation. This may or may not be the president.

6. How It All Fits Together

If you're new to all of this, the numerous components of a corporation may seem unduly complicated for a small business. Fortunately, it all fits together quite smoothly and easily.

EXAMPLE: Al, Bev, and Carla decide to form a corporation to run a fitness center. Their plan is to invest $10,000 apiece and be equal owners. Since state law requires only one person to sign the papers setting up the corporation, Bev signs the Articles of Incorporation for ABC Fitness Center Inc. and sends them to the secretary of state's office along with the filing fee. Bev is the *incorporator*.

Next, Bev adopts bylaws for the corporation calling for a three-person Board of Directors. She elects herself, Al, and Carla to serve as the first *directors*. The three of them then elect Bev to be the president, Al to be the secretary, and Carla to be the treasurer—so the three of them are then the *officers* of the corporation.

When Al, Bev, and Carla each pay $10,000 into the corporate bank account, they each receive a stock certificate for 10,000 shares of corporate stock; at that moment, they become shareholders.

All three are active in running the business, working 50 hours a week and receiving a salary. Al and Bev, who have experience as personal trainers, take charge of training customers and supervising a small staff of other workers. Carla, who studied business in college, looks after the finances—billing customers, marketing, ordering supplies. So in addition to their other roles in the corporation, Al, Bev, and Carla are employees.

B. Financing Your Corporation

It doesn't take an MBA degree to grasp the fundamentals of corporate finance in the typical small business. Assets come into the corporation in two forms: equity and debt. Let's look at each.

1. Funding Your Corporation With Equity

Basically, equity means shareholders contribute cash, valuable property, or services to the company in exchange for stock in the company. The number of shares issued is somewhat arbitrary, but the customary practice in some places is for new corporations to issue one share for each dollar invested.

The most common way to pay for stock is with cash. For example, you may put $5,000 into the company in return for 5,000 shares of corporate stock. But money isn't the only thing that you can invest in a company in return for stock. You may also transfer physical assets, such as real estate or equipment, or a copyright, patent, or trademark. Or you may receive stock in return for past services to the corporation.

Check before you transfer property for stock. *Before you transfer property to your corporation in exchange for stock, check with your tax advisor. If you receive stock for property that has increased in value since you bought it, you may owe taxes.*

In some states, you can receive stock in return for promising to perform services to the corporation, or in return for a promissory note. In other words, you might receive 5,000 shares of stock in return for your promise to work for the corporation for 200 hours or to pay the corporation $5,000 six months later. Not all states, however, permit stock to be issued based on a promise of future services or money, so check the rules of your state.

2. Funding Your Corporation With Debt

The other major way to fund a corporation is through debt—that is, by borrowing money. But you should know that if your corporation borrows from a bank or other outside lender, the lender will probably expect you to personally guarantee to repay the debt should the business be unable to.

⚠ Lending money to the corporation. *Until fairly recently, it was quite common for shareholders in some new corporations to lend money to the corporation or transfer assets from an existing sole proprietorship in exchange for a promissory note from the corporation. Shareholders gained tax benefits by dividing their initial investment between debt (represented by promissory notes) and equity (represented by stock certificates). Changes in the tax laws, however, have eliminated the shareholder loan as a viable option for purchasing equity in a new corporation.*

3. Leasing Property to the Corporation

Sometimes you'll want to retain ownership of property being used by the corporation. For example, maybe you own a garage or other small building your company will occupy. With real estate, it's usually better, from a tax standpoint, to have your corporation lease the property from you rather than to transfer the property to the corporation.

> **EXAMPLE:** Nino forms New Age Innovators Inc. to develop some practical new technologies for the plumbing industry. He plans to work out of his garage. He leases the garage to his corporation for $500 a month. On his own personal Form 1040, Nino will report the rent as income and will deduct interest expense (for the mortgage on the building) and depreciation. On its corporate tax return, New Age Innovators Inc. will deduct its rent payments and operating expenses for the garage.

If you lease property to the corporation, have the directors adopt a board resolution approving a lease. Then have the corporation sign the lease as tenant with you, of course, as the landlord. This will be helpful in establishing the existence of a lease if the arrangements are questioned by the IRS.

C. Compensating Yourself

I've just discussed how you put money into the corporation. Now let's get to the fun part—how you take it out.

1. Salary and Bonuses

As a corporate employee, you can receive a reasonable salary plus bonuses which, for tax purposes, are lumped in with salary. (Many corporate owners prefer to pay themselves conservative salaries and then to reward themselves with a year-end bonus if it makes sense economically.) Salaries and bonuses are treated as business expenses of the corporation, which means that the corporation owes no tax on what it pays you. You, in turn, report what you receive as income on your personal income tax return just as you would if you worked for any other employer. The IRS has rules on how much salary is appropriate—the primary one is that the salary must be reasonable. This is a pretty loose standard and, as a practical matter, doesn't affect most small business people, because their businesses can't afford to pay them the sort of stratospheric salaries the IRS might consider unreasonable.

2. Interest on Loans to the Corporation

If you lend money or property to the corporation when it's underway in exchange for a promissory note, you'll receive interest on your loans. Hopefully, the corporation will repay you the principal amount of the loans as well. But you'll have to pay tax only on the interest you receive—not on the principal portion.

⚠️ **Minimum interest.** *Any loan between a corporation and an employee or stockholder for more than $10,000 must carry a minimum interest rate. The rate is based on U.S. Treasury Bill rates. The loan type also determines whether other requirements must be met. Check with your tax advisor for details.*

3. Fringe Benefits

Another way to profit from your investment in the corporation is through fringe benefits. For example, your corporation may purchase health insurance for employees and set up a plan under which the corporation reimburses employees for medical expenses not covered by insurance. Health insurance premiums and medical reimbursements paid by the corporation are tax-deductible business expenses for the corporation—and aren't taxable to the employee as personal income. By contrast, if you were to pay for medical expenses with no corporate help, only a limited amount would be tax-deductible on your personal income tax return.

S Corporations Note. S corporations are treated differently under the tax laws. Fringe benefits for an owner-employee who owns more than 2% of the stock of an S corporation are not given this favorable tax treatment.

4. Dividends

You've probably heard about corporate dividends paid to shareholders. This is another way that funds can be removed from a corporation for the benefit of its owners. Perhaps surprisingly, it is rarely done in a small corporation. Because the corporation can't deduct dividends as a business expense, dividends add up to double taxation. (This doesn't apply to S corporations; see Chapter 1, Section C.) The corporation is subject to tax on money paid as dividends, and then the shareholder is taxed a second time. To avoid this double taxation, it's much better to take money out of the corporation through the means previously discussed.

D. Do You Need a Lawyer to Incorporate?

It's possible to form your own corporation without professional help. Every day, many entrepreneurs do exactly that by using an incorporation kit. If you're inclined to go this route, check out *How to Form Your Own California Corporation* or *Incorporate Your Business: A 50-State Legal Guide to Forming a Corporation,* both by Anthony Mancuso (Nolo). These books provide information about incorporating, even if you decide not to do it yourself.

The obvious motivating factor for setting up a corporation on your own is to save on legal fees, which can range from $1,000 to $2,000 or more, depending on where you live. But be aware that there's a tradeoff: you're subjecting yourself to bureaucratic hassles and, unless you do your homework carefully, possible errors. The paper-filing phase, by itself, isn't all that difficult. But tax and legal liability problems may not be obvious to the do-it-yourselfer. And if you plan to issue stock to other than a few people who will work in the business or are close friends and relatives, securities laws can be troublesome.

Still, dollars are often precious to people just starting out in business, and you may decide that it's worthwhile to attempt to form your corporation by yourself. If you choose that route, it's a good idea to have a lawyer experienced with small businesses look over the final documents before you file them. (Chapter 24 discusses finding, hiring, and working with a lawyer.) You should be able to find a lawyer willing to do this at a fraction of the cost of having the lawyer handle the matter from beginning to end.

⚠️ **Beware of securities law.** *If you'll have a number of shareholders—especially people who won't be working in the business and who are not close relatives living in your state—consult a lawyer to see that you're in compliance with federal and state securities regulations. (See Section E, below.) While most small businesses are considered to be closely held corporations and exempt from these potentially complicated regulations, it's worth spending a few bucks to find out for sure. Anthony Mancuso's how-to-incorporate books, mentioned above, discuss this issue in detail.*

E. Overview of Incorporation Procedures

While there are differences from state to state, the basic procedures that you or your lawyer will follow in creating a corporation are these:

- Prepare and file the articles of incorporation
- Select a board of directors
- Adopt bylaws
- Elect officers
- Issue stock
- Decide whether or not you want to elect S corporation tax status.

In a moment, we'll walk through the incorporation process. Before we do, let's look at one additional step to consider before starting to incorporate: a preincorporation agreement. It may be unnecessary if you're planning a one-person corporation or if your corporation consists only of family members. Similarly, a preincorporation agreement is less necessary if you and your associates are incorporating an existing business or if you've done business together before. However, if you're going into business with relative strangers, putting your agreement in written form will help you avoid disputes later or, if an argument does arise, will provide a basis for resolving it through arbitration or litigation. (See Chapter 22.) Your written agreement should include these key points:

- the name of the corporation
- its purpose
- how much stock each person will buy and how he or she will pay for it
- what loans each person will make to the corporation and the terms of repayment
- what offices (president, vice president, secretary, treasurer) each person will hold
- what compensation each of you will receive
- what expense accounts each of you will have
- what fringe benefits will be available.

If the corporation is going to lease real estate or other property from one of the owners, the agreement can also outline the terms of that transaction.

Another major topic to cover in either a preincorporation agreement or a separate buy-sell agreement is what happens if a shareholder wants to retire from the corporation or gets sick or dies or just wants to sell his or her stock. Will the corporation or the remaining shareholders be obligated to buy the stock? How will the price be set? Can the stock be sold to outsiders?

These are difficult and important issues—and it's much better to think them through and arrive at a written agreement at the beginning of the corporation's life rather than wait until a crisis arises. If you don't have an agreement in place, you risk the pain of personal and business discord, and possibly even expensive, disruptive litigation.

I cover buy-sell agreements more in Chapter 5. *Also, you can easily put together a solid agreement covering shareholder issues if you consult* Business Buyout Agreements: A Step-by-Step Guide, *by Anthony Mancuso & Bethany Laurence (Nolo).*

Chapter 2 of *Legal Forms for Starting & Running a Small Business* contains a preincorporation agreement.

Where to incorporate—beware the Delaware myth. *Many people are sold on the notion that there's something magical about incorporating in Delaware. The reality is that the best state to incorporate in is the state where your headquarters is located. For the vast majority of small business corporations, that means the state where you live. If you incorporate in Delaware you'll still have to register as an out-of-state corporation to do business in your own state.*

F. Twelve Basic Steps to Incorporate

The following outline will help you understand how to go about forming a corporation for your small business. The procedure for incorporating is similar—but not identical—in every state.

Step 1. Choose a Name

In Chapter 6, you'll find more detail about selecting a business name. But here are a few basics about naming a corporation.

In most states, to alert the public to your corporate status you must include certain words in your corporate name, such as *Incorporated, Corporation, Company*, or *Limited*, or the abbreviations *Inc., Corp., Co.,* or *Ltd*. And there are certain words you can't use in your name; for example, in California, the words *National, United States,* and *Federal* are prohibited. In New York, you need the approval of a department of state government to use the words *Benefit, Council, Educational,* or *Housing* in your corporate name.

The quickest way to learn what words are required or prohibited in your state is to call or write to the office where you file the articles of incorporation—usually the secretary of state or corporation commissioner's office. In the few states where they're unwilling to help you, the best approach (short of calling your lawyer) is to go to a law library and check the state statute ("code") sections dealing with corporations. For more on law libraries, see Chapter 24, Section D. Because you'll probably want to consult these laws frequently, you may want to buy a set from the state or a private publisher.

Most states will reject a corporation name that's the same as one already on file or one that's confusingly similar to the name of an existing corporation. But even if the Secretary of State accepts your corporate name (or tells you it's available in a prefiling name reservation procedure), this doesn't guarantee your legal right to use it. An unincorporated business may already be using it as its trade name, or a business may be using it as a trademark or service mark to identify products or services. In short, as is discussed in Chapter 6, there is a good deal more to do to check out the availability of a particular name.

Before you file your corporate papers, check with your state's corporate filing office. Generally they can make a preliminary check and tell you if the name is available. If you expect some delay before the papers are actually filed, find out whether your state permits you to reserve a name. Many will reserve a name for you for a month or more.

What happens if you've got your heart set on a name but find that it's too similar to one already in use? One approach is to change it slightly. Most state's name records are computerized, and often a fairly small modification will turn rejection to approval. Or you can ask the owners of the other business to let you use the similar name. In many states you can use such a name if you get the written consent of the corporation that was established earlier.

In many states, a corporation can do business under an assumed or fictitious name. For example, if you incorporate as Miller Manufacturing Company but want to market some of your products under a more specific business name, you can simply file an assumed name certificate for Miller Appliances. Some states require that you file this paper at the same state office where you filed the articles of incorporation (such as the secretary of state's office). In other states, you file your fictitious or assumed name certificate in the counties where your company does business. And some states require that you also publish notice of your assumed or fictitious name in a newspaper.

Using your corporate name as a trademark. *If you plan to use your corporate name as a trademark or service mark for products or services, you won't want a name that's very similar to someone else's. As explained further in Chapter 6, even if your name were approved by your corporate filing office, it might infringe the other user's trademark or service mark.*

Step 2. Prepare and File Articles of Incorporation

As noted above, in some states articles of incorporation are called certificates of incorporation, charters, or articles of association. Here I'll stick with the term "articles of incorporation."

In many states, the secretary of state can give you a printed form for the articles of incorporation; all you have to do is fill in some blank spaces. In other states, you must prepare the articles of incorporation from scratch.

Below is an example of articles of incorporation for a California corporation.

SAMPLE ARTICLES OF INCORPORATION

ARTICLES OF INCORPORATION
OF

_____

ONE: The name of this corporation is _____

TWO: The purpose of this corporation is to engage in any lawful act or activity for which a corporation may be organized under the General Corporation Law of California other than the banking business, the trust company business, or the practice of a profession permitted to be incorporated by the California Corporation Code.

THREE: The name and address in this state of the corporation's initial agent for the service of process is:

_____

_____

FOUR: This corporation is authorized to issue only one class of shares of stock which shall be designated common stock. The total number of shares it is authorized to issue is _____ shares.

FIVE: The names and addresses of the persons who are appointed to act as the initial directors of this corporation are:

Name   Address

_____   _____
_____   _____
_____   _____
_____   _____
_____   _____

SIX: The liability of the directors of the corporation for monetary damages shall be eliminated to the fullest extent permissible under California law.

SEVEN: The corporation is authorized to indemnify the directors and officers of the corporation to the fullest extent permissible under California law.

IN WITNESS WHEREOF, the undersigned, being all the persons named above as the initial directors, have executed these Articles of Incorporation.

Dated: _____   _____

                                     _____

                                     _____

                                     _____

                                     _____

The undersigned, being all the persons named above as the intial directors, declare that they are the persons who executed the foregoing Articles of Incorporation, which execution is their act and deed.

Dated: _____   _____

                                     _____

                                     _____

                                     _____

                                     _____

While details vary from state to state, the typical articles of incorporation include:

- the corporation's name
- its purpose
- the name of the "initial agent for service of process" (sometimes called a registered agent or resident agent)
- the number of shares authorized
- the names and addresses of the incorporators.

The purpose clause may seem confusing—it's as if you're being asked to define what your business will do until the end of time. Fortunately, this isn't necessary, because the statutes in many states allow you to use very general language, such as: "The purposes of this corporation shall be to engage in any lawful act or activity for which corporations may be organized under the business corporation law."

If such a statement is permitted in your state, it's usually best not to be any more specific. This leaves you free to change the nature of your business without amending the articles of incorporation. It also helps you avoid questions of whether you're acting beyond the scope of your stated purpose if you go into a new business.

Most states require you to designate somebody as a resident agent or registered agent in the articles of incorporation. This is the person who is authorized to receive official notices and lawsuit papers. Normally, you designate the corporate president as this person. If you change the person named or if there's a new address, you need to notify the secretary of state's office by filing a proper form.

It may take a few weeks for your articles of incorporation to be processed by the secretary of state's office. If you need quicker action, check to see if expedited handling is available. In some states, you can file your articles of incorporation in person and have the filing process completed within a day. Sometimes, articles of incorporation sent by UPS, Federal Express, or other overnight means are treated as in-person filings and given expedited treatment.

If you need to sign contracts, such as a lease, even before the corporation has been formed, it's a good idea to state in the contract that you're acting on behalf of a corporation to be formed and that the contract is subject to ratification by the board of directors of the new corporation. Then, if for some reason the corporation is never formed or if the directors fail to ratify the document, you're free from personal liability. Here is sample language for such a lease.

> Landlord acknowledges that Martin Green is signing this lease on behalf of XYZ Corporation (a corporation to be formed) and that this lease is subject to ratification by the corporation's Board of Directors. If the corporation is not formed or if the Board of Directors fails to ratify this lease within 30 days of the present date, this lease will be void. In no event will Martin Green have any personal liability under this lease.

If this approach is not acceptable to the person with whom you're contracting, another possibility is to sign the contract in your own name—thereby assuming personal liability temporarily—but to specifically reserve the right to assign it to the corporation later, as in the sample that follows.

Incorporation Fees

Each state imposes a fee or a combination of fees for incorporating. Some states also require an initial tax payment. The total amounts vary widely, from $50 to $1,000. To find out your state's fees, call the corporate filing office (usually a branch of the governor's office in your state capital). In some states the information is also available online: try exploring your state's website via www.50states.com. (Click on the name of your state, then, when an information screen pops up, click on the large box containing your state's name to be taken to your state's own government website.)

Landlord grants to Martin Green the right to assign this lease to XYZ Corporation, a corporation to be formed. Upon Landlord's receipt of written notice that such assignment has been made, Martin Green will automatically be released from any personal liability under this lease.

Step 3. Elect the First Board of Directors

In some states, initial directors are designated in the articles of incorporation. In other states, the incorporator or incorporators choose the first board of directors. If this is the practice in your state, be sure to document the appointment of directors with a statement or certificate signed by the incorporators. This statement or certificate, which will be inserted into your corporate record book, may look something like the one below.

SAMPLE DESIGNATION OF DIRECTORS BY INCORPORATOR

ACTION BY INCORPORATOR
OF XYZ CORPORATION

The Incorporator of XYZ Corporation, a Pennsylvania corporation, designates the following people to serve as the initial Board of Directors of the Corporation:

Joyce Barker
Lloyd Epstein
Norton Phillips

Dated:_____   _____

Joyce Barker, Incorporator

Step 4. Adopt Bylaws

The corporate bylaws contain much more detail than the articles of incorporation. They spell out the rights and powers of the shareholders, directors, and officers of the corporation.

Typically the bylaws state the time and place for the annual meeting of shareholders, how much notice of the meeting is given, and what constitutes a quorum. There are also provisions for special meetings to consider issues so important they can't wait for the next annual meeting and a statement about what actions the shareholders can take by written consent without a formal meeting. Bylaws provide how many directors there are, how they're elected, what their powers are, and if and how they're compensated. Titles of the corporate officers (generally, a president, secretary and treasurer) are listed in the bylaws.

The bylaws may also cover matters such as who is authorized to sign contracts, who has the right to inspect corporate books and records (and under what conditions), the fiscal year of the corporation, and how the bylaws can be amended.

In a few states the incorporators must adopt the bylaws; in others, the directors must adopt them. And in still other states, you can choose between the two methods. If the incorporators adopt the bylaws, be sure to document this in a signed statement or certificate. If the directors adopt the bylaws (see below), reflect this action in your minutes of the first directors' meeting; or, if you don't hold a meeting, in a written consent resolution of the directors.

Chapter 2 of *Legal Forms for Starting & Running a Small Business* contains sample bylaws.

Step 5. Hold a Directors' Meeting

The directors must do a number of things at the beginning to get the corporation on the right track. Historically, corporations have recorded these actions in a document called "minutes of first meeting of the board of directors." These minutes were written in language reflecting a formal parliamentary procedure that really doesn't match the less formal style of most small businesses.

Fortunately, in most states, there's a streamlined method for accomplishing this. You or your lawyer can prepare a consent form to be signed by the board of directors such as the one below.

SAMPLE CONSENT FORM FOR DIRECTORS

XYZ Corporation consent of the board of directors

The directors of XYZ Corporation consent to the following:

1. BYLAWS: The attached bylaws shall be the bylaws of the corporation.

2. OFFICERS: The following people are elected to serve as officers of the corporation for the next year, or until their successors are elected:

    President:_____

    Secretary:_____

    Treasurer:_____

3. ISSUANCE OF STOCK CERTIFICATES: The President and Secretary are authorized and directed to issue stock certificates in the following amounts upon receipt of payment from the designated shareholders:

Name	Number of Shares	Amount to be Paid
1. _____	_____	_____
2. _____	_____	_____
3. _____	_____	_____

4. LEASE: The President is authorized and directed to enter into a three-year lease of space in The Village Green on the terms set out in the attached memorandum.

    Dated:_____,20_____
    Director #1

    Dated:_____,20_____
    Director #2

    Dated:_____,20_____
    Director #3

What actions should the board of directors take at its first meeting, either in formal minutes or through a consent resolution? The following are typical:

- adopt bylaws
- designate corporate officers
- approve the form of stock certificate
- adopt the first fiscal year
- authorize issuance of stock
- approve lease
- approve employment contracts
- adopt a shareholders' agreement (buy-sell agreement—see Chapter 5).

Step 6. Set Up a Corporate Bank Account

Remember, your corporation is a legal entity separate from its shareholders, directors, and officers. For that reason, the corporation needs its own bank account so that its finances can clearly be kept separate.

If you're incorporating an existing business that already has a bank account, I recommend that you start fresh and set up a new bank account for the corporation. The bank will ask for a corporate board of directors' resolution authorizing the new account and an Employer's ID Number. (Employer's ID Numbers are discussed in Chapter 8, Section A.)

If you decide to simply continue the old account, do the following:

- Find out the bank's procedures for changing a sole proprietorship or partnership account into a corporate account. Most likely, the bank will want your directors to adopt a specific resolution, using language the bank will supply. The bank will want to see your articles of incorporation and a copy of the banking resolution. You'll also be asked to provide your Employer's Identification Number (issued by the IRS). You may not have this immediately, and the bank will probably let you start using the account for the corporation if you assure them that you've applied for the ID number.

- Keep detailed records showing exactly how much money was in the account when it was changed over to the corporation. Also keep track of any checks that were written by your existing business but haven't cleared yet. These checks should be treated as expenses of the unincorporated business and deducted from the amount considered transferred to the corporation. Preparing and retaining these records will save you headaches a year or two down the road when you try to figure out exactly what was transferred to the corporation.

Step 7. Issue Stock

The corporation should issue a stock certificate to each shareholder. The certificate is evidence of the shareholder's ownership interest in the corporation. Filling out the stock certificate is simple. Your main legal concern is whether you need to do anything to comply with federal or state securities laws.

Federal securities laws are administered by the Securities and Exchange Commission (SEC). In addition, each state has its own law regulating the sale of securities, intended to protect passive investors—people who put money into a corporation but are not active in the day-to-day operations of the business.

The bad news is that both the federal and state requirements are very complicated. The good news is that, as discussed earlier, the typical small corporation—consisting solely of investors who are actively involved in the day-to-day operation of the company, and often their close relatives—is completely exempt from the complicated requirements. Nevertheless, some paperwork may be involved. For example, it's frequently advisable to give a "shareholder representation letter" to each prospective shareholder, even though it isn't strictly required under the state's securities laws. The letter gives you a way to confirm the purchaser's reasons for believing the transaction is exempt from the state's securities laws.

EXAMPLE: Edgewater Inc. has been formed to build and operate a restaurant on the shore of a scenic lake. Chester, a wealthy investor who has been a partner in three major deals with Todd, the president of Edgewater Inc., is going to invest $75,000 in the new corporation and receive 75,000 shares of stock. To qualify a stock purchase as exempt under the state's "limited offering exemption," the purchaser must be one of the following: an insider shareholder (a director, officer, or promoter of the corporation); someone who's had a preexisting business or personal relationship with the corporation or one of its officers; or a "sophisticated investor." (Sophisticated investors are those who, because of their business or financial experience, are in a good position to protect their interests when buying stock in a new corporation.) Chester qualifies as both a sophisticated investor and one who's had a preexisting business relationship with the corporate president. Todd prepares a shareholder representation letter reciting these facts for Chester to sign.

Californians can obtain sample shareholder representation letters and reliable information on how to prepare them for their corporation (as well as blank stock certificates), from *How to Form Your Own California Corporation,* by Anthony Mancuso (Nolo).

Before you issue a stock certificate, make sure that the corporation has actually received payment for the shares. For example, if the shares are being purchased for cash, the corporation should receive the money before issuing the shares. If the corporation is issuing the stock in return for a promise of future payment by the shareholder (a practice allowed in some states but not others), the corporation should have in its possession a promissory note from the shareholder. If property is being transferred to the corporation in exchange for stock, the person transferring the property should sign a bill of sale for the property at the same time the corporate shares are issued.

Step 8. Complete Any Initial Financial Transactions

Tie up any other loose ends relating to the financing of the corporation. As noted earlier, your corporation may borrow some of its startup money from friends, relatives, or other lenders. The corporation should issue written promissory notes as evidence that loans have been made. In addition, if you're leasing a building or equipment to the corporation, sign a lease.

Step 9. Set Up a Corporate Record Book

You can create a corporate record book in an ordinary loose-leaf binder. A more official looking way to do it is to buy a corporate record book from Nolo or a local stationer. These usually come with stock certificates and an embossed corporate seal.

The main items that you'll keep in the corporate record book are the articles of incorporation, the bylaws, the minutes of meetings (or consent resolutions), and the stock certificate stubs or ledger sheets showing who received the stock certificates and when. In many small corporations, shareholders prefer the convenience of simply leaving the completed stock certificates in the corporate record book even though each shareholder is, of course, entitled to possession of his or her certificate.

Step 10. Follow Through on State Government Requirements

Your state may require that you file documents in addition to the articles of incorporation. For example, in New York, you need to file a stock registration certificate certifying that you "keep a place for the sale, transfer, or delivery of your corporate stock" at a certain address (normally your corporate offices). In California, you need to file a notice of stock transaction within 15 days after your first sale of stock and "an annual statement of domestic stock corporation" within 90 days after you file your articles of incorporation. To learn about requirements in your state, contact your corporate filing office.

Step 11. Comply With the Bulk Sales Act

If shareholders transfer assets of an existing business to the new corporation in return for stock, there may be some special requirements. Six states—California, Georgia, Indiana, Maryland, Virginia, and Wisconsin—have bulk sales laws designed to prevent business owners from secretly transferring their business assets to another company to avoid paying creditors. These laws apply mainly to retail, wholesale, and manufacturing businesses. Basically, bulk sales laws require you to notify creditors that the assets of the business are being transferred.

Fortunately, state laws usually provide for some exemption or shortcuts when the assets are being transferred to a new corporation that will be taking over and continuing an existing business. A key element generally is that your new corporation agrees to take over the business debts of the existing company. If you're forming a corporation to take over and continue a business formerly run as a sole proprietorship or partnership, compliance with the bulk sales law should be relatively easy.

Step 12. File S Corporation Election

As discussed in some detail in Chapter 1, an S corporation is simply a corporation that decides to be taxed as a partnership. That is, it's not a separate tax entity like a regular corporation. Instead, the profits and losses of the corporation flow through to the individual shareholders who report them on their individual tax returns.

For purposes of incorporating under state law, the procedure is the same whether you're a regular corporation or an S corporation. But to become an S corporation, you need to file a form with the IRS. This is Form 2553, *Election by a Small Business Corporation*. All of the shareholders must sign this form.

If you want to have S corporation status during the first tax year that your corporation exists, you need to file the election form before the 15th day of the third month of your tax year. In other words, you have a two-and-a-half month window during which you can file the election. When does your tax year start? For a new corporation, your tax year starts when your corporation (1) has shareholders, (2) acquires assets, or (3) begins doing business, whichever happens first. If you miss the deadline, you have to wait until the next tax year to file the election form.

G. After You Incorporate

This chapter concentrates on steps you need to take to form your corporation. What must you do after incorporating? Obviously, you need to comply with federal and state tax filing rules. (See Chapter 8.)

Your business may also need to get business licenses and permits. (See Chapter 7.) And it's smart to buy insurance before you begin doing business. (See Chapter 12.)

In addition, corporations must file an annual report with the state's corporate filing office. Typically this is a form sent to you by the corporate filing office which requires you to update information about corporate officers and location. Simply fill it out and return it with the necessary fee. If you forget to send the form back, your corporation may face fines and penalties and may even be automatically dissolved.

H. Safe Business Practices for Your Corporation

Last week you were the sole proprietor of a catering business you called Feasts On The Go. Today you own all the stock of a new corporation, Feasts On The Go, Inc. In addition, you're the corporation's director, president, secretary, and treasurer.

Or maybe last week you and Emily were partners in a used record shop called Around Again. Today you each own 50% of the stock in a new corporation called Second Time Around, Incorporated, which is running the old partnership business. Emily's the president, you're the secretary-treasurer.

What has changed? On a day-to-day level, not much. You still show up at the same place each day and do the same kind of work you did before you incorporated. In fact, your before- and after-incorporation lives will probably be so similar that it will be easy to forget the fact that you're now working for a corporation that is a separate legal entity.

But forgetting can be risky. If you're careless about maintaining the separation between the corporation and yourself, you can jeopardize your tax benefits or your freedom from personal liability—the main reasons to incorporate in the first place. While it's rare for a judge to disregard a corporation and impose personal liability on a shareholder, it does happen. When it does, it's almost always in a small corporation where the owners have allowed the line between the corporation and the shareholders to get very fuzzy or disappear.

Also, the IRS has the power to decide that a corporation is a sham if you fail to maintain it as a separate legal entity. Consider the following actual case:

> For 15 years, Walter Otto ran an export-import business in San Francisco. Then he incorporated his business. He filed articles of incorporation with the California Secretary of State for "Otto Sales Company Inc." Next he invested $50 in the corporation. A few years later, the business became insolvent. A salesman sued for unpaid commissions, naming both the corporation and Walter as defendants. After a trial, the judge ordered Walter himself to pay the salesman over $18,000. Doing business through a corporation didn't protect Walter from personal liability.
>
> *What Did Walter Do Wrong?* Several things:
> - He never issued any stock certificates to himself or anyone else.
> - He contributed only $50 to the corporation as his "equity" in the business. (For more on equity and how to structure the financial side of a corporation, see Section B, above.)
> - He continued to use the same sales contracts that he used before he incorporated. These contracts said "W.E. Otto" at the top. At the bottom (for seller's signature), the contracts said: "W.E. Otto, by
>
> _____, Sellers."

In the judge's view, Walter formed the corporation solely for his personal convenience and did not treat it as a real entity. So the judge "pierced the corporate veil" to make Walter personally liable for the debt. *Shafford v. Otto Sales Company,* 308 P.2d 428 (Cal. App. 1957).

Here are two more cases in which the owners of small corporations were found personally liable:
- J.C. Chou formed Oriental Fireworks Inc., a corporation that grossed from $230,000 to $400,000 annually. Its assets, however, never exceeded $13,000, and the company never bought liability insurance. Gregory Rice was seriously injured by fireworks distributed by the corporation. He sued and was awarded $432,000. Since the corporation lacked funds to pay the judgment—and didn't carry insurance—the court ruled that J.C. was personally liable.

  J.C.'s Main Mistake: Failing to provide even minimally adequate funds to the corporation (in legal lingo, failing to adequately capitalize the corporation) or to carry proper insurance. *Rice v. Oriental Fireworks Co.,* 707 P.2d 1250 (Or. App. 1985).
- Dusty Schmidt and Terry Ulven were partners in a business called Western Oregon Christmas Trees. At Christmas time, the partnership rented tents from the Salem Tent and Awning Company to display their trees. Later, Dusty and Terry formed a corporation—Western Oregon Christmas Trees Inc. They continued to rent tents from Salem but didn't sign rental agreements or checks as corporate officers. When several tents were destroyed by a storm, Salem sued the corporation and was awarded a judgment of $12,500. The court ruled that Dusty and Terry also were personally liable for the judgment.

  Dusty's and Terry's Main Foul-ups: Dusty and Terry made a $2,000 down payment on the tents using a check from their previous partnership—not from the corporation. Also, the pair commingled (mixed together) personal and corporate assets and failed to keep corporate records. *Salem Tent & Awning v. Schmidt,* 719 P.2d 899 (Or. App. 1986).

Even though these cases had unhappy endings for the owners of the small corporations, doing business as a corporation isn't all that dangerous. There are several simple steps you can take to preserve your corporate status so that you don't have to lie awake nights worrying about personal liability. These steps are not time-consuming—and they make good business sense.

1. Put Adequate Capital Into Your Corporation

Put in enough money and other assets to meet your foreseeable business requirements. The amount, of course, varies from business to business. What's reasonable to start a video store that requires a considerable inventory of films, a retail location, and several employees may be vastly different than what's reasonable to start a typing service, which may need little more than a personal computer, printer, modem, and copy and fax machines. See if you can get a recommendation from your accountant or someone in the same business.

2. Insure Against Obvious Risks

Try to determine whether there's a substantial risk of customers or others being injured because of your business. If so, it's wise to obtain a reasonable amount of coverage. (See Chapter 12 for more on insurance.) There have been some cases—not many—in which a judge has felt that the failure of owners of a small corporation to buy insurance that was reasonably available was so reckless that it was a factor in disregarding the corporation and holding its owners personally liable.

> **EXAMPLE:** Eunice owns all the stock in a corporation called Roadside Enterprises Inc. The corporation sells and installs tires. It's obvious that an improperly installed tire can cause a serious accident. What if a Roadside employee forgets to tighten the lugs on a newly installed tire and the tire falls off, causing the driver to swerve into a tree? If the driver is killed, his or her family will probably sue Roadside. And if the corporation doesn't have reasonable insurance coverage (and hasn't set up a reasonable reserve fund), a judge could rule that Eunice has some personal liability—even though she wasn't even at the tire store when the employee was inattentive.

Basically, it's a matter of exercising reasonable business judgment. If your business involves the risk of injury and you can buy liability insurance at a reasonable price, I recommend that you do so. On the other hand, if affordable insurance isn't available—an unfortunate reality in some industries today—it's highly unlikely that a judge would find fault with the owners of the corporation for not insuring against the risks.

3. Observe Corporate Formalities

Another way to protect yourself from the possibility that your corporation could be disregarded by a court is to always take it seriously yourself. Issue stock certificates to the shareholders before your corporation starts doing business. Keep a corporate record book containing your articles of incorporation, stock records, bylaws, and minutes of shareholders' and directors' meetings. Comply with state law requirements that you hold annual meetings of shareholders or act by signed consent actions or resolutions. Either way you should document all actions taken, such as election of officers for the next year.

Conference Calls. If it's not convenient for all the directors to meet at the same place, many states allow them to participate through a conference call. Follow up by documenting the telephone meeting in writing as soon as possible and sending a copy to each director.

Keep in mind that the annual meetings are minimum requirements. While it's not necessary or appropriate to write up minutes or consent actions for every conference you have with your colleagues, if you take significant corporate actions during the year, it's wise to document them through minutes of a special meeting or a consent action form. Keep the minutes and consent actions in your corporate record book.

Here are some types of business activities that you should document with minutes of a directors' meeting or a signed consent action form signed by the directors:

- authorizing corporate bank accounts and designating who is eligible to sign checks and withdraw funds
- determining salaries and bonuses of officers
- contributing to pension and profit-sharing plans
- acquiring another business
- borrowing money
- entering into major contracts
- buying, selling, or leasing real estate
- adopting or amending employee fringe benefits plans
- applying for trademark registration.

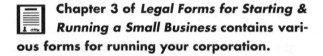 **Chapter 3 of** *Legal Forms for Starting & Running a Small Business* **contains various forms for running your corporation.**

4. Separate Your Personal Finances From the Corporation's

The corporation needs its own bank account. (See Section F, Step 6.) Don't use the corporate bank account to pay your personal expenses. Get salary checks on a regular basis from the corporation (deducting employee withholding taxes); deposit the checks in your personal account; and then pay your own bills.

If you use personal funds to pay business expenses—for example, you pick up a ream of typing paper while you're out for lunch—you can have the corporation reimburse you, but be sure the corporation keeps the receipt for the paper to justify the payment as a proper business expense.

To further preserve the distinction between you and the corporation, document all transactions as if you were strangers. If the corporation leases property from you, sign a lease. If the corporation borrows money from you, get a promissory note. If you sell property to the corporation or use your property to buy stock, sign a bill of sale or other legal document formally transferring legal title to the corporation.

5. Use the Correct Corporate Name

Suppose the name of your corporation is The A.B. Smith Fitness Store Inc. Use that full business name in all your business dealings—on your stationery, business cards, and phone book listings, on your signs, in catalogues, and on the Internet. Be careful not to use a different or abbreviated version (such as Smith Fitness Center) unless you file an assumed name certificate or fictitious name certificate as permitted by state law. (For more on corporate names, see Section F and Chapter 6.)

6. Sign Documents as a Corporate Officer

In correspondence and on checks, sign your name as William Jones, President, along with the full name of your corporation, rather than just William Jones. This makes it clear to those who deal with you that you're acting as an agent or employee of the corporation and not as an individual. Follow this practice on any other documents you sign, such as contracts, order forms, and promissory notes.

SAMPLE SIGNATURE OF CORPORATE OFFICER

JONES BAKERY INC.

By:_____

William Jones, President

In some cases, you may have to sign the contract or promissory note personally as a guarantor. For example, banks usually won't lend money to a small corporation without the personal guarantees of the principals, and some extra-cautious landlords may insist on similar guarantees for leases. But even if you have to accept personal liability for some corporate obligations, it's better to do this as a guarantor than as the main signer. The reason: The guarantee provides further evidence that you and the corporation are separate legal entities.

7. Assign Existing Business Contracts to the Corporation

If you incorporate an existing business (such as a sole proprietorship or a partnership), the old business may have contracts still in effect, which the corporation will take over. For example, maybe the prior business leased space and the lease still has a year to go. Or maybe you're a computer consultant and, as a sole proprietor, you'd just gotten started on a contract to design customized billing software for a medical clinic.

It's usually a good idea to formally transfer these contracts to the corporation. Generally, unless the contract expressly prohibits an assignment, you're free to transfer it to your corporation without getting the consent of the other party.

But bear this in mind: Unless you get that consent and a release of personal liability, or unless your contract already specifically permits you to assign it to a new corporation and be free from personal liability, you're still going to be legally responsible for performance of the contract. This means that the landlord can turn to you if the corporation doesn't pay the rent, and the medical clinic can hold you personally responsible if you don't deliver the software you promised.

Important tax note. *If your corporation will derive income from passive sources, such as rents, royalties, or dividends, or from the performance of personal services, get professional tax advice before you transfer contracts to the corporation. A transfer could lead to a personal holding company penalty—which could be quite substantial.*

To assign a contract, prepare a short document called "Assignment of Lease" or "Assignment of Computer Consultation Contract." A sample is shown below. Have the corporation agree to accept the assignment and to carry out the terms of the contract. From a business and legal standpoint, it makes sense to continue your business through a single entity—the corporation—rather than to do business simultaneously as a sole proprietor and as an employee of your corporation. Putting your eggs in one basket reduces the chances of blurring the distinction between the corporation and your personal business interests.

SAMPLE ASSIGNMENT OF CONTRACT

ASSIGNMENT OF RENOVATION CONTRACT

In consideration of the sum of $_____, receipt of which is acknowledged, Cecil Hardwick (d/b/a Hardwick Construction) assigns to Hardwick Building Company (a Nevada Corporation) all of his rights, duties, and obligations under his contract with Plaza Building Associates dated _____, 20____, concerning the renovation of the Plaza Building.

Hardwick Building Company accepts this assignment and accepts all of Cecil Hardwick's duties under the assigned contract.

Dated:_____, 20___

ASSIGNOR:

ASSIGNEE:

Hardwick Building Company,
A Nevada Corporation

By: _____

_____

Cecil Hardwick d/b/a
Hardwick Construction

Cecil Hardwick
President

***The Corporate Minutes Book, by Anthony
Mancuso (Nolo),*** *shows how to hold and
document necessary corporate meetings, and includes all forms on CD-ROM.* ■

CHAPTER

4

Creating a Limited Liability Company

C hapter 1 introduced the basic business entities—the sole proprietorship, the partnership, the limited liability company (LLC), and the corporation. This chapter tells you more about setting up an LLC.

As explained in Chapter 1, an LLC is often the best choice if you want to limit your personal liability as the owner of a small business. (Having limited liability means that being a member of an LLC doesn't normally expose you to legal liability for business debts and court judgments against the business.)

While forming a corporation will also give you and your co-owners (if you have any) limited liability, the structure of a corporation is somewhat more complicated than an LLC's. In even the smallest corporation, for example, you have a three-level organizational structure consisting of shareholders, a board of directors, and corporate officers.

It's true that the same people can fill all of these roles—in fact, in a one-person corporation, a single individual can do it all. But keeping track of what corporate hat you're wearing can be challenging when you have more pressing business matters to think about. And with an LLC, you may be able to avoid some of the legal and tax paperwork associated with a corporation. For example, an LLC needn't worry about getting signatures on stock subscriptions or issuing stock certificates or drawing up board of directors' resolutions—although an LLC whose members prefer a higher degree of formality are certainly free to issue membership certificates and to document all major company decisions. (See Section H8.)

And when it comes to taxes, a one-member LLC that prefers pass-through taxation (as in a sole proprietorship) rather than corporate-style taxation can remain what the IRS calls a "disregarded entity"—which means the LLC itself needn't file any tax documents at all.

In addition to requiring less paperwork, an LLC can be far more streamlined and flexible than a corporation. LLC owners can run their business with much less formality. For instance, the owners of an LLC (known as members) jointly manage the LLC (although they can instead designate one or more managers to manage it if they want to impose a separate level of management). And in most states, LLCs don't have to hold annual meetings of the members (although they can hold them if they choose). Finally, as discussed in Chapter 1, Section D, LLCs have the flexibility to choose to be taxed as corporations or as partnerships.

The paperwork requirements and legal rules governing LLCs are based on state laws. While these laws vary somewhat from state to state, LLCs do enjoy a surprising amount of consistency around the country. This chapter is based on the LLC state laws that are typical in most states. As you go through this chapter, you should keep in mind that the rules and practices for LLCs in your state may have some quirks that aren't covered here. It's your job to make sure that you're following the law in your state for creating an LLC.

 For comprehensive information and guidance on setting up an LLC: *Consult* Form Your Own Limited Liability Company, *by Anthony Mancuso (Nolo). Among other things, the book contains complete details on preparing your LLC articles of organization and LLC operating agreement. The book also contains a CD-ROM to help you prepare these documents. Also, Nolo's* LLC Maker *software, by Anthony Mancuso, walks you through the process of creating an LLC.*

A. Number of Members Required

Every state lets you form an LLC that has just one member.

B. Management of an LLC

As with any company, at least one person has to be in charge of managing the day-to-day business. In most states, unless you appoint one or more members or nonmembers to manage the LLC, you and all the other members are automatically responsible for managing the business. This is called "member-management." If you choose the other option and do appoint one or more people to manage the LLC, it's called "manager-management."

Chances are that your LLC will choose member-management rather than manager-management. That's because you probably won't want or need a separate level of management.

> **EXAMPLE:** Joyce, Phil, and Nora form Cyber Networking LLC, a small consulting firm. All three members are experienced computer experts who actively work in the business and participate equally in running it. They meet weekly to review new project proposals and to decide whether or not to take on the new work. They are all member managers. Nothing could be simpler.

There are situations, however, in which a manager-managed LLC is the better way to go. This is most likely to be the case if you have passive investors who will feel more comfortable if the LLC appoints an active managing member (or perhaps several managing members) whose duties are explicitly defined.

> **EXAMPLE:** Terry, Bill, and Chester form Wheel Wellness LLC, a bicycle repair business, built around Chester's years of experience in repairing exotic bikes. Terry and Bill contribute most of the money but, knowing little about bicycle repair, stay out of running of the business. Chester contributes a small amount of money to the LLC but his main contribution is his skill. Since Terry and Bill are passive investors, they agree that Chester will manage the company—

but they carefully spell out his duties in the operating agreement so he knows what decisions require input from the investors. All three are happy with their manager-managed LLC in which the lines of authority are clearly defined.

If your LLC chooses to designate managers, you'll need to specify this choice either in your articles of organization or your operating agreement (see below), depending on your state law.

C. Financing an LLC

Assets come into an LLC in two forms: equity and debt. Let's look at each.

1. Capital Contributions (Equity)

Ordinarily, you and the other LLC members will make an initial financial contribution to the business. In return, you'll each get a percentage (capital) interest in the LLC. Among other things, this capital interest determines the portion of the LLC assets each of you is entitled to receive if the business is dissolved or sold. Also, this percentage is frequently used to determine how profits and losses will be allocated while the business is in operation.

Under most state statutes, your capital contributions can consist of cash, property, or services—or the promise to provide any of these in the future.

⚠ **You may need to comply with securities laws.** *If an LLC membership is considered a "security," you'll need to register it at the federal or state level unless it's exempt from registration. Unfortunately, the rules for when LLC memberships are securities and when they're not haven't been well defined yet. Generally, if a member relies on his or her own efforts to make a profit—that is, the member actively engages in managing or working for the business—the interest probably won't be considered a security. It follows that most LLCs don't have to reg-*

ister before selling membership interests. If, however, a member relies on someone else's effort—that is, a member is a passive investor—that member's interest is probably a security, and must be registered.

Because the law on whether LLC interests are securities is in flux, you may want to see an experienced business lawyer before you sell membership interests in your LLC to people who won't be active in the day-to-day business. You may want to make sure that the membership interests are not considered securities or, if they are, that they're exempt from government registration.

Normally, a capital investment in an LLC is tax-free. You and the other members don't pay tax on the membership interests you receive, and the LLC doesn't pay tax on the cash or property it accepts in exchange. The tax effects of paying capital into an LLC are deferred until a later time; as an LLC member, you'll be taxed on any profit you make when you sell your interest or you dissolve the business.

> **EXAMPLE:** Wendy makes a capital contribution of $10,000 to her new pet supply business, Puppy Love LLC. As the sole member, she receives a 100% capital interest in the business. She pays no tax at this time. Five years later when Wendy sells the business and receives $50,000 after all expenses are paid, she pays tax on the $40,000 profit.

Attracting Financing for Your LLC

In the past, corporations sometimes had an edge over other business forms in attracting investment capital because the corporate stock structure easily accommodates the issuance of shares to investors. These days, however, a growing number of venture capitalists are investing in LLCs because LLCs can be taxed as corporations or partnerships and they offer flexibility in how they're managed.

For example, you can give majority voting power to a venture capital group in return for investing in your LLC. You simply amend your LLC operating agreement and issue voting membership interests to the group. What's more, if your LLC elects to be taxed like a partnership, the profits allocated to the investor-members won't be taxed twice (as corporate dividends are), but will pass through the LLC to the investors. They'll then report and pay taxes on the profits on their individual income tax returns.

2. Loans (Debt)

To supplement capital contributions, LLCs often borrow funds from time to time from their members or a member's family or friends. These loans help to increase the LLC's cash reserves or cover operational expenses. The money your LLC borrows isn't treated as business income—after all, it has to be paid back. As a result, neither the LLC nor the members pay tax on it.

These insider loans can benefit both the LLC and the lender. A loan payable with interest can result in an immediate investment return to the lender if repayments are made in monthly installments.

EXAMPLE: Phil's mother lends $10,000 to Phil's one-person LLC. The interest rate is set at 8%— less than Phil would pay to a bank but more than Phil's mother would earn from a government bond. The loan is repayable in monthly installments of principal and interest over a five-year period. Phil's mother receives a return on her money whether or not the LLC turns a profit in any given month or year.

To avoid IRS problems, your LLC should pay a lending member or other insider a commercially reasonable rate of interest—a rate that's close to what a bank would charge. When the LLC makes payments on the loan to the lending member, that member reports the interest payments received from the LLC on his or her individual income tax return, and pays taxes on them at the individual income tax rate.

Of course, the repayment of principal by the LLC to the lending member is simply a return of loan proceeds, and isn't taxable income. The LLC deducts the interest payments that it makes to the lending member as a business expense. These deductions reduce the net profit of the LLC, which in turn reduces the profits allocated and taxed to members at the end of its tax year.

D. Compensating Members

We've looked at how money gets put into an LLC. Now let's get to the fun part and look at how you take money out. We'll assume that your LLC has chosen the usual course and opted for partnership-style rather than corporate-style taxation (discussed in Chapter 1, and in Section G4, below).

LLC management can choose to pay active members a regular salary or a share of LLC profits. (If a member is inactive, the LLC can pay that member only a share of the profits—see directly below). If the LLC does choose to pay an active member a salary, the salary must be reasonable in light of the services performed by the member—the IRS has rules on what an LLC can pay to its members as salaries and what must be paid out as profits (see IRS Publication 535, Chapter 2).

A salary paid in return for the performance of services (one that is not tied to net income of the LLC) is classified as a "guaranteed payment." A guaranteed payment is taxed as ordinary income to the member, and the LLC will deduct it as a business expense before the net LLC income available for distribution to all members is computed.

EXAMPLE: Will and Peter each have 50% ownership interests in their home repair business, Fixer Upper LLC. Will works half time in the business and receives guaranteed payments (a salary) of $30,000 annually for his services. Peter works full time and receives guaranteed payments of $60,000 annually. During the year, the LLC earns $100,000 and has no expenses other than Will and Peter's salaries. After paying the salaries to the two members, the LLC is left with a $10,000 profit. That profit is allocated 50/50 between Will and Peter at the end of the year.

Now suppose you don't receive a "salary" for your services in the form of guaranteed payments during the year (or that you're an inactive member). In that case, your earnings are tied entirely to the net income of the LLC. An LLC's profits and losses are allocated to its members at the end of the LLC's tax year, according to the allocations in the LLC operating agreement.

Typically, the share of profits and losses allocated to each member is based on each member's percentage, or capital, interest in the LLC. So, going back to the above example, if Will and Peter didn't receive guaranteed payments for their services, the LLC's $100,000 profit would be allocated equally between them at the end of the tax year. The capital accounts of both Will and Peter would be credited with $50,000.

Sometimes members decide, and state in their operating agreement, that one or more members may receive what's called a "draw"—a periodic payment against future LLC profits. In this case, members do not have to wait until the end of the LLC's tax year to take profits from the LLC. Each member takes a draw each month or quarter; that draw, or distribution of future profit, is subtracted from the member's capital account. When profits are allocated to each member at the end of the LLC tax year, the member's capital account balance goes back up.

In tax lingo, profits that are allocated to an LLC member are known as the member's "distributive share." An LLC member must pay income tax on his or her distributive share whether it's actually distributed to the member or retained in the LLC coffers.

Self-Employment Taxes for LLC Members

As mentioned in Chapter 1, the IRS collects a 15.3% "self-employment" tax on the first $90,000 earned by a self-employed person and a 2.9% tax on earnings above that amount for Medicare alone. While owners of S corporations do not have to pay the self-employment tax on the profits passed through the corporation to them, according to proposed IRS regulations (which Congress has placed on hold), as an LLC member you would have to pay self-employment tax not only on money you receive as compensation for services, but also on all profits passed through the LLC to you, in the following situations:

- You participate in the business for more than 500 hours during the LLC's tax year.
- You work in an LLC that provides professional services in the fields of health, law, engineering, architecture, accounting, actuarial science, or consulting (no matter how many hours you work).
- You're empowered to sign contracts on behalf of your LLC.

The IRS says it won't challenge you if you use the proposed regulations to determine your liability for self-employment tax. If you fall into one of the three categories listed above, 100% of your income from the LLC will be subject to self-employment tax. Otherwise, you can apply the S corporation rules described at the end of Chapter 1.

E. Choosing a Name

Your LLC name will have to comply with state legal requirements. This usually means including an LLC designator such as "Limited Liability Company" or "Limited Company" in the LLC name. Many states allow abbreviations such as LLC or LC.

> **EXAMPLE:** You choose Andover Services as the name of your business. Depending on the state in which you're located, one or more of the following may be appropriate ways to indicate that your business is an LLC:
> - Andover Services Limited Liability Company
> - Andover Services L.L.C.
> - Andover Services LLC
> - Andover Services Limited Liability Co.
> - Andover Services Ltd. Liability Co.
> - Andover Services Limited Company
> - Andover Services Ltd. Co.
> - Andover Services L.C.
> - Andover Services LC.

You'll need to put the name of your LLC in the articles of organization that you'll file with your state's LLC filing office. If you pick a name that's already on file for an LLC in your state, your articles of organization will be rejected. The same thing will occur if your proposed name is not identical to but simply too close to one that's already on file. Some states will also cross-check your proposed name against names on file for existing corporations or limited partnerships.

By planning ahead, you'll avoid the annoying setback of having to choose another name. In many states, if you call the LLC filing office, the clerk will make an instant computer check and let you know if there's a name conflict. A few states will ask you to request the information in writing.

⚠️ **Name availability check is only preliminary.** *Until you've reserved an LLC name (as explained below) or filed your LLC articles of organization and had your filing accepted, your* *proposed name isn't yours to use. The information on name availability that you receive by phone or in response to a written request for a name check is just preliminary. Until you definitely have the name reserved or filed and accepted, don't spend money on business stationery, signs, or advertising using the proposed name.*

Be aware that even if your name is accepted by the LLC filing office, you may not have the full legal right to use that name to identify your products or services. The LLC filing office looks only at whether the name meets the requirements of the state LLC law and whether it's already in use by another LLC in the state. Some states will cross-check your proposed name against names on file for existing corporations or limited partnerships, but many will not even do that.

And, of course, legal conflicts may arise from other sources. Most important—especially if you'll use your name as a trademark or service mark to identify your goods or services—you'll need to make sure your proposed name isn't the same as or very similar to another well-known business name or trademark—Starbucks, Intel, or Borders, for example (see Chapter 6). If it is, the owner of the famous name will insist that you drop it; if you don't, the name owner will very likely go to court and win. To avoid this complication, you may want to do a national name search—and perhaps register your name as a trademark or service mark if the name is clear for your use.

To learn more about trademark law in general and name searches in particular (including how you can do a simple name search yourself): *Read* Trademark: Legal Care for Your Business & Product Name, *by Stephen Elias (Nolo).*

Suppose your LLC name is available but you're not quite ready to file your articles of organization. In most states, you can reserve the name for 30 to 120 days by paying a small filing fee. Many states have a preprinted form you can use for this purpose. After reserving a name, if you file your articles of organization within the reservation period, the name will be accepted by the LLC filing office.

You're not locked into your business name forever. *Your business can use a name that's different from the name used in your articles of organization. You can even use several alternative names. However, to use one or more alternatives with legal safety (in other words, to preserve the benefits of limited liability), you'll have to register each name as an "assumed" or "fictitious business name" at the state or county level or both. For more on this subject, see Chapter 6, Section B. It's also possible to change the name of your LLC by filing amended articles of organization.*

F. Paperwork for Setting Up an LLC

Setting up an LLC is simple. Typically, you must complete just two basic legal documents—the articles of organization (also called "articles of formation" or a "certificate of formation" in some states) and the operating agreement (called "regulations" in a few states).

Additional form for corporate-style taxation. *In the somewhat unusual event that you want to have your LLC taxed as a corporation, you'll also need to file a form with the IRS; it's IRS Form 8832, Entity Classification Election. See Section G4, below.*

1. Articles of Organization

In most states, preparing your articles of organization is surprisingly simple—especially if your LLC is a typical small business consisting of a handful of owners. Most states provide a printed form for the articles of organization; just fill in the blanks, sign the form, and file it with the LLC filing office. The task is made even easier in the states that include instructions for filling in the blanks.

Other states don't provide the actual articles of organization form but do furnish something almost as convenient: sample articles with instructions. You can prepare your own articles of incorporation by following the format and contents of the sample.

If your state is one of the few that provides neither fill-in-the-blank forms nor sample forms with instructions, you'll need to check your state's LLC statute to learn what to put into the articles of organization.

For step-by-step instructions on preparing articles of organization and other organizational documents for your LLC: *Consult* Form Your Own Limited Liability Company, *by Anthony Mancuso (Nolo).*

Typically, your articles of organization will not need to include anything more than the following information:

* *The name of your LLC.* (See Section E, above, for more on picking a name.)
* *The name and address of your LLC's initial registered agent and office.* You'll probably name one of your members as your registered agent—the person who receives official correspondence relating to the LLC and who gets served with lawsuit papers if someone sues the business. You'll generally use the LLC's business location or the registered agent's home as the registered office address.

* *Statement of purpose.* In most states, you don't need to describe your business activity—a general statement of purpose will suffice. Example: "Purpose: To engage in any lawful business for which limited liability companies may be organized in this state."
* *Type of management.* You usually need to say whether your LLC will be member-managed or manager-managed. The difference between the two is explained in Section B, above. In most states, if you don't specify the type of management, your LLC will be managed by all the members (that is, member-managed). Typically, you'll also need to give the names and addresses of your initial members and, for manager-managed LLCs, your initial managers. (Note: In some states, the type of management is specified in the operating agreement rather than the articles.)
* *Principal place of business.* You'll give the address of your main business location. For most small businesses, it's also the only location.
* *Duration of the LLC.* In many states, your articles must specify how long your LLC will be active. You may be able to choose between a "perpetual" (unlimited) duration or a specific number of years. Some states put an upper limit on the number of years you can choose—30 or 50 years, for example. These statutory limits should cause no problem because when the time is up, you or your LLC successors can extend the life of the business for another long term of years.
* *Signatures of people forming the LLC.* Usually, state law allows one person to sign the articles as the organizer of the LLC. But if your LLC is member-managed, you'll probably choose to have all the initial members sign the articles of organization to give everyone a sense of participation.

After preparing your articles, you file them with your state's LLC filing office—usually the secretary of state, located in your state's capital city. In a few states, before or after you file your articles of organization, you may need to put a legal notice in a local newspaper stating your intention to form an LLC.

⚠ There may be special requirements for licensed professionals. *In many states, if you're a licensed professional, you'll need to comply with additional rules for starting an LLC. For example, you may have to file special articles of organization for a professional LLC, and you may have to end your LLC name with special words or initials such as "Professional Limited Liability Company" or "PLLC." In a few states, such as California, many types of professionals, such as accountants, doctors, and physical therapists, to name a few, are not allowed to form LLCs. For more on professional LLCs, see Chapter 1, Section F2b.*

2. Operating Agreement

Once you've filed your LLC articles of organization with your state's LLC filing office and the document has been accepted, you're officially in business. But if you have more than one member, don't overlook another important piece of LLC paperwork: the operating agreement.

Although you can usually omit this document for a one-person LLC (except see "Ask your tax advisor about allocating goodwill payments in your operating agreement," below), it's very important to have one if your LLC has two or more members.

 Ask your tax advisor about allocating goodwill payments in your operating agreement. *If you plan to sell your LLC membership interest in the future, you may wish to specifically provide in your LLC operating agreement that part of the buyout price includes a reasonable payment for the selling member's share of the business's goodwill. (Goodwill is an intangible factor—often based on brand recognition or business reputation—that makes a business worth more than just the value of its physical assets.) You're probably aware that it's better to have income taxed as a capital gain rather than as ordinary income. By including such a goodwill allocation in an operating agreement, you ensure that the portion of the buyout price attributed to goodwill will be treated as a capital asset. This will save the selling member from having to pay tax on it at the higher, ordinary income tax rates. For this reason, if you set up a one-person LLC, you may want to create an operating agreement just for the purpose of making a goodwill allocation. See your tax advisor, as this is a complicated area of business tax law.*

The operating agreement serves a function similar to partnership agreements (Chapter 2) and corporate bylaws (Chapter 3). It sets the rules for how the owners will run th(9business and it defines their rights and responsibilities, such as the members' voting power and right to profits.

In a typical operating agreement for a member-managed LLC, provisions covering the following subjects are usually included:

- *Capital provisions.* One of the most important parts of an operating agreement sets forth how much money or property each member will contribute to the LLC and what additional contributions may later be required.
- *How a member's percentage interest is determined.* The operating agreement should state how members' percentage (capital) interests are computed. Typically a member's percentage interest will be based on how a member's capital account compares to the total of all

members' capital accounts. So if Ed has $25,000 in his capital account and the total of all capital accounts is $100,000, then Ed's percentage interest is 25%.

Capital Accounts Explained

In bookkeeping speak, a member's capital account represents the current value of that member's percentage of ownership interest.

When an LLC member contributes cash or property to the LLC, the member's capital account is credited with the cash amount or fair market value of the property contributed. Later, when profits are allocated at the end of the LLC tax year, the member's capital account balance goes up (the business owes the member this money); as distributions of profits are made, the capital account balance goes down (the business no longer owes this money to the member).

The capital account balance is also the amount of LLC assets that a member expects to be paid if the company is liquidated and split up among the members (assuming there's sufficient cash or other assets left after all creditors have been paid).

- *Type of management*. Your agreement may need to specify whether your LLC will be member-managed or manager-managed. Most small LLCs will opt for member-management, and in the majority of states, if you don't specify your choice, the law says that your LLC will be managed by all the members (that is, member-managed). Typically, you'll also need to give the names and addresses of your initial members and, for manager-managed LLCs, your initial managers. (Note: In most states, you can elect the type of management

either in your articles or your operating agreement.)

- *Membership voting*. Your agreement should also specify how issues will be voted on and decided. In the case of a member-managed LLC, you'll probably want a simple majority (51%) of membership interests to decide most issues, but you can also provide for a larger majority (two-thirds, for example) to decide some matters. You can also provide for per capita voting, where one member is given one vote.
- *Profits and losses*. Explain how profits and losses will be allocated to members. Typically, it will be on the basis of each member's percentage (capital) interest in the LLC.
- *Distribution of money*. You may decide to put language in your operating agreement spelling out who will decide if and when LLC profits will be distributed to members. For example, you might provide that all members must agree on a distribution or, perhaps, tfy4 a majority of members can make that decision.
- *Tax election*. As noted above, an LLC is taxed as a partnership unless it elects to be taxed as a corporation. It's a good idea to state in your operating agreement how the LLC will be taxed initially.
- *Transfer of a membership interest*. Your operating agreement should say how a member can withdraw from the business and whether a member can transfer his or her interest in the LLC to someone else.
- *Addition of new members*. Explain whether new members will be allowed into the LLC and how—that is, by a simple majority, a larger majority, or a unanimous vote.
- *Buy-sell provisions*. Chapter 5 covers the important subject of what happens if a member dies, moves away, gets sick, or simply wants to get out of the business. Can the LLC force the departing member to sell her interest to them? How will the interest of a departing member be valued? While you can cover

these issues in a separate buy-sell agreement, it makes better sense for LLC members to deal with them in the operating agreement.

- *Other businesses.* Your operating agreement can provide, for example, that members are free to own interests in or work for other businesses that don't compete with the business of the LLC.

As mentioned above, most small businesses that operate as LLCs will prefer to have the business member-managed rather than manager-managed. If your business chooses the less popular manager-managed option, you'll need a special section in your operating agreement dealing with how managers are selected and replaced, and what authority they have.

 For excellent guidance on preparing your LLC operating agreement: *Consult* Form Your Own Limited Liability Company, *by Anthony Mancuso (Nolo). It contains complete details for preparing an LLC operating agreement whether your LLC is member-managed or manager-managed. The CD that accompanies the book makes the task even easier.*

Have a lawyer review your operating agreement. *If you prepare your own operating agreement, it's a good idea to have an experienced small-business lawyer look it over before you and the other members sign it. That will help assure that the provisions are internally consistent and that you haven't made any technical errors that can cause legal, tax, or financial problems later. A lawyer's fees for reviewing the operating agreement should be a fraction of what they would be if the lawyer drafted the document from scratch.*

G. After You Form Your LLC

Once your LLC articles of organization have been accepted by your state's LLC filing office and you've signed an LLC operating agreement dealing with such important issues as managing the business, allocating profits and losses, and transferring membership interests, you're ready to start doing business. However, there are a few additional actions that are either legally required or worth considering to put your new company on a sound footing.

1. Set Up an LLC Bank Account

Remember, your LLC is a legal entity separate from its members and managers. For this reason, your LLC needs its own bank account so that its finances can clearly be kept separate.

If you're creating an LLC out of an existing business that already has a bank account—for example, your sole proprietorship or partnership business is now going to be run as an LLC—start fresh by opening a new bank account for the LLC. The bank may ask for a copy of your articles of organization and your Employer Identification Number (EIN), which is issued by the IRS. (EINs are discussed in Chapter 8, Section A.)

If you decide to simply continue the old account, you'll need to check with your bank to learn their procedures for moving a bank account from a prior business to a new legal entity. Again, the bank will probably want to see your articles of organization and your EIN. You need to keep detailed records showing exactly how much money was in the account when it was changed over to the LLC. Also, keep track of checks that were written by your prior business but haven't cleared yet. These checks should be treated as expenses of the prior business and deducted from the amount considered transferred to the LLC. If you don't prepare and retain these records, you can wind up with one big headache a few years from now when you try to reconstruct exactly what you transferred to the LLC.

2. Complete Any Initial Financial Transactions

Tie up any other loose ends relating to the financing of the LLC. For example, make sure that the members deposit their initial contributions of cash into the LLC bank account. If a member transfers property—computer equipment, for example—to the LLC in exchange for a membership interest, the member should sign a bill of sale confirming the transfer of property to the LLC.

And if your LLC is borrowing startup money from friends, relatives, or its members, be sure to issue promissory notes from the LLC stating the interest rate and other terms of repayment.

Finally, if you or another member will be leasing space to the LLC, prepare a lease as if the landlord were a complete outsider.

3. Comply With the Bulk Sales Law

If members are transferring assets from a preexisting business to the new LLC in exchange for membership interests in the company, you may need to comply with your state's bulk sales law. These laws, currently on the books in six states (California, Georgia, Indiana, Maryland, Virginia, and Wisconsin), apply mainly to retail, wholesale, and manufacturing businesses. They are intended to prevent business owners from secretly transferring their business assets to another company to avoid paying creditors. Typically, under these laws, you have to notify creditors that the assets of the business are being transferred.

While the details of bulk sales laws differ somewhat from state to state, these laws usually have an exemption or shortcut that applies when you transfer assets from an existing business to a new LLC that will continue the business. Typically, to qualify, your LLC needs to agree in writing to take over the business debts of the existing company.

4. Inform the IRS If Your LLC Chooses Corporate Taxation

An LLC is normally taxed as a partnership (explained in Chapter 1, Section D). This means that for federal income tax purposes, the LLC itself does not pay a tax on its income. Profits or losses pass through to the individual members, who include their share of LLC profits or deduct their share of LLC losses on their personal tax returns. This is the route that the members of most LLCs prefer. If that's what you want to do, you don't have to let the IRS know. You'll automatically be treated as a partnership for federal income tax purposes.

The other tax option is to have your LLC treated as a corporation for tax purposes. Your tax advisor may recommend this if you expect your LLC profits will be substantial and the members are prepared to leave some of the profits in the business. The funds can be used in a later year, for example, to pay for a new building or the purchase of additional equipment. With corporate tax treatment, the income retained in the LLC is taxed at lower corporate tax rates (15% and 25% for taxable net income up to $75,000), instead of the top individual tax rates of 35% and 38.6% that might apply to income allocated to members of an LLC that has elected partnership-style taxation.

If your members want to have your LLC taxed as a corporation, the LLC will need to file IRS Form 8832, *Entity Classification Election*, within 75 days of the formation of the company. Otherwise, you'll have to wait until a later tax year to make the change.

For more on complying with federal and state tax filing rules, see Chapter 8.

H. Safe Business Practices for Your LLC

In a small LLC consisting of just one member or a few members, it's sometimes hard to keep in the front of your mind the fact that the LLC is a separate legal entity from you and the other members. You and your business are not the same. In the eyes of the law, you are an agent of the LLC. For example, when you sign contracts and other documents, you're signing them (or should be signing them) on behalf of the LLC and not as an individual.

Remembering this distinction between you and your LLC can seem especially burdensome if you've done business in the past as a sole proprietorship or partnership and have just changed over to an LLC. On the day-to-day level, it's really business as usual and, in many respects, nothing at all has changed. Yet, if you want to get the maximum protection from personal liability for debts of the business, you need to carefully observe the legal distinction between yourself and your LLC. Fortunately, as you'll see shortly, that task isn't as tough as you may think.

The reason it's so important to always treat the LLC as a separate entity is that if you don't, a judge may decide that you're personally liable for a business debt or that you have to pay a lawsuit judgment out of your personal assets. It's becoming clear that in cases involving LLCs, judges will follow the same rules that they apply to corporations and will hold LLC owners personally liable for business debts if the owners haven't respected entity formalities. (See Chapter 3, Section H, for some examples of what courts have done when corporations have been sloppy.)

So if you ignore the fact that your business is organized as an LLC, and you operate it more like a sole proprietorship or a partnership, you will needlessly face the risk of personal liability. It follows that many of the precautions that I recommend for protecting corporate shareholders from personal liability should help to shield LLC members.

1. Put Adequate Capital Into Your LLC

Put enough money and other assets into your business to meet business expenses that are likely to come up. If you don't, and there's a lawsuit, a judge may rule that the LLC is a sham—that it really isn't a separate entity from its owners—in which case you and the other members may be personally liable.

Each business has different financial needs. You can often legally fund a small home-based business such as a computer consulting operation on a shoestring. But opening a pizza restaurant would require considerably more money, since you'd need to lease space, outfit a kitchen and dining area, and hire employees. Your accountant should be able to recommend a reasonable level of funding for your LLC.

2. Insure Against Obvious Risks

Think carefully about whether there's a substantial risk of customers or others getting hurt because of your business. If so, it's a good idea to buy a reasonable amount of liability insurance coverage. (See Chapter 12 for more on insurance.)

In a few cases, judges have felt that the owners of a small corporation were acting recklessly because the corporation didn't buy liability insurance that was reasonably available. This recklessness played a part in the judges' decisions to hold the owners personally liable to people injured by the corporations' employees or products. It's likely the same principle will be applied to LLCs. So if liability insurance is available at a reasonable price, see to it that your LLC gets the proper coverage.

3. Separate Your Personal Finances From Your LLC's Finances

The LLC needs its own bank account (see Section G1). Don't use that account to pay your personal expenses. If you receive checks from the LLC for salaries or draws (see Section D, above), deposit the checks in your personal account and then pay your personal bills from that account.

If you use personal funds to pay business expenses—for example, you pick up a business book on the way home from work—you can have the LLC reimburse you. Be sure the LLC keeps a receipt for your purchase of the book to justify deducting the cost as a proper business expense.

To further separate you and other members from the LLC, document all transactions as if you were strangers. If the LLC leases a building from you, sign a lease. If the LLC borrows money from you, get a promissory note. If you sell equipment to the LLC, sign a bill of sale to formally transfer legal ownership to the LLC.

4. Use the Official LLC Name

Suppose the name of your LLC is Kitchen & Bath Designers LLC. Use that full business name in all your business dealing—on your stationery, business cards, and phone book listings, on your signs, in catalogues, and on the Internet. Don't use a different name or abbreviation (such as Kitchen & Bath Designers, without the letters LLC) unless you file an assumed name certificate or fictitious name certificate as permitted by state law. For more on LLC names, see Section E, above, and Chapter 6.

5. Sign Documents as an LLC Member or Manager

In correspondence and on checks, sign your name as Paula Smith, Member, or Paula Smith, Manager, along with the full name of your LLC, rather than just Paula Smith. This makes it clear to those who deal with you that you're acting as an agent or employee of the LLC and not as an individual. Follow this practice on any other documents you sign, such as contracts, order forms, and promissory notes.

SAMPLE SIGNATURE OF LLC MEMBER OR MANAGER

> **Whole Grain Bakery LLC**
> **By:** _____
> Paula Smith, Member

OR

> **Whole Grain Bakery LLC**
>
> **By:** _____
> Paula Smith, Manager

In some cases you may have to personally sign an LLC document or promissory note as a guarantor. For example, a bank typically won't lend money to a small LLC unless the members personally guarantee repayment, and a super-cautious landlord may want you to guarantee the lease. But even if you have to accept personal liability for some LLC obligations, it's better to do this as a guarantor than as the main signer. The reason: The guarantee serves as further evidence that you and the LLC are separate legal entities.

6. File Annual State LLC Reports

In most states, you're required to file a one-page annual report on a form available from the LLC filing office. Usually, the form is automatically mailed to you. You'll have to pay a small filing fee in the range of $10 to $50—although the fee is higher in a few states. To avoid losing your legal status as an LLC and your protection from personal liability, it's important that you complete the form and return it along with the filing fee to the appropriate state office.

7. Assign Existing Business Contracts to Your LLC

If you've been doing business as a sole proprietorship or partnership and are now switching over to an LLC, you may have some ongoing contracts that you'd like the LLC to take over. For example, maybe your sole proprietorship signed a five-year lease for business space and there are still two years left to go under the lease. Or maybe the partnership you established for your lawn maintenance business has several contracts in force to service the lawns of major businesses in a local research park.

It makes sense to transfer these contracts to your LLC. You usually can do this without getting the consent of the other party to the contract, unless the contract specifically prohibits an assignment. But be aware that if you do assign a contract to your LLC, you'll still be personally liable for complying with it. There are basically only two situations in which this isn't true. The first is when the other party consents in writing to release you from liability. The second is when the contract contains language allowing you to assign it to a new LLC or corporation and be free from personal liability.

Unless you fall into one of these two exceptions, the landlord in the first example will be able to turn to you for the rent if the LLC doesn't pay it. Or in the second example, the businesses that contracted for your lawn maintenance services will be able to hold you personally responsible if your LLC doesn't perform and the businesses have to pay a higher price to get the work done by someone else.

Tax rules on passive investments are tricky. *If your LLC will receive income from passive sources (rents, royalties, or dividends, for example) or from the performance of personal services, get professional advice before transferring contracts to the LLC. A transfer could lead to a personal holding company penalty—which could be quite substantial.*

SAMPLE ASSIGNMENT OF CONTRACT

Assignment of Contract

In consideration of the sum of $_____, receipt of which is acknowledged, WordSmith Associates (an Indiana partnership) assigns to WordSmith Media Consultants LLC (an Indiana limited liability company) all of its rights and duties under the contract with Smoke Stack Industries, Inc., dated

_____, 20__, for advertising, marketing, and public relations services.

WordSmith Media Consultants LLC accepts this assignment and accepts all of WordSmith Associates' duties under the assigned contract.

Dated: _____, 20__

ASSIGNOR:	ASSIGNEE:
WordSmith Associates,	WordSmith Media Consultants LLC,
An Indiana Partnership	An Indiana Limited Liability Company
By:_____	By: _____
Cynthia Cardone	Cynthia Cardone
Partner	Member

8. Record Keeping

If someone goes to court and asks the judge to disregard your LLC and hold you personally liable, you may be able to bolster your position if you can produce a record book that shows you've consistently treated the LLC as a separate legal entity.

This is clearly the case when someone seeks to get behind a corporation and hold the owners (shareholders) personally liable. (See Chapter 3, Section H.) That's because by law and tradition, corporations are expected to observe a number of formalities such as holding annual meetings and documenting meetings of the board of directors. The paperwork requirements for an LLC are minimal compared with those for a corporation. Still, you may want to hold periodic meetings and document important LLC decisions—especially if you have more than two or three members.

Depending on the degree of formality you choose for running your LLC, I recommend that you keep an LLC record book containing important paperwork, such as:

- the articles of organization
- the operating agreement
- a membership register listing the names and addresses of your members
- a membership transfer ledger showing the dates of any transfers of membership interests by a member
- membership certificates and stubs (if your LLC decides to issue certificates to members), and
- minutes of LLC meetings and written consent forms (if your LLC decides to hold formal

meetings or to get written membership approvals for certain LLC decisions—see discussion directly below).

Even if your LLC has decided to proceed with a minimum amount of formal paperwork, you should consider documenting the members' approval of the most significant LLC actions, including:

- authorizing LLC bank accounts and designating who's eligible to sign checks and withdraw funds
- borrowing money, from a bank or from an LLC member
- amending the articles of organization or the operating agreement
- entering into major contracts
- buying, selling, or leasing real estate
- electing corporate-style taxation or a tax year other than a calendar year
- authorizing distributions of profits to members
- admitting new members
- authorizing the LLC purchase of the interest of a departing member.

By staying on top of this simple paperwork, you'll have a paper trail of important LLC decisions that will help satisfy courts, the IRS, and others that you've attended to all the legal and tax niceties and that you've treated the LLC as a separate legal entity.

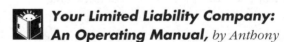 *Your Limited Liability Company: An Operating Manual,* by Anthony Mancuso (Nolo), explains ongoing record keeping requirements and provides minutes, written consent forms, and resolutions for a multitude of business decisions. ■

Preparing for Ownership Changes With a Buy-Sell Agreement

If you're in business with others, there's a good chance that there will be ownership changes as the years go by. That's true whether you organize your business as a partnership, a limited liability company (LLC), or a corporation. Ownership changes may be the last thing you want to think about when the business is brand-new. However, the fact is that many things can happen down the road—or maybe only a few steps away—to affect the ownership of your business. For example, you or a co-owner may:

- decide to move out of state to pursue a new line of work
- become physically or mentally disabled—or even die
- seek to buy out a co-owner's interest in the business, or
- want to sell to an outsider.

What happens then? Will the transition proceed smoothly and fairly? Or will there be discord and, possibly, lawsuits? The answer may depend on how well you've planned for the future. Without careful planning, the business itself may be in jeopardy. In an extreme case, all the time and money that you and the other owners have put into the venture may evaporate as the business falls apart.

Certainly, during the sunny, optimistic days when you're putting the business together, it's hard to focus on disruptive changes that you may face in the future. And it's equally difficult to do so when the business is humming merrily along. But planning ahead can save all involved from a ton of grief.

Most businesses with two or more owners should put together a buy-sell agreement. This principle applies regardless of the legal format you've chosen for your business. Partners in a partnership, shareholders in a corporation, and members of an LLC will all benefit from well-drafted buy-sell provisions.

First, let's get our terms straight. When I use the term buy-sell agreement, I'm not talking about a contract in which you promise to buy an outsider's business or an outsider promises to buy yours;

that's a separate topic, covered in depth in Chapter 10. The buy-sell agreement we're looking at here is a binding contract among the owners of your business that controls the buying and selling of ownership interests in that business. When a co-owner is thinking about selling or giving away his or her interest, a good buy-sell agreement steps in to give the continuing owners some control over the transaction. Often, the agreement will regulate who can buy the departing owner's interest and at what price, or sometimes whether the co-owner can sell at all.

Importantly, a buy-sell agreement helps assure that you and your co-owners aren't forced to work with strangers or other people you won't get along with. It can also help assure that if a co-owner leaves the business, that person will receive a reasonable sum in exchange for his or her ownership interest—or if a co-owner dies, that the heirs will be paid fairly.

Typically a buy-sell agreement also gives the business and its continuing owners a chance to buy out an owner who's stopped working for the business or has died. This eliminates the possibility that active owners will be forced to share profits with an inactive owner or an unsuitable new owner. Some buy-sell agreements also say that if an owner dies, the surviving owners can force the deceased owner's estate representative or inheritors to sell back the deceased owner's interest to the company or to its surviving owners. Similar provisions may apply when an owner decides to retire after a certain period of time, or becomes disabled and can't actively participate in the business.

 This chapter simply introduces you to the important concept of buy-sell agreements. *For comprehensive coverage of the subject and precise guidance on how to develop your own agreement, be sure to consult* Buy-Sell Agreement Handbook: Plan Ahead for Changes in the Ownership of Your Business, *by Anthony Mancuso and Bethany K. Laurence (Nolo). The book comes with a CD-ROM and a worksheet to walk you through the process.*

Check your agreement with an expert.
With the help of the comprehensive book and disk recommended above, you should be able to craft a respectable buy-sell agreement. However, as authors Mancuso and Laurence wisely note, even their book can't provide the depth of advice—especially in the tax and estate-planning realm—that a buy-sell or financial planner or tax expert can provide. And of course, their book can't customize an agreement for you that suits exactly your company's and each owner's individual needs. So if you do draft your own buy-sell agreement, be sure to take it to a small business tax or legal advisor before putting your finalized agreement into action.

A. Major Benefits of Adopting a Buy-Sell Agreement

If you *don't* have a buy-sell agreement, here are some things that can happen:

- You may be forced to work with and share control of the company with an inexperienced or untrustworthy stranger who buys the interest of a departing owner.
- You may be forced to work with the spouse or other family member of a deceased or divorced owner. While this might work out just fine, there's also a substantial possibility that the family member will lack the necessary business skills or the right personal qualities for working with you and the other co-owners.
- If you leave the company or die, you or your survivors may be stuck with a small business interest that no outsider wants to buy—and for which no insider will give you a decent price.
- You and your co-owners may argue with a departing co-owner or the inheritors of that co-owner over what price should be paid for

the interest that's changing hands. This can cause an angry deadlock that can wreak havoc on your business operations.

Now let's see how a buy-sell agreement can help your business avoid these situations.

1. Controlling Who Can Own an Interest in Your Company

An outsider who gains an ownership interest can disrupt the smooth flow of your business—especially in the case of major management decisions that require unanimous approval of the owners. Consider this example:

> **EXAMPLE 1:** Joe and Cindy form a small corporation. Each receives 50% of the corporate stock. They don't foresee problems down the road so they don't bother with a buy-sell agreement. A few years later, Joe and Cindy have a serious disagreement over how to expand the business. To avoid further hassles, Joe sells his shares to Albert, whom Cindy has never met before. The two quickly reach an impasse on management issues and the business comes to a standstill.

A buy-sell agreement can prevent this from happening, by giving the owners the power to prevent outsiders from buying in. Sometimes this is accomplished by giving the remaining owner or owners the opportunity to meet any outsider's offer for an interest in the company. This type of provision is called a "Right of First Refusal." To better understand its purpose, see what happens if Joe and Cindy had a buy-sell agreement:

> **EXAMPLE 2:** Joe and Cindy form a small corporation—and they wisely create a buy-sell agreement to deal with what happens if one of them wants to leave the business. A few years later

when they disagree on how to expand, Joe decides to sell his shares. Albert offers to buy the shares for $10 each. The Right-of-First-Refusal provision in their buy-sell agreement requires Joe to offer the shares to Cindy at the same price. Rather than share control of the business with a stranger, Cindy buys Joe's shares. The business continues to run smoothly and prospers.

A buy-sell agreement can also give the surviving owners the power to purchase the interest of an owner who's died if the surviving owners don't want the inheritors of the deceased owner to become co-owners of the business.

Who Doesn't Need a Buy-Sell Agreement?

Although a buy-sell agreement can benefit most small businesses, there are situations where one isn't essential.

You're the 100% owner of the business. If you have a one-person business, obviously you won't have much interest in an agreement that controls who may own interests in the company, since you can do that yourself. But consider the possibility that you may want to plan for the future by agreeing to sell the business to a valuable employee who is willing and able to take it over. In that situation, you might decide to sign a buy-sell agreement with the employee. This will assure the employee that he or she will be taking over some day, and you'll know that you or your inheritors will receive payment when ownership of the company is transferred to the employee upon your death.

You own the business with your spouse. If you've been married a long time and have a good, solid marriage, you probably won't need a buy-sell agreement. It's unlikely that either of you will want to leave the company unless you both do. And if one of you dies, the other one probably will inherit the ownership interest. On the other hand, if you haven't been married long, or your future with your spouse is unsure, a buy-sell agreement can make sense.

You own the business with one of your children. If you plan to transfer part or all of your business to your child, a buy-sell agreement isn't required. You can arrange the transfer through a regular contract or your will or a trust. But even here, you may want to sign a buy-sell agreement. It's always possible, for example, that your child will die or want to leave the business before you do. A buy-sell agreement can address this and other possibilities.

2. Providing a Guaranteed Buyer for Your Ownership Interest

As we've seen, a buy-sell agreement can protect your company by making sure that an outsider does not disrupt the business by becoming an owner without the approval of the owners. But a buy-sell agreement can also help you individually if you ever reach the point where you want or need to sell your ownership interest.

Obviously, it can be quite difficult to sell a less-than-100% share of a small business. There may be no market at all for a minority interest. A person interested in buying into a small business will normally not find it attractive to be in business with strangers and to have very little say in how the business is managed. This lack of a true market for your interest can be a problem for you and your family. The time may come when you want to leave the business but your co-owners may be unwilling to pay you a fair price for your interest. If that happens, you may be stuck with a share of the company you can't sell. The same thing can happen if your heirs inherit your piece of the company.

> **EXAMPLE:** Norm, Betty, and Phil form a small corporation, each receiving one third of the shares. They neglect to sign a buy-sell agreement. Three years later, Norm dies unexpectedly. His wife and two children inherit his shares. They'd like to sell the shares to raise money for college and other living expenses but can't find an outside buyer. Knowing this, Betty and Phil buy Norm's shares for a pittance, leaving Norm's family in dire economic straits.

A good buy-sell agreement can avoid an unfortunate outcome like this by requiring the company or the remaining owners to pay a fair price if your inheritors want to sell your interest in the business. You accomplish this by putting a "Right-to-Force-a-Sale" provision in your buy-sell agreement, which requires the company or the continuing owners to buy you out if you die, and sometimes under other circumstances. (The agreement can also provide that the company purchase life insurance on its owners, to fund the future purchase of a deceased owner's interest.) This can protect you and your inheritors from taking a financial hit if the company or continuing owners refuse to buy your interest at a fair price or from becoming embroiled in bruising negotiations over what will happen to your ownership interest.

Let's see how a buy-sell agreement could have changed the grim outcome for Norm's family in the above example.

> **EXAMPLE:** Norm, Betty, and Phil form a small corporation, each receiving one third of the shares. Wisely, they sign a buy-sell agreement containing a Right-to-Force-a-Sale clause, which kicks in if one of them dies. The clause requires the surviving owners to buy the interest of an owner who's died, assuming the estate representative, trustee, or inheritors want to sell it.
>
> Three years later, Norm dies unexpectedly. His wife, as representative of his estate, invokes the Right-to-Force-a-Sale clause. Since the agreement required the purchase of life insurance policies on each owner, Betty and Phil can easily buy out Norm's shares at the price in the agreement by using the insurance proceeds. Norm's wife spends the money for college expenses for the children and for other living expenses.

A buy-sell agreement can also require the company or remaining owners to buy your interest in other situations as well. For instance, you may want to retire or stop working, or you may become mentally or physically disabled. If you don't have a buy-sell agreement in these situations, there's no guarantee that you'll get a fair price for your business interest.

3. Setting a Fair Price and Providing a Workable Method for a Buyout

A well-prepared buy-sell agreement can set a price for interests in the business—or a formula for setting a price. This can eliminate lengthy disputes and unpleasant lawsuits about the value of an owner's interest. Equally important, the agreement can provide a mechanism for how the departing owner (or his or her family members) will be paid. Having to come up with a lump-sum payment for a departing owner's interest, for example, may create financial stress for the company or the remaining owners. As a solution, a buy-sell agreement may provide for payments to be made in installments over a number of years. Or maybe the payments will come from life or disability insurance that the company buys for each owner.

Be forewarned that figuring out a fair price in advance of a buyout scenario is no easy task. You and the other owners will be trying to arrive at a price that, years from now, will represent the true value of the company. You can't know today if your business will prosper in the years ahead or struggle to make a profit. And since there's no public market for small business interests, it's hard to make comparisons with interests in similar businesses—not that such information would be of great help anyway. Each industry and small business is different; comparative data from other companies has limited value. Still, picking a fair price— or a formula for setting the price—is essential if the buy-sell agreement is to do its job.

There are five basic methods for setting a buyout price—all of which are explained clearly and in great depth in *How to Create a Buy-Sell Agreement & Control the Destiny of Your Small Business,* by Anthony J. Mancuso and Bethany K. Laurence (Nolo). Typically, you'll set a price for the business as a whole—or a formula for determining that price, and the interest of an owner will usually be a percentage of that price. For example, if the entire business is worth $500,000, the interest of a 25% owner will be worth $125,000 for buy-out purposes. Let's briefly look at the most common methods for valuing a company for purposes of a buyout:

a. Valuation Method 1—Agreeing on a Fixed Price in Advance

Using this method, you simply agree on a price for the business as a whole and put that number in your buy-sell agreement. This agreed-value or fixed-price method is simple and certain. However, it's hard to pick a price that will reflect the value of the business throughout its life—the price you decide on today can quickly become outdated. So if you use this method, you will want to provide that the number will be updated each year.

b. Valuation Method 2—Book Value

The book value of a company is generally its assets minus its liabilities as shown on the company's most recent year-end balance sheet. Because the book value is basically a snapshot of the company's finances on a given day, it doesn't give information about the profitability of the business. Also, book value may not reflect assets such as customer goodwill that reflect the profit-making ability of the company. Compared to other formulas for determining value, the book value method usually results in the most conservative (lowest) value for a business.

c. Valuation Method 3—Multiple of Book Value

If a small business has been up and running for several years, its real value is probably greater than its book value. The multiple-of-book-value method takes into account intangible assets that add to the worth of the business—assets such as goodwill, patents, copyrights, brand names, and trade names.

You might decide that the price of the business should be, for example, two times its book value or three times its book value.

d. Valuation Method 4— Capitalization of Earnings

This method is best suited to established companies, since it measures the value of a business by its past profits. If your company is just starting out or hasn't been around very long, you can't use this method because you have no earnings history.

But after your company has produced a good profit for several years, you may want to shift over to this method. Here's how it works. You first determine the company's annual earnings, or profit, by subtracting the cost of doing business from gross revenues. Next you multiply the earnings by a number called a multiplier. The number you choose should depend, to some degree, on your company's industry and also on prevailing interest rates. Generally, you'll apply the multiplier to your company's average annual earnings for a "base earning period" of three years or longer.

e. Valuation Method 5—Appraisal Method

Your buy-sell agreement can simply provide that at the time of a buy-out, a professional business appraiser will establish the value of the business. Actually, you may want to provide for two appraisers. Typically, as part of the buy-out process, the buyer (usually the company or remaining owners) and the seller (for instance, the departing owner or the representative of a deceased owner's estate) each choose an appraiser to value the company. If they come up with the same price, that value is used. If they come up with close prices, the parties may be able to negotiate and agree on a price. But if the two appraisers are far apart on the price, the agreement may require them to choose a third appraiser

who will set the price. A drawback is that the appraisal method can be costly and time-consuming.

B. Where to Put Your Buy-Sell Provisions

You may be wondering what kind of document should hold your buy-sell provisions. Basically, you need to choose between putting the provisions in a separate buy-sell agreement and adding them to another document that may already be in existence— for example, your corporate bylaws, your LLC operating agreement, or your partnership agreement. Here are my recommendations.

1. Corporations

If you do business as a corporation, you can add your buy-sell provisions to your organizational documents—either your articles of incorporation or, more likely, your bylaws. Or, you can adopt a separate agreement, often called a shareholders' agreement in the corporate context. I believe that the latter approach—adopting a distinct agreement—is best. You're emphasizing the importance of these provisions, so that an owner can't later claim surprise when another owner asserts the terms.

If you follow this recommendation, it's a very good idea to refer to the separate buy-sell agreement in the bylaws. This can help head off a legal challenge by someone looking for a legal way to escape from the buy-sell terms.

Whichever approach you take, make sure your buy-sell provisions don't conflict with the existing provisions of your articles of incorporation or bylaws. You may want a lawyer to help you with this consistency check.

To make sure that potential buyers of your corporate stock as well as potential creditors know about the buy-sell agreement, add language to each stock certificate stating that the share is subject to the terms of a shareholders agreement. This statement is called a stock certificate *legend*.

2. LLCs and Partnerships

For a partnership—whether general or limited—the partnership agreement is the primary (and, usually, only) agreement among the business owners. Similarly, for an LLC, the operating agreement is the primary agreement between owners. So for partnerships and LLCs, I recommend that you place your buy-sell provisions in the partnership or LLC operating agreement itself. You'll want to make sure, of course, that the buy-sell terms mesh well with the other provisions of the agreement. A lawyer can help with this chore.

Perform a Consistency Check on Your Buy-Sell Provisions

Whether you adopt your buy-sell provisions as part of a separate agreement or add them to your bylaws, partnership agreement (discussed in Chapter 2), or LLC operating agreement (discussed in Chapter 4), make sure they do not conflict with the current provisions of those organizational documents.

Mostly, you want to check to make sure an existing provision in one of those documents does not prohibit, or impose addition rules on, any of the buy-sell provisions that you're adding. For example, if your partnership agreement prohibits the transfer of ownership interests to outsiders, but the buy-sell provision you want to use allows an owner to sell to an outside buyer under certain circumstances, you will want to amend your partnership agreement to delete the restriction on transfers.

⚠ Prevent legal termination of partnerships and LLCs. *One area that partnerships and LLCs need to cover in their buy-sell provisions is what happens to the company when an owner leaves (sells out, retires, or dies). Some state laws say that the part-nership or LLC automatically dissolves when an owners leaves unless the partnership agreement or LLC operating agreement says otherwise or unless the remaining owners vote to continue the company within 90 days. If the owners don't vote to continue the company in that period of time, the company is considered dissolved and must file dissolution papers with the state. To avoid risking the future of the partnership or LLC and having to take a vote after an owner leaves, as part of your buy-sell provisions state that the partnership or LLC continues without a vote of the owners when an owner leaves the company.*

C. When to Create a Buy-Sell Agreement

The key to a successful buy-sell agreement is coming up with a reasonable plan early on, before anyone knows who will be most affected by it. At the outset, when you're just getting started, your concerns and those of the other owners will be roughly the same because no one knows who will be the first to leave. Because at that early point no one wants to sell out, everyone has the same interest in crafting an agreement that's fair to everyone.

With a brand-new business, you and your co-owners can start by putting together a very simple buy-sell agreement. You can concentrate on giving your company or continuing owners the right to buy a selling or departing owner's interest at a fair price, or a price to be set according to a simple formula such as book or appraised value.

After you've been in business a few years, you may want to come up with a more complex agreement. The same holds true if your business's assets have become quite valuable or there's a concern about limiting estate taxes. While it's always a good idea to have a small-business lawyer look over your buy-sell agreement before it's final, it's especially important to get a lawyer's help in creating a more sophisticated agreement. ∎

Naming Your Business and Products

Trademark Terminology

Trademark: A word, phrase, design, or symbol that identifies a product brand—such as Compaq computers, Nike shoes, Kodak cameras, Xerox photocopiers, and Marathon gasoline.

Service Mark: A word, phrase, design, or symbol that identifies the provider of a service—such as Burger King (fast foods), Roto-Rooter (sewer-drain service), Kinko's (copy centers), and Blockbuster (video rentals).

Mark: Sometimes used to refer to both a *trademark* and a *service mark,* because the terms are nearly, but not completely, interchangeable.

Corporate Name: The name of a corporation as registered with one or more states. *Examples:* Time Inc.; Sony Corporation. The corporate name refers to the corporation only, and not to any product or services it offers.

Trade Name or Business Name: The name used to identify a business, as distinct from the product or service it offers. It may be the same as the product or service name; for example, Sony Corporation sells electronic equipment under the Sony trademark; McDonald's Corporation uses the service mark McDonald's on its fast-food service. Or the trade name or business name may be different— for example, General Motors Corporation sells cars under the Buick trademark.

Assumed Name or Fictitious Name: A business name different from the owner's name. *Example:* Laura does business as Coffee Express. Partnerships and (in many states) corporations may also use assumed or fictitious names. In most places, you must register a fictitious name. (See Section B3.)

Federal Trademark Register: A list of all trademarks and service marks registered with the federal government. To be accepted, a trademark or service mark must be distinctive and not confusingly similar to an existing mark. All states maintain trademark registers too, and some maintain service mark registers; preexisting federal trademark rights have priority.

N aming your business and products may not be as simple as it first appears. For one thing, you need to comply with legal procedures mandated by state law. If you incorporate, for example, or form a limited liability company, you must choose a corporate or LLC name acceptable to your state's business filing office. And all businesses—corporations, LLCs, partnerships, and sole proprietorships—must comply with laws dealing with the registration and possible publication of assumed names or fictitious names. (See Section B.)

Other legal procedures having to do with business names are not mandatory, but it nevertheless makes good sense to follow them. For example, before using a cool-sounding name—especially one that will also be used to identify your products and services—it's extremely smart to find out whether someone else already has rights to the name and, as a result, can legally limit how you use it or tell you not to use it at all. This normally involves at least two steps. To avoid a claim of unfair competition, your first step is to do a local name search to make sure that no local business in your field uses a similar name. Don't start Jimmy's French Laundry if there's already a Jenny's French Laundry a few miles away.

Step two involves making sure you gain maximum protection for your trademarks or service marks—names you'll use to identify your products or services. Especially if you're looking for comprehensive protection for a trademark or service mark, you'll want to first carefully check and then register the mark under federal and state trademark laws. (See Sections C, D, and E.)

Just how much effort and expense should you sensibly invest in protecting the name of your business, product, or service? The answer depends on many factors, such as: the size of your business, the size of the market that you'll operate in, the type of product or service, and your expectations for growth and expansion.

As a general rule, the more customers your business will reach, the more you need to be sure you have the exclusive right to use your chosen name within your business or product niche. For example, if you're starting a local computer repair service, you won't need as much business name protection as if you were planning to sell a new line of low-fat salad dressings in all 50 states. But be aware that because of the Internet and other electronic communication methods, the number of small businesses that compete with one another is rapidly growing, meaning the need to do in-depth name searches and to consider the implications of trademark law is also rapidly growing.

Business Names and Trademarks: They Are Not the Same

Legally, there are two main types of business names:

- the formal name of the business, called its trade name (Apple Computer Inc., for example), and
- the names that a business uses to market its products or services, called trademarks and service marks (Macintosh brand computer, for example).

Use of either type of business name can raise legal issues, but the most serious lawsuits tend to focus on the trademarks and service marks a business uses to market its products or services.

By being the first to use and register a trademark or service mark, a business can prevent another business from using the same or very similar mark. Laws that protect the integrity of trademarks and service marks are intended to prevent consumers from being unfairly confused about the source of products and services. A buyer should be able to rely on the fact that the source of a computer bearing the trademark "Macintosh" is Apple Computer Inc., which has registered Macintosh as a trademark.

Obviously, if you're choosing a name to use as a trademark or service mark, you need to conduct a full search to make sure no other business is already using that name as a trademark or service mark. What may be less obvious is that you need to make exactly the same kind of search if you plan to use your business name to identify your goods or services—as when Ford Motor Company markets cars under the brand name (trademark) Ford.

For a thorough discussion of business names: *See* Trademark: Legal Care for Your Business & Product Name, *by Stephen Elias (Nolo). That book discusses in great depth how to choose a legally protectable name and offers step-by-step instructions on how to file a federal trademark registration. Also check out the Nolo website (www.nolo .com) where you'll find extensive legal information on patents, copyrights, and trademarks.*

A. Business Names: An Overview

Complying with the few mandatory legal procedures for naming your small business is relatively simple. (See Section B.) For some very small, local businesses, meeting these requirements and doing nothing more may be adequate.

> **EXAMPLE:** Jeff wants to start a local word processing service called "Speedy Typing for All." He'll be a sole proprietor. Since his is a small, unincorporated local business, he is probably safe enough if he registers the name as an assumed or fictitious name. In most states, he will register it at the county level, but some states require registration at the state level and also require publishing the name in a newspaper. (See Section B for more on assumed and fictitious names.) Jeff probably doesn't need to spend time and money to register the name as a state trademark or service mark. With a descriptive name and a small local business, there's little likelihood that the customers of any other business would be misled, so there's not much

to protect. However, Jeff should check to be sure there are no other word processing services in his area using the same or a very similar name. If there are, Jeff should change his name or risk a claim of unfair competition. If Jeff wants to go the extra legal mile, he should check his state's Trademark Register and the Federal Register to see if other "Speedy Typing" businesses are registered. (See Section F for how to do a trademark search.)

Until quite recently, a wide range of local businesses—small retail stores, repair services, and craft studios, for example—didn't need to worry about registering a trademark or service mark. And to avoid possible claims that they were unfairly using another business's name, they could feel relatively secure if they checked for possible name conflicts in state and local business directories and Yellow Pages with no need to do a more formal state or federal trademark search.

But today, the rules of the game are dramatically different. The reason is that in the world of the Internet, mail order, and rapidly growing national chains, the idea of "local" isn't what it used to be. Today, even modest-sized businesses must consider taking name protection steps that used to be the sole concern of larger, more expansive enterprises. For example, you might think you have no problem if you're choosing a name for a shoe store in a small town. Think again. If you happen to pick a name that's similar to a shoe store that sells on the Internet, you are very likely to be accused of trademark infringement and probably forced to change your business name, even though the online store's headquarters is located 2,500 miles away.

Doing Business on the World Wide Web

Like many other business owners, you may decide to operate a website. If so, you'll need to select a domain name—a unique address that computers understand and customers can use to find you. The issues involved in choosing a domain name range from getting your hands on an available one to avoiding trademark lawsuits based on your choice of name.

A good domain name should be memorable, clever, and easily spelled. Unfortunately, many of the best names are already taken. To see if the name you have in mind has been registered, go to www.networksolutions.com. This site allows you to search for a particular name. For example, if you are starting a speed typing business, you might check "speedy.com." If you find that speedy.com is already taken, the www.networksolutions.com website allows you to peruse other possibilities. After you enter relevant keywords (such as quick, speedy, and typing), you'll get a list of related names that are still up for grabs.

Once you've found an available name, you'll need to make sure it doesn't conflict with someone else's trademark. If your choice will cause customer confusion between your company and another, you're safer choosing another name.

This is true even if the other business is halfway across the country. Once you've established a Web presence, you are in competition with businesses around the globe, and must address trademark issues equally broadly. A generic name such as "coffee.com" will keep you safest from lawsuits, but will also leave you unable to argue that other businesses cannot legally use a very similar business or domain name—you'll need to strike a balance.

After you've chosen an appropriate domain name, you can register it online with a service such as Network Solutions, at the website mentioned above. Some businesses register under more than one name, or register common misspellings of their names.

Courts are still grappling with the issues surrounding domain names and trademark law, and there's much more to know than I can cover here. For detailed and up-to-date information on choosing and registering domain names, as well as avoiding domain name conflicts, check out Nolo's free Internet Law Center at www.nolo.com. Also read *Domain Names: How to Choose & Protect a Great Name for Your Website*, by Stephen Elias and Patricia Gima (Nolo).

These days, about the only time you might be able to ignore thinking about trademarks and service marks is if you have a tiny, local business that uses your own name—or a very common name—to market goods and services locally. In short, if you plan to sell services using your own name (Harvey Walker Roof Repair) or if yours will be a one-person, home-based business such as a graphic design service (A+ Design), you're not likely to have a trademark problem.

But if your business is just a little bigger, such as a large camping equipment store (Wilderness Outfitters), or sells goods or services beyond a very local or industry-specific niche (Lamps.com Online Lamp Store), you really should take time to understand the basics of trademark law (Sections C, D, and E)—and conduct a name search to see if someone else in your field is already using your proposed name (Section F).

The reason to be absolutely sure you have the legal right to use your chosen business name is simple: You don't want to invest time and money in signs, stationery, and ads for your business and then get a nasty letter from a large company that claims a right to the name you're using and threatens you with a trademark infringement lawsuit. Just defending such a case in federal court can cost you upwards of $100,000, meaning that even if you're sure that you're in the legal right, you'll probably wind up changing your name just to duck the lawsuit—no fun, given the investment you've already made.

 If you decide that you want the protection of federal or state trademark registration: *See* Trademark: Legal Care for Your Business & Product Name, *by Stephen Elias (Nolo). You can probably handle the registration process yourself, but if you prefer to use a lawyer, the book will make you better able to take advantage of your lawyer's assistance.*

Relying on a State-Filing Search May Not Be Adequate

When you form a corporation or LLC, the state filing office will check to see whether your proposed business name is the same as or confusingly similar to one already on file. If so, your name will be rejected. But just because your name is accepted by the state filing office doesn't mean your business name is safe to use. That's because these offices don't check state or federal *trademark* registers. In short, even though a name may be available in your state to identify your business, you may run into costly trademark infringement problems if you also use it to identify your products and services.

EXAMPLE: Tony and Lars form a corporation that will design state-of-the-art sound systems for restaurants and jazz clubs. Their name—The Ears Have It Inc.—has been cleared by the secretary of state for their state. Can they now safely use this name as a service mark to market their services? No. When the secretary of state cleared the corporate name, it simply meant that the name didn't duplicate the name of another corporation in that state. Another company may have already been using the name as a trademark or service mark. This wouldn't show up in the secretary of state's corporate name records.

Since Tony and Lars are hoping to market their services in several states, they (or a name search company they hire) should do a thorough search, including checking federal and state trademark registers. If they don't, they may inadvertently find themselves in conflict with a company that's already using the name. If they find that their proposed name is clear, they should think about registering it as a federal trademark or service mark.

B. Mandatory Name Procedures

As mentioned, there are name-related legal tasks that every business must attend to.

1. Corporations

Part of the process of creating a corporation is choosing a corporate name. Most states require certain words or abbreviations in your corporate name, so the public can recognize that your business is a corporation. This puts them on notice that, in general, you're not personally liable for debts of the corporation. (See Chapter 1 regarding limitations on the liability of corporate shareholders.)

Each state has its own laws dealing with what words you must include in your corporate name, so check your own state's statute. Most states will send you an information packet along with a sample printed form for the articles of incorporation. Typically, the state will require one of the following in your official corporate name: *Incorporated, Corporation, Company,* or *Limited,* or the abbreviations *Inc., Corp., Co.,* or *Ltd.* If the name doesn't include one of the required terms, the state won't accept your corporate filing.

The law in your state will also likely list some words that can't be included in your corporate name or that can be used by only certain types of businesses.

Words That Are Typically Limited or Prohibited

Bank, banking, co-operative, engineering, trust, National, Federal, United States, insurance, acceptance, guaranty, pharmacy, credit union, medical, architect, indemnity, thrift, certified accountant, Olympic, surveyor.

This is by no means a complete list. For example, in New York you need the approval of a department of state government to use the words *Benefit, Council,* or *Housing* in your corporate name.

To learn about the prohibited or limited words in your state, start by calling the office where you file the articles of incorporation. This is usually the secretary of state or the corporate commissioner's office. If they can't or won't tell you, go to a law library or to Nolo's online legal research center (www.nolo.com) and look up the statute sections dealing with corporations.

Building Your Reference Library

Consider buying a copy of your state's corporation statutes; it will be handy for answering other legal questions as well. Of course, a lawyer can also let you know about your state's corporate name requirements.

Most states will reject a corporation name that's the same as one already on file or that's confusingly similar to the name of an existing corporation. If this happens to you and you've really got your heart set on the name you've picked out, there may be a way to get around the rejection. One approach is to change the name slightly or add something to it. Even a relatively small change may result in approval of the name.

Or in some states, you can use a similar (but not identical) name if the prior holder of the name consents in writing. The document in which the other company gives its consent will have to be filed with the office that accepts corporate filings. Obviously, you're most likely to get cooperation from the other corporation if your business involves a completely different product or service.

> **EXAMPLE:** Country Squire Inc. sells wood-burning stoves in the southern part of the state. It consents in writing to the use of the name "Country Squire Inn Inc." by a new corporation that will run a bed-and-breakfast in the northern part of the state. With the consent on file, the state corporations commissioner accepts the Country Squire Inn Inc. incorporation papers.

To avoid filing your corporate papers and then receiving word three weeks later that your name has been rejected, in many states you can call the government office that receives incorporation papers and ask whether your proposed name is available. They may give you preliminary clearance by phone if the records show that no other corporation in your state is using the same or a similar name.

⚠️ **Watch how you use the name.** *The fact that the state filing office accepts your corporate name doesn't assure that you have the exclusive right to use the name in your state. An unincorporated business may already be using it as its trade name in your state. Or another business—whether incorporated in your state or elsewhere—may be using the name as a trademark or service mark. Depending on the situation, the prior use often gives the user the right to legally prevent your use of the name if your use of the name would be likely to confuse customers. It's always prudent to check further to avoid conflicts with other users. (See Section F for how to conduct a name search. For how to protect a name as a trademark or service mark, see Section C.)*

If you expect some delay between the time you choose a name and the time you file your incorporation papers, find out if your state lets you reserve your preferred corporate name. Many states allow you to tie up a corporate name for two to four months by simply filing a form and paying a small fee.

2. Limited Liability Companies

The procedures for LLC names are very similar to the procedures for corporate names. When you prepare the Articles of Organization for your LLC, you'll need to include its name. If the proposed name—or one similar to it—is already in use by another LLC on file with the LLC filing office, your Articles of Organization will be sent back to you unfiled. To avoid this inconvenience, it's wise to check the availability of the name before you file the Articles.

Your LLC will have to include certain words or abbreviations that let people know its legal status. Examples include:

- Limited Liability Company
- Limited Company
- Ltd. Liability Co.
- L.L.C.
- LLC.

The list of words and abbreviations varies a bit from state to state, so check the law in your state to learn all the possibilities.

💡 **Here's a shortcut for picking a required LLC designator:** *Ending your LLC name with the words "Limited Liability Company" will meet the name requirements of all states except Florida and Iowa; in those two states, "Limited Company" or "L.C." is required.*

As with a corporation, your state law may prohibit you from using certain words in your LLC name—words, for example, that refer to banking, insurance, trust, or financial services. And again, as with a corporation, your state filing office won't accept your proposed LLC name if it's the same as or very similar to an LLC name that's already on file. Your state may also cross-check the name against the names of non-LLC entities—such as corporations and limited partnerships—that are required to register with the state. Your name will be rejected if it's too close to one of these.

For an in-depth discussion of choosing a name for your LLC: *See* Form Your Own Limited Liability Company, *by Anthony Mancuso (Nolo).*

3. Assumed and Fictitious Names

Sole proprietors sometimes choose to do business under names different from their own names, and partnerships usually select a partnership name other than the full names of all partners. Corporations and limited liability companies may also decide to do business under names different from their official corporate names. Depending on state law, these adopted business names will legally be called "assumed names" or "fictitious names." If your business uses such a name, you probably must register it.

a. Sole Proprietorships and Partnerships

If you're planning to do business as a sole proprietor or partnership, in most states you're required to file an assumed name or fictitious name certificate with the designated public office—usually at the county level—before you start doing business. Generally, there's a printed form for you to fill out, and you'll probably have to pay a small filing fee. In some states, the registration is good for a limited period, such as five years, and must be renewed. State law may also require that you publish notice of your business name in a local newspaper.

States require you to file the certificate for a simple reason: It lets members of the public know who is behind the name. If you don't register your assumed or fictitious name, you can have both legal and practical problems. For one thing, in many states, you may not be able to sue on a contract made or other transaction done under the business name. And in some states, you may be fined. In a number of states you can't open a bank account in the name of your business without filing.

Terminology

Some people refer to an assumed name or a fictitious name as a "DBA." That's short for "doing business as"—for example, Albert White doing business as Al's Cabinet Shop. On legal documents such as contracts and lawsuits, this may appear as: Albert White d/b/a Al's Cabinet Shop.

---

b. Corporations and LLCs

Most corporations and limited liability companies operate under their corporate or LLC name, which is of course on file with their state filing office. If, however, a corporation or LLC decides to do business under a different name, many states require it to file an assumed or fictitious name registration. This involves completing a simple form and sending it to the state filing office with a modest filing fee.

> **EXAMPLE:** Miracle Widget Manufacturing Company, a corporation, wants to do parts of its business under the name "Widco" and other parts under the name "Industrial Innovators." In many states, it will have to register both of these names as assumed or fictitious names.

It's important to use your correct corporate or LLC name, since this makes it more difficult for anyone to claim that your business entity is a sham (believe it or not, lawyers call this "piercing the corporate veil") and impose personal liability on you. (See Chapter 3 for more on corporate liability.) If you're going to do business under a name that deviates from the official name on your Articles of Incorporation or LLC Articles of Organization, it's essential that the name be properly registered. That way, you won't jeopardize the immunity from personal liability that's part of your reason for having a corporation or LLC.

If your state doesn't allow a corporation or LLC to register an assumed or fictitious name, there may be an easy way to reach this same end while complying with state rules. You can use a preferred business name in conjunction with your official corporate or LLC name.

> **EXAMPLE:** Contemporary Home Furnishings LLC is established in a state that doesn't allow registration of assumed or fictitious names. The company wishes to operate a lamp store called "Bright Lights." It does this by calling the lamp store "BRIGHT LIGHTS" and then in smaller print adding "a division of Contemporary Home Furnishings LLC" or by saying "BRIGHT LIGHTS, owned and operated by Contemporary Furnishings LLC."

This puts everyone on notice that the business isn't a sole proprietorship or partnership—so you continue to enjoy the benefits of limited personal liability.

When it comes to products and services, a corporation or LLC is completely free to use names that are unrelated to its corporate or LLC name (as long as these names don't infringe someone else's trademark, of course). In fact, this is common. Apple Computers, for example, sells products under the name Macintosh, and the Ford Motor Company sells Taurus automobiles.

C. Trademarks and Service Marks

A trademark or service mark consists of two parts. In reverse order, they are:

- The noun that specifies what kind of product or service you're talking about. *Examples*: automobile; health plan.
- The word or words that function as an adjective to identify a product or service as being different from all others. *Examples:* Buick automobile; Saab automobile; Blue Shield health plan; Kaiser health plan.

Think of these as the first and last names of products and services. The last name identifies the group; the first name uniquely specifies a member of that group. As such, the trademark is used as a proper adjective and is always capitalized.

Trademark law is the main tool that businesses use to protect the symbols and words that identify the origin of services and products. The basic premise is that the first user of a distinctive (that is, creative or unusual) name or symbol gets the exclusive right to use it. If you're the first user, you can make that right easier to enforce if you register the name or symbol with the federal trademark agency. The principal purpose of registration is to protect rights that already existed because you used the mark first. But registration can also confer other rights. For example, if you're using an unregistered mark without knowing that someone else used it first, federal registration can give you priority in areas outside the first user's market territory. The twin goals of trademark law are:

- to prevent businesses from getting a free ride off the creativity of others in naming and distinguishing services and products, and
- to prevent customers from being confused by names that are misleadingly similar.

From a legal protection standpoint, the best trademarks are coined words, such as Kodak or Yuban, or arbitrary words such as Arrow for shirts or Camel for cigarettes, which have nothing to do with the product. Nearly as good are suggestive trademarks—ones that hint at some aspect of the product. For example, Talon suggests the gripping power of a zipper.

Trademarks that consist of creative, unusual, or otherwise memorable terms are called "distinctive" and "strong." If you're the first to use such a name or symbol, you can legally stop others from using it in most situations.

Trademarks that consist of ordinary terms are called "weak," and competitors are free to use them. Merely descriptive words (such as Easy Clean for a cleanser) generally are not legally protectable. These weak marks can, however, become strong if they acquire a secondary meaning through prolonged usage. If that happens, they may be federally registered and may also be protected under the law of unfair competition if there's a local conflict with a similar mark. (See Section E, below.)

You can't acquire any rights in the name of the product itself; this is called a generic name. This means you can't adopt Bicycle or Refrigerator as your trademark for your version of those products. You can use the words as *part* of a distinctive name.

The law doesn't allow a business to claim the exclusive right to use descriptive words and generic names because competitors also need to describe their products. If you could tie up key words for your own exclusive use, your competitors would be unduly restricted in describing their goods. Also, descriptive terms aren't particularly memorable and don't further the purpose of trademarks and service marks.

D. Strong and Weak Trademarks

As noted earlier, with very few exceptions, only strong trademarks or service marks have the full protection of federal and state trademark laws. Remember, too, that trademark laws don't automatically protect a business name (the name of your company); to be considered a mark, a business name must be used to identify a product or service in the marketplace.

A trademark is considered weak when others can use it (or something similar) on products or services that don't compete directly with yours. Most ordinary trademarks are weak. *Examples:* Liquor Barn, Cuts Deluxe, Charlie's Auto Parts, 10-Minute Lube.

A trademark is considered legally strong when others can't use it or anything similar on related goods or services. There are two kinds of strong trademarks: ones that contain distinctive terms and ones that contain ordinary terms that have acquired distinctiveness through use.

1. Distinctive Terms

Distinctive trademarks are memorable, evocative, unique, or somehow surprising—for example, 7-Up, Lycra, or Cherokee apparel. The words themselves have little or no descriptive function; they serve to set the product or service off from others.

So if you're naming a service or product and want a strong mark, try for a name that is either unusual or used in an unusual way. A judge is likely to treat a distinctive name as a trademark or service mark and protect it from use by others—unless someone else has used a similar trademark on the same type of product or service first.

> **EXAMPLE:** "Buick" distinguishes a line of cars from others, and the name means nothing apart from its trademark use. It's a distinctive name. Conversely, "Dependable Dry Cleaners" merely tells you something about the business; it doesn't help you distinguish it from rivals who might also advertise their services as reliable or efficient. So the name would probably not qualify for trademark or service mark protection unless it had been in use for a long time and developed a sizable following—that is, a secondary meaning.

2. Ordinary Words

Generic terms can't be protected by trademark law; original and distinctive words can be protected. But what about other words used to identify products and services—ordinary words that are neither generic nor distinctive? This category covers place names (Downtown Barbers), surnames (Harris Sales), words that describe the product or service (Slim-Fast Diet Food) and words of praise (Tip-Top Pet Shop). Ordinary words receive limited legal protection as trademarks. It's more difficult to keep others from using them or something similar.

Even a weak trademark can acquire limited protection under unfair competition laws. For example, an ordinary name (a weak trademark) can be protected from someone else using the name in a confusing way. The law of unfair competition is generally based on state law (statutes and judge-made law) that supplements federal and state trademark laws. Owners of weak and unregistered names can get some relief from a rival's use of the identical name on the identical product or service in a competing market.

Weak trademarks can become strong ones through long use and extensive public familiarity with the mark. A trademark that starts out being ordinary or otherwise weak (like Dependable Cleaners) can sometimes, over time and through use, become identified in the public's mind with a specific product or service. When that happens, it can be transformed into a strong trademark.

> **EXAMPLE:** Chap Stick brand of lip balm was originally a weak trademark. It simply described the condition the product was designed to cure: chapped lips. But it became strong as advertising and word of mouth helped the public develop a clear association between the name and a specific product. Over time, the name developed distinctiveness based on familiarity rather than any quality inherent in the name.

Lawyers describe a trademark that has become distinctive over time as one that has acquired a "secondary meaning." McDonald's is another good example of a weak mark that developed a secondary meaning over the years—and now qualifies for broad protection.

E. How to Protect Your Trademark

What do the words aspirin, escalator, cellophane, and shredded wheat have in common? They are all former trademarks that have entered our language as product names. These words have lost their status as trademarks and are now generic terms. Other examples of former trademarks include harmonica, linoleum, raisin bran, thermos, and milk of magnesia. In each of these cases, a business lost its exclusive right to use a valuable trademark.

Here are some steps that your business can take to prevent this from happening to your trademark.

- Use your trademark as a proper adjective that describes your product. You'll notice that ads refer to a Xerox copier, Jell-O gelatin, and Band-Aid adhesive strips. If people continue to use the words Xerox, Jell-O and Band-Aid alone, these marks can easily go the way of other trademarks like nylon, mimeograph, and yo-yo.
- Always capitalize the first letter of your trademark. And at some place on each ad or package, say specifically that the trademark is owned by your company.
- If your trademark has been placed on the federal trademark register, consistently give notice of that fact by using the ® symbol. If a trademark isn't federally registered or is registered only by a state, you may use the letters "TM" or "SM" to give notice of your claims. You may not use ® unless your mark is in fact on the federal register.
- Take prompt legal action if other businesses use your trademark without permission. A trademark may become weakened or even generic if others use it to describe their prod-

ucts and you do nothing about it. You or your lawyer should send a letter by certified mail (return receipt requested) demanding that the infringement cease. If your demand is ignored, be prepared to go to court to seek an injunction—but first do a careful cost/benefit analysis to satisfy yourself that it's worth the expense.

- If you discover that a newspaper or TV program has improperly used your trademark, send them a letter. Keep a copy in your records as proof that you have consistently enforced your trademark rights.

F. Name Searches

There are compelling business and legal reasons to conduct a name search before you lock in the name of your business. As noted above, this is especially true if you choose an unusual or unique business name that will also be used to identify your products—Z Pop Inc., for example, will sell a new carbonated drink called Z. If someone else in your field is already using this name and may even have registered it as a state or federal trademark or service mark, you will really be an infringer if you start to use it (based on the fact that customers really are likely to be confused as to the source of two businesses' services and products). In such circumstances you can be forced to give up the name.

1. Conducting Your Search

Here are some self-help search techniques to see if others are using a business name like the one you have in mind:

- *Check state and county records where business names are filed.* To avoid a claim that you're unfairly competing with another local business by using their name, start with the records of your state's office where corporations and LLCs are registered—usually the secretary of state or corporations commissioner—as well as the state office (if any) that maintains a list of assumed or fictitious names for corporations, LLCs, partnerships, and sole proprietorships. In addition, if assumed or fictitious names are filed at the county or local level, check the lists for the counties and localities in which you plan to do business now or in the foreseeable future.
- *Check business directories and trade sources.* These include the phone books of all major metropolitan areas, general business directories, and trade magazines for your industry. A reference librarian should be able to help you. Also, take a look at all online search engines such as Google, Yahoo!, AltaVista, and Excite to see if anyone is using your name.
- *Check trademarks and service marks registered in your state.* The office that registers trademarks and service marks in your state should be able to tell you by phone if another business has registered a name that's the same as or close to the one you're thinking about. In some states, you may have to request the information in writing and pay a small fee for the search. It makes better sense, however, to mount an even broader search, checking on state registrations nationwide—a task made simple by using a computer database (see below).
- *Check the federal trademark register.* Since goods and services are widely marketed over

the Internet as well as through mail-order catalogues these days, your small business—even though you think it's local—may find itself competing with national companies. It makes sense to make sure you're not infringing on a trademark or service mark that's been federally registered. A large public library or special business and government library near you should carry the federal trademark register, which contains trademark and service mark names arranged by categories of goods and services. Check it for potential conflicts with your name. Also check the *Official Gazette* for the most recent filings.

Performing a full search of all registered and unregistered trademark sources involves time, effort, and some cost. Also, since there is considerable skill involved in doing an in-depth search, it often makes sense to engage professional help. But fortunately, there are three different levels of searches and a small, local business can often get by with a somewhat shallower search. The three levels are:

1. **A direct hit federal register search,** which compares your mark with identical or very similar federally registered (and pending) marks in one or more trademark classes. This is the quickest, cheapest, and most bare-bones type search. A direct hit search is especially helpful when you're trying to choose among several potential names or trademarks and want to narrow the field by discovering and eliminating obviously unavailable names or marks.

2. **An analytical search,** which compares your mark with all registered and pending marks (federal and state) that sound or look like your mark. The search also covers marks that mean the same thing or in some other way might lead to customers' confusion between them and your mark. This deeper type of search is more expensive and time-consuming than a direct hit search.

3. **A comprehensive trademark search,** which hunts for all possibly relevant unregis-

tered marks as well as for federal and state registered (and pending) trademarks. Because of its depth and breadth, this type of search is the trickiest to do well and, as a result, the most expensive and time-consuming.

For many businesses, especially those that plan to operate regionally or nationally, a direct hit search is only the first step to clearing a business name. If the proposed name is distinctive, a more thorough search—at least an analytical search—will be appropriate.

> **EXAMPLE:** Jamie is considering Geoscan as the name of her new company. She does a direct hit search and finds that no one else has registered that name. That's reassuring. But since Jamie plans to do business nationwide, she decides that she can't rely entirely on the direct hit search and needs to dig deeper.

Jamie has chosen a fairly distinctive name, so she is wise to take further steps. If your proposed name is less distinctive (a "weak" mark), or your business is small and local and you can live with the possibility that an undiscovered prior user will surface later, a direct hit search may suffice. A search firm can do a direct hit search for a reasonable fee. Or you can do the search yourself by using the federal government's trademark database, called TESS (for Trademark Electronic Search Service). You'll find it at the website of the U.S. Patent and Trademark Office, www.uspto.gov. On the left side of the home page under Trademarks, click "Search." To use TESS, you enter the business name you're interested in. The database will tell you if someone else is using the name, and if so, will give you the owner's name, the date of registration or application, and the goods or services it represents.

A deeper, analytical search looks for synonyms, phonetic equivalents, alternative spellings, anagrams (rearrangements of letters), and other similarities that may create a potential conflict.

EXAMPLE: Jamie embarks on an analytical search. She starts out by looking at the marks that immediately surround Geoscan alphabetically (it turns out that Geoport and Geoscope have been registered). Then she checks out all the marks ending in -scan and all marks with the sounds -eo or -osc in the middle. She also searches for all the synonyms she can think of (earthspan), and then anagrams (scanoge, canesog) and alternative spellings (gioscan, jeoscan, geoskan). This gives her a better idea of potential conflicts.

It's essential to perform this deeper search if you want to make sure your business name or mark isn't likely to be challenged as being confusingly similar to, or evocative of, an existing name or mark. While in theory it's possible for you to do an analytical search using the TESS database, I recommend you use another Internet resource, SAEGIS by Thomson & Thomson at www.saegis.com. True, even here, there's a considerable learning curve—and you will have to pay some fees. But the SAEGIS search engine is simply better suited to analytical searching than TESS.

Often, it's wise to go beyond a direct hit search *and* an analytical search. If you have a small, local business, you should, in addition to a direct hit search, check the Yellow Pages, newspapers, trade and product journals, and any other source that might show that another business is using the same or a similar name or mark locally.

If your business elects to do a more comprehensive search, you'd include not only an analytical search of registered and pending trademarks, but also an examination of Yellow Pages, trade directories, the Internet, product catalogues, and other industry sources. Because most disputes about names and marks are resolved in favor of the first actual user, you need to discover any actual use of the proposed name—whether or not it's officially registered.

Consider hiring a search firm. *You can reliably do a direct hit search yourself, but for an analytical or comprehensive search, a search firm is likely to produce more reliable results. It may be well worth the cost—especially if you have a strong and distinctive mark and will be investing heavily in promoting your products or services under that mark.*

Search firms—which, unlike lawyers, don't offer legal advice—generally charge as follows:
- *direct hit search (for identical marks)—from $30 to $100 per mark searched*
- *analytical federally registered trademark search (for similar or related marks)—from $85 to $300 per trademark*
- *common law search (for unregistered marks) —from $100 to $200 per mark searched*
- *comprehensive search (combining analytical federal, state and common law)—between $185 and $500 per mark searched.*

The ranges of rates reflect variations in search coverage, the type of report you get, the experience of the searchers, and economies of scale. Be on the lookout for firms that advertise an unusually low price to draw you in, but then add on charges so the overall cost becomes excessive. Shop sensibly to determine the true cost.

2. Analyzing Your Search Results

So now you've done your search, whether by hiring a search firm or performing the search yourself, and you have the results in hand. What do the results mean?

There are a few things you should look for when you read through the names that were found in your search. First, did your search turn up any names that are identical to the one you are using or plan to use?

Finding an identical name should make you pause, but doesn't automatically mean that you must scrap plans to use it. If the identical name is being used for a very different product or service from the one you are producing or plan to produce, then you have good reason to move forward with your plans to use the name and register it as a trademark or service mark. For example, just because a plumbing business in Coos, Oregon, calls itself Z-Pop doesn't mean you, in Arizona, can't use Z-Pop as the brand name for your soda pop. That plumbing business in Oregon is not your competitor and your use of Z-Pop for your soda pop will not likely confuse customers into thinking that your soda pop is related to that plumbing business.

On the other hand, if you find an identical name being used on an identical or closely related product or service, such as another soda pop product, then you really should consider choosing a different name. Even if the company using the name seems like a local outfit in a faraway place, it could have plans to expand its territory.

The second thing you should look out for is an identical (or very similar) name that is linked to a very famous company or product. This situation is often referred to, in trademark lingo, as dilution. Dilution occurs when a brand name has become so famous (like Coke) that not even noncompeting products or services can use the name. If it turns out that the mark you've had your eye on is famous

and highly marketed, don't touch it. Let it go. Find another name.

Finally, the third thing you should look for is a name that is very similar to the name you want to use. If you find a similar name *and* it is being used to market the same type of product or service that you are planning to create or offer, then you should seriously consider choosing a different name. How close is close? That is a very tricky issue and is often a matter of considerable subjectivity on the part of trademark examiners and the PTO. If you're not sure and really want to use the name, consider hiring an attorney specializing in trademark law for the sole purpose of helping you decide whether the two names are too close for comfort.

We've given you a few guidelines for evaluating your search results, but there is more to evaluating competing names than what we can provide in this chapter. If you think your situation is more complex, please consult the recommended book below.

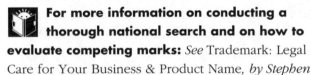 **For more information on conducting a thorough national search and on how to evaluate competing marks:** *See* Trademark: Legal Care for Your Business & Product Name, *by Stephen Elias (Nolo).* ■

Licenses and Permits

You'll probably need a license or permit—maybe several—for your business. In some locations, every business needs a basic business license. But whether or not that is required, your business may need one or more specialized licenses. This is especially likely if you serve or sell food, liquor, or firearms, work with hazardous materials, or discharge any materials into the air or water.

There are licensing and permit requirements at all levels of government—federal, state, regional, county, and city. It's not always easy to discover exactly what licenses and permits you'll need. But it's very important. You should thoroughly research this issue before you start a business, complete the purchase of a business, change locations, or remodel or expand your operation. If you don't, you may face huge expenses and hassles.

In a worst-case situation, you could be prevented from operating your planned business at a particular location—but still be obligated to pay rent or a mortgage. For example, what if you sign a five-year lease for business space and then discover that the location isn't zoned properly for your business? What if you buy a restaurant and then find out that the liquor license isn't transferable? Or suppose you rent or buy business space thinking that you can afford to remodel or expand it, without realizing that remodeling means you must comply with all current ordinances? You might have to pay for $15,000 worth of improvements to comply with the federal Americans with Disabilities Act (ADA) or $10,000 for a state-of-the-art waste disposal system.

Here are several examples that illustrate the types of licenses and permits many businesses need:

- Misook plans to open a new restaurant. Before doing so, she needs a permit from the department of building and safety for remodeling work and a license from the health department approving the kitchen equipment and ventilation system. She also needs a sign permit and approval of her customer and employee parking facilities from the city planning department. Finally, she has to get a sales tax license; even though in her state sit-down meals are not taxed, she must collect and report sales tax for take-out orders and miscellaneous items such as cookbooks.

- Leisure Time Enterprises, a partnership, buys a liquor store that also sells state lottery tickets. In addition to obtaining a basic business license issued by the city, the partners must have the state-issued alcoholic beverage license transferred to them. They also have to apply to the state lottery bureau for a transfer of the lottery license and to the state treasury department for a sales tax license.

- Electronic Assembly Inc., a corporation that assembles electronic components for manufacturers of stereo equipment, must obtain a conditional use permit from the planning and zoning board in order to conduct its "light manufacturing operation" in a commercial district. The company also needs clearance from a tri-county environmental agency concerned about possible air pollution and disposal of toxic chemicals. In addition, the new elevator must be inspected and approved by the state department of labor.

- Peaches and Cream, a new disco, has to get fire department clearance for its exit system and also must comply with the city's parking ordinance—which practically speaking means negotiating with the planning department for the number of off-street parking spaces the disco will provide for customers. The club also needs a liquor license from the state liquor control commission, a cabaret license from the city council, and a sales tax license.

- Glenda needs an occupational license from the state department of cosmetology before she can open up her beauty shop. Because she carries a line of shampoos, conditioners, and make-up, she needs a sales tax permit as well. In addition, because she's extending the front of her shop three feet into the front setback area, she needs a variance from the zoning board of appeals. Finally, because she's in an "historic preservation area," her sign must be approved by the local planning board.

If zoning requirements are too restrictive, you might decide to avoid the hassle and move somewhere you don't have to fight City Hall for the right to do business. Similarly, if building codes require extensive—and expensive—remodeling to bring an older building up to current standards, you might want to look for newer space that already complies with building and safety laws.

Each state has its own system of licensing as does each unit of local government. Obviously, it's impossible to provide a comprehensive list of every permit and license in the United States. Fortunately, I can give you some general principles and a positive approach to help you learn about and comply with the licensing requirements that affect your business.

⚠️ **Double check license and permit rules.** *When you investigate the type of licenses and permits you need for your business, check directly with the appropriate governmental agencies. Never rely on the fact that an existing business similar to yours didn't need a license or had to meet only minimal building code requirements. Laws and ordinances are amended frequently—generally to impose more stringent requirements. Often an existing business is allowed to continue under the old rules, but new businesses must meet the higher standards. Similarly, for obvious reasons, don't rely on the advice of real estate agents, business brokers, the seller of a business, or anyone else with a financial interest in having a deal go through.*

The Purposes of Licenses and Permits

Governments require licenses and permits for two basic reasons. One is to raise money; the whole point behind some licenses or permits is to levy a tax on doing business. In a way, these are the easiest to comply with—you pay your money and get your license.

The other basic purpose behind licenses and permits is to protect public health and safety and, increasingly, aesthetics. A sign ordinance that dictates the size and placement of a business sign or an environmental regulation that prohibits you from releasing sulphur dioxide into the atmosphere are two of many possible examples. Complying with regulatory ordinances can often be far more difficult than complying with those designed simply to raise money.

A. Federal Registrations and Licenses

Small businesses don't have to worry about federal permits and licenses, but all businesses must know about federal tax registrations.

1. Tax Registrations

On the federal level, there are two tax registrations that you should know about. The first is the application for an Employer Identification Number (Form SS-4), which should be filed by every business. The form is available online at www.irs.gov. If you're a sole proprietor, you may use your own Social Security number rather than a separate Employer Identification Number, but I generally recommend that even sole proprietors obtain an Employer Identification Number—especially if they plan to hire employees or retain independent contractors. It's one good way to keep your business and personal affairs separate. Employer Identification Numbers are covered in Chapter 8.

The second federal registration requirement applies if your business is a corporation and you want to elect status as an S corporation. In that case, you need to file Form 2553 (*Election by a Small Business Corporation*; also available at www.irs.gov). S corporations are discussed in Chapter 1, Section C2, and Chapter 3, Section A2; the requirements for filing Form 2553 are discussed in Chapter 8, Section B.

2. Federal Licenses and Permits

The federal government doesn't require permits from most small businesses, but it does get into the act when certain business activities or products are involved. Below is a list of the business operations most likely to need a federal license or permit, along with the name of the federal agency to contact.

Business	Agency to Contact
Investments advisors	Securities and Exchange Commission
Ground transportation business such as a trucking company operating as a common carrier	Federal Motor Carrier Safety Administration
Preparation of meat products	Food and Drug Administration
Production of drugs	Food and Drug Administration
Making tobacco products or alcohol, or making or dealing in firearms	Bureau of Alcohol, Tobacco, and Firearms of the U.S. Treasury Department

B. State Requirements

It may take a little effort to discover which business permits and licenses your state requires. Fortunately, small-business assistance agencies set up in every U.S. state can help you cut through the bureaucratic thicket. (See Appendix A.) Most offer free or inexpensive publications that list the required state registrations, licenses, and permits. Often the information is available online at the agency website.

Beyond contacting these general purpose agencies, it's wise to call all state agencies that might regulate your business and ask what they require. In addition, you can often get valuable information from the state chamber of commerce and from trade associations or professional groups serving your business, profession, or industry.

1. Licensing of Occupations and Professions

It should come as no surprise that states require licensing of people practicing the traditional professions, such as lawyers, physicians, dentists, accountants, psychologists, nurses, pharmacists, architects, and professional engineers. Most states also require licenses for people engaged in a broad range of other occupations. The list varies from state to state but typically includes such people as barbers, auto mechanics, bill collectors, private investigators, building contractors, cosmetologists, funeral directors, pest control specialists, real estate agents, tax preparers, and insurance agents. Since you can't always guess the occupations for which licenses are needed, you'll need to inquire.

Some licenses are taken out by the business entity (for example, your partnership or corporation), while others must be issued to the individuals who work in the business. For example, licensing laws for professionals—including lawyers, doctors, accountants, and architects—tend to place requirements on individual professionals rather than on the partnership or professional corporation that is the business entity.

The procedures vary, but to get a license for a profession or occupation, you'll probably have to show evidence of training in the field, and you may have to pass a written examination. Sometimes you must practice your trade or profession under the supervision of a more experienced person before you can become fully licensed.

For example, a real estate agent usually must work under the supervision of a licensed broker for several years before the agent is eligible to become a broker. Usually there's a formal application process, which may involve a background check. A license may be good for only a limited period, after which time there may be retesting before the license can be renewed. License laws for some occupations and professions require evidence of continuing education, usually in the form of short professional seminars.

2. Tax Registration

In all but the few states that still assess no taxes on income, chances are you'll have to register under your state's income tax laws in much the same way that you do under the federal laws. The state agency in charge (such as the treasury department or the department of revenue) can tell you what registrations are necessary. In addition, if you're engaging in retail sales, you may need to register for or obtain a sales tax license. There may also be registrations for other business taxes.

3. Employer-Employee Matters

As an employer, you may have to register with your state's department of labor or with agencies administering the laws on unemployment compensation and workers' compensation. As explained in more detail in Chapter 15, workers' compensation is a method of paying the medical bills and lost wages of employees injured in the course of their employment—regardless of who is at fault. Some state laws allow a business to be self-insured under some circumstances, but for most small businesses this isn't practical, so you'll have to carry workers' compensation insurance.

In addition, if your state has its own version of the federal Occupational Safety and Health Act (OSHA), your business may need to meet certain state-mandated requirements to protect your employees in the workplace.

Finally, a number of tax requirements relate to a business that has employees or works with independent contractors. For example, you'll need to get Employer ID Numbers from both the IRS and state tax authorities. And you'll have to withhold income taxes and Social Security taxes from the paychecks of employees, and report the figures to both the employee and the government.

With independent contractors, you need to report income annually on a Form 1099 which goes to the independent contractor and the government. For more on taxation, see Chapter 8. For more on employees and independent contractors, see Chapter 15.

4. Licensing Based on Products Sold

Some licenses for businesses are based on the type of products sold. For example, there often are special licenses for businesses that sell liquor, food, lottery tickets, gasoline, or firearms.

5. Environmental Regulations

Governmental regulation of environmental concerns continues to expand. As the owner of a small business, you may have to deal with regulators at the state or regional (multicounty) level. It's unlikely that you'll become involved with environmental regulations at the federal level.

Here are several activities that affect the environment and may require a special permit.

- *Emissions into the air for an incinerator, boiler, or other facility.* For example, if you're going to be venting your dry cleaning equipment into the outside air, you may need a permit.
- *Discharge of wastewater to surface or ground water.* For example, you may need a discharge permit if byproducts from manufacturing are being disposed of in a nearby pond. And you may need a storage permit if materials that you store on your site could contaminate ground or surface water.
- *Handling of hazardous waste.* If your business has any connection with hazardous waste, it's likely that the environmental agency will require you to at least maintain accurate records concerning the waste. You may need special disposal permits as well. Environmental regulations may also require you to register underground storage tanks holding gasoline, oil, or other chemicals. And if there's an underground tank on your business site that's no longer being used, you may be required to remove it.

⚠ **Permits aren't just for big factories.** *At first glance, the above list might suggest that only manufacturers or owners of large businesses need to worry about environmental regulations. Not so. Many small businesses need to obtain permits, or at least become informed about what they must do to avoid contaminating the environment. For ex-*

ample, if you create and sell leaded glass windows, you need to know whether you can dump your lead-laced wastewater down the nearby storm sewer or need a permit for some other means of disposal. Similarly, dry cleaners, photo processors, and others need to know the rules for handling and disposing of the hazardous substances used in their work.

C. Regional Requirements

Increasingly, some environmental concerns are being addressed by regional (multicounty) agencies rather than by an arm of the state or local government. If so, you may need a permit or license from that regional body.

1. Environmental Regulations

In many areas, control of air pollution is now handled by a regional (multicounty or state) agency that issues permits and monitors compliance. For example, in northern California, the Bay Area Air Quality Control District covers at least seven counties. A regional body with environmental responsibilities may also have jurisdiction over wastewater discharge or the storage or disposal of hazardous materials.

2. Water Usage

Questions affecting the use of water by a small business are usually dealt with at the local (city or county) level, but some issues may fall within the jurisdiction of a regional authority. For example, if your business is in a semirural area and plans to draw its water from a well rather than the public water supply, a regional health authority may test the purity of the water before you're allowed to use it. In scarce-water areas, a regional water management body may have authority to decide whether or not you may install a well or use an existing one.

Similarly, while regulation of septic systems typically is left to local health departments, in some areas permits may be under the control of a regional body.

D. Local Requirements

On the local level, begin by asking city and county officials about license and permit requirements for your business. A few larger cities that hope to attract economic growth may have a centralized office that provides this information. Otherwise, the city and county officials most likely to be of help are as follows:

- city or county clerk
- building and safety department
- health department
- planning (zoning) department
- tax offices (for example, tax assessor or treasurer)
- fire department
- police department
- public works department.

Nonofficial but often extremely helpful resources include local chambers of commerce, trade associations, contractors who have experience in building or remodeling commercial space, and people who have businesses like yours. You can also consult a lawyer who's familiar with small businesses similar to yours.

1. Local Property Taxes

Your city may impose a property tax on the furniture, fixtures, and equipment that your business owns. If so, you may be required by law to file a list of that property with city tax officials, along with cost and depreciation information. You may have to update this information annually. Sometimes there's also a tax on inventory—which leads many retail businesses to run a stock reduction sale a few weeks before the inventory-taking date mandated by the tax law.

2. Other Local Taxes

Some cities, especially larger ones, tax gross receipts and income. Check with the city treasurer for registration and filing requirements.

3. Health and Environmental Permits

If your business involves food preparation or sales, you'll need a license or permit from the local health department. The health ordinances may require regular inspections as well.

Whether you run a sit-down or a fast-food restaurant or a catering establishment, you can expect the health department to take a keen interest in the type of cooking equipment you use, the adequacy of the refrigeration system, and many other features of the business that can affect the health of your customers.

You may also run into health department regulations if you receive water from a well rather than a public water supply. In small towns or semirural areas, health departments routinely test well water for purity.

Also, where septic systems are used for sanitary sewer disposal, the health department supervises the installation of new septic systems to make sure that there's no health hazard. (As noted in Section

C, in some areas these matters are handled by regional rather than local authorities.)

Increasingly, local health departments are getting involved in environmental duties, including such things as radon tests and asbestos removal. Many other environmental problems, however, such as air and water quality, are still dealt with mainly at the state and regional level.

4. Crowd Control

If your business deals with large numbers of customers, you may need licenses or permits from the fire or police departments. These agencies are concerned about overcrowding and the ability of people to leave the premises in case there's an emergency.

The role of the fire department may overlap with that of the building and safety department in prescribing the number of exit doors, the hardware on those doors, the lighting to be used, and the maintenance of clear paths to the exits. The fire department will also be concerned about combustible materials used or stored on your business premises.

5. Building Codes

For anything but the most minor renovation (such as putting in track lighting or installing shelves), you're likely to need a permit—maybe several—from the building and safety department that enforces building ordinances and codes. Often, separate permits are issued for separate parts of a construction or remodeling project, including permits for electrical, plumbing, and mechanical (heating and ventilating) work. If you don't have experience in these areas, you may need a licensed contractor to help you discover the requirements for your construction or remodeling project.

Building codes are amended frequently, and each revision seems to put new restrictions and requirements on the building owner. Municipalities often exempt existing businesses from laying out money to retrofit their premises—at least for major items such as elevators, heating and ventilating systems, and overhead sprinkler systems. This is sometimes called "grandfathering"—slang for not imposing new rules retroactively.

Grandfathering can create surprises. You may look at space in an older building and figure that you'll have no problems in doing business there because the current business owner or the one who just vacated the premises didn't. But the prior occupant may have had the benefit of grandfathering language which didn't require him or her to bring the space up to the level of the current codes. A change in occupancy or ownership may end the benefits of grandfathering, and a new occupant or owner may be required to make extensive improvements.

An experienced contractor can help you determine the building and safety requirements that apply to a particular space—for example, a code section mandating that railings on outside stairs be 36 inches high.

If You Build or Remodel

For any building or remodeling project, it's essential that you learn the applicable rules. If your city uses all or part of the Uniform Building Code, get a copy of it.

Other municipal ordinances may be administered by the building and safety department or by another unit of local government. There's no uniformity in how the responsibility for administering these other ordinances is assigned. A large municipality or county might have several separate departments to act as the enforcing agency. A smaller city or county would probably leave everything to the building and safety department.

6. Zoning Ordinances

Before you sign a lease, you absolutely need to know that the space is properly zoned for your usage. If it's not, it's best to make the lease contingent on your getting the property rezoned or getting a variance or conditional use permit—whatever it takes under the ordinance to make it possible for you to do business there without being hassled by the city or county.

In some communities, you must get a zoning compliance permit before you start your business at a given location. Other communities simply wait for someone to complain before zoning compliance gets looked at. Keep in mind that by applying for a construction permit for remodeling or by filing tax information with the municipality, you may trigger an investigation of zoning compliance.

Zoning laws may also regulate off-street parking, water and air quality, and waste disposal, and the size, construction, and placement of signs. In some communities, historic district restrictions may keep you from modifying the exterior of a building or even changing the paint color without permission from a board of administrators.

Years ago, people tried to argue in court that such regulation of aesthetics wasn't a proper governmental function—that it wasn't related to the protection of the public health and safety. However, a carefully drawn ordinance seeking to preserve the special appeal of a historic district will very likely survive a legal challenge. So if you look at space in one of these protected neighborhoods, be prepared to suspend your freedom of choice and place the destiny of at least the exterior of the building in the hands of a panel of administrators.

In Chapter 14, dealing with home-based businesses, you'll find a discussion of zoning ordinances as they relate to businesses in the home. Take the time to review Chapter 14, Sections A and B, because zoning restrictions apply to all businesses.

E. How to Deal With Local Building and Zoning Officials

There's a certain amount of administrative discretion under building codes and zoning ordinances—enough, certainly, that it can help greatly to have the administrators on your side. Here are some ideas for accomplishing this.

1. Seek Support From the Business Community

If you employ local people and will contribute positively to the economy, it may pay to make contact with city or county business development officials or even the chamber of commerce. If they see your business as an asset and don't want you to locate in the next city, they may be helpful in steering you through the building and safety department and may even advocate on your behalf before zoning and planning officials.

Trade associations and merchants' associations may also come to your aid if you need building and safety officials to decide in your favor in areas in which they have some administrative discretion. Finally, contractors, lawyers, and others who are familiar with the system and the personalities often know how to get things done and can be helpful to you.

2. Appealing an Adverse Ruling

The decision of a zoning or building official isn't necessarily final. If you get an adverse decision from the local Planning Commission, for example, you may be able to have a board of zoning adjustment or board of appeals interpret the zoning ordinance in a way that's favorable to you. Alternatively, you may be able to obtain a variance (a special exception to a zoning law) if a strict interpretation of the ordinance causes a hardship. In some cases, you can get a conditional use permit, which lets you use the property in question for your kind of business as long as you meet certain conditions set down by the administrative panel.

In dealing with administrators and especially with appeals boards, it's important to have the support of neighbors and others in your community. A favorable petition signed by most other businesses in your immediate area or oral expressions of support from half a dozen neighbors can make the difference between success and failure at an administrative hearing.

Conversely, if objectors are numerous and adamant, you may not get what you're after. So if you sense opposition developing from those living or doing business nearby, try to resolve your differences before you get to a public hearing—even if it means you must make compromises on the details of your proposal.

LAW IN THE REAL WORLD
Strategic Planning Pays Off

Shelby, owner of Small Universe Books, is delighted to learn that the drugstore next door is going out of business. He immediately seeks to buy or sign a long-term lease for the building so he can expand his profitable business. The future looks rosy.

Not so fast. Shelby learns that for his new business use of the building, he'll have to supply eight parking spaces to get a permit. Doing this in his desperately crowded neighborhood is totally impossible at anything approaching an affordable price.

Instead of giving up, Shelby asks the city planning commission for a variance to waive the parking spaces rule. A public hearing is scheduled. Shelby knows he has to put on a persuasive case, so he:

- Calls hundreds of local writers, publishers, critics, educators, and book lovers to pack the hearing room and testify that an expanded book store will be a great community resource.
- Documents the prohibitive cost of buying or leasing the required parking spaces.
- Offers to validate parking at a lot four blocks away, just outside the worst of the congested area.
- Hires an architect who determines that a heavily used, nearby public garage can accommodate 20 more cars if the parking spaces are striped differently.
- Offers to pay for the restriping.

Shelby gets the variance.

3. Going to Court

Every day, hundreds if not thousands of interpreta-tions and applications of building and zoning laws are worked out through negotiation with adminis-trators and through administrative appeals. But if these channels fail, it's possible in many instances to go to court. This can be very expensive and time-consuming. What good is it if you win your battle for a permit to remodel your premises but you waste two years getting to that point?

Still, there are times when what you're seeking is so valuable and your chances of success are so great that you can afford both the time and money to get a definitive ruling from the courts. And in some instances, you can get a court to consider your dispute fairly quickly.

If, for example, you submitted plans to the city that complied with all building and safety codes, and the building official refused to issue a building permit unless you agreed to put in some additional improvements you believe are not required by the ordinance, you could quickly go to court asking for an order of "mandamus." Your argument would be that the administrator wasn't following the law.

Before you consider court action, however, get as much information as you can about the cost of litigation, how long it will take (you can win in the trial court, but the city might decide to appeal), and the likelihood of your ultimate success. This is a specialized corner of the law, so you're going to need someone who's had experience in the field—and there may not be that many to choose from in any given location. Look for a lawyer who's repre-sented a similar business in a dispute with the city or someone who formerly worked as a city attor-ney and knows all the ins and outs of the local ordinances. ■

Tax Basics for the Small Business

No matter whether your business is organized as a sole proprietorship, partnership, corporation, or limited liability company, you've automatically got a silent partner: Uncle Sam. The federal tax laws make this unavoidable. To guard against interest and penalties, you need to know what tax forms to file and when to file them. And to succeed in business, you need at least a basic, working knowledge of the tax system.

On a more positive note, by being aware of the fine points of the tax laws, you can often legally save a bundle of money—not to mention aggravation. For example, having a clear picture of what the IRS regards as a proper business expense will allow you to take deductions that otherwise might not occur to you.

Get detailed information. *The tax laws are vast and complicated, and you'll surely need much more information than you'll find in this chapter. Here I just hit the high points; it's up to you to deepen your knowledge. A good starting place is the IRS website at www.irs.gov.*

In addition to what you learn from books and other publications, you may have to hire a bookkeeper and an accountant. If you're operating a one-person word processing business out of your home, you may be able to keep your books and do your taxes with no professional help at all—or perhaps get help just the first time you file your annual tax return, to make sure you've correctly completed Schedules C (*Profit or Loss From Business*) and SE (*Self-Employment Tax*). On the other hand, if you've formed a corporation that's operating a good-sized dry-cleaning shop with eight employees, you may want an accountant to help set up your books and to prepare—or at least review—your business tax returns each year. And you may find that employing a part-time bookkeeper not only results in your records being well kept, but also frees you for more important tasks.

A word of caution about one other possible source of assistance: IRS employees. Most of them are hardworking and well-meaning, but their training and supervision are often inadequate. Unfortunately, it's common to receive poor oral advice in answer to questions. And if the advice proves to be so inaccurate that it results in your being assessed interest and penalties, the fact that you got it from an IRS employee won't get you off the hook. In short, it's often cheaper in the long run to rely on the advice of an experienced small business accountant than on a free oral opinion from the IRS.

State Taxes. In addition to federal taxes, you need to be aware of your state's tax scheme, which may include an income tax structured along the same lines as the federal version or one that has some major differences. Before you begin your business, contact your state's taxing authority to get detailed information. You'll also find helpful links at www.statetaxcentral.com.

A. Employer Identification Number

Even if your business has no employees, you must get an Employer Identification Number (EIN) from the IRS when you start a business that you've set up as:

- a partnership
- an S corporation
- a C corporation
- a limited liability company (LLC) with two or more members, or
- a single-member LLC that you've chosen to have taxed as corporation.

Technically, if you're a sole proprietor or the sole member of a limited liability company (LLC) that is not being taxed as a corporation (see Chapter 1, Section D) and you have no employees, you can use your personal Social Security number instead of an EIN. But even in those situations, it's a good business practice to get an EIN to differentiate cleanly between your personal and business finances.

You'll need your EIN before you file a tax return or make a tax deposit. In some cases, a bank will require you to have an EIN before you can open a business bank account.

APPLICATION FOR EMPLOYER IDENTIFICATION NUMBER

Form **SS-4**

(Rev. December 2001)

Department of the Treasury
Internal Revenue Service

Application for Employer Identification Number

(For use by employers, corporations, partnerships, trusts, estates, churches, government agencies, Indian tribal entities, certain individuals, and others.)

▶ See separate instructions for each line.   ▶ Keep a copy for your records.

EIN

OMB No. 1545-0003

Type or print clearly.

1 Legal name of entity (or individual) for whom the EIN is being requested

Alpha Bean Cromwell

2 Trade name of business (if different from name on line 1)	**3** Executor, trustee, "care of" name
ABCD Plumbing	

4a Mailing address (room, apt., suite no. and street, or P.O. box)	**5a** Street address (if different) (Do not enter a P.O. box.)
1234 Rooter Place	
4b City, state, and ZIP code	**5b** City, state, and ZIP code
Nowheresville, CA 95555	

6 County and state where principal business is located

Somewheres County, California

7a Name of principal officer, general partner, grantor, owner, or trustor	**7b** SSN, ITIN, or EIN
Alpha Bean Cromwell	

8a **Type of entity** (check only one box)

☒ Sole proprietor (SSN) 555 55 5555
☐ Partnership
☐ Corporation (enter form number to be filed) ▶ _____
☐ Personal service corp.
☐ Church or church-controlled organization
☐ Other nonprofit organization (specify) ▶ _____
☐ Other (specify) ▶

☐ Estate (SSN of decedent) _____
☐ Plan administrator (SSN) _____
☐ Trust (SSN of grantor) _____
☐ National Guard   ☐ State/local government
☐ Farmers' cooperative ☐ Federal government/military
☐ REMIC   ☐ Indian tribal governments/enterprises
Group Exemption Number (GEN) ▶ _____

8b If a corporation, name the state or foreign country (if applicable) where incorporated

State	Foreign country

9 **Reason for applying** (check only one box)

☒ Started new business (specify type) ▶_____
_____
☐ Hired employees (Check the box and see line 12.)
☐ Compliance with IRS withholding regulations
☐ Other (specify) ▶

☐ Banking purpose (specify purpose) ▶ _____
☐ Changed type of organization (specify new type) ▶ _____
☐ Purchased going business
☐ Created a trust (specify type) ▶ _____
☐ Created a pension plan (specify type) ▶ _____

10 Date business started or acquired (month, day, year)	**11** Closing month of accounting year
01/01/05	December

12 First date wages or annuities were paid or will be paid (month, day, year). **Note:** If applicant is a withholding agent, enter date income will first be paid to nonresident alien. (month, day, year) . . . . ▶

13 Highest number of employees expected in the next 12 months. **Note:** If the applicant does not expect to have any employees during the period, enter "-0-." . . . . ▶

Agricultural	Household	Other

14 Check **one** box that best describes the principal activity of your business.
☐ Construction ☐ Rental & leasing ☐ Transportation & warehousing
☐ Real estate   ☐ Manufacturing   ☐ Finance & insurance
☐ Health care & social assistance   ☐ Wholesale–agent/broker
☐ Accommodation & food service   ☐ Wholesale–other   ☐ Retail
☐ Other (specify)

15 Indicate principal line of merchandise sold; specific construction work done; products produced; or services provided.

16a Has the applicant ever applied for an employer identification number for this or any other business? . . . . ☐ Yes ☒ No
Note: If "Yes," please complete lines 16b and 16c.

16b If you checked "Yes" on line 16a, give applicant's legal name and trade name shown on prior application if different from line 1 or 2 above.
Legal name ▶   Trade name ▶

16c Approximate date when, and city and state where, the application was filed. Enter previous employer identification number if known.

Approximate date when filed (mo., day, year)	City and state where filed	Previous EIN

	Complete this section **only** if you want to authorize the named individual to receive the entity's EIN and answer questions about the completion of this form.	
Third Party Designee	Designee's name	Designee's telephone number (include area code) (510) 555-5555
	Address and ZIP code	Designee's fax number (include area code) (510) 666-6666

Under penalties of perjury, I declare that I have examined this application, and to the best of my knowledge and belief, it is true, correct, and complete.

Applicant's telephone number (include area code) ( )

Name and title (type or print clearly) ▶

Applicant's fax number (include area code) ( )

Signature ▶ *Alpha Bean Cromwell*   Date ▶ 1/1/05

For Privacy Act and Paperwork Reduction Act Notice, see separate instructions.   Cat. No. 16055N   Form **SS-4** (Rev. 12-2001)

1. How to Apply

To get an EIN, file Form SS-4, *Application for Employer Identification Number.*

The form isn't difficult to fill out if you follow the IRS instructions. Nevertheless, a few pointers may help.

Space 1. Insert your official corporate name if you're a corporation or your official company name if you're a limited liability company. If you're a partnership, use the partnership name shown in your partnership agreement. If you're a sole proprietor, insert your full name—the name you use on your personal tax return.

Space 11. Here you're asked to state the closing month of your business accounting year. Your answer, however, isn't binding. You make your binding election of a fiscal year-end on the first federal income tax return that you file for the business.

Sole proprietors, partnerships, S corporations, personal service corporations (see Chapter 1, Section F2a), and limited liability companies are generally required to use a calendar year—that is, a year ending December 31—for tax purposes. Personal service corporations have two basic characteristics:

- the professional employees of the corporation own the stock, and
- the corporation performs its services in the fields of health, law, engineering, architecture, accounting, actuarial science, performing arts, or consulting.

To use a tax year other than a calendar year, an S corporation must demonstrate to the IRS that there is a substantial business reason to do so, such as the seasonal nature of the business. Basically, the IRS wants to make sure that permitting you to claim a tax year other than the calendar year won't substantially distort your income.

See IRS Publication 589, *Tax Information on S Corporations,* and *IRS Publication 538,* Business Purpose Tax Year, *for details.*

A regular corporation that's not a personal service corporation is freer to choose a fiscal year. Most small businesses find that where there's a choice, the calendar year is the most convenient way to proceed. Sometimes, however, there are tax planning reasons for a business owner to choose a different tax year for the business.

EXAMPLE 1: Radcraft Inc., a regular corporation, selects the calendar year for its fiscal year. In December 2003 it pays a $30,000 bonus to Jill, the president and sole shareholder. The bonus is included on Jill's 2003 income tax return, and tax on the bonus is due in April 2004.

EXAMPLE 2: Jill selects a fiscal year of February 1 through January 31 for Radcraft Inc. (On Form SS-4, she lists January in space 11 for the closing month of the corporation's accounting year.) In January 2004, the corporation pays Jill a $30,000 bonus. The bonus is included in Jill's 2004 income tax return. The tax on the bonus isn't due until April 2005—although Jill must keep track of it when computing her quarterly estimates in 2004.

An accountant or other experienced tax advisor *can help you decide whether or not you and your corporation can realize a tax advantage by using a tax year other than a calendar year.*

Space 12. The IRS will send you computer-generated payroll tax forms based on your answer to this question.

Space 13. These numbers can be estimated. It's usually best to estimate on the low side.

Space 17a. This question refers to the business, not the owner. Normally, a partnership, corporation, or limited liability company has only one Employer Identification Number (EIN). A sole proprietor may have several businesses, each with a separate number.

After filling out the form, there are four ways to obtain the number.

- *By mail.* If you have enough lead time, you can mail Form SS-4 to the IRS and wait for the number to be mailed to you, which will take about four weeks.

- *By phone.* To get a Form SS-4 processed more quickly, use the TELE-TIN system operated by the IRS. Complete Form SS-4 and, before you mail it, phone in the information to the IRS at the phone number for your region. Phone numbers are listed in the form's instruction sheet. An IRS employee assigns an EIN, which you'll then insert in the upper-right corner of the form before sending it to the IRS.

- *Online.* The IRS has made it a snap to get your EIN online. Go to www.irs.gov. Click "Businesses," then "Employer ID Numbers," then "apply online." (You'll also find full instructions at the IRS site for completing the form—instructions that will be useful even if you prefer to fill out and file a paper form.)

- *By fax.* You can fax your Form SS-4. To obtain the fax number, inquire at the IRS office where you pick up your Form SS-4. You'll get your EIN in a day or two. This is slower than the phone method but it avoids the frustration of repeated calling because the TELE-TIN voice line is tied up.

Use your EIN on all business tax returns, checks, and other documents you send to the IRS. Your state taxing authority may also require your EIN on state tax forms.

2. When to Get a New Number

If your S corporation chooses to change to a regular corporation—or your C corporation chooses to change to an S corporation—it doesn't need a new EIN; the one you already have is still sufficient. However, you'll need to get a new EIN if any of these changes occur in your business:

- You incorporate your sole proprietorship or partnership.

- You convert your sole proprietorship or partnership to a limited liability company.

- Your sole proprietorship takes in partners and begins operating as a partnership.

- Your partnership is taken over by one of the partners and begins operating as a sole proprietorship.

- Your corporation changes to a partnership or to a sole proprietorship.

- You purchase or inherit an existing business that you'll operate as a sole proprietorship.

- You represent an estate that operates a business after the owner's death.

- You terminate an old partnership and begin a new one.

Filing Form SS-4 for an LLC

The IRS has some special rules applicable to LLCs completing Form SS-4, as follows:

- You have a single-member LLC, and you plan to run it as if you were a sole proprietor (using Schedule C to report business income). Your LLC won't need an Employer Identification Number (EIN). Therefore, you probably shouldn't file Form SS-4. Your name and Social Security number will normally be all you need to use for tax purposes. But if your LLC will have employees, you can, if you wish, get an EIN for the LLC for reporting and paying employment taxes. You can also get an EIN for nontax reasons (such as a state requirement) or simply as a bookkeeping preference. If you do decide to get an EIN for the LLC, check the "Other" box in space 8a and write in: "Disregarded Entity—Sole Proprietorship."

- You have a multimember LLC, and you plan to run it as if you were a partnership (using Form 1065 to report business income). You should apply for an EIN and, in space 8a, check the "Partnership" box.

- You have either a single-member or a multimember LLC, and you plan to run it as a C Corporation. You should apply for an EIN and, in space 8a, check the "Corporation" box. Then, below the "form number" line, write in "Single-Member" or "Multimember." Also be sure to file Form 8832 to elect corporate tax status, as explained in Chapter 4, Section G4.

B. Becoming an S Corporation

Many corporations derive tax benefits from electing S corporation status. The difference between a C corporation, which is a separate tax entity from its shareholders, and an S corporation, whose income is reported on the owners' tax returns, is described in some detail in Chapter 1. If you're not thoroughly familiar with this material, please reread it before going on.

To become an S corporation, all shareholders must sign and file IRS Form 2553 (*Election by a Small Business Corporation*) with the IRS by the 15th day of the third month of the tax year to which the election is to apply.

> **EXAMPLE:** Nancy, Jerry, and Agnes form a corporation, Phoenix Ventures Inc. They start to do business on September 1, 2004 and, like most businesses, use the calendar year for accounting and tax purposes. Their 2004 tax year will be a short one: September 1 through December 31. To obtain S corporation status for that first tax year, they need to file Form 2553 by November 15, 2004, which is the 15th day of the third month of that tax year. If they miss that deadline, their corporation won't qualify for S corporation status in 2004. But if they file Form 2553 by March 15, 2005 their corporation will get S corporation status for 2005.

A number of technical rules govern which corporations can elect to become S corporations. Your corporation must meet these requirements:

- It must be a "domestic" corporation—one that's organized under U.S. federal or state law.
- It must have only one class of stock.

- It must have no more than 100 shareholders.
- It must have as shareholders only individuals, estates, and certain trusts. Partnerships and corporations can't be shareholders in an S corporation.
- It can't have any shareholder who is a non-resident alien.

There are other technical rules, but the vast majority of new, small corporations may become S corporations if they choose to do so.

To elect S corporation status, you need the consent of all shareholders. Unless yours is a one-person corporation, you should agree on this election before you form your corporation.

An S corporation election doesn't have to be permanent. You can start out as an S corporation and then, after a few years, revoke your S corporation status and be taxed as a regular corporation. If you terminate your status as an S corporation, generally you'll have to wait five years until you can again become an S corporation—although you may be able to get permission from the IRS to shorten this waiting period.

Once the shareholders file a Form 2553, the corporation continues to be an S corporation each year until the shareholders revoke that status or it's terminated under IRS rules. What terminates S corporation status? For one thing, ceasing to qualify as an S corporation. For example, your corporation would no longer qualify if it had more than 75 shareholders or if you or another shareholder transferred some of your stock to a partnership.

C. Business Taxes in General

Three main categories of federal business taxes may apply to your business:
- income tax
- employment taxes
- self-employment tax.

This section looks briefly at each of these tax categories. Get IRS Publication 509, *Tax Calendars,* to see when to file returns and make tax payments. It's updated annually.

Excise Taxes. In addition to the three main business taxes, the federal government imposes excise taxes on a few specialized transactions and products. These taxes almost never are of concern to small businesses. To see whether your business is affected, see IRS Publication 334, *Tax Guide for Small Business.*

1. Income Tax

You must file an annual federal tax return reporting your business income. Below is a list of the forms to use.

Business Income Tax Forms

Type of Legal Entity	Form
Sole Proprietorship	Schedule C (Form 1040)
Partnership	Form 1065
Regular Corporation	Form 1120 or 1120-A
Single Member LLC	Schedule C (Form 1040)
S Corporation	Form 1120-S
Multimember LLC	Form 1065, 1120 or 1120-A

a. Sole Proprietorship

If you're a sole proprietor, your business itself doesn't pay income tax. You report your business income (or loss) on Schedule C, and file it with Form 1040. Your Schedule C income (or loss) is added to (or subtracted from) the other income you report on your personal Form 1040. If you have more than one business, file a separate Schedule C for each business.

b.   Partnership

A partnership Form 1065 is an informational tax return telling the IRS how much each partner earned. The partnership doesn't pay tax on this income. Each partner reports his or her share of income (or loss) on Schedule E, *Supplemental Income and Loss*, and files it with Form 1040.

This Schedule E amount is added to (or subtracted from) the other income the partner reports on Form 1040. In other words, a partner's income is treated like a sole proprietor's income on Form 1040: It's listed in a separate schedule and then blended with other income listed on the first page of the 1040.

⚠ **Passive losses.** *Losses from passive partnership activities—such as real estate investments or royalties, in which the partnership plays the role of a passive investor—can usually be taken as a credit only against income from other passive activities. This is explained in greater detail in IRS Publication 925.*

c.   S Corporation

The S corporation itself doesn't pay income tax. Form 1120-S filed by an S corporation is an informational return telling the IRS how much each shareholder earned. As a shareholder, you report your portion of income or loss on Schedule E and file it with Form 1040. Then you add that income to (or subtract a loss from) your other 1040 income.

d.   C Corporation

A C corporation reports its income or loss on Form 1120 or 1120-A and pays a tax if there is income. But in many small corporations, the shareholders are employees who receive all profits of the business in the form of salaries and bonuses, which are tax-deductible by the corporation as a business expense.

In that situation, the corporation would have no taxable income.

Not all small corporations, however, are able to pay out their income in the form of salaries and bonuses. If they don't, they must pay a corporate income tax.

EXAMPLE: Jenny and her twin sister Janet are the sole shareholders in Neptune Corporation, which manufactures swimming pool supplies. In the second year of their corporate existence, to encourage growth, Jenny and Janet decide to pay themselves minimal salaries and to plow most of the corporate income into inventory and the purchase of rehabilitated but serviceable equipment. The money that the corporation puts into inventory and equipment isn't available for distribution to Jenny and Janet; moreover, most of that money isn't a currently deductible business expense, so it is taxed at corporate income tax rates. (The equipment will be capitalized; depreciation deductions will be spread over several years.)

Tax Rates on Taxable Corporate Income		
Income Over	**But Not Over**	**Tax Rate**
$0	$50,000	15%
$50,000	$75,000	25%
$75,000	$100,000	34%
$100,000	$335,000	39%
$335,000	$10,000,000	34%
$10,000,000	$15,000,000	35%
$15,000,000	$18,333,333	38%
Over $18,333,333		35%

Note: Personal service corporations are subject to a flat tax of 35% regardless of the amount of income.

If you have a C corporation that expects to have taxable income, your corporation needs to make periodic deposits of its estimated income taxes. And if you're an employee of your C corporation (as is almost always the case with an owner of a small business corporation), taxes and Social Security payments must be withheld from your paychecks.

e. Limited Liability Company

A single-member LLC is normally taxed as a sole proprietorship, meaning that you'll report the income (or loss) on Schedule C and file it with Form 1040. The bottom line will be added to (or subtracted from) the other income you report on Form 1040.

An LLC that has two or more members, unless the owners choose to have the business taxed as a corporation, will be taxed as a partnership (tax liability passes through to the LLC members) and will use Form 1065—an informational return that tells the IRS how much each member earned. The LLC doesn't pay tax on its income but, as with a partnership, each member reports his or her share of income (or loss) on Schedule E, *Supplemental Income and Loss*, which is filed with Form 1040. This Schedule E amount is added to (or subtracted from) the other income the member reports on Form 1040.

An LLC that chooses to be taxed as a corporation will use Form 1120 or 1120-A. See Subsection d, above, for a discussion of corporate taxes.

New Tax Break for Manufacturing Businesses

Beginning in 2005, a manufacturing business can take an attractive deduction—and one that will get even better as it is phased in year by year. The tax law definition of manufacturing is broad enough to include income from farming and construction, but not from restaurants. Once the deduction takes full effect, you'll be able to deduct 9% of the lesser of:

- the business's production activities income, or
- its taxable income for a taxable year.

The deduction, however, can't be larger than 50% of your company's W-2 wages for the taxable year. In most cases this is the same as 50% of your company's payroll.

If your company is eligible, it can claim a 3% deduction in 2005 and 2006, and a 6% deduction from 2007 through 2009. In 2010, the full 9% deduction will kick in. The deduction applies to a wide range of entities—including sole proprietorships, partnerships, LLCs, C corporations, and S corporations.

Because this is a particularly complex area of tax law, you should talk to a tax pro to see how this tax break applies to your business.

2. Federal Payroll Taxes

There are several types of employment-related taxes the federal government exacts from businesses.

a. Federal Income Tax Withholding (FIT)

You must withhold income taxes from employees' paychecks based on:

- the employee's filing status (single, married, or married but withholding at the higher single rate)
- the number of dependents (withholding allowances) declared by the employee, and
- the size of the employee's salary.

Each employee should give you a signed Form W-4 stating his or her withholding allowance. Save these forms. You needn't send them to the IRS unless the employee:

- claims more than ten allowances, or
- claims to be exempt from withholding and also normally earns more than $200 a week.

Use the tables in Circular E (referenced below) to figure out how much income tax to withhold.

• IRS Publication 15, Circular E, *Employer's Tax Guide,* *published by the IRS, explains employment-related taxes clearly and in great detail. Updated whenever the tax rates change, Circular E is available at all IRS offices (or at www.irs.gov) and is mailed automatically to all businesses with an EIN.*

- *IRS Publication 334,* Tax Guide for Small Business, *and if you're just getting started, IRS Publication 583,* Starting a Business and Keeping Records, *are well worth reading. These publications are free from your local IRS office or can be obtained by calling the main IRS number: 800-829-3676, or by going to www.irs.gov.*
- Tax Savvy for Small Business, *by Frederick W. Daily (Nolo). An excellent guide to all the tax problems small businesses face. The audit material alone is well worth the price of the book.*

- Small-Time Operator, *by Bernard Kamoroff (Bell Springs Publishing), is a clearly written book that covers not only taxes but also many other practical aspects of doing business, including bookkeeping.*
- U.S. Master Tax Guide *(CCH, Inc.), is updated annually and available in law libraries, business school libraries, and the reference departments of major public libraries. It features in-depth explanations of tax complexities.*
- The Kiplinger Tax Letter, *published by the Kiplinger Washington Editors, is a biweekly newsletter that does an excellent job of keeping you up-to-date on what's happening in the tax field. The breezy—some would say breathless—style is fun to read. Go to www.kiplinger.com or call 800-544-0155.*

Also, there is software that handles payroll, including tax computations. Look into QuickPay, OneWrite, *and* Peachtree.

b. Social Security Tax (FICA)

You must withhold the employee's share of the Social Security tax and Medicare tax from the employee's pay. And you must also pay the employer's share. The amounts to be withheld are listed in the most current edition of Circular E. For 2005, for example, the employer and the employee are each required to pay 7.65% on the first $90,000 of the employee's annual wages; the 7.65% figure is the sum of the 6.2% Social Security tax and the 1.45% Medicare tax. There is no Social Security tax on the portion of the employee's annual wages that exceeds $90,000—only the Medicare tax; the employer and the employee each pay the 1.45% Medicare tax on the excess amount. The rates and the cutoff point for the Social Security tax change annually.

Withholding From an Owner's Paycheck

Money you earn from your corporation—whether it's an S or a C corporation—isn't limited to dividends you receive as a shareholder. If you perform substantial services for your corporation, you're considered an employee for tax purposes. This means you must complete and submit a Form W-4 to the corporation the same as any other employee, and the corporation must withhold income taxes and your share of Social Security and Medicare taxes from your paychecks.

These requirements may seem burdensome, but if you're an employee of a C corporation the time you spend completing the paperwork is well worth it because the money you take out as an employee is taxed only once rather than twice. (See Chapter 1, Section C2.)

c. Federal Unemployment Tax (FUTA)

Finally, you must report and pay the federal unemployment tax (FUTA). The employer is responsible for paying this tax; it's not withheld from the

employee's pay. The FUTA rate through 2007 is 6.2% of the first $7,000 of the employee's wages for the year. Employers are given a credit for participating in state unemployment programs. The credit reduces the FUTA rate to 0.8% for most employers—which translates into $56 for an employee earning $7,000 or more per year.

Use Form 940 or 940EZ to report federal unemployment tax. Sole proprietorships and partnerships don't pay the FUTA on the owners' compensation.

d. Periodic Deposits

You must periodically deposit the withheld income tax and the employer's and employee's shares of Social Security and Medicare taxes at an authorized financial institution—usually a bank. The IRS sends you coupons to use in making these deposits. It also provides instructions on how often you're required to deposit these funds, which depends on the size of your payroll and amounts due; a typical small business makes monthly deposits.

Deposit taxes on time. *Be sure to withhold taxes as required by the tax laws—and to deposit those taxes on time. There are substantial penalties if you don't. And if you're an owner of a small business and personally involved in its management, you can be held personally liable for these taxes and the additional penalties, even if the business has the funds to pay them. If your business suddenly runs into financial trouble, put the withheld taxes at the top of the list for payment. If that means not paying suppliers and others, so be it. The debts of the other creditors can be wiped out in bankruptcy if the business continues to go downhill. Not so with the withheld taxes. You can remain personally liable for these amounts even if the business goes through bankruptcy. However, passive investors—for example, those who merely own corporate shares and play no role in making business decisions—face very little risk of being personally liable for the taxes.*

Get a copy of **IRS Publication 509, *Tax Calendars,*** *to see when to file returns and make tax payments. It's available from your local IRS office, by calling the main IRS number: 800-829-3676, or by going to www.irs.gov. The publication is updated annually.*

Payroll Taxes Made Easy

If you're overwhelmed by the requirements for calculating payroll taxes and the fine points of when and where to pay them, you can pay a bank or payroll service to do the work for you. A reputable payroll tax service that offers a tax notification service will calculate the correct amount due, produce the checks to pay the employees and the taxes, and notify you when the taxes are due.

One big advantage of a payroll service over a bank is that the bank will normally withhold the amount of the tax from your account when the payroll is done, even though the tax isn't due yet. That means the bank, not you, gets the use of the money for a while. If your payroll service offers tax notification, it will prepare the checks and tell you when they must be deposited. Depending on how often you must make payments, that can give you the use of the money an extra month or more.

At the end of each quarter, the payroll service will produce your quarterly payroll tax returns and instruct you about how to file them. At the end of the year, the service will also prepare W-2 forms and federal and state transmittal forms.

Payroll services can be cost-effective as compared to the hours it will take to handle your own tax reporting (even for very small businesses). But when you look for one, it pays to shop around. Avoid services that charge setup fees—basically, a fee for putting your information into its computer—or extra fees to prepare W-2 forms or quarterly and annual tax returns.

3. Self-Employment Tax

The self-employment tax applies to income you receive from actively working in your business—but not as an employee of that business. Technically, it's not an employment tax, but it's so closely related that you should be aware of it to fully understand employment taxes.

If you're a sole proprietor or a partner (or an LLC member, probably—see note below), you must pay the federal self-employment tax in addition to regular income tax. The self-employment tax is equal to the employer's and employee's portion of the Social Security and Medicare taxes that you and your employer would pay on your compensation if you received it as an employee.

Compute this tax each year on Schedule SE, which you then attach to your personal Form 1040. Add the self-employment tax to the income tax that you owe. For example, in 2005, the self-employment tax is set at 15.3% on earnings up to $90,000 and 2.9% on earnings over $90,000. The tax law lightens the burden of the self-employment tax somewhat by allowing you to deduct one-half of this tax in computing your adjusted gross income. You take the deduction on the first page of your federal tax return.

You may not owe the full self-employment tax on all of your business earnings. If you have income from another job that's subject to withholding—common for people just getting started in business—the income from your other job will reduce the tax base for your self-employment tax. So in computing your self-employment for 2005, for example, you'd reduce the $90,000 figure to reflect any of your job earnings that were subject to employer withholding.

> **EXAMPLE:** Morton works ¾ time as a chemistry instructor at a local college, where he receives an annual salary of $60,000. He also does consulting, as a sole proprietor, for several chemical companies and earns an additional $40,000 a year after expenses. The $60,000 salary at the

college—which is subject to withholding by the employer—is used to reduce the $90,000 cap on income that's subject to the 15.3% self-employment tax. So Morton computes the tax at the rate of 15.3% on $30,000 of his consulting business income ($90,000 less $60,000 = $30,000). On the remaining portion—$10,000 ($40,000 less $30,000 = $10,000)—he computes the tax at the rate of 2.9%.

⚠ LLC members may have to pay self-employment tax. *As explained in Chapter 1 and Chapter 4, Section D, LLC members may have to pay self-employment tax on all income they receive from the LLC, whether in the form of salary or allocations of profit.*

Computing Your Estimated Taxes

Many taxpayers receive income from sources other than paychecks—for example, from investments and royalties. These taxpayers often owe surprising amounts of income taxes on April 15. Sometimes, that's because they had no employer to withhold income tax during the year. Other times, it's because even though there was an employer, the amounts withheld were insufficient to cover the taxpayer's non-employment income.

As you may know, the IRS doesn't want you to wait until April 15 to pay. Instead, the IRS requires you to pay your taxes in advance in quarterly estimated installments if not enough is being withheld from your salary to cover your full income tax bill. Every year, the IRS provides guidelines on how you can avoid interest and penalties for paying too little in estimated tax. For tax year 2004, for example, you would have avoided interest and penalties by paying 90% of your 2004 tax bill in advance, or an amount equal to 100% of your 2003 tax bill (or 110% of your 2003 tax bill if your adjusted gross income was over $150,000).

In figuring out what your tax bill will be and whether you need to pay any quarterly installments of estimated taxes, don't overlook the self-employment tax that is added to your regular income tax on your Form 1040 as part of your tax obligation. Make sure your quarterly installments are large enough to cover your self-employment tax as well as your usual income tax.

For more on this subject, see IRS Publication 505, *Tax Withholding and Estimated Tax,* available at the nearest IRS office or by going to www.irs.gov.

D. Business Deductions

Of all the federal taxes that may affect a small business, income tax is the one that business owners are most concerned about. The general formula is that you first figure out your gross profit—your gross receipts or sales less returns and allowances and the cost of goods sold. Then you subtract your other business expenses to find the net income or loss of your business. For an in-depth analysis of what business expenses can be deducted, see IRS Publication 535, *Business Expenses*.

In this section, we'll look at common categories of deductible business expenses.

Home-Based Businesses. If you have a home-based business, you'll find special tax pointers in Chapter 14.

1. IRS Guidelines for Business Deductions

The IRS has broad, general guidelines for what constitutes deductible expenses. For example, to be deductible, a business expense must be ordinary and necessary—something that's common in your type of business, trade, or profession. If you have an expense that's partly for business and partly personal, you must separate the personal from the business part. Only the business part is deductible.

So much for generalities. Here's a partial list of the kinds of expenses that your business can normally deduct:

- advertising
- bad debts
- car and truck expenses
- commissions and fees
- conventions and trade shows
- depreciation on property owned by the business (discussed in Section 2, below)
- employee benefit programs
- insurance
- interest
- legal, accounting, and other professional services

- office expenses
- pension and profit-sharing plans
- rent
- repairs to and maintenance of business premises and equipment
- supplies
- taxes and licenses
- trade publications
- travel, meals, and entertainment
- utilities
- wages.

This list isn't all-inclusive. You can also deduct any other expenses that you believe—and can convince the IRS—are ordinary and necessary business expenses.

Now let's look at the rules affecting a number of specific expenses (deductions) in more depth.

2. Depreciation

If you buy equipment or machinery that has a useful life longer than one year, the IRS generally won't let you deduct the full cost in the year you buy it. Instead, you deduct a portion each year over the term of the item's useful life by using depreciation.

Depreciation is the loss in the value of the property over the time the property is used—including wear and tear, age, and obsolence. IRS tables list the useful life of various types of equipment and machinery for the purpose of depreciation.

You don't need to depreciate inexpensive items. *Exceptions are made for inexpensive items for which the cost of detailed record keeping would be prohibitive. For example, your $75 desktop calculator may last for five years but you'd undoubtedly be allowed to deduct its entire cost in the year you buy it. You'd probably treat it as part of your office supplies.*

You may choose one of two methods—straight-line or accelerated—for figuring depreciation.

a. Straight-Line Depreciation

The straight-line method means that you deduct an equal amount each year over the projected life of the asset. Actually, that's a bit of an over-simplification; something called the "half-year convention" makes things slightly more complicated. That rule allows only a half-year's worth of depreciation to be deducted in the first year.

> **EXAMPLE:** Norbert buys a $1,000 fax machine in 2005 that can be depreciated over five years according to the IRS table. Under a strict application of the straight-line depreciation method, he'd deduct $200 each year for five years. But the half-year convention allows him to deduct only a half year's worth of depreciation—$100—the first year. So Norbert would deduct $100 the first year; $200 a year for the next four years; and the final $100 in the sixth year.

(Exceptions to the half-year rule are explained in IRS Publication 946, *How to Depreciate Property*.)

b. Accelerated Depreciation

Another method of depreciating assets—accelerated depreciation—is also available. Most small businesses will want to use the accelerated depreciation tables instead of the straight-line method. It allows them to write off a large amount of the purchase price in the years immediately following the purchase of the machinery or equipment. That, of course, makes the tax savings available sooner.

c. Immediate Write-Offs

Another tax rule—one especially helpful to small businesses—lets you get around the depreciation rules to a great extent. You can, if you choose, write off up to $102,000 of depreciable assets in the year of purchase. This figure will be adjusted annually for inflation in 2005 and future years. You can, if you choose, write off up to $100,000 of depreciable assets in the year of purchase.

> **EXAMPLE:** Bertha buys an $8,000 computer in 2005. Ordinarily, she'd have to use IRS depreciation tables and spread the cost over several years. But she has the option of deducting the cost all at once in the year 2005. This is known as a Section 179 capital-expense election.

There are a few important limitations to this deduction. The first, which doesn't affect many businesses that are just starting out, applies if you purchase more than $410,000 in depreciable assets in one year. If you do, the maximum amount you can deduct as a Section 179 capital-expense deduction is reduced, dollar for dollar, by the amount you exceed $410,000. For example, if you spend $415,000 on depreciable assets, you can write off—as an expense deduction—only $97,000 ($102,000 less $5,000). This $410,000 threshhold will be adjusted for inflation in 2005 and future years.

Second, the amount you write off can't exceed the total taxable income that your business received in that year. You may, however, carry forward any disallowed part of this write-off so that you get some tax benefit in future years.

Any depreciable assets that you don't write off under Section 179 can be depreciated and written off under the straight-line or accelearated methods of depreciation, above.

For further explanation of this complicated area: *See* Tax Savvy for Small Business, *by Frederick W. Daily (Nolo).*

To Take Business Deductions, You Need a Business

The tax laws don't allow you to take business deductions for a hobby. Sometimes, however, the line between a business and a hobby can get fuzzy. This can happen if your small business is more a labor of love than a dependable source of income. Let's say you're a chiropractor but your real passion is growing orchids. Occasionally, you sell your orchids to friends and neighbors. You can't possibly get rich doing this, but you are intrigued by the possibility of deducting the cost of your plant materials, gardening equipment, fertilizer, plant-related magazine subscriptions, and the expenses of attending an orchid-growers convention. Can you legitimately deduct these items? Maybe—or maybe not.

The answer lies in whether you're profit motivated. To test for a profit motive, the IRS relies mainly on a simple "3-of-5" test. If your business makes a profit in any three out of five consecutive years, you're presumed to have a profit motive. That's true even if during the profitable year the profit was only $1. If you don't pass the "3-of-5" test, you may still be able to convince the IRS that you have a profit motive—but the going will be tougher. You'll have to use your ingenuity to establish that you have a real business. Some things that may help: Business cards, letterhead, well-kept books, a separate bank account, a separate phone line, business licenses and permits, and expenses for marketing.

3. Employees' Pay

You can deduct salaries, wages, and other forms of pay that you give to employees as long as you meet certain IRS tests listed below. If you're both an em-

ployee and a shareholder of your business, your own salary must meet the same tests for deductibility as salaries paid to any other executive or employee.

For a salary to be deductible, you must show that:

- The payments are ordinary and necessary expenses directly connected with your business.
- The payments are reasonable. Fortunately, you have broad discretion to decide what's reasonable. Short of a scam—such as paying a huge salary to a spouse or relative who does little or no work—the IRS will almost always accept your notion of what's reasonable pay.
- The payments are for services actually performed.

If you use the cash method of accounting (very common among small businesses), you can deduct salaries and wages only for the year in which they were paid. However, you can deduct employee taxes your business withheld in the year your business withheld them; you can't deduct (until paid to the government) the employer's matching portion of these taxes. Businesses using the accrual method have more latitude as to when they can deduct salaries and payroll taxes.

You can also deduct bonuses you pay to employees if they're intended as additional payment for services and not as gifts; most bonuses qualify for deduction. If your business distributes cash, gift certificates, or similar items of easily convertible cash value, the value of such items is considered additional wages or salary regardless of the amount. If a bonus is considered as part of an employee's wages or salary, it's subject to employment taxes and withholding rules.

Certain noncash bonuses that *are* intended as gifts are deductible if they are less than $25 per person per year.

EXAMPLE: To promote employee goodwill, Pebblestone Partnership distributes turkeys, hams, and other items of nominal value at holidays. The value of these items isn't considered salaries or wages, but the partnership can deduct their cost as a business expense.

4. Employee Benefits

A number of employee benefits can be deducted, including:

- health and dental insurance
- group term life insurance
- moving expenses
- qualified employee benefit plans, including profit-sharing plans, stock bonus plans, and money purchase pension plans
- employee benefit plans that allow employees to choose among two or more benefits consisting of cash and qualified benefits.

If your business can afford these benefits, not only are they tax deductible by your business, but they are not taxed to the employee.

While these benefits sound attractive, there are two serious drawbacks. First, many small businesses—particularly those just starting out—can't afford them. Second, plans that mainly benefit the owners of the business are not tax-deductible. (See Chapter 1, Section C2b(2), for a more thorough discussion.)

5. Meals, Entertainment, and Travel

To be treated as a business deduction, travel expenses need to be ordinary and necessary in your type of business. Basically, these are any reasonable expenses you incur while traveling for business. You (or your business) can't deduct expenses for personal or vacation purposes, or any part of business expenses that is lavish or extravagant.

(And deductible travel expenses don't include expenses for entertainment such as sports events and concerts.)

But if you're on the kind of tight travel and entertainment budget common to most small business people, you won't have to worry about this last restriction. Here are examples of deductible travel expenses:

- air, rail, and bus transportation while traveling on business
- operating and maintaining your own car for business (see Section 6 for more on car expenses).
- taxi fares or other costs of transportation between the airport or station and your hotel, from one customer to another, or from one place of business to another
- baggage charges and transportation costs for sample and display material
- meals and lodging while traveling on business
- cleaning and laundry expenses
- telephone and fax expenses
- public stenographers' fees
- tips incidental to any of these expenses.

You cannot deduct expenses for transportation while you're not traveling. The IRS says that you're traveling away from home if (1) your duties require you to be away from the general area of your tax home substantially longer than an ordinary day's work, and (2) you need to get sleep or rest to meet the demands of your work. (Napping in your car doesn't count.) Generally, your "tax home" is your main place of business regardless of where your family home is.

If a trip is entirely for business, you can deduct all of your ordinary and necessary travel expenses. If your trip was primarily personal, you can't deduct any travel expenses—even if you did some business at your destination.

What if your trip was primarily for business but you took a vacation-like side trip? Then you need to allocate your expenses; see IRS Publication 463, *Travel, Entertainment, Gift, and Car Expenses*, for instructions. The IRS does give you one break; if you legitimately need to fly somewhere for business, you can write off the entire plane fare, even though you stay over for pleasure after your business is completed.

Meal and entertainment expenses have special rules and restrictions. You can generally deduct only 50% of your business-related meal and entertainment expenses. In addition, the IRS may disallow extravagant and excessive expenses.

But short of fraud or obvious gross excess, the IRS doesn't monitor where you go for your business meals. So in practice, for most small business people, 50% of all business-related meal expenses are deductible. As an employer, this 50% limit applies to your business even if you reimburse your employees for 100% of their meal and entertainment expenses.

If you're a sole proprietor, deduct the allowable portion of your own business travel, meals, and entertainment expenses on Schedule C of your Form 1040. Use Schedule C to also report the expenses that you reimburse or directly pay your employees. (Consult IRS Publication 463 for an in-depth treatment of this subject.)

If you're a partner or a shareholder of a corporation in which you play an active management role, it's usually best to have your partnership or corporation reimburse you for your business-related travel and entertainment expenses. The business can then deduct these amounts to the extent allowed by law.

⚠️ **Excessive expenses may trigger an audit.** *Your overall travel and entertainment budget may result in a tax audit if these expenses are out of proportion to what the IRS thinks is reasonable, given your type of business and income. For most honest small business people, this isn't usually a problem unless they have some extraordinary need to travel.*

EXAMPLE: *Ben starts a marble importing business and spends his first year visiting 200 prominent architects and interior designers from coast to coast to introduce his business. His high travel expense triggers an audit, but Ben is able to*

show that these trips were necessary to get his business off the ground.

If you are audited, you'll need to show the IRS complete and accurate records of your travel and entertainment expenses, including actual receipts. Also, since you need to tie each trip and meal to a specific business purpose, it makes good sense to keep a log stating the purpose. Otherwise, if challenged, you may have trouble recalling the details.

6. Automobile Expenses

If you use your car for business, you may be able to deduct some or all of your car expenses. Deductible items include:

- gas
- oil
- tolls
- tires
- garage rent
- lease fees
- rental fees
- parking fees
- repairs
- licenses
- depreciation.

The following discussion assumes you use your car more than 50% for business. Special rules apply if you use your car 50% or less for business. For complete information about deductions for your car, again see IRS Publication 463.

If you use your car for both business and personal purposes, you must divide your expenses between business and personal use. (This rule applies to all items you use for both business and personal use.) The miles you put on your car driving from your home to your main place of business are considered to be commuting miles—a personal use, not deductible. The same thing applies to fees you pay to park your car at your place of business.

EXAMPLE: Tricia has a catering business that requires her to call on customers. She drives 20,000 miles during the year: 12,000 for business and 8,000 for personal use (including her daily trips from home to her shop). She can claim only 60% of the cost of operating her car as a business expense (12,000 divided by 20,000). The coins she fed the parking meter in front of her shop each day would be a personal (commuting) expense and not deductible; fees paid for parking while calling on customers would, however, be deductible.

What about depreciation? As with other business assets, you can deduct the cost of a car (but only the portion used for business), but you must spread the deductions over several years. IRS depreciation tables have special schedules for cars. These schedules are updated periodically. For example, if you placed a car in service in 2004 and used it 50% or less for business, your first-year deduction was limited to $2,960 times the percentage of business use. If you used the car more than 50% for business, the maximum first-year depreciation was $10,610.

Depreciation for Employees' Cars. If your employees use their cars in their work, they can't take a depreciation deduction unless this use is for your convenience as their employer and you require it as a condition of employment.

If you don't want to keep track of your car expenses and you want to avoid the complexity of the depreciation rules, the IRS offers a second method for deducting car expenses. You can use the standard mileage rate for your business usage. In 2005, the rate is 40.5 cents per mile. The rate changes periodically, so check IRS publications for the latest figure.

If you're going to use the standard mileage rate, you must start by using it in the year you begin using the car for business. If you don't use the standard mileage rate that first year, you can't use it for that car later on. If you use the standard mileage rate, you can also deduct tolls and parking fees that were paid while on business.

If you take a deduction for car expenses, you must file Form 4562 with your tax return. If you give an employee a car for business and personal use, the employee must report as income the value of the personal usage. For example, an employee who keeps a company car at home and drives to and from work must report that commuting usage—and any other personal usage—as income.

If you lease rather than own your car, you can deduct the part of each lease payment that's for your business use of the car. If you use your leased car 60% for business, you can deduct 60% of each lease payment. You can't deduct any payments you make to buy the car even if the payments are called lease payments. A lease with an option to buy may be a lease or a purchase contract, depending on its wording.

Keep accurate records of your car usage so that if you're challenged by the IRS, you can demonstrate the extent of your business use. The best procedure is to keep a daily log in your glove compartment to record the following about each business trip:
- date
- destination
- mileage
- business purpose.

E. Tax Audits

As a small business owner, you're three times more likely to be audited by the IRS than a regular employee-taxpayer would be. If you're audited, you have the burden of proving that your tax return is accurate. In over 80% of audits, the taxpayer winds up owing more taxes—usually because of poor record keeping rather than dishonesty.

If your business is facing an audit: *You'll get excellent guidance from* Tax Savvy for Small Business, *by Frederick W. Daily (Nolo)— which is the source of much of the material in this section. The* Tax Savvy *book goes through the audit process step by step and in great depth. And if, as* *commonly happens, the business audit turns into a personal audit as well, refer to* Stand Up to the IRS, *which is also by Frederick W. Daily (Nolo).*

1. How the IRS Audits a Small Business

The IRS conducts two kinds of audits of small businesses and their owners: *office* audits and *field* audits. There's a difference not only in where the audit is held, but also in the intensity of the process.

If you're a sole proprietor and gross less than $100,000 per year, the IRS is likely to ask you to come to their office for the audit. Usually an office audit lasts from two to four hours, and a typical business taxpayer is hit for additional taxes averaging about $4,000.

If you have a partnership or corporation, or a sole proprietorship that grosses over $100,000 a year, the IRS will probably order a field audit. The process will be much more intensive than an office audit. Field auditors—called revenue agents—are much better trained in accounting than are IRS office tax auditors. The average amount owed by a business after going through a field audit is over $17,000, including additional tax, penalty, and interest.

An IRS field audit may be conducted at your business place, but doesn't have to be. If your business premises are very small, you might point out that having the audit conducted there would interfere with your operations. Ask that the audit be held elsewhere—at the IRS office, for example. Or if you plan to be represented by a tax professional—a lawyer or accountant with tax experience—you can request that the audit be conducted at the professional's office.

Even though you have the right to have an audit conducted elsewhere, an auditor has the power to enter your business if it's open to the public. But an auditor can't go into a private area—such as a storeroom or your private office—unless you consent. But if you have nothing to hide, there's no reason to raise suspicions by denying access. Offer the IRS auditor a complete tour.

If you have a home office, you don't have to let an auditor into your home unless there's a court order. But if you refuse entry, your home office depreciation or rental expense will probably be disallowed because you haven't proven you had a home office.

2. The IRS Inquiry

Wherever the audit is conducted, the auditor will want to see the business records you used to prepare the tax returns. This can include check registers, bank statements, canceled checks, receipts, invoices, and a formal set of books.

To get still more financial information about you and your business, an auditor can require records from your tax preparer, banks, suppliers, customers, and others.

3. Hiring a Tax Professional

Many small business owners can handle a run of the mill IRS office audit without professional representation. Often it's sensible to do this, since the cost of hiring professional help may be more than the IRS is likely to bill you. However, if you fear that some serious irregularity may come to light—perhaps you've taken a huge deduction and can't produce a receipt or canceled check to verify it—consult with a tax professional before the audit.

When it comes to a field audit, where more money will almost surely be at stake, it's usually wise to bring in a tax professional from the outset. The IRS uses experienced auditors to conduct field audits, so you may be overmatched if questions come up about your documents or interpretations of the tax law.

4. Preparing for Your Audit

Thoroughly review the tax return that's going to be audited.

Make sure you can explain how you came up with the figures. Identify problem areas, such as how you reported particular items of income or expense.

Then find all the records you need to substantiate your tax return and organize them logically and clearly for the auditor. Among the items to gather up for the audit are:

- bank statements, canceled checks, and receipts
- electronic records—for example, charge card statements
- books and records—which can range from a formal set of books to cash register tapes
- appointment books, logs, and diaries
- car records, and
- travel and entertainment records.

If records are missing, you may still be able to prove a deduction by offering an oral explanation or by reconstructing records in writing. Business-related expenses of less than $25 each don't require substantiation.

Neatness counts. *It can be tempting to dump a pile of receipts on the table and require the auditor to search through them. This is one temptation you'll want to avoid. Neatness helps build credibility with the auditor who, when presented with well-maintained records, may even give you the benefit of the doubt on questionable items.*

5. What Auditors Look For

In auditing your business, the IRS will try to determine if you

- failed to report all of your business sales or receipts (income)
- skimmed cash from the business
- wrote off personal living costs—family travel, for example—as business expenses
- failed to file payroll tax returns on time or to make the required deposits, or

- improperly classified some workers as independent contractors rather than employees.

This isn't a complete list—just the things the IRS auditor will most likely scrutinize.

Be prepared for an analysis of your bank accounts. Office auditors don't always take the time to do this, but field auditors do. This consists of adding up all the deposits in all your business bank accounts to see if the total is more than your reported income. The auditor will also want to see all of your personal account records to learn if the amounts deposited are consistent with your business cash flow.

It's smart to review your bank accounts in advance to try to spot and be able to explain deposits that weren't income and therefore weren't reported on your tax return—loan proceeds, for example, or proceeds from the sale of assets (other than the capital gain portion), transfers from other accounts, inheritances, gifts, or money held for relatives.

After confirming that your income figures are accurate, turn to your business expenses. The tax law makes you prove that your deductions were legitimate; the IRS doesn't have to disprove them. Be especially careful to have good documentation for deductions you took for travel and entertainment, a home office, thefts, bad debts, depreciation, and car expenses—all prime targets during an IRS probe.

If you can't produce thorough records to back up your deductions, don't despair. You may be able to reconstruct the missing documents. For guidance on how to do this, see *Tax Savvy for Small Business,* by Frederick W. Daily (Nolo).

6. How to Behave at an Audit

Keep small talk to a minimum. An auditor is trained to listen for clues about your lifestyle—which may not seem affordable on your reported income. Raising suspicions in an auditor's mind can prolong the agony of an audit.

If you're asked a direct question, try to answer "yes" or "no." Don't over-explain or answer questions that weren't asked. If you don't have a ready answer, it's OK to say, "I don't know" or "I'll get back to you on that," or "I'll have to check with my accountant." Often the auditor will let it go. At the very least, you've bought some time, which can work to your advantage.

Most auditors are businesslike, but now and then you run into one who's impolite, hostile—or maybe is just having a bad day. You're entitled to courteous treatment from IRS auditors. If your auditor gets out of line, mention your right to courteous treatment and politely ask the auditor to lighten up. If that doesn't work, ask to speak to the auditor's manager and describe the unfair treatment you're receiving.

 It's all right to ask for time out. *You can stop or recess an audit for just about any good reason—for a few minutes to go to the bathroom or eat lunch, or for the day because you feel ill or need to confer with a tax professional. If you ask for a recess, the auditor may find it more convenient to resume the audit in a week or two—giving you time to regroup or get professional advice.*

7. How to Negotiate With an Auditor

As Fred Daily explains in much greater depth in *Tax Savvy for Small Business* (Nolo), there's often room to bargain during the audit process—despite the official line that IRS auditors don't negotiate.

One approach is to suggest that a disputed item be resolved by applying a percentage figure. Suppose you claimed the costs of a trip as a business deduction. The auditor, believing it was a personal trip, wants to disallow the deduction. You might say: "Perhaps, in fairness, the trip can be seen as being both for business and pleasure. How about agreeing that 70% of the expenses were for business and 30% for pleasure?" This may work. On the other hand, IRS auditors are instructed not to talk about compromising the dollars—so you may not get as far by using a more direct approach and proposing, for example, to pay $5,000 to settle a $10,000 IRS claim.

Another tactic in negotiating is to take the offensive. An audit isn't a one-way street. Auditors must make adjustments in your favor when you're legally entitled to one. Maybe you missed a deduction or were overly conservative on your return. When the auditor's review has been completed, bring up the items that entitle you to an adjustment in your favor. This can help offset the amounts the auditor claims you owe. ■

Raising Money for Your Business

To succeed in business, you'll need money to get started and to keep afloat until you become profitable—and, assuming you're successful, you'll probably need more money to expand than you can generate internally. How much you'll need and when you'll need it will depend on the nature of the business. However, unless you have a good-sized nest egg put aside or are starting a tiny, home-based business on a shoestring, finding money to finance your new enterprise is likely to be a major concern.

Fortunately, there are many places to look for startup funds. If one source doesn't pan out, you can try another and then another.

And there's no requirement that you get all your money from a single source. Often, you can tap a combination of sources—for example, savings, loans, and equity investments—to provide the needed funds. In this chapter, we'll look at all of these sources—and the legal rules that apply.

⚠ Watch your pennies. *Although you may be chomping at the bit to get your new business going, it can be a mistake to pour in too much money at the beginning. You need time to learn whether the business is viable. Because a fair number of small businesses fail, raising and spending a pile of money for an untested business idea can lead to much grief—especially if you're personally on the hook for borrowed funds. While some small businesses require a great deal of cash or credit up front, my experience is that many others don't. Consider starting as small and cheaply as possible. If your concept works, more funds will become available. If not, you can move on and take advantage of the lessons you've learned—and you won't be burdened with a ton of debts.*

A Business Plan Can Help

Before you start searching for money, it's helpful to write a business plan—a statement that analyzes your proposed business and explains how it will become profitable. *How to Write a Business Plan,* by Mike McKeever (Nolo), offers step-by-step guidance. McKeever suggests that a simple plan include the following elements:

- business description
- your personal business-related accomplishments
- sales revenue forecast
- profit and loss forecast
- capital spending plan, and
- cash flow forecast.

For a more sophisticated plan, McKeever recommends that the following elements be added:

- marketing plan
- future trends
- risks your business faces
- personnel plan
- specific business goals
- your personal financial statement, and
- your personal background—including your strong and weak points.

A major part of your business plan should cover how much money you'll need to get started and how you'll pay it back. Be conservative in projecting income. It may take months before a significant amount of money starts flowing into the business. Obviously, you'll need sufficient funds to carry you through the startup period. A cash flow analysis can help you decide how much money you should start out with so you can weather the lean, early days of the business and give yourself a reasonable chance to find out if the business can turn a profit.

Putting numbers on paper also forces you to focus on where the money will be coming from and how it will flow through your business. This is a valuable reality test for you and—equally important—it's something that lenders and investors will want to look at before shelling out money.

A. Two Types of Outside Financing

If you're starting a small business, chances are that at least part of the initial funding will come from your own pocket—savings, an inheritance, or a severance check you received for taking early retirement. But you may also need to seek money from outside sources, so it's important to understand the two main categories of such funding and the differences between them. One category consists of loans; the other consists of equity investments.

1. Loans

As you know, a loan is based on a simple idea: someone gives you money and you promise to pay it back—usually with interest. Since you must pay back the lender whether your business is a fabulous success or a miserable failure, the entire risk of your new enterprise is placed squarely on your shoulders.

Of course, nothing in business—or in life, for that matter—is without risk. Nevertheless, a commercial lender will be unwilling to lend you money if the odds of your repaying the money look low. And to help keep the risk down, a lender will very likely ask for security for the loan—for example, a mortgage on your house so that the lender can take and sell your house if you don't keep up your loan payments.

But as compared to selling a portion of your business to investors, there's an obvious plus side to borrowing money: If your business succeeds as you hope and you pay back the lender as promised, you reap all future profits. There's no need to share them.

In short, if you're confident about the prospects of your business and you have the opportunity to borrow money, a loan is a more attractive source of money than getting it from an equity investor who will own a piece of your business and receive a share of the profits. Again, the downside is that if

the business fails and you've personally guaranteed the loan, you'll have to repay it. By contrast, you don't have to repay equity investors if the business goes under.

Loans are so common that you probably are familiar with the mechanics, but nevertheless it makes sense to review the basics.

a. The Promissory Note

A lender will almost always want you to sign a written promissory note—a paper that says, in effect, "I promise to pay you $XXX plus interest of XX%" and then describes how and when payments are to be made. (See Section C2 for a sample form.) A bank or other commercial lender will use a form with a bit more wording than our form, but the basic idea is always the same.

A friend or relative may be willing to lend you money on a handshake. This is a poor idea for both of you. It's always a better business practice to put the loan in writing—and to state a specific interest rate and repayment plan. Otherwise, you open the door to unfortunate misunderstandings that can unnecessarily chill a great relationship.

Sign only the original of the promissory note. When it's paid off, you're entitled to get it back. You don't want several signed copies floating around that can cast doubt on whether the debt has been fully paid. But you should keep a photocopy of the signed note—marked "COPY"—for your business records.

b. Repayment Plans

If the interest rate on the loan doesn't exceed the maximum rate allowed by your state's usury law, you and the lender are free to work out the terms of repayment.

Typically, a state's usury law will allow a lender to charge a higher rate when lending money for business purposes than for personal reasons—in fact, in several of these state laws, there's no limit at all on the interest rate that can be charged on business loans, as long as the business borrower agrees to the rate in writing.

In a few states, the higher limit or absence of any limit applies only when the business borrower is organized as a corporation. In other states, the higher rates permitted for business borrowers are legal even if the borrower is a sole proprietorship, partnership, or limited liability company.

⚠ **Check your state usury law.** *As a general rule, if your business is a corporation and the terms of repayment are in a promissory note, the lender can safely charge interest of up to 10% per year and not have to worry about the usury law. But because there's so much variation in usury laws from state to state, you or the lender should check the law. Look under interest or usury in the index to your state's statutes. (For more on doing your own legal research, see Chapter 24.)*

Assuming there are no usury law problems, you and the lender can agree on any number of repayment plans. Let's say you borrow $10,000 with interest at the rate of 10% a year. Here are just a few of the repayment possibilities:

- *Lump sum repayment.* You agree, for example, to pay principal and interest in one lump sum at the end of one year. Under this plan, 12 months later you'd pay the lender $10,000 in "principal"—the borrowed amount—plus $1,000 in interest.

- *Periodic interest and lump sum repayment of principal.* You agree, for example, to pay interest only for two years and then interest and principal at the end of the third year. With this type of loan plan—often called a "balloon" loan because of the big payment at the end—you'd pay $1,000 in interest at the end of the first and second years, and then $10,000 in principal and $1,000 in interest at the end of the third year.

- *Periodic payments of principal and interest.* You agree, for example, to repay $2,500 of the principal each year for four years, plus interest at the end of each year. Under this plan, your payments would look like this:
  End of Year One:
    $2,500 principal + $1,000 interest
  End of Year Two:
    $2,500 principal + $750 interest
  End of Year Three:
    $2,500 principal + $500 interest
  End of Year Four:
    $2,500 principal + $250 interest.

- *Amortized payments.* You agree, for example, to make equal monthly payments so that principal and interest are fully paid in five years. Under this plan, you'd consult an amortization table in a book, on computer software, or on the Internet to figure out how much must be paid each month for five years to fully to pay off a $10,000 loan plus the 10% interest. The table would say you'd have to pay $212.48 a month. Each of your payments would consist of both principal and interest. At the beginning of the repayment period, the interest portion of each payment would be large; at the end, it would be small.

- *Amortized payments with a balloon.* You agree, for example, to make equal monthly payments based on a five-year amortization schedule, but to pay off the remaining principal at the end of the third year. Under this plan, you'd pay $212.48 each month for three years. At the end of the third year after making the normal monthly payment, there'd still be $4,604.42 in unpaid principal, so along with your normal payment of $212.48, you'd make a balloon payment to cover the remaining principal.

⚠️ **Avoid loans with prepayment penalties.**
Whenever you borrow money, you'd like to be free to reduce or pay off the principal faster than called for in the promissory note if you have the wherewithal to do so, since this reduces or stops the running of interest. In other words, if you have a three-year loan but are able to pay it off by the end of year two, you don't want to pay interest for year three. By law, some states always allow such early repayment and you pay interest only for the time you have the use of the borrowed money. In other states, however, the law allows a lender to charge a penalty (amounting to a portion of the future interest) when a borrower reduces the balance or pays back a loan sooner than called for. Because it seems unfair to have to pay anything for the use of borrowed money except interest for the time the principal is actually in your hands, try to make sure any promissory note you sign says you can prepay any or all of the principal without penalty. If the lender doesn't agree, see if you can negotiate a compromise under which you'll owe a prepayment penalty only if you pay back the loan during a relatively short period, such as six months from the time you borrow the money.

c. Security

Lenders, with the possible exception of friends or relatives, will probably require you to provide some valuable property—called security or collateral—that they can grab and sell to collect their money if you can't keep up with the loan repayment plan. For example, the lender may seek a second mortgage or deed of trust on your house, or may ask for a security interest or lien on your mutual funds or the equipment, inventory, and accounts receivable of your business. Again, the reason for doing this is if you don't make your payments, the lender can sell the pledged assets (the security) to pay off the loan.

But it's important to realize that a lender isn't limited to using the pledged assets to satisfy the loan. If you don't make good on your repayment commitment, a lender also has the right to sue you.

Typically, a lender will seize pledged assets first and then sue you only if the funds realized from those assets are insufficient to pay off the loan—but that's not a legal requirement. A lender may decide to sue you before using up the pledged assets. If the lender wins the lawsuit and gets a judgment against you, assets you haven't specifically pledged as security are at risk—as is a portion of your future earnings.

In short, before you borrow money—under either a secured or unsecured promissory note—think about what will happen if you run into financial problems.

d. Cosigners and Guarantors

If you lack sufficient assets to pledge as security for a loan, a lender may try other methods to attempt to guarantee that the loan will be prepaid. One is to ask you to get someone who is richer than you to cosign or guarantee the loan. That means the lender will have two people rather than one to collect from if you don't make your payments.

When asking friends or relatives to cosign or guarantee a promissory note, be sure they understand that they're risking their personal assets if you don't repay it.

If you're married, the lender may insist that your spouse cosign the promissory note. Be aware that if your spouse signs, not only are your personal assets at risk, but also those assets that the two of you jointly own—a house, for example, or a bank account. What's more, if your spouse has a job, his or her earnings will be subject to garnishment if the lender sues and gets a judgment against the two of you because the loan isn't repaid as promised.

Community Property States

If you live in a community property state— Arizona, California, Idaho, Louisiana, Nevada, New Mexico, Texas, Washington, or Wisconsin—you'll need to do a bit of research or consult briefly with a business lawyer to learn the legal effect of your spouse cosigning a promissory note. (See Chapter 24.) In researching Wisconsin law, you'd look under marital property, but the concept is the same as community property for all practical purposes.

In a community property state, debts incurred by one spouse are usually the legal responsibility of both—meaning that a couple's community property is at risk if the debt isn't paid.

In addition to community property, you or your spouse may have separate property— which, depending on the law of the particular community property state, is usually property owned by a spouse prior to marriage or acquired after marriage by gift or inheritance. The effect of your spouse cosigning a promissory note for a business loan is to obligate his or her separate property, as well, to repay the loan.

⚠️ **Forming a corporation or LLC may not protect you from personal liability on a loan.** *As explained in Chapter 1, a virtue of doing business as a corporation or a limited liability company (LLC) is that corporate shareholders and LLC members aren't personally liable for paying business debts, including loans made by the corporation or LLC. But a small corporation or LLC—especially one just starting up—will find it impossible to borrow money from a bank or other sophisticated lender unless the shareholders or members personally guarantee repayment. And if this guarantee is made, the shareholders or members are just as obligated to repay the loan as if they signed as personal borrowers*

in the first place. Typically, lenders will continue to require that shareholders or LLC members guarantee repayment of a corporate or LLC loan—at least until the business is well established and has a long record of being profitable.

2. Equity Investments

Equity investors buy a piece of your business. They become co-owners and share in the fortunes and misfortunes of your business. Like you, they can make or lose a bundle. Generally, if your business does badly or flops, you're under no obligation to pay them back their money.

However, some equity investors would like to have their cake and eat it too; they want you to guarantee some return on their investment even if the business does poorly. Unless you're really desperate for the cash, avoid an investor who wants a guarantee. It's simply too risky a proposition for someone starting or running a small business.

a. Limiting Risk

Because equity investors are co-owners of the business, they may be exposed to personal liability for all business debts unless your business is a corporation, limited partnership, or limited liability company. If you recruit equity investors for what has been your sole proprietorship, your business will now be treated as a general partnership. This means your equity investors will be considered to be general partners, whether or not they take part in running the business. And, as explained in Chapter 1, as far as people outside of the business are concerned—people who are owed money or who have a judgment against the business—general partners are all personally liable for the debts of the partnership.

Equity investors often want to limit their losses to what they put into the business. An investor who puts $10,000 into a business may be prepared to lose the $10,000—but no more. In short, the investor doesn't want to put the rest of his or her assets at risk. The investor will want to avoid being—or being treated as—a general partner.

Fortunately, there are three common ways to organize your business so that you can offer an investor protection from losses beyond the money being invested.

- *Corporation.* Form a corporation and issue stock to the investor. A shareholder who doesn't participate in corporate activities and decision making is virtually free from liability beyond his or her original investment. A shareholder who does help run the company is liable to outsiders for his or her own actions—for example, making slanderous statements or negligently operating a piece of equipment—but isn't liable for corporate debts or the actions of corporate employees.
- *Limited Partnership.* Form a limited partnership and make the investor a limited partner. A limited partner's freedom from liability is similar to that of a shareholder, as long as the limited partner doesn't become actively involved in running the business.
- *Limited Liability Company.* Form a limited liability company and make the investor a member. The investor will be protected in much the same manner as a shareholder or limited partner.

Each of these business formats is described in much greater detail in Chapter 1.

⚠ Encourage investors to determine their own degree of risk. *As mentioned, an investor in a business organized as a corporation, limited partnership, or limited liability company usually stands to lose no more than his or her investment. However, state laws must be followed carefully to achieve this result. To avoid having investors accuse you of giving misleading assurances, recommend that they check with their own financial and legal advisors to evaluate whether their investment exposes them to the possibility of incurring additional losses.*

b. Return on Investment

Someone who invests in your business may be willing to face the loss of the entire investment and not insist that you guarantee repayment. But to offset the risk of losing the invested money, the investor may want to receive substantial benefits if the business is successful.

For example, an investor may insist on a generous percentage of the business profits and, to help assure that there are such profits, may seek to put a cap on your salary. The terms are always negotiable—there's no formula for figuring out what's fair to both you and the investor.

Here are just a few possibilities:

- John, a former police detective, decides to start a business to offer security training seminars to midsized manufacturing companies. He forms STS Limited Liability Company and invests $10,000, which is only part of his $20,000 start-up budget. His aunt Paula, recently widowed, invests $10,000 of her inheritance in the company. The STS operating agreement states that John will be in full control of day-to-day operations. John and Paula agree in writing that John will receive a salary of no more than $4,000 a month from STS for the first four years, and that Paula will receive 60% of STS profits during that period. After that, John's salary will be tied to gross receipts, and John and Paula will share profits equally.
- Stella wants to start a travel agency. She approaches Edgar, a friend from college days, who has just sold a screenplay to a major studio and is looking for investment opportunities. They agree that Stella will form a limited partnership and act as the general partner. Edgar will invest $60,000 in the business and become a limited partner. Stella will work for $3,000 a month and use the first profits of the travel agency pay back Edgar's $60,000 investment. After that, the profits will be split 50/50.
- Larry, an experienced carpenter, wants to become a general contractor so he can build cus-

tom homes and do major remodeling jobs. He's able to invest his savings of $30,000 in his new venture, but needs another $20,000 to get started. Larry forms a corporation, Prestige Homes Inc., and invites his friend Brook, who owns a building supply business, to invest $20,000 in return for a 40% interest in Prestige Homes. Brook agrees, on the condition that the new corporation will buy all its lumber and other building materials from Brook's company—and, in addition, pay Brook $5,000 for each home that's built by Prestige Homes. They sign a shareholders' agreement containing those terms.

c. Compliance With Securities Regulations

The law treats corporate shares and limited partnership interests as securities. Issuing these securities to investors is regulated by federal and state law. In some cases, an investor's interest in a limited liability company may also come under these laws.

This means that before selling an investor an interest in your business, you'll need to learn more about the requirements of the securities laws. Fortunately, there are generous exemptions that normally allow a small business to provide a limited number of investors an interest in the business without complicated paperwork. Chances are good that your business will be able to qualify for these exemptions.

In the rare cases in which the exemptions won't work for your small business and you have to meet the complex requirements of the securities laws—such as distributing an approved prospectus to potential investors—it's probably too much trouble to do the deal unless a great deal of money is involved.

 For a first-rate introduction to securities laws and the exemptions for small businesses: *See* Incorporate Your Business: A 50-State Legal Guide to Forming a Corporation, *or* How to Form Your Own California Corporation, *both by Anthony Mancuso (Nolo).*

B. Thirteen Common Sources of Money

While there are many sources of money for a small business, some are more accessible than others. There are 13 that entrepreneurs tend to rely on most frequently.

1. Salary

"Don't give up your day job." That's the advice commonly given to aspiring actors and musicians—but it's equally applicable to many entrepreneurs who are testing the waters. If you start small enough, you may be able to stay afloat for many months by continuing your full-time job or cutting back to part time. This steady source of income can reduce your need for turning to others for start-up funds and can help keep you solvent if the business doesn't succeed.

2. Personal Savings

Putting your own money into your business is the simplest way to get started or to expand your business. You avoid entanglements with others, keep your business affairs private, and steer clear of possible legal complications.

If your business takes off, you'll own business assets—such as inventory, equipment, and furniture—free of debt, making it easier to borrow money later or bring equity investors into the business.

Your money may come from savings that you've carefully accumulated over the years. Or it may come from a lump sum of money that's available all at once. For example, you may have received an inheritance from a relative or an attractive severance package from a job you've just left. Or perhaps you've sold your house and will be living in a less expensive one or in rented quarters. Investing this money in your own business may yield a bigger return than you could ever expect to receive by investing it in someone else's business.

⚠ **Try to keep some cash in reserve.**
Since no business is risk-free and the cash flow is usually unpredictable, it makes sense not to commit every last dollar to your business. Yes, this can be extremely hard to do. But if you can plan well enough to keep a reasonable amount of cash on hand to cover several months' worth of living expenses and possible medical emergencies, you'll improve your odds of succeeding in business. And you'll receive an added bonus of not having to worry constantly about how to pay personal bills.

If You're the Beneficiary of a Trust Fund

Another possible source of funds can be a trust fund established on your behalf at the death of a parent, grandparent, or other relative. Often these funds provide the beneficiary with income for a number of years before the trust ends and all remaining funds are turned over to the beneficiary in a lump sum. However, in the meantime, the trustee often has the discretionary power to take additional money out of the trust for a good reason, such as education, health needs, and possibly starting a business.

Since the trustee's discretion will be tied to the specific wording of the trust document, you'll want to start by reading it carefully. But assuming that distributing money for a business venture would qualify as a proper purpose under the trust, you should present your business plan to the trustee. If the trustee agrees that your plan has merit, this can magically free up the cash you're looking for.

3. Equity in Your Home

If you own a home, you may be able to tap into a portion of the equity to raise cash. As you know, equity is the difference between what the home is worth and how much is left on the mortgage. Let's say you bought your home several years ago for $150,000 by paying $30,000 down and getting a $120,000 mortgage. Today, the house would sell for $200,000 and the mortgage balance is down to $100,000. You have $100,000 in equity—some of which you can use to help finance your business.

There are two ways to get your hands on a portion of the equity. One is to get a new, larger mortgage that will pay off the earlier one and still yield some cash. For example, if you get a new mortgage for $160,000—which is 80% of the home's current value and likely to be approved by a conservative lender—you'll have $60,000 after the earlier mortgage balance of $100,000 is paid off.

Unfortunately, the actual amount you'll end up with will be significantly less because the bank will require you to pay some hefty costs for processing the mortgage. These transaction costs typically include an application fee, document preparation fees, closing costs known as points, fees for a personal credit check, an appraisal of the home, and mortgage title insurance.

⚠ Plan carefully before applying for a new mortgage. *If your purpose in getting a new mortgage is to raise a relatively small amount of money for your business, make sure you understand all of the costs involved. Obviously, unless it's your only way to raise money, you don't want to plunk down $2,000 in expenses to get your hands on $10,000 that, of course, will also require you to pay interest. Before applying for a mortgage, ask the lender to itemize the costs involved. Also, if you're planning to quit your job or cut back to half-time to run the business, it may be wise to wait until after the mortgage loan has been made—especially if you don't have a spouse or significant other earning a decent income. This is because before approving the new mortgage, the lender will be looking at your ability to repay. Having a steady source of income from a job when you apply for and receive a mortgage loan can help convince the lender to approve the loan.*

The second approach is to apply for a line of credit based on your home equity. The bank will have a second mortgage on your home. Using the assumptions in the example, you may be able to obtain a line of credit for $60,000. Typically, the bank will give you a checkbook that you can use to write checks against the line of credit. Your monthly payment to the bank will depend on how much of the credit line you've used.

Deciding which method to use can be difficult. A line of credit will likely cost less to set up—perhaps there will simply be a $250 upfront fee rather than a few thousand dollars in closing costs for a mortgage—but the interest rate will likely be higher or, if the loan has a variable interest rate, the bank will have the right to increase the interest rate if interest rates in the overall economy rise.

💡 Don't overdo borrowing against your house. *Whichever method you use to borrow against your house, you put your home at risk if you can't meet the repayment schedule. You don't want to lose your house to the lender or be forced to sell under pressure of an imminent foreclosure to save a portion of the equity. So don't borrow more than you absolutely need. Also, take time to figure out how you'll make the mortgage payments if your business is slow to get off the ground or you end up closing it. One good approach is to look for a loan with a long repayment window and, hence, lower monthly payments. If your business does well, you can always repay the loan sooner.*

4. Retirement Savings

If you have money in a retirement savings plan where you work, you may be able to borrow some of that money. As you know, income tax on the money you contribute to an IRS-qualified plan—such as a 401(k) plan—is deferred, allowing your retirement to grow faster.

Check the plan language to see whether loans are allowed for business purposes. If so, you should be able to borrow up to one-half of what you have in the plan—but no more than $50,000. Also check other conditions, such as the maximum term allowed for a loan (typically, five years), the interest rate, and the loan fees. You will have to pay interest on the money you borrow from your plan, but that's not all bad. Because the money you're borrowing is yours, the interest goes back into your plan.

Generally, unless you've reached the age of 59½, you wouldn't be wise to simply take rather than borrow money from the tax-deferred plan. Early withdrawals are subject to a penalty tax. After age

59½, however, IRS rules allow you to withdraw funds without paying a penalty tax.

⚠ **Don't borrow from an IRA.** *Unfortunately, if you borrow money from an Individual Retirement Account (IRA), it will be treated as a withdrawal and you'll have to pay a penalty tax if you're not yet 59 ½ years old.*

5. Credit Cards

You can use your credit cards to help finance your business. Plastic can quickly get you a computer and fax machine—and probably other business equipment and furniture as well. And for expenses such as rent, phone bills, or money to pay employees, you can usually get a cash advance.

Credit cards are a convenient way to arrange for short-term financing because they're so easy to use. Over the long haul, however, they're less attractive—mainly because the interest charges are relatively high, often as much as 20% or more per year. If you're going to succeed in business, you shouldn't need me to tell you not to borrow very much for very long at those rates.

6. Buying on Credit

The companies from which you're buying goods or services may offer favorable credit terms to capture your business. Often this will mean you don't have to pay your bill for 30 or 60 or more days. Or you may be able to spread payments for a purchase over a period of several months with no finance charges as long as you pay each installment on time. And the interest rate that's charged may be substantially lower than that charged by a credit card company.

Don't be discouraged by the fact that the best credit terms usually go to established businesses and that new businesses typically have to pay up front. Credit decisions are somewhat subjective,

leaving you room to convince the seller that your new business deserves special consideration.

Especially if you'll need starting inventory, as in the case of a retail store, call suppliers and ask for help. Show them a copy of your credit history and business plan. If they look good and you're persuasive, you may be able to get a fair amount of your inventory on favorable terms.

7. Leasing

If you need equipment—anything from computers and copiers to forklifts and trucks—consider leasing it. True, leasing doesn't put money directly in your hands but, almost as good from a cash flow point of view, it does reduce the amount of cash you'd have to come up with if you were to instead buy the same equipment. And many leases offer you the option to acquire the equipment for a nominal amount when the lease period is over.

Over the long term, leasing usually costs a bit more than buying—but if the cash flow from your business will be tight for a few years, leasing can be an effective way to get the equipment you need now.

8. Friends, Relatives, and Business Associates

Those close to you can often lend you money or invest in your business. This helps you avoid the hassle of pleading your case to outsiders and enduring extra paperwork and bureaucratic delays—and can be especially valuable if you've been through bankruptcy or had other credit problems that would make borrowing from a commercial lender difficult or impossible.

Some advantages of borrowing money from people you know well are that you may be charged a lower interest rate, may be able to delay paying back money until you're more established, and may be given more flexibility if you get into a jam. But once the loan terms are agreed to, there's one thing that borrowing from friends, relatives, or business associates doesn't do. It doesn't legally diminish your obligation to meet those terms.

In addition, borrowing money from relatives and friends can have a big downside. There's always the possibility that if your business does poorly and those close to you end up losing money, you'll damage a good personal relationship. So in dealing with friends, relatives, and business associates, be extra careful to not only clearly establish the terms of the deal and put it in writing, but also make an extra effort to explain the risks. In short, it's your job to make sure your helpful friend or relative won't suffer a true hardship if you're unable to meet your financial commitments.

⚠ **Don't borrow from people on fixed incomes.** *Don't borrow or accept investment money from folks who can't afford to lose money. It's fine to borrow needed money from your Mom if she's well enough off that lending you $20,000 won't put her in the poorhouse if things go wrong and you can't repay the loan. But if your Mom lives on Social Security, don't borrow her last $10,000 no matter how badly you need it. If you do and your business fails, you'll be about as miserable as it's possible to be.*

Gifts Can Save Taxes

If you're likely to inherit money from a parent or grandparent in the future, it can make sense for them to make a gift now. Why? Because if a family member's estate exceeds a certain amount ($1.5 million in 2005, rising to $2 million in 2006), the excess will be heavily taxed by the federal government when that person dies.

By contrast, up to fairly generous limits, there will be no estate or gift tax on the money the relative gives away while alive. Specifically, an individual can make a gift of up to $11,000 per year per person free of any federal gift or estate tax—and a couple can give twice that amount.

For example, your mother and father can each give $11,000 to you and $11,000 to your spouse—a total of $44,000—in one year. This has the effect of removing this money from their estates with neither a federal estate or gift tax. Obviously, gifts of that size can be a big boost to any small business since there is no worry about the need to repay.

💡 **How to promote family harmony.** *If your parents give you money for your business, it may make sense for them to make equal gifts to the other children. Or if the parent isn't financially able to do this, he or she can even things out by leaving the other children more in a will or trust. If this is done, the reason for the discrepancy can be explained in the will or trust, or in a separate letter.*

📖 **For detailed information on gifts and the tax laws:** *See* Plan Your Estate, *by Denis Clifford and Cora Jordan (Nolo).*

9. Supporters

As Mike McKeever points out in *How to Write a Business Plan* (Nolo), many types of businesses have loyal and devoted followers—people who care as much about the business as the owners do. A health food restaurant, a women's bookstore, an import car repair shop, or an art studio, for example, may attract people who are enthusiastic about lending money to or investing in the business because it fits in with their lifestyle or beliefs.

Their decision to participate is driven to some extent by their feelings and is not strictly a business proposition. These people can also be a source of great ideas—ideas that can be as valuable as money—and they'll be happy to share these with you at no charge.

The rules for borrowing from friends and relatives apply here as well. Put repayment terms in writing—and don't accept money from people who can't afford to risk it.

10. Banks

Banks are in the money business, so it's natural to look to them for startup funds. It's hard to predict, however, whether the banks you approach will be willing to lend you money on reasonable terms.

Historically, banks were reluctant to lend substantial sums to a new business, even if the owner was willing to pledge a house or other valuable asset as security for repayment (for example, by giving the bank a second mortgage). Often this reluctance to lend was attributable to the fact that loan officers were looking for an established record of business profitability which, of course, a new business couldn't provide.

Fortunately, that standoffish attitude is starting to crumble. Many banks, in fact, have departments geared especially to the needs of small businesses—and some are even eager to establish a banking relationship with those just getting started. With a little luck, you may be able to locate such an enlightened, small-business-oriented bank in your community. As you might imagine, banks offer their best terms to businesses that appear the least risky and that are likely to maintain sizable deposits as the business grows.

Banks tend to respond more favorably to loan applications when the requested loan has been guaranteed by the Small Business Administration (SBA). Two SBA loan programs are particularly worth a look:

- **Basic 7(a) Loan Program.** If you qualify, the SBA will typically guarantee up to 85% of a loan of $150,000 or less, and up to 75% of a loan above $150,000. You can use the loan proceeds for most sound business purposes, such as working capital, equipment, and buying or renovating a building. You get the loan from a commercial lender, and the SBA supplies the guarantee.
- **Microloans.** These are short-term loans to let you buy inventory, supplies, furniture, fixtures, and equipment. You can borrow up to $35,000, but the average loan is about $10,500. You apply through a local intermediary lender—a nonprofit organization with experience in lending and in giving technical assistance. The funds are provided by the SBA.

 Check out the SBA's loan prequalification program. *SBA-affiliated experts are available to analyze your loan application, as long as you're not applying for more than $250,000. The program focuses on your character, credit, experience, and reliability, rather than on your assets. The expert will work with you to strengthen your loan application and improve your chances of qualifying for an SBA loan or guarantee.*

Want more information on SBA loans? *The best starting point is the SBA website, www.sba.gov.*

11. Other Commercial Lenders

If you can't get a bank loan, consider applying to other commercial lenders, such as Allied Capital Corp., the Money Store, or GE Capital. More than one third of the money loaned to small businesses comes from these nonbank sources. They're often less tightfisted than banks and may give more weight to intangible factors like your business vision and personal integrity. You'll be in an especially good position to borrow from a nonbank lender if your loan qualifies for SBA backing.

The Five C's of Credit

Bankers like to speak of the five C's of credit analysis—factors they look at when they evaluate a loan request. When applying to a bank for a loan, be prepared to address these points.

- **Character.** Bankers lend money to borrowers who appear honest and who have a good credit history. Before you apply for a loan, obtain a copy of your credit report and clean up any problems.
- **Capacity.** This is a prediction of the borrower's ability to repay the loan. For a new business, bankers look at the business plan. For an existing business, bankers consider financial statements and industry trends.
- **Collateral.** Bankers generally want a borrower to pledge an asset that can be sold to pay off the loan if the borrower lacks funds.
- **Capital.** The borrower's net worth—the amount by which assets exceed debts—is scrutinized.
- **Conditions.** The current economic climate can influence whether a loan is given and the amount of the loan.

---

12. Venture Capitalists

There are companies and individuals looking to invest in extraordinary companies that will reward them with large profits. See if your city has a venture capital club which helps introduce new businesses to venture capitalists. If so, get in contact and find out how you can meet potential investors.

Often you'll be afforded a chance to make a short presentation which can make an impression on someone with deep pockets. Your local or state chamber of commerce should be able to direct you to the closest club, or you can check with the instructor of a business school that offers courses in entrepreneurship.

13. The Seller of an Existing Business

If you're buying an existing business, you may be able to negotiate favorable payment terms—which can reduce the amount of cash you have to come up with. You have a number of variables to work with. Try to keep the down payment low and see if the seller will agree to below-market interest rates or will even charge no interest for the first year or two.

Try, too, to extend the payments over as many years as possible. As with a bank loan, you can always pay the debt off early if your business prospers. (For more on buying a business, see Chapter 10.)

C. Document All Money You Receive

In raising money for your business, you should be familiar with the basic paperwork and other legal requirements, a number of which I've already mentioned in this chapter.

Chapter 4 of *Legal Forms for Starting & Running a Small Business* contains several promissory note forms and a security agreement.

1. Gifts

If a family member gives you money for your business, it's smart to put it in writing. Strictly speaking, this isn't a legal requirement, but nevertheless I highly recommend that you do so. For one thing, it can help with taxes. An individual can make a gift each year of up to $11,000 to any number of people. These gifts won't be subject to either the federal estate or gift tax. (See "Gifts Can Save Money," in Section B8.) If the giver states in writing that the money is a gift and not a loan, it will be clear to the IRS that no tax is owed.

A second reason to document the gift is to avoid possible future misunderstandings with other people who eventually inherit from the giver. Incredible as it may seem, brothers and sisters have sometimes gone to court to argue that a sum of money that a parent advanced to one child should be treated not as a gift, but as a loan to be repaid to the estate. And even where siblings haven't resorted to such drastic action, doubts about a parent's intentions can simmer beneath the surface for years, hurting the relationship.

2. Loans Without Security

The way to document a loan is through a promissory note. (See Section A1.)

Banks and other commercial lenders will have their own forms for you to sign. The following forms can be used if you borrow money from a relative or friend.

SAMPLE PROMISSORY NOTE FOR INSTALLMENT PAYMENTS THAT INCLUDE PRINCIPAL AND INTEREST

September 1, 20XX

For value received, I promise to pay to Leo Lender

$10,000 and interest at the rate of 10% per annum on the unpaid balance as follows:

1. I will pay 60 monthly installments of $212.48 each.

2. I will pay the first installment on October 1, 20XX, and a similar installment on the first day of each month after that until principal and interest have been paid in full.

3. Payments will be applied first on interest and then on principal.

4. I will pay the entire amount of principal and interest within five years from the date of this note.

5. I may prepay all or any part of the principal without penalty.

6. If I am more than 10 days late in making any payment, Leo Lender may declare that the entire balance of unpaid principal is due immediately, together with the interest that has accrued.

_____

Bob Borrower

SAMPLE PROMISSORY NOTE FOR ANNUAL INTEREST PAYMENTS AND BALLOON PAYMENT OF PRINCIPAL

September 1, 20XX

For value received, I promise to pay to Leo Lender

$10,000 and interest at the rate of 10% per annum on the unpaid balance as follows:

1. I will pay interest on September 1 each year for five years beginning in 20XX.

2. I will pay the principal five years from the date of this note.

3. I may prepay all or any part of the principal without penalty.

4. If I am more than 10 days late in making any payment, Leo Lender may declare that the principal is due immediately, together with the interest that has accrued.

_____

Bob Borrower

SAMPLE PROMISSORY NOTE FOR LUMP SUM REPAYMENT

September 1, 20XX

For value received, I promise to pay to Leo Lender

$10,000 and interest at the rate of 10% per annum on the unpaid balance on [_Insert date when the entire $10,000 plus interest is due_]. I may prepay all or any part of the principal without penalty.

_____

Bob Borrower

 For additional promissory notes that cover several common transactions: _See_ 101 Law Forms for Personal Use (with CD-ROM), _by Robin Leonard and Ralph Warner (Nolo). You'll find promissory notes that can be used for a loan repayable in a lump sum with no interest, a lump sum with interest, installments without interest, installments with interest, a lump sum secured by real or personal property, and installments secured by real or personal property._

3. Loans With Security

If you're pledging property as security for a loan, you can start with one of the sample forms given in Section C2, above—but the promissory note should also state that it's a secured loan and that additional documents have been prepared and are being signed to fully protect the lender.

Commercial lenders will generally prepare these additional documents. When you're borrowing from a friend or family member, however, and pledging security for the loan, you and the lender will need to follow through on these details.

a. Note Secured by Personal Property

Personal property is property that's not real estate—equipment and inventory, for example. If you're pledging personal property as security, here is sample language to include in a promissory note:

SECURED INTEREST PROVISION

I agree that until the principal and interest owed under this note are paid in full, the note will be secured by a security agreement signed today giving (_lender's name_) a security interest in the equipment, fixtures, inventory, and accounts receivable of the business known as (_name of borrower's business_).

You should prepare and sign a security agreement that gives the lender the right to take the specified assets if you don't repay your loan as agreed. Also prepare and sign a Uniform Commercial Code Financing Statement—sometimes called Form UCC-1. This form should be available at office supply stores that serve lawyers.

Generally, there will be a statewide office where the lender should file this form. In addition, in many states, the lender should also file a copy at the county office that keeps records of liens on personal property. The form notifies future creditors that the lender is a secured creditor and holds a lien on the listed assets. When you pay off the loan, the lender should release the lien—and, as with real estate liens, the release should be filed at the same public office where the Form UCC-1 was filed.

If you pledge a car or truck, check with the office in your state that handles motor vehicle titles to learn how to record the fact that the lender is obtaining a security interest in the car or truck.

b. Note Secured by Real Estate

Here is sample language to include in a note secured by real estate:

SECURED INTEREST PROVISION

```
    I agree that until the principal and
interest owed under this note are paid in
full, the note will be secured by a mort-
gage [or deed of trust] to real estate
commonly known as ___(address or other
description)___, owned by
_____(name)_____ signed on _(date)_
and recorded at ___(place recorded)___.
```

You'll probably need professional help in preparing the mortgage or deed of trust. This is routine stuff for an experienced real estate lawyer, so you should be able to get it done by paying for a half-hour or less of a lawyer's time.

The mortgage or deed of trust will have to be witnessed and notarized, and then get recorded for a small fee at a government office that handles real estate registrations. To learn the name and location of the correct government office, call the county clerk or inquire at a title insurance company.

⚠ **Be sure the security interest gets canceled.** *You don't want to face problems ten years from now when you go to sell the real estate. So when you pay off the loan, don't forget to get a paper signed by the lender that releases or discharges the mortgage or deed of trust. The document, which will need to be witnessed and notarized, must be filed at the same place where the mortgage or deed of trust was filed. Again, you'd be wise to consult briefly with a lawyer or check with a local title insurance company to make sure you're doing this correctly.*

4. Equity Investments

Equity investments in a limited partnership, corporation, or limited liability company are usually treated as securities and may be regulated by federal and state laws. (See Section A2.) It's unlikely that this will be a problem for a small business with just a few owners and investors. Investments in these businesses are usually exempt from the regulations. If that's so in your case, you won't have to deal with the sometimes burdensome paperwork.

If, however, you decide to go public—make a public offering of an interest in your business—then you definitely need to seek detailed legal advice.

Whether or not you must meet special requirements under federal or state laws regulating securities, you should always have a written agreement with an equity investor. The mechanics will depend on the legal structure of your business.

- **Sole Proprietorship.** By definition, a sole proprietorship is owned by just one person. Anyone else who invests in your business and acquires equity in it becomes a co-owner—

which means that, legally, your sole proprietorship is converted into a partnership. It makes sense to sign a partnership agreement outlining your responsibilities and those of the investor (see Chapter 2).

- **Partnership.** An equity investor in a partnership is a partner, so you should amend your partnership agreement to include your new partner and specify the financial relationships. All partners—old and new—should sign it. (Again, see Chapter 2 for help on partnership agreements and consult *The Partnership Book,* by Denis Clifford and Ralph Warner (Nolo).)

- **Limited Partnership.** Assuming that the investor will play a passive role and won't be actively involved in running the business, he or she will be a limited partner. The limited partnership agreement will define how a limited partner gets money from the business. The limited partner will receive a certificate recognizing his or her interest in the limited partnership.

- **Corporation.** The equity investor will be a shareholder. You, the equity investor and all other shareholders should sign a shareholders' agreement—or amend the existing agreement if there is one—to spell out the corporation's obligations to the investor. The corporation should issue a stock certificate in the investor's name.

- **Limited Liability Company.** The equity investor will be a member. You, the equity investor, and all other members of the LLC should sign an operating agreement—or amend the existing operating agreement if there is one. ■

Buying a Business

For those who would like to own their own business, buying an existing business may be a better approach than starting from scratch. After all, there's something attractive about letting someone else find a location and sign a lease; test the market and develop a customer base; buy furniture, fixtures, equipment, and inventory; hire employees; and perform the countless other chores that go with starting a business. In short, you'll have let someone else prove that the business works.

If you find yourself looking for an existing business to buy, keep an open mind. It's not always possible to buy a business you'll be happy with at a price you can afford. Many people who buy existing businesses do very well, but others, having explored the opportunities and finding nothing to their liking, return to the idea of starting their own business. And some people pay too much money for a poor business or one they may never really enjoy operating.

This chapter first looks at how to find a business to buy. Then it turns to the nuts and bolts of actually buying a business, including how to structure the purchase, what to investigate before closing the deal, and the legal documents needed for a business to change hands.

Selling a Business. This chapter focuses on buying a business, but a seller's concerns are also discussed briefly in Section I.

A. Finding a Business to Buy

Before you look for a business to buy, narrow your field of possible choices. First, decide whether you want to be in a service, manufacturing, wholesale, retail, or food service business. Once you make this choice, consider the specific type of business you're interested in—perhaps a desktop publishing center, a management consulting business, a direct-mail processing business, a dance studio, a flower shop, or a used book store.

Your choice of business should be motivated by the type of work you've done in the past, courses you've taken, special skills you've developed through a hobby, or perhaps just a strong yearning to work in a particular field. It's almost always a mistake to consider buying a business you know little about, no matter how good it looks. For example, if you're confused by mechanical and electronic equipment, buying an auto tune-up shop or a business that installs security systems makes little sense even if the business looks irresistible from a financial point of view.

If you're currently employed by a small business you like, what are the chances of that business becoming available to you? Maybe the current owner wants to retire, is in bad health, is moving out of the city, or is just getting bored. If you know the inner workings of the business and are sure that it's doing well—or at least that it has the potential to flower under your able leadership—that would be an ideal place to start. Failing that, perhaps business associates or friends can provide you with leads to similar businesses that may be available.

Here are some other time-tested ways to search for an available business:

- *Newspaper ads*. This is a traditional starting point and can quickly put you in touch with people who are actively seeking a buyer for their business. Unfortunately, ads are only the tip of the iceberg. Many of the best business opportunities never get into the papers but surface by word of mouth.

- *Professionals who advise small businesses.* Bankers, lawyers, accountants, insurance agents, and real estate brokers who regularly work with small businesses often know about available businesses before they go on the market. Think about who you know who is plugged into this network and get on the phone. A few well-placed phone calls may be enough to identify likely candidates in your area.

- *Business suppliers.* Another great way to tap into the grapevine is to contact the network of suppliers for that business. For example, if you're thinking of opening a flower shop, a floral wholesaler in your area will probably know who is thinking of retiring or selling out for other reasons.

- *Trade associations.* Almost every business has a local or regional trade association—for example, the Northern California Booksellers Association or the Michigan Pest Control Association. The secretary or a longtime employee of such a group may have heard about a business owner who's thinking of retiring.

- *The direct approach.* If there's a business that you've admired from afar, simply drop in and politely ask if the owner has ever thought about selling. Who knows? Maybe he or she has been thinking about moving to another part of the country or changing to a different type of business. Once in a while, you'll be in the right place at the right time. A long shot? Probably—but you have nothing to lose by trying it.

- *Business brokers.* Finally, there are business brokers—people who earn commissions from business owners who need help finding buyers. As is true in all endeavors, not all business brokers are created equal. A few are honest, ingenious, and hardworking. Many more are adequate but nothing special when it comes to competence, energy, and integrity. More than a few are sleazy, incompetent, and interested almost exclusively in earning a commission. In short, before working with a broker, it pays to carefully check out his or her reputation. Several glowing recommendations from a banker, accountant, or fellow small business person should raise your confidence level. On the other hand, if the feedback you get is lukewarm, look for someone else.

It's foolish to rely on a broker—who gets paid only if the deal goes through—for advice about the quality of the business or the fairness of its price. If you do, he or she is almost sure to paint an unrealistically rosy picture. Also, because the seller typically pays the broker, the broker's loyalty will be to the seller—not to you. Use a broker only to find a business, not to negotiate the purchase price and

other terms. See Section G on drafting the documents involved, particularly the purchase agreement.

B. What's the Structure of the Business You Want to Buy?

If you find a business you're interested in, one important question is: What kind of legal entity owns the business—a sole proprietorship, partnership, corporation, or limited liability company (LLC)?

1. Buying From a Sole Proprietor or Partnership

When you buy a business from a sole proprietor or a partnership, you never acquire the old legal structure of the business, only its assets (and possibly its liabilities, depending on how your deal with the seller is structured).

Legally, it's simplest to buy a business from a sole proprietor, because one person owns the business and the assets are in his or her name. Buying from a partnership is almost as simple, although a partnership agreement typically requires the consent of all owners before the business can be sold. If you're dealing with only one partner in a partnership, to avoid disappointment, promptly ask to see the partnership agreement. Then make sure that the person negotiating the deal has received proper authority from the other owners. Beyond that, get a clear understanding early on about whether you'll only be buying the assets of the business, or whether the seller is also trying to get you to assume responsibility for all liabilities.

⚠️ **It's best to avoid assuming business liabilities.** *A major issue in buying any business is whether you'll be purchasing only its assets, or if, as part of the deal, you'll also be taking on its liabilities. You'll avoid many potential legal and debt entanglements if you insist on buying the assets only (even if this means you pay a higher price). But whatever you and the seller decide, it's vital that you clearly record your understanding in the purchase documents.*

💡 **Changing a business's structure.** *A new owner is free to change the legal form of a business. For example, you can buy a business from a sole proprietor and then operate it through a partnership or corporation.*

2. Buying From a Corporation

When you buy a business owned by a corporation, you run into a special problem: figuring out the best way to structure your purchase. You can buy the corporate entity itself (the stock) or you can buy only its assets, leaving the seller still owning the corporation minus the assets you purchased.

In almost any purchase of a business, you'll be much better off buying the assets rather than the corporate stock (but see Subsection c, below). Most sales of small businesses—a whopping 94%—involve the sale of assets rather than corporate stock. Buying assets has four distinct advantages:

- It helps you avoid the liabilities of the existing business.

- It gives you significant tax advantages.
- You can avoid acquiring unwanted assets from the corporation.
- You generally can get a higher tax basis for depreciable assets, which means there's less taxable gain to report if you later sell the assets.

EXAMPLE OF STOCK PURCHASE: Brown Manufacturing Inc. is a small corporation owned by Joseph Brown and his two sons. The company, which makes specialized computer circuit boards, owns a small factory, several machines, raw materials, an inventory of completed items, office furniture and equipment, and two delivery trucks. The corporation owns all of the assets of the business. In a stock purchase, you'd buy 100% of the stock of the corporation from Joseph Brown and his sons. As the new owner, you'd elect yourself (and anyone else you choose) to the board of directors; the board would then typically appoint you to the office of president.

EXAMPLE OF ASSET PURCHASE: You want to buy the business operated by Brown Manufacturing Inc., but instead of buying the corporate stock, you have the corporation sell you all or most of its assets, such as the factory, the machines, the trucks, and several patents and trade secrets associated with circuit board assembly. The seller would continue to own Brown Manufacturing Inc. minus its assets. You would use these assets to run the manufacturing business as a sole proprietorship or partnership (if you have one or more business associates), or perhaps you would choose to place the assets in a new corporation of your own.

Get the Consent of Shareholders When You Purchase Corporate Assets

Remember that a corporation is a separate legal entity from its owners—the shareholders. When you purchase the assets of a small corporation, you want to avoid the possibility of having to deal with disgruntled minority owners. Even though the corporation's bylaws or shareholders' agreement may permit the sale of its assets with the consent of a majority (or more) of the shareholders, it's legally far safer for you if you insist that all shareholders agree with the sale of the corporation's assets. Get this consent in writing by following a two-step process:

- Require that all shareholders sign the purchase contract.
- Ask that all of the corporation's shareholders and directors sign and give you a copy of an official Corporate Resolution Authorizing Sale of Assets.

A big bonus that comes with insisting that all shareholders sign the purchase contract is that they then become personally liable for the warranties and representations in the contract. Without their signatures, should things go wrong, your only recourse would be against the corporation, which by that time would probably be without funds. You can also include language committing each shareholder to any noncompetition clause in the agreement—but as with other noncompete covenants, you must pay the signer something to make the covenant legally binding.

a. Liabilities of the Corporation

If you buy the stock of a corporation, you're buying not only the assets but any liabilities as well. This is fine if there aren't any, but this can be difficult to determine. Maybe the corporation owes federal income taxes that you don't know about or has a huge balance to pay on a bank loan. Or maybe a customer slipped in the entryway of the business three months ago, broke his leg, and is right now visiting a lawyer to prepare a million-dollar lawsuit. Or maybe there's an underground storage tank quietly leaking into the earth below the corporation's main office. Hidden liabilities can surface for injuries caused by defective products, discrimination against employees, or environmental or safety violations, to name but a few.

In addition, the business may have contracts that you don't want to assume. For example, the corporation may have a five-year maintenance contract for service on the computers it owns—and there may be four more years to go, at a rate you consider exorbitant.

You can protect yourself against some unknown liabilities. A good investigation will uncover many (though not all) potential liabilities. And personal warranties from the seller guaranteeing payment of any liabilities not disclosed can give you someone to turn to if unknown or undisclosed liabilities suddenly surface. Insurance may cover some of these risks, such as claims for injuries caused by defective products. But the point remains—if you buy a corporation, it's almost impossible to get 100% protection from its obligations.

In contrast, by buying the assets of the corporation rather than the corporate stock, you can avoid virtually all of these liability problems as long as you notify creditors of your purchase under the terms of your state's bulk sales statute (see Section G10) and you don't lead creditors to believe that you're picking up the liabilities of the corporation.

It's important to realize, however, that under some circumstances, if you continue the business of the prior corporation, you or your new corporation may still be subject to some liabilities incurred by the old corporation even if you only purchase assets. Known in legal lingo as "successor liability," the most common area of concern is product liability—liability to a person injured by a defective product.

This is particularly likely to arise if you buy the assets of a corporation that manufactured a potentially hazardous consumer product and you directly continue the business. Each state has its own legal rules governing what constitutes a sufficient link (often called continuity) between the first manufacturer and the second to hold the second liable. One court ruled that there may be such a link if:

- There is a continuation of the management, personnel, physical location, assets, and general business operations of the selling corporation.
- The selling corporation quickly ceased its ordinary business operations and then liquidated and dissolved.
- The purchasing company assumed the liabilities and obligations of the seller ordinarily necessary for continuing the business operations of the selling corporation.

In addition, depending on state law, a company that's just a continuation of an earlier corporation may be liable for other legal problems of the earlier corporation—for example, a wrongful discharge case brought by an ex-employee—or even for contractual obligations such as a union contract.

The good news is that if you're fully informed about the law in your state, you can usually anticipate any successor liability problems and structure your purchase to avoid them. Or you may be able to buy insurance—often called "tail coverage"—to protect you from the long tail of the old corporation's liabilities.

b. Tax Advantages

You may be able to get several kinds of tax advantages in an asset purchase because you can allocate the purchase price among various assets you buy. As long as this allocation is based on an arm's-length negotiation between you and the seller, it's likely to be upheld by the IRS.

You want to allocate the greater portion of the purchase price to assets you can quickly write off or depreciate on your tax returns. These include things like the inventory of the business, supplies, machinery, equipment and vehicles, furniture, and fixtures.

Normally, you'll also want to assign some value to the seller's noncompetition agreement. The value of the promise not to compete is spread over its duration (often three to five years), and an equal amount is deducted each year.

On the other hand, you'll want to assign minimally reasonable values to assets that can't be deducted as current expenses, depreciated, or amortized. This includes such assets as goodwill, trademarks, customer lists, and trade names. (How to allocate purchase price to different assets you're buying is discussed in Section G.)

In addition, by buying assets rather than corporate stock, you can depreciate assets that the seller has already fully depreciated.

> **EXAMPLE:** Arthur is buying a dry cleaning business. The business has dry cleaning equipment that's ten years old but in excellent condition. The owner has fully depreciated it. Arthur and the seller allocate $30,000 of the purchase price to the equipment. That way, Arthur can start to depreciate it a second time. If Arthur bought the corporate stock, he wouldn't be able to take any depreciation for this equipment.

c. Exceptions: When You Must or Should Purchase Stock

In some situations you may not be able to swing a deal in which you buy only corporate assets. This can occur, for example, if the seller insists on a stock sale—perhaps because he or she believes there's a tax advantage in going this route. If you agree to this, see Subsection d, below, "How to Protect Yourself If You Buy Corporate Stock."

In some limited circumstances where the corporation has a uniquely valuable asset that can't be transferred, it may actually be better to buy the stock of the corporation rather than its assets. For example, the corporation may have tax benefits such as a net operating loss carryover (NOL) that you want to take advantage of. The NOL carryover would be lost if you purchased the assets rather than the corporate stock. Also, if a store had a favorable five-year lease with a five-year option to renew that wasn't freely assignable, that could provide an incentive to you to buy the corporate stock. Or suppose a computer retail business had a hard-to-get distributorship for a particular brand of popular computers. If the distributorship contract couldn't be assigned to you and you weren't sure you could qualify for a similar contract yourself, you might consider buying the corporate stock because the corporation would likely continue to have the rights to be a distributor.

⚠️ **Investigating distributorships.** *Even in a stock purchase, you'd want to read the distributorship documents carefully and check with the manufacturer to confirm that the manufacturer didn't reserve the right to cancel the distributorship if the corporate stock changed hands.*

d. How to Protect Yourself If You Buy Corporate Stock

If you do decide to purchase a corporation's stock instead of its assets, protect yourself to the maximum extent possible. Conduct an in-depth investigation of the corporation's financial affairs. Try to get a strong personal guarantee from the shareholders that things are as stated.

You could also get a warranty from the seller that he or she will pay for certain types of problems such as tax liabilities, obligations to former employees, or damage claims by the landlord. Then arrange to pay for the business in installments spread over a number of years. Most liabilities will come to light in the first few years after you purchase the business. If the seller fails to make good on his or her warranty, you can pay for these liabilities and then withhold the amounts from the balance you owe the seller.

Also, as mentioned earlier, insurance may be in place or obtainable to protect against product liability and other personal injury claims.

3. Buying From an LLC

In buying a business from an LLC, you'll have to start by making the same decision as when buying from a corporation: Should you purchase the whole entity (the LLC) or just its assets? In my opinion, you're much better off buying the assets rather than the en-

tity, for the reasons I listed in Section B2, above, "Buying From a Corporation."

Buying the Entity. If you buy the LLC entity, you won't be buying shares of stock as you would with a corporation. An LLC doesn't issue stock. Instead, you'll purchase the membership interests of all the LLC members. By doing so, you'll wind up owning the LLC, which in turn owns the company's assets.

Buying the Assets. If you simply buy the business's assets, the LLC will transfer the assets to you, leaving the current LLC members with ownership of the LLC shell. (The shell is a company without any assets, except possibly your promissory note for the balance of the purchase price.) To avoid possible problems with dissatisfied LLC members, I recommend that you require all members to sign the sales agreement.

C. Gathering Information About a Business

Buying a business takes weeks or months. During that time you'll need to diligently gather information—lots of information—about the business so that you don't get stung on the purchase price or have surprises later about income, expenses, or undisclosed liabilities. Eventually, this information will help you structure a sound sales agreement.

In most small business purchases, the buyer learns everything possible about the business before signing the sales agreement. By contrast, business brokers sometimes advise making a quick formal offer to purchase with a number of contingencies that allow you to terminate the deal if all the facts don't turn out as represented by the seller. I recommend against this approach.

Why invest your time, effort, and money in a complete investigation of the business if the preliminary review of records convinces you that this isn't the business for you or that the price is too high? Better to request early access to financial records that will help you decide whether you're really interested in the business. Then if you're satisfied with the finances you can sign a sales agreement with appropriate contingency clauses or wait until closing (legal lingo for the transfer of the business) to sign.

If you and the seller are strangers to one another, however, the seller may be reluctant to turn over sensitive business information until he or she is confident that you're a serious buyer. The seller may suspect you have some secret plan in mind, like using the information in a competitive business or some other improper purpose. To allay these fears, consider giving the seller a confidentiality letter like the one below.

SAMPLE CONFIDENTIALITY LETTER

```
Carlos Mendez, President
Mendez Furniture Company Inc.

Dear Mr. Mendez:

   As you know, I am looking into the pur-
chase of your furniture business. Our con-
versations have been helpful but I'm now at
the stage where I would like to see your
company's financial records, including your
tax returns, for the past five years.

   I know that the information that I'm
requesting is confidential and that im-
proper use of the information could damage
your business. Consequently, I will use
this confidential information only to help
me decide whether I want to purchase your
business and the terms of that purchase. I
will disclose this confidential informa-
tion only to my co-investors, my lawyer,
and my accountant. I'll make sure that each
of these people knows that this information
is confidential, and I'll ask them to sign
confidentiality agreements before I re-
lease the information to them.

   If I don't buy your business, I will
return all of the confidential informa-
tion, including any copies, to you and
will continue to treat in confidence the
information you have disclosed to me.

   I look forward to receiving this infor-
mation.

Sincerely yours,


Suzanne Gerstein
```

That kind of letter will satisfy many sellers. But a few sellers may prefer a longer, more formal confidentiality agreement drafted by a lawyer. That's okay, but you (and perhaps your lawyer as well) should make sure that the proposed document contains no binding commitment to buy the business. It should be limited to your agreement to treat the information as strictly confidential and use it only to investigate the purchase of the business, and to the other terms set out in the letter. If the proposed agreement goes farther than that, find out why and get legal advice.

Don't be surprised if the seller wants to learn about your own financial status, job, or business history. Remember that most purchases of a small business are usually done on an installment basis, where the seller receives a down payment and payments over a period of time. The seller is interested in your financial stability, your reputation for integrity, and your general business savvy because the seller, in effect, will be extending credit to you.

D. Valuing the Business

Does it sound impossibly demanding to determine a fair purchase price for a business? It's really not—especially if you take the sales price with a grain of salt. Most sellers ask for way too much, and far too many inexperienced buyers don't bargain aggressively enough. Lots of little businesses are worth no more than the fair current value of inventory and equipment. Goodwill, over and above the value of the continuing hard work of the owner, is commonly a myth.

1. What Are You Buying?

Generally, the assets of a business consist of inventory, fixed assets (furniture, fixtures, equipment), and intangible assets (such as a lease, trade name, customer list, and goodwill). The most important factor in establishing the fair market value of these assets is this: Given the realities of the business and the industry in which it operates, what kind of return would a buyer reasonably expect on his or her investment? To arrive at this number, an appraiser will look both at the business's earnings and what similar businesses typically earn.

2. Goodwill Can Be a Myth

Be very careful about what you pay for goodwill—the portion of the purchase price attributed to such intangible factors as the reputation of the business, its location, and the loyalty of its customers. Despite what sellers will almost surely tell you, many small businesses have little or no value beyond the value of the hard assets such as furniture, fixtures, and equipment.

How can this be, if a business earns a good yearly profit? Easy. Most of the profit is commonly attributable to the hard work, clear vision, and good judgment of the owner, not to the inherent value of the business. Think of it this way: Most rug cleaning businesses, hardware stores, print shops, and restaurants don't make a substantial profit. Those that do are usually run by uniquely talented people. When these people move on, many of those businesses quickly lose their luster.

> **EXAMPLE:** Joe and Monte own Caretti Brothers, a highly successful produce store that they've operated for 20 years. They sell the business to Anna Marie, who pays $200,000, including $100,000 for goodwill. Anna Marie continues to run the business as Caretti Brothers and does her best to preserve the store's distinctive atmosphere. Nevertheless, in her first year she earns only one-third the profits generated by the former owners.
>
> Unhappily, she realizes that Joe and Monte succeeded because customers valued their extroverted personalities and their rare ability to select only the freshest and tastiest tomatoes and grapefruit. Too late, she understands that she should have paid little or nothing for goodwill, which was largely personal to the Carettis and couldn't be transferred to her.

Goodwill isn't always a myth. Some profitable businesses—usually those that have been established for years and have strong name recognition—are worth significantly more than the value of their tangible assets, because they have a good reputation. Even if the owner retires or sells out, this reputation will continue to bring in business.

Unfortunately, deciding that a business has goodwill is easier than deciding how much. One approach is for buyer and seller to try to agree on a multiplier—the number by which earnings (or sometimes sales) must be multiplied to determine the value of the business.

Where does the multiplier come from? In some industries, there are rough norms. For example, certain types of businesses typically sell for five times earnings, while other often sell for ten or more. Construction companies, retail stores, and restaurants are examples of businesses where you can often obtain standard multipliers from business evaluators or appraisers who specialize in that industry.

⚠ **Be critical of all multipliers.** *Never accept a multiplier without loads of caution. The facts of a particular business, the state of the local economy, and industry trends change so quickly that last year's sensible multiplier can be completely off base this year.*

3. Evaluating the Business's Financial Health

To properly evaluate the business, ask for access to the following documents:

- tax returns, profit and loss statements, and balance sheets for the last five years
- loan documents, if you're going to assume any obligations of the business
- papers relating to specific assets; for example, the lease if you're taking over seller's space or title documents if you're purchasing the seller's building
- patents, trademarks, copyrights, and licenses
- documents that relate to lawsuits, administrative proceedings, and claims against the corporation
- all accountants' reports, including compilation reports, reviews and audit reports. (See "Types

of Accountants' Reports," below.) A full-fledged audit report is the best, but not all small businesses have one available. Whatever type report the business has, specifically ask for a list of all assets and the depreciation schedules.

In addition, if you're purchasing corporate stock, ask for:

- corporate contracts with major suppliers, as well as contracts obligating the corporation to deliver goods or services
- employment agreements, union contracts, and any other documents concerning wage levels and fringe benefit obligations.

Types of Accountants' Reports

Reports from Certified Public Accountants come in three basic varieties:

Compiled. The CPA compiles the balance sheet of the company and the related statements of income and retained earnings and cash flows for a specified year. The compilation simply presents, in the form of a financial statement, the information gathered by the owners of the company. The accountant doesn't audit or review the information or offer an opinion about it.

Reviewed. The CPA goes a step farther by asking questions of company personnel and analyzing the financial data presented by the owners. Short of a full-scale audit, the CPA certifies only that he or she isn't aware of any material modifications that should be made to the financial statements to conform to generally accepted accounting principles.

Audited. Here, the CPA examines, on a test basis, evidence supporting the amounts and disclosures in the financial statements. For example, the CPA may visit the warehouse to see if it really contains the inventory that's claimed. Also, the accountant assesses the accounting principles used by the owners and evaluates the overall financial statement. If everything is in order, the CPA signs an opinion that the financial statements are accurate and maintained in conformity with generally accepted accounting principles.

Once the books are in your hands, have an experienced small business accountant study them. You and your accountant should look especially hard at the years before the last one. It's relatively easy for a business owner to pump up earnings and depress expenses for a year or two, so assume that the results for the last year at least have been manipulated.

Tips for spotting exaggerated earnings:
One way to see if earnings have been exaggerated is to see if there are fewer employees now than previously—almost any business can operate shorthanded for a limited time. Also, check to see whether equipment maintenance or replacement has been deferred by comparing maintenance and replacement costs for the last year with those of the years before.

4. Expert Help

Consider hiring an experienced appraiser to appraise the business as a whole as well as the individual assets. Check references and be sure the person you pick understands the type of business you are entering.

For example, if you're thinking of buying a traditional typesetting business, work with someone who thoroughly understands the mostly negative implications that the rapid improvement of desktop publishing techniques holds for this business. Appraisals do cost money, but it's money well spent if it saves you from overpaying for the business.

Where can you turn for an accurate assessment of the value of a business? Here are three suggestions:

- Consult a member of the American Society of Appraisers who specializes in business valuations. For a list of such appraisers, call 800-ASA-VALU or visit www.appraisers.org.
- Check with a respected firm of certified public accountants. Many CPA firms offer business valuation services.
- Seek guidance from an experienced business broker. But use caution. Brokers are best at making deals. They often lack the technical training needed for placing a value on a business.

E. Other Items to Investigate

Now let's look at some other items that are worth investigating before you close on the purchase of a business.

1. Title to Assets

If real estate is included in the sale, ask to see the deed and the title insurance policy. The title should be rechecked to make sure no new encumbrances appear, and the title insurance policy will need to be updated. Also ask to see ownership documents for any cars and trucks.

It's a good idea to check with the appropriate county or state offices to see if there are liens on any of the vehicles or other equipment or merchandise. Lenders who have taken a security interest in the business or suppliers who have extended credit may have filed a UCC (Uniform Commercial Code) financing statement with the appropriate state agency to record the fact that they have a security interest in some assets of the business.

Any bank lending officer, small business lawyer, or accountant should be able to tell you where and how to check in your state.

2. Litigation

Ask to see copies of any lawsuit papers and letters from any people threatening lawsuits. Also check with the court clerk in the main counties in which business is conducted. What you're looking for are actual or threatened lawsuits involving injuries or claimed breaches of contract.

This type of investigation is particularly important when you're buying the stock of a corporation, but you may also turn up information that will be valuable to an asset purchase. For example, if the business manufactures or distributes aluminum stepladders, finding product liability lawsuits pending will help you determine whether the ladders are safe or need to be redesigned. Also, remember that in a few circumstances even those who purchase assets of a corporation may be held liable for the existing business's liabilities. (See Section B2.)

3. Warranties and Guarantees

If you buy the stock of a corporation, you want to know what types of warranties the corporation has extended to its customers so you can anticipate claims. For example, if you buy a business that writes customized computer software, you'll want to know what promises have been made should bugs be discovered in already-installed programs.

4. Workers' Compensation Claims and Unemployment Claims

Check with the workers' compensation insurance carrier to learn the claims history of the business and current insurance rates. Also check with the state office handling unemployment affairs to learn what rate is currently applied to the payroll of the business. These facts will be primarily of concern if you're planning to purchase the stock of a corporation, because they'll indicate how much you'll probably have to pay for workers' compensation insurance or unemployment coverage. But in some states, even purchasers of corporate assets may have their future workers' compensation insurance rates affected if it looks like the new business is simply a continuation of the old one.

5. Employee Contracts and Benefits

This is a concern primarily if you're buying the stock of a corporation and will be subject to its contracts. However, if you intend to keep the same employees, you need this information for other purchases as well so that you'll know the employees' expectations when they come to work for your new business entity. They won't be happy campers if you offer them less pay or benefits than they're currently getting.

If it's a concern, ask the seller for permission to talk to key employees to see if they'll stick with you after you buy the business. (Strictly speaking, permission isn't required, but being polite helps bring about a smooth transition.)

6. Maintenance of Trade Secrets

Not every business has trade secrets, but if the one you're purchasing does—and those secrets are a valuable asset for which you're paying—you want to be sure they've been properly safeguarded. Ask what the business has done to protect its trade secrets and other proprietary information such as customer lists. Has this information been disclosed only to key employees? Have those employees signed confidentiality agreements and covenants not to compete? If not, and key employees leave and set up a competing business, you may be buying a lot less than you bargained for.

7. Taxes

Again, this applies primarily to a purchase of corporate stock because you want to know what tax liabilities are hanging over the head of the corporation. But whatever kind of purchase you're making, you can gain valuable information about the income and expenses of the business, including the kinds of items that have been tax-deductible in the past. Check on state and local property taxes and sales taxes, federal and state income taxes, and any special taxes levied by federal and state governments.

8. Leases

Look carefully at all space and equipment leases. How long does the lease have to run? Is it renewable? And, most important, if you're purchasing the assets, is it transferable? If the lease isn't clearly assignable, check with the landlord or equipment lessor about taking over the lease. If they respond favorably, get a commitment in writing. (For more on real estate leases, see Chapter 13.)

9. Other Contracts

If the business has contracts with suppliers or customers, become familiar with their terms. In the case of an asset sale, the important question is whether or not the contracts are assignable by the seller. Often, you need the consent of the supplier or customer. For example, if you're buying a gas station, does the oil company have to approve your taking over the contract for that brand of gasoline? Where a contract is freely transferable if all the conditions have been met, make sure the seller isn't in default or otherwise in noncompliance. If he or she is, you may not be able to enforce the contract.

10. Patents and Copyrights

Many small businesses don't own patents or copyrights, but as information becomes a more and more valuable part of many businesses, they are cropping up fairly often. Of course, if you're interested in buying a book, software, or music publishing company, you can be pretty sure that the business's most valuable assets will be its intellectual property.

If patents or copyrights are involved, get hold of the basic registration documents and any contracts that give the business the right to exploit these rights. If you're not fully familiar with these matters, have the documents and contracts reviewed by a lawyer who specializes in this area of law. These lawyers are usually listed in a separate category in the Yellow Pages under "Patent and Trademark."

11. Trademarks and Product Names

Trademarks, service marks, business names, and product names may be important business assets. If so, make sure that you'll have the continuing right to use them. Ask about the extent of any searches for conflicting marks and names, and what has been done to register or otherwise protect the marks and names you'll be taking over. (See Chapter 6 for more on business and product names.)

12. Licenses and Transferability

Check into any special licenses that you'll need to continue the business. For example, if you're buying a restaurant with a liquor license, is the license transferable? Has the existing business obtained an environmental permit for disposal of its wastes? If so, what about transferability? (If not, look into your potential liability.) The same goes for other special permits the existing business has, such as a health department license, or a federal license for trucking or broadcasting. (For more on licenses and permits, see Chapter 7.)

13. Zoning

The existing business may be operating under a temporary zoning variance or a conditional use permit that has important limitations. Learn exactly what the requirements and conditions are and whether you can continue operating under the variance or conditional use permit.

Also, if you buy the business assets rather than corporate stock, you may find that you're no longer covered by prior zoning or building preferences; you may, for example, need more parking, better access, and different signs. (See Chapter 7, Section D, and Chapter 14, Section A, for more on zoning and related requirements.)

14. Toxic Waste

If the business must dispose of toxic waste, or if its activities have any possible adverse impact on the purity of water and air, look into what licenses or permits are needed. Also, especially if your purchase involves real property, check carefully to see how toxic waste has been handled in the past. You could find yourself stuck with liability for past improprieties.

15. Franchisor Approval

If you're looking at a business that's operating under a franchise, the seller undoubtedly will need the approval of the franchisor before assigning the franchise to you. Look at the franchise agreement to see exactly what's involved in obtaining the franchisor's approval and then speak directly to the franchisor to see how the approval process can be expedited. (For more on franchises, see Chapter 11.)

16. Availability of Credit

Find out whether banks and major suppliers will be willing to extend credit to you. Credit may mean the difference between success and failure.

17. Scuttlebutt

Never rely entirely on documents and public records. You can learn a lot simply by talking to people who have had contact with the existing business—bankers, key customers, suppliers, neighboring businesses, and former employees. When talking to key people, take your time and pay attention to subtleties. Many people may be reluctant to talk frankly until they've sized you up, and others will have ties of friendship to the seller or be worried about their own possible legal liability if they divulge unfavorable information about the business.

F. Letter of Intent to Purchase

If all goes well, you and the seller may eventually agree on most major aspects of the purchase. But you still may not be quite ready to put together a formal sales agreement. Perhaps you need time for additional investigation, or maybe your lawyer, business advisor, or key lender is out of town for a week or two.

One device that can be helpful to keep momentum is a nonbinding letter of intent to purchase. The same objective can be accomplished through a more formal "memorandum of intent to purchase"—but a memorandum usually turns out to be more legalistic and, therefore, more threatening to a seller.

Giving the seller a modest, earnest money deposit along with the letter of intent is also helpful, because it shows you're sincerely interested in pursuing the purchase and are not wasting the seller's time. But because details of the purchase have not solidified at this point, be sure to provide that the deposit is to be refunded if the purchase falls through.

A sample nonbinding letter of intent is shown below.

LETTER OF INTENT TO PURCHASE

Robert Tower, President
The Tower Mart Inc.
25 Glen Blvd.
Arlington Heights, IL

Dear Bob:

Thanks for meeting with me again last week. I continue to be interested in purchasing the assets of the Tower Mart Inc. If we reach an agreement regarding my purchase, I plan to transfer these assets to a new corporation that I'm forming. My new company would then run a convenience store similar to what you're currently operating.

I'm interested in purchasing the following assets: the inventory, fixtures, equipment, leasehold improvements, and business name. In addition, I will need all necessary licenses and permits transferred to me. I will expect you to give me a covenant not to compete stating that for three years, you won't open a similar store in our city. The purchase price for all of the assets as well as the goodwill and your covenant not to compete would be $150,000, as we have already discussed.

[*Before referring to a covenant not to compete, see the discussion of such covenants in Section G5, below*]

As an indication of my good faith in pursuing this matter, I am enclosing a check for $1,000 as earnest money. I would pay an additional $49,000 in cash at closing. The balance of $100,000 would be amortized in equal monthly installments over a period of 10 years with interest at the rate of 10% per annum.

Regarding the inventory, we will check this at the time of closing. If the inventory is valued at less than $45,000, the purchase price would be reduced accordingly. Also, as you and I discussed, your corporation would remain responsible for all liabilities of the present business and these would not be assumed by my new corporation.

Before I have my lawyer draft a sales agreement, there are some things I need to investigate:

1. I want to meet with your landlord to make sure that I can take over the existing lease and that I can get an option to extend it for another five years.

2. I need to have my accountant review all of your tax returns and business records for the past five years so that I can satisfy myself regarding the financial condition of your business.

3. I want to make sure that the state liquor board will approve a transfer of the beer and wine retail license to my new corporation.

Assuming that I'm satisfied with these items and all other aspects of the proposed purchase, I will have my lawyer draft a sales agreement and then we can close approximately 45 days from now.

This letter states my intent but it is not a legally binding contract or commitment on either my part or yours. Upon further investigation I may change my mind. If the deal doesn't go through for any reason, I'd be entitled to my earnest money back.

If my letter has captured the essence of what we talked about and you're still interested in pursuing the sale, please let me know. I believe that we are moving toward a transaction that can be advantageous to both of us.

Sincerely,

Mary Beyer

⚠️ **Don't commit yourself.** *Make it clear in a letter of intent that it is not intended to be a binding contract. You may or may not need your lawyer's assistance in writing a letter of intent, but I do recommend that you call your lawyer to at least check on the adequacy of the language you use to describe the nonbinding nature of the letter.*

G. The Sales Agreement

The sales agreement is the key legal document in buying business assets or an entire corporation or LLC. You should create a written outline of the terms that you and the seller have agreed on. Next, you may want to have your lawyer review it and help draft the next version of the agreement. Once you and your lawyer are satisfied, present the agreement to the seller.

Why take on the document drafting yourself, rather than letting the seller do it? Because even though it's more time consuming, this approach will almost surely give you more control over the overall shape of the transaction. By seizing the initiative, you may well wind up with 95% or more of what you want.

This section briefly reviews the principal types of clauses in a business sales agreement. Remember, as discussed earlier (Section B2), it's almost always better to buy the assets from the corporation than to buy its stock. Accordingly, these clauses are geared primarily to an asset purchase. If for some reason you decide to buy corporate stock, make corresponding changes in your sales agreement.

📄 **Chapter 5 of *Legal Forms for Starting & Running a Small Business* contains various forms for buying a business.**

1. Names of Seller, Buyer, and Business

Your sales agreement will start with the name and address of the seller and the buyer. It will also identify the business by its current name.

- *Purchase from or by a sole proprietor.* Name the sole proprietor, adding the business name if it's different from the individual's. *Example:* Mary Perfect doing business as Perfect Word Processing Service.
- *Purchase from or by a partnership.* Use the partnership's legal name and the names of all partners. *Example:* Ortega Associates, a Colorado partnership of William Ortega and Henry Cruz.
- *Purchase from or by a corporation.* Simply use the corporate name and identify it by the state where it's registered. *Example:* XYZ Enterprises Inc., a Massachusetts corporation.
- *Purchase from or by an LLC.* Just use the LLC name and the state where it's registered. *Example:* ABC Associates LLC, an Illinois limited liability company.

If you're going to operate the business you're purchasing as a new corporation or LLC, I recommend either of two procedures: Set up the new corporation or LLC before signing the purchase agreement and name the new entity as the purchaser. Or list the purchaser as yourself as the agent of a corporation or LLC to be formed. Using either of these methods, the assets can go directly into your new corporation or LLC rather than having a two-stage process in which you receive the assets and then transfer them to the new entity.

If you're going to be putting the assets into a corporation or LLC, the seller undoubtedly will want you (and probably your spouse as well) to personally guarantee the payment of any part of the purchase price that's being paid on an installment basis.

2. Background Information

Often, before a sales agreement gets into the terms of the transaction, it outlines some background facts. For example, the sales agreement might state that "Mildred Johnson currently owns a business in Cincinnati that produces ice cream, sorbet, and other dessert products" and that the sales agreement "applies only to the portion of the business operated at seller's west side location at 123 Maple Street."

You can also include some statements about the buyer; for example, "The buyer is a building contractor licensed under the laws of the state of Maine." These statements aren't usually a key section of a purchase agreement, but if they are included, it's important to be accurate.

3. Assets Being Sold

This is where you list what you're purchasing. You can put the details, such as lists of equipment, on a separate page, which is sometimes referred to in the body of the agreement as a schedule or exhibit and specifically made part of the contract. Here's an example of how a sales agreement might list assets being sold:

a. All furniture, trade fixtures, equipment, and miscellaneous items of tangible personal property owned by seller and used in the business, listed and described in Exhibit A, which is hereby made a part of this agreement.

b. Customer lists and all other files and records of the business.

c. Assignment of the seller's interest (as tenant) in the lease dated March 1, 2005 for the building located at 123 Main Street owned by Central Property Associates (landlord).

d. Assignment of the seller's interest (as lessee) in the computer equipment lease with CompuLease dated March 1, 2005.

e. All telephone numbers of the business and the right to use the business name, "The Tower Mart." Seller will cease using that name on the day of closing.

If you have so agreed, also include a statement that you're not acquiring any of the liabilities of the business or that you're acquiring only those that are specified.

> Except as otherwise specified in this agreement, buyer is not assuming responsibility for any liabilities of the business. Seller will remain responsible for all liabilities of the business not specified in this agreement, and will indemnify buyer and save buyer harmless from and against such liabilities.

4. Purchase Price and Allocation of Assets

After stating the purchase price, allocate the price among the different categories of assets. Some typical allocations are shown below.

Allocation for a Retail Business

Merchandise on Hand	$ 75,000
Tangible Personal Property	$ 30,000
Assignment of Lease Agreement	$ 4,000
Trade Name and Goodwill	$ 8,000

Allocation for a Small Computer Company

Inventory (Computers and Software)	$100,000
Trade Name and Goodwill	$ 20,000
Patents and Copyrights	$ 5,000
Building Owned by Seller	$100,000
Land	$ 30,000

For tax reasons, as a buyer, you want most of the price assigned to the assets that give you the fastest recovery of your investment. You want the least allocated to items like goodwill, which can't be depreciated and gives you no tax benefits until you sell the business. Here's a summary of the write-off rules:

Type of Asset	Normal Write-Off Period
Inventory	As sold
Furniture, Fixtures, and Equipment	5 to 7 years
Trade Name and Goodwill	15 years
Buildings	39 years
Patents and Copyrights	Remaining Term of Patent or Copyright
Lease Assignment	Remaining Term of Lease
Land	No Write-off

Because you and the seller will have differing tax priorities, you may have to negotiate the allocation of the purchase price. The seller will want the bulk of the purchase price to be assigned to categories that are taxed at long-term capital gains rates rather than ordinary income rates—for example, buildings and goodwill. You'll be more interested in tilting the allocation toward items you can start to write off or depreciate—like equipment. If you wind up allocating the price in a way that saves you a ton of taxes but costs the seller a fair bit of change, you may need to raise the purchase price a little to help even things up. Similarly, if the allocation favors the seller, it's reasonable to work out a modest price reduction. A tax pro can help you crunch the numbers.

In the first example above, inventory and merchandise on hand are given as high a value as can be reasonably supported. In the second example, the seller's building and land could reasonably be valued at anywhere from $130,000 to $160,000 depending on whose appraisal is used. I've assigned the lowest reasonable value to the building and land because, under IRS guidelines, the building must be depreciated over a period of 39 years and the land can't be depreciated at all.

If the seller is going to provide consulting services to you for a year or so, consider assigning a portion of the purchase price to those services so that you can write off that amount quickly as a business expense. Better yet, remove an appropriate amount from the purchase price and put it in a separate agreement for consulting services.

5. Covenant Not to Compete

Especially if the seller is well known and would be a threat to your business if he or she opened a rival outfit, you want a covenant (promise) not to compete. In such a covenant, the seller agrees not to compete directly or indirectly with you in the operation of the type of business that you've purchased. If the seller violates the covenant, judges or arbitrators will usually enforce it unless it unreasonably limits the seller's ability to earn a living.

To increase chances that your agreement will be enforced, it's wise to place a reasonable geographic limitation on the seller's right to run a similar business (for example, within 25 miles of your business) and also a reasonable time limit (for example, three years). If you're purchasing a business from a corporation, have the individual operators of the business sign their own personal promises not to compete.

Obviously, whatever geographic limitations you and the seller agree on should fit the area. In New York City, a 25-mile zone would take in a huge chunk of New Jersey and some 15 to 20 million people—probably an unreasonable restraint on the seller's future ability to earn a living. In drafting a covenant not to compete, get help from a savvy lawyer who knows what the state courts enforce.

An example of a covenant not to compete is shown below.

Covenant Not to Compete

Seller shall not establish, engage in, or become interested in, directly or indirectly, as an employee, owner, partner, agent, shareholder, or otherwise, within a radius of ten miles from the city of _____, any business, trade, or occupation similar to the business covered by this sales agreement for a period of three years. At the closing, the seller agrees to sign an agreement on this subject in the form set forth in Exhibit B.

LAW IN THE REAL WORLD
Why You Need a Covenant Not to Compete

Sid is buying a travel agency from Mary Jones, who has been in the travel business for 25 years and is well known in the community. Part of the reason Sid is buying her business is the excellent reputation and following her business has earned.

Two months after Sid takes over the business, Mary—who quickly tired of retirement—opens a new travel agency four blocks away. Inevitably some, perhaps many, of her old customers will abandon Sid and patronize Mary's business. Sid should have included a covenant not to compete in the sales agreement to protect himself against this possibility.

---

6. Adjustments

You'll probably need to adjust the sales price slightly at closing. For example, you should reimburse the seller for payments the seller has made for such items as rent, utilities, or insurance for periods after you take over. On the other hand, if salaries and wages are paid every two weeks and you take over the business halfway through that period, the purchase price should be reduced at closing to reflect the fact that you'll be paying salaries for a period when the seller still owned the business.

Adjustments may also be made for license fees, maintenance contracts, equipment leases, and property taxes. Your sales agreement should contain a clause spelling out what items will need to be adjusted at closing and the method for making the adjustments.

7. Terms of Payment

Nearly 80% of small business purchases are handled on an installment basis, with the seller extending all or most of the credit. Typically, a buyer puts down about one third of the purchase price and pays the balance over four or five years. For example, in the purchase of a $250,000 business, you may negotiate a contract that requires you to make a $50,000 down payment at closing with the balance paid in five annual installments of $40,000 each plus interest at 10% per year.

At the closing, you'll sign a promissory note for the unpaid portion of the purchase price. The seller generally will want to retain an ownership (security) interest in the equipment and other assets of the business until the purchase price has been paid. Sometimes called a "lien," this is akin to a mortgage on your home. Just as the bank could sell your home to pay off your loan if you fell behind in your payments, the seller of a business who retains a lien on or security interest in your business assets could, if you were delinquent in making payments, take possession of those assets and sell them to cover the balance owing.

Here's a sample terms of payment clause:

Purchaser will pay seller $_____ at closing and will pay the balance of $_____ according to the terms of a promissory note purchaser will sign at the closing, in the form set forth in Exhibit __. The promissory note will provide for monthly payments of $_____ each. The payments will include interest on the unpaid balance at the rate of ____% per annum from and after the date of closing. The first installment will be due on the first day of the month following the closing and the remaining installments will be due on the first of each month after that until the principal and interest is fully paid. Payments will be applied first on interest and then on principal. The unpaid principal and interest shall be fully paid no later than ____ years from the date of the note. There will be no penalty for prepayment.

Until purchaser has paid the full balance of principal and interest on the debt, seller will retain a security interest in the business assets being purchased. As evidence of such security interest, purchaser, at closing, will sign a security agreement in the form set forth in attached Exhibit __ and will also a sign a Uniform Commercial Code Financing Statement, to be recorded at the appropriate county and state office.

It's a good idea to attach the proposed promissory note as well as the proposed security agreement as exhibits to the sales agreement.

Tax and Usury: Charge Reasonable Interest

The IRS will accept the interest rate agreed to by the seller and buyer if it is reasonable in terms of the current financing market and the risk involved in extending credit. If the interest rate is outside the reasonable range, the buyer may not be able to deduct the excess interest paid. To avoid this, stick close to prevailing interest rates.

Also be aware that state usury laws limit the rate of interest that can be charged. Here, it's the seller rather than the buyer who runs the risk of running afoul of the law. Not only may the seller not be able to collect excessive interest, but he or she may also face criminal penalties.

8. Inventory

Because the inventory of salable merchandise is likely to fluctuate between the time you sign the sales agreement and the closing, consider putting a provision in the sales agreement that allows for adjustment. For example, you might say that you'll pay up to $75,000 for merchandise on hand at the closing based on the seller's invoice cost. You might also provide that if there's more than $75,000 worth of merchandise on hand when you close, you have the right to purchase the excess at the seller's cost, or to choose $75,000 worth and leave the rest in the hands of the seller.

Here's another way to handle this problem. Simply provide that a physical count of all merchandise will be made on the day of sale or another mutually agreeable date. You might define the word merchandise to include only unopened and undamaged merchandise. In a retail business, you can agree to value the merchandise at its current wholesale cost, or at the seller's current retail price less a certain percentage.

If you don't have experience doing an inventory, you might also put in the sales agreement that you and the seller will split the cost of hiring an inventory service company to determine the amount of the purchase price of the merchandise.

In a manufacturing or service business, you may have the analogous problem of placing a value on work in progress.

9. Accounts Receivable

The business you're buying may have sold goods to or performed services for customers who haven't yet paid. These unpaid sums are called "accounts receivable." Usually the accounts receivable of an existing business remain the property of that business and aren't transferred to the buyer. But a seller who prefers to be free of collection problems may want to include them.

Be very careful. When a business changes hands, accounts can be hard to collect. A considerable percentage will probably never be collected, so you should get a substantial discount. How much depends on how collectable these accounts are. By now you should know this through your close examination of the seller's books and, if most of the money is owed by only a few accounts, by checking with them personally.

10. Bulk Sales Compliance

If the business you're buying involves the sale of merchandise from a stock you'll keep on hand, you may have to comply with a "bulk sales" law. Every state used to have such a law, but today only a handful still do. These laws apply to transfers of a major part of the seller's materials, supplies, merchandise, or other inventory. Generally, they don't apply to transfers where the seller's business consists primarily of selling personal services rather than merchandise.

Typically, a seller covered under the bulk sales law must give you a list (sworn to under penalty of perjury) of all business creditors and tell you the amounts due each one. Also, the seller must tell you about any claims made by potential creditors, even if the claims are disputed. Then you send notice to the creditors so that they'll know that the business is changing hands.

If these things are not done, the creditors of the old business will continue to have a claim against the merchandise that you're buying. Sending proper notices protects you from such claims.

Sometimes, to avoid the need to comply with the bulk sales law, a contract will say that the seller will pay all outstanding debts of the business before the closing, or out of the proceeds of the sale at the time of closing, and will furnish an affidavit to that effect at closing.

For more information on your local bulk sales law and the legal forms used to comply with it, the best place to look is a legal newspaper or other major newspaper that publishes legal notices.

11. Seller's Representation and Warranties

In the sales agreement, the seller should guarantee the basic facts of your transaction. Here's an example of the guarantees when the seller is a corporation:

Seller and seller's shareholders represent and warrant that:

1. Andover Corporation is in good standing under the laws of Wisconsin.

2. Andover Corporation's board of directors has authorized (through board resolutions to be delivered to buyer at closing) the signing of this sales contract and all of the transactions called for in the contract.

3. Andover Corporation has good and marketable title to the assets that are being sold and will convey them to buyer free and clear of all encumbrances, except for the assets listed in Exhibit A, which will remain subject to the encumbrances listed there.

4. The balance sheet that Andover Corporation gave buyer correctly reflects the assets, liabilities and net worth of the business as of October 31, 2005, and there will be no material changes between the balance sheet date and the closing.

5. The income statement that Andover Corporation gave buyer accurately reflects the income and expenses of the company during the period covered, and no significant changes in the level of income or expense will occur between the contract date and the closing.

6. The lease under which Andover Corporation occupies space at 789 Oak Avenue is in full effect and is assignable to buyer. Andover Corporation will take all necessary steps to assign the lease to buyer.

7. Between the contract date and the closing, And—over Corporation will operate the business as usual and will take no action out of the ordinary.

8. Andover Corporation has complied with all applicable laws and regulations of the federal, state, and local governments.

9. There are no lawsuits or claims pending or threatened against Andover Corporation other than those listed in Exhibit __, and Andover Corporation does not know of any basis for any other lawsuit or claim against the business.

10. Andover Corporation has disclosed to buyer all material facts that would reasonably affect a prudent investor's decision to purchase the assets covered by this agreement.

In addition, if the seller made specific statements to you about the business and these influenced your decision to buy it, have the seller reiterate these statements in writing in this section of the agreement.

⚠ Don't rely on the seller's promises.
Never use the seller's warranties and represen-tations as an excuse for not thoroughly checking all important facts yourself, as discussed in Section C, above. Enforcing a warranty against the seller or suing for a misrepresentation can involve a long and expensive lawsuit.

If you're buying a business or the assets from a corporation, have the principal owners sign the war-ranties as individuals in addition to signing them as officers of the corporation. That way, you'll be able to go after their personal assets if they've misrepre-sented facts or if their warranties are violated.

The contract should also say that the warranties survive the closing. This gives you the right to sue if you discover some unpleasant facts about the busi-ness several years after you purchase it. Here's some wording to consider:

> The representations and warranties of the parties to this agreement and those of the seller's shareholders shall survive the closing. The act of closing shall not bar either party from bringing an action based on a representa-tion or warranty of the other party.

12. Buyer's Warranties and Representations

The seller may expect the buyer to sign representa-tions and warranties as well. For example:

> Buyer represents and warrants that:
>
> 1. Buyer is a corporation in good standing under the laws of Wisconsin.
>
> 2. Buyer has the authority to enter into and perform the buyer's obligations under the sales agreement.
>
> 3. Buyer has had an opportunity to inspect the assets of the business and agrees to accept the assets as is, except for the items referred to in Exhibit C.

The first representation in this example assumes you've established a corporation. You wouldn't in-clude this statement if you were buying as a sole proprietor or signing on behalf of a partnership.

In the second representation, a corporate buyer would agree to furnish the seller with a board of directors' resolution approving the terms of the sales agreement and authorizing the signing of the purchase documents.

The third representation says that you're accepting the assets "as is." If it turns out that some of the assets are defective, that will be your problem and not the seller's—unless the seller knew about and failed to disclose some hidden defect that you couldn't be expected to discover through an inspection. Before signing a sales agreement, make sure you have actually inspected all the assets. If there are some that you haven't looked at carefully or which you're *not* willing to take as is, list them in an exhibit that specifically excludes them from the "as is" clause.

13. Access to Information

By the time you sign the sales agreement, you should have seen a lot of financial information involving the business, but you may still want to see more to verify that everything is as promised. So it's a good idea to include a paragraph or two in the sales agreement covering your right to get full information. In exchange, the seller will probably want to include language assuring that you'll deal with the information in a responsible manner—that is, that you won't make unnecessary disclosures. (For a discussion of sellers' concerns about confidentiality, see Section C, above.)

Here's some language you might place in the sales agreement:

> Before the closing, seller will provide to buyer and buyer's agents, during normal business hours, access to all of the company's properties, books, contracts, and records, and will furnish to buyer all the information concerning the company's affairs that buyer reasonably requests.
>
> Buyer acknowledges that the company's books, records, and other documents contain confidential information, and that communication of

such confidential information to third parties could injure the company's business if this transaction is not completed. Buyer agrees to take reasonable steps to assure that such information about the company remains confidential and is not revealed to outside sources. Buyer further agrees not to solicit any customers of the company disclosed from such confidential information.

> The confidential information that may become known to buyer includes customer lists, trade secrets, channels of distribution, pricing policy and records, inventory records, and other information normally understood to be confidential or designated as such by seller.

14. Conduct of Business Pending Closing

Unless the sales agreement is signed at the closing, be sure that the seller doesn't make any detrimental changes in the business between the time you sign the sales agreement and the time you close. We considered some commitments along this line in Section G11 dealing with the seller's warranties and representations.

In addition, if you're purchasing the stock of a corporation, get a commitment that no change will be made in the Articles of Incorporation or in the authorized or issued shares of the corporation. Also, if you're dealing with a corporation, get a commitment that no contract will be entered into by or on behalf of the corporation extending beyond the closing date, except those made in the ordinary course of business.

Finally, have the corporation agree that it won't increase the compensation paid to any officer or employee and won't make any new arrangements for bonuses.

15. Contingencies

A contingency clause is a safety valve that lets you walk away from the transaction if certain things don't pan out. For example, if the location of the business is a crucial part of your decision to buy, you'll want to reserve the right to cancel the deal if you find out that the lease can't be assigned to you. The same thing might be true of a required license; if you're buying a bar, you would make the deal contingent on the state transferring the liquor license to you. If you plan to expand the business or move to a new location, make the deal contingent on your being able to get approval from the local zoning and building officials.

Here's a sample contingency clause:

> This agreement is contingent upon buyer receiving approval, by _____ , 20____ from the landlord and the city's building and safety department for a remodeling of the premises leased by the business as shown in the plans and specifications attached as Exhibit __.

16. Seller to Be a Consultant

Sometimes it pays to have the seller stay on for a few months as a consultant or employee to help ease your transition into the business and reassure long-time customers and suppliers that the business is in good hands. If you make these kinds of arrangements with the seller, be sure to capture them in the sales agreement, using language such as the following:

> _____, as an independent contractor engaged by buyer, will provide consultation, customer relations, general assistance, and information to buyer pertaining to the company for up to 20 hours per week as requested by buyer for a period of eight weeks

> following closing. For such services, buyer will pay _____ $_____ per week.

The consulting fees are tax deductible as current business expenses.

17. Broker Fees

If a business broker is involved, specify who is responsible for paying the fee, unless you independently hired the broker to help you locate the business. Normally, the seller is responsible.

18. Notices

It's customary to state addresses for both the seller and the purchaser where any notices and demands can be sent—for example, if a payment is late or another contract term is not met. Typically, sales agreements provide that notices can be given by first-class mail, but it is appropriate to require notice by registered mail with a return receipt requested.

19. Closing Date

Include a date for the closing. That's when you'll make your down payment, and both parties will sign any documents that are necessary to transfer the business to you.

H. The Closing

Finally, the big day has arrived—you're about to become the owner of a business. In an ideal world, you'd simply give the seller a check and the seller would give you the keys. Unfortunately, there's lots of additional paperwork involved.

There's also a certain amount of stress and pressure at a closing (after all, it's not every day that you buy a business). Working with your lawyer or other advisor, make a checklist in advance listing all documents to be signed and other actions to be taken at the closing. Review this carefully a couple of days before the closing and be sure you have all your paperwork ready to go. If anything is unclear or doesn't make sense to you, ask your lawyer to redraft the language in plain English so that you and everyone else can understand it.

Checklist for a Typical Closing

☐ *Adjust purchase price* for prorated items such as rent payments or utilities, or changes in the value of inventory.

☐ *Review documents promised by seller*—for example, a corporate board resolution authorizing the sale or an opinion of the seller's lawyer stating that the corporation is in good legal standing and that the sale has been properly approved by the shareholders and/or directors.

☐ *Sign promissory note* if you're not paying all cash for the business. The seller may require your spouse's signature as well so that your joint bank account will be a source of repayment if the business doesn't produce enough income.

☐ *Sign security agreement* giving the seller a lien on the business assets if you don't pay the full price in cash at closing. (If you fail to keep up your payments as promised, the seller can take back the assets subject to the security agreement.)

☐ *Sign assignment of lease* if you're taking over an existing lease. If the landlord's approval is required, be sure it has been obtained before the closing.

☐ *Transfer vehicle titles* if cars or trucks are among the business assets.

☐ *Sign bill of sale* transferring ownership of other tangible business assets.

☐ *Sign transfer of patents, trademarks, and copyrights* if included in the sale.

☐ *Sign franchise transfer documents* if you're buying a business from a franchisee. This should include the signed approval of the franchisor.

☐ *Sign closing or settlement statement* listing all financial aspects of the transaction. Ideally, everything in the closing or settlement statement should be based on clear language in the sales agreement so that nothing need be negotiated at the closing table.

☐ *Sign covenant not to compete* if seller agreed to one.

☐ *Sign consultation or employment agreement* if the seller has agreed to stay on as a consultant or employee.

☐ *Complete IRS Form 8594, Asset Acquisition Statement,* indicating how the purchase was allocated among the various assets. You and the seller will attach a copy of the form to your respective income tax returns.

I. Selling a Business

Obviously, when you're just starting out in business, selling it isn't at the forefront of your mind. But there's a good chance that, sooner or later, you'll need to or want to sell. The reasons can vary widely—from not liking working for yourself, to a need to relocate, to one spouse selling to the other as part of a divorce, to retirement.

Let's look at some things you can do get a good price for your business and protect your legal position.

For in-depth guidance on how to sell a business: *See* Sell Your Business: A Step-by-Step Legal Guide, *by Fred Steingold (Nolo). The CD-ROM that accompanies the book contains a full set of forms.*

1. Valuing Your Business

When you contemplate selling all of a business or only part (which might occur if you take in a partner or sell out to your co-owner spouse as part of a divorce), your first task is to determine the value of your business.

> **EXAMPLE:** Pauline has built a thriving retail business with three locations and 24 employees. Now she's getting divorced. She and her husband have agreed that she'll keep the business rather than liquidate it. Pauline must put a value on the business so that she and her husband can arrive at a reasonable property settlement.

You can get help from an appraiser (see Section D, above) or a business broker. If you do use a broker to sell your business, carefully read the listing agreement. Consider these issues:

- Does the broker have the exclusive right to sell your business or can you sell it directly without paying a commission?
- Do you have the right to reject a proposed purchaser because of the purchaser's credit history or for other reasons without having to pay the broker's commission?
- If there's an installment sale, will the broker receive his or her total commission out of the down payment or in installments as you're paid?

If you do business through a corporation, you'll probably be selling only the assets the corporation owns—not the corporation itself—although, from a tax and liability standpoint, it's more advantageous for you to sell the corporate stock.

Timing of a sale can be critical to getting the best price. Suppose your company has had earnings of $400,000 per year for the past three years. And suppose, too, that you have good reason to believe you'll jump to $600,000 next year. You can, of course, tell a prospective buyer why you expect an increase in profits. But there's often a better tactic: hang on to the business for another year so that you have actual numbers to point to—not just a theory.

Would-be buyers will have much more confidence in your figures if you can show them several years' worth of financial statements audited or reviewed by a CPA. (The distinctions between the types of CPA reports are discussed in Section D, above.) Also, keep detailed schedules of expenses so that buyers can compare your business with others in your industry.

Getting a Good Price for Your Business

- *Show steadily increasing profits at or above the industry average.* Plan ahead. To show strong profits, you may need to give up some hidden perks. Don't fret; you'll be handsomely rewarded at sale time.
- *Put your business in good general condition.* Everything should be neat, tidy, and in good working order. Machinery should be in good repair; your inventory should be well balanced and current.
- *Maintain adequate personnel.* A buyer will be put off—and discount the price—if the first chore in running the business is to recruit and train new employees.
- *Get a written appraisal supporting your sales price.* This can help persuade the buyer that the price is right.

These suggestions are from *Valuing Small Businesses and Professional Practices,* by Shannon Pratt (Dow Jones–Irwin).

2. Read Your Lease

Your lease may say that a new business owner can't take over your space without the landlord's consent. If so, such consent will be needed if you signed the lease as a sole proprietor or partner. It will also be needed if the purchaser is buying the assets of your corporation or LLC rather than its stock or membership interests. Find out early whether your landlord will be an obstacle to selling the business and, if so, how you can get his or her support.

3. Protect Your Privacy

A prospective purchaser will want to investigate your business thoroughly before signing a purchase agreement. To protect your privacy, use a confidentiality or nondisclosure agreement in which the potential purchaser promises not to use or disclose confidential information about your business—unless, of course, he or she decides to buy it. (A sample agreement is shown in Section C, above.) A prospective purchaser who violates this agreement can be sued for damages and injunctive relief.

4. Sign a Letter of Intent

In Section F, we looked at the nonbinding letter of intent from the standpoint of a buyer. There's no reason why such a letter can't be drafted by a seller who wants to summarize the terms of the proposed transaction as part of testing whether a potential buyer is serious.

5. Draft a Sales Agreement

To understand the elements of a sales agreement, read the previous sections of this chapter, particularly Section G. Here are some points to consider from the seller's viewpoint:

a. Structure of the Sale

The sales agreement structures the sale. As noted in Section B1, if you're doing business as a sole proprietor or partnership, the structure of the sale is a foregone conclusion: You'll sell the assets of the business to the buyer. But if you're doing business as a corporation or LLC, the matter is more complicated. It's almost always better for you to sell your corporate stock or LLC membership interests than to have your business sell its assets. But for tax and liability reasons, buyers prefer to buy assets rather than stock or membership interests.

b. Excluded Assets

If you're selling the assets of the business or the business itself—whether it be a sole proprietorship, a partnership, a corporation, or an LLC—the purchase agreement lists the assets being transferred. Typically, this includes furniture, fixtures, equipment, inventory and vehicles, and the business name. Equally important, specify any items excluded from the sale, for example: cash, accounts receivable, life insurance policies, or your personal desk or computer.

c. Allocation of Purchase Price

In Section G, we focused on the allocation of the purchase price from the buyer's standpoint. The buyer typically wants to assign a relatively high value to items that can be quickly written off or depreciated for tax purposes. The seller generally prefers to place a high value on assets that will provide long-term capital gain treatment; the tax on such gain is lower than the tax on ordinary income. A tax pro can help size up your particular sale and recommend how to allocate the purchase price. Also, a tax pro can suggest ways to adjust the purchase price up or down to reflect whoever takes the tax hit.

d. Adequate Security for Installment Sales

When a small business is sold on an installment payment basis, the buyer typically makes a down payment of 20% to 40% of the purchase price and pays the balance in monthly installments over three to five years. Plan ahead in case the buyer doesn't keep up the payments as promised. Insist that the buyer's spouse sign all closing documents jointly with the buyer. That way, if you need to sue the buyer because of nonpayment, you have a chance of collecting the judgment out of a house owned jointly by the buyer and spouse, or from bank accounts in their joint names. If the couple's credit is weak, insist that the documents be signed by an outside guarantor.

The purchase agreement should require the buyer to give you a security interest (also called a lien) in the business assets. A financing statement that's filed with county or state officials will give public notice that you have a claim on the business assets.

If you're doing business as a corporation and are selling your stock, consider placing the stock certificates in escrow. That way, the buyer won't receive the certificates until the purchase price has been paid in full.

e. Looking to the Future

The buyer may want to hire you for several months or years as a consultant or employee. If so, spell this out in the sales agreement or in a separate document signed at the same time. Be specific about the types of services you'll be expected to render, the amount of time you're committing, and the amount you'll be paid. Sometimes, compensation for a seller's post-sale services is simply folded into the purchase price so the seller receives no additional payment.

If you've agreed not to compete with the buyer, the terms should be specified in a covenant not to compete. Cover such matters as precisely what business or activities you won't engage in, being careful not to burn all of your bridges. Think carefully about how long you're willing to refrain from working in a competing enterprise and how large a geographical area should be barred during the noncompetition period. (See Section G5.)

f. Warranties

Sales agreements typically contain numerous warranties and representations by the seller and a few by the buyer. (See Sections G11 and G12 for examples.) Read your warranties and representations carefully to make sure they don't go too far.

For example, suppose the proposed warranty language says: "Seller warrants that the business name does not conflict with the name of any other business." What happens if, the day after the sale, a business that you didn't know about surfaces and complains that it had the name first? With the warranty wording given here, you could be liable for damages whether or not you knew about the other company.

If you see a warranty that's too far-reaching, have it rewritten. In our example, you might say something like "Seller warrants that, to the best of seller's knowledge, . . ." Or perhaps you could say: "Seller warrants that it has received no notice that its business name conflicts with that of any other business." ■

Franchises: How Not to Get Burned

America's landscape is dotted with franchises: Take the first exit off any freeway, and you're likely to spot familiar ones offering fast food, gasoline, groceries, lodgings, and more. So, you might conclude, they must be making money, or they'd pack up and disappear. And why shouldn't you buy into an established chain to get a jump on the learning curve and tap into an existing customer base?

Not so fast. For most people hoping to own a small business, buying a franchise is a poor idea. Most of the franchises you see on the road—or on Main Street or at the mall—are just barely eking out a profit beyond the percentage they must pay to the franchise vendor (the "franchisor"). Worse yet, some of their owners would like to sell, but can't. Because of the legal and economic rules exerted by the franchisor, you may end up feeling more like an indentured servant than an entrepreneur. In my view, you'll be happier and farther ahead financially if you start a business from scratch or buy an existing one.

In this chapter, I'll explain how franchises work, and delve deeper into their pitfalls. Then I'll introduce you to the two most important legal documents that are involved in the purchase of a franchise: the Uniform Franchise Operating Circular (UFOC) and the Franchise Agreement.

 For more insight into the perils of franchise ownership: *Read the chapter titled "Don't Buy a Franchise" in* How to Run a Thriving Business, *by Ralph Warner (Nolo). Also see* The Franchise Fraud: How to Protect Yourself Before and After You Invest, *by Robert L. Purvin, Jr. (John Wiley & Sons, Inc.). You'll find additional information on the websites of two organizations dedicated to promoting the rights of franchises: The American Franchisee Association (www.franchisee.org) and The American Association of Franchisees & Dealers (www.aafd.org). Both contain valuable information to help you protect your legal and financial interests. Also, the website of the U.S. Small Business Adminis-*

tration (www.sba.gov) offers a helpful download, "Evaluating Franchise Opportunities."

Get professional advice before you plunge in. *Don't wait until you find yourself trapped in a costly and frustrating relationship with a franchisor—at which time you may have little legal recourse. It's worth paying for some sound legal and financial advice before you get locked into a contract or pay the franchisor a cent.*

A. What Is a Franchise?

The most convenient analysis and definition of a franchise comes from the Federal Trade Commission (FTC)—the one government agency that has nationwide regulatory power in this field. The FTC recognizes two types of business relationships that qualify for regulation as franchises:

- *The Package Franchise.* The franchisor licenses you to do business under a business format it has established. The business is closely identified with the franchisor's trademark or trade name. Examples include car washes, fast food outlets, motels, transmission centers, tax preparation services, and quick copy shops.
- *The Product Franchise.* You distribute goods produced by the franchisor or under the franchisor's control or direction. The business or goods bear the franchisor's trademark or trade name. Examples include gasoline stations and car dealerships.

This chapter deals primarily with package franchises, which are more common.

The FTC definition is broad. It covers all of the businesses that you and I would ordinarily think of as franchises. Generally, the FTC (and many state agencies that regulate franchises) will classify your business relationship as a franchise if three conditions exist:

- You have the right to distribute goods or services that bear the franchisor's trademark, service mark, trade name, or logo.
- The franchisor significantly assists you in operating your business or significantly controls what you do. For example, your franchisor might assist in site selection, train you and your employees, or furnish you with a detailed instructional manual. A franchisor might exercise control by telling you where your business must be located and how your shop must be designed, or by dictating your hours, accounting and personnel practices, and advertising program.
- You pay a fee to the franchisor of more than $500 for the first six months of operations. (In the real world, you're going to be paying a franchisor much more—probably anywhere from $10,000 or $20,000 to $1 million.)

All of this can add up to a complex and expensive relationship between you and the franchisor.

EXAMPLE: Lila loves the idea of selling doughnuts, and buys a franchise from Munchin Donuts International. She pays Munchin Donuts $50,000 as a franchise fee plus an additional $5,000 for training for herself and an assistant. Lila and her assistant must travel to the Munchin Donuts headquarters in another state for the training. Munchin Donuts helps her find a suitable location for a doughnut shop, then prescribes the store layout and décor. Lila makes the necessary improvements, but can't use her favorite contractor—she must use one on Munchin Donuts' approved list. She buys the doughnut-making equipment and shop furnishings directly from Munchin Donuts, as required by her franchise contract. Munchin Donuts provides Lila with a 500-page operating manual called *Making Donuts the Munchin Way*. Lila is also given the right to use the Munchin Donuts logo in her signage and advertising. Lila must buy all of the doughnut mixes directly from

Munchin Donuts, and each month she must pay Munchin 8% of her gross sales, plus a hefty fee for participation in Munchin's co-op advertising program. She must keep the shop open from 7 a.m. to 9 p.m., six days a week, as required by the Munchin Donuts operating manual.

B. The Downsides of Franchise Ownership

During your negotiations to buy a franchise, while everyone is still smiling, the franchisor is likely to assure you that you won't be in business all by yourself, but will be part of a team selling a recognized product or service. Franchisors typically also tout three other supposed benefits:

- *A proven plan for running the business.* The franchisor will furnish an operations manual that can serve as a roadmap to get you started.
- *Help from the franchisor if you run into problems.* The franchisor promises to make people available who are experienced in real estate, personnel policies, accounting, and day-to-day operations.
- *A national or regional marketing program to attract customers.* The franchisor promises to advertise in print and on radio and TV so that the brand will become famous and customers will flock to your door.

Even if the franchisor makes good on all of these commitments—and many won't—the price you'll pay to get these benefits may be backbreakingly high. Do you really need to pay a company month after month, year after year, in order to master the fundamentals of making pizza or cleaning houses? As for business help from the franchisor, can't you simply hire advisors on an as-needed basis to help you with real estate, marketing, or accounting issues? (As a matter of fact, you can probably learn the basic management skills you'll need by taking a course or two at a nearby community college.) And will the franchisor really invest enough money to build the kind of brand recognition that translates into huge profits for you? It's highly unlikely.

It's true that some small business people have signed on for a franchise and found prosperity and happiness, but many more have lost their shirts and feel bitter about their franchise experiences. So before you're seduced by the glitter of the franchisor's glib promises, take a hard look at the downsides of investing in a franchise.

It takes money to make money. *Some franchises may have a high profit potential—but the better ones tend to be well beyond the reach of the small operator. As Ralph Warner convincingly explains in* How to Run a Thriving Business: Strategies for Success & Satisfaction *(Nolo), national hotel and motel groups may offer fine franchise opportunities, since they provide a real service through their 800 phone numbers and reservation booking services. Ditto for auto rental franchises since they, too, offer something of value. And franchises with famous and respected brands such as McDonald's and Pizza Hut may be worth the high cost. But these blue-chip opportunities are expensive to buy into. If you're an ordinary entrepreneur with possibly $50,000 or $75,000 to invest, you'll probably be looking at lesser-known franchises for which the prospects are not nearly so bright.*

Let's look at some reasons why franchises are usually a worse option than starting your own business or buying an existing one.

1. The Franchisor Gets a Huge Chunk of the Pie

The franchisor will almost certainly insist on getting a thick slice of your financial action—often the lion's share. Franchisors have figured out many ways to make money on your business, including:

- *Franchise fees.* You must always pay up front for the right to be a franchisee. These buy-in fees can verge on the astronomical, especially for a successful, nationally established franchise.
- *Royalties.* Commonly, the franchisor gets a percentage of the income your franchise earns. Income usually means gross sales, not profits. If your franchise takes in $200,000 from gross sales and your contract calls for a 10% royalty, the franchisor will be entitled to receive $20,000 whether or not your business earns a profit. Other operating expenses can easily eat up the remaining $180,000 of gross income, leaving nothing—or even less.
- *Markups on equipment, goods, and supplies.* The franchisor may add dollars to the cost of equipment, goods, and supplies that the franchisor furnishes. Many franchise agreements require you to buy certain items from the franchisor rather than from outside suppliers; others let you buy through outside sources if the items meet the franchisor's specifications. If, for example, you're required to purchase cooking equipment from the franchisor, you may pay a bundle more than you'd pay a restaurant supply store.
- *Training fees.* Often you must pay the franchisor to train you and your employees—whether or not you need the training.
- *Co-op ad fees.* These fees cover advertising for the entire group of franchises or a regional group. For example, you may have to contribute to a fund for national advertising or for advertising for all the franchisees in your metropolitan area—whether or not any of your customers are likely to see the ads.

- *Interest on financing.* You may have to pay for deferring payment of a portion of the franchise fee, the cost of improving your business premises, or buying equipment.
- *Leases.* Your franchisor may charge you rent on real estate or equipment. Typically, the franchisor does not lease real estate or equipment to you at the franchisor's cost but adds on a profit factor. But because relatively few franchisors own the premises where their franchisees do business, real estate lease charges are relatively uncommon.

If it appears that I'm painting a grim picture, I am. After you've made all the required payments to the franchisor, there may be very little left for you.

LAW IN THE REAL WORLD
Going It Alone

Phil, a real estate broker, wanted to open his own shop. He first considered going it alone, but then decided he might do better by purchasing a franchise from one of the national organizations. He contacted several and was amazed to find that he couldn't buy a one-office franchise directly from them. Instead he was told that in his region a "master" franchise had already been sold and that he would have to contact this company to purchase a subfranchise.

When he did, he learned that his region had been divided into hundreds of subregions or territories, each of which was for sale through a local real estate office. All training, quality control, and recruiting was done by the master franchise holder, not the national organization.

Eventually, Phil decided not to purchase any of the local franchises he was offered, concluding that the territories had been divided too narrowly. In the meantime, he has opened his own office and is doing fairly well. He might still affiliate with a franchise organization, but only if he can find one that sells good-sized territories at a reasonable price.

---

2. The Franchisor Can Tell You What to Do

If you're like many entrepreneurs, part of the attraction of owning a business is that you're free to make your own business decisions, test new ideas, and change and improve the products and services you offer. Unfortunately, when you're a franchisee, you give up a great deal of that freedom. The franchisor typically prescribes a formula for running the business and, for the most part, you're locked into using it. Don't be surprised if you soon become frustrated and bored.

But the consequences of signing on as a franchisee can go much farther than just stifled creativity. There's a real chance that your bottom line will be affected. Small businesses normally enjoy a huge advantage over multistate giants: they're nimble enough to respond quickly to local conditions.

By contrast, large organizations can't react nearly as fast, meaning that opportunities for adding profits—or avoiding losses—can be missed. For example, if you own a pizza franchise and notice that everyone in town is going crazy for fresh shiitake mushrooms, you could wait years before your franchisor lets you put any mushroom atop your pizza that isn't straight from a can. You're just a cog in a huge machine.

3. The Franchise Contract Will Favor the Franchisor

When you buy a franchise, you'll need to sign a contract with the franchisor. Contracts aren't bad in and of themselves—they're useful tools for spelling out all the terms and conditions of the relationship. However, the contract that you'll be handed will have been drafted by a team of skilled lawyers hired by the franchisor and will most likely contain dozens of clauses aimed at giving the franchisor every conceivable advantage. And you'll probably be told to "take it or leave it," with no opportunity to negotiate any of the contract terms.

To give you an idea of how one-sided these contracts can be, here are some clauses you're likely to find in the typical franchise contract.

- **Competition.** The franchisor will usually protect its freedom to grant additional franchises without restriction. This means that if your operation is successful, the franchisor may decide to sell a franchise to someone else right down the street, cutting into your market share. By contrast, you'll be required to agree that after the franchise relationship ends, you won't compete with the franchisor—either directly or indirectly. This stops you from working or investing in a similar business. While it's reasonable for the franchisor to want to protect its trademarks and trade secrets, the franchisor already has plenty of legal protection in this area. The franchisor has no solid justification for interfering with your ability to earn a living doing similar work after you've stopped being a franchisee—but it has superior bargaining power. It can usually force even unreasonable restrictions on you as part of the price of buying the franchise.

- **Selling Your Franchise.** When you own your own business, you're free to sell it to whomever you wish. Not so with a franchise. Typically, you can't sell your franchise unless the franchisor approves of the buyer. This means that if you want to retire or move to another state or shift to a different line of work, you're at the mercy of the franchisor. If the franchisor is picky, you may be left with few—if any—prospective buyers, and you may have to settle for a fraction of what the business is worth. Worse yet, the buyer will have to sign a new franchise contract, which may call for even higher royalty charges than you've been paying, making it all the more difficult to sell the business.

- **Disputes.** The contract may require you to resolve any disputes with the franchisor in the courts of the franchisor's home state. If you do business in Oregon and the franchisor's headquarters are in New Jersey, that's a long and expensive trip.

- **Goods and Services.** The contract may force you to buy all your goods and services from the franchisor. If you have to buy your milkshake mix from the franchisor, and your marketing services as well, you'll probably end up paying much more than if you were free to buy from vendors of your choice.

For more on franchise agreements, see Section E.

4. The Government Won't Protect You

Franchisors become very adept at selling franchises—but aren't known for following through on what they promise in the sales presentations. Some franchisors are notorious for misrepresenting key facts about their organization. Many deftly inflate your expectations of the profits you'll bring in. And some are fly-by-night outfits operating entirely by smoke and mirrors.

Don't assume you can go running to the government for help if the franchisor's promises turn out to be puffery. Neither the state nor the federal government is going to thoroughly investigate the accuracy of information in the offering circular or bail you out if things go wrong. True, you may get limited help from a government agency to close down or even prosecute an operator whose actions constitute outright fraud. But even in the case of blatant dishonesty by the franchisor, you'll be pretty much on your own in trying to get back your money.

The time to be cautious is at the beginning, while you listen to the sales banter from the franchisor. Remember that you're almost surely not receiving a balanced, objective point of view. No matter what they say about peace, brotherhood, and all prospering together, most franchisors look at their job as simply to sell as many franchises as possible, as fast as possible, at the highest price possible.

Some Sobering Statistics

Benefits touted by the franchise industry may be overblown. Timothy Bates, an economics professor at Wayne State University, studied the numbers for a four-year period. Here's his comparison of what happened to those who started an independent business from scratch versus those who started a franchised business:

	Started an Independent Business	Started a Franchised Business
Maintained Ownership	62%	54%
Shut Down	32%	38%
Gave up Ownership	6%	8%

Professor Bates also found that after four years, people who bought an independent on-going business were doing better than those who bought an ongoing franchise business. He cites these figures:

	Bought Into an Independent Business	Bought Into an Ongoing Franchise Business
Maintained Ownership	68%	52%
Shut Down	18%	32%
Gave up Ownership	16%	15%

Professor Bates concluded that whether someone starts a new business or buys one that's already in existence, the risk of having to shut down is greater if the owner takes the franchise route.

Source: *Inc. Magazine*, July 1995

C. Investigating a Franchise

If you've done your research and have identified a few businesses in which you believe you could be successful as a franchisee, investigate the franchisors. A good track record counts. Find out how many franchises each franchisor has in actual operation—information that's readily available in the offering circular. (See Section D20.)

Next, carefully evaluate whether the specific franchise operation you're thinking about makes economic sense. Is there really a demand out there for the product or service that you'll be selling? Can you make a decent profit given how much you can charge and your cost of doing business?

Don't forget to count all those franchise fees. The franchisor may give you actual or hypothetical projections of how much money a typical franchisee can earn. Distrust these. Chances are they're full of hype. Ask for financial details about individual franchise operations that are geographically and demographically similar to the one that you're considering.

Most important, speak to a number of other franchisees. The names and addresses of those in your state will be listed in the offering circular. (Again, see Section D20.)

The more you know about the franchisor, the better. Visit the home office, even if it's in another city or state. Get to know the people you'll be dealing with if you buy. What's the background of the owners, officers, and management staff of the franchisor? Do they have the experience and competence to give you the promised technical support?

Be especially suspicious of franchises that promise big profits for little work and offer a money-back guarantee. Rarely do you get something for nothing in this world and almost never do you get your money back when business deals go awry.

Learn how much help you can expect from the franchisor in:

- selecting a site
- negotiating a lease
- writing and placing help wanted ads for employees

- interviewing prospective employees
- getting the necessary business licenses, and
- ordering equipment.

Make sure all key promises are in writing. Oral statements don't count: Often they're not legally enforceable, but even where they are, proving in court what someone said years before may be impossible. One good way to get things in writing is to take notes when you talk to the franchisor. Then write up your notes, review them with the franchisor, and ask for the signature of someone in authority.

With a larger franchisor, many of your contacts will be with a district or regional manager. Meet these people and find out what they're like.

Ask about whether any franchise operations have closed. Obviously, this is a sensitive topic for a franchisor. Ideally, the franchisor will be honest in discussing failures with you, but you can't count on this. If the franchisor seems to be stonewalling, try to get the names of franchisees whose operations failed from existing franchisees and talk to them directly.

Investigate the area where your franchise will be located. Talk to people who work or live nearby to learn more about the behavior and tastes of potential customers. What do other business owners have to say about your customer base? How do they think your franchise will fit into the community?

D. The Uniform Franchise Offering Circular

The Federal Trade Commission requires franchisors to give prospective franchisees an offering circular containing details about the franchise. In addition, the franchisor must give you a copy of the proposed franchise agreement and related documents. But FTC rules don't dictate the terms of the deal you and the franchisor agree to. As long as there's full disclosure, the deal can be very one-sided in favor of the franchisor and still be legal.

The FTC does list the items that a franchisor must include in an offering circular and provides a format for the franchisor to follow. Most states that regulate franchise sales prefer a slightly different format called the "Uniform Franchise Offering Circular." Since the FTC says it's okay for a franchisor to use that format, practically every national franchisor does.

Although the FTC requires the disclosure, it doesn't verify or vouch for the information the franchisor discloses. It's up to you to check out anything you don't understand or that sounds too good to be true.

Under FTC rules, if you're a prospective franchisee, the franchisor must give you the offering circular at the earliest of either:

- your first in-person (face-to-face) meeting with the franchisor, or
- ten working days (not counting Saturdays and Sundays) before you sign a contract or pay money to the franchisor.

If a franchisor violates these or other FTC rules, it may face heavy civil penalties. Also, the FTC may sue the franchisor, on your behalf, for damages or other relief, including cancellation of a franchise contract and refunds.

State laws often provide other avenues of relief for violation of disclosure and other requirements. For example, in some states, you may have the right to sue a franchisor who fails to make disclosures properly. In other words, you won't have to rely on the state to make your case for you.

Knowing that these legal avenues are open to you may give you some peace of mind—but don't relax your guard too much. If the franchisor becomes insolvent or goes into bankruptcy, chances are you'll recover only a minuscule part of your loss, or maybe nothing at all.

Here are the 23 items included in the Uniform Franchise Offering Circular and brief comments about how to think about each:

1. The Franchisor, Its Predecessors and Affiliates

Here you'll learn the name of the franchisor and its predecessors and affiliates, as well as the name under which the franchisor does business. You'll also find out if the franchisor is a corporation, a partnership, or some other type of business.

The franchisor then describes its businesses and the franchises being offered, and lists the business experience of the franchisor and its predecessors and affiliates. You can find out how long the franchisor has operated the type of business you'd be franchising. You can also learn whether the franchisor has offered franchises in other lines of business and the number of franchises sold.

Finally, the franchisor must describe any regulations that are specific to the industry in which the franchisee operates.

2. Business Experience

The franchisor must list its principal officers. For each officer, his or her job for the past five years must be disclosed.

3. Litigation

This is where you learn the legal history of the franchisor. If the franchisor or its associated people have a history of legal problems, watch out. If the franchisor follows the FTC rule, you'll discover, for example, whether or not there are administrative, criminal, or civil cases alleging:

- violation of any franchise, antitrust, or securities law
- fraud
- unfair or deceptive trade practices, or
- comparable misconduct.

If any such actions are pending, the offering circular must provide full information.

Furthermore, the franchisor must disclose whether, in the past ten years, the franchisor or its people have been convicted of a felony, pleaded no contest to a felony charge, or have been held liable in a civil action involving any of the offenses listed above.

And there's more: If the franchisor or associated person is subject to an injunction (court order) relating to a franchise or involving any laws on securities, antitrust, trade regulation, or trade practice, the franchisor must disclose this information. This can provide an early warning of potential problems.

Don't rely on the franchisor's explanations of lawsuits involving the company. You can look at the court files, which are open to the public and will name all of the participants on both sides. Call the people on the other side and get their version of events.

4. Bankruptcy

The franchisor must state whether the franchisor or its officers have gone through bankruptcy or been reorganized due to insolvency during the past ten years. The information required is far-reaching. The franchisor must disclose if any officer or general partner was a principal officer of any company or a general partner of any partnership that went bankrupt or was reorganized due to insolvency within one year after the officer or general partner was associated with the company or partnership.

5. Initial Franchise Fee

Read this section carefully to learn how much you'll be charged before you open for business and whether you'll have to pay it in a lump sum or installments. The franchisor must also explain under what conditions your money will be refunded.

If the franchisor doesn't charge identical initial fees to each franchisee, the franchisor must tell how fees are determined, or state the range of fees charged in the past year.

6. Other Fees

Here's where you get detail about any required fees. Using a simple chart, the franchisor must tell you the formula used to compute fees and the conditions for refunds.

When any fees are set by the vote of a cooperative organization of franchisees—for advertising, for example—the franchisor must disclose the voting power of franchisor-owned outlets. If franchisor outlets have controlling voting power, the franchisor must disclose a range for the fees.

7. Initial Investment

These are estimates (or a high-low range) of expenses you'll be responsible for. You'll be told who the payments must be made to, when the payments are due, and the conditions for refunds. If part of your initial investment may be financed, you'll learn the details, including interest rates.

Listed expenses include those for:
- real estate, whether it's bought or leased
- equipment, fixtures, other fixed assets, construction, remodeling, leasehold improvements, and decorating costs
- inventory required to begin operation
- security deposits, utility deposits, business licenses, other prepaid expenses, and working capital required to begin operation, and
- any other payments you must make to start operations.

⚠ **Don't invest everything in a franchise.** *These fees can add up to far more than you first expected and dangerously stretch your budget. Never put every last cent into a franchise. Even with an honest franchisor, there's a good chance you won't make any money the first year. Keep enough money in reserve to live on during the startup phase. And always be wary about pledging your house for a loan needed to buy a franchise. It's one thing to risk your savings; it's quite another to risk the roof over your family's head.*

8. Restrictions on Sources of Products and Services

Here, the franchisor states whether you're required to purchase or lease from the franchisor—or from companies designated by the franchisor—any of the following: goods, services, supplies, fixtures, equipment, inventory, computer hardware and software, or real estate.

The franchisor also must say if and how it may earn income from these required purchases or leases. As mentioned in Section B, many franchisors mark up the products they require their franchisees to buy from them.

9. Franchisee's Obligations

In a simple table, the franchisor lists each of your obligations and tells you where each is spelled out in the franchise agreement and offering circular.

10. Financing

Look for the terms and conditions of any financing arrangements offered to help franchisees afford the purchase. Also review the statement of your liability if you can't make the payments.

As you review these, bear in mind that after signing onto a promissory note or financing contract requiring you to make payments to the franchisor, you may find that some other company has acquired the right to collect the debt from you. This can happen if the franchisor sells or assigns (transfers) the promissory note or financing contract to the other company.

In the offering circular, the franchisor needs to state whether or not it plans to handle the financing arrangement this way. It may seem like a minor detail, but it can affect you down the road. Here's why: If you're dealing directly with the franchisor in making your payments, you may be able to withhold payment if the franchisor isn't meeting its obligations to you. By contrast, if the note or financing contract has been transferred to somebody else, you'll probably be obligated to pay regardless of how poorly the franchisor is performing.

⚠️ **Beware of finance charges.** *Paying finance charges and interest on notes held by the franchisor is a real financial burden. If you can't afford to pay all of the franchise fees up front, maybe you shouldn't buy the franchise. Think long and hard before you pledge your house as security for these obligations—and before you ask your spouse or a relative to be a cosigner or guarantor of the debt.*

11. Franchisor's Obligations

What are the franchisor's obligations to you before you open your franchise business? For example, will the franchisor select a location for your business? Will the franchisor help you:

- negotiate the purchase or lease of the site?
- make sure the building you'll occupy conforms to local codes?
- obtain required building permits?
- construct, remodel, or decorate the premises?
- purchase or lease equipment, signs, and supplies?
- hire and train employees?

And what kind of assistance will the franchisor give you once your business is operating?

Look for detailed answers to these questions as well as a description of the training program the franchisor will provide, including: the location, length, and content of the training program; when the training program will be conducted; experience that instructors have had with the franchisor; any charges for the training; the extent to which you'll be responsible for travel and living expenses of people enrolled in the training program; and whether any additional training programs or refresher courses are available or required.

12. Territory

Here the franchisor describes whether or not you have any territorial protection. Check to see whether the franchisor has established another franchisee or company-owned outlet in your territory, or has the right to do so in the future. Obviously, your business will be in trouble if the franchisor defines your exclusive territory very narrowly and then floods the market with outlets offering similar products or services.

Even if you have exclusive rights within a territory, you may not be safe from direct competition. Some franchisors require you to achieve a certain sales volume or market penetration to keep those exclusive rights. Make sure you understand under what conditions your area or territory can be altered.

13. Trademarks

Most likely your franchise will require you to use the franchisor's trademarks, service marks, trade names, logos, or other commercial symbols. Fine. In many ways, these represent much of the value of a franchise. In fact, you'll want to research whether the franchisor itself has an ongoing right to use these marks and symbols.

For starters, the franchisor must tell you in the offering circular whether or not the franchisor's trademarks and symbols are registered with the U.S. Patent and Trademark Office. The franchisor must also describe any agreements, administrative proceedings, or court cases that may affect your right to use these trademarks and symbols.

Franchisors should stand behind their trade names and trademarks. Even if a trademark is properly registered, it can still be challenged in court by a company that used it before the franchisor used it or registered it. Make sure that your franchisor is obligated in writing to defend any challenges against its names and trademarks and to indemnify you against any damage awards for using them. The franchisor should also agree to reimburse you for out-of-pocket expenses if you have to replace signs and print new supplies because of an adverse court ruling regarding names or trademarks.

14. Patents, Copyrights, and Proprietary Information

The franchisor must give full details about any patents or copyrights that relate to the franchise and the terms and conditions under which you can use them. Let's say, for example, that a tire store franchisor has published an excellent copyrighted booklet telling consumers how to choose the right tires for their cars. The franchisor needs to disclose whether there have been any administrative or other claims filed that might affect the continued use of the booklet. And the franchisor needs to state whether it can require its franchisees to discontinue use of the booklet in running their franchisees.

Also, the franchisor must state if it claims proprietary rights in confidential information or trade secrets.

15. Obligation to Participate in the Actual Operation of the Franchise Business

Some franchisors permit someone to own a franchise without actively participating in the operation of the business. Other franchisors want the owner to be fully involved. The franchisor must state whether or not it will obligate you to participate

personally in operating the franchise business. It must also state whether or not it recommends that you participate.

If the franchisor doesn't require you, as a franchise owner, to personally be present and run the business, it may require that you employ an on-site manager who has successfully completed the franchisor's training program.

16. Restrictions on What the Franchisee May Sell

If you're going to be restricted in the goods or services you can offer or the customers you can sell to, this must be spelled out in the offering circular. Find out if you'll be required to carry the full range of the franchisor's products. For example, with a food franchise, do you have to offer the full menu? Can you add items to the menu?

Also, check whether the franchisor has the right to change the types of goods and services you're authorized to sell.

17. Renewal, Termination, Transfer, and Dispute Resolution

You're entitled to know the conditions under which you may renew, extend, or terminate your franchise and also the conditions under which the franchisor may refuse to deal with you. (See Section E8 for more on termination.)

Look, too, for information on whether disputes must be submitted to mediation or arbitration in place of going to court.

Mediation or arbitration is usually a plus. *Fighting a franchisor in court can be prohibitively expensive for a franchisee. The franchisor usually has very deep pockets and can better afford to finance—or even drag out—the litigation. If a legal*

dispute can't be settled through negotiation, it's al-
most always better for you to submit the matter to
mediation or arbitration rather than go to court.
Mediation and arbitration proceedings are much
less expensive than lawsuits—and speedier to boot.
There's a trade-off, however: In a lawsuit you can
compel the franchisor to show you key documents
and to answer questions under oath (in what's
called a pretrial deposition). Mediation and arbitra-
tion offer only very limited opportunities for this type
of information gathering. For more on resolving le-
gal disputes, see Chapter 22.

18. Public Figures

Some franchisors use celebrities to promote franchise
operations. The franchisor must disclose any compensation or other benefit given or promised to any
public figures for using their names or endorsements.
You also need to be told the extent to which celebrities are involved in the actual management or control
of the franchisor and how much—if anything—they
have invested in the franchise operation.

19. Earnings Claims

The franchisor has a choice. It can disclose the actual or potential sales, profits, or earnings of its
franchisees. Or it can say nothing on the subject—
which is what most franchisors choose to do. If the
franchisor does make any earnings claims, the offering circular must describe the factual basis and material assumptions that underlie these claims.

For earnings claims to make sense, you need to
know the franchise locations that the numbers are
based on and the number of years that they have
been in operation. Actual figures are, of course,
more helpful than hypothetical projections. Before
you buy a franchise, have your accountant go over
the numbers with a fine-tooth comb. Also check
with a number of existing franchisees to see how
they're doing.

20. List of Outlets

The information in this part of the circular can be a
gold mine if you take advantage of it. The franchisor must list the total number of franchise locations
and state how many of them were in operation
when the offering circular was prepared, as well as
how many are covered by franchise agreements but
are not yet in operation. The franchisor must also
list the names, addresses, and telephone numbers of
all its franchises in your state.

A company with a hundred franchises up and
running has had a chance to test its business formula and has experience in helping franchisees get
started. A company with only eight or ten units in
operation is relatively young and still has a lot to
learn. But be leery of a franchise that's merely on
the drawing board and isn't yet in actual operation.
It may never open and, even if it does, may not
prosper. Obviously, a franchise that's not yet open
can't give you hard information about sales or profitability.

The franchisor must also tell you how many
franchises it has canceled or terminated in the last
three years; how many it has not renewed; and how
many the franchisor has reacquired.

Contact franchisees in your state or in nearby
states. Ask questions: "How's it working out? Was it
a good deal? Would you do it again? Are you making a profit? How much?" Franchisees sometimes
feel locked in and are reluctant to admit that they
made a mistake in buying a franchise, but they
might level with you if you ask, "Would you feel
comfortable recommending that I put my life savings into this deal?"

Ask franchisees whether they get help and support from the home office and how often they see
someone from headquarters. Spend a day or two at
a few franchises. Picture yourself in that setting.
How does the system seem to be working? If there's
a franchisee organization, see if you can attend
meetings and get old newsletters. Don't rely on
what one or two franchisees tell you—they could
have unrevealed ties to the franchisor or be unreal-

istically positive because they're trying to unload their own franchise or will be paid a commission if they help reel you in.

21. Financial Statements

The franchisor must file audited financial statements showing the condition of the company. Unless you have experience in interpreting financial statements, get an accountant with experience with franchises to interpret the figures and help you develop tough questions. You want a franchisor to be financially strong enough to follow through on training commitments, trademark protection, and support services. If a franchisor is financially weak—many are—and folds overnight, your franchise may not be worth much.

To find an accountant with the right experience, seek recommendations from owners of successful local franchises who have been in business for a while.

22. Contracts

The franchisor must attach to the offering circular a copy of all agreements that you'll sign if you purchase the franchise. This includes lease agreements, option agreements, and purchase agreements. Read them carefully and don't sign until you understand everything.

23. Receipt

The last page of the offering circular is a detachable receipt, which you sign as evidence that you received the offering circular.

E. The Franchise Agreement

If you buy a franchise, you and the franchisor will sign a long document called a franchise agreement. There probably will be other documents to sign at the same time, but the franchise agreement is far and away the most important. Whether or not any terms of the agreement are negotiable depends on whether the franchisor is new or long established and on prevailing market conditions. A new franchisor eager to penetrate the market may be more flexible and willing to make concessions than an established franchisor whose franchises are in high demand.

Again, if the franchisor has made any promises to you, make sure that they're in the franchise agreement. Otherwise, chances are you won't be able to enforce them.

Joan, a legal secretary, inherited $200,000. To achieve her goal of financial independence, she decided to start a business. Drawing on the experience of her cousin Max, who had done very well running several franchised taco stores, Joan decided to look at franchise opportunities.

Because she couldn't afford a major franchise, she narrowed her search to small outfits. One, a Belgian waffle shop, particularly intrigued her. When she expressed interest and her solvency was documented, she was quickly:

- flown to corporate headquarters
- assigned to two enthusiastic "vice presidents"
- shown an exciting video featuring a waffle shop overflowing with happy customers
- taken on a tour of a "typical" waffle franchise outlet, and
- told there were only a few franchises left and she had to decide quickly.

It almost worked. But at literally the last minute before signing she decided she had better call her cousin Max. He yelled "stop" so loudly that she told the franchise she wanted a few days to investigate, even if it meant losing out on the deal.

The investigation showed that the franchise was almost broke, three lawsuits from disappointed franchisees were pending, and the supposedly successful franchise was owned by the parent company and looked successful because prices were kept artificially low to bring in customers. And, oh yes, the "vice presidents" who dealt with Joan were really sales reps working on commission.

Let's look at a few sensitive areas of a franchise deal that you must be aware of before you plunk down your money and sign an agreement.

1. Franchise Fee

The extent of your personal liability for the franchise fee and other franchise obligations is a crucial consideration for you in making this deal.

Does the franchise agreement allow you to avoid personal liability for franchise-related debts by forming a corporation to serve as the franchisee? Or does the franchisor require you (and perhaps your spouse as well) to be personally responsible for all franchise obligations?

At the risk of being repetitive, I strongly recommend against pledging your house or other assets as security for payment of the franchise fee. (See Section D5 for how the franchise fee is dealt with in the offering circular.)

2. Advertising Fees

If the franchise agreement requires you to pay an advertising fee to the franchisor, make sure that part of that fee is earmarked for local advertising over which you'll have some control. Perhaps the franchisor will agree to match any money you spend on local advertising. This is especially important if your franchise will be in an area where there are only a few other franchise locations. Otherwise the franchisor may spend all the advertising money 1,000 miles away where there are more franchisees—and you'll essentially be paying to support someone else's business.

Be alert for arrangements that allow the franchisor to reap profits from the advertising fees it charges you. In one case, a federal court said it was legal for Meineke Mufflers to set up its own in-house ad agency and hire it to handle franchise system advertising—a scheme that profited Meineke to the tune of millions of dollars in fees. (*Broussard v. Meineke Discount Muffler Shops,* 155 F.3d 331 (4th Cir. 1998).)

3. Royalty Fees

Typically, the royalty fees you pay the franchisor are a percentage of your gross sales. (See Section B.) They may, however, be a flat weekly or monthly charge. Be cautious about a franchisor who charges a small initial franchise fee but then charges you a high percentage of monthly sales.

> **EXAMPLE:** Compare two fast food operations. Franchisor A charges an initial fee of $5,000 and monthly royalties of 8% (in addition to advertising fees). Franchisor B charges a franchise fee of $20,000 and monthly royalties of 5% (not including advertising). Let's say that each franchise has annual sales of $500,000. In the first year, each franchisee will pay $45,000 to the franchisor. But look at succeeding years. Franchisee A will pay $40,000 each year to its franchisor, while Franchisee B pays only $25,000.

⚠️ **Franchise royalties are costly.** *Remember that many franchises simply are bad business deals. In a world where it's very hard for any small business to make a 10% profit, giving a huge chunk of money to the franchisor as a royalty rarely makes sense.*

4. Hidden Costs

Read the franchise agreement carefully to uncover any hidden costs—many of which are mentioned earlier in this chapter. (See Section B1.) It's to your advantage if the income received by the franchisor is primarily based on royalties. That way, the franchisor has a direct interest in making your business profitable. The franchisor's incentive to promote your profitability is somewhat reduced if the franchisor begins to see itself as primarily your landlord or supplier rather than as a business partner.

If you must buy equipment, supplies, or inventory from the franchisor, make sure that the prices you'll pay are competitive with those charged by outside sources. You don't want to sign up with a franchisor who plans to gouge you on these items—especially if they're of iffy quality.

Yes, the franchisor has a legitimate interest in seeing that all franchisees run standardized operations, and this can require that certain items such as food supplies be exactly the same. But this need for specialization should be balanced against your need to make a decent profit. Franchisors often allow you to buy equipment and goods through an approved supplier, as long as the franchisor's specifications are met.

5. Quotas

Some franchise agreements require you to meet sales quotas. For example, your agreement might state that if you don't maintain a certain volume of business, you'll no longer have the right to an exclusive territory. In some cases, the franchisor may also reserve the right to terminate your franchise if quotas aren't met.

Watch out for this one. If the quotas aren't realistic or if it takes you longer than you expected to master the business, you face the horrible prospect of losing some or all of your investment.

6. The Franchise Term

Typically, a franchise agreement provides for a term of five to 15 years. Beware of an agreement that states that the franchise can be terminated "at will" by the franchisor upon written notice. See Section E8 for a further discussion of termination provisions.

Also carefully study your renewal rights. Is renewal entirely in the hands of the franchisor? If you do renew, will a renewal fee be charged? Will you have to sign a new franchise agreement containing whatever terms are in effect when you renew? This could change the whole ball game, because ten years from now, when you go to renew, a new franchise agreement could have higher royalties or advertising fees.

Under some franchise agreements, the franchisor can require a franchisee to install expensive improvements in the business premises—even beyond the startup installations. If the franchise agreement doesn't grant you the automatic right to renew your franchise on the same terms, seek language limiting the franchisor's right to force you to put expensive improvements into the business beyond the initial alterations. You want to be sure that if you're forced to put more money into the premises, you have enough time to recover that investment.

7. Assignment

Usually, a franchise agreement says that you must get the written approval of the franchisor before you transfer or assign your franchise agreement to someone else. But what happens if you have a serious health problem that prevents you from running the franchise? Could you transfer the franchise to a family member? Or, if you were to die, would your spouse automatically be able to continue the business for you?

And if you die, is there a deadline (such as 90 days or six months) during which the franchise must be transferred to a new owner to avoid termination of the franchise by the franchisor? Find out how long it takes, if someone wants to buy your franchise, to learn whether the franchisor approves or disapproves of the sale.

One way of dealing with your possible death as an owner of a franchise is a clause allowing your survivors a period of time to elect to keep and operate the business, as long as they meet the franchisor's training requirements.

Assuming you remain hale and hearty, but want to be able to get out of the franchise, some franchisors may be willing to give you the right to sell,

subject to the franchisor's right to match any bona fide offer (called a right of first refusal). For example, if someone comes to you with an offer to buy your franchise, you would have to give the franchisor 30 or 60 days to meet the terms of the purchase.

8. Termination

Study carefully what the franchise agreement says about the franchisor's right to terminate the franchise. If the franchisor can terminate your franchise because you have supposedly defaulted upon or breached the agreement, you want to be notified in writing of the franchisor's intent and given at least 30 days in which to clear the defaults or correct the breaches. On the other side of the coin, you may want to have the right to terminate the agreement yourself if the franchisor is in default.

Commonly, the franchisor has the right to terminate the franchise if you either fail to operate the business, understate your gross revenues, don't pay royalties when due, or participate in a competing business.

Termination without good cause. *Watch out for franchise agreements that give the franchisor the right to terminate the franchise whether it has a good reason or not. Such clauses are harsh and unfair—so much so that several states have enacted statutes limiting the right of a franchisor to unilaterally terminate a franchisee. Typically, under such statutes, the franchisor would have to show "good cause" before terminating you.*

9. Competition

It's critical to know where you stand in terms of competition with other franchisees. Typically, the franchisor grants you a protected territory for your franchise operations. Within your territory, your franchisor agrees not to grant another franchise or to operate its own competing business. If you don't have a protected territory, will the franchisor at least give you first crack at buying any proposed new location near yours?

A franchise agreement also usually restricts you from competing in a similar business during the term of the franchise and for several years after its termination. Generally, courts enforce these restrictive covenants if they're reasonable as to time and geographic scope. Franchisors want to make sure their trade secrets aren't misused. You, on the other hand, don't want to give up your right to earn a living in the field that you know best. So take a close look at the noncompetition language and make sure that it doesn't restrict you too severely. Maybe you can live with a provision that says that you won't go into a competing business in the same county as your franchise for two years after a termination; but maybe you can't.

F. Resolving Disputes With Your Franchisor

If you do opt for a franchise, try to keep the lines of communication with your franchisor open. Talk about problems as soon as they begin to emerge. If you wait until a lawsuit is your only option, you'll discover how expensive, time-consuming, and often frustrating or even hopeless litigating with a franchisor can be.

A better option may be for you to band together with other franchisees to try to work out your mutual grievances with the franchisor. You'll gain negotiating power by presenting your concerns as a group.

Some franchisees even form a separate franchisee's organization to negotiate on their behalf. If such negotiation doesn't work, look into whether the FTC—or perhaps the attorney general who enforces the franchise laws in your state—will take up the cudgels for you.

As a final resort, hire a lawyer familiar with franchisee rights to evaluate your prospects of winning a lawsuit. Be aware that franchise law is a relatively specialized area; not all business lawyers are experienced in this field. ■

CHAPTER

12

Insuring Your Business

A well-designed insurance program can protect your business from many types of perils. Consider the following:

- A fire destroys all the furniture, fixtures, and equipment in your restaurant.
- Burglars steal $75,000 worth of computer equipment you use in your book publishing business.
- A customer visiting your yogurt store slips on the just-washed floor and shatters her elbow.
- On the way to an office supply store to pick up some fax paper, one of your employees runs a stop sign and injures a child.
- A house painter has a severe allergic reaction to a solvent that your company manufactures and distributes.
- One of your employees is hospitalized for four weeks with a severe back injury she received while trying to lift a heavy package.
- The building where you're located is severely damaged by a windstorm. You're forced to close your doors for two months while repairs are made. In addition to having to pay $35,000 for continuing business expenses, you lose the $25,000 of profits you expected for that period—a total loss of $60,000.
- A client installs a lawn sprinkling system based on specifications you recommended as a landscape architect. Because you hadn't checked soil conditions carefully, the system malfunctions, flooding your client's basement and ruining the antique furniture stored there. Your client sues you for professional negligence.

Maybe none of these will happen to your business—but unless you consider yourself permanently exempt from Murphy's Law ("If anything can go wrong it will"), don't bet on it. Fortunately, insurance is available to cover each of these events and for many, if not most of them, is reasonably cost-effective.

Not every small business needs every type of coverage. In fact, a business that tried to buy insurance to cover all insurable risks probably wouldn't have money left over to do anything else. Deciding on insurance coverage usually involves some difficult choices. Here are some general rules to start with:

- Get enough property and liability coverage to protect yourself from common claims. These are the most important kinds of insurance for a small business.
- Buy insurance against serious risks where the insurance is reasonably priced.
- Keep costs down by selecting high deductibles.
- Self-insure if insurance is prohibitively expensive or the particular risk is highly unlikely.
- Adopt aggressive policies to reduce the likelihood of insurance claims, particularly in areas where you're self-insured.

Sections B, C, and D look at the standard types of insurance available to small businesses and how you can put together a reasonable insurance program.

A. Working With an Insurance Agent

Find and work with a knowledgeable insurance agent—one who takes the time to analyze your business operations and to come up with a sensible program for your company.

Generally, it's best to work with a single insurance agent for all your business needs so that coverages can be coordinated. But be sure to find out whether any agent you're speaking to is locked into one insurance company. If so, it may be wise to look elsewhere. The agent you choose should be willing to obtain quotes from several companies so that you don't pay more than is necessary.

To find a competent insurance agent or broker, talk to local business people, particularly those in your line of work. Other people in the same field should be able to give you good leads on insurance agents. Working with an agent who knows your business is advantageous because that person is already a fair way along the learning curve when it comes to helping you select an affordable and appropriate package.

> **EXAMPLE:** Louisa, who owns a plant nursery, wants insurance coverage for risks associated with bugs and toxic substances. She finds an insurance agent who already works with similar businesses. The agent knows what insurance is available for a plant nursery and how to tailor the coverage to Louisa's business so that it will be affordable.

Insurance Terminology

In some parts of the country, the term "insurance agent" refers to a person who represents a specific company, and "insurance broker" refers to a person who is free to sell insurance offered by various companies. Elsewhere, the term "insurance agent" is used more broadly to cover both types of representatives—and that's how it's used in this chapter.

Steer clear of an agent who, without learning the specifics of your business, whips out a package policy and claims it will solve all your problems. Yes, the insurance industry has developed some excellent packages that cover the basic needs of various businesses. For example, there are packages offered for offices, retail sales operations, service businesses, hotels, industrial and processing companies, and contractors. One of these may meet your needs, but neither you nor your insurance agent will know for sure until the agent asks you a lot of questions and thoroughly understands your business. If the agent is unable or unwilling to tailor your coverage to your particular business, find someone else.

Be frank with your agent when discussing your business. Reveal all areas of unusual risk. If you fail to disclose all the facts, you may not get the coverage you need or, in some circumstances, the insurance company may later take the position that you misrepresented the nature of your operation and, for that reason, deny you coverage for exceptional risks.

Make sure you have a clear understanding of what your insurance policy covers and what's excluded. Does the policy exclude damage from a leaking sprinkler system? From a boiler explosion? From an earthquake? If so, and these are risks you face, find out if they can be covered by paying a small extra premium.

Also ask how much the agent will help in processing claims if you do have a loss. Ideally, the insurance company should have a local or regional office that's readily accessible to you. That's normally a better arrangement and more personal than dealing with an insurance company that hires an independent claim service to investigate and deal with claims.

It's a good idea to talk to several agents before making a final selection. Ask for written recommendations on comparable coverage and what the cost will be. There should be no charge for providing this information, because the agents will be eager to get your business.

Is the Company Solvent?

In recent years, many insurance companies have become insolvent. If you wind up with a company that goes broke and you have a loss covered by a policy, you may receive only a paltry portion of the coverage that you paid for or none at all. The best way to minimize this risk is to work with a company that appears in good financial shape.

You can check out insurers in these standard reference works, which rate insurance companies for financial solvency:

- *Best's Insurance Reports* (Property-Casualty Insurance Section)
- *Moody's Bank and Financial Manual* (Volume 2)
- *Duff & Phelps* (Insurance Company Claims-Paying Ability Rating Guide)
- *Standard & Poor's.*

Each publication has strengths and weaknesses. In my opinion, the best overall sources on the list are *Moody's* and *Duff & Phelps*. Some commentators think that *Best's* is too lenient in its ratings. And *Standard & Poor's* is sometimes incomplete because some companies prefer not to pay the huge fee it takes for a listing. Your insurance agent should be able to give you the latest ratings from these publications. You can also check the reference department at a public library.

Also consider the services offered by Weiss Inc., which is reputed to be tougher (more conservative) in its ratings. Weiss offers a variety of low-cost reports on the solvency of an insurance company. You can call Weiss toll-free at 800-289-9222 or go to its website at www.weissratings.com.

B. Property Coverage

In considering property coverage, there are four main issues to think about:

- What business property should you insure?
- What perils will the property be insured against? In other words, under what conditions will you be entitled to receive payment from the insurance company?
- What dollar amount of insurance should you carry? (Obviously, the higher the amount, the higher the premiums. You don't want to waste money on insurance but you do want to carry enough so that a loss wouldn't jeopardize your business.)
- Should you buy coverage for replacement cost or for the present value of the property?

Section B6 outlines property insurance from a renter's point of view. *Renters may want to skip ahead, then return here and read the general information on how property insurance works.*

1. Property Covered

Your insurance policy will contain a section called Building and Personal Property Coverage Form, which lists exactly what property is covered. If you own the building you're occupying, be sure the building is covered, including:

- completed additions
- permanently installed fixtures, machinery, and equipment
- outdoor fixtures (such as pole lights)
- property used to maintain or service the building (such as fire extinguishing equipment).

The policy may also cover additions under construction as well as materials, equipment, supplies, and temporary structures on or within 100 feet of the main building.

Be sure that your business personal property is also covered. A typical policy covers the following items located on the business premises:

- furniture and fixtures

- machinery and equipment
- inventory
- all other personal property used in the business (such as technical books and cassette tapes)
- leased personal property, if you're contractually obligated to insure it
- personal property of others that's in your custody.

⚠️ **Be sure that everything is covered.**
Check carefully to be sure the policy covers all the types of personal property that you own or expect to own: furniture, equipment, goods that you sell, products that you manufacture, and raw materials used in the manufacturing process.

Typically, various items are excluded, such as accounting records, currency, deeds, and vehicles held for sale. If you need coverage on excluded items, you can usually arrange it, for an additional premium.

2. Perils Covered

More than 90% of the time, property insurance for small businesses is written in one of three forms: Basic Form, Broad Form, and Special Form. Special Form coverage is the most common and affords the best protection.

Whichever policy you decide on, read it carefully before you pay for it—not just when you've suffered a loss. You may discover that some coverage is narrower than it first seemed. For example, smoke loss may refer only to loss caused by a faulty heating or cooking unit; it may not cover smoke damage from industrial equipment. Similarly, an explosion may not include a burst steam boiler.

Fortunately, most insurance policies today are written in plain English so you should have little problem in understanding what's covered and what isn't. If you need coverage not provided in the policy, talk to your agent about how to add it on.

Basic Form coverage includes losses caused by fire, lightning, explosion, windstorm or hail, smoke, aircraft or vehicles (but not loss or damage caused by vehicles you own or operate in the course of your business), riot, vandalism, sprinkler leaks, sinkholes, and volcanoes. The policy defines these perils—and also lists some exclusions, such as nuclear hazards, power failures, or mudslides.

Broad Form coverage contains everything that's in the Basic Form and adds protection from a few more perils, including breakage of glass (that is part of a building or structure), falling objects, weight of snow or ice, and water damage. Again, these terms are defined in the policy and, again, exclusions are listed.

Special Form policies are constructed differently than Basic and Broad Form policies and offer wider and slightly more expensive coverage. Instead of listing specific perils such as fire and lightning, Special Form policies simply say that your business property is covered against all risks of physical loss unless the policy specifically excludes or limits the loss. This type of policy offers the most protection. For example, it's a convenient way to insure against loss by theft, which isn't covered by Basic and Broad Form policies. (Section D2 discusses theft insurance.)

⚠️ **If you need additional coverage.** *If you're concerned about property loss caused by perils not covered or, in the case of a Special Form policy, excluded from an insurance policy, you can often get the additional coverage through an endorsement (add-on page) to the policy by paying an additional premium. For example, such coverage is usually available for losses due to earthquakes and floods.*

 Consider getting insurance coverage for damage caused by terrorists. *The Terrorism Risk Insurance Act of 2002 requires insurance companies to offer such coverage. True, you'll be*

charged an additional premium, but it should be relatively small. The law that requires insurers to offer this coverage will be in effect through 2005, but Congress may extend it beyond that. If your business had an insurance policy in effect on November 26, 2002, and the policy excluded damage caused by terrorists, that exclusion has been temporarily suspended—in other words, the insurance company must pay for such damage. But the insurer can reinstate the exclusion if you don't pay the increased premium for terrorism coverage within 30 days after the insurer bills you for it.

Earthquake and Flood Insurance

Earthquake insurance can be handled through a separate policy or an endorsement to Basic, Broad, or Special Form coverage. Deductibles in an earthquake endorsement are typically stated as a percentage—such as 10%—rather than as a dollar amount. This means that the higher your policy limit, the bigger the deductible. As a result, some business people choose a $200,000 policy with a $20,000 deductible rather than a $400,000 policy with a $40,000 deductible. They reason that the deductible on the latter policy is so high they're unlikely to ever collect anything.

Flood insurance, by contrast, is usually handled through a separate policy called "Difference in Conditions."

Combining property and liability insurance in one policy. You can purchase property insurance as a stand-alone and buy a separate stand-alone policy for liability coverage (discussed in Section C), or you can buy a policy that combines both coverages. It's often—but not always—cheaper to buy a combination policy. Here's where comparison shopping definitely pays off.

3. Amount of Coverage

Be sure to carry enough insurance on the building to rebuild it. But there's no need to insure the total value of your real property (the legal term that includes land and buildings), because land doesn't burn. Especially if you're in an area where land is very valuable, this is a big consideration.

If you're in doubt as to how much it would cost you to rebuild, have an appraisal made so you know that your idea of value is realistic. Because the value of the building and other property may increase, it's wise to get a new appraisal every few years. Your insurance agent should be able to help you do this.

Usually it's best to insure your property for 100% of its value. If doing this is prohibitively expensive, consider a policy with a higher deductible rather than underinsuring.

Underinsuring to get a reduced premium is a false economy for several reasons. Not only are you not covered if you suffer a total loss, but it may also reduce your ability to recover for a smaller loss. This is because most insurance policies carry a coinsurance clause which states that to recover the full policy amount, you have to carry insurance to cover at least 80% (this percentage may vary) of the property's replacement cost or actual cash value. If you don't, you become a coinsurer if there's a loss, even if it's less than the policy maximum; the policy will only pay off a percentage of its face value.

EXAMPLE 1: Fluoro Corporation owns a $100,000 building. If Fluoro carries $80,000 worth of insurance or more, the insurance company will pay Fluoro for the full amount of any loss up to the policy limit. For example, if the loss is $50,000 Fluoro will get the full $50,000. If the loss is $90,000, Fluoro will receive only $80,000, the policy limit.

EXAMPLE 2: Pluto Associates owns a similar $100,000 building. To get a reduced premium, the partners decide to carry only $40,000 worth of insurance. If there's a fire and Pluto has a loss of $20,000, its insurance company will pay only $10,000. Because Pluto carried only half of the 80% figure mentioned in the policy, it's entitled to only a proportional payment.

4. Replacement Cost vs. Current Value

Historically, in case of a loss, a basic fire insurance contract covered the actual current value of the property, not its full replacement value. Today, policies are routinely available with replacement cost coverage. This is the coverage you want.

> **EXAMPLE:** Sure-Lock Corporation owns a 20-year-old building. The current cash value of the building (the amount someone would pay to buy it) is $150,000. But if the building burned down, Sure-Lock would have to pay $200,000 to replace it. If Sure-Lock buys insurance based on the building's cash value and the policy has an 80% coinsurance clause, the company will need to insure the building for $120,000. If Sure-Lock buys insurance based on replacement cost, it will need to insure for $160,000, which is 80% of $200,000.

The real cost of insurance is reduced when you consider that insurance premiums for a business are a recognized business expense—which means they are tax deductible.

5. Ordinance or Law Coverage

If you're purchasing insurance for an older building—either because you own it or your lease requires it—understand that a normal Basic Form, Broad Form, or Special Form policy designed to replace your existing building should it be destroyed probably won't be adequate. The problem is that legal requirements adopted since the building was constructed will normally require that a stronger, safer, more fire-resistant building be constructed. Doing this can cost far more than simply replacing the old building. To cope with this possibility, you want a policy that will not only replace the building but pay for all legally required upgrades. This coverage is called "Ordinance or Law Coverage."

> **EXAMPLE:** Time Warp Inc. sells antique furniture and building materials removed from old homes. In keeping with its image of days gone by, Time Warp does business in a 100-year-old building in a historic part of town. Time Warp carries insurance for the full replacement cost, $100,000. One day a fire destroys 50% of the building. The insurance pays $50,000 toward reconstruction, but the Time Warp owners learn to their dismay that rebuilding will cost much more and that the additional costs are not covered by their insurance policy. The items excluded by their typical property insurance policy include the following:
>
> • *The cost of meeting current health and safety codes.* The old building was of wood frame construction and lacked an elevator and sprinkler system. That was okay before the fire. The building predated the health and safety ordinances and was "grandfathered"—specifically exempted from the new construction requirements. After the fire, it's a whole new ball game. In rebuilding, Time Warp must spend an additional $100,000 for masonry construction, an elevator, and a sprinkler system required by current health and safety codes.
>
> • *The cost of rebuilding the undamaged portion of the building.* The local ordinance requires that if a building built before current codes is destroyed by fire to the extent of 50% or more, the entire building must be replaced. The cost of replacing the undamaged 50% of the building is another $200,000.

- *The cost of demolition.* The local ordinance requires that, because of the extent of damage, the entire building—both the damaged and undamaged portions—must be torn down before reconstruction begins. That will cost another $25,000.

"Ordinance or Law Coverage" would pay for all of these items.

6. Tenant's Insurance

If you're a tenant, read the insurance portion of your lease. You may have agreed to insure the building and protect the landlord against any liability suits based on your activities, in which case you'll need the type of coverage an owner would carry. This is available through a renter's commercial package policy, which also provides routine product liability coverage for businesses not involved in hazardous activities and allows you to name your landlord as an additional insured.

Even if you haven't agreed to provide insurance coverage in your lease, a renter's commercial policy can make excellent sense. Not only will it cover any of your "leasehold improvements," such as paneling and partitions, but it will also cover damage to the premises caused by your negligence.

For example, if the building you rent suffers fire or water damage as a result of an employee's negligence (a fire in an area where food is prepared spreads and damages the walls and ceiling), you may be liable. This is true even if the building owner is insured and recovers from his or her insurance company, because the owner's insurer has the right to try to recover.

What the insurer will pay you for loss to leasehold improvements is based not on replacement value but on what's called the "use interest" in the improvements. Basically, the insurance company looks at how long you would have had the use of the improvements and reimburses you for the use you lose.

EXAMPLE: Court Reporting Associates (CRA) installs $20,000 worth of paneling in their rented offices. They have a five-year lease with an option to renew for five more years—which, for insurance purposes, is treated as a ten-year lease. Two years into the lease, a fire destroys the paneling. Because CRA used up 20% of the lease before the fire, it will receive payment for only 80% of value of the paneling.

Insurance clauses in leases vary widely. (See Chapter 13, Section D13, for more on such clauses.)

C. Liability Insurance

The second major category of insurance coverage for a small business is liability insurance. Your business can be legally liable to people injured and for property damaged because you or your employees didn't use reasonable care. For example, if a customer falls on a slippery floor and then sues you, you may be liable because you negligently failed to provide safe premises.

As you probably know, when it comes to personal injuries, judges are broadening the scope of what people can sue for—and juries are increasingly generous in awarding damages. Because an injured person can collect not only for lost wages and medical bills but also for such intangibles as pain, suffering, and mental anguish, a single personal injury verdict against your business has the potential to wipe it out. For that reason, unless you have a very unusual business that has no personal contact with customers, suppliers, or anyone else, your insurance program should include liability coverage.

Some intentional acts not involving bodily injuries are also usually covered under the liability portions of an insurance policy. Examples are libel, slander, defamation, false imprisonment, and false arrest.

Toxic Waste Cleanup

Suppose the government orders your company to clean up a toxic waste problem on your property. This can and regularly does occur even if the pollution occurred years before you bought the property. Will your liability insurance policy cover the cleanup costs (called the "response costs")?

Most courts that have considered this question ruled that response costs are covered by a liability insurance policy, but a significant minority have ruled otherwise. If you have a business or own property that by any stretch of the imagination could become involved in a toxic waste or pollution problem, try to find out exactly how far your liability coverage extends in environmental situations. You may need to buy supplementary coverage (if available and affordable) to cover this risk.

Keep yourself informed on this subject. It's likely that, faced with court decisions saying that general liability coverage requires insurance companies to pay for response costs under cleanup orders, insurance companies will tighten up their policy language to exclude these expenses. You may need to buy special coverage if your business faces the possibility of a cleanup order.

1. General Liability Policies

Liability policies are designed to protect you against lawsuit judgments up to the amount of the policy limit plus the cost of defending the lawsuit. They provide coverage for a host of common perils, including customers and guests falling and getting mangled by your front door or otherwise being injured.

Liability policies usually state a dollar limit per occurrence and an aggregate dollar limit for the policy year. For example, your policy may say that it will pay $500,000 per occurrence for personal injury or a total of $1 million in any one policy year.

⚠ **Excluded claims.** *Punitive damages— damages intended to punish your business for willful or malicious behavior rather than compensate the injured person—are not covered by the typical general liability policy. And liability coverage won't protect your business if an employee intentionally assaults a customer. In addition, a general liability policy doesn't cover injuries caused by defective products or motor vehicles, or by an employer's liability for injuries received by workers on the job. Special coverage for these types of liability is discussed in the next three subsections.*

As noted, both building owners and tenants may purchase liability coverage separately or as part of a package policy that also provides a number of other types of insurance, including fire insurance for the building itself.

2. Product Liability Insurance

Product liability insurance covers liability for injuries caused by products you design, manufacture, or sell. You may be liable to a person injured by a defective product or one that came without adequate instructions or warnings.

Product liability insurance can be very expensive, but if your business manufactures, distributes, or sells a product that may injure people, you should seriously consider buying it. For example, if you manufacture medical instruments or chemicals, you'll probably want this coverage. If you're a retailer and sell products in their original packages and provide no product assembly or service or advice, your exposure is drastically reduced; the manufacturer is primarily liable and the product liability coverage provided by standard renter's commercial policies should be adequate.

The amount of product liability insurance that you need depends on the nature of your product and not on your gross sales. Obviously, a company that sells $2 million of paper clips a year will need less coverage than a firm that manufactures gauges critical to the safe operation of heaters and also has $2 million worth of sales annually.

3. Vehicle Insurance

Make sure your business carries liability insurance not only on its own cars and trucks but also on employees' cars and trucks when those vehicles are used for business purposes. This coverage is known as Employer's Non-Owned Automobile Liability and is relatively inexpensive—a premium of $65 to $100 may buy you coverage of $1 million for one year. Vehicle insurance isn't provided under general liability policies.

It wouldn't hurt to check your employees' driving records before you entrust company vehicles to them or send them on business errands using their own cars, but failure to check won't be a problem under most vehicle policies unless the insurance company has listed that employee as an excluded driver. To do this, insurance companies periodically ask businesses for the names of employees who are driving on company business. They then check the names against state driving records. If this results in the discovery of a poor driving record for a particular employee, the insurer will likely exclude that driver from coverage and notify you.

Coverage for injury or property damage while using leased vehicles can be added to either your motor vehicle policy or your general liability policy—which is what a company would do if it owned no vehicles. This is known as Hired Vehicle coverage.

Most vehicle policies also cover physical damage to the car or truck caused by collision, fire, or theft.

4. Workers' Compensation Insurance

As the name implies, workers' compensation insurance covers your liability for injuries received by employees on the job. All businesses with employees are required to provide for some kind of workers' compensation coverage.

Usually, an injured worker can't sue your business for negligence. But as a trade-off, he or she can collect specified benefits from your business for work-related injuries whether or not the business was negligent. All the worker must prove is that the injury came about in the course of employment—a concept that has a very broad definition in many states. For example, an employee injured at a company picnic may have a valid workers' compensation claim.

The amount of money that the employee can recover is limited. The worker can recover for medical treatment and lost wages and, in serious cases, for impaired future earning capacity. But there are no awards for pain and suffering or mental anguish. A growing portion of workers' compensation claims, however, result from mental or emotional stress.

As a sole proprietor, you usually can't be personally covered by workers' compensation insurance for any work-related injuries you sustain; only your employees can be covered. Workers' comp coverage of a partner or of an officer of a small corporation usually isn't required but can be obtained if you choose.

Each state has a law setting out what an employer must do to provide for workers' compensation benefits. Sometimes an employer can self-insure. Usually, that isn't practical for small businesses because they can't afford the type of cash reserve required by state law. Most small businesses buy insurance through a state fund or from a private insurance carrier. Insurance rates are based on the industry and occupation, as well as the size of the payroll. Your business's safety record can also influence the rate; if you have more accidents than are usually anticipated, your rate is likely to be increased.

Although workers' compensation laws cover virtually all injury claims by an employee against an employer, in a few instances employees can still sue an employer for pain and suffering resulting from a work-related injury. For example, in some states, an employer whose gross negligence or intentional conduct caused an injury can be sued. A second part of a workers' compensation policy (sometimes called Coverage B or employer's liability) insures the employer against liability for these types of claims. I recommend policy limits of $500,000 for most businesses for this coverage.

Workers' compensation insurance is required only for employees—not for independent contractors. (Independent contractors are covered in greater detail in Chapter 15, Section P.) Small businesses sometimes buy services from independent contractors to save money on workers' compensation insurance, as well as taxes and other expenses normally associated with employees. That's fine as long as you correctly label people as independent contractors rather than employees. But if you make a mistake, and a person improperly labeled as an independent contractor is injured while doing work for your business, you may have to pay large sums to cover medical bills and lost wages that should have been covered by workers' compensation insurance.

In addition, you can sometimes have a problem with a properly classified independent contractor who hires employees to perform some work for you. If you hire an independent contractor who has employees, insist on seeing a certificate of insurance establishing that the employees are covered by workers' compensation insurance.

EXAMPLE: You hire Sharon, who is doing business as Superior Painters, to paint your store. Sharon will be doing the work along with two of her employees. If Sharon doesn't carry workers' compensation insurance for her employees, and any of them are injured on the job, they may be treated as your employees, which would increase your own workers' compensation premiums. Also, have Sharon show you that she has general liability coverage; if she or one of her employees injures one of your customers while painting your store, such injuries may not be covered by your own insurance.

The Expanding Boundaries of Workers' Comp

Premiums for workers' compensation insurance are on the rise—partly because judges are extending the types of claims for which workers can receive payment. A key factor in many cases is stressful working conditions. Money has been awarded to:

- A worker who suffered a heart attack after an argument with his boss.
- A truck driver who blacked out while driving and was then unable to drive because of anxiety that he might black out again.
- A worker who fainted, fell, and suffered a head injury after his supervisor told him he would be transferred to a new department and had to take a pay cut.

Judges have also expanded the right to receive workers' comp in other situations. For example, benefits were awarded to the family of a convenience store clerk who died after getting into a fist fight with a disorderly customer. And a woman who bought a cold tablet from her employer received payments when the tablet caused her to have tremors due to a congenital condition.

In another case, a cocktail waitress at a resort was on her way home when she stopped to help a resort guest who was having car trouble. The guest sexually assaulted her. The waitress was awarded workers' comp for injuries she received in the assault. The court's reasoning: The waitress had been told to be "very cordial and nice to guests." Therefore, her offer of assistance on the road was related to her employment.

D. Other Insurance to Consider

There are many forms of business insurance on the market today. You won't need them all, but some specialized coverage may make sense for your business.

1. Bonds Covering Employee Theft

If you're seriously concerned that employees might embezzle money from the business, look into bonds that cover all workers, including those hired after the bond goes into effect. Then, if an employee steals from you, the bonding company reimburses you for the loss.

2. Crime Coverage

Crime insurance covers losses when the criminal isn't connected with your business. Your policy should cover not only burglary and robbery but also other thefts and loss or disappearance of property. Depending on the kind of business and the part of the country you're in, you may be more concerned about losses by theft than from fire. Computers and other high-tech equipment are relatively lightweight and easy to carry away. A midsized publisher or word processing company, for example, could easily suffer a $100,000 loss in a night if its computers were stolen.

Usually, your company's business insurance covers only property owned by the company, not your personal property.

> **EXAMPLE:** Management Concepts Inc., a small consulting firm, is using an expensive computer that's the personal property of Patricia, the corporation's president. If the computer is stolen from the corporate offices, the corporation's insurance policy normally won't cover it. To protect against this kind of problem, Patricia should sign a Bill of Sale formally transferring legal title to the computer to the corporation. Or she should make sure that the corporation has an insurance policy that specifically protects property of officers or employees that's used in the business.

Probably the most convenient way to insure your business against loss by theft is to purchase the Special Form of property insurance, which includes such coverage. (See Section B2.)

If property is stolen from your business, you will, of course, have to document the loss. I recommend that you keep a computerized list of your business property, updated periodically. And keep a copy at home or in a fireproof box in case the computer and your records get stolen or destroyed.

3. Business Interruption Insurance

If your business property is damaged or destroyed and you can't use it, your business losses will far exceed the cost of repairing or replacing the damaged property. Your business may be unable to function until you can find a new location and purchase more goods. For example, if you're in California and an earthquake levels your retail warehouse, or if your business is in Indiana and a tornado rips the roof off your store, or a fire burns you out, you may be out of business for weeks or months while your inventory is replaced and new buildings are located.

Business interruption insurance—a valuable but often overlooked kind of insurance—is intended to cover your lost income while your business is closed, as well as the expenses you incur in keeping your business going while the lost property is repaired or replaced. This insurance coverage also pays the cost of renting temporary quarters. It's also possible to guard against losses if your business is interrupted because disaster strikes someone else.

> **EXAMPLE:** Tom operates a small bakery. Half of his income comes from supplying bread, rolls, and pastry to a large restaurant. If the restaurant burns down, Tom's income will be drastically reduced. He might sensibly look into business interruption insurance that covers not only losses that would occur should his property be damaged but also those that would result if a major supplier or customer were suddenly forced to stop or curtail operation.

Before you buy business interruption insurance, run through a contingency plan of what you'd do in case of a disaster. Let's say that your warehouse was destroyed by fire. Assuming the contents of the warehouse were covered by your fire or multiperil insurance, you need worry only about how much it will cost you to be out of business until you can set up a temporary warehouse and get more merchandise. Could you replace key merchandise quickly and take other steps to minimize the harm? If it's reasonable to believe that you'll be partially back in business in a couple of weeks and be in fairly good shape within 30 days, business interruption insurance might not really be worth the cost.

⚠️ **Business interruption coverage is site-specific.** *If, for example, you have two retail stores and a warehouse, you need to make sure that each location is covered.*

Will Your Customers Come Through?

Ben runs a successful bookstore. His inventory is covered, by a multiperil contract, from loss from most hazards. But he worries that if he is burned out of his historic building, it might take a year or more to get repairs approved and made. Ben asks his insurance broker whether or not business interruption insurance makes sense.

After establishing that Ben could get new merchandise within a couple of weeks because book wholesalers and publishers would be anxious to help (Ben's credit is good), the broker recommends against it, pointing out that within a mile of Ben's building there are a dozen empty stores that Ben could rent very reasonably and be back in business almost immediately. The fact that Ben's loyal customers would likely support him after a disaster might even mean that sales would go up.

4. Industry-Specific Insurance

Supplementary insurance policy packages are often available for retail or manufacturing businesses, or even for specific types of businesses—a bookstore, barber shop, or restaurant—and can be well worth looking into. For example, a manufacturing policy may have broader coverage for losses caused by malfunctioning equipment and machinery than a standard Special Form policy.

📖 **These additional resources might be helpful:**
• Insuring Your Business: What You Need to Know to Get the Best Insurance Coverage for Your Business, *by Sean Mooney (Insurance Informa-*

tion Institute Press). This is a well-written and comprehensive resource that contains many helpful suggestions. The Insurance Information Institute also offers other publications and free online information—see its website at www.iii.org.
• Insurance Law in a Nutshell, *by John F. Dobbyn (West Wadsworth), is a concise statement of the basic legal principles. It's written primarily for law students, but useful to business people as well.*

E. Saving Money on Insurance

This chapter is based on the sensible premise that few businesses can really afford to adequately insure themselves against every possible risk. You need to decide what types of insurance are really essential and how much coverage to buy. While this is no easy task, here are some guidelines that should help.

1. Set Priorities

Start by looking at what coverage is required by state law. For example, there may be minimum requirements for coverage on business-related vehicles, and you will almost surely be required to carry workers' compensation insurance if you have employees.

Next, if you rent, you'll need to purchase any insurance required by your lease. See Section B6, above, and Chapter 13, Section D13, for a discussion of insurance language in a lease.

Beyond the required coverages for your business, ask these questions: What types of property losses would threaten the viability of my business? What kinds of liability lawsuits might wipe me out? Use your answers to tailor your coverage to protect against these potentially disastrous losses.

Be less concerned about insuring against smaller losses. For example, if you're in the self-help publishing business, consider a package especially tailored to printers and publishers that includes liability coverage for errors and omissions (such as leaving some vital information out of an instruction booklet you publish), but be less concerned about protecting yourself against claims of libel—after all, your material never comments on personalities.

2. Increase the Amount of Your Deductibles

Deductibles are used primarily for real and personal property insurance, including motor vehicle collision coverage. The difference between the cost of a policy with a $250 deductible and one with a $500 or $1,000 or even higher deductible is significant—particularly if you add up the premium savings for five or ten years.

For example, the difference between a $250 and a $500 deductible may be 10% in premium costs, and the difference between a $500 and $1,000 deductible may save you an additional 3% to 5%. Most businesses can afford to be out of pocket $500 or even $1,000—especially if taking this risk means you pay significantly lower premiums.

Consider using money saved with a higher deductible to buy other types of insurance where it's really needed. For example, the amount you save by having a higher deductible might pay for business interruption coverage.

3. Initiate Loss Prevention and Risk Reduction Measures

Good safety and security measures may eliminate the need for some types of insurance or lead to lower insurance rates. Ask your insurance agent what you can do to get a better rate. Sometimes something simple like installing deadbolt locks or buying two more fire extinguishers will qualify you for a lower premium. Here are some other ideas to cut losses and premiums.

- Install a fire alarm system, if one can be found at a reasonable cost.
- Install fireproofing materials to minimize fire damage in susceptible areas of the premises.

- Isolate and safely store flammable chemicals and other products.
- Provide adequate smoke detectors.
- Install a sprinkler system.

Ideas for preventing theft include:

- Install tamper-proof locks.
- Purchase a secure safe.
- Install an alarm system.
- Install better lighting.
- Hire a security service to patrol your property at night.

Also consider placing bars on doors or windows. This may create a negative impression; an innovative architect or contractor may be able to help you design and install these security devices in ways that are not unsightly.

To prevent injuries to customers, employees, or members of the public, you might:

- Check each applicant's driving record and not hire people to drive who have poor records.
- Give additional training to drivers you do hire.
- Set up a system for safer operation of machinery.
- Conduct fire drills.
- Give your employees protective clothing and goggles if necessary.

Although how to protect against some types of risks may be obvious to you, how to protect against many others won't be. Get help from people who are experienced in identifying and dealing with risks. One excellent resource is your insurance company's safety inspector; your insurance agent can tell you whom to contact.

Another good approach is to ask your employees to identify all safety risks, no matter how small. Also ask them to propose cost-effective ways to eliminate or minimize them—they may have cheaper and more practical ideas than you do.

EXAMPLE: Adventure Apparel Corporation sells recreational and travel clothing by mail order from its well-stocked warehouse. The 25 employees of the corporation all take turns serving on the safety committee, which meets regularly to discuss safety issues ranging from the best way to operate computer terminals to reduce the possibility of repetitive motion injuries to making sure that the electric pallet lifters are run only by trained people. The system works because the employees are in a unique position to monitor safety hazards and to suggest practical solutions.

In the long run, a safety program will reduce your losses and, in turn, lower your insurance rates. In the short term, simply putting these practices into effect and letting insurance companies know about them may put you in a lower rate category. And of course, your employees will appreciate the care you show for their well-being—a significant plus in a world where keeping good employees is a real business asset.

4. Comparison Shop

No two companies charge exactly the same rates; you may be able to save a significant amount by shopping around. But be wary of unusually low prices—it may be a sign of a shaky company (see Section A for information on how to check out an insurance company). Or it may be that you're unfairly comparing policies that provide very different types of coverage. Make sure you know what you're buying.

Review your coverage and rates periodically. The insurance industry is cyclical, with alternating phases of low prices and high prices. When competition for insurance customers increases in a particular field, you really can achieve savings. But don't dump a loyal agent for a few cents. Ask your agent to look around and meet or come close to meeting the competition.

You can make the cyclical nature of the insurance industry work for you. If you're shopping for insurance during a time when prices are low, try

locking in a low rate by signing up for a contract for three or more years.

5. Transfer Some Risks to Someone Else

Here are some possibilities:
- *Indemnification by manufacturer.* Suppose you run a store that sells exercise equipment, and primarily from one manufacturer. If you're buying a significant amount of equipment, the manufacturer may be willing to provide insurance that indemnifies your business from any claim by a customer injured by the equipment.
- *Leasing employees.* Some businesses lease employees at least in part because the leasing company takes care of carrying workers' compensation and liability insurance on the employees (among other things); but be cautious—the overall cost of leasing employees may be greater than if you hire directly. You may also to be able to transfer some risks by simply engaging independent contractors to handle the more hazardous aspects of your business operations. (See Chapter 15.)

6. Find a Comprehensive Package

Look for a small business package that includes a full range of coverage. This is often much cheaper than buying coverage piecemeal from several different companies. Group plans often offer these packages.

7. Seek Out Group Plans

Is there a trade association in your industry? If so, it may be a source of good insurance coverage. Trade associations often get good affordable insurance rates for the members because they have superior bargaining power.

8. Self-Insure

Using this technique, you simply don't buy insurance and hope to maintain your own reserve fund to cover likely losses or liabilities. There are two drawbacks. First, despite good intentions, most small businesses don't have enough funds to set aside for this purpose. Second, unlike insurance premiums, money put into a reserve fund isn't tax deductible until or unless you spend it.

F. Making a Claim

As soon as a loss occurs, gather and preserve evidence to help prove your claim if it becomes necessary. (If you followed my suggestion and have a comprehensive list of your property, get it out now.) Take pictures of any damaged property. Collect documents such as receipts showing what you paid for the lost property. If you can, secure the damaged property in a safe place so that it will be available for inspection later and for possible use in a lawsuit. Gather names of any witnesses who can help substantiate how the loss occurred and the extent of the damage.

Your next step is to request a claim form from your insurance agent. For small, routine losses you or someone else in your company can probably complete the form, with a little help from your agent. If more money is at stake, a lawyer can help you structure and justify your claim. (See Chapter 24 for information on how to find and hire a good lawyer.)

Damage to Rented Space. If you're renting the space your business occupies, start by figuring out whose insurance policy covers the loss—yours or the building owner's. For example, if a pipe breaks, you'll have to look at both insurance policies to see which one covers this risk.

Ideally, your insurance company will pay you for damage to your inventory and equipment, and the owner's insurance company will pay for damage to the building. To make this happen and avoid squabbles, it helps to have a "mutual waiver of subrogation" in your lease. Without it, you can get caught in the crossfire between two insurance companies. (See Chapter 13, Section D13.)

Often there's a time limit on filing your claim, but you may need more time to analyze all of your damages. Don't feel rushed. Simply file the claim form within the required time limit, listing the losses you're sure of at that time. Indicate that the list of losses is partial and that you're still gathering information.

If you're served with a lawsuit or are informed that an injured person is going to make a claim against your business, get the lawsuit papers and related information to your insurance company as soon as possible. Contact your agent promptly. ■

13

Negotiating a Favorable Lease

lmost all small businesses start out in leased premises; many businesses prefer to use leased space throughout their business lives. By leasing rather than owning, you avoid tying up valuable working capital. Also, it's easier to move to new quarters if your space needs change. This chapter looks at how to find the right place for your business and how to negotiate your lease.

For more information on commercial leases: *See* Leasing Space for Your Small Business, *by Janet Portman and Fred S. Steingold (Nolo).*

A. Finding a Place

Your first step is to find the right space. Begin by analyzing the specific needs of your business. Real estate professionals are fond of saying that the three most important factors in choosing a business space are location, location, and location. For certain types of retail stores and restaurants, this may be true. For example, a sandwich shop requires a location with a high volume of foot traffic. Or maybe you'll benefit if you're near other businesses that are similar to yours; restaurants often like to locate in a restaurant district.

But for many other businesses, where you're located doesn't matter much. For example, if you repair bathroom tile, run a computer-based information search business, import jewelry from Bali, or do any one of ten thousand other things, it won't help you to be in a high-visibility, high-rent district. Chances are your business can efficiently operate in a less pricey area, where you can negotiate a lower rent and the

landlord is likely to be far more flexible on other lease terms as well.

After you've analyzed what you need, it's time to begin searching for the right spot. Go to the neighborhoods where you might like to locate; spend a day or two driving or walking the streets to see what may be available. Don't just look for vacant space. A store, office, studio, or workshop that's good for your business may be occupied by a tenant who is going out of business—or moving to larger quarters in a few months. If you find a desirable location, call the landlord to see if the space will be coming on the market soon. There's a lot of turnover among small businesses, and you may get lucky.

Because some of the best opportunities come to light through word of mouth, ask friends, associates, and other business people if they know of available space. Business owners—particularly those in the part of town that you're interested in—may know of businesses that are moving or going out of business long before these vacancies are announced. And if you get there early, the landlord, relieved that he or she can avoid a period of vacancy and uncertainty, may offer you a favorable lease.

For-rent ads in newspapers are an obvious place to look. If the selection there is limited, call a real estate office that deals primarily with business space. The agent's fee—usually, a percentage of the rent that you'll be paying—is generally paid by the landlord. If your space needs are special, consider hiring an agent to search the market for you. But if you follow this somewhat unusual approach, you'll probably have to pay the agent's commission.

B. Leases and Rental Agreements: An Overview

A lease is a contract between you and the landlord. A lease can be for a short term (as little as one month) or long term, and it can be written or oral—although a lease for more than a year must be in writing to be legally enforceable. Some people use the phrase "rental agreement" to describe a short or oral lease for which rent is typically paid once a month and the tenancy can be terminated on a 30-day written notice. (See Section C, below, for more on short-term leases.) To avoid confusion, I'll stick to the word "lease."

Terminology

Sometimes a written lease talks about the "Lessor" and the "Lessee." The lessor is the landlord; the lessee is the tenant. If you have a choice in terminology, go with the plain English "landlord" and "tenant"; you'll reduce the risk of typos!

In theory, all terms of a lease are negotiable. Just how far you can negotiate, however, depends on economic conditions. If desirable properties are close to full occupancy in your city, landlords may not be willing to negotiate with you over price or other major lease terms.

On the other hand, in many parts of the country where commercial space has been overbuilt, landlords are eager to bargain with small businesses to fill empty units. Even in a tight market you may come across some acceptable space that, for one reason or another, the landlord is anxious to fill, giving you greater bargaining power. This is often true where there's a new building or one under construction and the landlord needs cash. Also, if you're one of the first tenants in the building, you may get an especially attractive deal, because your presence may help the landlord attract other tenants.

If you find a landlord willing to negotiate, what should you ask for? After you read Section D, you'll have a good understanding of the kinds of terms that usually go into a lease. Since you're not likely to get everything you want, it's important to get your priorities straight in your own mind and concentrate on achieving what's most important. What do you really care about? What would be nice to have but not essential? What benefits can you offer the landlord for things you really need?

A lower rent is likely to be high on everybody's bargaining list. But how about physical changes in the building? Would you want the landlord to redesign the entryway? Add some office space at the back of the warehouse? Customize the interior for your needs? More or better parking for your customers might be worth more than slightly lowered rent. Your priorities may be unique to your business, so think them through carefully before making proposals and counterproposals to the landlord.

Let's look at how you might approach the matter of rent. A landlord who is reluctant to lower the basic rent may be willing make other adjustments—which may be even more valuable. The landlord might do this so he or she can truthfully tell other prospective tenants that you're paying a high dollar amount per square foot. (It may sound silly, but some landlords do play this game.) For example, in a slack market, the landlord may be willing to give you a move-in allowance. Also, check out what the landlord is willing to do in paying for improvements (often called build-outs) to the space. (See Section D9.)

C. Short-Term Leases (Month-to-Month Rentals)

Once you've found the space you want, the next step, usually, is to sign a lease. (See Section D.) Occasionally, a small business that's just starting out prefers an oral lease permitting the tenant to occupy the space from month to month. This might seem attractive if you just want to test the waters, have great uncertainty about the prospects for your business, and wouldn't mind leaving on short notice if the landlord terminated the lease. But even if you want to make only a very short-term commitment, it almost always makes far more sense to negotiate a written month-to-month lease or rental agreement. A written lease clarifies what's been agreed to and helps avoid disputes.

Whether oral or written, the key feature of a month-to-month lease is that you can move—or the landlord can require you to move—on short notice.

You can negotiate how notice is required, but if you don't, the law in your state will dictate the amount of time.

In many states, this is 30 days, although states don't always compute the time period in the same way. Some, such as California, allow either the landlord or tenant to give notice at any date during a month; the 30 days runs from the notice date. Other states require that the notice be given at least 30 days before the first day of the next monthly rental period; furthermore, the termination date must coincide with the beginning of a new period.

EXAMPLE: Albert is a tenant under an oral month-to-month lease in Michigan. He and the landlord haven't agreed on a specific notice period, relying instead on the law in their state, which requires a 30-day notice. Albert pays his rent on the first of each month. On July 15, Albert's landlord notifies him that he's terminating the lease as of August 15. Does Albert have to move by August 15? No. He can stay until September 1. That's because under the court interpretations in his state, he's entitled to notice 30 days in advance of a full rental period. Because Albert's rental period begins on the first day of each month, he can't be kicked out in the middle of a month. He's entitled to stay for at least one full rental period. If the landlord wanted Albert out by mid-August, he should have given Albert his notice before July 1.

Notice requirements vary from state to state. *For information about what's required in your state, you'll need to check the statutes or case law. (Chapter 24 suggests ways to do basic legal research.)*

The clauses in a month-to-month lease, other than those dealing with the length of the tenancy, are much the same as those in any other written lease, so be sure to consult the following sections of this chapter.

D. Written Long-Term Leases

Many small businesses and landlords prefer the protection of a written lease that lasts a year or more. But when you talk to the landlord, you'll probably be presented with a typed or printed lease prepared by the landlord or the landlord's lawyer. Because the terms typically favor the landlord, consider it as no more than the starting point. Chances are excellent that you'll be able to negotiate at least some significant improvements.

Keep in mind that you have two sometimes conflicting goals: to get a favorable lease and to have a good long-term relationship with your landlord. In the interest of long-term harmony, there are times when it makes sense not to fight for the last scrap of a concession as if you were a starving pit bull.

To eliminate a proposed lease's one-sidedness, ask for equal treatment for you and the landlord for all clauses where this is relevant. For example, if the lease requires you to cure your lease defaults within ten days after you receive notice from the landlord, it should also require the landlord to cure his or her defaults within ten days after you give notice. Similarly, if you're required to pay for your landlord's attorney fees in enforcing the lease, the landlord should be required to pay for your attorney fees if you have to enforce the lease.

Now let's look at some common lease terms and how you might approach them.

Chapter 6 of *Legal Forms for Starting & Running a Small Business* contains various commercial lease forms.

1. Who Should Sign the Lease?

Leases begin by naming the landlord and the tenant. Make sure that the person, partnership, or corporation named as landlord is the owner of the property. Although this may seem to go without saying, believe me, it often doesn't. A husband may not have legal authority to sign leases for space in a building owned solely by his wife. A management company or onsite manager may have only day-to-day management powers that fall short of the right to approve new leases. Or if they can sign a lease, they may be able to offer only certain terms and concessions. If you have any doubts about whom you're dealing with and what authority they have, ask to see a deed or title insurance policy to verify that the named landlord really owns the building. Here are the rules about who's authorized to sign a binding lease on behalf of the landlord:

- If a building owned is by an individual, that person (or an authorized agent) should sign the lease.
- If a building is owned by a general partnership, insist on the signature of one of the partners.
- If a building is owned by a limited partnership (not uncommon for rental properties), require the signature of a general (managing) partner; a limited partner usually lacks the power to bind the partnership.
- If a building is owned by a corporation, get the signature of a corporate officer or an executive with authority to sign leases.
- If you're dealing with a rental agent who will be negotiating the lease and signing it on behalf of the owner, ask for written confirmation from the owner that the agent has that authority. Obviously, you need to worry less about this step if the rental agent is part of an established and respected real estate management company, but it never hurts to request documentation.

Who should be named as the tenant? Before you sign a lease as an individual or a partner, be aware that you'll be personally liable for the rent if your business runs into financial problems. If your business fails, the landlord can (and probably will) go after your personal assets such as your car, home, and bank account. To avoid this exposure, consider incorporating. Then you can sign the lease as President of XYZ Inc.—and you're personally off the hook. (Personal liability for business debts is discussed in Chapter 1.)

⚠ **Beware of personal guarantees.** *In addition to signing in your corporate capacity, you may be asked to personally guarantee the lease. Doing this makes you personally responsible for the rent and means that the corporation doesn't shield your personal assets. One approach is to offer to guarantee the lease only up to a maximum amount—say, three months worth of rent. For even greater protection, see if the landlord is willing to release you from your personal guarantee if all rent is paid on time during the first year.*

2. Defining the Space You're Leasing

The lease should identify the space that you'll be occupying. If you're leasing the whole building, that's easy: simply give the street address. If you're leasing less than the whole building, specify your space more precisely. One way is to refer to building or floor plan drawings. For example, you might say "Suite 2 of the Commerce Building as shown on the attached drawing" or "The south half of the first floor of the Entrepreneur Plaza."

In describing the space you'll be occupying, don't overlook the common areas—space you'll be sharing with other tenants. This often includes hallways, rest rooms, elevators, storage space, and parking. Spell out in your lease that your business (and your customers) have the right to use these additional spaces and facilities.

If your business keeps unusual hours, remember to define when you have access to your space and the common spaces. You don't want to find yourself locked out some evening or weekend.

Because commercial space is often priced by the square foot, find out what method is used to compute square footage. Sometimes it's measured from the exterior of the walls or from the middle of walls' thickness. If this is the case, you'll be paying for some space that's not really usable. This isn't necessarily bad. But you need to find out about it in advance, because it affects rent negotiations.

The square footage rate is usually stated in annual terms—$20 a square foot means $20 per square foot per year. However, it's sometimes stated by the month—$.60 a square foot means 60 cents per square foot per month. Obviously you need to know exactly what any numbers you're quoted mean.

Also find out if the quoted figure applies only to the space occupied by your business or whether you're expected to pay for a proportionate share of the common areas. If your rent is computed on the basis of dollars per square foot, and if you're asked to pay for a share of the common areas, it's reasonable to seek a lower square-footage rate for common areas.

If your landlord has agreed to set aside some parking spaces for your business or to let you use a storage building or other outbuilding, get it in writing in the lease. Also specify whether indoor storage space will be shared or is reserved exclusively for your use.

3. Starting Date of the Lease

Your lease should clearly state its starting date. This can sometimes be a problem, especially if you're renting space in a building that's still under construction or space currently occupied. If you sign a lease before ground has been broken or if the building is only partially complete, what happens if your space isn't ready by the time you need it? This too should be addressed in your lease. Otherwise there may be little pressure on the landlord to meet deadlines.

One possibility is to negotiate a cutoff date by which you have the right to cancel the lease if the building (or your unit) isn't ready for occupancy. You may also be able to collect damages from the landlord if you suffer losses because your space isn't ready on time. But in negotiating such a clause, remember it's always hard to prove lost profits—particularly if you're just starting out in business—so it's better to negotiate a preset amount for your damages.

Also, with a building to be constructed or under construction, state in your lease that until local building officials have issued a certificate of occupancy for the building, no rent will be due. You may think that this is so obvious it doesn't need to be spelled out in your lease, but some landlords have actually tried to collect rent even before building officials have approved the building for occupancy.

In a slight variation on this problem, some leases call for the landlord to erect a shell building. Then you, the tenant, finish off your own space. Obviously, you want to avoid having to install improvements in a partially constructed building, which may not be completed for many months. One good solution: a lease clause saying you don't have to start work on your space until the building is enclosed and the common areas—such as hallways and rest rooms—are done.

The lease could also require the landlord to have the building and safety department make a preliminary inspection of your space before you start making improvements. The inspection would make sure the landlord has correctly installed the electrical and plumbing lines, and heating, ventilating, and air-conditioning facilities within your leased space. You don't want to risk the possibility that you'll have to rip out and redo your interior work because the landlord's contractor made a mistake.

With space that's currently vacant, ask the landlord to agree to let you have immediate access to decorate and install equipment. That way, you'll be ready to do business when you start paying rent. Spell this out in the lease.

4. Ending Date of the Lease

The lease should state its termination date, although you may have an option to renew. (See Section 5.) Some leases state that if the tenant remains in possession after the termination without exercising an option to renew, the tenancy is from month to month during the holdover period. (See Section C for information on month-to-month tenancies.)

5. An Option to Renew a Lease

When you first negotiate a lease, you can often bargain for a clause that gives you the right to renew or extend your lease when its term ends. Let's say you're negotiating a new two-year lease. You like the location, the rent is favorable, and you'd like the right to stay for an extended period if your business is doing well. But at the same time, you're nervous about signing a four-year lease in case your business doesn't prosper.

A two-year lease that includes an option to renew for two more years may be ideal. Typically, you exercise an option to stay by notifying your landlord in writing a set number of days or months before the lease expires. The amount of notice required is negotiable.

Getting the landlord to include an option in your lease may not be easy. Put yourself in the landlord's shoes. You might well go for a firm commitment from the tenant for eight years with adequate rent increases built in. You'd find it less attractive to grant a series of successive two-year options, which introduce an element of uncertainty—they allow the tenant the right to stay if the location turns out to be profitable but to leave if it's a dud. Not surprisingly, as a landlord, you'd look for some economic incentive to make the deal more attractive.

Now that you understand the landlord's point of view, you won't be too surprised if you find that the rent rate for a short lease with an option to renew is more than the rate you can lock in with a long-term lease. Also, the landlord will likely want a higher rent for the renewal period, either in a fixed amount or an increase tied to a cost-of-living index.

⚠ **Drawbacks of options to renew.** *An option to renew isn't always a good idea. If your business isn't particularly sensitive as to its location (maybe you publish a newsletter on how to raise fish or sell advertising for trade shows), think twice before you waste bargaining clout or pay extra for an option to renew. Sure, you may have to move, but in a high-vacancy climate, you might even find space with a lower rent.*

LAW IN THE REAL WORLD
Know the Fine Print

Charlie bought a copy shop in a high-traffic location. There was only one year left on the three-year lease, but the lease contained an option to renew for an additional three years at a slightly higher—though still favorable—rent. The landlord consented to an assignment of the lease and Charlie took over the business. Things went well. Charlie decided to stay at the location.

Nine months after Charlie took over the business, the landlord came by for a casual chat. Charlie mentioned his plans for the coming year, including some marketing ideas. "Sounds good," the landlord said, "but you'll have a new address. I'm planning to move you to a spot around the corner on the second floor." Charlie was stunned. The new space would be much less visible to the public—and Charlie's business depended on walk-in customers.

Fortunately, Charlie had the presence of mind to dig out his lease. There, nestled in the fine print, was an option clause. All that Charlie had to do was to notify the landlord in writing, at least 60 days before the original lease expired, that he was exercising his option to stay on in the same space. A quick look at the calendar confirmed that Charlie had more than enough time to give the written notice. To be on the safe side, he quickly sent his notice to the landlord by certified mail (return receipt requested)—and thereby averted a financial disaster. For Charlie, the option clause meant the difference between success and failure.

6. The Right to Expand

If future expansion is a good possibility, you may want the lease to give you the right to add adjacent space or to move to larger quarters in the building.

Sometimes this is done through a right of first refusal—the landlord promises in the lease that before any other vacant space is rented to someone else, the landlord must offer it to you on the same terms and conditions.

7. Rent

Leases usually state the rent on a monthly basis; for example, $1,000 per month; and indicate when payment is due—typically the first of the month in advance. The lease may also say that the rent for your two-year lease is $24,000 payable in monthly installments of $1,000 per month on the first of the month. Sometimes there's a late charge if you're more than a few days late.

This isn't the only way to compute rent. Depending on the type of building and local custom, here are the main ways that the rental amount is set:

- *Gross leases.* These require the tenant to pay a flat monthly amount. The landlord pays for all operating costs for the building—taxes, insurance, repairs, and utilities. Under one common variation, the tenant pays for its own electricity, heat, and air-conditioning; if your lease uses this method and you are in a building with other tenants, see if there are separate meters available so that you can control these costs. If not, ask to see copies of the bills—you don't want to agree to pay for utilities if someone else in the building runs up huge bills.

- *Net leases.* The tenant must pay a monthly base rent plus some or all of the real estate taxes. If you sign this kind of lease and you're leasing just a portion of the building, make sure that the portion of the real estate taxes allocated to your space is fair.

- *Net-net leases.* This type goes farther and requires the tenant to pay the base rental amount plus real estate taxes and the landlord's insurance on the space you occupy (which is different from your own liability insurance,

discussed in Chapter 12). In a standard lease, the landlord insures the entire building against property damage caused by fire, flooding, and the weather, as well as negligence and vandalism. The landlord's insurance also covers claims against the landlord brought by people injured on the property. In a net-net lease, the cost of this insurance is allocated among the tenants, usually on the basis of the proportion of space each one occupies.

- *Net-net-net ("triple net") leases.* The tenant pays the base rental amount plus the landlord's operating costs, including taxes, insurance, repairs, and maintenance. Such leases are not often used for space rented by a small business, but there are exceptions, such as storefronts in popular areas of large cities.

- *Percentage leases.* These leases are used most commonly for retailers in a shopping mall. The tenant pays base rent plus a percentage of gross income. (See Section F for a discussion of shopping center leases.)

If the lease is for more than one year, the landlord may want to build in a rent increase for future years. For example, a three-year lease may provide for rent of $1,000 per month in year one, $1,100 in year two, and $1,200 per month in year three. Sometimes the increase is tied to some external measure, such as the Consumer Price Index. If the CPI increases 5% during the base year, so does your rent in year two.

Some landlords want the rent to be increased if their taxes or maintenance costs go up. If you're moving into a new building and the landlord proposes this last kind of formula, be particularly careful. No one really knows what operating costs will be in this situation—they may jump 50%. You'll at least want to negotiate a cap on how much the rent can go up because of increased operating costs.

As emphasized throughout this chapter, leases are normally negotiable. For example, depending on market conditions, you may be able to convince the landlord to turn a triple net lease into a gross lease. Or the landlord may be willing to put a cap on the amount of taxes, insurance, and maintenance costs you'll have to pay. If vacancies rates are high, the landlord may be willing to give you a few months of free rent in return for your agreeing to take the space on a triple net basis.

8. Security Deposit

Landlords commonly request a security deposit in the amount of the last month's rent plus an additional amount equal to a half month's or full month's rent. So if your rent is $1,000 per month, you may have to cough up $2,500 to $3,000 before you take possession—$1,000 for the first month and $1,500 to $2,000 for the security deposit. This is all negotiable.

Ask the landlord to hold the security deposit in an interest-bearing bank account for your benefit. If you're concerned about the landlord's solvency, you might go farther and suggest that the security deposit be held in escrow by a third party—but don't be surprised if the landlord balks at either suggestion.

The security deposit is intended to cover unpaid rent if you move out early and any damage you cause during your occupancy over and above normal wear and tear. Usually, your right to be free from liability for normal wear and tear is recognized under state law; you don't have to worry about this unless the lease the landlord proposes tries to make you responsible for it. So if your lease obligates you to return your space "in tip-top condition," you'll want to ask for a change. Similarly, it's normally considered unreasonable for the landlord to require you to pay to repaint the space before you move out or install new carpeting—unless, of course, you caused an unusual amount of damage.

9. Improvements by the Landlord

Unless you rent a recently remodeled space designed for a business such as yours, the space will often need to be fixed up or modified before it's suitable for your use. At the inexpensive end of the spectrum, you may need only a few coats of paint on the walls, or perhaps to have the carpet cleaned. At the big bucks end of the spectrum, you might need hundreds of thousands of dollars' worth of improvements before you could open an elegant new restaurant (for up-to-date kitchen equipment and an appealing decor) or a small manufacturing facility (pollution control equipment and a loading dock).

In between these two extremes, your business might need more lighting and electrical outlets, air-conditioning, or perhaps a partitioned office or work area. Who's going to pay for these things— you or the landlord? It's all negotiable.

Your lease should specify the improvements the landlord is to make. Ideally, the landlord should agree to have improvements in place before your move-in date. The next best thing is a stated deadline within the first months of your lease.

Try to get the landlord to agree to pay for all or most of these improvements. But be forewarned that the landlord's willingness to pick up the tab will depend on a number of factors including the condition of the building, your type of business, the extent and cost of the improvements, whether the improvements would be useful to a future tenant, the length of your lease, and—very important—how much rent you'll pay. For example, if you're starting a fancy restaurant, the landlord isn't likely to make $200,000 of improvements—but this might change if you're a famous chef whom the landlord is counting on as an anchor tenant. But if you're opening a bookstore, the landlord may agree to install shelving for you. If the building is in bad repair, you can probably convince the landlord to put it in decent shape for you and maybe to make needed modifications in the process. If you're paying a hefty rent for five years, you can expect more than if you're signing up for one year at a low rent.

Improvements to leased space usually become the property of the landlord. (See the discussion of fixtures in Section 10.) This means that after you move out, future tenants will continue to use the space in its improved condition, and the landlord will continue to collect rent for the improved space. In other words, if your improvements are sensible, the economic benefits to the landlord will outlast your lease. This is a good negotiating point; you shouldn't be expected to bear the major financial burden for improvements that have a long useful life.

On the other hand, if you have specialized needs—for example, you're running a photo lab or a dance studio—and your darkroom or hardwood floor would be of limited value to most future tenants, don't expect the landlord to willingly pick up the costs of the improvements. The landlord may even want to charge you something to cover the cost of remodeling the space after you leave.

After you agree with the landlord on improvements, make sure the lease is clear on what's being done. Attach drawings and specifications so later there can be no doubt about what was promised. If extensive improvements are to be made, insist on drawings and specs prepared by an architect or construction specialist. Think about all your needs: partitions, special lighting, soundproofing, special floor coverings, painting, wall coverings, woodwork, cabinetry, and so on. Many landlords can be very flexible and open to making improvements if you approach them before the lease is signed.

Here is some language you might include in the lease:

> Before the beginning of the lease term, Landlord, at its expense, will make improvements to the premises as set forth in Exhibit A (Plans and Specifications for Improvements). These improvements will be completed in a workmanlike manner and comply with all applicable laws, ordinances, rules, and regulations of governmental authorities.

Improvements to raw space—particularly in a new building—are often called the "build-out." Sometimes the landlord offers a standard build-out to every tenant. For example, the build-out might include a certain grade of carpeting or vinyl floor covering; a particular type of drop-ceiling; a certain number of fluorescent lighting panels per square feet of floor space; and a specified number of feet of drywall partitions, with two coats of paint. Once you understand the landlord's standard build-out, see if you can get some upgrades or extras thrown in. You may wind up with better carpeting, more lighting, or fancier woodwork.

If the landlord offers a build-out allowance based on the cost of the improvements (for example, up to $30 per square foot of rented space), see if you can negotiate a higher figure. Generally, the longer the lease, the better the deal you can negotiate on the build-out. This makes sense. With a lease of three or five years, the landlord has an incentive to do far more for you than if you sign up for only 12 months.

10. Making Improvements Yourself

You may want to make improvements or alterations that go beyond what the landlord is willing to provide. The lease proposed by the landlord may require the landlord's permission before you can make improvements or alterations to the premises. Meet this clause head on by submitting your plans to the landlord before you sign the lease—and don't sign unless you get approval.

Also, provide that the landlord won't unreasonably withhold consent to future improvements you may wish to make.

At the end of the lease, you may want to remove some of the items you've installed and take them to a new location. Leases sometimes prohibit the removal of improvements. The landlord has a legitimate concern in preventing you from removing items in a way that damages the space or impedes renting to a new tenant. If your lease doesn't spell out your rights, the state law on "fixtures" will normally say that anything you've attached has become part of the real estate and is therefore the landlord's property. This can lead to arguments. For example, who owns the window air-conditioner that you attached with metal brackets?

The best way to avoid argument is to specify what you can remove and what belongs to the landlord. List all items you'll want to remove—either in the lease itself (if there's room) or on an extra sheet attached to the lease. (See Section G for how to do this.)

Even if you have permission to remove certain items, make sure that you install them so they can be removed later without damage to the building. It may cost a little more to install easy-to-remove shelves, cabinets, light fixtures, and air-conditioning units. In the long run, however, it will be well worth it, because you can keep these items without having to make extensive repairs to the landlord's property.

11. Compliance With the ADA

The federal Americans with Disabilities Act (ADA) makes both you and your landlord responsible for making the premises accessible to disabled people. You can work out the details in your lease. Here are some suggestions on how to proceed:

- Ask the landlord to state (lawyers say "warrant") that the building complies with the ADA, based on an ADA survey or audit performed by an engineer or architect.
- If the landlord will be making improvements, see if the landlord will agree to pay for fully complying with the ADA.
- Make sure that the costs of bringing common areas into compliance aren't passed along to you as part of the "CAM" (common area maintenance) charges.

To comply with the ADA, you or the landlord may need to provide accessible parking, and install ramps, wide entry doors, and specially designed rest rooms. Since some of these improvements may be costly, you'd like the landlord to foot as much of the bill as possible.

Your obligations don't end with access to the building. *To meet ADA requirements, you may have to redesign your business's interior space to improve access for disabled customers and employees. For example, you may need to widen aisles so that people using wheelchairs, walkers, and electric scooters have ample room to maneuver, and you may need to lower service counters for ease of access. Be sure to budget enough to cover these improvements—your landlord isn't likely to cover these costs. For more information on ADA compliance for business premises, check the U.S. Department of Justice website, www.usdoj.gov, where you can view or download several helpful publications.*

12. Zoning Laws, Permits, and Restrictions on Use of the Space

If the lease says nothing about the use of the space, you can use it for any lawful purpose. However, leases are often quite specific about what you can and can't do. For example, if your business sells and repairs bicycles, the landlord may insist that the lease limit you to these activities. This may seem okay now, but what if you want to do other things in the future? Define the permitted uses broadly enough to encompass any needs you anticipate. A poster business, for example, might want to provide that the space can also be used for classes on making and framing posters. A private post office might want to be free to do photocopying, fax transmissions, and the retail sale of greeting cards.

No lease or landlord can give you the right to do something that's prohibited under the zoning laws. So it's an excellent idea to check with your local building or zoning department to be sure your anticipated uses are permitted under the local zoning ordinance. A bicycle shop may not be permitted in an office zone, for example.

In addition to zoning ordinances, other planning, building, safety, and health ordinances can affect your intended use. An ordinance may require a certain number of offstreet parking spaces for some types of businesses, an entrance accessible to handicapped people, or a restroom for customers—a common requirement for a restaurant. (For more on this subject, see Chapter 7, Section D6.)

13. Required Insurance

Most landlords want their tenants to carry insurance to cover damage the tenant does to the building and injuries suffered by customers and other visitors on the premises. This is something that any business would be wise to do even if it weren't required by a lease. (Chapter 12 covers the types of insurance you should consider.) But when you get down to specifics, it can be one of the most complicated parts of the lease.

Look carefully at the policy limits the landlord wants you to carry. Is a $2 million liability policy reasonable for your business? Some landlords want you to buy a policy to cover the landlord's liability for injuries as well as your own. This is often considered unreasonable; bargain to eliminate such a requirement, if you can.

At the very least, your landlord should agree to pay for casualty insurance on the building so that funds are available to repair it if it's destroyed or damaged by a fire or windstorm. And if you're in an area where floods or earthquakes are common, insist that the landlord also include these nonstandard coverages.

With both you and your landlord buying insurance, there's always the possibility of unnecessary duplication of coverage. Ask for a copy of your landlord's policy and review it with your agent.

When a landlord and tenant each carry property insurance, you can run into complications because of the legal concept of "subrogation." Ordinarily, if an insurance company pays an insured business for damaged property, the company has the right to turn around and sue any third party that caused the damage. The insurance is said to be subrogated to the rights of the insured business to collect damages—in other words, the insurance company steps into the shoes of the insured business.

EXAMPLE: Pericles Corporation is a tenant in a building owned by Town Development Associates. Pericles carries insurance on its property and Town Development carries insurance on the building. One evening, employees of Pericles forget to turn off the coffeemaker before leaving.

The coffee boils away, the machine overheats, and a fire breaks out, seriously damaging the building, furniture, and equipment of Pericles. Pericles' insurance company pays for replacement of the damaged furniture and equipment, and Town Development's insurance company pays for repair of the building. However, since the fire was caused by the negligence of a Pericles employee, Town Development's insurance company steps into the shoes of Town Development and sues Pericles to collect the money paid out to repair the building. In doing so, the insurance company is exercising its right of subrogation.

You can head off this kind of headache by including a clause such as the following in your lease:

Mutual Waiver of Subrogation

Landlord and Tenant release each other from any and all liability to each other for any loss or damage to property, including loss of income and demolition or construction expenses due to the enforcement of ordinance or law, caused by fire or any of the Extended Coverage or Special Coverage perils, even if such fire or other peril has been caused by the fault or negligence of the other party or anyone for whom such party may be responsible.

If you don't have such a clause in your lease and try to waive subrogation rights after a loss occurs, you may be out of luck. Most insurance policies provide that a waiver of rights is effective only if it is made in writing before a loss.

14. Subletting Your Space or Assigning the Lease

Someday you may want to share your space with another business. For example, if you run a toy store, you might want to rent a portion of your floor space to someone who sells children's books. You'd do this by subletting the space. When you sublet, you're still responsible to the landlord for paying the entire rent and honoring all other provisions of the lease. Obviously, subletting is of more concern with a long lease than with a short one.

Another possibility is that you'll want to move out of the space during the term of the lease, because you've found better space or you've decided to go out of business. If you found another tenant to take over your space, you could sublease the whole space to the new tenant; in that case, you'd still be responsible to the landlord under the lease. But ideally, you'd want to assign your lease to the new tenant. Assigning your lease takes you out of the picture entirely. The new tenant pays the landlord directly and you have no further liability under the lease.

Landlords often are reluctant to give tenants an unlimited right to assign their lease or sublet their space. They're afraid of winding up with an occupant who is a deadbeat or who may damage the property or who runs a business that will adversely affect the image of the building, making it harder to attract good tenants. A typical provision drafted by a landlord looks like this:

> Tenant agrees not to assign or transfer this lease or sublet the premises or any part of the premises without the written consent of Landlord.

In my opinion, such a clause is unfair from a tenant's point of view. To make it fairer, ask to add the following wording:

> Consent of Landlord will not be unreasonably withheld.

With this additional wording in your lease, if you find a reasonable occupant to sublet to, and the landlord refuses to let you sublet, courts will generally rule that you're off the hook for rent after you move out.

⚠️ **Uncooperative landlords.** *If you find yourself with a landlord who objects to a subtenant you've found, check with your lawyer or do some research to learn your legal rights in your state.*

LAW IN THE REAL WORLD
When Corporate Status Comes in Handy

Elena formed a corporation called Elena's Mediterranean Deli Inc. As president of her new corporation, she signed a five-year lease for space in a popular food court. Buried in the lease's small print was a sentence that said the lease couldn't be assigned and the space couldn't be sublet without the landlord's permission.

A few years later, Elena wanted to sell her business to Arnold for a handsome profit. Arnold planned to continue running the business at the same location. Elena told the landlord about her plans to sell and sublet. The landlord, who wanted to install his nephew in Elena's space, objected, saying he wouldn't let Elena assign the lease or sublet the space. The landlord was willing to excuse Elena from the rest of the lease—but this wouldn't allow her to reap the profit from a sale of her business.

What to do? Fortunately, because the corporation rather than Elena was the tenant, the lease was legally a corporate asset. Elena realized that she didn't need to sublet or assign her lease. She sold the corporation to Arnold, which meant that the corporation—although owned by a new shareholder—was still the tenant. Elena used the profits to go to grad school.

15. The Landlord's Right to Enter Your Space

Some leases give the landlord a broad right to enter your premises at all times to make inspections or repairs. This is an unnecessary invasion of your privacy, and most landlords will settle for a more limited right of entry. It's reasonable to provide that the landlord can enter your leased space only during normal business hours, unless there's a genuine emergency, such as a burst pipe or electrical hazard.

Because repairs can be disruptive, you might also require the landlord to consult you before making repairs and schedule them for a mutually convenient time. For many businesses, this won't be a problem. But if repairs could be disastrous—for example, you're a doctor renting space for your allergy practice or the owner of a shop that assembles delicate electronic components—you'll want to tightly control when the landlord can repaint or install new carpeting.

A related issue comes up near the end of a lease. Does the landlord have an unlimited right to enter your place to show it to prospective tenants? Depending on the type of business you have, this can be disruptive and annoying. It's a good idea for your lease to limit this type of intrusion to a slow period (say, 9 a.m. to 11 a.m., Monday through Friday) and to require 24 hours' notice.

16. Signs

Many types of businesses need one or more external signs. Check the lease to see if it gives your landlord the right to disapprove signs before they go up. One way to be sure the landlord won't be unreasonable is to have your signs approved when you sign the lease. If you do, attach a drawing or photo of the signs to the lease so that there can't be any argument later about what you agreed on.

⚠ Don't forget municipal sign ordinances.
In some communities, signs are heavily regulated by ordinances that restrict their size, number, color, and location. In a few communities, there are even limitations on the content of signs—for example, in a few places in Southern California, there are limits on the number of non-English words you can use. So besides providing for your signs in your lease, check with local building and planning officials to see what ordinances and regulations may affect you.

17. Cancelling Your Lease

In general, you can't cancel your lease before it runs out without pointing to a specific reason stated in the document itself—unless, of course, your landlord agrees to end the lease early. The right to end your lease early is definitely something you should think about during your negotiations. The future of your business may look rosy, but especially with a new business, no one knows for sure.

One approach for a new business is to propose a provision that allows you to cancel your lease if your gross income projections haven't reached a stated level by a certain time—say, six months after you take occupancy. Although this would be a somewhat unusual clause, a landlord with vacant space and no other tenants in prospect might accept it.

An even more compelling reason for ending your lease early would be that the building has been damaged by a fire or flooding and you can't conduct your business there. In most states, if you rent space in just a portion of a building, the law provides that you can terminate your lease if the building is destroyed.

But what if it's only heavily damaged? If the landlord doesn't make repairs promptly, state law may allow you to terminate based on "constructive eviction"; the landlord's inaction, you would argue, constitutes an eviction. But if the landlord disputes this, you'll be stuck with what a judge rules. A better approach is to provide in your lease that if you can't run your business in your space for 30 days because of damage that you didn't cause, you can cancel the lease. Also, if relevant, make sure your 30-day provision covers the possibility that you and your customers can't get access to your space because of damage to another part of the building.

For more information on getting out of a lease, see Section I.

18. Mediation or Arbitration

I recommend that all small business leases have a clause requiring mediation or arbitration of landlord-tenant disputes. With mediation, an outside party helps the disputants arrive at their own settlement, which can then be recorded as a legally binding agreement. Arbitration is more like a private court action with the arbitrator in the role of a judge listening to the dispute and rendering a decision. But because no court is involved, it tends to be far faster and cheaper than a full-blown lawsuit. (Mediation and arbitration are covered in Chapter 22.)

19. The Fine Print

Study the lease thoroughly so that you're sure your responsibilities and those of the landlord are clear and reasonable. In addition to the major items already discussed, make sure the lease deals with all possible costs, including any of the following that concern you:

- *Real estate taxes.* If nothing is mentioned in the lease, this is normally the landlord's responsibility.
- *Utilities—water, electricity, natural gas, heating oil, etc.* These are usually the tenant's responsibility if not specifically mentioned in the lease.
- *Maintenance of the building and of your premises.* Without a lease provision to the contrary, the landlord must pay for maintaining the building; you pay for maintaining your own space. If you're leasing an entire building, you are normally responsible for all maintenance unless the lease specifies otherwise.
- *Repair and maintenance of the interior walls, ceiling, and floors in your space.* This is normally the tenant's problem in the absence of a lease provision.
- *Repair of malfunctioning plumbing, electrical, and mechanical systems (heating, ventilation, and air-conditioning—commonly called HVAC).* Without a lease provision, payment responsibilities are debatable. Generally, the landlord is responsible for systems that affect the entire building—although the opposite is

usually true if you lease the entire building. When you rent less than an entire building, the responsibility for mechanical or electrical facilities within the four walls of your space isn't always clear; you could find yourself arguing over who must pay for replacing a defective light fixture or a thermostat that goes haywire if the lease doesn't cover it.

- *Janitorial services.* These are normally the tenant's responsibility unless the lease says otherwise. Landlords usually provide janitorial services for bathrooms and other areas used in common by several tenants.
- *Window washing.* Without specific lease language, the landlord normally doesn't have to wash windows. In smaller buildings, leases usually leave window washing to the tenant, with the possible exception of windows serving common areas such as hallways, entryways, and storage areas. In larger, multistoried buildings, the landlord usually accepts responsibility—at least for the exterior of the windows.
- *Trash removal.* Without lease language to the contrary, this is the tenant's chore.
- *Landscape care and snow removal.* This is generally the landlord's duty unless you lease the entire building, in which case the burden shifts to you. It's always wise to address this issue in the lease—particularly if you're a tenant in a professional or other building where projecting the right image is important.
- *Parking lot maintenance.* This is something the landlord usually must pay for unless the whole parking lot is under your control, in which case it's usually your job unless the lease provides otherwise. In addition to maintenance, be sure the lease is clear regarding the landlord's duty to make a certain number of spaces available, keep the lot or garage open during normal business hours, and provide security.

On service items such as janitorial services and window washing, specify how often this will be done. If the landlord is responsible for heating and air-conditioning, will these services be available weekends and at night? If your business keeps long hours, you want your space to be comfortable at all times.

Regarding repairs, you and your landlord may find it convenient to allow you to make certain minor repairs not exceeding a fixed sum (say $300) and to deduct those outlays from your next month's rent.

E. Additional Clauses to Consider

Most of the above lease clauses are relatively common. Here are a few more, which are seen less often but which can be valuable to you as a tenant.

1. Option to Purchase the Building

If the situation warrants, consider a clause giving you an option to buy the building someday. It could give you the right to buy at a specified future time at a specified price, or a right of first refusal, in which if your landlord receives an offer from someone else to purchase the building, you'll be given a chance to match that offer. Many landlords will give you this right because it doesn't cost them anything. If you decide not to exercise your right of first refusal, the landlord simply sells the property to the person who made the offer.

2. The Right to Withhold Rent

Suppose your landlord violates the lease by not furnishing air-conditioning for a sweltering July—or heat for a frigid January. Can you withhold rent? The traditional legal view is that your obligation to pay rent is independent of the landlord's obligation to perform under the lease. In other words, tenants are expected to quietly pay their rent except in the most extreme circumstances.

But in the last 25 years, a tenants' rights revolution has taken place—mainly in the area of residential leases. For example, in the case of housing, many states recognize an "implied warranty of habitability." This means that regardless of what the lease obligates

the landlord to do, the landlord must put dwelling units in a habitable condition—and keep them that way throughout the lease. If the landlord fails to do so, the tenant can withhold all or part of the rent without fearing eviction. Unless the parties come to an accommodation, a judge will ultimately decide how much of a rent reduction (the technical term is "abatement") the tenant is entitled to.

Commercial tenants, however, have not fared as well. The courts in most states still say that a commercial tenant must continue to pay rent despite the landlord's failure to meet implied or expressed duties. But this may be changing. Courts in several states have shown concern for the rights of commercial tenants. For example, a Texas court ruled that there is an implied warranty by a commercial landlord that leased premises are suitable for their intended purpose. The ruling came in a case where the landlord didn't provide adequate air-conditioning, electricity, hot water, janitorial services, or security to a business tenant. The tenant stopped paying rent and moved out. The court upheld the action of the business tenant. *Davidow v. Inwood North Professional Group–Phase I*, 747 S.W.2d 373 (Tex 1988).

How far the courts will go to protect your rights as a commercial tenant is still uncertain. Certainly a one-day failure to provide air-conditioning wouldn't be enough to let you withhold rent or move out. But what if you and your customers have to sweat it out for two weeks? Or six weeks? That may be enough in some states, assuming you've given the landlord prompt notice of the problem and a chance to make repairs.

I recommend that you deal with all this legal uncertainty by requesting a lease clause giving you the right to withhold rent if, after reasonable notice, the landlord violates the lease in a way that seriously interferes with your ability to do business. Here's a sample clause:

> If, within ten days after notice from Tenant, Landlord fails to cure a default by Landlord that materially affects Tenant's ability to conduct its business, Tenant shall be entitled to a reason-

able abatement of rent for the period of default and may withhold all rent until Landlord has cured the default.

F. Shopping Center Leases

Leases for space in a shopping center are a special breed of animal. They often charge a percentage of sales as part of the rent and restrict competing businesses, to mention just two major differences.

It can be hard to read a shopping center lease and decide whether it offers a square deal or not. So, in addition to reading the lease language carefully, one of your first steps should be to check whether the shopping center has a tenants' association; many shopping centers have them, and it can be a source of invaluable information. If there's no formal association, drop in on some current tenants. Either way, learn as much as you can about the center's management and how tenants are really treated. Also, try to find out which lease clauses the owner considers negotiable. This sort of information as to problems and opportunities will give you a definite advantage in your lease negotiations.

Now let's look at a typical shopping center lease. Many of the lease clauses discussed earlier in this chapter also appear in a shopping center lease, but there are likely to be a number of different wrinkles you should know about.

1. Percentage Rent

Retail businesses moving into a shopping center often find that the landlord expects to receive a percentage of gross sales in addition to a fixed "base rent." For example, the lease might provide:

a. The landlord will receive $2,000 a month as base rent.

b. In addition, if your gross sales exceed $200,000 a year, the landlord will receive 5% of the amount of your gross sales over the $200,000 figure.

c. The amount received by the landlord under the percentage rent clause won't exceed $25,000 a year.

In addition to trying to negotiate more favorable terms, be specific in how you define gross sales. Depending on your type of business, certain items should be deducted from gross sales before the percentage rent is determined. Here are some possibilities:

- returned merchandise
- charges you make for delivery and installation
- sales from vending machines
- refundable deposits
- catalogue or mail-order sales
- sales tax.

In short, make sure your lease excludes all items that overstate your sales from the location you're renting.

2. Anchor Tenants

You may be attracted to a certain shopping center because one of the tenants is a major department store or supermarket. These superstars, known as anchor tenants, attract customers to the shopping center. Insist on a provision letting you out of the lease if an anchor tenant closes or, with a new shopping center, if the center never opens.

Also seek the right to cancel your lease if center occupancy falls below a certain percentage. There's nothing worse than having a store in a half-empty mall.

3. Competing Businesses

How many record or running shoe stores can a mall support? You may want to negotiate a limit on the number of competing businesses allowed in the mall. Similarly, the landlord may want you to agree not to open a second store within a two-mile radius of the mall; the fear is that a second store too close might decrease gross sales from your mall location—thereby reducing the money the landlord gets under the percentage rent clause. At any rate, remember that these issues are usually negotiable. Many shopping centers (especially older ones) can no longer afford to dictate coercive terms to small businesses, and you may find much more landlord flexibility than you expect.

4. Duty to Remain Open

Your lease may compel you to remain open for business during all mall hours—typically 10 a.m. to 9 p.m. Monday through Saturday, and noon to 5 p.m. on Sunday. With a small business, think about whether you can afford to run your business during all of those hours or if it's appropriate to do so. For example, not many people buy children's shoes at 8:45 on Tuesday evening, but there is often a line on Saturday morning that justifies opening at 8:30 or 9 a.m. instead of 10, when the rest of the mall opens. If you need reasonable changes, ask for them.

G. How to Modify a Lease

As discussed in this chapter, there are a number of constructive ways to modify the lease presented by the landlord. The most important thing is to put the changes in writing. Never rely on oral understandings. In this day of computers and word processing software, the simplest method for making changes may be to have the landlord or landlord's lawyer print out a revised version of the lease—or you can make small changes on the lease itself by crossing out unacceptable wording and adding new language. You and the landlord should initial each of these changes.

If changes are extensive and it's not practical for the landlord to include them in a fresh draft, it's best to prepare an addition to the lease—in legal parlance, an "addendum." The addendum should refer to the main lease and state that in case of any conflict, the terms of the addendum supersede the original lease. A sample addendum is shown below.

Addendum

This is an Addendum to the Lease dated

_____, 20__ between

_____ (Landlord) and _____

_____ (Tenant) for commercial

space at

_____.

The parties agree to the following changes and additions to the Lease:

[*Insert changes and additions*]

In all other respects, the terms of the original Lease remain in full effect. However, if there is a conflict between this Addendum and the original Lease, the terms of this Addendum will prevail.

Keep in mind that a lease can be modified even after it's been signed. For example, if six months into your lease your landlord agrees to install some partitions for $2,000, you can sign an addendum then.

H. Landlord-Tenant Disputes

There's almost no limit to the kinds of disputes that landlords and tenants can have. Your landlord may claim that you're damaging the building, or that you're consistently late paying rent, or that you or your customers or visitors park in other tenants' spaces. You may feel that your landlord hasn't been furnishing services that were promised, such as security, janitorial, or landscaping, or that your landlord is failing to attend to the leaky roof or having the windows washed frequently enough.

No matter what the cause, it's usually best to compromise a landlord-tenant dispute through negotiation. Sometimes a frank discussion and a little give and take by each side can resolve what seems like an impossible problem.

If the dispute is serious and not amenable to face-to-face negotiations, have your lawyer help you analyze your legal rights. They may be stronger than you think. Legal trends in many parts of the country have improved the tenant's position.

If your lease has a mediation or arbitration clause, this is the obvious next step. But even if it doesn't, you may wish to suggest one or both of these approaches. Going to court can be expensive and time-consuming—something the landlord probably wants to avoid. In short, a sensible landlord has good reason to listen to your complaints and to mediate or arbitrate disputes. (See Chapter 22 for more on mediation and arbitration.)

1. Put Your Complaints in Writing

If you think your landlord has violated the lease, put your concern in writing in a straightforward, nonhostile way. State specifically what the violation is and what part of the lease it involves. Deliver your notice or letter to the landlord either in person or by certified mail (return receipt requested). Putting a landlord on early notice can help bolster your legal position if the dispute ever goes to court.

If rent withholding is allowed in your state or by a specific clause in your lease (see Section E), you may want to write a letter or two to the landlord before you hold back on the rent. An example of such a letter is shown below.

SAMPLE LETTER TO LANDLORD

August 5, 20____

Arnold Ace
Ace Real Estate Associates
1234 Main Street
Anytown, U.S.A. 12345

I am writing to you about some problems we are having with our store space at 567 Enterprise Drive.

As you know, paragraph 12 of our lease specifically says that Ace Real Estate Associates will maintain the heating and air conditioning system and keep it in good repair. I have called your office twice this week and left word that the air conditioning is not working. No one has come to fix it or given us a date by which the work will be done. Our customers have complained, and on Tuesday we had to close early.

Also, under paragraph 14 of our lease, the Landlord agreed to replace the broken floor tiles in the entry area within two weeks after we took possession. We have been here for six weeks now and nothing has been done about the tiles. The broken tiles are hazardous.

These are serious violations of our lease. I am requesting that you immediately repair the air conditioning and promptly replace the broken floor tiles. We cannot operate without the air conditioning during this hot weather. Its lack has already caused us to lose substantial revenues and has damaged customer relationships.

If you do not take care of these matters within five days, I plan to have the work done myself and to deduct the cost from next month's rent.

If the cost of fixing the air conditioning is excessive, I may choose to terminate the lease and to sue your company for damages caused by your breaching the lease, including moving expenses and lost profits.

I hope that this will not be necessary. Please proceed at once to make the repairs as required by the lease.

Very truly yours,

Peter Olsen

2. Coping With the Threat of Eviction

Many leases contain stern language that appears to give the landlord the right to enter your space and regain possession if you don't pay your rent on time or fail to live up to some other lease obligation. Don't be intimidated. No matter what the lease says, in most states a landlord can't evict you without going to court and getting a court order first. This process requires that you be given notice and an opportunity to present your side of the dispute.

A hearing by a judge—or, if your lease so provides, by a mediator or arbitrator—gives you a chance to explain any legal defenses you have. For example, perhaps the reason you didn't pay your rent by the first of the month was that the landlord failed to repair the air-conditioning as required by the lease. The right to a court hearing also gives you valuable time to develop your case and perhaps resolve the dispute. Court hearings don't take place instantly. You usually have some breathing space in which to build your legal response.

I. Getting Out of a Lease

Suppose that your business doesn't work out or—more optimistically—that you outgrow the space that you've leased. How free are you to simply vacate the space and walk away from the lease? Unless your landlord has done something to make your space unusable, you're legally responsible for the entire rent for the remaining portion of the lease if the landlord can't find another suitable tenant.

But especially if you have desirable space and a favorable lease, getting out of it—or most of it, anyway—may be less difficult than you think. If you find that you need to move out, you have two options:

- *Buy your way out.* Try working out a deal in which the landlord keeps all or a part of your security deposit (including, perhaps, the last month's rent) in return for releasing you from the lease. If the lease still has a fairly long time to run or it will be hard to find a new tenant, you might need to sweeten the deal by offering an additional month or two of rent.

- *Find a new tenant.* Find a new tenant to take over the space. Present the new tenant to the landlord along with information about the person's credit and business history. Especially if your lease says that your landlord can't unreasonably refuse to consent to a sublease, you're in a strong legal position if the new tenant has good financial credentials and runs a business of a type permitted by your lease. But again, even without this provision (or if your lease flat out prohibits subletting or assignment), the law in your state may recognize the landlord's duty to mitigate damages—that is, try to find a replacement tenant and minimize his or her loss. If so, you're in a pretty good legal position. If the landlord accepts a new tenant who agrees to pay as much or more than you do, you're free of the lease at no further cost. If the landlord turns down the new tenant and then sues you for lost rent, you can argue that the landlord acted unreasonably and that the landlord—not you—should absorb any losses.

In addition, in states that recognize the landlord's duty to mitigate damages, usually the landlord must make a good faith effort to fill the space. Some landlords claim to meet this duty by placing a few ads in the newspaper and listing the property with a real estate agent (why should they do more since you're still obligated?). You're better off to use your own efforts to find a new tenant if possible.

J. When You Need Professional Help

A basic lease that sticks to routine clauses like those listed earlier in this chapter and is written in clear English should be no problem to negotiate yourself. However, it still may be prudent to have a lawyer with small business experience look over the final draft of the lease before you sign it. A visit of one-half hour or less should be sufficient.

A real estate or small business expert may also be able to assist you. But make sure the person you check with doesn't stand to profit from putting the deal together—a circumstance that all but guarantees you won't get objective advice.

For nonroutine leases, seek assistance earlier in the game. You may need considerable help in negotiating and drafting some critical clauses. This may cost a few dollars, but compared to a confusing or landlord-slanted lease, a fair, well-drafted lease that contains the provisions you need is almost always a bargain.

For more on leases, see Leasing Space for Your Small Business, *by Janet Portman and Fred Steingold (Nolo);* Every Tenant's Legal Guide, *by Janet Portman and Marcia Stewart, (Nolo);* Every Landlord's Legal Guide, *by Marcia Stewart, Ralph Warner, and Janet Portman (Nolo); and* Leases & Rental Agreements, *by Marcia Stewart and Janet Portman (Nolo).* ■

CHAPTER

14

Home-Based Business

Ah, Home Sweet Home. Or is it Home Sweet Workplace? One of the major business trends is the dramatic increase in the number of consultants, artists, craftspeople, therapists, mail order specialists, professionals, and others who use their homes as a business base.

One reason for this trend is the amazing array of electronic equipment that makes it possible to be productive and in touch with the rest of the world without leaving the comforts of home. By investing in a computer, a copier, a fax, and an extra phone line or two, you can now duplicate conditions that until recently were practical only in leased commercial space.

But the upsurge in home-based businesses also reflects a new emphasis on the quality of life. Working at home gives you the chance to spend more time with your family, be more flexible in the hours that you work, and avoid the gridlock of the highway.

From a legal standpoint, a home-based business isn't much different from any other business. You still need to pick a business name; decide whether to be a sole proprietor or to form a partnership or corporation; purchase insurance; pay taxes; sign contracts; and collect from customers. But a few special legal issues are peculiar to the at-home business, including land use restrictions, insurance, and special tax provisions.

A. Zoning Laws

Planned communities and condominiums often have their own detailed rules affecting home-based businesses. Typically, these rules are stricter than local zoning ordinances. Skip ahead to Section B if your home is subject to these rules.

Is it legal to run a business in your home? The answer depends on where you live and what you do. To understand how this works, let's start with the case of Bob Mullin, (*Metropolitan Development Commission v. Mullin,* 339 N.E.2d 751 (Ind. App. 1979), whose plight made its way into the lawbooks.

Bob ran his insurance business from his two-bedroom home in Indianapolis. He thought he was on safe legal ground. After all, unlike in some cities, the local zoning ordinance allowed people to use their homes for "home occupations." As long as a home was used primarily as a residence, it could also be used for "professions and domestic occupations, crafts or services." The ordinance specifically allowed homes to be used for such occupations as law, medicine, dentistry, architecture, engineering, writing, painting, music lessons, and photography. Also, people could use their homes for such businesses as dressmaking, tailoring, hair grooming, washing, ironing, and cabinetmaking. So why not an insurance business?

Bob Mullin used his living room as a reception room and office, complete with a secretary's desk and filing cabinet. He put his own desk in the dining room in place of a dining room table. The photocopier stood in the kitchen next to the stove and refrigerator, and he converted one of the bedrooms into an office.

The zoning board took Bob to court, claiming he'd gone too far. The Indiana Court of Appeals agreed. The court ruled that it was okay for Bob to conduct an insurance business at home, but that Bob's usage was excessive. The business had taken over the house to the point that the primary use was no longer residential. The court told Bob to cut back or close down.

This case demonstrates but one of the many ways that local zoning ordinances can have a devastating effect on a home-based business. The good news is that by learning the law and using discretion, you may find that zoning isn't a real problem for your business.

1. How Zoning Ordinances Are Organized and Applied

Most cities have zoning ordinances. Areas outside of cities are usually covered by zoning ordinances adopted by county, village, or township governments.

Zoning ordinances come in many shapes and sizes, but they all do basically the same thing: they divide the area into districts in which various types of activities are allowed or prohibited. For example, there are usually residential districts for single-family and two-family homes and other districts for apartments. Other areas or zones are earmarked for commercial usage. Ordinances often break down the types of commercial usage; in some zoning districts, only offices or retail and service businesses are allowed. Usually some part of town is reserved for manufacturing operations, which are typically broken down into light and heavy industrial.

In some areas, more than one use is allowed in a district; for example, commercial and light industrial, or residential and commercial. Outside of cities, zones allow various types of agricultural activities.

Some zoning ordinances, especially in affluent areas, exclude home-based businesses. More commonly, zoning ordinances restrict—but don't prohibit—using a home for a business. An ordinance might say, for example, that in general you can't run a business from your home, but then go on to list several types of business that are permitted. The Indianapolis ordinance mentioned earlier specifically allowed professions such as law, medicine, and architecture, as well as painting, music lessons, and

photography. Some ordinances are vague, simply allowing "customary home occupations"—a term that must be interpreted by a judge if a given use is challenged.

Zoning ordinances that regulate home businesses frequently also limit:

- the amount of car and truck traffic
- outside signs
- on-street parking
- the number of employees
- the percentage of floor space devoted to the business.

It's not always easy to tell whether or not a particular business is allowed in a home under the zoning ordinance you're looking at. Some zoning ordinances were written years ago and don't adequately deal with many contemporary businesses that people wish to operate from home—especially sophisticated businesses that depend on high-tech communications equipment.

The level of enforcement varies widely. In more enlightened communities, zoning officials recognize that residential zoning is intended primarily to preserve the residential character of a neighborhood—not to prohibit low-profile businesses. Officials don't go out looking for violations but take their cues from the neighbors: If people living near a home-based business don't complain, why search for a possible technical violation? Even where it's clear that there's a violation, these officials work with the business owner to see whether changes can be made to make the business conform to the ordinance before ordering the owner to end the business or taking administrative or court action.

On the other hand, you may have the misfortune of living in a community that strictly enforces of all ordinances. If so, your home-based business may be at the mercy of fairly rigid bureaucrats—although, as we'll see, you may fight arbitrary or unreasonable action.

If municipal officials are determined to close down your home-based business, their first step is to write you a cease and desist letter. If you ignore this, you'll probably get another letter or two followed eventually by a misdemeanor prosecution (seeking a fine or, in an extreme case, a jail term) or a civil lawsuit requesting an injunction—a court order prohibiting future violations of the ordinance. If you violate such an injunction, the judge can fine you for contempt of court or even put you in jail.

2. Investigating Zoning Laws

Before setting up a home-based business, it's a good idea to learn not only what your local zoning ordinance provides but also to find out about enforcement attitudes. If you're in a strict enforcement community and you file for a local business license or tax permit, this may trigger an inquiry about whether you comply with the zoning ordinance. Talk to people who run other home-based businesses, local contractors, your city's business development office, small business advisors, and lawyers about how to make the fewest legal waves.

You may find yourself in a gray area. Your planned home-based business may or may not violate a vaguely worded local ordinance—for example, a computerized information searching business in an area that allows traditional home-based businesses. It's hard to predict whether the local zoning officials will take action against you or not.

One approach is to just go ahead and chance it. If you're simply planning to set up your desk and computer in an unused room in a home you already own, you have little to lose.

This approach is far less sensible if you plan to buy or renovate a house to accommodate your business. Before you spend a significant sum to house your business, you want assurance that you won't be closed down. It's best to approach the city, explain your plans, and ask for an official green light. If a purchase is involved, put a clause in your offer making the deal contingent on getting approval from the zoning authorities. Then, if your use isn't approved, you're free to cancel your purchase.

If you plan to operate out of your existing residence and decide that your business is doubtful legally, or that you could be closed down if the ordinance were strictly enforced, you can minimize the risks. Start by being a good neighbor. Make sure that your business has little if any impact on the people who live around you.

For example, if all you do is convert one room to an office equipped for a consulting business, it's unlikely that anyone will complain—as long as you have no employees and see only an occasional client or customer at your home. This is true even if you generate $1 million a year in gross income. You'll also be in a better position if you cleared your plans with your neighbors or if several of them also have home-based businesses.

What kinds of things are most likely to get you in trouble? Anything that a neighbor can see, hear, or smell outside of your home that causes inconvenience or smacks of a commercial venture. Increased traffic, parking problems, signs, outside storage of supplies, noises, or unpleasant odors emanating from your home—any of these can lead to neighborhood complaints. Pollution is another red flag.

EXAMPLE: A craftsman who worked at home with stained glass and even taught classes there was doing quite well until he started dumping lead-laced fluids down a storm drain. The neighbors properly insisted that the city attorney put him out of business.

Look for alternatives to frequent deliveries. *A daily procession of FedEx, UPS, and U.S. Post Office trucks making deliveries to your house can annoy the neighbors. Consider having mail and packages sent to a private mailbox service such as the one run by Mail Boxes Etc. or a similar operation—especially if there's one located nearby.*

Ted operates a business in his home helping nonlawyers prepare their own divorce and bankruptcy forms. Several customers come and go each day, often in the early evening and on Saturdays. One of Ted's neighbors, who has no idea of what Ted is doing, jumps to the conclusion that he's dealing drugs.

She calls a meeting of other neighbors and convinces the others that there can be no other explanation for all the coming and going. They complain to the police and zoning board. When the truth comes out, the police laugh and leave.

The zoning officials are another matter. They cite a local ordinance prohibiting businesses that generate traffic and tell Ted to close down. Eventually, when Ted gets all his chagrined neighbors to sign a statement saying a few cars a day aren't a problem, the zoning officials reverse their position.

Ted could have avoided this time-consuming, anxiety-producing process if he'd simply told folks what was going on when he began his business.

3. Dealing With Zoning Officials

Suppose you receive a complaint from the city. What steps can you take? Start by going to City Hall and talking to the person who administers the zoning law—someone in the Zoning or Planning Department. There are both practical and legal reasons for attempting to resolve zoning matters without filing a lawsuit. On the practical level, administrative (agency) relief is quicker, less expensive and often more flexible than a judicial solution. And the law usually requires you to pursue your available administrative solutions before you go to court; this is known in legal lingo as "exhausting your administrative remedies."

The kind of response you can hope for at City Hall depends greatly on community attitudes. If some home-based businesses are allowed, you clearly want to show that yours meets the spirit of the criteria for allowing businesses. Emphasize how small and unobtrusive your business is. When faced with the facts, the city may become more reasonable. Or you may be able to negotiate a settlement under which you scale down your operations. For example, you might agree to limit your business to weekdays from 8 a.m. to 5 p.m. and to provide off-street parking for your one employee.

If you can't negotiate with the city staff, there are more formal approaches. Most places have a planning or zoning board with power to grant exceptions (variances or conditional use permits) if compliance with an ordinance would cause unreasonable hardship. For example, a zoning board might allow a physically handicapped person to operate a therapy practice at home even though some traffic is generated.

The board may also have power to overturn a zoning official's interpretation of an ordinance. If you appeal to a local zoning or planning board, try to get neighbors to attend the hearing to speak on your behalf. If that is too inconvenient, ask as many neighbors as possible to write letters or sign a petition stating that they support your business use. Neighborhood support or opposition is likely to be crucial to the success or failure of your appeal. Also, come to the hearing with any photographs or documents that accurately show the nature and extent of your business.

In many cities, if you're turned down by a zoning or planning board or commission, you can appeal to a second board—often the city council itself. While it's less likely that you'll prevail at this level, it does happen.

Going beyond administrative channels, you may be able to get the zoning ordinance amended by the city council or county legislative body. For example, in some communities moves are afoot to change ordinances that allow "traditional home-based businesses" to include those based on the use of computer and other high-tech equipment—businesses that are unobtrusive, but hardly traditional.

To push through an ordinance change, you'll probably have to lobby some city council members or planning commissioners. You may also need to enlist the local chamber of commerce and other groups representing business people. With increased use of homes for businesses, the time may be ripe in your community for ordinance revisions of this sort. It's politically attractive to revamp an archaic ordinance to allow more home-based businesses, especially if the city is struggling with traffic and parking problems.

Also consider trying to get your property re-zoned. This works best if your home is on the edge of a commercial district. Ask the city to move the boundary line separating the two zoning districts so that your home falls within the commercial district—which, of course, would give you much greater latitude to run your business out of your home.

4. Going to Court

If you decide municipal officials are being unreasonable in attempting to close down your home-based business and you can't get administrative relief or an ordinance amendment, you may want to take the matter to court yourself—before the city starts a prosecution or requests an injunction. By acting first, you have a chance to frame the factual and legal issues more favorably, putting the municipality on the defensive.

At this stage, you'll probably need a lawyer's help; zoning cases are relatively complicated and specialized. Consulting and perhaps hiring a lawyer

who works in this area regularly will be well worth the fee. Make sure you find a lawyer who's familiar with zoning practices (see Chapter 24 for more on finding and working with lawyers). You needn't turn the whole case over to a lawyer—there's plenty you can do to organize support from neighbors and other home-based businesses as well as researching how courts have decided other similar cases.

You can assert several legal theories in a zoning lawsuit, including the following:

- The city's legal interpretation of its zoning ordinance was incorrect. For example, you might claim that your word processing business is a "home occupation" even though the zoning officials decided that it isn't. You'd ask the judge to issue a judgment declaring that your business does qualify as a home occupation.

EXAMPLE: Dr. William Brady lived in Beverly Hills, California. He wrote a syndicated column and, with the help of secretaries, mailed out 150,000 pamphlets a year from his home office. The city tried to close his business because the local zoning ordinance prohibited home businesses that involved the purchase or sale of materials for profit. But the court ruled that the doctor wasn't violating the zoning ordinance; sending out the pamphlets was basically the same as a person answering his or her mail. *City of Beverly Hills v. Brady,* 215 P.2d 460 (Cal. 1950).

- The ordinance is invalid because it violates the state statute (called an "enabling law") that gives cities authority to enact zoning ordinances. For example, you might claim that the zoning ordinance is invalid because it doesn't permit homeowners to have "reasonable accessory uses" or "home occupations" as required by the state enabling law.
- The ordinance is invalid because the city didn't use proper procedures in adopting or

enforcing it. For example, the city may not have held the necessary public hearings before it amended the zoning ordinance to prohibit certain types of home-based businesses.

- The authorities have acted in a discriminatory manner by enforcing the ordinance against you. For example, they've allowed similar home-based businesses for years but now have singled you out for special treatment.

You aren't limited to just one legal theory. Your lawsuit can allege as many theories as apply.

Lawsuits are expensive, but yours may be settled before there's a full-scale hearing or trial. The city may agree on an acceptable compromise to avoid the expense or inconvenience of fighting your lawsuit, or may not want to put its zoning ordinance in jeopardy just for the sake of closing down one in-home business.

B. Private Land Use Restrictions

Zoning ordinances are not the only source of potential problems for a home-based business. You must also check out private restrictions on your use of your home, condo, or co-op unit. Depending on the part of the country and the type of ownership arrangement, use restrictions commonly are found in the following documents:

- property deed (the restrictions are called "restrictive covenants")
- a subdivision's declaration of building and use restrictions or covenants, conditions, and restrictions (CC&Rs)
- planned unit development (PUD) rules
- condominium regulations
- co-op regulations
- leases.

Language in these and similar documents is likely to restrict or even prohibit business uses. If your residence is covered by a title insurance policy (virtually every piece of real estate is), use restrictions may be identified there. If you've lost your deed or your subdivision, condo, or co-op restrictions, get a copy from your association or go to the county office where title papers are recorded (usually the county recorder or register of deeds) and purchase a copy.

If your neighbors believe you're violating these restrictions, they may take action to stop you. Often—especially for condo, co-op, or PUD units—they can take you before an owners' association board empowered to enforce regulations. If you don't come into compliance, you may lose privileges and face other penalties. Beyond these private sanctions, your neighbors can take you to court and try to stop your business. Judges can be very strict in enforcing these private restrictions. Here are three real-life instances where a judge sided with the neighbors.

EXAMPLE 1: Salvador, a field manager for a brush manufacturer, supervised a staff of door-to-door salespeople and supplied them from his residence in Metairie, Louisiana. He interviewed prospective salespeople at his home and received stored merchandise in his garage. The court ruled that merely receiving samples wouldn't violate the restrictive covenants in the deed to Salvador's property. But Salvador had a problem because he used his home to hire and outfit new employees with samples stored at home. He wasn't using his home "for residential purposes only" as required by the restrictive covenants. *Woolley v. Cinquigranna,* 188 So.2d 701 (La. App. 1966).

EXAMPLE 2: Sheldon and Raye practiced psychotherapy in their home in Illinois. The subdivision restrictions covering their home said that "No lot shall be used except for single residential purposes." Their neighbors took them to court, claiming a violation of that restrictive rule. The judge ordered Sheldon and Raye to discontinue their professional use of their home even though the exterior appearance of the home as a single-family home hadn't been altered. *Wier v. Isenberg,* 420 N.E.2d 790 (Ill. App. 1981).

EXAMPLE 3: Myrtle operated a part-time beauty parlor in her Sunnyvale, California, home, receiving six customers per day. Myrtle didn't advertise her services, there was no external evidence of her business, and neighbors weren't inconvenienced. Still, the judge ruled that Myrtle violated the subdivision restriction that said "No lot shall be used except for residential purposes." *Biagini v. Hyde,* 3 Cal. App. 3d 877, 83 Cal. Rptr. 875 (Cal. App. 1970).

If you're taken to court, you have two main lines of defense. The first is that your neighbors or the condo association are misinterpreting the restrictions and that your business use is allowable. Second, if the neighbors did not object to prior business uses, they have, in legal effect, waived the right to do so now. In other words, their inaction in the past has nullified the restrictions.

Judges are often sympathetic to homeowners seeking to enjoy the use of their property. If neighbors have been lax or the restriction is vague, you have a good chance of getting a favorable ruling if your business use doesn't really hurt your neighbors or change the residential character of your neighborhood. On the other hand, if the legal restrictions are tightly drafted and your neighbors acted swiftly to enforce them whenever a violation came to their attention, even a sympathetic judge won't be able to help you.

But slugging it out in court should be a last resort. If you're both dogged and diplomatic, you may be able to find a way to operate your home-based business. Look first at the rule to see how restrictive it is. Some specifically allow certain types of home-based businesses while others simply adopt the standard in your municipality's zoning ordinance (see Section A, above), which in turn may be fairly permissive. If you don't qualify under the rules, consider trying to change them. Other people in

your subdivision may also feel they are too restrictive. Often the document creating restrictive covenants says that restrictions can be changed if a certain number—say 70%—of the homeowners in the subdivision agree. Similarly, condo regulations can often be changed by agreement of a specified number of owners.

Leases. If you live in a rented house or apartment, read your lease carefully. Your landlord may have the right to evict you if you use the premises for business. It's best to get clearance in advance and have it written into the lease. Most landlords won't care if you use the property partly for business as long as you don't cause any damage or create any problems with your neighbors.

C. Insurance

Chapter 12 discusses insurance coverage for small businesses. The same general principles apply to home-based businesses, but there are also some special considerations you should be aware of.

Never rely exclusively on your normal homeowner's policy. If you do, bad things can happen:

- After your computer is stolen, you may find out that it's not covered by your homeowner's policy because business property is excluded.
- After your house burns down, you may find that the fire coverage is void because you didn't disclose your business use to the insurance company.
- After the UPS delivery person slips on your front porch and breaks his back, you may find you're not covered for injuries associated with business deliveries.

It's easy to avoid these nasty surprises. Sit down with your insurance agent and fully disclose your planned business operations. It's relatively inexpensive to add riders to your homeowner's policy to cover normal business risks. You may need separate policies for other business-related coverage.

When it comes to business equipment and furnishings, figure out how much it would cost for replacements after a fire, theft, or other disaster. Don't overlook things such as the specialized business software you run on your computer. Depending on the nature of your business, replacing equipment and furniture could run into many thousands of dollars. Ask your insurance agent what it takes to insure this valuable property, allowing for a good-sized deductible to keep costs down. (See Chapter 12, Section E, on how to buy affordable insurance.) Make sure that the coverage on equipment and furnishings is for the full replacement cost—not just the depreciated value, as can be the case in some homeowner's policies.

Your homeowner's policy also may not adequately protect you from liability to business visitors. Accidents—such as people getting hurt when they trip and fall—are more likely to happen at home than in a well-planned office building. Your homeowner's policy probably protects you if you're sued by a social guest or someone at your home for a nonbusiness purpose—a florist's truck driver delivering flowers or the meter reader who's checking on gas usage. But it may not cover a business associate, employee, customer, or delivery person who is injured on your property.

Some home-based businesses need special kinds of insurance. If you render professional services, look into professional liability insurance. If you manufacture, distribute, or sell products that may hurt someone, think about product liability insurance. Also, if you have employees, you'll need to provide workers' compensation coverage. (All this is covered in Chapter 12.)

If you do some business away from your home, be sure that your car insurance covers injuries that occur while you're on business errands. And see about the extent of your general liability coverage if you should accidentally injure someone or damage their property while away from home on business. You may need a rider or special policy to cover this risk. The Insurance Information Institute reports that many insurance companies are offering such riders for less than $200.

Policies to cover both your home and home business. *Several insurance companies have developed special policies that cover both your home and a business run from your home. Typically, these policies cover your computer equipment and other business property—whether used in your house or elsewhere—and protect you from business liability lawsuits and loss of income. These policies can be less expensive than either adding riders to your home insurance or buying separate policies for home and business. But check the coverage carefully, as these policies tend to primarily address home offices and may not adequately insure you if, for example, you're a small manufacturer or a wholesaler who stores inventory in the basement.*

Operating as a separate entity can affect your insurance coverage. *While the typical home-based business is organized as a sole proprietorship or partnership, you may have organized yours as a corporation or an LLC to get the benefit of limited personal liability. That's fine, but remember that your homeowner's policy—even if it has riders—insures you personally and may not insure a separate business entity. This can present a coverage problem if your corporation owns the $3,000 computer that gets stolen or the delivery person falls down your front stairs while delivering an overnight letter to your LLC. Check with your insurance agent or broker to make sure your business entity is covered in the insurance policy—as well as yourself. It's usually just a simple matter to have your business added as an insured party.*

D. Deducting Expenses for Business Use of Your Home

You may be able to take a tax deduction for business use of your home. The deduction is available not only for a home office but for other business uses as well, such as a workshop or studio at home.

Basically, if you meet the technical requirements of the tax law, you can deduct the cost of utilities, rent, depreciation, home insurance, and repairs when you use part of your home for business. For a detailed explanation, see IRS Publication 587, *Business Use of Your Home,* which also spells out the limitations on the amount you can deduct. It's available online at www.irs.gov.

Keep in mind that whether or not you can deduct expenses that relate specifically to your home, such as rent, utilities, home insurance, and repairs, you can still take a deduction for regular business expenses, such as photocopies, stationery, paper clips, wages, travel, equipment, professional memberships, and publications. (See Chapter 8.) You can also deduct the cost of long-distance calls you make from home and a separate phone line used for business calls.

According to the IRS, your "home" can be a house, condo, or apartment unit—or even a mobile home or boat. But wherever you live, before you can deduct expenses for using part of your home as a business, you must meet two tax law requirements.

Requirement #1: You must regularly use part of your home exclusively for a trade or business (see Section 1).

Requirement #2: You must be able to show that:
- you use your home as your principal place of business (see Section 2), or
- you meet patients, clients, or customers at home (see Section 3), or
- you use a separate structure on your property exclusively for business purposes (see Section 4).

For more coverage of tax issues for home-based businesses: *See* Tax Savvy for Small Business, *by Frederick W. Daily (Nolo) and* Home Business Tax Deductions: Keep What You Earn, *by Stephen Fishman (Nolo).*

1. Regular and Exclusive Use

The first requirement for taking deductions related to your home is that you regularly use part of your home exclusively for a trade or business. The notion of regular use is a bit vague. The IRS says it means you're using a part of your home for business on a continuing basis—not just for occasional or incidental business. A few hours a day on most days is probably enough to meet this test.

Exclusive use means that you use a portion of your home only for business. If you use part of your home for your business and also use it for personal purposes, you don't meet the exclusive use test.

> **EXAMPLE:** Brook, a lawyer, uses a den in his home to write legal briefs and prepare contracts. He also uses the den for poker games, watching TV, and hosting a book club. Result: Brook can't claim business deductions for using the den.

Ways to Document Your Home-Business Deduction

Here are some steps you can take to help establish your legal right to deduct home-related business expenses.
- Photograph your home office and draw a diagram showing the location of the office in your home.
- Have your business mail sent to your home.
- Use your home address on your business cards and stationery and in all business ads.
- Get a separate phone line for the business.
- Have clients or customers visit your home office—and keep a log of those visits.
- Keep track of the time you spend working at home.

2. Principal Place of Business

In addition to using part of your home regularly and exclusively for business (see Section 1), to take deductions relating to your home, your home must be your "principal place of business"—or, alternatively, if your home isn't your principal place of business, you can qualify for the deduction if you meet clients or customers at home (see Section 3) or if you use a separate structure on your property exclusively for business purposes (see Section 4).

Establishing that your home is your principal place of business is simple if you have only one type of business and conduct it only at home. It gets more complicated if you have several businesses or conduct a business from more than one location.

The IRS says that you can have a principal place of business for each trade or business in which you engage. This means that if you use your home for a part-time enterprise, it may qualify as a "principal place of business" for that business.

> **EXAMPLE:** Alma teaches school. As a teacher, her principal place of business is the school where she teaches. She also runs a public relations consulting company and uses a part of her home as the headquarters for that business; her expenses for this business use of the home should be deductible.

If you have more than one business location, including your home, for a single trade or business, you must figure out whether your home is your principal place of business for that enterprise. Again, if it isn't, you can't take a deduction for the business use of your home.

Your home qualifies as your principal place of business if:

- you conduct the administrative or management activities of your business there, and
- you have no other fixed location where you conduct those activities.

Your home doesn't have to be the place where you generate most of your business income. It's enough that you regularly use it to do such things as keeping your books, scheduling appointments, doing research, and ordering supplies. As long as you have no other fixed location where you do such things—for example, an outside office—you can take the deduction.

> **EXAMPLE:** Ellen, a wallpaper installer, performs services for clients in their homes and offices. She also has a home office which she uses regularly and exclusively to keep her books, arrange appointments, and order supplies. Ellen is entitled to deduct expenses for that part of her home.

⚠️ **Home-connected expenses.** *As noted earlier, the IRS rules discussed in this chapter apply only to home-connected expenses such as utilities, rent, depreciation, home insurance, and repairs. You needn't conform to these rules in order to deduct other business expenses. If you have a bona fide business and don't qualify for deducting home-connected expenses, you can still deduct many other business expenses—for example, the cost of supplies, postage, advertising, and long-distance phone calls.*

3. Meeting Clients or Customers at Home

If your home isn't your principal place of business, you may still be entitled to deduct expenses for business use of your home if you regularly use part of your home exclusively to meet with clients, customers, or patients. Doing so even one or two days a week is probably sufficient. You can use the business space for other business purposes as well—doing bookkeeping, for example, or other business paperwork—but you'll lose the deduction if you use the space for personal purposes, such as watching movie DVDs.

EXAMPLE: Julie, an accountant, works three days a week in her downtown office and two days a week in her suburban home office, which she uses only for business. She meets clients at her home office at least once a week. Since Julie regularly meets clients at her home office, she can take a home office deduction. This is so even though her downtown office is her principal place of business.

Keep a log of the clients or customers you meet at home. *Good records can be key if the IRS challenges your right to deduct home-related business expenses. Maintain an appointment book in which you carefully note the name of the client or customer and the date and time of each meeting at your home. Save these books for at least three years; they can be crucial to documenting business usage if your tax return is audited by the IRS.*

4. Using a Separate Building for Your Business

If your home isn't your principal place of business, and you don't meet clients or customers at home, you can deduct expenses for a separate, freestanding structure that you use regularly and exclusively for your business.

This might be a studio or a converted garage or barn, for example. The structure doesn't have to be your principal place of business or a place where you meet patients, clients, or customers. But be sure you use the structure only for your business: you can't store garden supplies there or, at least in theory, even use it for the monthly meeting of your investment club.

EXAMPLE: Norm is a self-employed landscape architect. He has his main office in a professional center near a shopping mall, but most weekends he works in his home office, which is located in a converted carriage house in his backyard. Since Norm uses the carriage house regularly and exclusively for his landscape architect work, it qualifies for the home office deduction.

Storing Inventory or Product Samples at Home

If you sell retail or wholesale products and you store inventory or samples at home, you can deduct expenses for the business use of your home. There are two limitations, however: First, you won't qualify for the deduction if you have an office or other business location away from your home. Second, you have to store the products in a particular place—your garage, for example, or a closet or bedroom. It's okay to use the storage space for other purposes as well, as long as you regularly use it for inventory or samples.

EXAMPLE: Jim sells heating and air conditioning filters to small businesses. His home is the only fixed location of his business. Jim regularly stores his inventory of filters in half of his basement. He sometimes uses the storage area for working on his racing bikes. Jim can deduct the expenses for the storage space even though he doesn't use that part of his basement exclusively for business.

5. Amount of Deduction

If you meet the tests for deducting expenses for business use of your home, you need to figure out how much you can deduct. The tax law lets you deduct only a portion of your home expenses—not 100%. Begin by determining how much of your home you use for business. There are two common methods for doing this.

Square-Footage Method. Divide the number of square feet of space used for your business by the total number of square feet in your home. For example, if your home contains 1,200 square feet and you use 240 square feet for your business, then your business percentage is 20%.

Number of Rooms Method. If the rooms in your home are about the same size, figure the business percentage by dividing the number of rooms used for business by the number of rooms in the home. If you use one room in a four-room home for business, then 25% of the total area is used for business.

The deduction for business use of your home has several components. Using the percentage arrived at by either of the above methods, you can deduct from your gross income the business portion of:

- your rent, if you rent your home, or
- depreciation, mortgage interest, and property taxes on your house, if you own your home —although you may prefer to deduct all of your mortgage interest and property taxes as part of your itemized personal deductions.

In addition, as either an owner or renter, you may deduct this same percentage of other expenses for keeping up and running an entire home. The IRS calls these *indirect expenses.*

They include:

- utility expenses for electricity, gas, and heating oil
- service expenses for snow removal and trash pick-up
- homeowner's or renter's insurance

- home maintenance expenses that benefit your entire home, such as roof and furnace repair and exterior painting
- casualty losses if your home is damaged—for example, in a storm
- security system maintenance.

You may also deduct the entire cost of expenses you incur for the part of the house you use for business. The IRS calls these *direct expenses.* They include, for example, painting your home's business area or paying someone to clean it. If you pay a housekeeper to clean your entire house, you may deduct your business percentage of the expense.

EXAMPLE: Rudy rents a 1,600-square-foot apartment and uses a 400-square-foot bedroom as a home office for his newsletter publishing business. His percentage of business use is 25% (400 divided by 1,600). He pays $12,000 in annual rent and has a $1,200 utility bill for the year. He also spends $200 to paint his home office. Rudy can deduct 25% of his rent and utilities and 100% of the painting expenses, allowing him to write off a total of $3,500.

 You're always able to deduct the normal business expenses not associated with your home use. *Remember that this section addresses only the expenses you can deduct for business use of your home. As discussed earlier, whether or not you qualify for or take a home-business deduction, you're able to claim as business expenses—and deduct from gross income—the cost of such items as supplies, postage, long-distance charges, and so on. You don't need to qualify to take deductions for your business use of your home in order to write off these items. And you can also depreciate or expense (under Section 179) the cost of office furniture, computers, copiers, and other tangible property you use for your business and keep at home.*

New rules affect home-business owners who sell the home. *The IRS has changed the rules for what happens if you sell a home that you've been using, in part, for your business. In the past, there was a tax trap if you took a home office deduction for more than three of the past five years before selling the home; you had to pay capital gains taxes on part of the profit. For example, let's say your home office occupied 20% of the house. If you sold the house for a $50,000 profit, you'd owe tax on $10,000 of your profits (20% x $50,000 = $10,000).*

That's no longer the case. Now, if you live in your home for at least two of the five years before you sell it, the profit you make on the sale—up to $250,000 for single taxpayers and $500,000 for married tax-payers—isn't taxable. (See IRS Publication 523, Selling Your Home).

You will, however, have to pay a capital gains tax on any depreciation deductions you took after May 6, 1997 for your home office. These are the deductions you may have taken each year for the decline in value due to wear and tear on the business part of your home. The IRS taxes these "recaptured" deductions at a 25% rate (unless your income tax bracket is lower than 25%). As Stephen Fishman points out in Home Business Tax Deductions: Keep What You Earn *(Nolo), this may not be a bad deal. The tax is probably no more—and is often less— than the tax you'd have paid if you didn't take the depreciation deductions and, instead, paid tax on your additional taxable income at ordinary income tax rates.*

- • Working From Home, *by Paul and Sarah Edwards (Jeremy P. Tarcher Inc.). This encyclopedic volume by the reigning gurus of home-based businesses covers everything from how to live with computers, faxes, and voicemail to juggling family, friends, children, and work.*
- • The Home Office and Small Business Answer Book, *by Janet Attard (Owl Books). Using a reader-friendly question-and-answer format, this hefty book guides you through such essential issues as how to find customers, manage your home-based business, and—most important of all—get paid.* ■

Employees and Independent Contractors

This chapter deals with how to hire and fire employees and how to comply with laws that affect them. We'll also look at hiring independent contractors, instead of employees, for certain tasks.

As we go through the technical legal rules for hiring and firing, don't lose sight of three even more important concepts:

- hire qualified people
- treat them well, and
- create a workplace where employers and employees cheerfully combine their energies for the common good.

 Chapter 9 of _Legal Forms for Starting & Running a Small Business_ contains forms for hiring employees and independent contractors.

For an in-depth treatment of your legal obligations: _See_ The Employer's Legal Handbook, _by Fred S. Steingold (Nolo)._

A. Hiring Employees

You can steer clear of most of the legal perils of hiring employees by following the guidelines outlined below.

1. Avoid Illegal Discrimination

Federal and state laws prohibit you from discriminating against an applicant or employee because of race, color, gender, religious beliefs, national origin, physical disability—or age if the person is 40 years old or older. Also, many states and cities have laws prohibiting employment discrimination based on marital status, sexual orientation, and a variety of other characteristics.

But antidiscrimination laws don't dictate whom you must hire. You remain free to hire, promote, discipline, and fire employees and to set their salaries based on their skills, experience, performance, and reliability.

Some illegal practices should be obvious, such as advertising a job for people ages 20 to 30 only—which on its face violates age discrimination laws—or paying lower wages to women than men for the same work in violation of equal pay laws. But more subtly, antidiscrimination laws also can bar employment practices that seem innocent but end up having a disproportionate and discriminatory impact on certain groups. For example, if your main means of seeking candidates is through word of mouth and your workforce consists entirely of white men, the word-of-mouth recruitment can be illegal discrimination if it produces only white male applicants.

To avoid violating antidiscrimination laws at the hiring stage:

- advertise job openings in widely read newspapers so they come to the attention of diverse people
- determine the skills, education, and other attributes that are truly necessary to perform the job so that you don't impose requirements that unnecessarily exclude capable applicants, and
- avoid screening techniques that have an unfair impact on any group of applicants.

2. Respect the Applicant's Privacy Rights

While it's wise to screen potential employees, there's a potential problem in mounting intensive background checks. Your attempt to assess applicants by gathering information about their past can conflict with their right to privacy. Before you send for high school or college transcripts and credit reports, obtain the applicant's written consent. If the applicant won't consent, you're free to drop him or her from further consideration—as long as you follow that policy with all applicants.

3. Avoid False Job Security Promises

Employees have no legal rights to their jobs. This harkens back to a doctrine holding that an employee's continued employment is at the will or discretion of the employer, meaning that the employer can fire the employee at any time for any reason—or for no reason at all—absent a written or implied contract guaranteeing a fixed term of employment. The flip side is that the employee is free to quit at any time.

Of course, the at-will employment doctrine doesn't free you from complying with antidiscrimination laws. You can't fire someone for an illegal reason—because of the color of the employee's skin, for example, or because you prefer to put a younger person in the job.

The at-will relationship gives you considerable freedom to fire employees, but it may take some planning to preserve that freedom. One reason for this is that courts in many states have ruled that as a result of promises made at an employment interview or in an employee handbook, an employer has implied that an employee has a long-term work contract and will be fired only if there's a good reason such as poor performance or excessive absenteeism. Fortunately, if you follow commonsense business practices, you normally can retain a great deal of control over the firing process.

Don't give an applicant or employee any long-term assurances about employment that you may not be able to honor. Make sure your application forms, employee handbooks, and offers of employment state that the job is at will and that oral statements can't act as a binding contract. Have the applicant acknowledge this in writing. Then you'll have an excellent chance of choosing whether and when to fire an employee on your own terms and without legal repercussions.

Full disclosure in hiring. *Recent legal developments indicate that in some circumstances you may have some legal responsibility to provide new employees with some measure of job security even if your employee handbook and other written statements say there is none. Specifically, if you're encouraging an applicant to leave an existing job or to move to your city from elsewhere, some courts have ruled that you have an affirmative duty to disclose negative information about the future of your business. Failure to do so may allow an employee who suffers adverse consequences from your failure to tell the whole truth to sue and recover damages. For example, if your business is in shaky financial shape or you're planning to downsize and eliminate many jobs, it's your responsibility to tell job candidates about it before they leave their presently secure jobs or move from New York to Los Angeles to work for you. Be especially forthright if you're already planning or considering eliminating the position you're hiring for.*

4. Prevent Negligent Hiring Claims

You have a legal duty to protect your customers, clients, visitors, and the general public from injuries caused by employees who may harm others. When you hire someone for a position that may expose customers or others to danger, you must use special care in checking references and making other background checks. If someone gets hurt or has property stolen or damaged by an employee whose background you didn't check carefully, you can be sued for negligent hiring.

Be especially vigilant when hiring maintenance workers and delivery drivers, whose jobs give them easy access to homes and apartments.

If you hire people for sensitive jobs, investigate their backgrounds as thoroughly as possible and look for any criminal convictions. If an employee will be driving, make sure he or she is currently licensed and has a decent driving record. And where state laws require an occupational license—for asbestos removal, for example, or tending bar—check to see that the applicant is properly licensed.

Contact all previous employers. Insist that the applicant explain any gaps in employment history. Consider turning over the prehire investigation to professionals with experience in screening job applicants.

To learn more about negligent hiring cases: *See* Employer's Guide to Workplace Torts, *by Ronald M. Green and Richard J. Reibstein (Bureau of National Affairs).*

5. Protect Against Unfair Competition

Employees sometimes leave to start a competing business or go to work for a competitor. Obviously, you needn't be too concerned about the employee you hire to scoop ice cream or the clerk you hire to work behind the counter at your dry cleaning shop. But employees who have access to inside information about product pricing or business expansion plans, for example, may pose competitive risks. The same goes for employees who handle valuable and hard-won customers—a salesperson, perhaps, who handles a $200,000 account.

Consider asking new hires to sign agreements not to take or disclose trade secrets or other confidential information. Also, you might ask selected employees to sign covenants not to compete with your business. (See Subsection b.)

a. Trade Secrets

Some business owners need to protect their unique assets from misuse—assets such as:

- a restaurant's recipes for a special salad dressing
- muffins that draw people from miles around
- a heating and cooling company's list of 500 customers for whom it regularly provides maintenance, or
- a computer company's unique process for speedily assembling computer boards.

If they are treated as such, the recipes, the customer list, and the assembly process are all trade secrets. Other examples are an unpatented invention, engineering techniques, cost data, a formula, or a machine. To qualify for trade secret protection, the business information you seek to protect must meet two requirements:

(1) The information must truly be secret.
The information must not be freely available from other sources. If the recipe for a restaurant's award-winning custard tart can be found in a standard American cookbook or recreated by a competent chef, it isn't a trade secret. On the other hand, if the restaurant's chef found the recipe in a medieval French cookbook in a provincial museum, translated it and figured out how to adapt it to currently available ingredients, it probably would be considered obscure enough to receive trade secret protection. That's because the recipe isn't available to other American restaurants.

(2) You must have protected the secrecy.
You must show that you've taken steps to keep the information secret—for example, by:

- keeping it in a secure place such as a locked cabinet
- giving employees access to it on a need-to-know basis, and
- having employees acknowledge in writing that the information is a trade secret.

EXAMPLE: Sue works at Speedy Copy Shop. She has daily access to the list of larger accounts that are regularly billed more than $2,000 per month. She quits to open her own shop. Before she does, she copies the list of major accounts. One of her first steps in getting her new business going is to try to get their business away from her former employer. Speedy sues Sue for infringing on its trade secret. At trial, Speedy shows that it keeps the list in a secure place, permits access only to selected employees who need the information, and has all employees—including Sue—sign nondisclosure agreements. In light of these precautions, the judge orders Sue not to contact the customers on the list and requires her to compensate Speedy from any profits she's already earned on those accounts.

b. Covenants Not to Compete

It's always disappointing and often quite costly when a high-level employee leaves your business and begins competing with you—especially if you've trained the employee and shared valuable, inside information. Consider having high-level employees sign a covenant not to compete. In a typical covenant, the employee agrees not to own or work in a business that competes with yours for a specific time and within a specific distance from your established business.

The best time to secure a covenant not to compete is when you hire an employee. An employee who is already on the payroll may be more reluctant to sign anything—and you'll have less leverage to negotiate the agreement.

Battles over the legality of these agreements must usually be resolved in court. Judges are reluctant to deprive people of their rights to earn a living, so the key to a legally enforceable covenant not to compete is to make its terms reasonable. Focus on three questions.

- **Is there a legitimate business reason for restricting activities of the particular employee?** There probably is if you expect to spend significant time and money training a high-level employee and plan to trust him or her with sensitive contacts or lucrative accounts.
- **Is the covenant reasonably limited in time?** Courts tend to favor short covenants—the shorter the better. A one-year covenant may be reasonable for a particular employee. A three-year limit might not be.
- **Is the covenant reasonably limited as to geographical scope?** For a local business, a 50-mile limit or one that excludes competition in a few counties may be reasonable. For a regional business, a limit spanning several states may be deemed reasonable.

EXAMPLE: When Mary hires Sid to be the office manager for her profitable travel agency, she realizes that Sid will have access to major corporate accounts and daily contact with the corporate managers who make travel arrangements. Mary also knows that she'll spend considerable time in training Sid and invest more than $4,000 in specialized seminars that she'll require Sid to attend. She has Sid sign a covenant not to compete, in which Sid promises that while working for Mary and for two years afterwards, he won't work for or own a travel agency within 50 miles of Mary's agency. After six months, Sid quits and starts a competing agency one mile from Mary's. The judge enforces the covenant not to compete by issuing an injunction forbidding Sid from operating his new business and by awarding damages to Mary as well.

 Computers may defeat geographical limits. *As the travel and other industries begin doing more business through computer linkups, geographical limits will become a less effective way to control competition by former employees. Through computer technology, a former worker may be able to compete with you from halfway across the country.*

 For a guide on creating noncompete covenants for your employees to sign: *See* How to Create a Noncompete Agreement, *by Shannon Miehe (Nolo).*

B. Job Descriptions

Write a job description for each position. This will make the hiring process more objective, which in turn will reduce the possibility that you can be successfully accused of discrimination. Focus on qualifications, such as necessary skills, education, experience, and licensure.

Be careful in setting requirements for education and experience. If set at an unnecessarily high level, your requirements may have the unintended effect of excluding a disproportionate number of racial minorities or other applicants who are part of other groups protected by antidiscrimination laws. Requiring a high school diploma or college degree may be discriminatory in some job categories because members of some minority groups are less likely than members of the general population to have completed high school or college. To require evidence of educational attainment may create an unnecessary barrier to getting a job. Of course, in many cases, a diploma, degree, certificate, or license is a legitimate requirement because the job requires more than basic skills.

Also, specify the essential job functions. The Americans with Disabilities Act (ADA) forces you to decide what really is the core of each job so you don't exclude someone simply because he or she can't perform some marginal duties. Suppose your job description for a file clerk includes answering the phone, but the basic functions of the job are to file and retrieve written materials. Other employees usually answer the phone. Someone whose hearing is impaired may have trouble handling phone calls but be perfectly able to file and retrieve papers. Phone answering isn't an essential job function and shouldn't be listed as one.

C. Job Advertisements

After you write a job description, summarize it in a job advertisement. Be careful, because nuances in an ad can be used as evidence of discrimination against applicants of a particular gender, age, or marital status.

There are a number of semantic pitfalls to avoid in job ads.

Don't Use	Use
Salesman	Salesperson
College Student	Part-time Worker
Handyman	General Repair Person
Gal Friday	Office Manager
Married Couple	Two-Person Job
Counter Girl	Retail Clerk
Waiter	Wait staff
Young	Energetic

In any ad, stick to the job skills needed and the basic responsibilities. Some examples:

"Fifty-unit apartment complex seeks experienced manager with general maintenance skills."

"Midsized manufacturing company has opening for accountant with tax experience to oversee interstate accounts."

"Cook trainee position available in new vegetarian restaurant. Flexible hours."

D. Job Applications

Develop a standard application form to make it easy to compare applicants. Use the form to let the jobseeker know the basic terms and conditions of the job. Because the applicant signs the application, it can be a valuable piece of evidence if a question comes up later about what you actually promised.

You can also use the job application to obtain the employee's consent to have you conduct a background investigation and reference check. If the applicant consents to your investigation, he or she will have a tough time later claiming an invasion of privacy. (See Section G.)

Limit the form to job-related information that will help you decide who's the best person for the job. Consider requesting the following information:

- Name, address, and phone number
- Are you legally entitled to work in the United States?
- What position are you applying for?
- What other positions would you like to be considered for?
- Can you work overtime?
- If you are hired, when can you start work?
- Education—high school, college, graduate, and other (including school names, addresses, number of years attended, degree, and major)
- Employment history—including name, address, and phone number of each employer, supervisor's name, date of employment, job title and responsibilities, and reason for leaving, and
- Special training or achievements.

If the job involves handling money or calling on customers at home, ask whether the applicant has ever been convicted of a crime and the details of the conviction. Similarly, in an application for a job which requires driving, ask about the applicant's driving record.

1. Preemployment Inquiries

The chart below outlines the type of information you can ask for in applications and during job interviews as specified in federal laws. The chart may also be sufficient for complying with the laws of your state, but double check with your state's civil rights department.

In addition to the areas covered in the chart, the Americans with Disabilities Act (ADA) prohibits you from asking any preemployment questions about a disability—including medical history or treatment—or requiring a medical exam. However, before you make a job offer, you may ask questions about an applicant's ability to perform specific job functions.

PREEMPLOYMENT INQUIRIES

SUBJECT	LAWFUL PREEMPLOYMENT INQUIRIES	UNLAWFUL PREEMPLOYMENT INQUIRIES
Name	Applicant's full name. Have you ever worked for this company under a different name? Is any additional information relative to a different name necessary to check work record? If yes, explain.	Original name of an applicant whose name has been changed by court order or otherwise. Applicant's maiden name.
Address or Duration of Residence	How long have you been a resident of this state or city?	
Birthplace	None	Birthplace of applicant. Birthplace of applicant's parents, spouse, or other close relatives. Requirements that applicant submit birth certificate, naturalization, or baptismal record.
Age	Are you 18 years old or older? This question may be asked only for the purpose of determining whether applicants are of legal age for employment.	How old are you? What is your date of birth?
Religion or Creed	None	Inquiry into an applicant's religious denomination, religious affiliations, church, parish, pastor, or religious holidays observed.
Race or Color	None	Inquiry regarding applicant's race, complexion, or color of skin.
Photograph	None	Any requirement for a photograph prior to hire.
Height	None	Inquiry regarding applicant's height.
Weight	None	Inquiry regarding applicant's weight.
Marital Status	Is your spouse employed by this employer?	Requirement that an applicant provide any information regarding marital status or children. Are you single or married? Do you have any children? Is your spouse employed? What is your spouse's name?
Gender	None	Mr., Miss, Ms., or Mrs. or an inquiry regarding gender. Inquiry as to the ability to reproduce or advocacy of any form of birth control. Requirement that women be given pelvic examinations.

PREEMPLOYMENT INQUIRIES (continued)

SUBJECT	LAWFUL PREEMPLOYMENT INQUIRIES	UNLAWFUL PRE-EMPLOYMENT INQUIRIES
Disability	These [*provide applicant with list*] are the essential functions of the job. How would you perform them?	Inquiries regarding an individual's physical or mental condition which are not directly related to the requirements of a specific job and which are used as a factor in making employment decisions in a way which is contrary to the provisions or purposes of the Civil Rights Act.
Citizenship	Are you legally authorized to work in the United States on a full-time basis?	Questions below are unlawful unless asked as part of the federal I-9 process. Of what country are you a citizen? Whether an applicant is naturalized or a native-born citizen; the date when the applicant acquired citizenship. Requirement that an applicant produce naturalization papers or first papers. Whether applicant's parents or spouse are naturalized or native-born citizens of the United States: the date when such parent or spouse acquired citizenship.
National Origin	Inquiry into language applicant speaks and writes fluently.	Inquiry into applicant's lineage; ancestry; national origin; descent; parentage, or nationality (unless part of I-9 process). Nationality of applicant's parents or spouse. Inquiry into how applicant acquired ability to read, write, or speak a foreign language.
Education	Inquiry into the academic, vocational, or professional education of an applicant and public and private schools attended.	
Experience	Inquiry into work experience. Inquiry into countries applicant has visited.	
Arrests	Have you ever been convicted of a crime? Are there any felony charges pending against you?	Inquiry regarding arrests which did not result in conviction. (Except for law enforcement agencies.)
Relatives	Names of applicant's relatives already employed by this company.	Address of any relative of applicant, other than address (within the United States) of applicant's father and mother, husband or wife, and minor dependent children.
Notice in Case of Emergency	Name and address of person to be notified in case of accident or emergency.	Name and address of nearest relative to be notified in case of accident or emergency.
Organizations	Inquiry into the organizations of which an applicant is a member, excluding organizations the name or character of which indicates the race, color, religion, national origin, or ancestry of its members.	List all clubs, societies, and lodges to which you belong.

Source: *The Employer's Legal Handbook*, by Fred Steingold (Nolo).

2. Postoffer Inquiries

After you make a conditional job offer, you're free to gather more details on health matters. You can at that point require a medical exam or ask health-related questions—but only if you require this for all candidates who receive conditional offers in the same job category.

E. Interviews

Before interviewing applicants for a job opening, write a set of questions focusing on the job duties as listed in the job description (see Section B) and the applicant's skills and experience. Some examples:

"Tell me about your experience in running a mailroom."

"How much experience did you have making cold calls on your last job?"

"Explain how you typically go about organizing your workday."

"Have any of your jobs required strong leadership skills?"

By writing down the questions and sticking to the same format for all interviews for the position, you reduce the risk that a rejected applicant will later complain about unequal treatment.

During an interview, focus on job requirements and company policies. Suppose you're concerned that an applicant with young kids may spend too much time talking with them on the phone. You can't ask: "Do you have children?" or "Who watches the kids when you're at work?"

But you can say to the applicant: "We don't allow personal phone calls during work hours. Do you have a problem with that?" The applicant then knows the ground rules and will let you know if a problem exists. Just make sure you apply your phone policy to all employees.

For additional suggestions on interviewing: *See* Stay Out of Court: The Manager's Guide to Preventing Employee Lawsuits, *by Rita Risser (Prentice-Hall).*

F. Testing

Testing job applicants—which can include skills testing, aptitude testing, honesty testing, medical testing, and drug testing—is most common in larger businesses. But even if your business is small or midsized, you may have needs you feel could best be met by testing. If so you should know the legal limitations.

1. Skills Tests

Most small businesses—especially new ones—operate on a slim profit margin and need to know that employees will be up to speed from day one. If you're hiring a computer operator, you may want to test the applicant for speed and accuracy in entering information. If you're hiring a person to be a clerk in your bookstore, you may want to test the applicant's knowledge of literature. If you're hiring a driver for a delivery van, a road test would be appropriate—and a cooking test for a chef is quite reasonable. As long as the skills you're testing for are genuinely related to job duties, a skills test is generally legal.

2. Aptitude Tests

Few small employers are tempted to use written tests to get additional insight into an applicant's abilities or psyche. That's fortunate, because these tests are usually a poor idea. A written aptitude test may discriminate illegally against minority applicants because it really reflects test-taking ability rather than actual job skills.

A personality test can be even riskier. In addition to its potential for illegal discrimination, such a test may invade an applicant's protected privacy rights—by inquiring, for example, into religious beliefs or sexual practices.

If you do decide to use aptitude or personality tests, make sure they've been screened scientifically for validity and are related to job performance.

Get professional advice. *Because testing is such a sensitive legal issue and it's easy to make mistakes, it makes sense to check with an experienced employment lawyer before testing applicants. (See Chapter 24.)*

3. Honesty Tests

Lie detector or polygraph tests—rarely used by small businesses anyhow—are virtually outlawed by the federal Employee Polygraph Protection Act. With just a few exceptions, you can't require job applicants to take lie detector tests and you can't inquire about previous tests. The only private employers who can use lie detector tests to screen applicants are businesses that offer armored car, alarm, and guard services or that manufacture, distribute, or dispense pharmaceuticals—and even in those situations there are restrictions on which applicants can be tested and how the tests must be administered.

About the only time the typical employer can use a lie detector test is when an employee is reasonably suspected of being involved in a workplace theft or embezzlement.

Some employers are intrigued by written "honesty tests" as a way to screen job applicants. Because these tests are often inaccurate and sometimes invade an applicant's privacy or have a discriminatory impact on some minority groups, their legality is doubtful in most states.

4. Drug Tests

You have a legal right to insist on a drug-free workplace. Most small employers don't test for drugs, preferring to use background checks and personal interviews to try to screen out serious drug users. However, some employers want to be sure employees are drug-free and want to test.

The only problem is that testing to weed out drug users may conflict with workers' rights to privacy. The laws on drug testing vary widely from state to state and are changing quickly. Statutes regulating drug testing are summarized in the chart below. In states having such statutes, your right to test for drugs may turn on whether or not the employee's job poses an unusual risk of danger to the employee, coworkers, or the public.

Check your state law on drug testing. *Before you initiate any program of testing job applicants or employees, be sure you know exactly what your state law provides. Like all laws, the laws summarized on the chart are subject to amendment—and states currently without drug-testing laws may decide to adopt them. A trade association may have information about the current status of the drug-testing laws in your state or you can do your own legal research. A brief consultation with an experienced employment lawyer should also give you the information you need. (See Chapter 24.)*

State Drug and Alcohol Testing

Note: The states of Colorado, Delaware, Kansas, Kentucky, Massachusetts, Michigan, Missouri, New Hampshire, New Jersey, New Mexico, New York, Pennsylvania, South Dakota, Washington, West Virginia, Wisconsin, Wyoming, and the District of Columbia are not included in this chart because they do not have drug and alcohol testing laws governing private employers. Check with your state department of labor if you need more information. (See Appendix for contact list.)

Alabama

Ala. Code §§ 25-5-330 to 25-5-340

Employers affected: Employers who establish a drug-free workplace program to qualify for a workers' compensation rate discount.

Testing applicants: Must test upon conditional offer of employment. Must test all new hires. Job ads must include notice that drug and alcohol testing required.

Testing employees: Random testing permitted. Must test after an accident that results in lost work time. Must also test upon reasonable suspicion; reasons for suspicion must be documented and made available to employee upon request.

Employee rights: Employees have 5 days to contest or explain a positive test result. Employer must have an employee assistance program or maintain a resource file of outside programs.

Notice and policy requirements: All employees must have written notice of drug policy. Must give 60 days' advance notice before implementing testing program. Policy must state consequences of refusing to take test or testing positive.

Drug-free workplace program: Yes

Alaska

Alaska Stat. §§ 23.10.600 and following

Employers affected: Voluntary for employers with one or more full-time employees. (There is no state-mandated drug and alcohol testing.)

Testing employees: Employer may test:
- for any job-related purpose
- to maintain productivity and safety
- as part of an accident investigation, or
- upon reasonable suspicion.

Employee rights: Employer must provide written test results within 5 working days. Employee has 10 working days to request opportunity to explain positive test results; employer must grant request within 72 hours or before taking any adverse employment action.

Notice and policy requirements: Before implementing a testing program employer must distribute a written drug policy to all employees and must give 30 days' advance notice. Policy must state consequences of a positive test or refusal to submit to testing.

Arizona

Ariz. Rev. Stat. §§ 23-493 and following

Employers affected: Employers with one or more full-time employees.

Testing applicants: Employer must inform prospective hires that they will undergo drug testing as a condition of employment.

Testing employees: Employees are subject to random and scheduled tests:
- for any job-related purpose
- to maintain productivity and safety, or
- upon reasonable suspicion.

Employee rights: Policy must inform employees of their right to explain positive results.

Notice and policy requirements: Before conducting tests employer must give employees a copy of the written policy. Policy must state the consequences of a positive test or refusal to submit to testing.

Drug-free workplace program: Yes

Arkansas

Ark. Code Ann. §§ 11-14-105 to 11-14-112

Employers affected: Employers who establish a drug-free workplace program to qualify for a workers' compensation rate discount.

Testing applicants: Must test upon conditional offer of employment. Job ads must include notice that drug and alcohol testing required.

Testing employees: Employer must test any employee:
- on reasonable suspicion of drug use
- as part of a routine fitness-for-duty medical exam
- after an accident that results in injury, or
- as follow-up to a required rehabilitation program.

Employee rights: Employer may not refuse to hire applicant or take adverse personnel action against an employee on the basis of a single positive test that has not been verified by a confirmation test. An applicant or employee has 5 days after receiving test results to contest or explain them.

Notice and policy requirements: Employer must give all employees a written statement of drug policy and must give 60 days' advance notice before implementing program.

Drug-free workplace program: Yes.

California

Cal. Lab. Code §§ 1025, 1026

Employers affected: No provisions for private employer testing. An employer with 25 or more employees must reasonably accommodate an employee who wants to enter a treatment program. Employer is not, however, required to provide paid leave. Employer may fire or refuse to hire an employee whose drug or alcohol use interferes with job duties or workplace safety.

Employee rights: Employer must safeguard privacy of employee who enters treatment program.

State Drug and Alcohol Testing (continued)

Connecticut

Conn. Gen. Stat. Ann. §§ 31-51t to 31-51bb

Employers affected: Any individual, corporation, partnership, or unincorporated association.

Testing applicants: Employer must inform job applicants in writing that drug testing is required as a condition of employment.

Testing employees: Employer may test:

- when there is reasonable suspicion that employee is under the influence of drugs or alcohol and job performance is or could be impaired
- when authorized by federal law
- when employee's position is dangerous or safety-sensitive, or
- as part of a voluntary employee assistance program.

Employee rights: Employer may not take any adverse personnel action on the basis of a single positive test that has not been verified by a confirmation test.

Florida

Fla. Stat. Ann. §§ 440.101 to 440.102

Employers affected: Employers who establish a drug-free workplace program to qualify for a workers' compensation rate discount.

Testing applicants: Must inform job applicants that drug and alcohol testing is required as a condition of employment.

Testing employees: Must test any employee:

- on reasonable suspicion of drug use
- as part of a routine fitness-for-duty medical exam, or
- as part of a required rehabilitation program.

Employee rights: Employees who voluntarily seek treatment for substance abuse cannot be fired, disciplined, or discriminated against, unless they have tested positive or have been in treatment in the past. All employees have the right to explain positive results within 5 days. Employer may not take any adverse personnel action on the basis of an initial positive result that has not been verified by a confirmation test.

Notice and policy requirements: Prior to implementing testing, employer must give 60 days' advance notice and must give employees written copy of drug policy.

Drug-free workplace program: Yes.

Georgia

Ga. Code Ann. §§ 34-9-410 to 34-9-421

Employers affected: Employers who establish a drug-free workplace program to qualify for a workers' compensation rate discount.

Testing applicants: Applicants are required to submit to a substance abuse test after they have been offered employment.

Testing employees: Must test any employee:

- on reasonable suspicion of drug use
- as part of a routine fitness-for-duty medical exam, or
- as part of a required rehabilitation program.

Employee rights: Employees have 5 days to explain or contest a positive result. Employer must have an employee assistance program or maintain a resource file of outside programs.

Notice and policy requirements: Employer must give applicants and employees notice of testing, and must give 60 days' notice before implementing program. All employees must receive a written policy statement; policy must state the consequences of refusing to submit to a drug test or of testing positive.

Drug-free workplace program: Yes.

Hawaii

Haw. Rev. Stat. §§ 329B-1 and following

Testing applicants: Same conditions as current employees.

Testing employees: Employer may test employees only if these conditions are met:

- employer pays all costs including confirming test
- tests are performed by a licensed laboratory
- employee receives a list of the substances being tested for
- there is a form for disclosing medicines and legal drugs, and
- the results are kept confidential.

Idaho

Idaho Code §§ 72-1701 to 72-1714

Employers affected: Voluntary for all private employers.

Testing applicants: Employer may test as a condition of hiring.

Testing employees: May test as a condition of continued employment. An employer who follows drug-free workplace guidelines may fire employees who refuse to submit to testing or who test positive for drugs or alcohol. Employees will be fired for misconduct and denied unemployment benefits.

Employee rights: An employee or applicant who receives notice of a positive test may request a retest within 7 working days. If the retest results are negative, the employer must pay for the cost; if they are positive, the employee must pay.

Drug-free workplace program: Yes (compliance is optional).

Illinois

775 Ill. Comp. Stat. § 5/2-104(C)(3)

Employers affected: Employers with 15 or more employees.

Testing employees: Employer may prohibit all employees from using or being under the influence of alcohol and illegal drugs. Employer may test employees who have been in rehabilitation. Employee may be held to the same standards as other employees, even if the unsatisfactory job performance or behavior is due to drug use or alcoholism.

State Drug and Alcohol Testing (continued)

Indiana

Ind. Code Ann. §§ 22-9-5-6(b), 22-9-5-24

Employers affected: Employers with 15 or more employees.

Testing employees: Employer may prohibit all employees from using or being under the influence of alcohol and illegal drugs. Employer may test employees who have been in rehabilitation. Employee may be held to the same standards as other employees, even if the unsatisfactory job performance or behavior is due to drug use or alcoholism.

Iowa

Iowa Code § 730.5

Employers affected: Employers with one or more full-time employees.

Testing applicants: Employer may test as a condition of hiring.

Testing employees: Employer may test employees:

- as a condition of continued employment
- upon reasonable suspicion
- during and after rehabilitation, or
- following an accident that caused a reportable injury or more than $1,000 property damage.

Employee rights: Employee has 7 days to request a retest. Employers with 50 or more employees must provide rehabilitation for any employee who has worked for at least one year and has not previously violated the substance abuse policy; no adverse action may be taken if employee successfully completes rehabilitation. Employer must have an employee assistance program or maintain a resource file of outside programs.

Drug-free workplace program: Yes (compliance is optional).

Louisiana

La. Rev. Stat. Ann. §§ 49:1001 and following

Employers affected: Employers with one or more full-time employees. (Does not apply to oil drilling, exploration, or production.)

Testing applicants: Employer may require all applicants to submit to drug and alcohol test. Employer does not have to confirm a positive result of a pre-employment drug screen, but must offer the applicant the opportunity to pay for a confirmation test and a review by a medical review officer.

Employee rights: Except for a pre-employment test, employer may not take adverse personnel action on the basis of an initial screen. Employees with confirmed positive results have 7 working days to request access to all records relating to the drug test. Employer may allow employee to undergo rehabilitation without termination of employment.

Maine

Me. Rev. Stat. Ann. tit. 26, §§ 681 to 690

Employers affected: Employers with one or more full-time employees. (Law does not require or encourage employers to conduct substance abuse testing.)

Testing applicants: Employer may require applicant to take a drug test only if offered employment or placed on an eligibility list.

Testing employees: Employer may test for probable cause, but may not base belief on a single accident; must document the facts and give employee a copy. May test when:

- there could be an unreasonable threat to the health and safety of coworkers or the public, or
- an employee returns to work following a positive test.

Employee rights: Employee who tests positive has 3 days to explain or contest results. Employee must be given an opportunity to participate in a rehabilitation program for up to 6 months; an employer with more than 20 full-time employees must pay for half of any out-of-pocket costs. After successfully completing the program, employee is entitled to return to previous job with full pay and benefits.

Notice and policy requirements: All employers must have a written policy approved by the state department of labor. Policy must be distributed to each employee at least 30 days before it takes effect. Any changes to policy require 60 days' advance notice. An employer with more than 20 full-time employees must have an employee assistance program certified by the state office of substance abuse before implementing a testing program.

Maryland

Md. Code Ann., [Health-Gen.] § 17-214

Employers affected: Law applies to all employers.

Testing applicants: May use preliminary screening to test applicant. If initial result is positive, may make job offer conditional on confirmation of test results.

Testing employees: Employer may require substance abuse testing for legitimate business purposes only.

Employee rights: The sample must be tested by a certified laboratory; at the time of testing employee may request laboratory's name and address. An employee who tests positive must be given:

- a copy of the test results
- a copy of the employer's written drug and alcohol policy
- a written notice of any adverse action employer intends to take, and
- a statement of employee's right to an independent confirmation test at own expense.

State Drug and Alcohol Testing (continued)

Minnesota

Minn. Stat. Ann. §§ 181.950 to 181.957

Employers affected: Employers with one or more full-time employees. (Employers are not required to test.)

Testing applicants: Employers may require applicants to submit to a drug or alcohol test only after they have been given a job offer and have seen a written notice of testing policy. May test only if required of all applicants for same position.

Testing employees: Employers may require drug or alcohol testing only according to a written testing policy. Testing may be done if there is a reasonable suspicion that employee:

- is under the influence of drugs or alcohol
- has violated drug and alcohol policy
- has been involved in an accident, or
- has sustained or caused another employee to sustain a personal injury.

Random tests permitted only for employees in safety-sensitive positions. With two weeks' notice, employers may also test as part of an annual routine physical exam.

Employee rights: If test is positive, employee has 3 days to explain the results; employee must notify employer within 5 days of intention to obtain a retest. Employer may not discharge employee for a first-time positive test without offering counseling or rehabilitation; employee who refuses or does not complete program successfully may be discharged.

Notice and policy requirements: Employees must be given a written notice of testing policy which includes consequences of refusing to take test or having a positive test result. Two weeks' notice required before testing as part of an annual routine physical exam.

Mississippi

Miss. Code Ann. §§ 71-7-1 and following; 71-3-205 and following

Employers affected: Employers with one or more full-time employees. Employers who establish a drug-free workplace program to qualify for a workers' compensation rate discount must implement testing procedures.

Testing applicants: May test all applicants as part of employment application process. Employer may request a signed statement that applicant has read and understands the drug and alcohol testing policy or notice. (Must test applicants if drug-free workplace.)

Testing employees: May require drug and alcohol testing of all employees:

- on reasonable suspicion
- as part of a routinely scheduled fitness-for-duty medical examination
- as a follow-up to a rehabilitation program, or
- if they have tested positive within the previous 12 months.

Employee rights: Employer must inform an employee in writing within 5 working days of receipt of a positive confirmed test result; employee may request and receive a copy of the test result report. Employee has 10 working days after receiving notice to explain the positive test results. Private employer who elects to establish a drug-free workplace program must have an employee assistance program or maintain a resource file of outside programs.

Notice and policy requirements: 30 days before implementing testing program employer must give employees written notice of drug and alcohol policy which includes consequences:

- of a positive confirmed result
- of refusing to take test, and
- of other violations of the policy.

Drug-free workplace program: Yes.

Montana

Mont. Code Ann. §§ 39-2-205 to 39-2-211

Employers affected: Employers with one or more employees.

Testing applicants: May test as a condition of hire.

Testing employees: Employees may be tested:

- on reasonable suspicion
- after involvement in an accident that causes personal injury or more than $1,500 property damage
- as a follow-up to a previous positive test, or
- as a follow-up to treatment or a rehabilitation program.

Employer may conduct random tests as long as there is an established date and all personnel are subject to testing.

Employer may require an employee who tests positive to undergo treatment as a condition of continued employment.

Employee rights: After a positive result, employee may request additional confirmation by an independent laboratory; if the results are negative, employer must pay the test costs.

Notice and policy requirements: Written policy must be available for review 60 days before testing.

Nebraska

Neb. Rev. Stat. §§ 48-1901 and following

Employers affected: Employers with 6 or more full-time and part-time employees.

Testing employees: Employer may require employees to submit to drug or alcohol testing and may discipline or discharge any employee who refuses.

Employee rights: Employer may not take adverse action on the basis of an initial positive result unless it is confirmed according to state and federal guidelines.

State Drug and Alcohol Testing (continued)

Nevada

Nev. Rev. Stat. Ann. § 608.156

Employers affected: All employers who offer health benefits.

Employee rights: Employee health benefits must include treatment for drug or alcohol abuse. Limits are $1,500 per year for treatment for withdrawal; $9,000 per year for inpatient facility; $2,500 for outpatient counseling. Maximum of $39,000 per lifetime.

North Carolina

N.C. Gen. Stat. §§ 95-230 to 95-235

Employers affected: Law applies to all employers.

Testing employees: Employer must preserve samples for at least 90 days after confirmed test results are released.

Employee rights: Employee has right to retest a confirmed positive sample at own expense.

North Dakota

N.D. Cent. Code § 34-01-15

Employers affected: Any employer who requires a medical exam as a condition of hire or continued employment may include a drug or alcohol test.

Testing employees: Employer may test following an accident or injury that will result in a workers' compensation claim, if employer has a mandatory policy of testing under these circumstances, or if employer or physician has reasonable grounds to suspect injury was caused by impairment due to alcohol or drug use.

Ohio

Ohio Admin. Code §§ 4123-17-58, 4123-17-58.1

Employers affected: Employers who establish a drug-free workplace program to qualify for a workers' compensation rate discount.

Testing applicants: Must test all applicants and new hires within 90 days of employment.

Testing employees: Must test employees:
- on reasonable suspicion
- following a return to work after a positive test, or
- after an accident which results in an injury requiring offsite medical attention, or property damage over limit specified in drug and alcohol policy.

Employee rights: Employer must have an employee assistance plan. Employer must offer health care coverage which includes chemical dependency counseling and treatment.

Notice and policy requirements: Policy must state consequences for refusing to submit to testing or for violating guidelines. Policy must include a commitment to rehabilitation.

Drug-free workplace program: Yes.

Oklahoma

Okla. Stat. Ann. tit. 40, §§ 551 to 565

Employers affected: Employers with one or more employees. (Drug or alcohol testing not required or encouraged.)

Testing applicants: Employer may test applicants as a condition of employment, and may refuse to hire applicant who refuses to undergo test or has a confirmed positive result.

Testing employees: Before requiring testing, employer must provide an employee assistance program. Random testing is allowed. May test employees:
- on reasonable suspicion
- after an accident resulting in injury or property damage over $500
- as part of a routine fitness-for-duty examination, or
- as follow-up to a rehabilitation program.

Employee rights: Employee has right to retest a positive result at own expense; if the confirmation test is negative, employer must reimburse costs.

Notice and policy requirements: Before requiring testing employer must:
- adopt a written policy
- give a copy to each employee and to any applicant offered a job, and
- allow 30 days' notice.

Oregon

Or. Rev. Stat. §§ 659.840, 659A.300, 438.435

Employers affected: Law applies to all employers.

Testing applicants: Unless there is reasonable suspicion that an applicant is under the influence of alcohol, no employer may require a breathalyzer test as a condition of employment. Employer is not prohibited from conducting a test if applicant consents.

Testing employees: Unless there is reasonable suspicion that an employee is under the influence of alcohol, no employer may require a breathalyzer or blood alcohol test as a condition of continuing employment. Employer is not prohibited from conducting a test if employee consents.

Employee rights: No action may be taken based on the results of an on-site drug test without a confirming test performed according to state health division regulations. Upon written request, test results will be reported to the employee.

Rhode Island

R.I. Gen. Laws §§ 28-6.5-1 to 28-6.5-2

Employers affected: Law applies to all employers.

Testing employees: May require employee to submit to a drug test only if there are reasonable grounds, based on specific observations, to believe employee is using controlled substances that are impairing job performance.

Employee rights: Employee who tests positive may have the sample retested at employer's expense and must be given opportunity to explain or

State Drug and Alcohol Testing (continued)

refute results. Employee may not be terminated on the basis of a positive result, but must be referred to a licensed substance abuse professional. After referral, employer may require additional testing, and may terminate employee if test results are positive.

South Carolina

S.C. Code Ann. §§ 41-1-15, 38-73-500

Employers affected: Employers who establish a drug-free workplace program to qualify for a workers' compensation rate discount.

Testing employees: Must conduct random testing among all employees. Must conduct a follow-up test within 30 minutes of the first test.

Employee rights: Employee must receive positive test results in writing within 24 hours.

Notice and policy requirements: Employer must notify all employees of the drug-free workplace program at the time it is established or at the time of hiring, whichever is earlier. Program must include a policy statement that balances respect for individuals with the need to maintain a safe, drug-free environment.

Drug-free workplace program: Yes.

Tennessee

Tenn. Code Ann. §§ 50-9-101 and following

Employers affected: Employers who establish a drug-free workplace program to qualify for a workers' compensation rate discount.

Testing applicants: Must test applicants upon conditional offer of employment. Job ads must include notice that drug and alcohol testing is required.

Testing employees: Employer must test upon reasonable suspicion; must document behavior on which the suspicion is based within 24 hours or before test results are released, whichever is earlier; and must give a copy to the employee upon request. Employer must test employees:

- who are in safety-sensitive positions
- as part of a routine fitness-for-duty medical exam
- after an accident that results in injury, or
- as a follow-up to a required rehabilitation program.

Employee rights: Employee has the right to explain or contest a positive result within 5 days. Employee may not be fired, disciplined, or discriminated against for voluntarily seeking treatment unless employee has previously tested positive or been in a rehabilitation program.

Notice and policy requirements: Before implementing testing program, employer must provide 60 days' notice and must give all employees a written drug and alcohol policy statement.

Drug-free workplace program: Yes.

Texas

Tex. Lab. Code Ann. § 411.091

Employers affected: Employers with 15 or more employees who have a workers' compensation insurance policy.

Notice and policy requirements: Must adopt a drug abuse policy and provide a written copy to employees.

Utah

Utah Code Ann. §§ 34-38-1 to 34-38-15

Employers affected: Employers with one or more employees.

Testing applicants: Employer may test any applicant for drugs or alcohol as long as management also submits to periodic testing.

Testing employees: Employer may test employee for drugs or alcohol as long as management also submits to periodic testing. Employer may also require testing to:

- investigate an accident or theft
- maintain employee or public safety, or
- ensure productivity, quality, or security.

Employee rights: Employer may suspend, discipline, discharge, or require treatment on the basis of a confirmed positive test result.

Notice and policy requirements: Testing must be conducted according to a written policy that has been distributed to employees and is available for review by prospective employees.

Vermont

Vt. Stat. Ann. tit. 21, §§ 511 and following

Employers affected: Employers with one or more employees.

Testing applicants: Employer may not test applicants for drugs or alcohol unless there is a job offer conditional on a negative test result, and applicant is given written notice of the testing procedure and a list of the drugs to be tested for.

Testing employees: Random testing not permitted unless required by federal law. Employer may not require testing unless:

- there is probable cause to believe an employee is using or is under the influence
- employer has an employee assistance program which provides rehabilitation, and
- employee who tests positive and agrees to enter employee assistance program is not terminated.

Employee rights: Employer must contract with a medical review officer who will review all test results and keep them confidential. Medical review officer is to contact employee or applicant to explain a positive test result. Employee or applicant has right to an independent retest at own expense. Employee who

State Drug and Alcohol Testing (continued)

successfully completes employee assistance program may not be terminated, although employee may be suspended for up to 3 months to complete program. Employee who tests positive after completing treatment may be fired.

Virginia

Va. Code Ann. § 65.2-813.2

Employers affected: Employers who establish drug-free workplace programs to qualify for workers' compensation insurance discount.

Drug-free workplace program: State law gives insurers the authority to establish guidelines and criteria for testing.

Current as of January 2004

You generally have much more leeway in screening job applicants than in testing employees who are already on board. If your state permits testing applicants or employees and you plan to do such testing, use the job application form to inform applicants of this policy.

In addition, it's a good idea—and required by the law of some states—to give applicants a written drug testing policy statement that's separate from the application. When applicants are told up front about drug testing, it's harder for them to later claim that your drug testing program is a violation of their privacy.

Once an applicant becomes an employee, drug testing gets stickier. Testing is usually permitted when employees have been in an accident or you've seen them bring illegal drugs to work. Your legal right to test at random and without prior notice is unclear—and questionable.

Drug Testing and the ADA

The Americans with Disabilities Act (ADA) forbids you from testing an applicant for drugs until you've made a conditional offer of employment.

After you've made a conditional offer of employment and as part of a pre-employment medical screening, you may discover that the applicant had a drug problem in the past. The ADA prohibits you from discriminating against people because of past drug problems. This includes people who no longer use drugs illegally and are receiving treatment for drug addiction and those who have been rehabilitated successfully.

To make sure that drug use isn't recurring, however, you may request evidence that a person is taking part in a drug rehab program. You may also ask for the results of a drug test.

You can refuse to hire someone with a history of alcoholism or illegal drug use if you can show that the person poses a direct threat to health or safety. You must show that there's a high probability that the person will return to the illegal drug use or alcohol abuse, and a high probability of substantial harm to the person or others—harm that you can't reduce or eliminate by making reasonable changes in the workplace. Unfortunately, the EEOC offers no guidance on the type of evidence that would suffice to show the high probability of a problem arising.

G. Investigating Job Application Information

Since some people give false or incomplete information in their job applications, it's a good idea to verify their application information. To reduce the risk of an invasion of privacy claim, inform the applicant in the job application that you will be requesting information from former employers, schools, credit reporting sources, and law enforcement agencies.

Ask the applicant to sign a consent form as part of the application process.

1. Former Employers

Contact as many former employers as possible to get the inside story about an applicant. But understand that former employers are often reluctant to say anything negative for fear that if they speak frankly, they may be hit by a lawsuit for defamation.

In speaking with former employers, you'll often have to read between the lines. If a former employer is neutral, offers only faint praise, or repeatedly overpraises a person for one aspect of a job only—"really great with numbers" or "invariably on time"—there's a good chance some negative information is hiding in the wings. Ask former employers: "Would you hire this person back if you could?" The response may be telling. If the person pauses or equivocates, you have your answer.

If references aren't glowing and don't take in all aspects of the job, consider calling the applicant back for a more directed interview.

Reference checks may become more informative. *States are starting to pass laws that allow employers to speak more frankly about their former employees without fear of being sued. Under a Kansas law, for example, an employer is presumed to be acting in good faith when responding to reference checks. The Kansas law says that to collect damages, a former employee must show by "clear and convincing evidence" that the former employer acted in bad faith in providing job-related information. Laws such as this help the former employer cope with a troubling legal bind: the possibility of being sued by the former employee for speaking too freely or, alternatively, being sued by the potential new employer for not disclosing seriously negative information.*

Find out whether your state has a law or a court decision requiring employers to disclose seriously negative information about a former employee or absolving employers from liability for doing so in good faith. If so, don't assume that the former employers you call for reference checks know about it. Telling them about their responsibility and the protection they have under your state's law may lead to your getting a fuller picture of a prospective employee.

2. School Transcripts

On-the-job experience generally is more relevant to employment than an applicant's educational credentials. Still, you may have good reasons for requiring a high school diploma or college degree for some jobs—especially for younger employees who don't have a lot of job experience. If so, you may want to see proof that the applicant really received the diploma or degree or took the courses claimed in the job application.

3. Credit History

Credit information may be relevant in the rare cases when you hire someone who will handle money. Someone with large debts, for example, may be inclined to skim money from your business. And an applicant who can't keep his or her personal finances in order is probably not a good choice for a job requiring management of your company's finances. For these types of jobs, a credit check is sensible.

In most situations, however, a credit check is an unnecessary intrusion into an applicant's personal life. What's more, unless you have a good reason for doing a credit check for a particular job, you may run afoul of antidiscrimination laws. According to the EEOC, requiring an applicant to have good credit may subtly discriminate against some minority groups. State laws, too, may limit your use of credit information in deciding whether to hire someone.

Assuming that you have a good business reason to order a credit report on a job applicant, it's always a good idea to get the applicant's consent first. Some states, in fact, require such consent. In addition, the federal Fair Credit Reporting Act requires you to let an applicant know if he or she has been denied employment because of something in a credit report.

 Authoritative information about the Fair Credit Reporting Act *is available at the Federal Trade Commission's website, www.ftc.gov.*

4. Criminal History

Asking an applicant about his or her arrest record or making a hiring decision based on that record can violate state and federal antidiscrimination laws. Criminal charges are often dropped or found to be without merit.

Convictions are another matter. Antidiscrimination laws generally allow you to inquire about an applicant's conviction record and to reject an applicant because of a conviction record that suggests the applicant wouldn't be a good fit for the job. If you're hiring a delivery truck driver, for example, it wouldn't violate antidiscrimination laws to reject an applicant based on a drunk driving conviction.

In some states you can't ask about convictions for minor offenses or misdemeanors that go back more than five years if the applicant has had a clean slate since that time.

5. Driving Records

When a job requires an employee to drive, it's wise to inform applicants that you'll be checking on their driving record—and to actually do so. You usually can obtain driving records for a modest cost from the state authority that issues driver's licenses.

Check, too, with your insurance company to be sure you meet the requirements for bringing new employees under your vehicle insurance coverage.

H. Immigration Law Requirements

Immigration laws, enforced by the Department of Homeland Security (DHS), prohibit hiring aliens who don't have government authorization to work in the United States. There are specific procedures you must follow when hiring employees—even those who are born and raised in the town where your business is located. Specifically, you and the new employee must complete Form I-9, *Employment Eligibility Verification*. This one-page form is intended to ensure that the employee can work legally in the United States and has proof of his or her identity.

 Form I-9 and further information *are available on the website of DHS's U.S. Citizenship & Immigration Services (USCIS) at www.uscis.gov.*

I. Personnel Practices

The vast majority of job disputes can be resolved within the workplace if you listen patiently to what employees have to say and are prepared to make adjustments when legitimate complaints surface. However there's always the chance a dispute will get out of hand and that an employee will sue your small business for some perceived abuse of his or her rights. Or an unhappy employee may file a complaint with a government agency alleging that you violated a statute or an administrative regulation.

If that happens, you'll have to prove to a judge, jury, arbitrator, or investigator that you met your legal obligations to the employee. That can be harder than you think. Key paperwork may have been lost—or never prepared in the first place. And

witnesses may have forgotten what happened or have moved on and not be locatable.

To maintain a solid, legal footing, establish good written policies and then maintain a paper trail indicating how they are implemented. Written policies and an employee handbook explaining employee benefits and responsibilities provide cogent points of reference when you discuss problems with an employee—and increase the likelihood of reaching an amicable resolution.

1. Employee Handbooks

An employee handbook can be of practical help in running your business. Once you give it to an employee, there can be no dispute over whether you gave the employee a list of paid days off or explained your vacation policies. It's all there in writing and everyone has the same information. If yours is a very small business, keep your handbook short and sweet at the start. At that stage, it's easy to involve all employees in writing it so that it accurately covers their concerns. Then, as your business grows, the framework necessary for a more detailed version will be in place.

If your handbook is good, you get a bonus: a measure of legal protection if you're challenged by an employee in a court or administrative proceeding. A handbook can be an objective piece of evidence showing that you've adopted fair and uniform policies and have informed your employees of exactly where they stand in their employment.

A good handbook should tell your employees how to let you know if they have a workplace problem. This gives you a chance to react before a small misunderstanding erupts into a full-blown legal dispute.

Even a tiny business with six to ten employees can benefit from an employee handbook—and you can produce one quickly and cheaply by using a self-help book or software program as a starting point. Modify the sample wording to fit your own needs.

Then check with your state department of labor to make sure your handbook complies with the laws in your state. Keep the handbook up to date as laws change. If you have specific legal questions, a brief consultation with a lawyer should be sufficient to clear them up.

 Make sure your handbook doesn't promise more than you can deliver. *Your handbook may be treated as a contract that can actually limit your right to fire employees. To avoid that result, state in the handbook that:*

- *employees don't have employment contracts— and can't have them in the future—unless they're in writing and signed by the company president, and*
- *your company reserves the right to terminate employees for reasons not stated in the handbook or for no reason at all.*

 Want an easy way prepare a professional, legally safe handbook? *See* Create Your Own Employee Handbook: A Legal & Practical Guide, *by Lisa Guerin and Amy DelPo (Nolo). The included CD-ROM eliminates the heavy lifting.*

2. Employee Performance Reviews

Most large companies review and evaluate their employees periodically. This is a sound management practice and one which many small companies should consider—especially for new employees.

Evaluating new employees periodically gives them a chance to improve if they're not performing well. If you later find it necessary to discipline or fire an employee, it won't come as a surprise to the employee. By putting your evaluations in writing and saving them in the employee's file, you normally have a credible history of documented problems you can use if an employee claims that he or she was fired for an illegal reason.

If your business has fewer than half a dozen employees, formal evaluations may be unwieldy—but it's still important to let employees know if they're not measuring up to what's expected of them. Keeping a short note of what you told the employee and when can be helpful as evidence that you gave the employee a chance to improve before you fired him or her.

J. Illegal Discrimination

To give workers a fair opportunity to get and keep jobs, Congress and state legislatures have passed laws prohibiting discrimination in the workplace.

1. Title VII of the Civil Rights Act

Title VII (42 USC § 2000 and following) applies to your business if you employ 15 or more people— either full time or part time. State laws, with similar prohibitions against discrimination, generally cover smaller employers, too.

Under Title VII, you can't use race, color, religion, gender, or national origin as the basis for decisions on hirings, promotions, dismissals, pay raises, benefits, work assignments, leaves of absence—or just about any other aspect of employment. Title VII applies to everything from Help Wanted ads, to working conditions, to performance reviews, to giving references to other prospective employers.

2. Sexual Harassment

Sexual harassment in the workplace is a form of prohibited sexual discrimination. Illegal sexual harassment occurs when unwelcome sexual advances, requests for sexual favors, and other verbal or physical conduct of a sexual nature create a hostile or abusive work environment. The harassed employee is entitled to legal relief even without proof that the offending behavior has injured the employee psychologically.

Under federal law, it's clearly sexual harassment for an employer or a manager to make unwelcome sexual advances or to demand sexual favors in return for job benefits, promotions, or continued employment.

But sexual harassment in the workplace can consist, as well, of many other activities including:

- posting sexually explicit photos that offend employees
- telling sex-related jokes or jokes that demean people because of their gender
- commenting inappropriately on an employee's appearance
- requiring employees to dress in scanty attire
- repeatedly requesting dates from a person who clearly isn't interested
- having strippers perform at a company gathering, and
- stating that people of one gender are inferior to people of the other gender or can't perform their jobs as well.

In short, any hostile or offensive behavior in the workplace that has a sexual component can constitute sexual harassment—and is illegal.

Your business can also be held responsible for sexual harassment if you or a supervisor know, or should know, it's being committed by one co-worker against another—or even by customers or vendors on your premises.

You're also under a legal duty to take all necessary steps to prevent sexual harassment. No matter the size of your business, start by adopting a formal policy stating clearly that sexual harassment won't be tolerated. Post it on a bulletin board and place it in your employee handbook. Let employees know who within your company they can complain to if they've been sexually harassed.

Common Sense From the Supreme Court

People sometimes have taken extreme positions on the laws prohibiting sexual harassment. Fortunately, in 1998, the U.S. Supreme Court offered some practical advice to both employers and employees: Act reasonably and use common sense.

For example, in a case involving claims of same-sex harassment, the Court suggested that drawing the line between horseplay or flirtation and discrimination on the job isn't all that hard, even though men and woman may play differently. The Court said: "Common sense and an appropriate sensitivity to social context will enable courts and juries to distinguish between simple teasing or roughhousing among members of the same sex, and conduct which a reasonable person in the plaintiff's position would find hostile or abusive."

In other decisions, the Court has said that people who know about sexual harassment should let the employer know so that steps can be taken to stop it. An employee who doesn't cooperate with an employer's attempts to take corrective action may have a relatively weak case. The Court recognizes that, as an employer, you can defend against sexual harassment charges by showing you used reasonable care to address the problem—by having a strong written antiharassment policy, for example, and a sound procedure for receiving and investigating complaints. Three cheers for common sense!

For an excellent in-depth explanation: *See* Sexual Harassment on the Job: What It Is & How to Stop It, *by William Petrocelli and Barbara Kate Repa (Nolo).*

3. Age Discrimination

The Age Discrimination in Employment Act or ADEA (29 USC § 623(a)) prohibits discrimination against those 40 years old or older. It applies to businesses with 20 or more employees—but similar state laws generally apply to businesses with fewer employees. As with the rest of Title VII, age discrimination is prohibited in all aspects of employment—hiring, firing, compensation, and all other terms of employment.

Another law, the Older Worker's Benefits Protection Act, makes it illegal to use an employee's age as the basis for discrimination in benefits. Like the ADEA, this act covers employees who are 40 years old or older. Under this law, you cannot, for example, reduce health or life insurance benefits for older employees, nor can you stop their pensions from accruing if they work past their normal retirement ages. The law also discourages your business from targeting older workers when you cut staff.

The law also regulates the legal waivers that some employers ask employees to sign in connection with early retirement programs. For details, see *The Employer's Legal Handbook*, by Fred S. Steingold (Nolo).

4. Pregnancy

The Pregnancy Discrimination Act or PDA (92 USC § 2076) applies to businesses with 15 or more employees. Under the PDA, it's a form of gender discrimination to treat an employee differently because of pregnancy, childbirth, or related medical conditions. If a woman is affected by such a condition, you must treat her the same as you treat other people in the workforce who are either able or unable to work.

You violate the PDA, for example, if you fire a woman whose pregnancy keeps her from working, but you don't fire other workers who are temporarily unable to do the job because of other physical problems. Similarly, if a pregnant worker is able to do the job, you can't lay her off because you think it's in her best interests to stay home. On the other hand, you don't violate the PDA if you apply medically based job restrictions to a pregnant woman—as long as you apply those same policies to employees who are not pregnant but who are under medical restrictions.

5. National Origin

The Immigration Reform and Control Act of 1986 makes it illegal to discriminate against a person because he or she isn't a U.S. citizen or national. The law forbids you from discriminating against aliens who have been lawfully admitted to the U.S. for permanent or temporary residence—and aliens who have applied for temporary residence status.

6. Gay and Lesbian Workers

Federal law doesn't specifically prohibit workplace discrimination based on sexual orientation, but several states have such laws—including California, Connecticut, the District of Columbia, Hawaii, Massachusetts, Minnesota, Nevada, New Hampshire, New Jersey, Rhode Island, Vermont, and Wisconsin. Over 120 cities prohibit discrimination based on sexual orientation. If you're not sure what the local law is, call the municipal clerk where your company does business, or your state labor department or fair employment office.

K. Wages and Hours

Federal and state statutes regulate workplace wages and hours, imposing strict requirements on employers. Since fines and back wage awards can be expensive, it pays to know the law.

1. The Fair Labor Standards Act

The main law affecting worker's pay is the Federal Fair Labor Standards Act or FLSA (29 USC §§ 201 and following) which Congress passed in 1938. In addition to setting a minimum wage, the FLSA requires premium pay for overtime work and equal pay for men and women doing the same work. The law also contains special rules for hiring young workers.

Virtually all businesses and employees are covered. There are just a handful of specific exemptions, including most small farms. For details, check with the nearest office of the U.S. Labor Department's Wage and Hour Division. Even though your business is covered by the FLSA, some employees may be exempt from that law's minimum wage and overtime pay requirements.

Most employees who are exempt from the minimum wage and overtime pay requirements fall into one of five categories:

- executive employees
- administrative employees
- professional employees
- outside salespeople, and
- people in certain computer-related occupations.

There are a few miscellaneous categories of workers who are exempt as well.

Need to learn more about exempt employees? *The fine points of these exemptions are detailed at the website of the U.S. Department of Labor, www.dol.gov. Click "Employers," then "Fair Labor Standards Act," then "Fact Sheets," and you'll come to a page providing dozens of explanations. Fact Sheet # 17a is a good starting point.*

Who's Exempt and Who Isn't?

Job titles alone don't determine whether someone is an exempt executive, administrative, or professional employee. The actual work relationship is what counts. Still, it's possible to make some generalizations about who's exempt and who isn't. Typical exempt jobs include such positions as department head, financial expert, personnel director, credit manager, account executive, and tax specialist. Typical nonexempt jobs include such positions as clerk, bank teller, secretary, warehouse worker, errand runner, data entry person, bookkeeper, inspector, and trainee.

2. Pay Requirements

If your business is covered by the FLSA, you must pay all covered employees at least the minimum wage—$5.15 an hour. Federal law allows you to pay a "training wage" of $4.25 an hour to employees under 20 years of age during their first 90 days on the job.

The amount will be higher if your state has established a higher minimum wage. In Alaska, for example, the minimum wage must remain 50 cents higher than the federal minimum. In California, the minimum wage is $6.75 an hour. In the few states that have a lower minimum, the federal rate controls. Each state has its own—often complex—rules for who's covered by its minimum wage law. A person who's exempt from the federal minimum wage requirements may be entitled to a minimum wage under the state law. To learn the details, call your state's department of labor.

The Equal Pay Act, an amendment to the FLSA, requires you to provide equal pay and benefits to men and women who do the same jobs, or jobs that require equal skill, effort, and responsibility. Job titles aren't decisive in assessing whether two jobs are equal; it's the work duties that count. The Act makes it unlawful, for example, for the owner of a hotel to pay its janitors (primarily men) at a different pay rate than its housekeepers (primarily women) if both are doing essentially the same work.

The Equal Pay Act doesn't prohibit pay differences based on:

- a seniority system
- a merit system
- a system that pays a worker based on the quantity or quality of what he or she produces, or
- any factor other than the worker's gender— starting salaries, for example, that are based on the worker's experience level.

3. Overtime Pay

The FLSA requires you to pay nonexempt workers at least one and one-half times their regular rates of pay for all hours worked in excess of 40 hours in one week. The FLSA doesn't require you to pay an employee at an overtime rate simply because he or she worked more than eight hours in one day. Generally, you calculate and pay overtime by the week. Each workweek stands alone; you can't average two or more workweeks. And you can't manipulate the start of the workweek merely to avoid paying overtime.

According to overtime rules that took effect in August 2004, you don't need to pay overtime to the following exempt employees:

- **White-Collar Employees:** Salaried employees who earn $23,660 a year or more, and

primarily perform executive, administrative, or professional work, as defined by the U.S. Department of Labor.

- **High Earners:** Salaried employees who earn $100,000 or more, whose primary duties include office or nonmanual work, and who also regularly perform at least one executive, administrative, or professional function.
- **Outside Salespeople:** Employees who work away from your place of business to make sales or obtain orders.
- **Computer Professionals:** Computer analysts, programmers, software engineers, and similarly skilled workers who earn at least $27.63 an hour, or are paid a salary of $455 a week or more.

Note that no exemptions are allowed for manual laborers or others who perform repetitive operations with their hands, or use physical skill and energy, regardless of how much they're paid. Such workers are always entitled to overtime pay.

⚠️ **Congress may tinker with the exemption and overtime rules.** *They're somewhat controversial and subject to change. For the latest information, check the U.S. Department of Labor website at www.dol.gov.*

📖 **Looking for more information on the overtime rules?** *Go to www.dol.gov and click "Employers." Then click "FairPay Overtime Rules," and you'll be given links to several in-depth fact sheets to help keep you on the right track.*

4. Compensatory Time Off

The practice of granting hour-for-hour compensatory time—for example, giving a worker six hours time off one week as compensation for six hours of overtime work the previous week—isn't usually allowed for private sector employees covered by the FLSA. The rule is different for public employees.

Employers and employees are often puzzled when they learn that comp time isn't permitted in the private sector, because it seems like a sensible and mutually beneficial way to handle overtime in many situations. You do, however, have a few options for avoiding premium overtime pay by giving a worker time off instead of money. One way is to rearrange an employee's work schedule during a workweek.

EXAMPLE: Margaret, a paralegal at the law firm of Smith and Jones, normally works an eight-hour day, Monday through Friday. One week, Margaret and the lawyers need to meet a deadline on a brief due in the court of appeals. So that week, Margaret works ten hours a day, Monday through Thursday. The law firm gives Margaret Friday off and pays her for a 40-hour week at her regular rate of pay. This is legal because Margaret hasn't worked any overtime as defined by the FLSA; only the hours over 40 hours in a week count as overtime hours.

If an employee works more than 40 hours one week, it's sometimes possible to reduce the worker's hours in another week so that the amount of the employee's paycheck remains constant. This is legal if:

- the time off is given within the same pay period as the overtime work, and
- the employee is given an hour and a half of time off for each hour of overtime work.

EXAMPLE: Frames and Things, a shop that specializes in framing pictures, employs Jared and pays him $560 at the close of each two-week pay period. Because a week-long street art fair is expected to generate a great demand for framing services, the shop's owner wants Jared to work longer hours that week. However, the owner doesn't want to increase Jared's paycheck. She asks Jared to work 50 hours during art fair week and gives him 15 hours off the next week. Since Jared is paid every two weeks, Frames and Things may properly reduce Jared's hours the second week to keep his paycheck at the $560 level.

Since state regulations may further restrict the use of comp time, check with your state's labor department and get a copy of all publications touching on wages and hours.

5. Calculating Work Hours

You must pay covered employees for all of their time that you control and that benefits you. In general, time on the job doesn't include the time employees spend washing themselves or changing clothes before or after work, or meal periods when employees are free from all work duties.

You needn't pay employees for the time spent commuting between their homes and the normal job site, but you do have to pay for commuting time which is actually a part of the job. If you run a plumbing repair service, for example, and require workers to stop by your shop to pick up orders, tools, and supplies before going out on calls, their work day begins when they check in at your shop. Otherwise, just about the only situation in which you must pay workers for commuting time is when they've completed a day's work and are then called at home to do an emergency job for one of your customers.

You must count as payable time any periods when employees are not actually working, but are required to stay on your premises while waiting for work assignments. If you require employees to be on call, but you don't make them stay on your premises, then two rules generally apply.

- You don't count as payable time the on-call time that employees can control and use for their own enjoyment and benefit.
- You do count as payable time the on-call time over which employees have little or no control and which they can't use for their own enjoyment or benefit.

EXAMPLE: AirTec provides mechanical services for small private planes at a local airfield. The company designates one of its mechanics to be on call each Saturday. A mechanic who is on call must remain at home near the phone and, for safety reasons, can't drink any alcohol. Since designated mechanics aren't free to use their on-call time as they please, it's payable time.

Unless there's an employment contract that states otherwise, you can generally pay a different hourly rate for on-call time than you do for regular work time. But keep in mind that employees must be paid at least the minimum amount required under the wage and hour regulations.

Nearly half the states have laws requiring employers to provide meal and rest breaks and specifying minimum times that must be allowed. You don't have to pay a covered employee for time spent on an actual meal. But the key is that the employee must be completely relieved from work during that period so that he or she can enjoy a regularly scheduled meal. If, for example, you require employees to remain at their desks during the meal period or keep an eye on machinery, you must pay for the meal time.

6. Child Labor

The FLSA (29 USC § 206) has special rules for younger workers. Those rules are designed to discourage young people from dropping out of school too soon and to protect them from dangerous work such as mining, demolition, wrecking, logging, and roofing. Check with the local Wage and Hour office of the U.S. Department of Labor for the current rules and a list of jobs that are considered to be hazardous to young people. State laws—available from your state department of labor—may impose additional restrictions in hiring young workers.

L. Occupational Safety and Health

The Occupational Safety and Health Act or OSHA (29 USC §§ 651 to 678) is designed to reduce workplace hazards. It broadly requires employers to provide a workplace free of physical dangers and to meet specific health and safety standards. Employers must also provide safety training to employees, inform them about hazardous chemicals, notify government administrators about serious workplace accidents, and keep detailed safety records.

Although there can be heavy penalties for not complying with OSHA, such penalties are usually reserved for extreme cases in which workplace conditions are highly dangerous and the employer has ignored warnings about them. If your workplace is inspected, OSHA will work with you to eliminate hazards. Inspections of small businesses are rare unless the business is especially hazardous—an auto paint shop, for example, or a welding business.

The OSHA law won't apply to your workplace if you're self-employed and have no employees, or if your business is a farm that employs only your immediate family members. Similarly, you won't be covered if you're in a business such as mining that is already regulated by other federal safety laws.

OSHA requires that you provide a place of employment that's "free from recognized hazards that are causing or likely to cause death or serious physical harm to employees." The Occupational Safety and Health Administration—also called OSHA—enforces the OSHA law and has set additional, more specific, workplace standards covering concerns such as:

- exposure to hazardous chemicals
- first aid and medical treatment
- noise levels
- protective gear—goggles, respirators, gloves, work shoes, ear protectors
- fire protection
- worker training, and
- workplace temperatures and ventilation.

Most small businesses are inspected by OSHA only if:

- an employee has complained to OSHA
- a worker has died from a job-related injury, or
- three or more employees have been hospitalized because of a workplace condition.

In each state, there's an agency funded mostly by the federal office of OSHA that offers free, on-site consultations about how you can comply with the law. In addition to consultants, a trade association in your industry may often be able to provide advice on complying with OSHA.

M. Workers' Compensation

The workers' compensation system provides replacement income and medical expenses to employees who suffer work-related injuries or illnesses. Benefits may also extend to the survivors of workers who are killed on the job.

Workers' compensation is a no-fault system, meaning an employee is usually entitled to receive stated benefits whether or not the employer provided a safe workplace and whether or not the worker's own carelessness contributed to the injury or illness. But the employer, too, receives some protection, because the employees are limited to fixed types of compensation—basically, partial wage replacement and payment of medical bills. The employee can't get paid for pain and suffering or mental anguish.

Each state has its own workers' compensation statute. While the details differ among those laws, one thing is clear: If you have employees, you generally need to obtain workers' compensation coverage. Your state workers' compensation office can tell you about any legal requirements for informing employees of their rights—generally by displaying a poster.

To cover the cost of workers' compensation benefits for employees, you usually are required to pay for insurance—either through a state fund or a private insurance company. While self-insurance is a possibility in some states, the technical requirements usually make this an impractical alternative for a small business.

Premiums are based on two factors: industry classification and payroll. If your premium is above a certain amount—$5,000 in many states—your actual experience with workers' compensation claims will affect your premiums. Your rate can go up or down, depending on how your claims compare with other businesses in your industry. The number of claims filed by your employees affects your premium more than the dollar value of the claims. That's because if you have a lot of accidents, it's assumed that you have an unsafe workplace and the insurance company eventually will have to pay out some large claims.

To keep your workers' compensation costs down, try to prevent accidents in the workplace by emphasizing safety. Provide proper equipment, safety devices, and protective clothing. Make sure desks, chairs, and keyboards are up to ergonomic standards and that employees know how to use them properly. Train and retrain your employees in safe procedures and in how to deal with emergencies. Consider setting up a safety committee made up of both managers and workers. And promote employee health by offering wellness and fitness programs.

You may also be able to save money by reclassifying a worker—which may involve slightly changing the worker's job duties. For example, if you have five people in a warehouse assembling and packing products, consider assigning two as assemblers (perhaps in a separate area) and three as warehouse workers. The cost of workers' compensation for the assemblers should be lower since they don't need to lift heavy loads or work with equipment.

N. Termination

Firing someone—even a person who is demonstrably incompetent—can be a risky endeavor. Do it for the wrong reason or in the wrong way and you can be obligated to pay substantial money in damages, or to rehire the worker.

Cases in which former employees claim they were terminated for an improper reason or that an employer bungled the process are known as wrongful discharge cases—and they're based on such legal theories as violation of an antidiscrimination law, breach of contract, failure to deal in good faith with an employee, and violation of public policy.

1. Guidelines for Firing Employees

As noted in Section A3, the at-will doctrine theoretically gives you the right to fire an employee at any time as long as it's not for an illegal reason. Even so, the safest approach any time you fire someone is to make sure that you have a legitimate business reason for the termination—a reason that you have thought out and documented.

If a fired employee sues you and the case goes to trial, jurors won't be too impressed if your main defense is, "I own the business and I don't have to give a reason for firing anyone." Most jurors feel that the at-will doctrine is unfair and they'll look for ways to hit you with damages if there's a way they can do it and still comply with the judge's legal instructions.

Another reason to always have a good, legitimate basis for firing someone is that a former employee—shocked by the firing—may be looking for a way to retaliate against you. The employee may claim that your business ignored a sexual harassment complaint or that the firing was motivated by racial discrimination. When challenged on a firing, you should be able to show, for example, that the employee did not adequately perform specific job duties or violated a clearly stated company policy.

Some Employees Have Contract Rights

Before you fire an employee, check into whether you've made an oral or written contractual commitment that may limit your right to fire. Consider the following:

- Is there a written or oral contract that promises the employee a job for a fixed period of time?
- When you hired the employee, did you make any oral commitments about job security?
- Have you assured the employee that you'd only fire him or her for good cause?
- Have you listed causes for termination—in a contract, employee handbook, or elsewhere—in a way that limits you to those specified causes?
- Does your employee handbook or do other written policies or memos make any promises about job security?
- Does your company have written or customary procedures that must precede firing?

Your answers to these questions will help you identify whether you've limited your ability to fire the individual. If your employee handbook or your handouts to new employees restate your right to fire a worker at any time and say that all contracts must be in writing, you're usually in good shape.

Written employment contracts can be a two-way street. *While they may limit your right to fire an employee, the flip side is that they usually spell out the employee's obligations to your business. If the employee isn't performing well, chances are that he or she is in breach of the contract, giving you the legal right to terminate the relationship. Because the interpretation of contract terms can involve legal subtleties, consider having a brief conference with a lawyer before firing an employee who has a written contract.*

To head off the possibility that an employee may try to base a wrongful termination action on alleged illegal conduct or motives in your workplace, be prepared to show the real reason for the firing.

Reasons that may support a firing include:
- performing poorly on the job
- refusing to follow instructions
- abusing sick leave
- being absent excessively
- being tardy habitually
- possessing a weapon at work
- violating company rules
- being dishonest
- endangering health and safety
- engaging in criminal activity
- using alcohol or drugs at work
- behaving violently at work
- gambling at work, and
- disclosing company trade secrets to outsiders.

Depending on the nature of your business, you may have other legitimate reasons to fire employees as well. Whatever reasons you use as a basis for firing people, it's absolutely essential that you treat your employees evenhandedly. That is, if you regularly let some employees engage in prohibited conduct, you'll be on shaky legal ground if you claim good cause for firing others for the same reason.

EXAMPLE: Andrew, a black patient attendant, is a half-hour late for work three days in a row. His employer, a medical clinic, fires him. In suing for wrongful discharge based on illegal discrimination, Andrew shows that two white attendants had been similarly tardy in recent weeks, but received only a verbal warning to shape up. Even though excessive tardiness is a valid business reason for firing someone, the jury awards damages to Andrew because the employer applied the rules unevenly and unfairly.

2. Final Review

Since firing is such a drastic and traumatic step—and one having potentially serious legal consequences for a small business—it makes sense for the owner or president to have the final say. If you're unsure about any aspect of the firing, seek advice from an experienced employment lawyer—especially if the employee may claim illegal discrimination or other legal violation.

Your final review should verify that:
- the firing wouldn't violate antidiscrimination or other statutes
- the firing wouldn't be a breach of contract, including oral assurances of job security or statements made in an employee handbook
- your company has given the employee adequate and documented warnings that he or she faced being fired—except where the conduct would clearly warrant immediate firing
- you have followed your stated personnel practices, and
- you have followed the same procedures in similar situations involving other employees.

For more on firing practices: *See* Dealing With Problem Employees: A Legal Guide, *by Amy DelPo and Lisa Guerin (Nolo).*

O. Unemployment Compensation

State laws generally require employers to contribute to an unemployment insurance fund. Your rate is normally based on the size of your payroll and the amount of unemployment benefits paid from your account. Employers with smaller payrolls and low levels of unemployment claims will, over time, pay lower taxes.

Employees who are terminated because of cutbacks or because they are not a good fit for a job are generally entitled to payments from the unemployment fund. Employees who are fired for serious misconduct—stealing or repeated absenteeism, for example—or who voluntarily leave a job without good cause are not entitled to unemployment payments.

Applying these categories to a particular termination isn't always easy. For example, suppose you and an employee get into an argument and she leaves shortly afterward. If she has quit, benefits are not legally due. If she was fired, however, she's entitled to unemployment benefits absent truly bad conduct such as selling illegal drugs in the workplace. It's sometimes difficult to discern whether a termination is a quitting or a firing.

The details of the claims process vary in each state. Pick up the applicable rules at the unemployment office closest to you. Typically, the process starts when a former employee files a claim with the state unemployment agency. You receive written notice of the claim and can file a written objection—usually within seven to ten days.

The state agency makes an initial determination of whether the former employee is eligible to get unemployment benefits. You or the former employee can appeal the initial eligibility decision and have a hearing before a referee—a hearing officer who is on the staff of the state agency. Additional appeals may also be available.

⚠ Serious charges may be raised. *The referee's decision sometimes influences what happens in a related civil lawsuit. For example, if the referee rules that the employee quit because he or she was being sexually harassed, that ruling may be decisive in a later case that the employee brings against your business. Consult a lawyer if you anticipate that complicated legal issues—such as sexual harassment, illegal discrimination, or retaliation for complaining about a workplace hazard—may surface at the hearing.*

Think Twice Before Fighting Claims

Contesting all questionable claims may not be the wisest policy. Lots of claims you think are questionable probably are allowed under unemployment compensation laws, which are made deliberately lenient to give unemployed workers a transitional source of income and keep them off welfare. Unless there's strong evidence that the employee pilfered from the company or engaged in other fairly extreme conduct such as quitting for no reason, he or she will usually win in a claims contest.

What's more, fighting a claim can be time consuming, emotionally draining, and costly for you—especially when balanced against the fact that a few unemployment claims spread over several years are unlikely to greatly increase your insurance rate.

Perhaps most important, fighting an unemployment claim will guarantee an angry former employee—a person far more likely to file a lawsuit or harm you or your business in some other way, such as bad-mouthing you among friends who remain on your payroll. This might happen anyway. But your challenge to the employee's right to receive unemployment benefits may be the irritant that prompts the former employee to strike back.

Balance the benefits of saving on unemployment taxes against the trouble it takes to fight the claim and the risk of inviting a lawsuit against your business.

P. Independent Contractors

Independent contractors differ from employees in two main ways:

- Independent contractors control not only the outcome of a project but also how the job gets done.
- Independent contractors control their own economic destiny to a large extent, making decisions and business investments that affect how much profit they'll earn and whether they'll suffer a loss.

Typically, a small business hires many independent contractors. Common examples are a lawyer or accountant, a painter who spruces up your office, or a computer consultant who installs specialized software at your store and teaches employees how to use it.

Generally, independent contractors have special skills that you need to call on only sporadically. But sometimes your company may have ongoing needs that can be filled equally well by an employee or an independent contractor. (Section 1, below, describes the advantages and disadvantages of independent contractor status.) If you weigh both possibilities and conclude that you can save money and reduce paperwork by using an independent contractor rather than an employee, fine. But be sure he or she really qualifies for independent contractor status.

The IRS strongly prefers that workers be treated as employees and not as independent contractors. This is because employers must collect taxes on employee earnings through payroll withholding, assuring that the funds flow quickly and surely to the government. By contrast, an independent contractor receives his or her entire earnings without taxes being withheld and is responsible for paying taxes on those earnings. Contributing to the IRS bias against independent contractor status is a belief that some independent contractors may underreport or even fail to report their earnings, which results in a loss of tax revenue. State tax agencies, as well, tend to

discourage businesses from classifying workers as independent contractors.

If you classify a worker as an independent contractor when the worker should have been treated as an employee, and the IRS or a state unemployment or labor commissioner's office investigates and rules against you, you can wind up having to pay the taxes that should have been withheld, together with interest and penalties. Section 2, below, discusses how you can reduce the risk of being challenged by the IRS—and other agencies—over whether you properly classified someone as an independent contractor.

Hiring Independent Contractors, by Stephen Fishman (Nolo), provides clear and comprehensive guidance on all aspects of using independent contractors in your business.

1. Advantages and Disadvantages of Independent Contractor Status

By hiring a person as an employee, you assume financial burdens that you don't have if you hire the same person as an independent contractor. For example, you must make an employer's contribution for the worker's Social Security. You're also responsible for withholding federal and state income taxes, and for keeping records and reporting these items to the federal and state governments. Each year, you must send the employee a Form W-2 showing how much he or she earned and how much was withheld. (See Chapter 8, Section C2, for details on an employer's tax responsibilities.)

That's not all. As an employer, you must carry workers' compensation insurance for the employee and may have to make payments into an unemployment protection fund. Health insurance, retirement plans, and other fringe benefits may add to the cost. Finally, although not legally required, most employers provide paid vacations and sick leave for employees, further driving up costs.

Now, contrast this situation with hiring an independent contractor. When you use an independent contractor, you're not required to withhold taxes from the amount you pay the worker, and you don't have to pay any portion of the worker's Social Security taxes. Your only responsibility is to complete a Form 1099-MISC at the end of the year if you paid the independent contractor $600 or more during the year. The form is sent to the IRS and the employee.

By hiring an independent contractor rather than an employee, you normally also save the expense of providing an office or other work space for the worker and the ongoing expenses of fringe benefits and insurance. Furthermore, if you become unhappy with the person's work, you can turn to another independent contractor without going through the trauma often associated with firing an employee who works each day on your premises.

Another benefit of hiring someone as an independent contractor is that your company generally won't be liable for the negligence of the person you hire. If you hire employees, however, you would be liable if, for example, the employee carelessly injured someone while at work.

Of course, there are tradeoffs. A business doesn't enjoy as much day-to-day control over the work of an independent contractor. And not having the person always available may also be inconvenient. Furthermore, because an independent contractor must charge enough to cover the costs of doing business and still make a profit, he or she may charge a higher price for services than the hourly rate paid to an employee. And if an independent contractor is injured because of some dangerous situation at your business premises or in a place that you have control over, the independent contractor can sue your business, claiming negligence. By contrast, an employee in the same situation would be limited to often lower workers' compensation benefits. But if you carry adequate liability insurance to protect you from claims by any injured person who is not an employee, this isn't a significant drawback.

Given a choice, many workers prefer to be treated as independent contractors rather than employees. Some like the fact that there's no withholding of taxes; they feel that they have a better cash flow, even though they're ultimately responsible for paying their taxes, and the employer isn't picking up any part of the Social Security tax. Workers may also see benefits in being treated as independent contractors because of the opportunity it affords them to charge a higher rate and to deduct business expenses, including money spent on cars, home offices, and travel and entertainment.

On the other hand, some workers prefer employment status that gives them paid vacations, medical care, and other fringe benefits at the employer's expense—and freedom from worry about the paperwork required of people who are in business for themselves.

2. How to Avoid Classification Problems

Because the IRS is the government agency most likely to challenge your classifying a worker as an independent contractor, we'll focus here on how to stay within the IRS guidelines. Fortunately, a worker who qualifies as an independent contractor under the IRS tests will almost certainly qualify as well under the rules of most state agencies, even though the state rules may be slightly different.

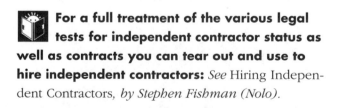 **For a full treatment of the various legal tests for independent contractor status as well as contracts you can tear out and use to hire independent contractors:** *See* Hiring Independent Contractors, *by Stephen Fishman (Nolo).*

It may surprise you to learn that there's no law or court case to precisely guide you in deciding whether it's legally safe to treat a worker as an independent contractor for federal tax purposes. In fact, the most authoritative guidance is found in an unlikely place —the manual the IRS uses to train its audit examiners. Fortunately, by following a few basic rules derived from the principles discussed in this manual, you're likely to steer clear of most problems.

a. The Easy Cases

As a practical matter, you can hire a wide range of independent contractors with virtually no worries about whether they should be treated as employees. These "no sweat" situations involve workers who clearly are in business for themselves, demonstrated by the fact they share most of the following characteristics:

- The worker is available to perform services for many businesses.
- The worker has a fixed base of operations—a commercial or office location perhaps, or a room at home—and ongoing business expenses.
- The worker lists the business in the phone book and may also drum up business through newspaper ads, radio commercials, and circulars.
- The worker undertakes a job based on the results the client wants, but remains free to decide how to get the job done.
- The worker hires and pays for assistants, as needed.
- The worker has invested significant money in the business for equipment, vehicles, and supplies.
- Depending on how the business goes, the worker may earn a large profit, a small profit, or none at all—perhaps even suffering a loss.
- The worker incurs expenses in doing a job that won't be reimbursed by the client.

A few examples will help you identify what a classic, easy-case independent contractor looks like.

EXAMPLE 1: Lydia runs a billing service for a number of law firms. She purchases a speedy computer for her home office, along with sophisticated billing software, which she upgrades from time to time. Lydia advertises her business in a newspaper that serves lawyers, does work for several law firms, and is continually looking for more clients. She goes to lawyers' offices weekly to collect their time and expense records so she can enter them into her computer system and produce bills and reports. During these visits, she sometimes consults with the managing partners about their special problems and needs, but she's free to devise solutions to meet the lawyers' needs. She pays for billing paper and other supplies and for her transportation to and from the lawyers' offices—and isn't directly reimbursed for these expenses.

EXAMPLE 2: Joe does lawn maintenance work in the summer and snow removal in the winter for local businesses, advertising for clients by sending out a circular twice a year to members of the chamber of commerce. He owns a truck, two lawn mowers, a leaf blower, fertilizer spreader, two shovels, and a snow blower, as well as a scraper that attaches to the front of his truck. Joe has a schedule of charges based on the size of the grounds to be serviced and the number of times he provides his services. Sometimes, to meet his commitments to clients, Joe hires his brother to help mow grass or remove snow, paying him as his part-time employee. During a mild winter, when Joe gets fewer calls, he may have trouble covering his expenses.

EXAMPLE 3: Elsie, a catalogue designer, works out of a studio in her apartment. She does freelance work for three local ad agencies, who have major retail clients. The ad agencies pay her a flat fee for each catalogue she lays out. The agencies send her basic materials to be featured and suggest a theme for each catalogue, but rely on Elsie's judgment on how best to present the material. She uses her own cameras, computers, and art supplies to produce the camera-ready pages for the catalogues. In busy times, she farms out some of the artwork to colleagues in a nearby town, and pays them herself.

In each of these examples, the small business people (Lydia, Joe, and Elsie)—not the companies that hire them—determine how to do the work. In addition, Lydia, Joe, and Elsie control how they run their business. It's highly unlikely that a business hiring any of these three as an independent contractor would have any difficulty justifying its position if challenged.

b. The Tougher Cases

Other workers may be harder to classify as independent contractors. Not infrequently, a worker may be in an ambiguous area where the distinction between an employee and an independent contractor gets fuzzy. While you may see some advantages in treating the worker as an independent contractor, you may at the same time feel nervous about the legal risks involved, since any penalties for misclassification will fall squarely on your shoulders and not those of the worker.

The possible ambiguity in a worker's status can be seen in the following examples.

EXAMPLE 1: During the week, Rocco is employed as a custodian at a research firm. Hoping to earn additional money, he checks the help-wanted ads, where he sees that a small company is looking for someone to come in every Sunday to perform janitorial services. Rocco applies for the work and learns that the company would provide mops, brooms, and pails, but that Rocco would be expected to bring his own vaccuum cleaner. The company would pay Rocco $100 per cleaning session, and would reimburse him up to $10 per session for cleaning supplies. The company would provide Rocco with a checklist of cleaning duties and the sequence in which they were to be performed. If the company president were to decide that the work on a given Sunday wasn't satisfactorily performed, Rocco would have to come back on Monday night to touch up.

EXAMPLE 2: Alice is offered work delivering flowers and plants for a local florist shop from 2 p.m. to 5 p.m., Monday through Friday. The deal is that Alice will drive her own van and be responsible for gas and maintenance, which is offset by the fact that she'll earn $13 an hour for her work. The business owner will give Alice a delivery list each day, indicating the priority deliveries which need to be accomplished first. Otherwise, Alice will be free to decide the timing of the deliveries and to choose what route to follow. The business will also provide Alice with a cellular phone to take with her on her deliveries so she can call in periodically to see if she needs to return to the shop to pick up last-minute orders. While making deliveries, Alice will have to wear a jacket bearing the name of the florist shop.

EXAMPLE 3: Edgar teaches art and design at a community college. He is approached by a clothing store owner who has a highly visible downtown location and is known for eye-catching window displays that change weekly. The store owner wants Edgar to come in each Tuesday—a day when Edgar doesn't teach—and change the window display under the owner's supervision. This is similar to work that Edgar is already doing for a bookstore on Saturday mornings. Edgar would be expected occasionally to construct some of the displays in his basement shop, since there's limited space at the clothing store to do so. He'd be reimbursed for the supplies used in the displays, but not for the tools he'd need to do the work.

In these three examples—and thousands of similar cases—the work arrangements share some characteristics of an employment relationship and some characteristics of an independent contractor relationship. It's difficult to predict whether the IRS would agree with the business owner's decision to treat the worker as an independent contractor. The IRS pronouncements are not exact enough to allow you to accurately predict the outcome.

In these ambiguous situations, you have two safe ways to proceed—and a third way that involves a measure of risk.

Treat the worker as an employee. If you want to be super-safe and avoid any risk that the IRS—or other governmental agencies—will determine that you've mistakenly classified the worker as an independent contractor, follow a policy of always treating the worker as an employee. This will protect you from possible penalties. The problem is that both you and the worker will lose the advantages that can flow from an independent contractor relationship.

Require the worker to incorporate. If you and the worker are both motivated to go the independent contractor route in an ambiguous situation, there's a way to do it that's virtually as free from problems as hiring the person as an employee: simply have the worker incorporate. The IRS will almost always treat this as a valid arrangement and accept the fact that the worker isn't your employee but an employee of his or her own corporation. As described in Chapter 1, it's legal in every state to form a one-person corporation—and the process can be simple and relatively inexpensive.

Here are the details about how this strategy works:

- The worker forms a corporation under state law and obtains an Employer Identification Number from the IRS.
- You sign a contract with the corporation under which the corporation agrees to provide specified services for your business.
- The corporation hires the worker (who owns the corporate shares) as an employee to perform the services required by your contract with the corporation.
- The corporation bills you as services are performed for your business under the contract.
- You pay the corporation—not the employee—for the services billed to your business.
- Each time the corporation issues a paycheck to its employee, the corporation withholds federal income taxes, along with the employee's share of Social Security and Medicare taxes, as outlined in Chapter 8.
- Periodically, the corporation (using its own Employer Identification Number) pays the IRS the withheld taxes along with the employer's share of Social Security and Medicare taxes.

You'll find numerous easy-to-use contracts in: *Hiring Independent Contractors, by Stephen Fishman (Nolo). In filling out these contracts, be sure to indicate that you're hiring the corporation as an independent contractor. The corporation's owner should sign the contract in a corporate capacity (as president, for example) rather than as an individual.*

Accept a measure of risk. Suppose the worker's status as an independent contractor is ambiguous and, for one reason or another, the safer courses of action—treating the worker as an employee or requiring the worker to incorporate—are not practical. Then you must recognize that if you move ahead and hire the worker as an independent contractor, you're opening yourself up to some legal risk.

One way to reduce the risk is to get professional advice. See a tax expert—a lawyer or accountant who's familiar with the worker classification issues.

Another way to reduce the risk is to follow as many of the following suggestions as you can:

- Sign a contract with the independent contractor spelling out the responsibilities of each party and how payment is to be determined for each job. The contract should allow the independent contractor to hire his or her own assistants and to have as much say as possible as to how the work is to be performed. A sample contract is shown below.
- Require the independent contractor to furnish all or most of the tools, equipment, and material needed to complete the job.
- Avoid a commitment to reimburse the independent contractor for his or her business expenses; if necessary, pay the independent contractor a little more, but have him or her assume that responsibility.
- If feasible, arrange to pay a flat fee for the work rather than an hourly or weekly rate.
- Don't provide employee-type benefits such as paid vacation days, health insurance, or retirement plans.
- Make it clear that the independent contractor is free to offer services to other businesses.

- Specifically state in your contract that the contractor will carry his or her own insurance, including workers' compensation coverage.
- Keep a file containing the independent contractor's business card, stationery samples,

ads, and Employer Identification Number. These items can help show that the contractor has an established business.

SAMPLE CONTRACT WITH INDEPENDENT CONTRACTOR

AGREEMENT

This AGREEMENT is made on _____, ____, between _____
                                                                                    Client

of _____ and _____
                    Business Address   Contractor

of _____.
                    Business Address

1. Services to Be Performed. Contractor agrees to perform the following services for Client:

   [*Description of services*]

2. Time for Performance. Contractor agrees to complete the performance of these services on or before

_____, _____.

3. Payment. In consideration of Contractor's performance of these services, Client agrees to pay Contractor as follows:

   [*Description of how payment will be computed*]

4. Invoices. Contractor will submit invoices for all services performed.

5. Independent Contractor. The parties intend Contractor to be an independent contractor in the performance of these services. Contractor shall have the right to control and determine the method and means of performing the above services; Client shall not have the right to control or determine such method or means.

6. Other Clients. Contractor retains the right to perform services for other clients.

7. Assistants. Contractor, at Contractor's expense, may employ such assistants as Contractor deems appropriate to carry out this agreement. Contractor will be responsible for paying such assistants, as well as any expense attributable to such assistants, including income taxes, unemployment insurance, and Social Security taxes, and will maintain workers' compensation insurance for such employees.

8. Equipment and Supplies. Contractor, at Contractor's own expense, will provide all equipment, tools, and supplies necessary to perform the above services, and will be responsible for all other expenses required for the performance of those services.

CONTRACTOR   CLIENT

_____   _____

Date _____

⚠️ **Trade secrets.** *In some situations, you may disclose trade secrets of your business to an independent contractor. If so, include a clause in the agreement prohibiting the independent contractor from disclosing or making any unauthorized use of the trade secrets.*

3. Special Categories of Workers

In most situations, the status of a worker is determined by the guidelines described in Section 2 above. Certain workers, however, fall into special categories, and the usual IRS criteria don't apply to them. For example, the federal tax law says that the following workers are automatically treated as employees as far as Social Security taxes, Medicare taxes, and federal unemployment taxes (FUTA) are concerned:

- officers of corporations who provide service to the corporation
- food and laundry delivery drivers
- full-time salespeople who sell goods for resale
- full-time life insurance agents working mainly for one company
- at-home workers who are supplied with material and given specifications for work to be performed.

For these workers, you must withhold the worker's share of Social Security and Medicare taxes and you must also pay the employer's portion of those taxes. But you may or may not have to withhold income taxes for a statutory employee; it depends on whether the worker qualifies as an employee or independent contractor under the usual IRS guidelines.

Federal law also provides that for tax purposes, licensed real estate agents and door-to-door salespeople are generally treated as "nonemployees"—which is another way of saying they're independent contractors. People in these occupations may, however, be treated as employees for the purpose of state payroll taxes and workers' compensation coverage.

As a sole proprietor or partner in your own business, you're neither an employee nor an independent contractor. You're responsible for paying your own income tax and Social Security self-employment tax. If you're a shareholder in a corporation but provide services to the corporation, you're generally an employee.

4. Additional State Rules

The IRS analysis of who qualifies as an independent contractor is similar to the standards followed in most states for state taxes and unemployment rules, but there can be some differences. For example, in California, a person working for a licensed contractor who performs services requiring a license (for example, erecting a building) is considered to be an employee unless the worker also has a valid contractor's license. In short, if you plan to hire independent contractors, check with the employment office in your state to see if special rules are in effect.

5. The Risks of Misclassification

There are at least three ways for the IRS to learn about your hiring and classification practices. First, the IRS may look into the affairs of an independent contractor who hasn't been paying his or her income taxes. Second, disgruntled employees may complain to the IRS if they think independent contractors are getting favored treatment. Third, during tax audits, the IRS routinely checks to see if workers have been misclassified as independent contractors.

The presumption is that the worker is an employee unless proven otherwise. If the status of a worker is questioned, it's up to you to prove that the worker is an independent contractor rather than an employee.

If it turns out that an employee was in fact misclassified, the cost to your business will be heavy. You'll be responsible for paying the employee's Social Security tax, federal income tax, and federal unemployment insurance for up to three years. In addition, the IRS can add penalties and interest.

State government officials are also interested in businesses that misclassify employees as independent contractors. A state employment office may audit your business to see if there's been any misclassification. The audit can be the result of a spot check by the state employment office or a request by an independent contractor for unemployment or workers' compensation benefits. You may wind up owing money to a state unemployment insurance fund. And if the IRS learns of the state's action, you'll probably face a federal audit as well.

A Worker's Status Might Change

Don't assume that once you've determined that a worker is an independent contractor, you can forget about the matter. If there's a shift in the working arrangements, you may have to reclassify the worker.

EXAMPLE: John operates a small desktop publishing shop specializing in writing and designing brochures, flyers, and other promotional materials for small businesses. At first, John does most of the work himself, turning any overload over to others with similar skills. John collects from the customer and pays these people as independent contractors. So far, so good.

As John's business grows, he arranges for part-time help on a fairly regular basis. Sue, Ted, and Ellen regularly handle the overflow, working in John's offices under his broad supervision an average of about two days per week each. The rest of the time they work for themselves. John continues to treat them as independent contractors. By law, he shouldn't.

Since John is exercising significant control over these workers and using their services in-house on a regular basis, he's tempting fate—and the IRS. To be safe, John should treat them as part-time employees, which requires that he withhold income taxes and pay the employer's share of Social Security taxes as well as carry workers' compensation insurance and pay into the state's unemployment fund.

The Importance of Excellent Customer Relations

Customers (you may call them clients or patients) are the lifeblood of any small business or professional practice. To thrive, you not only need a steady stream of people who keep coming back for more goods or services; you also need them to enthusiastically recommend your business to their friends. To build a loyal following, you must do more than just give people what the law requires. Yes, knowledge of your legal rights and those of your customers is important, but it's even more important not to let legal technicalities take priority over a key objective of your business: to keep happy customers coming back and sending other people your way.

EXAMPLE: When Sandra brought her white wool blazer home from the dry cleaner's, she was dismayed to see that it had a very slight pink tint. Sandra reported the problem to Milt, the owner of the cleaning shop. Milt could have legally responded in a number of ways, including the following:

- "The problem is scarcely noticeable. You're being fussy."
- "How do I know the blazer wasn't like this when you brought it in?"
- "Didn't you see our sign? We're not responsible for any problems once you take the cleaned garment from the shop."
- "That's a two-year old blazer. Used clothing isn't worth much. I'll pay you $20 for the damage—not a penny more."
- "I've never had this type of complaint before. I want to send the blazer to an independent testing lab to see if the fabric is substandard. If it is, it's your problem—not mine."

But Milt was a wise businessperson. He didn't stand on his legal rights. Instead he told Sandra: "I'm sorry this happened. We use state-of-the-art cleaning processes, but apparently something went wrong. In any case, we guarantee your complete satisfaction. Since we can't fix this type of damage, let me know the purchase price of an equivalent new blazer." Sandra did, and Milt reimbursed her the full amount.

As a result of his enlightened attitude, Milt had a happy customer. In the two years since the blazer problem, Sandra and her husband have taken more than $500 worth of cleaning business to Milt's shop. They not only continue to be loyal customers, but—even more important—every time Sandra wears her new blazer, she tells the story of how Milt bought it for her and she recommends his business. Because Milt treated Sandra well, the blazer now ranks as one of Milt's all-time best investments.

Now consider what would have happened if Milt had responded with a strictly legalistic approach, offering Sandra the value of a two-year-old blazer. Sandra might have grumbled and accepted the $20 payment, or she might have taken Milt to small claims court and perhaps have won a few dollars more. But this much is certain: Sandra and her husband would never have taken any more cleaning to Milt's place. Even worse, they'd likely have told others about Milt's inadequate service for years to come and might have complained to local better business and state regulatory agencies. So while Milt was thinking of himself as a tough businessperson who knows his legal rights and never lets customers rip him off, he actually would have foolishly lost many thousands of dollars of business.

Whether you run a restaurant, a hardware store, or a sand and gravel business, if a customer complains about your product or service, don't quibble. It's much smarter to point to your customer satisfaction policy as you eliminate or reduce the charges—and maybe even give the customer something extra as a reward for putting up with the problem. Maybe you won't make any money on that transaction; you'll probably even take a small loss. And yes, once in a blue moon someone will take unfair advantage of your policy. So what? When you consider the good feelings that customers will have about your business—and the fact that you'll receive positive rather than negative word-of-mouth from everyone you treat generously—it's a bargain. Consider, too, that a customer whose problem you resolve is unlikely to complain to any agency or board with power to license or otherwise oversee your business. Anyone who has had to cope with an investigation knows that even if the complaint that triggered the inquiry has no merit, the process can be worrisome and, if lawyers are involved, expensive.

Legal relationships with customers are covered in the next three chapters. Chapter 17 covers the legal rules for handling advertising, retail pricing, returns, warranties, and other customer transactions. In Chapter 18, you'll find information about checks and credit cards. Chapter 19 explains how to extend credit and get prompt payment.

A. Developing Your Customer Satisfaction Policy

Whether you're selling products or services, go farther than is legally required in anticipating and responding to the problems of your customers. How you do this depends in part on the nature of the products or services you offer. But for starters, consider the policy of Eddie Bauer—a highly successful national company that sells outdoor goods through its catalogue and retail outlets:

OUR GUARANTEE

Every item we sell will give you complete satisfaction or you may return it for a full refund.

OUR CREED

To give you such outstanding quality, value, service, and guarantee that we may be worthy of your high esteem.

Over the years, my family and I have bought many items from Eddie Bauer. We've never had to return anything for a refund. But just knowing that the company stands behind what it sells has given us confidence in Eddie Bauer products. And that, of course, is the point: By reassuring customers in advance that they control the resolution of any problems, Eddie Bauer's good customer service is a marketing advantage.

Some department store chains such as Nordstrom's have also built solid businesses based in large part on their guarantee of customer satisfaction. But it's not just the big-time operators who successfully use a customer recourse policy as a business-building technique. Nolo—the small California company that published this book—has more than held its own in the highly competitive book business in part because of consumer-oriented policies such as this one:

OUR NO-HASSLE GUARANTEE

Return anything you buy directly from Nolo for any reason and we'll cheerfully refund your purchase price. No ifs, ands, or buts.

Short and simple. No legal technicalities. No complicated rules. As additional evidence of its desire to serve its customers, Nolo offers another customer satisfaction policy almost unheard of in the industry: Nolo gives people 35% off on any current title if they return the cover of a prior, out-of-date edition. Why? Because out-of-date law books can be dangerous, and a customer who uses them is poorly served.

Businesses that treat customers generously can reap an unexpected dividend: higher morale among workers. Employees are not robots. They hate defending miserly policies that result in stressful confrontations with customers. They make great ambassadors for businesses they truly feel good about.

LAW IN THE REAL WORLD
Listening to Your Employees

Rose, the owner of a retail store, overhears clerk Ned tell an unhappy customer that there is nothing he can do—the time to return a particular item ran out yesterday. Rose intervenes to solve the customer's problem by graciously taking the merchandise back. Now, Ned is unhappy. "I was just following your policy," he tells Rose. "You undercut me and made me feel really stupid." Rose realizes it is unwise to adopt a strict policy and then throw it out on a whim. After all, if she hadn't overheard the conversation, she would have lost a customer and made an employee feel bad about being a tough guy. Rose meets with her employees, and together they come up with a much more customer-friendly policy. They post it conspicuously in the store so that everyone knows what the new, fairer rules are.

Businesses that offer services have different problems than restaurants and retail outlets. But they still have many opportunities to enhance customer satisfaction and favorable word-of-mouth. On longer-term jobs, you can set time-performance standards in advance so that both you and the customer can judge whether everyone's expectations are being met. Often this consists of little more than committing yourself to meeting interim deadlines.

For example, a toxic materials contractor removing asbestos from heating ducts in a three-story building might agree to get the entire job done in 30 days with the first floor clean and ready to reoccupy in ten days and the second floor in 20 days. A home remodeling or painting company might go farther and commit to meticulously cleaning up its work area each day.

Another good approach is to regularly ask for feedback from customers or clients. For example, if you run a bookkeeping service, a copy shop, or a janitorial service that does regular business with larger accounts, ask your customers from time to time whether your high standards—and the customer's needs—are being met. I was favorably impressed when the landlord who owns the building where my law firm practices asked me to evaluate the interior and exterior maintenance services we were receiving. There's currently a glut of office space in my town. When my lease is up I'll have a choice of many new buildings. But I'll remember that my current landlord seemed sincerely concerned about keeping this building spic and span.

You may think that a business offering a service as intangible as a seminar would have a hard time developing an effective customer satisfaction policy—but you'd be wrong. Here's a guarantee from the American Management Association that serves as an excellent model:

A SIMPLE GUARANTEE FOR A COMPLEX BUSINESS WORLD

At AMA, we guarantee the quality of our seminars. It's that simple. More than 98% of our seminar attendees say they would recommend the course they have taken to their colleagues. But if for any reason you are not satisfied with a seminar for which you have paid, AMA will give you credit toward another course of comparable price or will simply refund your fee. That's it! No hassles. No loopholes. Just excellent service. That's what AMA is all about.

Here are some other examples of service businesses that use guarantees as a way of building a customer base:

- If you're unhappy with your hotel room, Hampton Inn will refund your money.
- If you get transferred from phone to phone while seeking an answer to an insurance question, Delta Dental Plan of Massachusetts will send you a $50 check.
- If your mini-pizza takes more than five minutes to be served, Pizza Hut gives you a free one.
- If you're not satisfied with a lawn treatment applied by Green Valley Lawn Care, the company will reapply the treatment at no cost—or, if you prefer, refund the cost of the treatment.
- If an item you buy from Eddie Bauer doesn't give complete satisfaction, you can return it for a full refund.

Elements of an Effective Customer Satisfaction Policy

The following ideas for developing your customer satisfaction policy come from *Marketing Without Advertising,* by Michael Phillips and Salli Rasberry (Nolo):

- Customers should be encouraged to tell you about any problems.
- Customers should know their rights and responsibilities from the beginning.
- Customers should know the circumstances under which they are entitled to get their money back and how to take advantage of other rights.
- Customers—not you—should feel in control. It's far better to provide a full refund if the customer is dissatisfied than to demand that the customer come up with a "good reason" for the refund.
- A refund, or any other recourse you offer, should be prompt.

B. Telling Customers About Your Policies

Every communication between you and your customers is an opportunity to let them know that you're sincerely interested in their complaints and comments. Show your concern through signs in your business place, questionnaires and surveys mailed to them, and by simply inquiring from time to time whether their needs are being met.

Use your imagination. Labels, receipts, catalogues, and packaging afford you the chance to let people know what their rights are and exactly how you'll deal with any problems. And don't use small print. Although it's sometimes hard to accept, you want your customers to know that you welcome the chance to fix problems. Also see Chapter 17, Section E, for advice on how your website can best convey your policies to customers.

And now, a few words on how not to communicate with customers. We've all seen stores that have negative signs next to the cash register, with unfriendly messages like:

No returns without receipt

No cash refunds

No out-of-town checks

Often, the owner has then added a few Scotch-taped signs with more negative messages such as "$10 is charged for every returned check—no exceptions" or "If you break it, you own it." Not only is this offensive—it's stupid. Your statement of a customer's responsibilities doesn't have to be put in confrontational language. To take one example, even if you decide not to give cash refunds (a policy you may want to rethink), there are friendlier ways to state your policy, such as:

We are pleased to accept all returns

within 30 days for full store credit.

This statement has a positive tone but makes the customer responsible for returning the goods within 30 days to receive credit.

The law in many cities and a few states requires that you post your policies on returns and other customer recourse. In many of those locations, if you don't post your policy, your customers have the right to a full cash refund. But even if the law doesn't require you to post your policy, it makes excellent business and legal sense.

Get Help to Solve Customer Disputes

Sometimes, despite your best efforts to treat customers fairly, a dispute starts to get out of hand. At that point, consider bringing the Better Business Bureau or other respected third party into the picture. I recommend the BBB because according to various national polls, it's usually the first agency that consumers turn to for help when they're trying to solve a problem with a business.

Your local government may also offer mediation as a means of resolving consumer-business disputes without going to court. This is true, for example, in many counties in California. Also, many communities have neighborhood dispute programs that may be helpful for some types of small business disputes.

For more on dispute resolution techniques, including negotiation, mediation, arbitration, and litigation, see Chapter 22.

Legal Requirements for Dealing With Customers

Many legal problems can be avoided by adopting enlightened policies for dealing with your customers. Customer-friendly policies, however, can't anticipate every problem. Consequently, you must understand the legal rules that apply. This chapter covers advertising, retail pricing and return practices, warranties, and consumer protection laws.

A. Advertising

Before we get into the legal rules for advertising, consider a more fundamental question: Do you really need to advertise?

1. Is Advertising Necessary?

People starting a small business often assume they must advertise to attract customers. This always made good sense to me—until I read and thought about some eye-opening ideas in *Marketing Without Advertising,* by Michael Phillips and Salli Rasberry (Nolo). Phillips and Rasberry argue convincingly that for small businesses, most money spent on conventional advertising—radio and TV

spots and display ads in newspapers—is wasted. You're competing with thousands of other advertisers, and your message is unlikely to be noticed by enough potential customers to produce a profitable level of sales.

Here's more from *Marketing Without Advertising:*

> The best and most economical way to attract and hold customers is through personal recommendation. A customer who is prescreened and prepared for what you have to offer is far more likely to appreciate you and use your business than is someone responding to an ad offering a low price. The essence of marketing without advertising is to encourage personal recommendation. How do you do this? Lots of ways, all of which start with creating an atmosphere of trust. Central to doing this is to run an honest business.

Phillips and Rasberry recommend marketing strategies that don't rely on traditional advertising. For example, they discuss the importance of the physical appearance of your business (insist on scrupulous cleanliness and avoid clutter and unpleasant smells). They point out that listing your products or services where customers expect to find them—such as the Yellow Pages, local business directories, trade publications, and, depending on the business, the classifieds—is often extremely cost-effective.

Interestingly, Phillips and Rasberry distinguish between advertising and listings not on the basis of cost (although advertising does usually cost considerably more), but on whether customers are prescreened to see your message. For example, someone who checks the Yellow Pages or a local free classified newspaper for a drain cleaning service needs that type of business. By contrast, someone who reads a display ad or hears a radio spot for the same business is unlikely to need that service immediately or to remember the ad months or years later when the need does arise.

2. Legal Standards for Advertising

Advertising is regulated by both federal and state law. Under the law, your ad is unlawful if it tends to mislead or deceive. This means the government doesn't have to prove (at an administrative hearing or in court) that the ad actually fooled anyone—only that it had a deceptive quality. Your intentions don't matter either. If your ad is deceptive, you'll face legal problems even if you have the best intentions in the world. What counts is the overall impression created by the ad—not the technical truthfulness of the individual parts. Taken as a whole, your ad must fairly inform the ordinary consumer.

In addition, if your ad contains a false statement, you have violated the law. The fact that you didn't know the information was false is irrelevant.

The Federal Trade Commission (FTC) is the main federal agency that takes action against unlawful advertising. State and local governments also go after businesses that violate advertising laws; usually this is the responsibility of the state attorney general, consumer protection agency, and local district attorney. Consumers and competitors may also be able to proceed directly against the advertiser.

Over the years, the FTC has taken action against many businesses accused of false and deceptive advertising. A significant number of those administrative actions have been tested in court. By and large, courts have upheld even the most stringent FTC policies. For the most part, the FTC relies on consumers and competitors to report unlawful advertising. (See Appendix B for addresses and phone numbers of FTC offices.)

If FTC investigators are convinced that an ad violates the law, they usually try to bring the violator into voluntary compliance through informal means. If that doesn't work, the FTC can issue a cease-and-desist order and bring a civil lawsuit on behalf of people who have been harmed. The FTC can also seek a court order (injunction) to stop a questionable ad while an investigation is in progress. In addition, the FTC can require an advertiser to run corrective ads—ads that state the correct facts and admit that an earlier ad was deceptive.

Most states have laws—usually in the form of consumer fraud or deceptive practices statutes—that regulate advertising. Under these laws, state or local officials can seek injunctions against unlawful ads and take legal action to get restitution to consumers. Some laws provide for criminal penalties—fines and jail—but criminal proceedings for false advertising are rare unless fraud is involved.

Consumers often have the right to sue advertisers under state consumer protection laws. (See Section D.) For example, someone who purchases a product or services in reliance on a false or deceptive ad might sue in small claims court for a refund or join with others (sometimes ten of thousands of others) to sue for a huge sum in another court.

A competitor harmed by unlawful advertising, or faced with the likelihood of such harm, generally has the right to seek an injunction and possibly an award of money (damages) as well, although damages are often difficult to prove. Such cases usually are based on one of two legal theories: unfair competition or commercial disparagement.

3. How to Stay Out of Trouble

The following rules will help keep your ads within safe, legal limits.

Rule 1—Be Accurate

Make sure your ads are factually correct and that they don't tend to deceive or mislead the buying public. Don't show a picture of this year's model of a product if what you're selling is last year's model, even if they look almost the same.

Be truthful about what consumers can expect from your product. Don't say ABC pills will cure headaches if the pills offer only temporary pain relief. Don't claim a rug shampooer is a wizard at removing all kinds of stains when in fact there are some it won't budge.

Waterproof or fireproof means just that—not water resistant or fire resistant under some circumstances. The term polar, when attached to winter gear, suggests that it will keep people warm in extreme cold, not that it's just adequate when the temperature drops near freezing.

Rule 2—Get Permission

Does your ad feature someone's picture or endorsement? Does it quote material written by someone not on your staff or employed by your advertising agency? Does it use the name of a national organization such as the Boy Scouts or Red Cross? If so, get written permission.

Under U.S. copyright law, the "fair use" doctrine allows limited quotations from copyrighted works without specific authorization from the copyright owner. In some circumstances, this doctrine provides legal justification for the widespread practice of quoting from favorable reviews in ads for books, movies and plays—and even vacuum cleaners. However, with the exception of brief quotes from product or service reviews, you should always seek permission to quote protected material. For more on the fair use doctrine and many other aspects of copyright law and practice, see *The Copyright Handbook: How to Protect & Use Written Works,* by Stephen Fishman (Nolo).

Rule 3—Treat Competitors Fairly

Don't knock the goods, services, or reputation of others by giving false or misleading information. If you compare your goods and services with those of other companies, double check your information to make sure that every statement in your ad is accurate. Then check again.

Rule 4—Have Sufficient Quantities on Hand

When you advertise goods for sale, make every effort to have enough on hand to supply the demand that it's reasonable to expect. If you don't think you can meet the demand, state in your ad that quantities are limited. You may even want to state the number of units on hand.

State law may require merchants to stock an advertised product in quantities large enough to meet reasonably expected demand, unless the ad states that stock is limited. California, for example, has such a law. In other states, merchants may have to give a rain check if they run out of advertised goods in certain circumstances. Make sure you know what your state requires.

Rule 5—Watch Out for the Word "Free"

If you say that goods or services are "free" or "without charge," be sure there are no unstated terms or conditions that qualify the offer. If there are any limits, state them clearly and conspicuously.

Let's assume that you offer a free paintbrush to anyone who buys a can of paint for $10.95 and that you describe the kind of brush. Because you're disclosing the terms and conditions of your offer, you're in good shape so far. But there are pitfalls to avoid.

- If the $10.95 is more than you usually charge for this kind of paint, the brush clearly isn't free.
- Don't reduce the quality of the paint that the customer must purchase or the quantity of any services (such as free delivery) you normally provide. If you provide a lesser product or service, you're exacting a hidden cost for the brush.
- Disclose any other terms, conditions, or limitations.

For more information on the use of the word "free," see Section B1, below.

Rule 6—Be Careful When You Describe Sales and Savings

You should be absolutely truthful in all claims about pricing. Because this point is so important, I discuss it in more detail in Section B1, below.

Rule 7—Observe Limitations on Offers of Credit

Don't advertise that you offer easy credit unless it's true. A business that's not careful in this area can be charged with engaging in an unfair or deceptive practice that violates the FTC law. You don't offer easy credit if:

- You don't extend credit to people who don't have a good credit rating.
- You offer credit to people with marginal or poor credit ratings but you require a higher down payment or shorter repayment period than is ordinarily required for creditworthy people.
- You offer credit to poor risks, but once all the fine print is deciphered, the true cost of credit you charge exceeds the average charged by others in your retail market.
- You offer credit to poor risks at favorable terms but employ draconian (although legal) collection practices against buyers who fall behind.

If you advertise specific credit terms, you must provide all relevant details, including the down payment, the terms of repayment, and the annual interest rate.

B. Retail Pricing and Return Practices

In addition to regulating advertising, the federal government and most state governments have laws and rules that address several types of retail practices.

1. Deceptive Pricing

The Federal Trade Commission (FTC) has jurisdiction over deceptive pricing practices. At the state level, usually the attorney general's office or, in bigger cities, the district attorney's consumer fraud unit enforces laws dealing with deceptive trade practices. The two biggest problems they encounter concern retailers who (1) make incorrect price comparisons with other merchants or with their own "regular" prices, and (2) those who offer something that is supposedly "free" but in fact has a cost. (See Section A.)

Offering a reduction from your usual selling price is a common and powerful sales technique. But to satisfy legal requirements, it's essential that the former price be the actual, bona fide price at which you offered the article. Otherwise, the pricing is misleading.

> **EXAMPLE:** WizWare Inc. produces computer software and announces a new product for $129. But the company sells the product to wholesalers as if it were a $79 product and similarly discounts it to direct customers. The $129 price has never really existed, except to mislead customers into thinking they were receiving a discount.

Price comparisons often use words such as "Regularly," "Usually," or "Reduced." For example, it's common to see a price tag that says, "Regularly $200, Now $150." Or sometimes a sign says "⅓ off our regular price." These comparisons are fine legally—if you in fact offered the sale merchandise at the old price for a reasonable length of time. They're not okay if you've brought a special batch of merchandise especially for the sale and created a fictional "regular" price or one you adhered to for only a day or two.

If your ad compares your price with what other merchants are charging for the same product, be sure of two things:

- The other merchants are selling the identical product; and
- There were a sufficient number of sales at the higher price by merchants in your area so that you're offering a legitimate bargain.

In other words, make sure that the higher comparison price isn't an isolated or unrepresentative price.

Regarding offers of "free" products or services, you can offer gifts only if there are no strings attached. (See the discussion of "free" offers in Section A.)

2. Sales Away From Your Place of Business

A customer has three days—a "cooling-off period"—to cancel any sale not made at a normal business place. For details, see the FTC's trade regulation rule called "Cooling Off Period for Door-to-Door Sales," 16 CFR § 429. Here's how the FTC defines a door-to-door sale:

> The sale, lease, or rental of consumer goods or services with a purchase price of $25 or more, whether under single or multiple contracts, in which the seller or his representative personally solicits the sale, including those in response to or following an invitation by the buyer, and the buyer's agreement or offer to purchase is made at a place other than the place of business of the seller.

Pay attention to the words "other than the place of business of the seller." They cover a lot of ground. Legally, a door-to-door sale is one made at a customer's home, but it's also one made at a sales presentation at a friend's home, a computer fair, hotel, restaurant, convention, or similar site.

If you do any selling covered by the FTC definition, you must do two things. First, give the buyer a fully completed receipt or a copy of the sales contract. These documents must contain everything that you promised orally, as well as the date of the transaction and your name and address. Also, you must have the following words in large boldface type near the signature on the contract or the front of the receipt:

> You, the buyer, may cancel this transaction at any time prior to midnight of the third business day after the date of this transaction. See the attached notice of cancellation form for an explanation of this right.

LAW IN THE REAL WORLD
Selling at Trade Shows

Do you sell consumer goods at trade shows or fairs? If so, you should give customers notice about their right to cancel their purchases. Otherwise, you may be violating the FTC's three-day cooling-off rule.

The FTC devised the rule to protect homebound, unsophisticated consumers from fast-talking door-to-door salespeople. (If you've seen the movie *Tin Men*, you know what I mean.) At the time, most transactions at trade shows and fairs were business-to-business; the cooling-off period didn't apply. Over the years, however, trade shows and fairs have expanded considerably. In fact, many shows—featuring everything from computer software to outdoor equipment and housewares—are geared primarily toward consumer sales.

The FTC has "prosecutorial discretion" in pursuing merchants who sell at trade shows and fairs without giving customers a notice of cancellation rights. In most instances, the FTC doesn't stroll the halls of convention centers to shut down noncomplying businesses. But it has that power. And an unhappy (and savvy) customer could report you to the agency, which would investigate and could take action against you.

Second, you must give the buyer at the same time a completed form, in duplicate, labeled "NOTICE OF CANCELLATION." It must be attached to the receipt or contract and be easily detachable. Here's what the notice must say:

NOTICE OF CANCELLATION

(Enter date of transaction)

You may cancel this transaction, without any penalty or obligation, within three business days from the above date.

If you cancel, any property traded in, any payments made by you under the contract or sale, and any negotiable instrument executed by you will be returned within ten business days following receipt by the seller of your cancellation notice, and any security interest arising out of the transaction will be canceled.

If you cancel, you must make available to the seller at your residence, in substantially as good condition as when received, any goods delivered to you under this contract or sale; or you may if you wish, comply with the instructions of the seller regarding the return shipment of the goods at the seller's expense and risk.

If you do make the goods available to the seller and the seller does not pick them up within 20 days of the date of your notice of cancellation, you may retain or dispose of the goods without any further obligation. If you fail to make the goods available to the seller, or if you agree to return the goods to the seller and fail to do so, then you remain liable for performance of all obligations under the contract.

To cancel this transaction, mail or deliver a signed and dated copy of this cancellation notice or any other written notice, or send a telegram to [*name of seller*], at [*address of seller's place of business*] not later than midnight of _____.

I hereby cancel this transaction.

_____   _____

Date   Buyer's Signature

⚠️ **State laws and regulations.** *Most states also have laws and regulations dealing with door-to-door sales. Some of them go beyond the federal requirements. For example, in some states, the cooling-off period is five days. Also, some states require that the notice of cancellation and contract be in the same language as the oral presentation.*

3. Refunds

Strictly speaking, once a sale (other than a door-to-door sale) is complete, you don't have to give a refund to a customer who changes his or her mind. This is based on traditional contract law, which says that a sale is a completed contract. In short, unless there's been a significant breach of the contract (for example, the goods or services you sold were seriously flawed), or some provision allows one of the parties to cancel, you're both stuck. So a customer who buys a product from you doesn't have the legal right to cancel the "contract" later and automatically get a refund. By the same token, if you discover that you could have charged a higher price, you can't cancel the sale either.

So much for the legalities. In real life, most retailers give customers the option of returning merchandise for either a cash refund or at least a store credit. Sometimes retailers impose conditions. For example, the customer must return the merchandise within a certain number of days; the merchandise must be unused; the customer must show a receipt or other proof of purchase.

A liberal refund policy can give your customers confidence in your business and can be an effective marketing technique. (See Chapter 16.) Whatever you decide to do about a customer recourse policy, word your rules as positively as possible and post them conspicuously in your store.

California's Refund Statute

In what appears to be the beginning of a trend, California (which is often a legal leader) has adopted a statute about refunds. New York, Virginia, and Florida also have refund posting laws.

Under California Civil Code § 1723, a business is not required to give a cash refund or even a store credit to a customer who wants to return a product. You must, however, conspicuously post your policies if you don't meet the following minimum standards for merchandise returned within seven days after the sale:

- You don't give either a cash refund or credit refund; and
- You don't allow an equal exchange for such merchandise.

The California law doesn't apply to sales of food, plants, flowers, or other perishable goods. And it doesn't apply to merchandise marked "as is," "no returns accepted," or "all sales final," or goods used or damaged after purchase, special goods received as ordered, goods not returned in their original package, or goods which can't be resold due to health reasons.

4. Mail Orders

If you take orders by mail, telephone, fax, or the Internet, you need to become familiar with the Federal Trade Commission's rule dealing with this subject. The best source is the booklet *A Business Guide to the Federal Trade Commission's Mail or Telephone Order Merchandise Rule*. It's available at the FTC website, www.ftc.gov. Once there, click "For Business," then "Business Publications," then "Telemarketing," and look for a link to the guide (a somewhat mistitled link; it calls it "Businessperson's

Guide"). Here are some important features of the FTC rule:

- You must ship the merchandise within 30 days after you receive a properly completed order and payment, unless your ad clearly states that it will take longer.
- If there's going to be a delay, you must notify the customer in writing. You must give the customer the option of a new shipment date (if known) or the opportunity to cancel the order and receive a full refund. You must give the customer a postage-free way to reply. You may assume that a customer who doesn't reply has agreed to the delay.
- If the customer cancels, you must refund the customer's money within seven days after you receive the canceled order. If the customer used a credit card, you must issue the credit within one billing cycle.
- A customer who consents to an indefinite delay can still cancel the order any time before it's shipped.
- A customer who cancels or never receives the ordered merchandise doesn't have to accept a store credit in place of a refund, but is entitled to a cash refund or credit on the charge card.

The mail order rule doesn't cover:

- services such as mail order photo finishing
- spaced deliveries such as magazines (except for the first shipment)
- sales of seeds and plants
- COD orders, or
- transactions covered by the FTC's Negative Option Rule, such as book and music clubs.

5. Unordered Merchandise

With only two exceptions, federal law (and the law in most states) makes it illegal to mail unordered merchandise. The exceptions:

- free samples that you clearly and conspicuously mark as such
- merchandise mailed by a charitable organization to solicit contributions.

It's illegal to send the recipient a bill or dunning letter for any unordered merchandise. The FTC applies this law as well to unordered merchandise delivered by means other than the mail. A person receiving unordered merchandise can treat it as a gift.

C. Warranties

Basically, a warranty is a guarantee. It's a commitment that the manufacturer and retailer will stand behind a product. Sometimes a warranty is made through an oral or written statement of the seller. This is called an express warranty.

Even if you don't make an express warranty, however, a warranty may be imposed by law; this is called an implied warranty. In other words, the law holds the manufacturer or retailer responsible for some warranties even if they've said nothing on the subject. Sometimes you can get rid of an implied warranty by making a disclaimer.

The law of warranties comes from two main sources. The first is a law called the Uniform Commercial Code (UCC), which has been adopted in every state. The second is the Magnuson-Moss Warranty Act, a federal law designed to protect consumers. In addition, some states have laws that go beyond the provisions of the UCC or Magnuson-Moss.

Although I focus on the sale of goods, it's also possible for services to be warranted. For example, a TV fix-it service may warrant that a repair job will be good for at least six months; an auto mechanic may warrant the repairs on a car's electrical system for one year; and a lawn maintenance company may warrant that certain weeds won't reappear during the current season. Warranties for services are almost always express and not implied, and they're not widely regulated by statute.

Plan Ahead to Avoid Warranty Problems

If you're a retailer who sells big-ticket items, try to work out a procedure with manufacturers for handling repair and replacement of defective products and making refunds. Obviously, you'll have better customer relationships if you deal quickly and smoothly with warranty problems.

If you're a retailer and you help customers select, assemble, or install products, or give advice or instructions about their use, carry product liability insurance. (See Chapter 12.)

---

1. Express Warranties

Express warranties are statements and promises that a manufacturer or retailer makes about a product or about a commitment to remedy defects and malfunctions in the product. If the statements are untrue or if the stated commitments are not honored, the manufacturer or retailer may be legally liable to the buyer for breach of warranty.

Express warranties take a variety of forms, from advertising claims to a printed certificate that accompanies the product and specifically guarantees it. Express warranties can be made either orally or in writing.

a. Oral Warranties

If a seller makes an oral promise to a buyer, that is an express warranty.

EXAMPLE: A seller says, "This TV set is new" or "This oven heats to over 600 degrees." If the TV set is used, or if the oven heats only to 500 degrees, the seller will be liable for breach of warranty, whether or not the seller knew that the claims were false.

If the seller shows a customer a sample or a model of goods being sold, there's an express warranty that the goods the customer purchases will be basically indistinguishable from the sample. For example, if a salesperson shows a customer some samples of fax paper and the customer orders a dozen packages based on the sample, the entire order must conform to that sample. And if a dealer shows a customer a small scale model of a garage door, the door the customer receives must look like and be constructed like the model.

But not everything that a seller says as part of a sales transaction is a warranty. Merely giving an opinion about the goods or praising them doesn't create a warranty.

- Martha is at a drugstore looking at hair coloring products. The clerk says: "I recommend this brand. It works very well, and I believe you'll be satisfied with it." Martha uses the product and develops a severe allergic reaction on her scalp.
- Phillip tries on a new suit. The store owner says: "It looks good on you. You'll be wearing it for a long time." In fact, the suit is a size too big and wears out after a year.

These statements would be considered opinions, not promises or statements of fact. They wouldn't constitute express warranties.

b. Written Warranties

A statement doesn't have to be called a warranty or guarantee to be legally treated as such. And warranties needn't be part of a formal written contract. Statements made in product literature distributed by the manufacturer or retail store, in advertisements, or orally by salespeople can constitute binding warranties.

If a sales contract or order form contains a description of the goods, that constitutes an express warranty by the seller that the goods will be as described. So if the product is described as an Ear Play Model 400 stereo receiver and it turns out to be a different brand or model, the seller has breached an express warranty.

Written warranties on consumer products are covered by state laws and a federal law, the Magnuson-Moss Warranty Act. That law is designed to make it easier for consumers to understand and deal with warranties. It doesn't replace state warranty laws but does add certain requirements.

The Magnuson-Moss Warranty Act covers consumer products normally used for personal, family, or household purposes. It doesn't require a manufacturer or seller to give any written warranty at all. But if a written warranty is given, it must comply with the statute and with rules of the Federal Trade Commission.

For a product costing the consumer $15 or more, the written warranty must be in simple, understandable language. Also, the seller must make the terms of the warranty available to the buyer before the sale occurs. There are four ways you can comply with this requirement:

- Clearly and conspicuously display the warranty "in close conjunction to" the warranted product.
- Keep copies of warranties in readily available loose-leaf binders in each department of your store.
- Display packages so that the warranty is clearly visible to customers at the point of sale.
- Place a notice containing the warranty near the product in a way that clearly tells prospective buyers the product to which the warranty applies.

If a product costs $10 or more, the written warranty must state either that it's a full warranty or limited warranty. Naturally, a consumer who sees the words "full warranty" believes that he or she is getting a large measure of protection. To qualify as a full warranty, a written warranty must include at least the following coverage:

- A defective product will be repaired or replaced for free (including removal and installation, if necessary) during the warranty period.
- The product will be repaired within a reasonable time.
- The consumer won't have to do anything unreasonable to get warranty service (such as return a heavy product to a store or service center).
- The warranty is good for anyone who owns the product during the warranty period.
- If the product hasn't been repaired after a reasonable number of tries, the customer gets a replacement or a refund.
- The customer doesn't have to return a warranty card for the warranty to be valid.
- Implied warranties can't be disclaimed or denied or limited to any specific length of time.

Any written warranty that doesn't qualify as a full warranty must be labeled as a limited warranty. You can restrict the duration of implied warranties, as long as the restrictions are not unconscionable (that is, shockingly unfair). Restrictions must be stated clearly, and the implied warranties must last for a reasonable time.

The Magnuson-Moss Warranty Act doesn't supersede state laws that give consumers even greater rights and laws that permit people to recover damages for injuries caused by defective products, despite a disclaimer of liability. For example, in California the Song-Beverly Consumer Warranty Act contains more stringent warranty provisions than the Magnuson-Moss Warranty Act. Among other things, the California statute provides that a manufacturer who provides a written warranty (full or limited) must maintain service and repair facilities in California reasonably close to all areas where its products are sold. The manufacturer can delegate repair and service facilities to retailers or independent repair shops. Repairs must be completed within 30 days, except in unusual circumstances.

2. Warranties Imposed by Law

Implied warranties don't come from anything a seller says or does. They arise automatically when a product is sold. Under the Uniform Commercial Code, there are two kinds of implied warranties:

- that the product is fit for its ordinary use, and
- that the product is fit for any special use the seller knows about.

Each of these is explained below.

a. Fitness in General

A seller automatically makes an implied warranty that new (not used) goods sold "are fit for the ordinary purposes for which such goods are used"—in other words, that the product will work the way similar products ordinarily work. This implied warranty is also called a warranty of merchantability. Here are some examples:

- A lawnmower will cut grass that is four inches tall.
- A stepladder will support a 275-pound person.
- A toaster will make both dark and light toast.
- A bicycle's brakes will work in a light rain.
- A bottle of ginger ale won't have loose glass in it.

The manufacturer and retailer of a product that's not fit for ordinary purposes are liable to the purchaser for breach of the implied warranty.

b. Fitness for a Particular Purpose

There's a special implied warranty if the seller has reason to know that (1) the goods are required for a particular purpose, and (2) the buyer is relying on the seller's skill or judgment to select suitable goods. In that situation, the seller is bound by an implied warranty that the goods will be fit for that purpose.

- Joanne goes to a paint store and asks for two gallons of white paint that will work well on plaster walls. The store owner selects paint for her. Unfortunately, it's intended solely for metallic surfaces and ruins her walls.
- Morton asks an air-conditioning contractor to pick out and install an air-conditioning unit for a part of his plant. He explains that the room contains extensive electronic equipment and must be kept at 55 degrees or cooler at all times. The air-conditioner is installed but leads to costly problems, because in hot weather it can't keep the temperature below 62 degrees.
- Wilma goes to a sports retailer and asks for a sleeping bag that will be adequate to 10 degrees Fahrenheit. The retailer selects a certain model for Wilma, and she buys it, but it won't keep a normal person warm below freezing.

In these examples, each seller is liable to the buyer for breach of the implied warranty of fitness for a particular purpose. That's because each seller knew the buyer needed the goods for a particular purpose and that the buyer was relying on the seller's skill or judgment to furnish suitable goods.

This is different from the implied warranty of general fitness discussed in the preceding section. An air-conditioner that cooled a room to 62 degrees in hot weather would be fit for the ordinary purposes for which an air-conditioner is used. It wouldn't violate the implied warranty of general fitness. But because the seller in the second example knew the buyer had special requirements and was relying on the seller to meet them, this special implied warranty took effect.

c. Disclaimers of Implied Warranties

The Uniform Commercial Code allows sellers, in many cases, to disclaim implied warranties through a conspicuous written notice. Typically, to disclaim implied warranties, you must inform consumers in a conspicuous manner, and generally in writing, that you won't be responsible if the product malfunctions or is defective and that the entire product risk falls on them. To do this, you must specifically state that you don't warrant "merchantability," or use a phrase such as "with all faults" or "as is."

There are, however, major exceptions to the general rule, which may make it impossible to make a disclaimer.

Exception 1: State Law Restrictions. In some states, you may not be able to avoid implied warranties. Despite its name, the Uniform Commercial Code isn't completely uniform; several state legislatures have tinkered with parts of it, including the part about disclaiming implied warranties. Some states (including Connecticut, Massachusetts, and Kansas) don't let you sell consumer products "as is."

Exception 2: Injuries. A disclaimer of implied warranties won't shield you from legal liability if your product is so defective it injures someone. Courts consider such a disclaimer "unconscionable."

Exception 3: Federal Law Restrictions. If you offer a written warranty for a consumer product or offer a service contract on it, you can't disclaim any implied warranty. (This restriction is imposed by the Magnuson-Moss Warranty Act.)

⚠️ **Implied warranties are difficult to disclaim.** *If you're going to enter this legal thicket, you'll likely need a lawyer's advice on whether you can disclaim implied warranties in your situation and, if so, how best to do it. Even if the law permits a disclaimer of warranties, if you and a customer slug it out in court, you'll find that judges often tend to be proconsumer—that is, to rule that unless a seller is absolutely clear, this warranty disclaimer will be disallowed.*

Sometimes a seller is interested not in getting rid of implied warranties entirely but only in limiting the remedies in case of a breach. For example, the seller may want to say that in case of a product defect, the buyer can either (1) return the goods and get a refund, or (2) have any defective parts replaced or repaired—but not collect monetary damages. But while a limitation on damages is normally effective, this isn't always true, especially where the limitation is found to be highly unreasonable. Suppose the seller of a $2,000 stereo set puts this language in the warranty: "Seller is obligated only to replace defective parts." After Mildred buys a stereo, a protective circuit fails, causing it to overheat. This destroys several key parts and ruins the stereo. Will a court allow the seller merely to replace the $5 part that didn't work? Perhaps not. The buyer may be able to convince the court that the limitation shouldn't be enforced because (under these circumstances) the limitation deprived her of the "substantial value of her bargain" or because the limitation is unconscionable (that is, shockingly unfair). And remember that a disclaimer can't shield you from liability for personal injury to a consumer hurt by a defective product.

3. What Happens If a Warranty Is Breached

Federal and state laws give consumers certain rights when an express or implied warranty is breached.

a. The Buyer's Options

Under the Uniform Commercial Code, if there's a breach of warranty, the customer usually can return the merchandise and get a full refund. The manufacturer or retailer bound by the warranty, however, has the right to cure the breach by fixing the merchandise or replacing it with nondefective merchandise. A customer who prefers to keep the merchandise can do so and sue for the direct economic loss—generally, the reduced value of the product because it's defective.

In addition to damages for the reduced value of a defective product, a buyer is also entitled to damages for:

- Consequential economic losses (such as lost profits) resulting from the product's failure to meet requirements and needs that were foreseeable at the time of sale.

EXAMPLE: Meadowbrook Golf Course buys 12 golf carts, all of which are defective. As a result, Meadowbrook loses $20,000 in profits over the eight-week period it takes to get the carts fixed. (It proves impractical to get substitute carts on short notice.) It can successfully recover these losses.

- Injury to people and damage to property caused by the defective product.

EXAMPLE: Millie buys a CutAbove power lawnmower. One day when her teenage son Reggie is mowing the lawn, the mower propels a small stone into one of his eyes. Reggie loses his sight in that eye. Because the mower doesn't contain normal safety features, Reggie is entitled to collect damages for his injury.

b. Who Is Liable?

Who is liable if a customer buys a product from a retailer and the product fails to live up to the warranty? Sometimes the manufacturer, sometimes the retailer, and sometimes both. Although liability depends on the circumstances, here are some general rules:

- *Manufacturer's Express Warranty.* If an express warranty made by the manufacturer was breached, the manufacturer is responsible for making good on the promise. The retailer usually isn't liable, unless it "adopts" the manufacturer's warranty by its conduct at the time of sale.

EXAMPLE: Maria goes to Pete's Fitness Mart and looks at HomeBody, a $3,000 set of exercise machines manufactured by Health Horizons Inc. She's interested, but wants to be sure it's backed by a broad warranty. To clinch the sale, Pete calls the president of Health Horizons and has the company send an extensive written warranty.

Nine months after Maria buys the HomeBody, it fails; meanwhile, Health Horizons has gone out of business. Pete's Fitness Mart is bound by the warranty, because it was part of the inducement that Pete used to convince Maria to buy HomeBody.

- *Retailer's Express Warranty.* If the warranty was made independently by a retailer, the retailer is liable. The manufacturer isn't bound unless the retailer was acting under the authority (in legal lingo, as an agent) of the manufacturer in making the warranty.
- *Breach of Implied Warranty of General Fitness.* If there is a breach of the implied warranty that the goods are fit for ordinary purposes, both the manufacturer and the retailer are liable—but if the customer sues the retailer, the retailer in turn will usually have the right to recover against the manufacturer for supplying a defective product.
- *Breach of Implied Warranty of Fitness for a Particular Purpose.* If the customer relied on the retailer to select the goods for a particular purpose and the goods aren't satisfactory for that purpose, the retailer is liable.
- *Personal Injury.* A buyer who's injured by an unfit product can usually sue the manufacturer, even though the injured person didn't deal directly with the manufacturer. What's more, not only the buyer can sue for personal injuries from a defective product. In most states, members of the buyer's family or household, or house guests who are injured, can also sue the manufacturer if it's reasonable to expect that these persons would use or be affected by the product.

Whether or not an injured person can sue the retailer as well as the manufacturer depends on court decisions in your state and the extent of the retailer's involvement in the sale. In many states, a retailer who simply sells an unopened box and makes no statements about the product is immune from liability if the product later injures someone. But some states hold the retailer liable even under these circumstances.

⚠️ **Get legal advice.** *Liability for breach of warranties is one of the most complex areas of commercial law. Because liability depends on many factors and because the law is somewhat unsettled, use this book for general background only. Also, it's important to understand that in a lawsuit, a person who has suffered a serious injury or significant economic loss because of a defective product will probably assert additional theories of legal liability (such as negligence and strict liability) besides breach of warranty. See a lawyer for specific legal advice.*

D. Consumer Protection Statutes

Remember "caveat emptor"—let the buyer beware? That used to be the law of the marketplace. Not anymore. Today, consumers have clout.

Case 1. In Florida, a Chevrolet dealer promised a "free four-day, three-night vacation to Acapulco" to anyone who bought a car or van. Relying on this special promotion, Peter bought a van from the dealer. When the vacation voucher arrived, Peter found that the so-called free vacation was really a time-share sales promotion. The vacation trip was loaded down with conditions, restrictions, and obligations. Believing he'd been cheated, Peter sued the dealer. The jury awarded Peter $1,768 in compensatory damages (the value of the trip) plus $667,000 in punitive damages. (*Bill Branch Chevrolet, Inc. v. Burkert*, 521 So. 2d 153 (Fla. App. 2 Dist., 1988.)

Case 2. In New Jersey, Kenneth ordered some furniture from a store. When it arrived, Kenneth noticed numerous defects. He rejected the order and demanded a return of his deposit. The furniture store refused, and Kenneth sued. The jury awarded him three times the amount of his deposit and ordered the furniture store to pay his attorney fees. (*DiNicola v. Watchung Furniture's Country Manor*, N.J., Middlesex County Superior Court, No. L-80734-35, 1988.)

Both cases were brought under state consumer protection statutes. These statutes are meant to protect consumers from unfair or deceptive practices and often go beyond the traditional legal remedies available for breach of warranty. Laws like these are on the books in nearly every state, although the details vary.

Consumer protection laws place a potent weapon in the hands of buyers. In an ordinary lawsuit, a plaintiff can recover only his or her actual losses. For example, without the benefit of a consumer protection law, the man who sued to get back his furniture deposit would be entitled to no more than his $600 deposit. But under the statute in his state, he received triple damages plus attorney fees. Similarly, the man who sued the car dealer about the free vacation won punitive damages amounting to many times the value of his trip. The potential for large verdicts gives buyers and their lawyers an incentive to sue if it looks like a law has been violated.

"Big deal," you may say. "I'm an honest and ethical business person. None of this affects me." Well, that may not be so. For one thing, you need to know the details of your state's consumer protection laws so that you can tell your employees about practices that could get you in trouble. Furthermore, these state laws often allow a customer to sue even if the violation was not intentional. If you sell a product manufactured by a U.S.-based company (say, a Schwinn bike) and mistakenly advertise that the product was made in the U.S. when in fact it was made in Taiwan, you may be liable under the statute.

Hundreds of cases have been brought under consumer protection laws, including these:

- A man sued a department store that ran out of an advertised waffle iron and didn't give him a rain check—a violation of the consumer protection law in his state.
- A homeowner sued a roofing contractor who falsely advertised that it could arrange financing for roof repair jobs.
- A woman sued a health spa that reneged on its promise to return her deposit and cancel her contract if she changed her mind within three days.

Health spas, incidentally, have been singled out for special regulation; if you're going to start one, get the FTC pamphlet on this subject.

Most consumer protection laws contain a broad prohibition on "unfair or deceptive practices." In addition, many statutes list specific practices that are forbidden, such as bait-and-switch and deceptive pricing, discussed above in Sections A3 and B1.

E. Dealing With Customers Online

For the most part, the same legal rules apply when you do business online as when you sell to customers in a brick-and-mortar store or by mail. As long as you don't overstep federal and state statutes and regulations, you have quite a bit of latitude in establishing your business policies and making them legally binding on your customers. You can set rules covering issues such as what sort of currency you accept, when and how customers can return items, and what warranties you offer.

In a store, you might do this by posting your policies in a prominent place or by having customers agree to them on an order form. When selling by mail, you can include your policies in your catalogue or, again, on an order form. But obviously,

the mechanics of informing customers of your policies are different when you're selling over the Internet.

In this section, I'll provide information to help you establish legally enforceable policies for your website. These online policies go by many different names, such as: *Terms and Conditions, Customer Conditions,* or *Terms of Service.* The label you attach to them is not important; the content is.

For more on this subject: *See* How to Get Your Business on the Web: A Legal Guide to E-Commerce, *by Fred S. Steingold (Nolo). The book also explains how to choose and protect a domain name, how to create a website, and how to limit your legal liability when doing business online.*

1. Why Bother to Post Policies?

With just one major exception, there are no laws requiring e-commerce websites to post their terms and conditions or mandating how and where such conditions should appear. The exception is the Children's Online Privacy Protection Act (COPPA), which requires you to post a privacy policy if your Web content is directed at children. The Federal Trade Commission enforces COPPA, so check its website for more information (www.ftc.gov).

Even with no general requirement that a business post its policies, posting can offer both business and legal benefits. On the business side, being straight with visitors and customers builds trust, credibility, and loyalty. On the legal side, a well-thought-out set of terms and conditions can help limit your legal liability and avoid disputes over the details of transactions.

True, if a disgruntled customer sues you, your terms and conditions may not give you 100% protection, but at least you and your lawyer should have some solid arguing points to present to the judge.

2. Policies Worth Posting

If you'll be selling goods or services online, here are some topics you may want to cover in the policies you post:

Credit card use. If your website will offer direct sales via credit cards, it's wise to reassure customers that their credit card information will be kept confidential. Advise them of any steps you've taken to ensure the security of their credit card purchase. Also, under federal law, a credit card user is liable only for the first $50 of unauthorized purchases—assuming that the user promptly notifies the credit card issuer about the unauthorized use. Some businesses offer to pay up to the $50 limit if the credit card issuer fails to do so.

Warranties. You may already be offering a warranty that explains what you will and will not do for the customer if there's a problem with the produ ts you sell. Your warranty can both reassure the customer and limit your liability, so I recommend that you post your warranty on your website. When you sell goods that carry a *manufacturer's limited warranty* and the goods sell for more than $15, federal law requires you to post the warranty or tell customers how they can view it.

Returns and repairs. It's important to develop a return and repair policy and post it online. For example, perhaps you're prepared to give a full refund, but only if the product is returned within 30 days and is in salable condition. If customers know this in advance, they won't be surprised if you refuse to give a refund 45 days after the purchase. While you have a great deal of discretion in how you deal with returns and repairs, a generous policy can build tremendous goodwill among present and prospective customers.

Legal jurisdiction. Since people from all over the country—or the world—may buy from you online, you may want to say that the law of your state will apply to any dispute, and that the courts of your state will have exclusive jurisdiction. Be aware, however, that some judges balk at enforcing this type of restriction, especially in a consumer transac-

tion involving a claim of $50 or more. Still, posting this type of provision can do no harm.

Sales limited to USA. You may wish to limit your exposure to laws (and lawsuits) in distant places by selling only to people in the United States. If so, you can post a notice to that effect—but also take polite and reasonable steps to reject orders from people outside the country.

Limited liability. You can use your postings to limit the financial damages for which your business will be legally responsible if there's a problem with the products, services, or information you offer online. Understand that language limiting your liability won't always have the desired effect; judges may balk at limitations that are grossly unfair or that try to cut off the amount a person can receive for bodily injuries. But in most situations, judges do enforce limitations that customers have agreed to. Your posting may include language such as this: "Protobiz LLC will not be liable to a customer for any damages beyond what the customer has actually paid to Protobiz."

 Do some no-cost research: read the terms and conditions posted on websites that you respect. *The sites that you've personally used and come to trust will probably have well-written, customer-friendly policies that you can adapt for your own site. If you've never studied their fine print before, now's the time to do so. Then, after you've drafted your own set of policies, consider having a lawyer look over your handiwork and possibly tweak it for maximum legal impact.*

3. How and Where to Post Your Terms and Conditions

Easy navigation will be important throughout your website, and access to your terms and conditions is no exception. You'll want to provide prominent links that take customers right to your postings. This, by itself, provides a reasonable level of legal protection. If you want a higher degree of confidence that your terms and conditions will be binding, add an "I Accept" button by which customers must agree to your terms.

a. How to Link Prominently

Linking to your terms and conditions on your site's home page is a good place to start. You might also add links on other important pages, including the order page. You can call your link *Terms and Conditions* or anything else that's reasonably descriptive—for example, *Our Policies, Customer Policies,* or *Terms of Service*.

Here are some other ways to make your links and other information grab the customers' attention:

- Put the home page link where users can see it without having to scroll down.
- Put the link in large type and a distinctive color.
- Include a link on all other pages, if possible. But at a minimum, put the link on the pages where customers place orders so they can read your terms and conditions first.

- Write your terms and conditions in plain English so customers can easily understand their meaning.
- Put your terms and conditions in large type that's easy to read.

b. Requiring Actual Assent

If a dissatisfied customer sues you, you'd like the judge to treat your terms and conditions as a binding contract. Some judges will find a contract if you've followed the above guidelines—the assumption being that the customer read and accepted your terms. But other judges may rule that a conspicuous posting is not enough. They'll find a contract only if the customer specifically accepted your terms.

Currently, the most practical way to protect yourself is to present your terms to your customers, then require them to click a button at the end that says "I Accept" or "I Agree" before they can complete the transaction. That way, if a dispute ever ends up in court, you'll have evidence that the customer not only could have read your terms and conditions by clicking a link, but presumably did read them, right before actually agreeing to them. ■

Cash, Credit Cards, and Checks

This chapter considers the three most common ways that businesses get paid for the goods and services they sell: cash, credit cards, and checks. If you extend credit directly to customers, clients, or patients, you should also read Chapter 19, which explains how to avoid collection problems.

A. Cash

Cash includes not only currency but also equivalents that are as good as cash—certified checks, cashier's checks, traveler's checks, and (less common these days) money orders. Personal and business checks are quite another matter. (See Section C.)

If you have very large cash transactions, you may have to report them to the IRS. The reporting requirements are intended primarily to deter money-laundering schemes by customers (often drug dealers) who want to conceal income.

If you receive more than $10,000 in cash—or in traveler's checks or money orders—in one transaction or two or more related transactions, you must provide information about the transaction to the IRS. (Certified, cashier's, or business or personal checks aren't covered by this requirement.) The necessary information includes the name, address, and Social Security number of the buyer. In addition, if you're a retail merchant, you must report:

- cash transactions in which you receive more than $10,000 in installment payments in one year
- transactions of more than $10,000 in which part of the payment is in cash, traveler's checks, or money orders; and

- any "suspicious transaction," no matter what the amount.

In calculating whether a transaction or related transactions involve more than $10,000 in cash, you must include not only cash, but also each cashier's check, traveler's check, bank draft, or money order that's made out for $10,000 or less.

> **EXAMPLE 1:** Gloria buys a boat from Todd, a boat dealer, for $16,500. She pays Todd with a $16,500 cashier's check payable to him. The cashier's check isn't treated as cash because the face amount is more than $10,000. Todd doesn't have to report this sale to the IRS as a cash transaction.

> **EXAMPLE 2:** Donald buys gold coins from Maryanne, a coin dealer, for $13,200. Donald pays Maryanne $6,200 in $100 bills and a $7,000 cashier's check that he's purchased. Because the cashier's check is less than $10,000 it's treated as cash, so Maryanne must report this to the IRS as a cash transaction.

Use IRS Form 8300 (*Report of Cash Payments Over $10,000 Received in a Trade or Business*). You must also provide a copy of the completed form to the customer. The form must be filed within 15 days after a $10,000 or more transaction occurs, or within 15 days after a customer's transactions over a 12-month period add up to $10,000.

B. Credit Cards

Depending on the business you're in, your customers or clients may want to pay with plastic—the familiar Visa, MasterCard, Discover, American Express, and other cards. Technically, there's a distinction between "credit cards" (such as Visa or MasterCard) and "travel and entertainment cards" (such as American Express and Diners Club) also called "charge cards." Credit cards are administered through banks; charge cards are usually administered through the issuing company. For most practical purposes, the same legal concepts apply, so I'll simply use "credit card" to cover both types.

In deciding which credit cards to recognize, take into account the preferences of your customers and clients, as well as the size of the discount exacted by the credit card issuer and how quickly you get paid.

When a customer charges goods or services using a bank-administered credit card, the bank credits your account with the amount of the sale less a discount—usually 3% to 5%—which is the bank's fee for handling the transaction and accepting the risk that the customer doesn't pay. In addition, the bank may charge you a startup fee and an annual rental fee for the imprinting machine you use to record credit card information on sales slips.

If you're in a retail or other business where customers or clients expect to pay on credit, credit cards are often more cost-effective than directly extending credit. In general, if you follow the bank's rules—such as checking the credit card to make sure it hasn't expired and getting approval for all or at least larger transactions—the credit card issuer (not you) absorbs the loss if the customer doesn't pay up. Some of the newer electronic systems used by credit card issuers do most or all of the checking for you and get the money into your bank account almost immediately.

But whether you check credit cards the old-fashioned phone-in way or rely on the new systems, there are still a few exceptions to this general rule that if you follow the bank's procedures, you're sure to get your money. For example, if the goods are defective and the customer refuses to pay the bank, you may have to bear the loss. This will be spelled out in your contract with the bank. Read it carefully.

About a dozen states restrict your ability to record personal identification information about a credit card holder. The laws on this subject differ from state to state, but the California statute provides a good illustration of the kinds of restrictions that may apply to you. In California, in most cir-

cumstances you can't require the cardholder to give you personal identification information such as an address or phone number. There are, however, a few exceptions. You can require the cardholder to provide this information if:

- The bank or other agency that issued the credit card requires it to complete the transaction; or
- You need the information for a special purpose related to the transaction, for example, shipping, delivery, servicing, or installation of the merchandise, or for special orders.

There can be hefty penalties for violating these statutes, so learn the rules in your state and make sure that your employees know them.

But even if your state does permit you to record this information, ask yourself if you really need it. After all, if the customer doesn't pay the bill, it's a problem for the bank that issued the credit card, not for you. And because some customers regard the request for personal information as an invasion of their privacy, doing so may be poor marketing. If your main reason to gather this information is to build a mailing list, it's better simply to ask your customers if they'd like to be added to your list.

⚠ **Don't unwittingly aid the identity thieves.**
As you know, if a credit or debit card receipt with the full account number and card expiration date falls into the wrong hands, it can lead to misery for the customer. An important provision of the Fair and Accurate Credit Transactions Act deals with this problem. It requires you to shorten the information

on the credit and debit card receipts you print up. You can't include more than the last five digits of the card number, and you must omit the expiration date. (Up-to-date receipt printers are programmed to meet this federal law.) You needn't comply with this provision if you give only handwritten receipts or receipts that imprint or copy the card—methods that are becoming less common.

C. Checks

In any business—and especially in a service or wholesale business—you're likely to find that many customers or clients want to pay for goods and services using personal or business checks. Obviously, accepting payment by check is riskier than accepting payment by cash or credit card. Approximately 450 million bad checks are written each year.

1. Avoiding Bad Check Problems

Checks can be no good for a number of reasons. Here are the main ones:

- There are insufficient funds in the account to cover the amount of the purchase. Unless the check writer has overdraft protection, the check will be returned to you unpaid.
- The account has been closed—or perhaps it's a fictitious account that never existed.
- The signature of the person who signed the check is a forgery, in which case the bank will refuse payment.
- In the case of a third-party check (such as a paycheck) names or dollar amounts on the check have been altered, or the endorsement is a forgery.
- A person signing or endorsing a check on behalf of a partnership or corporation doesn't have legal authority to sign for the business.

Faced with these many possibilities for losses, some retail businesses adopt a simple policy: No

checks. But such a policy often carries its own risks—mainly that you may lose perfectly solvent customers or clients who like the convenience of writing checks. After all, it's customary for most retail, wholesale, service, and manufacturing industries to accept checks. And because with checks the bank doesn't keep a percentage of each transaction (as is the case with credit cards), you may actually want to encourage regular customers to pay by check rather than credit card.

No matter what type of business you're in, the best way to approach the potential bad check problem is to adopt sensible rules and stick to them. How stringent you want to be depends on the nature of your business, and how well rules will be accepted by your customers and clients. It boils down to a business decision about how much risk you're willing to accept.

If yours is a retail business, here are some policies to consider:

- Require that checks be written and signed in your presence.
- Accept checks drawn on local banks only.
- Be sure the checks have the customer's name, local address, and phone number preprinted on them.
- Don't accept checks written for more than the purchase price; in other words, don't give change for a check. (Some small businesses, such as grocers, build customer loyalty with minimal losses by issuing check-cashing cards allowing regular customers to write a check for up to $20 more than the price of goods purchased.)
- Wait until the check has cleared before giving a cash refund for returned goods.
- Don't accept third-party checks—paychecks, Social Security checks, and other checks that someone else has made out to the customer who then endorses them.

EXAMPLE: Laurie offers you a check made out to her from her employer, Amalgamated Products. She endorses it on the back. The check may be a forgery, or maybe the company doesn't have funds in the account to cover the check.

- Don't accept post-dated checks.
- Set a limit on the check amount you will accept. Or at least call the bank and verify that larger checks are good.
- Require a manager's approval for checks over a certain amount. Better yet, hire clerks whose judgment you trust.
- Write the customer's phone number on the check, if the law in your state allows it.
- Ask to see ID—including something that contains a photo and signature. A driver's license is a good choice. Record key information (such as the driver's license number) on the check; it will help you locate the customer if the check is no good.

Restrictions on ID requirements. *Find out if your state has a law restricting the kind of ID you can require. In some states, for example, you can't require a customer to show you a credit card as condition of accepting a check. However, if a customer voluntarily shows you a credit card as ID, state law may permit you to record the type of card, the issuer, and the expiration date—but you can't write down the card number. If you violate laws of this type, you may face a fine, a civil lawsuit, or both. No matter what your state law is, avoid using credit cards as a form of ID. For one thing, you can't charge the client's credit card account if the check bounces. For another, bank personnel or others seeing a credit card number may use this information improperly. Why subject your customers to this risk?*

If you're presented with a check drawn on a business account, be sure that the person signing it has authority to do so. If a check is signed by someone other than the owner, a partner, or a corporate officer, call the bank to see if the person presenting the check is an authorized signer.

Some businesses post a sign saying that they charge a specified fee for any check that bounces. The legal reasoning is that in many states you can't collect such fees without advance warning to customers. And some business owners think that such notices deter bad-check writers. Still, I generally recommend against posting signs. It's insulting to the customer, and there's no evidence that it will cut down the bad checks you receive. And remember, your main goal is to avoid getting bad checks in the first place—not to try to collect them later plus a $10 fee. But if you do post such a sign or charge such a fee, check the law in your state to see how much you can legally charge.

 Solve Your Money Troubles: Get Debt Collectors Off Your Back & Regain Financial Freedom, by Robin Leonard (Nolo), is addressed primarily to people who owe money, but the information on bad-check laws is also helpful to businesses receiving money.

Once you accept a check, stamp it with an endorsement stamp (available from your bank) and deposit it in your business account the same day. Every day you wait increases the chances that the check-writer will have emptied or closed the account. Under the Uniform Commercial Code, a statute adopted in every state and which governs most banking transactions, there's a presumption that a check becomes "stale" six months after the date it's signed. The bank may refuse to honor it after that period—although in actual practice, they'll usually honor older checks as long as the account is solvent.

2. Dealing With Bad Checks

Even though you take all reasonable precautions, a bad check will occasionally slip through your system. A bank may return a check to you with the notation "insufficient funds" or "NSF," which means the same thing: the customer has an active account but there's not enough in it to cover the check. Or a bank may inform you that the account has been closed.

Here are some steps you can take—many of which apply primarily to bad checks from individuals. Other techniques may be more appropriate when the bad check comes from another business. (See Chapter 19.)

Step 1. Call the Customer

Call the customer and ask that he or she make the check good or pay you in cash. (This is one reason it's good to write down the customer's phone number when you take a check, if permitted by state law.) But be careful about when you call the customer—and how often. Laws in several states limit what you can do to collect debts. (See Chapter 19, Section D.) To avoid problems, call only between 8 a.m. and 9 p.m., don't discuss the debt with the customer's employer, and make sure your request for payment is polite. Threatening a debtor that you'll publicize his or her name or notify his or her employer is illegal.

Step 2. Write a Letter

Send a certified letter—return receipt requested—making the same demand. This sets the stage for a possible criminal prosecution if the check-writer intentionally attempted to defraud you. Also, 35 states (including Arizona, California, Colorado, Florida, Illinois, Montana, New York, and Washington) have bad-check laws that are particularly favorable to businesses. In such states, if you send a written demand for payment, you may be able to collect extra damages in court (often two or three times the value of the check) if the check-writer doesn't come through.

> **EXAMPLE:** Monica, the owner of a Florida gift shop, receives a bad check from Norbert. She sends Norbert a notice demanding payment in full plus a service charge of $15 or 5% of the check, whichever is greater. If Norbert doesn't pay within seven days, Monica can sue him under Florida law for the amount of the check plus additional damages of three times the amount of the check (at least $50). This is in addition to court costs, reasonable attorney fees, and any bank fees that she incurs.

The sample notice and demand for payment shown below here is derived from the Florida bad-check statute (Crimes, § 832.07). Because the law in each state is different, find out the specific requirements where you do business. To see your state's bad-check law, go to www.uslegalforms.com/lawdigest/bad-checks-law-digest.htm.

Sample Bad Check Notice (Florida)

You are hereby notified that a check, numbered _____, issued by you on _____, ___, drawn upon _(name of bank)_ , and payable to _____, has been dishonored. Pursuant to Florida law, you have seven days from receipt of this notice to tender payment of the full amount of such check plus a service charge of $15 or an amount of up to 5% of the face amount of the check, whichever is greater, the total amount due being $_____ and _____ cents. Unless this amount is paid in full within the time specified above, the holder of such check may turn over the dishonored check and all other available information relating to the incident to the state attorney for criminal prosecution. You may be additionally liable in a civil action for triple the amount of the check, but in no case less than $50, together with the amount of the check, a service charge, court costs, reasonable attorney fees, and incurred bank fees, as provided in Florida Statutes Title VI, Civil Practice and Procedure, § 68.065.

Step 3. Contact the Bank

If the customer's bank account is still active, wait a few days and then inquire to see if the check is now good (the customer may have deposited a paycheck after the check was dishonored). You can normally check the status of an account by calling the bank and saying you hold a check for a certain dollar amount and asking whether there is enough in the account to cover it. If so, take the returned check to the bank and draw out the cash. Another alternative is to ask the customer's bank for "enforced collection." If the bank offers this service, the bad check will be held in a special category. The next money deposited in the customer's account will go to you. Procedures and costs vary; get details from the bank.

Step 4. Request Prosecution

Intentionally writing a bad check is a crime. As noted above, before you contact the local district attorney's or prosecuting attorney's office to request prosecution, you may have to give the check-writer a written notice. After all, the bad check may have been an innocent mistake. The police department or district attorney can tell you whether you must send a notice as a prelude to a prosecution (generally you must) and what the notice must contain. But again, in any oral or written communication with the customer who passed the bad check, avoid the temptation to threaten prosecution. Such a threat may constitute harassment or extortion under some state statutes.

What are the chances of law enforcement officials taking action? Some police departments and prosecuting officials drag their feet on these kinds of cases, saying that they don't want to be used as a collection agency. Others are far more cooperative. Some of the best have bad-check programs under which the person who has written the check is contacted and given a chance to avoid being prosecuted by making the check good and, in some counties, by attending special classes under a "diversion" program.

Step 5. Use Small Claims Court

If you still haven't been paid, consider suing in small claims court, as long as the check is less than the maximum amount you can sue for in small claims—or close enough that you don't mind waiving the excess. Most states have limits between $3,000 and $15,000. (See Chapter 23 on how to represent yourself in small claims court.) As noted in Step 2, if you've followed the bad-check procedures in your state, you may be entitled to two or even three times the amount of the check as damages as well as your court-filing and service-of-process costs. And if the check-writer has a job, you'll generally be able to use post-judgment proceedings to get paid out of the worker's wages—although it's difficult to collect from the wages of low-income people. You might also be able to collect from bank or other deposit accounts. In most states, you can also cheaply and easily put a lien against the debtor's real estate. Chances are you'll ultimately be paid when the property is voluntarily sold or refinanced.

Step 6. Use a Collection Agency

Turning a bad check over to a collection agency is often worth considering. For smaller checks, going to small claims court may not be worthwhile. Or perhaps, despite the huge cut a collection agency takes, you might want to put your time and energy elsewhere. And while some states make small claims court fairly friendly to businesses (for example, you may be able to send an employee to court with business records), other states require that the business owner appear to testify in person. That may make suing the check writer more trouble than it's worth. So if you want to keep to a minimum your personal involvement in the collection process, keep open the possibility of letting a collection agency do most of the work.

When the Customer Stops Payment

Sometimes a customer stops payment on a check, claiming that the goods you sold were defective. If there's a legitimate dispute, the customer's good faith will be a valid defense to a prosecution or a civil lawsuit for multiple damages. And if it turns out that the goods were in fact defective, the customer will be entitled to a reduction of the amount owed—or even, in extreme cases, a cancellation of the debt. But if the customer's allegations are a trumped-up excuse to get something for nothing, you'll be entitled to your full legal remedies in court. Often, however, in dealing with a customer who is unhappy with the merchandise purchased, the best policy is simply to have the customer return the goods and to call it a day.

Payment in Full

Be careful about accepting and depositing checks that say "Payment in Full" or something similar. If the check writer owes more, you may be barred from collecting the additional amount.

Where there's a good-faith dispute about how much the check writer owes you, depositing a full-payment check usually means that you accept the check in complete satisfaction of the debt. Crossing out the words "Payment in Full" generally won't help you. You'll still be cut off from suing for the balance.

However, a number of states have changed this rule to help creditors. In those states, if you cash a full-payment check and explicitly reserve your right to sue for the balance, you can go after the check writer in court. States that have this modified rule include Alabama, Delaware, Massachusetts, Minnesota, Missouri, New Hampshire, New York, Ohio, Rhode Island, South Carolina, South Dakota, West Virginia, and Wisconsin.

If your state has modified the rule, you normally can preserve your right to sue for the balance by writing the words "Under Protest" or "Without Prejudice" with your endorsement. California simply lets you cross out the full-payment language, cash the check, and sue for the balance—but the check writer may be able to get around this by following certain procedures specified in the statute (California Civil Code § 1526). The statute was created to protect creditors, not debtors, however, so in most instances you can defeat a "Payment in Full" check.

Extending Credit and Getting Paid

In this chapter, you'll find out how to establish credit practices that help ensure that you get paid when you should. You'll also learn how to comply with federal and state credit laws and what to do if customers, clients, or patients don't pay when they're supposed to.

A. The Practical Side of Extending Credit

Some businesses give customers 30 or 60 days to pay for goods and services. They may even let customers make installment payments over a longer period. For example, a small wholesaler of children's music products might require retail customers to pay at the time of sale, but extend 30 days' credit to wholesale customers. Similarly, many professionals and other service providers extend short-term credit to clients and customers, who are expected to pay after receiving a monthly invoice.

If you extend credit, you need to set up a well-organized, accurate, easy-to-use system of accounts, send out bills periodically and keep after those who pay slowly or not at all—all of which takes time, money, and effort.

Many small business people fantasize about avoiding the whole mess by requiring customers to pay cash. Unfortunately, this sort of daydreaming is normally just that; in many businesses and professional practices it's almost impossible to operate if you don't extend credit.

1. Professional and Personal Service Businesses

In many professional or consulting practices, it used to be considered unusual to require a client or patient to complete a formal credit application. No longer. Today, credit applications are becoming routine, because businesses simply can't afford to work for deadbeats. But if you shy away from a formal application, you can still gather much pertinent information from your new client or patient intake sheet. Ask where the person works and banks. Ask for the name of the "nearest relative not living with you"—useful information if the client or patient skips out.

Health care professionals will, of course, want to inquire about insurance or Medicaid/Medicare coverage. Consider offering a modest discount (say, 5%) for payment at the time services are rendered—it usually leads to prompt payment. And think about posting a dignified sign saying: "If it's convenient, payment is appreciated when the bill is presented." If you accept credit cards, there's really no reason for the patient not to pay on the spot.

Lawyers, accountants, appraisers, engineers, dentists, and other professionals may appropriately ask for advance payment to be applied against the first batch of services, especially if a new client or patient needs extensive services. One way to do this is to present a fee letter to each new client. The letter might state that new clients are asked to pay a retainer and that future payments are due ten days from billing. (See "Putting Professional Relationships on a Sound Financial Footing," below.)

Another positive thing a professional or consultant can do is to routinely record bank account data about the client or patient as payment is received. Then, if you have to sue the client or patient, you have one more place to turn to try to satisfy your judgment.

If you're worried that someone isn't creditworthy—particularly if the bill is likely to mount rapidly—you can run a quick credit check with a credit reporting agency. Credit checks are so routine these days that this won't drive away business. However, you should notify the client or patient beforehand. Also, before using credit reports, familiarize yourself with the federal Fair Credit Reporting Act and similar state laws. (See Section B.) For example, if you reject credit for a client or patient based on a credit report, you need to disclose this to the person, as well as the name, address, and phone number of the credit reporting agency that gave you the negative information.

Putting Professional Relationships on a Sound Financial Footing

If you have a professional practice or run a consulting or personal service business, consider giving each client or patient a written statement of your billing procedures, so that they know what to expect.

It is also businesslike and inoffensive to prepare a letter of retention spelling out the services you'll be performing, how much you'll be charging, when you'll be billing, and when payment is due. Such letters may even be legally required. In California, for example, lawyers and clients must sign a fee agreement if the expected fee is more than $1,000 or the fee is contingent on the outcome of a lawsuit.

You could even take the retention letter one step farther by providing payment envelopes for the patients to use in sending their monthly checks. This approach works for professionals where fairly predictable services are delivered over a defined time period.

Your letter should state when you expect to be paid—usually within ten days of the statement date. Also, list the amount of any interest or finance charges you'll assess (as permitted by state law) if payment is late, and reserve your right to stop rendering services. (In a few professions, rules of professional ethics may affect how and when you can terminate the relationship.) Have the client or patient acknowledge in writing that he or she has received your letter and agrees to its terms.

To find out legal limits on interest or finance charges, check the index to the annotated statutes (sometimes called a "code") for your state—available in any good law library. Look under the terms "interest," "usury," or "finance charges." Also, your professional or trade organization should have helpful information.

2. Wholesale and Manufacturing Businesses

If you're a shoe wholesaler, software company, or clothing manufacturer—or if you're in any other wholesale or service business—you should have a credit policy, and you should insist that customers complete a formal application for credit. The details of your credit policy will depend on the kind of business you're in and the type of customers you serve. Here are some issues to think about:

- How many days after billing is payment due?
- Is there a discount for early payment?
- Do you require prepayment or COD terms for certain classes of customers?
- Do you add interest or finance charges? If so, how much?
- When are credit checks required? (For example, you obviously wouldn't require a credit check if the customer is the government, and probably wouldn't for a major, well-established company. On the other hand, you likely would want to check on the credit of a new small business or an individual making a large purchase.)
- How are credit limits determined?
- When and how often do you send past due notices and follow up with phone calls?
- Do you keep selling to a customer whose account is overdue?
- At what point will you begin aggressive credit efforts?

When you approve credit for new trade accounts, let them know the maximum credit you're allowing and when they're expected to pay—as well as other relevant features of your credit policy.

Should You Charge Interest?

Most businesses don't charge interest or impose finance charges in exchange for granting credit. More typically, interest is charged when bills aren't paid within the agreed time, often between ten and 30 days. If you decide to impose these charges, you must inform the customer how the charges will be computed. The Truth in Lending Act (see Section B), which applies primarily to sales to consumers, prescribes the disclosures you must make—but not the rates you can charge. That's done by state law.

One reason to consider adding interest or finance charges after a certain date is that customers who are short of cash tend to pay first the bills that carry such charges. Other incentives for early payment include:

- Discounts for prompt payment—for example, 5% off if the customer pays his or her bill on the spot or within ten days.
- Free shipping and handling (a big item these days) for customers who prepay.
- Making the customer responsible for paying for court costs and reasonable attorney fees required to enforce collection if the customer doesn't pay as agreed. The customer must agree to this, either in a credit application or a separate contract.

A sample credit application form designed for trade accounts is shown below.

SAMPLE CREDIT APPLICATION

CREDIT APPLICATION

The undersigned company is applying for credit with ABC ELECTRICAL INC. and agrees to abide by the standard terms and conditions of ABC ELECTRICAL INC. as printed on the reverse side.

Company Name _____

DBA (if different) _____

Contact Person _____

Address _____

Phone ( )_____ Fax ( ) _____

Federal Tax ID or Social Security No. _____

Type of Business _____ No. of Employees_____

Date Business Established _____

Types of Products You Will Purchase _____

Amount of Credit Requested $ _____

Are You a:

☐ CORPORATION

State of Incorporation _____

Names, Titles, and Addresses of Your Three Chief Corporate Officers _____

Name and Address of Your Resident Agent _____

☐ LIMITED LIABILITY COMPANY (LLC)

State Where Formed _____

Names, Titles, and Addresses of Your Three Chief Managers or Members_____

_____

_____

_____

Name and Address of Your Resident Agent _____

_____

☐ PARTNERSHIP

Names and Addresses of the Partners

_____

_____

_____

☐ SOLE PROPRIETORSHIP

Are you sales-tax exempt? Yes ___ No ___

Have you ever had credit with us before? Yes ___ No ___

If yes, under what name? _____

Authorized Purchasers _____

_____

Purchase Order Required? Yes ___ No ___

SAMPLE CREDIT APPLICATION (continued)

TRADE REFERENCES

Reference #1   Name _____

                 Address _____

                 Phone (   ) _____

Reference #2   Name _____

                 Address _____

                 Phone (   ) _____

Reference #3   Name _____

                 Address _____

                 Phone (   ) _____

BANK REFERENCES

Bank #1   Account # _____ Phone (   ) _____

            Contact Person _____

            Name of Bank_____

            Address _____

Bank #2   Account # _____ Phone (   ) _____

            Contact Person _____

            Name of Bank_____

            Address _____

I represent that the above information is true and is given to induce ABC ELECTRICAL INC. to extend credit to the applicant. My company and I authorize ABC ELECTRICAL INC. to make such credit investigation as ABC ELECTRICAL INC. sees fit, including contacting the above trade references and banks and obtaining credit reports. My company and I authorize all trade references, banks, and credit reporting agencies to disclose to ABC ELECTRICAL INC. any and all information concerning the financial and credit history of my company and myself.

I have read the terms and conditions stated below and agree to all of those terms and conditions.

Authorized Signature: _____

Printed Name: _____

Title: _____   Date: _____

GENERAL TERMS AND CONDITIONS AND PERSONAL GUARANTEE

1.   Bills are sent on the first day of each month. You may take the 5% discount as indicated on the bill if you pay the invoice by the 10th of the month.

2.   All bills become payable in full on the 11th day of the month and, if not paid by the end of the month, are considered past due.

3.   A service charge of 2% per month will be added to all amounts billed if not paid by the end of the month.

4.   No additional credit will be extended to past due accounts unless satisfactory arrangements are made with our credit department.

5.   PERSONAL GUARANTEE: If the credit customer is a corporation or LLC, then those signing this application, whether or not signing as an officer or manager, personally guarantee payment for all items purchased on credit by the corporation or LLC.

Personal guarantees can be a problem. *See the discussion in Section 3, below.*

3. Extending Credit to Businesses

When the customer is another business, it's wise to get information about whom you're really dealing with—especially if the business wants a substantial amount of credit. Is the customer a sole proprietor? A partnership? A corporation? The answer determines who's liable for the debt. If the business is owned by an individual (for example, Bill Jones doing business as Jones Products), the owner's own assets—as well as those of the business—are available to satisfy the debt. With a general partnership, you can go after the assets of the individual partners, if necessary, so it's a good idea to have the names of all the partners listed on the credit application. A limited partnership, on the other hand, consists of general partners and limited partners; only the assets of the general partners are available to satisfy the debts of a limited partnership. (See Chapter 1, Section B.)

With a corporation, you usually are limited to collecting from the business assets. Because you can't collect from the personal bank accounts of the officers and shareholders, there's good reason to seek personal guarantees when dealing with a new or small corporation that wants substantial credit. In some businesses, however, it's completely against trade practices to ask for a personal guarantee. It's your job to learn the practices in your industry before using a clause like number 5, in the sample credit application above. If you do decide to seek personal guarantees, check out whether or not a signature on a credit application is sufficient in your state. The law may require that you obtain a new guarantee each time you extend credit to a company.

You may also want to ask for the personal guarantees of others if someone who applies for personal credit has a weak financial status. Maybe a friend or family member will agree to be responsible if the customer doesn't pay on time. This is often called cosigning. You can obtain the personal guarantee or cosignature on the credit application form or on a separate document called "Guarantee of Payment."

As noted above, in some states, a personal guarantee on an application form or a one-time separate document may not suffice. You may need to get a signature from the guarantor each time you extend credit.

4. References and Credit Checks

Your credit application should provide space for the applicant to list several other businesses who will vouch for the fact that the applicant pays on time. Check these references carefully, even though the credit applicant is sure to list people who will say positive things. Your job is to try to penetrate the facade many credit applicants are sure to present that everything is just fine. One way to do this is to ask offbeat questions such as, "You mean ABC's credit is so good you'll take me to lunch if they stiff me?"

If the amount of credit you're extending is large, don't stop with checking a few references. Purchase a credit report on an individual from a national credit reporting agency such as Trans Union, Experian, or Equifax or, on a business, from Dun & Bradstreet. You'll find them listed under "Credit Reporting Agencies" in the Yellow Pages, or check for a toll-free number or website.

To get a report on an individual, most agencies want the name, address, phone number, Social Security number, and date of birth, if possible, of the person you're asking them to search—information you should get on your credit application form.

Be wary of negative information in credit reports, which may be inaccurate or out of date. If an individual seems to be otherwise well qualified for credit, consider giving him or her a chance to explain the negative stuff before you deny credit.

5. Signatures for Receipt of Goods

Have customers sign receipts when they receive merchandise on credit. If you provide services, have customers sign an acknowledgment of services performed. This avoids arguments about whether or not the customer actually received the goods or services.

B. Laws That Regulate Consumer Credit

Many small businesses don't extend credit directly to consumers. With the widespread availability of credit cards, this is often the safest and most cost-effective way to go. However, if yours is a business where credit must be granted, you must comply with federal laws affecting credit sales to consumers for personal, family, or household purposes. States are also beginning to adopt consumer credit laws that mirror many provisions of federal law.

Here's an introduction to the major federal laws that affect consumer credit:

1. The Truth in Lending Act

This statute requires you to disclose your exact credit terms to people who apply for credit, so they'll know what they're expected to pay. It also regulates how you advertise consumer credit. Among the items you must disclose to a consumer who buys on credit are the following:

- the monthly finance charge
- the annual interest rate
- when payments are due
- the total sale price—cash price of the item or service plus all other charges
- the amount of any late payment charges and when they'll be imposed.

2. The Fair Credit Billing Act

This law dictates what you must do if a customer claims you made a mistake in your billing. The customer must notify you within 60 days after you mailed the first bill containing the claimed error. You must respond within 30 days after you receive the letter unless the dispute has already been resolved. You must also conduct a reasonable investigation and, within 90 days after getting the customer's letter, explain why the bill is correct or correct the error. If you don't follow this procedure, you must give the customer a $50 credit toward the disputed amount—even if your bill was correct. Until the dispute is resolved, you can't report to a credit bureau that the customer is delinquent.

> **EXAMPLE:** Ron notifies CompuCo that he wasn't properly credited for a payment he sent in on his computer system. Under the Fair Credit Billing Act, CompuCo must acknowledge Ron's notice within 30 days. And within 90 days, CompuCo must either agree with Ron and correct his account or, after conducting a reasonable investigation, send Ron a letter explaining why the company feels his bill was correct. While this is happening, Ron doesn't have to pay the disputed amount. And he can't be penalized for withholding payment. During this period, CompuCo can't tell a credit reporting agency that this is a delinquent bill. CompuCo can charge interest on the disputed bill, but if Ron turns out to be right, the interest must be dropped.

State laws may also deal with billing disputes. Generally, if a state law on this subject conflicts with the federal statute, the federal statute will control—but there's one exception: a state law will prevail if it gives a consumer more time to notify a creditor about a billing error. For example, as explained above, the federal law gives a consumer 60 days after receiving a bill to notify you of a billing error. If a state law gives a consumer 90 days to notify you, the consumer will be entitled to the extra 30 days.

In addition to telling you how to handle billing disputes, the Fair Credit Billing Act requires you, in periodic mailings, to tell consumers what their rights are.

3. The Equal Credit Opportunity Act

You may not discriminate against an applicant on the basis of race, color, religion, national origin, age, sex, or marital status. The Act does leave you free to consider legitimate factors in granting credit, such as the applicant's financial status (earnings and savings) and credit record. Despite the prohibition on age discrimination, you can reject a consumer who hasn't reached the legal age in your state for entering into contracts.

4. The Fair Credit Reporting Act

This law deals primarily with credit reports issued by credit reporting agencies. It's intended to protect consumers from having their eligibility for credit thwarted by inaccurate or obsolete credit report information. The law gives consumers the right to a copy of their credit reports. If they feel something is inaccurate, they can ask that it be corrected or removed. If the business reporting the credit problem doesn't agree to a change or deletion or if the credit bureau refuses to make it, the consumer can add a 100-word statement to the file explaining his or her side of the story. This becomes a part of any future credit report.

5. The Fair Debt Collection Practices Act

This statute addresses abusive methods used by third-party collectors—bill collectors you hire to collect overdue bills. Small businesses are more directly affected by state laws that apply directly to collection methods used by a creditor. (See Section D3.)

 Want to learn more about consumer credit? *An excellent resource is* Consumer Law: Sales Practices and Credit Regulation, *by Howard J. Alperin and Roland J. Alperin (West Publishing Co.). It should be available at most law libraries. Also helpful is* Manual of Credit and Commercial Laws *(National Association of Credit Management).*

A fine Nolo book discusses these issues from the perspective of the consumer: Solve Your Money Troubles, *by Robin Leonard.*

Also very helpful are two booklets published by the Federal Trade Commission:

- How to Advertise Consumer Credit: Complying With the Law
- How to Write Readable Credit Forms.

Both are available at www.ftc.gov. See Appendix B for additional FTC contact information.

Finally, you may find helpful information in Bankruptcy and Other Debtor-Creditor Laws in a Nutshell, *by David G. Epstein (West Publishing Co.).*

You may be able to get information from a local trade association (such as a contractors', restaurant, or tax preparers' association) or Chamber of Commerce.

C. Becoming a Secured Creditor

If you sell major amounts of merchandise or equipment to a customer on credit, look into becoming a secured creditor. If the debt is secured by property of the customer, you can seize that property if the customer doesn't pay the debt as promised. A common arrangement is for a business to take a security interest in the goods it sells on credit.

For example, a store that sells furniture on credit keeps a security interest in the furniture. If the buyer gets behind on payments, the store can take the furniture back. Under federal and state laws dealing with billing problems, you may be subject to penalties for failing to comply with the required procedures.

1. Sales of Merchandise or Equipment

The Uniform Commercial Code (UCC), which has been adopted by all states, provides a method for you to acquire a legal (security) interest in the property that you sell to the customer—or in other property of the customer—that will let you sell or take back the property if the customer doesn't pay. Typically, you have the customer sign a financing agreement and a UCC Financing Statement. You then file the UCC Financing Statement with the appropriate public office, such as the county clerk or the secretary of state (it varies from state to state).

Also, if the customer files for bankruptcy, you'll have a big advantage over general (unsecured) creditors—those who didn't take a security interest in the customer's property. The property in which you have a security interest will be earmarked for your benefit. Unsecured creditors get only a share of the bankrupt's unsecured assets—which may repay only a tiny portion of what's owed or (often) nothing at all.

Obviously, it takes time and requires some paperwork and expense to create a security interest. It may not be worth it if you sell someone a $500 washing machine (it's a lot easier to take credit cards and require full payment)—but definitely worth doing when the product is a $10,000 computer system. Banks routinely obtain a security interest when they lend money to a customer to purchase equipment.

Incidentally, as an alternative to extending credit on larger purchases, one option is to refer the customer to a bank or leasing company—particularly one with whom you've established a working relationship. These organizations are in business to take credit risks and can absorb losses better than you can.

2. Special Rights for Those in the Construction Business

A lien is a legal claim on someone's property. Under state law, you may have a mechanic's, materialman's, or construction lien on real estate if you provided materials or labor on a construction or renovation project—for example, if you supplied the lighting fixtures or installed the roofing for a new house. If your bill isn't paid, you can foreclose on your lien. This means the real estate can be sold to pay your bill.

Unfortunately, in many states to take advantage of this powerful weapon to protect your rights, you have to file certain legal documents claiming (perfecting) a lien within a short time after you complete your work or supply the materials. Speak to a construction industry trade association or, if necessary, a lawyer about how to do this.

D. Collection Problems

Despite your best efforts to screen your customers, if you extend credit, sooner or later you're going to run into people or businesses who are slow in paying. It can be one of the most frustrating aspects of running a business. Part of the reason is that you may be pursuing several objectives that are not compatible. Here's what I mean:

- You want to be paid in full, of course, but—
- You'd also like to continue doing business with the customer, if possible. What's more—
- You don't want to run afoul of laws that restrict or prohibit aggressive collection tactics, and—
- You don't want waste your resources on a wild goose chase.

It's not an easy problem, but a number of techniques can help keep your losses to a minimum.

1. Strategies for Avoiding or Reducing Losses

Following these suggestions should help you hold down your losses on credit transactions:

- Send bills promptly and rebill at least monthly. There's no need to wait for the end of the month.

- Make sure your bills clearly state the goods sold or the services provided. It's a great idea to include on the bill a request to the customer to contact you if there are problems with the goods or services. If the customer fails to do so and later tries to excuse the failure to pay by claiming the goods or services were unsatisfactory, you have a good argument that the customer is fabricating a phony excuse. Another benefit is that if your goods or services are in fact prone to problems, you open up lines of communication and usually can keep the customer happy.

- Enclose a self-addressed envelope (preferably stamped) to facilitate payment.

- Keep a record of the checking account that the customer uses to pay you.

- Send past-due notices promptly when an account is overdue. Ask clearly for payment. Many people worry that the word "pay" sounds too blunt. Here are a few alternate phrases, courtesy of collection expert Leonard Sklar, author of *The Check Is NOT in the Mail* (Baroque Publishing):

  "We'd appreciate it if you would *clear your account.*"

  "You can *take care of this* by cash or check, whichever you prefer."

  "Please *bring your account current.*"

- If this doesn't work, promptly telephone to ask what's wrong. The customer needs to know that you follow these matters closely. Do not extend more credit, no matter what the hard luck story. This is particularly important. Lots of businesses facing tight finances pay only when they need more merchandise.

If you let them have it without payment, you're teaching them that you're a pushover.

- Have a series of letters to use in routine cases. These letters should escalate in intensity as time goes by. (See the discussion of collection letters later in this section.)

- If the customer has genuine financial problems, find out what the customer realistically can afford. Consider extending the time for payment if the customer agrees in writing to a new payment schedule. Call the day before the next scheduled payment is due to be sure the customer plans to respect the agreement.

- Save copies of all correspondence with the customer and keep notes of all telephone conversations.

- Watch out for checks for less than the full amount that say "Payment in Full." In some states, if you deposit the check—especially if the amount owed is in dispute—you may have wiped out the balance owing. (See Chapter 18, Section C2.) Learn the law in your state before you deposit such a check.

- Continue to keep in contact with the customer—but don't harass him or her. (See Section D3.)

- If an account is unpaid for an extended period and you're doubtful about ever collecting, consider offering in writing a time-limited, deep discount to resolve the matter. This way, the customer has the incentive to borrow money to take advantage of your one-time, never-again offer to settle.

- When collection starts to put heavy demands on your time, and your chances of recovery are slim because you know the customer is on the skids, consider turning the debt over to a collection agency so you can get on with more productive activities. (But first consider the collection alternatives described in Section E.)

2. Collection Letters

You may find it useful to develop a set of past-due notices to use when customers fall behind. Although these are form letters, it's easy to customize them using your computer and word processing software. In writing to an individual customer, use the customer's name. In writing to a company, address your letter to the owner or chief operating office. It's less effective to start out with "Dear Customer" or "Dear Accounts Payable Supervisor."

Your first letter may suggest that perhaps the bill was overlooked, and that payment should be sent now so that the customer can maintain a good credit rating. Your second and third letters should be polite but increasingly firm. Vary the format of your letters. Each one should look a little different. Samples are shown below.

Letter 1

```
            Account No. _____


    Dear _____:


    Our records show that you have an outstanding balance with our company of $450.00.
This is for  (describe the goods or services) .

    Is there a problem with this bill? If so, please call me so that we can resolve the
matter. Otherwise, please send your payment at this time to bring your account current.
I'm enclosing a business reply envelope for you to use.

    Until you bring your account current, it's our policy to put further purchases on a
cash basis.

    Sincerely,




    P.S. Paying your bill at this time will help you to maintain your good credit rating.
```

Letter 2

Re: Overdue Bill ($_____)

Account No._____

Dear _____:

    Your bill for $450.00 is seriously overdue. This is for the _(describe the goods or services furnished)_ we supplied to you last _(state the month)_. More than 60 days have gone by since we sent you our invoice. You did not respond to the letter I sent you last month.

    We value your patronage but must insist that you bring your account up to date. Doing so will help you protect your reputation for prompt payment.

    Please send your check today for the full balance. If this is not feasible, please call me to discuss a possible payment plan. I need to hear from you as soon as possible.

    Sincerely,

Letter 3

Re: Collection Action on

Overdue Bill ($_____)

Account No._____

Dear _____:

    We show an unpaid balance of $450 on your account that is over 90 days old. This is for the _____ that we supplied you over _____ days ago.

    I have repeatedly tried to contact you, but my calls and letters have gone unheeded.

    You must send full payment by _(date)_ or contact me by that date to discuss your intentions. If I do not hear from you, I plan to turn over the account for collection.

    As you know, collection action can only have an adverse effect on your credit rating, and, according to our credit agreement, you will be responsible for collection costs. I hope to hear from you immediately so that the matter can be resolved without taking that step.

    Sincerely,

3. Prohibited Collection Practices

Because of abuses, Congress passed the Fair Debt Collection Practices Act to regulate the activities of collection agencies. The federal law doesn't cover small businesses that collect their own bills. Many state laws, however, do crack down on the aggressive collection techniques of such businesses. And in states where the legislature hasn't yet acted, court decisions often penalize businesses that harass debtors or use unfair collection tactics.

Most business owners know intuitively the kind of behavior that's out of bounds. Here are some debt collection practices specifically outlawed by California's Fair Debt Collection Practices statute:

- Using or threatening to use physical force to collect a debt.
- Falsely threatening that the failure to pay a consumer debt will result in an accusation that the debtor has committed a crime.
- Using obscene or profane language.
- Causing expense to the debtor for long distance calls.
- Causing a phone to ring repeatedly or continuously to annoy the debtor.
- Communicating with the debtor so often as to be unreasonable and to constitute harassment.
- Communicating with the debtor's employer regarding a consumer debt unless the communication is necessary or the debtor has consented in writing. (A communication is necessary, according to the statute, only to verify the debtor's employment, to locate the debtor, or to carry out a garnishment of wages after you have sued and won a judgment.)

The list goes on and on. If there's a similar statute in your state, get a copy and read it carefully. Like California's, most state laws in this field are modeled on the federal law. Some statutes, however, are more specific than others; for example, some list specific hours during which you can call the debtor.

E. Collection Options

Suppose you can't get the customer to pay up voluntarily. What next? If you're not willing to write off the debt (which is sometimes the wisest thing to do), you have three collection options:

- sue in small claims court
- hire a lawyer
- turn the account over to a collection agency.

Each choice has pros and cons.

Small claims court (see Chapter 23) is inexpensive and speedy. The downside is that it can take a good chunk of your time. Furthermore, any judgment that you receive may be worthless if the debtor lacks a job or bank account.

Lawyers can be effective, but they're expensive. Consider using a lawyer to write dunning letters. Many lawyers are willing to do this for a nominal charge.

Collection agencies are good at tracing elusive debtors, but they take a big percentage of what they collect for you. ■

Put It in Writing: Small Business Contracts

As the owner of a small business, it's likely that you'll often encounter both written and oral contracts. The most important piece of advice about contracts is obvious: Put all important agreements in writing. This chapter shows you how, and tells you what to do if something goes wrong.

A. What Makes a Valid Contract

A valid contract requires two and sometimes three elements:

- An agreement (meeting of the minds) between the parties
- "Consideration"—a legal term meaning the exchange of things of value
- Something in writing, if the contract covers certain matters, such as the sale of real estate and tasks that can't be completed in one year. (See Section D.)

For example, suppose you're opening a new store. You meet with Joe, a sign maker, to discuss the construction and installation of a five-foot by three-foot sign. Joe offers to do the work for $450 and to have the sign ready for your grand opening on June 15. "It's a deal," you say. You now have a legally binding contract, enforceable in court or by arbitration. All the necessary elements are present:

- **An Agreement.** Joe offered to build and install the sign at a certain price by a certain date. You accepted the offer by telling Joe, "It's a deal."
- **Consideration.** The two of you are exchanging something of value. You're giving your promise to pay $450. Joe is giving his promise to build and install the sign.
- **Written Agreement Not Required Here.** Normal business contracts that can be performed in less than a year don't have to be in writing to be enforceable.

To understand why "consideration" is important, let's explore the difference between a contract and a gift. Assume that Joe installs the sign on time and

you pay him $450 as agreed. Impressed by the high quality of his work, you say: "Joe, to thank you for the great job you did, I'm going to send you a $100 bonus next week." Can Joe enforce your promise to pay the bonus? No. He got what he bargained for— the $450 payment. He didn't promise you anything (consideration) for the extra $100 payment. If you pay it, fine. If not, Joe can't force you to.

1. Negotiations

Negotiations, which may or may not lead to an agreement, do not constitute a contract. So if instead of meeting face to face with Joe, you call him and describe the job, and he says he can probably do it for about $450, you don't have a contract.

2. Offer and Acceptance

If after negotiations, two people reach an agreement, a contract is formed. Say that after discussing the job with you by phone, Joe promptly sends you a letter in which he says: "I can build and install the sign shown on the enclosed sketch for $450. I'll have it in place by June 15 when you open. You can pay me then." You send back a fax saying: "Sounds good. Go ahead." This is a valid contract. Joe has made a clear offer. You've just as clearly accepted that offer. The fact that you and Joe didn't meet face-to-face and didn't even use the same type of communication medium doesn't alter this conclusion.

In this example, you accepted Joe's offer promptly. But what if you'd waited two weeks or two months to accept? The legal rule is that an offer without a stated expiration date remains open for a reasonable time. What's reasonable depends on the type of business and the facts of the situation. If you're offered a truckload of fish or flowers, it might be unreasonable to delay your acceptance more than a few hours or even minutes, while an offer to sell surplus wood chips at a time when the market is glutted might reasonably be assumed to be good for a month or more. But there's really no need to tolerate any uncertainty in this regard. Include a clear deadline for acceptance when you present an offer. If you want to accept an offer, do it as promptly as possible.

3. Counteroffers

In the real world, negotiations aren't usually as simple as making an offer and having it accepted. And until an agreement is reached, there's no contract.

For example, say Joe sends you the letter offering to provide your sign for $450. You call his office and leave a message on his voice mail saying: "Go ahead, but I can only pay $400." So far, there's no contract. By changing the terms of Joe's offer, you've rejected it and made a counteroffer. The two of you are still negotiating. If Joe calls back and says, "Okay, I'll do it for $400," you now have a binding contract. Joe has accepted your counteroffer. Again, the fact that you and Joe weren't in the same room or never spoke to each other isn't significant. What is key is that one of you made an offer (in this case, in the form of a counteroffer), and the other accepted it.

4. Revoking an Offer

Until an offer is accepted, it can be revoked by the person who made it. So if you're about to write Joe a letter accepting his offer, and Joe calls to revoke his offer because he's decided $450 isn't enough, you're out of luck. Joe revoked his offer before you accepted it, so there's no contract.

How an Offer to Contract Ends

- The person who made the offer revokes it before it's accepted.
- The offer expires.

  EXAMPLE: "This offer will expire automatically if I don't receive your acceptance by noon on May 10." But unless you've been paid something to keep the offer open (as is common for an option to buy real property—see next section), you (the offeror) can still revoke the unaccepted offer before the period for acceptance expires.

- A reasonable time elapses. As discussed in Section 2, above, there are no hard and fast rules as to what's reasonable. It all depends on circumstances and the practices in your industry.
- The offer is rejected. If you reject an offer and then change your mind, it's too late. To get the deal going again, you'll need to make an offer to the other party.
- Either party dies before the offer is accepted.

5. Option to Keep Offer Open

If you want someone to keep an offer open while you think about it, you may have to pay for the privilege. If you do, and the person who made the offer agrees to keep it open, your agreement (which is itself a contract) is called an "option." Options are commonly used when real estate or businesses are sold.

To stay with our sign example, say that when Joe sends you the letter offering to provide your sign, you tell him you're not ready to respond yet, but you want to be sure the offer will stay open while you think about it. Joe responds that if you pay $100 now, he'll keep his offer open for two more weeks. You pay the $100 and accept the offer within the two-week period. The resulting contract would be valid even if Joe tried to withdraw his offer before the end of the two-week period. You and Joe already have a contract (an option), which consists of your right to purchase his services at the $450 price if you act within the two-week period. He received something of value (your $100) in return for granting you this option.

6. How Offers Are Accepted

Usually, offers are accepted either in writing or orally. But that's not always necessary. It is an area of considerable legal complexity, but generally an offer can be accepted by a prompt action that conforms with the terms of the offer. For example, you might leave the sign builder Joe a note at his workshop, saying "Please add a red border to this sign today; I'll pay you an extra $100." Joe comes back that afternoon and adds the red border. You're obligated to pay him.

7. An Advertisement as an Offer

Under traditional contract law, ads are considered only invitations to negotiate or to make an offer;

you have no obligation to go through with the deal just because someone offers to meet your advertised price. So if a customer appears and says she wants to buy the house, land, or business that you advertised in the classifieds for $200,000, there's no binding contract. One major exception to this rule involves rewards. Generally, an ad offering to pay a reward is binding if someone performs the requested act.

Consumer protection laws have also changed this traditional rule. For example, the law in many states requires merchants to stock advertised items in quantities large enough to meet reasonably expected demand, unless the ad states that stock is limited. And some states require the merchant to give a rain check allowing the consumer to purchase the same merchandise at the same price at a later date. (See Chapter 17 for more on consumer transactions.)

B. Unfair or Illegal Contracts

What if a person makes a bad bargain? Suppose you agree to pay $800 for a used laser printer that's worth only $200. Can you call off the deal on the ground that the contract was grossly unfair? Probably not. As long as there's a valid contract, it doesn't usually matter whether or not the item is objectively worth the price paid for it.

Sometimes, however, a court sets aside a contract if the terms are unconscionable—that is, shockingly unfair. For example, a judge or arbitrator may release an unsophisticated consumer (say a recent immigrant with a language problem) from a grossly unfair contract extracted by a sophisticated, high-pressure salesperson. Applying this principle of law, a contract to sell a $500 television for $5,000 might be set aside. But even though a judge might cite contract law, the decision would probably be based more on the doctrine of fraud or misrepresentation. Or the decision might be based on a state consumer protection statute that prohibits taking advantage of someone who can't protect his or her interests because of disability, illiteracy, or a language problem. (See Chapter 17, Section D, for more on this type of statute.)

When it comes to reasonably experienced businesspeople working out contracts with each other, however, unfairness is rarely if ever a legal ground for setting aside a contract. Usually, a party who negotiates a bad deal is stuck with it.

If a contract clause is illegal or against public policy, a judge or arbitrator won't enforce it. For example, a remodeling contract stating that neither party will obtain a legally required building permit would be void as a violation of public policy, as would a similar contract obligating a party to bribe a building inspector.

C. Misrepresentation, Duress, or Mistake

If before you sign a contract the other person tells you a false statement about something important, and you rely on that statement in signing the contract, you can go to court and have the contract rescinded (canceled). This is so even if the other person doesn't realize that the fact is untrue. For example, say you buy a pickup truck for your business, relying on the seller's assertion that the truck can carry loads up to two tons. It turns out that the

seller got the numbers wrong, and the truck can only carry one-ton loads. You can have the contract rescinded. If you have a contract rescinded, you must return any benefits you already received. In this example, you'd have to return the pickup truck to the seller to get your money back.

If you accept "an offer you can't refuse"—because, for example, the offer is made at gunpoint—the contract isn't legally enforceable. The same is true of any other contract made as a result of unlawful threats. For example, if one party threatens to report the other party to the IRS or a state agency if a one-sided contract isn't signed, the contract isn't enforceable.

A mistake is the other ground for rescission of a contract. You thought you were buying a two-year-old computer. The seller thought you were buying her five-year-old computer. If you were both acting in good faith and simply miscommunicated, a judge or arbitrator would probably set aside the contract. But you can't avoid liability if you simply used bad judgment and paid too much for a five-year-old computer that doesn't provide the quality or speed you need.

Breach of Warranty

Sometimes a buyer can return goods to the seller and get a refund based on a breach of warranty. While the practical result in such cases may be the same as setting aside a contract for the reasons mentioned in this section, a different legal concept is at work.

An action for breach of warranty assumes that there's a valid contract. When a buyer seeks a refund based on breach of warranty, he or she is saying: "I acknowledge that we have a binding contract. I want to enforce my rights under that contract for breach of warranty." (See Chapter 17.)

D. Must a Contract Be in Writing?

Unless a contract falls into one of several specific categories, it is binding even if it's not in writing. You should put all important contracts in writing anyway. Otherwise, you run the risk of a dispute as to exactly what was promised, how much was to be paid, when the contract was to be performed, and on and on and on. And if you argue so long that you end up in court, it can be somewhere between difficult and impossible (not to mention expensive) to prove the existence and terms of an oral contract.

1. Contracts That Must Be in Writing

Each state has a statute (usually called the Statute of Frauds) listing the types of contracts that must be written to be valid. A typical list includes:

a. Contracts Involving the Sale of Real Estate or an Interest in Real Estate

Examples are a contract to purchase a building or parking lot or a contract to sell someone the right to use part of your land for a certain purpose (an easement).

Chapter 7 of *Legal Forms for Starting & Running a Small Business* contains forms for buying real estate.

b. Leases of Real Estate Lasting Longer Than One Year

An example is a three-year lease for retail space in a neighborhood shopping plaza.

Chapter 6 of *Legal Forms for Starting & Running a Small Business* contains forms for commercial leases.

c. A Promise to Pay Someone Else's Debt

This generally involves guarantees of payment. Examples are the president of a corporation personally guarantees to pay for any goods you sell to the corporation; or an uncle guarantees to pay the rent for his nephew's new store.

d. Contracts That Will Take More Than One Year to Perform

This provision of the Statute of Frauds applies only to contracts that cannot be performed within one year; for example, a contract to provide landscaping services to a hotel for a two-year period.

If performance of a contract is possible within one year, the contract doesn't have to be in writing. How about a contract to plant three maple trees within the next two years? Since the trees could be planted right away, the contract doesn't have to be in writing to be enforceable. Here are several more examples of oral contracts performable within one year (and therefore enforceable):

- A contract to teach four new employees within the next 18 months how to use a software program.
- A contract to cater a total of ten sales banquets for a corporation at dates to be selected by the corporation during the next three years.
- A contract to remove debris from the sites of five new homes to be completed within the next two years.

e. Contracts for the Sale of Goods (Tangible Personal Property) Worth $500 or More

A contract to sell you a notebook computer for $2,000, for example, must be in writing to be enforceable. If you call a computer store and they agree over the phone to sell you the computer for $2,000 but raise the price to $2,500 when you get there, you don't have an enforceable contract.

Under the Uniform Commercial Code (UCC), however, the written contract doesn't have to state the price or time of delivery—only that the parties agree on the sale of goods and the quantity of goods being sold. And in some cases, if the seller simply sends a written confirmation of an oral order and the buyer doesn't promptly object, a contract has been formed. These UCC exceptions are very important; be sure to read Section 3, below, which explains them in more detail.

There's an important exception to the rule that contracts for the sale of goods worth $500 must be in writing. If an oral contract is partially performed, the whole contract becomes binding. For example, say a salesperson offers to sell you a notebook computer for $2,000 and to throw in a modem when the store gets its next shipment in a week. You pay the $2,000 and take the computer home. When you return to the store the next week to pick up your modem, the store denies that it owes you one. You could sue successfully for breach of contract even though you don't have a written contract for a sale of goods over $500. The reason is that partial performance of the oral contract (your payment and the store's partial delivery of the merchandise) removes the transaction from the written contract (Statute of Frauds) requirements. Of course, as a practical matter, it would have been better to get the whole deal in writing.

📄 **Chapter 8 of *Legal Forms for Starting & Running a Small Business* contains forms for buying, selling, manufacturing, renting, and storing goods.**

2. What Constitutes a Written Contract

When state law does require a contract to be in writing, it doesn't mean you need a long-winded document labeled "contract" or "agreement" and signed by both parties. Especially in a business context, judges recognize and enforce writings that contain few details. All that's typically required is a letter, memo, or any other writing signed by the party against whom the contract is being enforced. The writing must identify the parties and generally describe the subject and the main terms and conditions of the agreement. That's all. The rules for what the writing must contain are even more relaxed for transactions covered by the Uniform Commercial Code, which automatically fills in many missing details. (See Section 3, below.)

I don't recommend that you settle for the bare-bones legal requirements. Because businesspeople's memories—like everyone else's—are imperfect, and because putting a contract in writing tends to highlight erroneous assumptions, and because not everyone you deal with is completely trustworthy, you want important contracts to contain a reasonable amount of detail.

> **EXAMPLE:** Arnie, a fish shop operator, meets Phyllis, a phone equipment salesperson, at a trade show. Arnie becomes enthusiastic about purchasing a new telephone system for $3,000, which he believes covers the installation, including all wiring and control panels. Phyllis, the sales rep for FoneTek, thinks her company is providing just the phones themselves. If they go ahead on the basis of an oral contract, disaster clearly looms. If, however, Arnie and Phyllis sit down to write up a contract, the issues that haven't really been agreed on are sure to come out, and Arnie and Phyllis will have ample opportunity to make necessary adjustments or call the deal off.

See Section E, below, for suggestions on writing a business contract.

3. The Sale of Goods: Special Uniform Commercial Code Rules

The Uniform Commercial Code (UCC) contains special rules affecting contracts for the sale of goods. It loosens up the requirements for creating a binding contract when goods are being sold.

The UCC requires you to produce something in writing if you want to enforce a contract for a sale of goods and the price is $500 or more. However, the UCC says that this writing can be very brief—briefer than a normal written contract. Under the UCC, the writing need only:

- indicate that the parties have agreed on the sale of the goods, and
- state the quantity of goods being sold.

If items such as price, time and place of delivery, or quality of the goods are missing, the UCC fills them in based on customs and practices in the particular industry.

Don't rely on sketchy contracts. *Just because the UCC makes legal some very sketchy contracts for the sale of goods doesn't mean it's a good idea to routinely use such contracts. It's far better to follow the outline in Section E, below, to put together a good written contract.*

Remember, if a customer comes to a store, pays for merchandise, and takes it away, there's no need for a formal written contract—the deal is done. (For larger purchases, it makes sense for the retailer to have the customer sign a receipt acknowledging delivery of the goods.) Under the UCC, having some writing is important when the seller merely promises to deliver the goods.

In most situations, the UCC requires that when a contract must be in writing to be enforceable, it must be signed by the person against whom the other party is seeking to enforce the contract. Stated another way, if A wants to sue B for breach of contract and a writing is required, A must show that B signed something showing an intent to be contractually bound.

But when merchants—people who sell goods—are involved, there doesn't always have to be a signed document. If a seller sends a confirmation of an order and the buyer doesn't object in writing within ten days after receiving it, nothing more is required to satisfy the written contract requirement.

EXAMPLE: Nandita owns a retail store that sells shoes. Runner's Choice Inc., a manufacturer, sends Nandita a notice saying: "This is to confirm that you agreed to buy 1,000 pairs of men's jogging shoes from this Company." Under normal written contract rules (see Section B, above), this wouldn't be enough to permit Runner's Choice to enforce a contract against Nandita, because she's signed nothing. But under the UCC, if Nandita doesn't object in writing within ten days after receiving the notice, she can't complain about the lack of a written document bearing her signature.

In this example, the notice from Runner's Choice satisfies the requirement that the contract be evidenced by a writing. However, if Runner's Choice sues Nandita for rejecting the shipment of shoes, it will still have to convince the judge or arbitrator that before Runner's Choice sent Nandita the notice, the parties actually reached an oral agreement regarding the shoes. In short, the notice, by itself, is not conclusive evidence that the parties reached a meeting of the minds. A contract signed by both sides is always preferable.

Where the UCC Came From

In 1940, someone came up with a brilliant idea: Why not put together a comprehensive code (statute) covering all the branches of commercial law and get it adopted in all states? That way, businesses in Michigan, Illinois, Georgia, and Oregon would all follow the same rules.

It took 11 years to carry out this proposal, which resulted in a set of model statutes called the Uniform Commercial Code, or UCC. Every state except Louisiana has adopted it; Louisiana has adopted key portions of it. It covers these areas of law:

- Sales (including Warranties; see Chapter 17, Section C)
- Commercial Paper (drafts, checks, certificates of deposit, promissory notes)
- Bank Deposits and Collections
- Letters of Credit
- Bulk Transfers
- Warehouse Receipts, Bills of Lading, and Other Documents of Title
- Investment Securities
- Secured Transactions.

Checking Out the UCC

Your state laws (statutes) should be available in any law library in your state, in the reference section of many public libraries, and via Nolo's website at www.nolo.com. The Uniform Commercial Code is probably indexed under Uniform, Commercial, or Commerce. Another good Web source is www.law.cornell.edu/uniform/ucc.html. For most small businesses, the section on Sales (Article 2) is the most helpful part of the UCC. The UCC changes fairly often; be sure you have the latest version that's been adopted in your state.

Valid contracts with no writing at all. Where specially manufactured goods are ordered, the UCC says you don't need something in writing to enforce a sales contract if the seller has already made a significant effort toward completing the terms of the contract.

> **EXAMPLE:** A restaurant calls and orders 500 sets of dishes from a restaurant supply company. The dishes are to feature the restaurant's logo. If the supply company makes a substantial beginning on manufacturing the dishes and applying the logo, the restaurant can't avoid liability on the contract simply because it was oral.

E. Writing Business-to-Business Contracts

Whatever your business, you'll need to write contracts from time to time. You'll probably need a written contract if you want to:

- buy or sell goods
- perform services as an independent contractor or consultant
- lease real estate or equipment
- manufacture, distribute, or license products
- enter into joint ventures
- grant credit
- advertise.

1. Checklist of Contract Clauses

The content of a contract depends, of course, on the type of transaction you're getting into. This checklist includes items to consider when you draft a contract:

☐ *Names and addresses of the parties.*

☐ *Date that the contract is signed.* (See Section F for suggestions about signing a contract.)

☐ *A short preamble ("recitals").* This provides some of the background of the agreement. For example, a contract might recite that Discs Unlimited is a retailer of compact discs and has three stores in the metropolitan area; that Stewart has an inventory management business; and that Discs Unlimited wishes to retain Stewart as an independent contractor to establish and maintain the company's computerized inventory control system.

☐ *What each party is promising to do.* Pay money, provide a service, sell something, build something, or so on. Often this section of the contract—particularly if it involves a product or a construction project—is labeled "specifications." In many situations, such as designing software, constructing a building, or providing consulting services, the specifications require lengthy attachments that may include drawings, formulas, or charts. (See Section 3, below, for how-to information.)

☐ *When the work will be done or the product delivered.* If strict compliance with contract deadlines is important, be sure to include the words, "Time is of the essence." Otherwise, a judge would probably allow reasonable leeway in enforcing the deadlines.

☐ *How long the contract will remain in effect.*

☐ *The price—or how it will be determined.*

☐ *When payment is due.* Will there be installments, and will interest be charged? In contracts for consulting and other services, it's common to have a payment schedule tied to interim completion deadlines. For example, a contract for architectural services might provide for payment of one-third of the architect's fees when drawings and specifications are finished and approved; one-third after bids have been received on the construction project and a contract signed with the general contractor; and one-third when the project is completed and a certificate of occupancy is issued by the building department.

☐ *Warranties.* If one party guarantees labor and materials for a certain period of time, what steps will be taken to correct warranty problems?

☐ *Conditions under which either party can terminate the agreement.*

☐ *"Liquidated damages" if performance is delayed or defective.* In cases where actual damages for breach of contract would be difficult to compute, the parties can establish in advance a fixed dollar amount (called liquidated damages) to be paid by a party who fails to perform its contractual obligations properly. (See Section H, below.)

☐ *Whether or not either party can transfer (assign) the contract to another person or company.* A contract that allows assignment of contract rights may be okay if it involves just the right to receive money, but not if it means that some other, unknown party will wind up performing skilled services called for by the contract.

☐ *Arbitration or mediation of disputes.*

☐ *Whether or not a party who breaches the contract is responsible for the other party's attorney fees and legal costs.*

☐ *Where notices of default or other communications concerning the contract can be sent.* Typically, the notices are sent to the business headquarters of the contracting parties.

☐ *What state law applies if questions about the contract arise.* If the parties have operations in different states or the contract is to be performed in more than one state, you may avoid potentially knotty legal issues if you specify in advance which state law applies.

2. Additional Requirements for Specialized Contracts

Many states require specific provisions in contracts that cover certain types of transactions. Areas where special requirements are likely include:

- sales of new and used vehicles and mobile homes
- home improvement services
- motor vehicle repairs
- apartment and home rentals
- door-to-door sales
- funerals, burials, and cremations.

If you're in one of these regulated businesses, you not only need to use a written contract—you also need to make sure it conforms to your state's legal rules. Among other things, you may have to put certain information or warnings in type of a certain size, including a statement about the customer's right to cancel the deal under certain conditions. In some states, you may have to print the contract in Spanish as well as English.

EXAMPLE: In Michigan, a statute requires a funeral director to insert the following language in boldface type in every prepaid funeral contract:

"This contract may be canceled either before death or after death by the buyer or, if the buyer is deceased, by the person or persons legally authorized to make funeral arrangements. If the contract is canceled, the buyer or the buyer's estate is entitled to receive a refund of __% of the contract price and any income earned from investment of the principal less administrative or escrow fees."

3. How to Design Your Contracts

You need contract forms that reflect the specialized nature of what you do, be it creating software, selling produce, publishing books, or cleaning buildings. This is especially true if your business is subject to consumer laws that require specific contract language. Typically, you'll need several basic types of contract for your business, each with spaces to fill in the details of the specific transaction.

EXAMPLE: Brian is setting up a direct mail consulting business. He plans to work with local businesses to show them how to stay in better contact with customers by announcing sales, new merchandise, and seasonally extended hours. Brian needs a contract that covers what he'll do, when he'll do it, what he expects his small business clients to provide, warranties, responsibilities for proofreading and signing off on mailings, and payment.

Brian will also need to hire independent contractors, graphic designers, artists, and computer wizards to help him carry out his contracts, so he'll also need a basic "work-for-hire" contract. Finally, Brian plans to use his experience to develop customized software for sale to similar businesses and so will need a basic software licensing agreement.

If you're new to your business, start by gathering copies of contracts used by other people in your field. Some kinds of contracts, such as commercial leases, are widely available. For other kinds, you may have to dig a bit. Trade associations, which commonly publish material containing sample contracts, are one good source. Other people in your line of work may be willing to share their contracts with you. Form books published for lawyers are an excellent starting point for developing your own specialized contract. Talk to the librarian at any major law library to find some suitable books. (See Chapter 24 for tips on finding and using a law library.)

Once you find a simple contract that's more or less suitable, make sure that you understand every word. Obviously, contracts written in plain English are better than those filled with legalese—but if the latter type is all you can find, it may not be too difficult to rewrite it. Next, write a rough draft of any additions you may need.

⚠ Professional help. *If you plan to use a form contract for major transactions, consider reviewing it with a lawyer who has small business experience—ideally, one who knows something about your field. It can help you see whether or not the contract does what you want it to do and includes everything you need. Because you have done most of the work, your advisor's advice should be reasonably priced. (See Chapter 24 for how to hire and work with a lawyer.)*

4. Attachments to Contracts

It's common to use attachments (often called exhibits) to your contract to list lengthy details that don't fit neatly into the main body of the contract. For example, in drawing up a contract with a sign maker, you could attach a sketch of the sign and a list of detailed specifications, including materials to be used. Simply refer in the main contract to Attachment A or Exhibit A and note that you "hereby incorporate it into your contract." By referring to the attachment in the contract itself, you make it a part of the contract.

If you're a consultant or routinely contract for your services, consider using a short basic contract and then adding your performance specs in an attachment. That way you can use the same basic contract form over and over with only slight modifications.

 Materials Written Primarily for Individuals
• 101 Law Forms for Personal Use, *by Robin Leonard and Ralph Warner (Nolo). This book, which includes promissory notes and agreements to sell, lease, and store property, also contains contracts for service providers (child care, home repair contractors) that are of use to small business people in these fields.*

Materials Written Primarily for Business People
• Legal Forms for Starting & Running a Small Business, *by Fred S. Steingold (Nolo). The book, accompanied by a CD-ROM, will make it easy for you to prepare a variety of business contracts and legal forms, including leases, contracts for the purchase of a business or real estate, and contracts for hiring employees and independent contractors.*

Materials Written Primarily for Lawyers and Law Students
• Contracts in a Nutshell, *by Claude D. Rohwer and Gordon D. Schaber (West Publishing Co.). An overview of contract law.*
• Sales and Leases of Goods in a Nutshell, *by John M. Stockton and Frederick H. Miller (West Publishing Co.). Legal analysis of the Uniform Commercial Code sections dealing with sales.*
• Basic Legal Forms with Commentary, *by Clifford R. Ennico and Marvin Hayman (West Publishing Co.). Clear and comprehensive forms. This one-volume work is found in many law offices. It's more expensive than the other books on the list, but well worth the price if you draft a lot of contracts.*

F. The Formalities of Getting a Contract Signed

Many contracts take the form of a single document containing a series of numbered clauses. Both parties sign in duplicate, and each keeps a copy. But as discussed throughout this chapter, some written contracts are much less formal. Commonly they're in two—or more—parts. For example, A sends B an offer; B accepts by a separate letter or fax. Or A sends B an offer; B sends back a counteroffer; A accepts the counteroffer by letter or fax. As pointed out in Section A, as long as there's a genuine meeting of the minds, a contract contained in several documents is valid.

Another form of contract is a letter that pulls together the details of your deal and is accepted by the other person by a signature at the bottom. This is typical when you and the other party (perhaps someone you've worked with often) have worked out the deal over lunch or through a series of phone calls and don't feel the need for a formal contract. An example is shown below.

September 10, 20__

Dear Mary:

   I'd like to summarize our agreement for you to redecorate our store at 123 Main Street. We agreed that for $2,000 you'll apply wall covering to the south wall of our sales areas and apply two coats of paint to the remaining walls. The paint will be XYZ brand latex semigloss, and the wall covering will be ABC brand vinyl, pattern #66.

   In addition to the $2,000 payment, I'll promptly reimburse you for the paint and wall covering at your cost (when you present invoices from RacaFrax Wall Coverings), but you'll be responsible for the cost of all other tools, equipment, and supplies.

   I'll pay you $1,000 before you start work and the balance within 7 days after the work is completed. You'll do the work on the next two Sundays so that our business isn't interrupted. The quality of your work will meet or exceed the job you recently completed for the Ski Shoppe next door.

   We also agreed that if any problems come up about this job and we can't resolve them ourselves, we'll submit our dispute to Metro Mediators Inc. for mediation and, if that doesn't resolve the problem, to binding arbitration—and we'll split the cost 50/50.

   If I've accurately stated our agreement, please sign the enclosed copy of this letter and return it to me by noon Wednesday.

   Sincerely,

Jim Dalton
d/b/a Jim's Fitness Shop

The above terms are acceptable to me.

Date: Mary Walz

Be sure to read Section D3, above, *for special rules affecting contracts governed by the Uniform Commercial Code.*

1. Revising a Contract Before You Sign

In negotiating a contract, it's common for the parties to go back and forth through several drafts, refining the language. Using a computer with word-processing software, it's simple to crank out a fresh version of the contract each time revisions are made. But that's not the only way to handle changes in wording. For minor changes, you can simply cross out the old wording and write in the new, using a typewriter or pen. If you use this method, each party should initial each change when the contract is signed, to establish that the changes were properly consented to and not illegally added later.

Still another way to handle changes—particularly if the changes are extensive—is to put them in an addendum. If you use an addendum, state that in case of a conflict between the addendum and the main contract, the wording in the addendum prevails. Both parties should sign the addendum and the main contract.

If a contract has gone through several revisions, it's a good idea to have both parties initial each page so that you're sure everyone has a correct copy of the final draft.

2. Signatures

Business people are sometimes confused as to how best to sign a contract. It depends on the legal form of your business.

- **A Sole Proprietor** can simply sign his or her name, because a sole proprietorship isn't a separate legal entity. But there are two other ways to do it, either of which is just as legal.
  Method 1:

Jim Dalton
D/B/A Jim's Fitness Shop
[*D/B/A means "doing business as."*]
Method 2:
Jim's Fitness Shop
By:_____
   Jim Dalton

- **For a Partnership,** the following format is commonly used:
  ARGUS ELECTRONICS,
  A Michigan Partnership
  By: _____
     Randy Argus, a General Partner

Only one partner needs to sign on behalf of a partnership.

Chapter 2, Section B, *contains a discussion of the authority of a single partner to bind the partnership and each of the individual partners.*

- **For a Limited Liability Company,** use this format:
  REALTY APPRAISAL SERVICES, LLC
  By:_____
     Shela Martin, Member [*or Manager*]
- **For a Corporation,** use this format:
  KIDDIE KRAFTS INC.,
  A California Corporation
  By: _____
     Madeline Arshak, President

A person signing as a corporate officer doesn't assume personal liability for meeting contractual obligations. (See Chapter 1, Section C, for a discussion of how using the corporate form of doing business can limit the personal liability of people operating the corporation.) If the other party to a contract is a corporation, you may (particularly in a major transaction) want to see a board of directors' resolution or corporate bylaws authorizing the particular officer to sign contracts on behalf of the corporation. You can omit this step if the contract is signed by the corporate president; a president is presumed to have authority to sign contracts for a corporation.

If you're entering into a contract with a corporation and want someone (such as a corporate officer or major shareholder) to sign a personal guarantee, you can use a clause like this one at the end of the contract:

> In consideration of Seller entering into the above contract with Starlight Corporation, I personally guarantee the performance of all of the above contractual obligations undertaken by Starlight Corporation.

_____

Liz Star

Chapter 1 of _Legal Forms for Starting & Running a Small Business_ contains additional information on signing business contracts.

3. Witnesses and Notaries

Notarization means that a notary public certifies in writing that:

- You're the person you claim to be, and
- You've acknowledged under oath signing the document.

Very few contracts need to be notarized or signed by witnesses. The major exceptions to this rule are documents that are going to be recorded at a public office charged with keeping such records (usually called the county recorder or registrar of deeds). These documents are described in the next section. Occasionally—but very rarely—state laws require witnesses or notaries to sign other types of documents.

4. Recording

The great majority of business contracts don't have to be publicly recorded—and, in fact, are usually ineligible for recording. Here are the exceptions:

- Documents that affect title to or rights in real estate. This includes deeds, mortgages, trust deeds (a form of mortgage used in many states), and easement agreements.
- Long-term real estate leases, or memoranda summarizing them.
- Some documents dealing with tangible personal property, such as UCC financing statements or chattel mortgages, when the seller or a third party is financing part of the purchase price and receiving a security (contingent ownership) interest in the property. Banks, for example, routinely record security interests when making equipment loans.

5. Dates

When you sign a contract, offer, counteroffer, or acceptance, include the date—and make sure the other person does too. This helps to establish that there was agreement (remember, a meeting of the minds is an essential element of any valid contract). A simple way to do this is to always put a date line (Date: _____, 20__) next to the place where each person will sign. Don't worry if the dates of signing differ by a few days or even a week, as is common when the parties exchange documents by mail.

> **EXAMPLE:** If you sign on Monday and the other party signs a week later, you have a valid contract unless (1) you revoked your signature before the other person signed, or (2) you stated in the contract or offer that the other person must accept the offer before that date.

6. Originals and Photocopies

A contract is an "original" as long as the signatures are originals. So a photocopied document which both parties then sign is an original. So is a carbon copy or computer-printed copy which both parties sign.

If you enter into a traditional written contract—one document that contains the full agreement of the parties and is signed by both of them—it's best if each party has a copy of the contract with the original signatures of both parties. This is easy if you sign at the same session; simply sign two originals, so each party can keep a fully signed one.

A photocopy or faxed copy of a signed contract can still be enforced as long as the judge or arbitrator is convinced that what you have is an accurate reproduction of the original.

Storing Contracts

Store your contracts and other important documents in a fireproof safe or file cabinet. Another precaution is to keep photocopies of all important documents at another location. This may seem like overkill—but not if you have to prove what's in a contract and all copies have been destroyed, stolen, or lost.

7. Revising a Contract After Both Parties Sign

Once a contract has been signed, any changes must be agreed to by both parties. In essence this means they're forming a new contract. The simplest way to make fairly minor revisions to a signed contract is through an addendum—or a second or third addendum if necessary. When you write an addendum, follow these steps:

- Refer to the earlier contract by date, names of the parties, and subject matter.
- State all of the changes.
- State that in case of a conflict between the terms of the original contract and the addendum, the terms of the addendum prevail.
- Make it clear that all terms of the original contract, except those that you're changing, remain in effect.
- Sign and date the addendum and keep it with the original.

LAW IN THE REAL WORLD
Writing Contracts the Simple Way

Galen owns a small publishing company that specializes in local guide books. Henry, one of Galen's long-time authors, is late in delivering a manuscript for a book on 50 offbeat family adventures in the Northern Rocky Mountains. When he finally turns it in, the computer-printed manuscript is full of nearly incomprehensible handwritten additions.

Galen calls Henry and points out that their contract requires Henry to submit the manuscript neatly typed. Henry is furious. "You told me to get it done fast, no matter what," he says. "I stayed up half the night for two weeks to make the deadline and this is the thanks I get."

Galen prudently waits a few days and then invites Henry to lunch. Once both men look at the plain language of the contract, "Author shall submit all manuscript material neatly typed," Henry has to agree that Galen is right. Galen then offers to have someone on his staff do the typing work and subtract the cost from Henry's future royalties. They scribble the contract addendum on a paper placemat and both sign it. Later, Galen photocopies the placemat and mails it to Henry.

G. Enforcing Contracts in Court

Often, if there's a dispute about a claimed breach of contract, you can resolve it through negotiation. If that doesn't work, you'll need to use one of the other methods of resolving legal disputes: mediation, arbitration, or litigation. (See Chapter 22 for an overview on how each works.)

Here is how a contract dispute is likely to be resolved if mediation doesn't work and you resort to more formal proceedings—arbitration or a lawsuit.

Most lawsuits and arbitrations involving contracts focus on two basic questions:

- Was there a breach of contract?
- If so, what relief should be awarded to the nonbreaching party?

We'll tackle the first question here, and the second one in Section H.

Suppose your business sues or is sued for an alleged breach of contract or such a claim is taken to arbitration. What defenses can the defendant assert? Here are the main ones:

- **No valid contract was formed.** If there was no meeting of the minds (no legally binding offer and acceptance) in the first place, or no consideration was given in exchange for one party's promise, no contract even exists. (See Section A.) It's a lot easier to establish such a claim if neither side has begun to follow and rely on the so-called contract.

- **There's no written contract, and because of the subject of the contract, one is required by law.** (See Section D.)

- **The contract is void because it's illegal or against public policy.** Contracts that call for criminal or immoral conduct may be unenforceable. (See Section B.)

- **The contract should be rescinded (canceled) because the other side misrepresented the facts in inducing you to sign it.** (See Section C.)

- **The contract was induced by duress.** (See Section C.)

- **There was a mutual mistake.** (See Section C.)

- **There was no breach of contract.** The defendant admits entering into a valid contract with the plaintiff, but fully complied with its terms.

- **The other party suffered no damages.** The breach of the contract was minor or technical and didn't cause the plaintiff any actual loss or damage. For example, if your store delivered a conference table and six chairs to a lawyer's new office a week later than promised, there's likely been minor inconvenience but no real damage—nothing serious enough to make you liable for breach of contract.

- **The plaintiff failed to limit (mitigate) the damages.** All parties to a contract have a legal duty to act reasonably and keep any damages to a minimum (called "mitigation of damages" in legalese). Or, put another way, it's not legally permissible to sit back and let damages add up when reasonable steps could be taken to stop or limit them. For example, suppose your company services refrigerators, and you signed a two-year contract with a butcher. While you're on vacation, the butcher calls your company and requests that you immediately repair a breakdown in his refrigerator. Your chief assistant is sick, so the job doesn't get done until you return ten days later. The butcher sues for damages, claiming he lost $5,000 worth of meat due to lack of refrigeration. You can point out that the butcher could have mitigated his damages by calling another company to fix his refrigerator. Had he done this promptly, his loss might have been limited to $500 of particularly temperature-sensitive meat plus $300 for the extra service charged. You should be responsible for $800 in damages and not the full $5,000.

Chapter 13, Section I, *explains how the concept of mitigation of damages applies where a lease is involved. This information is generally applicable to all contracts.*

Enforcing Lost Contracts

What if a party wants to legally enforce a written contract, but neither party can find a signed copy? The contract is still legally enforceable if you can prove to the satisfaction of an arbitrator or judge that:

- A written agreement was actually signed, and
- It contained the specific terms you're seeking to enforce.

You may be able to reconstruct the terms from an unsigned photocopy or from a final draft stored on your computer.

H. What Can You Sue For?

In a breach-of-contract case, the court may award the plaintiff money damages and may also, in some cases, order the defendant to do—or stop doing—something.

1. Compensatory Damages

If a plaintiff proves that a defendant breached a contract, the usual approach is for the judge or arbitrator to award the plaintiff "compensatory damages." The goal is to put the parties in the same position as they would have been in if the contract had been performed—or to come as close to that as possible.

Let's return to the contract with Joe, the sign maker we discussed in Section A. If Joe failed to build the sign for your business, and it cost you $750 to have someone else do it, you'd be entitled to recover $300 from Joe for breach of contract. This is the difference between the contract price you and Joe agreed on ($450) and what you had to pay to get the job done ($750). This assumes that you made a reasonable effort to limit or mitigate your damages. In this situation, you'd have to show that you made a reasonable attempt to find a second sign maker to do the job at a fair price. You couldn't just go to the most expensive sign maker in the state and expect Joe to reimburse you for the top dollar. (Mitigation of damages is discussed in Section G, above.)

2. Consequential Damages

A plaintiff may also be entitled to "consequential damages." These are damages that arise out of circumstances that the breaching party knew about or should have foreseen when the contract was made.

For example, what if Joe built your sign for you but didn't get around to installing it until a month after your business's grand opening? Can you sue for the profits you lost because potential customers

didn't know your store was there? The usual rule is that you can recover for lost profits only if this issue is covered by your contract or if it was foreseeable to both parties when you signed the contract that you'd lose profits if the other person didn't carry out the contact. Whether or not a judge will award you damages for Joe's failure to install your sign on time is anybody's guess—unless you specifically dealt with the issue in the contract.

If the contract did provide for lost profits, there's another problem: The amount of lost profits you claim must be ascertainable with reasonable certainty. With a new store, you have no earnings history. This makes it difficult to prove and recover lost profits. But you may able to show how much similar stores at similar locations earned when they first started and get a judge to accept this as a reasonable estimate of your losses.

Let's look at one more example. Say that the sign you ordered from Joe was to contain your store name plus the name of a major manufacturer of merchandise you planned to carry. You had a deal with the manufacturer that entitled you to a 10% discount if you put the manufacturer's name on your sign. Because Joe put up the sign a month after the store opened, you didn't receive the discount on the first batch of merchandise, which cost you an extra $1,000. Can you collect this money from Joe? Only if Joe knew about your deal with the manufacturer when you and he entered into your contract. Otherwise, Joe would have no reason to expect you to suffer this additional loss if he installed the sign late.

3. Liquidated Damages

In addition to or in place of compensatory and consequential damages, a plaintiff may be able to recover "liquidated damages." These are damages that the parties agree in the contract will be paid if there's a breach. That is, instead of trying to determine the money damages for a breach of contract after the fact, you do it in advance.

For example, because actual losses caused by late installation of your sign would be difficult to determine, you and Joe could agree in your contract that for each day of delay, Joe would owe you a $25 late fee. If the liquidated damages are a reasonable attempt to estimate the losses you'd suffer and are not intended as a penalty, a judge or arbitrator will enforce this clause.

Contracts for the purchase of real estate commonly contain a liquidated damages clause. For example, if you put down $5,000 in "earnest money" when you sign a contract to purchase a building, the contract will likely allow the seller to retain the $5,000 as liquidated damages if you later back out for no good reason.

4. Injunctions and Other Equitable Relief

In addition to monetary damages, a judge may order "equitable" relief in some circumstances. This can come in a variety of forms, depending on the facts of the case and the ingenuity of the judge. The idea is to reach a fair result and do justice in a way that can't be done simply by an award of money. Here are some equitable remedies that a judge may order:

- **Injunctions.** An injunction is an order issued by a judge prohibiting a person from performing specified activities. Occasionally, a judge issues an injunction to prevent a party from violating a contract. When time is of the essence, a judge may issue an emergency injunction (sometimes called a temporary restraining order) without a hearing to freeze matters until a court hearing can be held.

EXAMPLE 1: Aggie accepts a job as the accounts manager for DDS Innovations, a dental supply house. As part of her employment contract, she signs a covenant not to compete in the same business in a four-county area for two years after leaving the company. After 18 months on the job, Aggie quits and starts a business in the same city, competing directly with DDS Innovations. The company sues Aggie for breach of her covenant not to compete. The judge, after conducting a trial, finds that the covenant not to compete is reasonable and legally valid, and enjoins Aggie from continuing in that business for two years.

EXAMPLE 2: Maurice and Albert are business partners who have a falling out. Unable to resolve the dispute, Maurice sues Albert, claiming a breach of the partnership agreement. Albert countersues. The judge holds a preliminary hearing and issues a preliminary injunction—in force while the lawsuit is pending—prohibiting both partners from removing any property from the offices of the partnership and from taking any money from the partnership bank account.

EXAMPLE 3: Gilda and her landlord Archie have a dispute over who is to pay for electricity to Gilda's restaurant. On Friday afternoon, Archie threatens to shut off the power to Gilda's restaurant, which would ruin a private banquet for 200 guests that night. Based on Gilda's affidavit (sworn statement) showing the likelihood of immediate damage, the judge issues a temporary restraining order (TRO) prohibiting Archie from shutting off Gilda's power. The judge schedules a hearing for 9 a.m. Monday, at which time the TRO may be dissolved or continued. Because a TRO is usually issued based on the statements of one party only ("ex parte" in legal lingo), such an order is signed only if there's an emergency. A court hearing is always scheduled promptly.

- **Specific Performance.** If a contract concerns a unique or special asset—such as a piece of real estate, a work of art, or a uniquely valuable item of jewelry—the judge may order the losing party to deliver the property to the other party to carry out the agreement. This remedy is rarely used in any other type of commercial transaction.

- **Rescission.** In an appropriate case a judge may rescind (cancel) a contract and order restitution of any money already paid. This unusual remedy is generally reserved for situations where one party's breach has completely frustrated the objectives of the other party, making enforcement of the contract unfair. To obtain rescission, the party getting a refund must give up any benefits already received. (Grounds for rescission of a contract are discussed in Sections B and C.)

If a judge orders you to perform a contract or stop doing something that violates a contract, you can find yourself in deep trouble if you don't obey the order. You can be held in contempt of court, which is punishable by fines and even time in jail. ■

The Financially Troubled Business

A new business doesn't come with a guarantee. Even with the best planning, there's a possibility that your business will go through hard times and maybe even fail. Many an entrepreneur has weathered a number of shaky ventures before landing in a business that proved solidly successful. So if your business becomes troubled, or even if it needs to be put out of its misery, it shouldn't be viewed as the end of the world.

And, although it's always unpleasant—and can be heartbreaking—to have your business go bad, it's important to understand that there are many steps you can take to limit your losses so that you can get back on your feet and move on to other, more productive ventures. Especially if faced promptly, business troubles don't have to be long-term financial disasters.

A key economic preservation strategy is to protect your personal assets from business debts to the greatest extent possible. How you organize and run your business can make a decisive difference in whether you're able to do this. (See Section A.)

In addition, if your enterprise should find itself in financial trouble, your day-to-day management decisions should be guided at least in part by your knowledge of what legal and business actions can help or hurt your personal situation. (See Section B.)

Finally, if your financial troubles become so severe that you consider ending your business and maybe even declaring bankruptcy, you'll need to know exactly what legal options and protections are available.

A. Thinking Ahead to Protect Your Personal Assets

Perhaps you personally own a home, a valuable car, stocks and bonds, or a savings account. Or maybe you own a second business or other valuable assets. Whatever you own, one thing is sure: You don't want to see everything you've acquired gobbled up by debts resulting from a failed business. Fortunately, with some advance planning, you can often protect many of your personal assets from your business creditors.

⚠ **Early planning is essential.** *It's crucial that you develop your asset protection plan as early as possible—preferably before rather than after you begin doing business. Once your business is in operation—and especially after it runs into financial trouble—you'll be greatly restricted in the steps you can take to protect your personal assets.*

1. Choice of Business Entity

As discussed in Chapter 1, when you start your business, insulating yourself from personal liability for business debts and liabilities is one important consideration. This is especially true if there's a strong possibility that failure of the business would leave a huge stack of bills or lawsuits for uninsured liabilities. If you organize your business as a sole proprietorship or partnership, you'll be personally liable for all obligations of the business. If, however, you organize your business as a corporation or a limited liability company (LLC), your personal liability will be substantially limited. Or to put this more bluntly, corporations and LLCs offer the greatest opportunity for protecting your personal assets from business obligations.

2. Beware of Penniless Partners

Another good reason to start your business as a corporation or LLC rather than a general partnership—or to switch your existing partnership to a corporation or LLC—is to protect yourself from the possible insolvency of any co-owners that could leave you stuck with all the business liabilities. The potential problem of working with co-owners in the context of a partnership is that if your business goes bad, you and your partners will be liable "jointly and severally" for business debts. This legal jargon means if one partner can't pay his or her share of business debts, the others will each owe the whole amount. So if you operate as a partnership, at least make sure your partners have enough assets to pay their share of any partnership debts.

> **EXAMPLE:** Ginny has two partners when her partnership business fails, leaving $30,000 in unpaid bills. Creditors get a judgment for $30,000 against all three partners. Unfortunately, Ginny's partners don't have any assets. Under the doctrine of joint and several liability, Ginny is legally on the hook to pay the entire judgment.

Assuming that Ginny pays the entire $30,000 judgment and the partnership agreement makes all the partners equally liable for business debts, she'll be able to collect $10,000 from each of the other partners if they come into some money in the future.

3. Personal Loan Guarantees

Even if you form a corporation or LLC to insulate your personal assets from business debts, you're likely to find yourself asked to put your personal assets on the line if your business applies for a bank loan or line of credit. Commercial lenders particularly won't make a loan or extend a line of credit to new corporations or LLCs unless the business owners personally guarantee to repay it. Unfortunately, if you agree to do this and your business later is unable to make payments as they come due, the lender has a right to get a judgment and collect it from your personal assets exactly as if you hadn't formed a corporation or LLC in the first place.

In some cases, the requirement that you personally guarantee a potential loan may be enough to dissuade you from borrowing the money in the first place. In unusual circumstances, a lender may agree to put a cap on the amount of your guarantee so your assets aren't fully at risk. Or, if you can't sell that idea, try for a written commitment that your personal guarantee will expire after a preestablished period of time—perhaps two years—if the corporation or LLC has made all payments on time and is profitable.

4. Having Your Spouse Sign Too

If a lender asks you to personally guarantee a line of credit or a loan for your corporation or LLC, the lender may also ask for your spouse to be a co-guarantor. A lender may make a similar request if you open a line of credit or take out a loan as a sole proprietor or partner. Be aware of the additional risk this entails.

In most states—except for the nine that follow the community property system—if you alone sign for a line of credit or a loan and don't pay on time, the creditor can get a judgment against you but not against your spouse. This means that, ordinarily, a creditor will be able to reach the property that you own in your own name, but not the property that you and your spouse own in both your names.

If you and your spouse both sign on the dotted line, the creditor's rights will be much greater. Now if you and your spouse own property in your joint names—a home or bank account, for example—the creditor will be able to sue and get a judgment against both of you if the debt isn't paid. In addition, the creditor can then enforce the judgment by seizing your joint bank account or jointly owned securities or home in addition to property you own in your name alone. The creditor will also be able go after property that's in your spouse's name alone—and even be able to garnish your spouse's paycheck.

> ⚠️ **Both spouses are liable for most debts in community property states.** *Nine states follow the community property system: Arizona, California, Idaho, Louisiana, Nevada, New Mexico, Texas, Washington, and Wisconsin. In those states, a married couple's property accumulated after marriage is primarily community or jointly owed property regardless of the names in which it's held. Each spouse can also own separate property but, especially in longer marriages, this tends to be less important. In most instances, the rights of creditors vary, depending on the type of property involved.*

- **Community Property.** *Usually, property earned or acquired by either spouse after marriage—except by gift or inheritance—is at risk for a debt incurred by either spouse. This means a creditor can go after the community property of you and your spouse to pay off a debt, even if only you signed for the loan. In other words, you can't shield the community property from a creditor by not having your spouse sign for the loan.*

- **Separate Property.** *This usually is property a spouse owned before getting married, acquired later by gift or inheritance, or agreed in writing would be kept separate. It's also property—such as a business—acquired from separate assets. If, for example, someone gets married owning a piece of real estate, sells it and uses the proceeds to open a business, the business is separate property. If your spouse has separate property and signs for a loan, his or her separate property will be at risk if you default—but if your spouse declines to sign, his or her separate property will normally be beyond the creditor's reach. Your own separate property, of course, will be at risk whether or not your spouse signs.*

5. Pledging Collateral for Loans

In addition to asking you to personally guarantee a loan by signing a promissory note, a lender may ask you to pledge a personal asset—typically, your home—as collateral for a business loan. In the case of your home, this would be done through a second mortgage or deed of trust. Think long and hard before you agree to do this, since it means you'll lose your home if you can't repay the money and the lender exercises its right to foreclose.

A key point is to understand that there can be a big difference between simply putting your personal signature on a promissory note (see Section A3, above) and giving the lender a security interest

in property such as your home. The reason is that states have debtor protection laws (called homestead laws) that protect your investment in your home. This means that being unable to pay a personal debt—one, for example, based on a promissory note that's not secured by your home—won't automatically put you at risk of losing your home. By comparison, however, if you pledge your house as security for a loan, these homestead laws won't protect you.

! Check the law in your state. *In many states the homestead exemption is low—or even nonexistent. This means that if an unsecured creditor sues and gets a judgment, the creditor could possibly force the sale of your home to collect.*

So much for the law. In the cold world of trying to raise money for your business, you may have no practical alternative to putting your home at risk. The truth is that the equity in your home may be your most accessible source of cash. The point is to ponder seriously what you and your family would do if you lost your home due to business reverses.

! Be careful in using a home equity line of credit to finance your business. *A home equity line of credit, of course, amounts to a second mortgage. Don't overlook the fact that if you write a $15,000 check against your line of credit to cover business expenses and can't later make your payments on time, the bank can enforce its lien rights and force sale of your home.*

6. Maintain Adequate Insurance

You never know when an injured person may sue your business, claiming that you or an employee acted negligently—for example, a customer who falls in your parking lot and fractures her hip may claim that you were negligent in not keeping the area properly lighted. A jury may agree that you were negligent and sock your business with a huge judgment. There are many other risks as well—such as an injured consumer suing your manufacturing business for producing a defective product or a suit by a pedestrian injured by one of your employees who was driving a company truck. In short, you absolutely need to carry adequate insurance because if you don't, your investment in the business could be wiped out by a huge verdict. Even if your personal funds or house aren't at risk, you'll have suffered a stunning financial loss.

If you're a sole proprietor or partner, be especially careful to carry adequate business risk insurance, since you're personally liable for paying the judgment. Another way to say this is if insurance proves too expensive or difficult to get, you'll almost certainly want to form a corporation or LLC to at least limit your personal liability. (For more on insurance, see Chapter 12.)

B. Managing the Financially Troubled Business

So far this chapter has reviewed things small business owners can do in advance to limit potential liability. Now let's shift gears and assume your business is currently facing financial problems. My focus here is to present several practical strategies that will help legally protect both you and your personal assets.

1. Keep Taxes Current

Rule Number One for the owner of any struggling business is to meticulously pay on time all taxes withheld from employees' paychecks. (See Chapter 8, Section C.) Even if you operate your business as a corporation or LLC, the IRS and state tax authorities can hold you personally liable for these taxes—plus penalties—if they're not paid. And you're still legally on the hook to pay these taxes, even if the business goes bankrupt.

So if your business starts having financial problems, stave off the other creditors as best you can—and use whatever cash is available to take care of employment taxes. Paying these taxes is so crucial that if your business is financially disorganized, you should pay for any accounting help you need to be sure these taxes are computed accurately and paid on time.

And remember that you don't have to wait until the last day to deposit employment taxes. It's often wise to deposit the employment taxes as soon as you know the figures so the money will be out of your bank account and legitimately beyond the reach of any other creditor who is attempting to collect a court judgment against your business.

⚠ **Don't pay employment taxes with a charge card.** *If possible, use a check or cash to pay employment taxes, since this means they're really paid. By contrast, if you use your personal charge card and can't pay the bill later, you'll continue to be responsible to the charge card company for the amount you charged for taxes—even if you go through personal bankruptcy. A discharge in bankruptcy won't cancel your personal liability for the portion of your credit card debt that's attributable to the tax payments.*

2. Don't Lie About Debts

When a business starts to have financial troubles, its owner may frantically try to borrow more money.

Before doing this, think carefully about whether your business is really likely to do better in the near future or if you're only likely to compound your debt problems. If you apply for a new loan or to consolidate old ones, be forthright in disclosing the financial condition of your business. If you misrepresent your debts to get a loan, you may not be able to get rid of your personal liability for the debt—even if you go through bankruptcy—because the law will regard your new debt as being obtained by fraud. Where big bucks are involved, the debt could haunt you for many years.

The key to avoiding trouble with lenders is to be very careful that all facts appear—and appear accurately—on any financial statement you give a potential creditor. Even if you borrow money or have credit extended to you without having to fill out a financial statement, it can be treated as fraud if you knew that the business was having financial trouble and didn't make all the facts clear to your creditor.

⚠️ **Don't rely on shortcuts suggested by the lender's agent.** *Some finance company employees have been known to deliberately tell people—orally, of course—that they don't need to list all their debts. Often this is done because the person in the finance company office is under pressure to make loans and therefore has a motive to bend the rules to qualify you. Don't fall for this. If you later default on the loan and the company claims you obtained the money by fraudulently withholding information about your finances, chances are the employee will either be long gone or will say, "Of course I didn't say to deliberately omit debts." Either way, chances are you'll be unable to discharge the "fraudulent" debt in bankruptcy.*

Also, be aware that the bankruptcy laws take a broad view of what constitutes fraud. Not disclosing negative financial information may be considered fraudulent even if you acted with the best of intentions.

EXAMPLE: Jimmy, a sole proprietor, owns a secondhand furniture store. One day, the landlord raises the store rent by 50%. Based on past performance, Jimmy knows that with the rent increase, he'll have difficulty making a profit. Nevertheless, he decides to stay at that location because it would cost even more money to move elsewhere. At this time, he has a line of credit for $25,000 with a local bank of which only $10,000 has been used. A month later, already feeling the sting of the higher rent, he draws against the additional $15,000 and uses it to keep afloat. Because Jimmy neglected to tell the bank about the significant rent increase that put his business in a precarious financial condition, the additional draws can be considered to be a fraudulent use of credit and may well not be discharged in bankruptcy. If the bank sues Jimmy in bankruptcy court after he's gone through bankruptcy, Jimmy may still be liable for the $15,000.

This doesn't mean that drawing on a line of credit to meet the ordinary ebb and flow of business constitutes fraud. It doesn't. After all, the bank expects that you'll use your line of credit to cover leaner times. But you do need to disclose significant changes in your business such as a lawsuit or the bankruptcy of your largest customer that threatens the financial well-being of your business.

3. Be Careful About Transferring Business Property

Occasionally, out of desperation, a business owner will consider trying to protect personal assets by hiding them. Since creditors are used to ferreting out such tactics, by and large they prove ineffective and are likely to give rise to civil and perhaps even criminal charges of fraud. Specifically, a business owner shouldn't:

- transfer assets to friends or relatives in any effort to hide them from creditors or from the bankruptcy court, or
- conceal property or income from a court.

4. Avoid Preferential Payments to Creditors

The Bankruptcy Code frowns on your preferring certain creditors over others by making what are called "preferential payments." If you file for bankruptcy, all payments you make during the year before the filing will be scrutinized by creditors to make sure that some creditors weren't given an unfair advantage by being paid while others received little or nothing. If you did improperly single out some creditors for more favorable treatment by paying money or transferring property to them, the bankruptcy judge can order those creditors to return the money or property so it can be added to the total (called your bankruptcy estate) available to all of your creditors.

Fortunately, most payments you make as part of your business's ordinary operations won't be considered to be illegal preferences should you declare bankruptcy. Here's a brief overview of the types of payments that are safe and those likely to cause problems.

- *Payments in the ordinary course of business.* Neither you nor the payee has to worry about the payments you make in the ordinary course of business. These payments are considered to be safe and won't be undone—even if you made them the day before you filed for bankruptcy. Examples of payments you can safely make include:
  - utilities
  - rent
  - payroll deposits
  - retirement plan contributions
  - insurance premiums
  - payments to suppliers whom you pay on delivery or with 30- to 60-day terms, and

  - salaries—as long as they're kept at the same level you've been paying right along.
- *Payments to family members or insiders.* If you repay money or transfer property to a family member or insider and then you file for bankruptcy within one year after the payment or transfer, the family member or insider will probably have to return the money or property to the bankruptcy court so it can be divided among your creditors. (An insider is someone who's in or close to your business such as a partner, a corporate director, or a corporate officer.)
- *Payments to other creditors.* When you repay money or transfer property to someone who's neither a relative nor an insider and the payment isn't in the ordinary course of business, the 90 days before you file for bankruptcy are crucial. (Example: Paying off a bank loan that's not due for six months.) If you make such payments or transfers of property during the 90-day period, the recipient may have to return the money or property to the bankruptcy court to be added to the pool of funds available to your creditors.

5. Protect Your Bank Account

If you face serious financial problems and owe money to a bank, it's often wise to keep most of your checking and other accounts elsewhere. This is because typically your loan agreement gives the bank the right to take your funds without prior notice if the bank thinks you're in financial trouble. (This is called a setoff.) To put it mildly, it can be a rude surprise to learn that your favorite lender has suddenly drained your account.

6. Plan for Ongoing Insurance Coverage

If your business winds up in a Chapter 11 or Chapter 13 reorganization under the Bankruptcy Code (see

Section F), you may have a tough time finding a carrier that's willing to renew your business coverage or one that's willing to issue a new policy. So if you're planning to seek protection under either of those bankruptcy sections, make sure you have insurance in place that extends at least 12 months into the future. You'll need to make payments on the policy as payments become due, but as long as you pay on time, the insurance can't be canceled and you'll enjoy some peace of mind as you continue in business.

7. Don't Panic About Utilities or Your Lease

If you declare bankruptcy, the utility companies can't use your filing as an excuse for shutting off services—although they can require you to post a reasonable deposit if you want to keep the lights, phone service, and heat.

Similarly, as long as you continue to pay your rent, your landlord can't kick you out. Don't be spooked by the scary clause commonly placed in commercial leases that says you're automatically in default if you file for bankruptcy. You can't believe everything you read. These clauses are not enforceable.

8. Consider Returning Some Leased Property

If you're leasing equipment and know you won't want to retain it after you file for bankruptcy, consider giving it back to the leasing company before you file. If you do so and the equipment is currently worth less than what you owe under the lease, the deficiency will get discharged in bankruptcy.

On the other hand, if you prefer to keep the leased property, you'll need to continue making your lease payments on time. When you choose to hang onto leased property, the obligation to make lease payments isn't discharged by your going through bankruptcy.

C. Seeking an Objective Analysis

A business can get into financial trouble for a long list of reasons. One of the most common is simply that the business owner, over time, becomes less attentive to the needs of the business—perhaps as a result of getting tired of dealing with problems which have become tedious. It may help to think of a business much as you would a child: No matter how much work you put in early in life, both continue to need constant attention and are unlikely to thrive if that attention is absent for any extended time.

Early signs of financial trouble usually include the following:

- You've routinely begun to ask creditors for more time to pay bills.
- Creditors are beginning to require you to pay COD.
- Your bank line of credit is routinely maxed out.
- You need to delay cashing your own paycheck a few days because the money isn't there.

And red flags are obviously flying if:

- Impatient creditors are calling you repeatedly.
- You're getting cash advances on your credit card to keep your business afloat.
- You're starting to miss payments to your landlord.
- You're being sued or threatened with lawsuits.
- You're having trouble paying employment taxes.
- Other tax bills are piling up.

The fact that your business is having financial problems doesn't mean it will fail. Even a seriously ailing business may be savable if you recognize the true extent of its problems and seek help soon enough. One good approach is to get objective advice to help you determine how deep your financial problems are and what options are open to you. Maybe you're just facing a temporary downturn that you should be able to weather by cutting costs and fine-tuning your business operations. But it's also possible that your problems may be more serious, requiring you to take more drastic steps to avoid a complete financial disaster that eats up not only your investment in the business but your personal assets as well.

Turn first to an experienced accountant. A small business accountant can usually review your business numbers—your debt-to-equity ratio, for example, or the time it's taking you to collect receivables—and quickly take your business's financial temperature. Then, he or she will try to identify some problem areas—such as overhead that's too high given your volume of sales. And an experienced business accountant often can provide practical advice for getting the business back on a solid financial track by suggesting, for example, ways to collect more of your receivables or quickly convert assets to needed cash.

If you conclude your financial problems are especially serious, you'll also normally want to consult an experienced small business lawyer or self-help law book. For starters, the lawyer will probably have a good idea about what the creditors are thinking—insights that can be very valuable in managing these strained relationships. In addition, after information about your business's financial problems and legal structure is on the table, an experienced lawyer should be able to help you sensibly decide whether it's best to try to buy more time through negotiations with creditors, try to sell the business, use a bankruptcy proceeding to keep creditors off your back while you try to rebuild the business, or simply shut the business down and liquidate any remaining assets.

Seek out a good small business consultant. *If you can find the right one, a small business consultant can often suggest more meaningful business operation strategies than an accountant or lawyer—new strategies, for example, for your product mix, marketing, location, and pricing. But check references carefully to be sure the person you're considering working with really helped others in similar circumstances. Almost anyone can set up shop as a business consultant and the last thing you want is bad advice.*

It May Pay to Have Your Business Appraised

It can often make sense to hire an appraiser to place a value on the business's real estate, equipment, and inventory. For one thing, a solid appraisal will provide realistic values for your business assets and therefore help you and your accountant analyze your financial predicament. Especially if you're considering trying to sell your business, this information can be extremely helpful.

An appraisal may also be helpful if you try to negotiate a nonbankruptcy "workout" with your creditors. Even though you're not legally required to disclose the results of an appraisal at this stage, doing so can definitely be in your interest if the appraisal shows you have valuable assets. This information is likely to reassure unsecured creditors and convince them to give you some breathing room. (See Section D on workouts.)

What's more, knowing the value of business assets can be extremely helpful in making decisions about bankruptcy, if matters come to that. You'll have a good idea, for example, of how much debt will remain if the assets are liquidated in a Chapter 7 business bankruptcy and whether the remaining debt—which you may be responsible for paying—will force you into personal bankruptcy.

How a Good Consultant Can Help

Ben opens an instant typography business, borrowing from his family to purchase necessary phototype equipment and software and leasing the rest. Although his business is busy from the start and Ben is working long hours, after nine months it's obvious he's losing money. Trying to figure out what to do, Ben considers increasing his sales or cutting his overhead. But since he and his employees are already overworked, this doesn't promise to solve the problem.

Finally, Ben turns to Sarah, a local small business consultant highly recommended by a neighboring business owner. After examining Ben's books for less than two hours, Sarah spots the problem. Ben isn't charging enough for his services.

After listening to Ben explain that producing type for local businesses is a very competitive business and that he will lose customers if he institutes a general price increase, Sarah helps Ben come up with a plan that involves keeping his current prices in effect for about one-half of his volume. But she also suggests that he raise prices significantly for rush orders and specialty work. With some adjustments over time, Sarah's plan works brilliantly. Customers remain loyal, since prices for routine work haven't changed. On rush orders and specialty work, it turns out that Sarah's insight that customers focus more on speed and quality and less on price is correct. Ben's customers pay his higher prices without much complaint and within a month his business is making money.

D. Workouts

In developing a plan of action for your financially troubled business, your objectives probably include one or more of the following:

- keeping the business alive
- salvaging as much as possible from your investment
- minimizing or eliminating your personal liability for business debts
- avoiding personal liability for IRS or other tax penalties
- retaining certain property—such as your house—that's been pledged as security to a creditor
- preserving your ability to get personal or business credit in the future, and
- protecting the assets of relatives and friends who have helped you financially.

Fortunately, several nonbankruptcy ways to try to cope with a failing business are worth considering. In this section I explain one of these, which is commonly called a workout. This normally involves developing a voluntary plan under which your creditors and others make concessions so you can keep your business in operation. The idea is that you will continue to zealously address its financial problems so that eventually your creditors can hope to receive all or most of their money.

But workouts aren't your only choice. Section E, below, briefly covers two other nonbankruptcy possibilities: selling your business or simply shutting it down.

Finally, Section F summarizes the bankruptcy alternatives of liquidating your business under Chapter 7 of the Bankruptcy Code or keeping it in operation under the protection of Chapter 11 or Chapter 13. You'll want to read all of these sections for an overview of the full range of choices available.

Sometimes it's hard to remember this when your business is going badly: There are bound to be a number of people who are pulling for your business to succeed—people such as creditors, suppliers, employees, customers, and even neighboring business owners who will benefit if you can stay in operation. Bruce Ballenger, a Los Angeles CPA, refers to these people as "stakeholders," since they have a stake in whether your company lives or dies. Given their long-term self interest, some of these folks may be willing to lend a helping hand. To take an example, creditors may be willing to make some financial concessions—usually as part of a well-defined business recovery plan (the workout)—to help you through your financial difficulties.

Creditors who will give you more time to pay or otherwise help you probably won't do it for altruistic reasons but because they understand that their chances of getting paid on past debts are better if they cut you some slack, such as extending the time for debt payment or even agreeing to forgive a portion of your debt. Valued customers who rely on the availability of your goods and services may also be willing to help out. For example, they may be willing to speed their payments to you so they won't have to turn to a less satisfactory business to fill their needs. Similarly, suppliers may realize that they need your future business as much as you need their supplies. As long as you can convince them that your business can be viable in the long run, they may extend the time for you to repay old debts and even extend more credit.

Your employees are obviously among your business's key stakeholders. Some may agree to work reduced hours or accept reduced wages and benefits until your business gets healthy again. After all, a job in the hand is worth two in the want ads.

Finally, local authorities may be willing to give you more time to pay property taxes—a better alternative than trying to squeeze cash from a defunct business, unless there are statutory tax-sale deadlines.

To get all your stakeholders to work together, you typically need to create a "workout plan." This is an out-of-court agreement under which your major creditors agree to hold off on suing your business, collecting on court judgments they've already obtained, or forcing you into bankruptcy. Possibly,

creditors may even agree to extend more credit while you try to jointly devise a realistic payment schedule. For creditors to go along with your proposal, they must at a minimum be convinced that they're likely to come out better financially under your workout plan than they would if they sued you or pushed you into bankruptcy.

To prepare a workout package, you'll need to start by opening your books to your creditors. A good way to begin the full disclosure process is to prepare a list of all creditors and how much each is owed. Then, list the assets of your business along with estimates as to their value both if you liquidate and if you stay in business. It makes sense to include financial statements—and property appraisals if you have them—in your workout package so that creditors can see what you're worth and what your problems are. Also, if you have created a business turnaround plan either on your own or working with a small business advisor, include it in your package.

Next, you'll normally want to compare what the creditors will receive if you have to liquidate the business in a Chapter 7 bankruptcy with what they're likely to receive if your workout plan succeeds. To do this, you may need some help from a bankruptcy lawyer or experienced accountant in putting together the liquidation scenario.

Give time and thought to showing why your alternative proposal—your long-term workout plan—is likely to eventually put far more money in each of your creditor's pockets as compared to the meager returns they are likely to receive if you go through bankruptcy. While it makes sense to emphasize why your plan to turn around your business has a good chance of succeeding, you'll also want to be realistic. Creditors will be justly suspicious of any plan that's based on wishful thinking.

Put the facts on bankruptcy forms.

For extra psychological leverage in trying to get creditors to negotiate a livable workout plan, you may want to prepare official bankruptcy forms (available from an office supply store) as if you actually planned to file. The filled-in forms will list your business debts and the value of your business assets. Show the forms to your creditors along with your workout plan. This sends the message that you're really prepared to file for bankruptcy if you can't achieve a compromise. It also dramatically highlights how little the creditors will wind up with if they push you into bankruptcy.

In negotiating with creditors who have a mortgage or other security interest in real property, vehicles, or business equipment in your possession, be prepared to show them that you're continuing to keep the property in good condition. Otherwise, they'll likely conclude that they're better off to move quickly to repossess it. Also realize that while suppliers may be willing to extend your time for paying past debts, most will expect you to pay in advance or COD for any new goods delivered to your business. To avoid this inconvenience, you'll need to convince them that your business is in the black on the basis of current operations and that you're routinely paying all new bills promptly.

Be sure your employees support you. If your long-time managers and other key employees are willing to take a temporary pay cut, it will go a long way towards convincing creditors that your business can slim down enough to become profitable. Also be sure that disgruntled employees aren't badmouthing your recovery plan. Remember that most long-term creditors will almost surely know some of your employees and are very likely to contact them for the true lowdown on your business.

Try to get 100% of your major creditors to agree to your plan. Unfortunately, if there are a significant number of holdouts among your major creditors, your workout plan is probably doomed to failure. The holdouts will drain your time and energy—not to mention your checking account—as they push ahead with lawsuits and other collection efforts.

Once your creditors agree to your plan, quickly put the terms in writing. Each written agreement should state specifically that if you make agreed workout payments on time, the creditor will hold off on filing lawsuits and will terminate collection actions. In addition, if the creditor has agreed to accept less than 100% of what's owed, there should be a clear statement that if you pay the agreed amount, you and your business will be fully released from the debt.

Make your peace with the IRS first.

If you owe back taxes, pay them or come to terms with the IRS before you approach the other creditors. They're unlikely to agree to a workout if there's a chance the IRS may close down the business.

Ideas for Business Workouts

Here are a number of common elements of workout packages.

- *Partial Liquidation of Assets.* You agree to sell specific business assets that are not essential to your current business and to use the money to partially pay creditors on a pro rata basis.

- *A Creditor Takes the Collateral.* You turn over to a secured creditor the property you pledged as security for the loan or line of credit. The creditor agrees that your total obligation is wiped out—even if the property is worth less than you still owe. Normally, the creditor will do this only if he or she concludes that repossessing and selling the used property is likely to net more than letting you keep it and holding onto your debt. Or put another way, if the creditor really sees you as a long-term deadbeat, he or she will be more likely to take the property and forget about the debt.

- *Lump Sum Payback.* The creditor accepts a lump sum payoff that's less than the full debt and in full satisfaction of the entire debt. This scenario can particularly make sense when you have a family member or friend who will lend you some new money only if your creditor will accept a partial payment. The important thing is to make creditors realize they may get little or nothing if they don't agree.

- *Monthly Payments.* You agree to make monthly payments on your debts and the creditors agree to hold off on lawsuits and other collection actions. The total amount they agree to accept may be less than the amount owed—but if the debt is reduced, the creditors will probably want a larger monthly amount than they'd settle for on a lump sum payoff.

- *Creditors Become Owners.* In unusual situations, creditors may agree to take ownership rights—such as stock in your corporation—in exchange for forgiving some or all debts owed to them.

Source: *Holding Onto the American Dream: How Small Businesses Can Conquer Financial Problems,* by Marguerite M. Kirk (Odenwald Press).

E. Selling or Closing the Business

Although selling your financially troubled business may seem like a long shot, it's always worth a try. (See Chapter 10, Section I.) Naturally, you won't get top dollar for your business when it's in distress—but if you arrange a sale, it may give you enough to pay creditors and come away with a few bucks. Selling an operating business, even one that's in trouble, almost always brings more money than closing it down and selling off the assets.

Before you give up and conclude that no one will buy your business, consider that people buy businesses—even those with financial problems—for all sorts of reasons, including:

- The buyer may have lower personal financial needs and expectations and may be willing to squeak by on a modest return that's wholly unacceptable to you.

- The buyer may have a similar business and by combining the two operate more efficiently than you can.

- The buyer may be extremely anxious to take over one or more of your business assets—its location, key employees, or name.

- The buyer may have better access to needed financing than you do and therefore be able to stay the course until your good business idea ultimately proves itself.

- The buyer may have greater expertise in your business than you do and see a way to turn a profit by changing how the business is run.

- The buyer may conclude that it's cheaper to buy your business and turn it around than to start a similar business from scratch.

Value is in the eye of the beholder.

Even if you believe it is an illusion, the fact that the buyer merely thinks that he or she has greater expertise than you do or that the business has unrecognized potential may be enough to produce a purchase offer. Don't let your ego get in the way of making the deal by defending your business decisions and strategy so forcefully that you talk the potential purchaser into withdrawing his or her offer.

If you have an opportunity to sell your business but the proceeds of the sale won't yield enough money to pay off all the business debts, look carefully at what remaining debts you'll be personally responsible for and what personal assets have been pledged as security for the business debts. Merely selling the business won't be enough to relieve you from your personal liability to creditors or the risk that creditors may take property that you've pledged as security.

To reduce or eliminate your personal liability or the danger of losing pledged property, there are some solutions worth looking into. On debts for which you're personally liable, see if the bank or other creditor is willing to substitute the purchaser of your business on the indebtedness and release. The creditor may be willing to do this if the person buying your business is financially stronger than you are or, in the case of a currently unsecured debt, is willing to pledge security. A buyer who's enthusiastic about the prospects of the business may be willing to be substituted for you.

If the creditor won't let you off the hook, another way of dealing with unsecured debts that you'll be personally liable for is to ask the buyer to agree in writing to pay the specified debts and to indemnify and save you harmless from those obligations. This means that if the bank or other creditor comes after you because the debt isn't paid, the buyer guarantees to pay the debt and protect you from any liabil-

ity. Of course, this kind of guarantee is only as good as the buyer's financial condition, so you won't want to rely on such a guarantee if you have any reason to believe the buyer is financially shaky.

Where you've secured a business debt by pledging your personal property as collateral—for example, your home, car, or stocks—see if the creditor is willing to release your property as security if the buyer substitutes property of equal or greater value. The buyer, for example, may have as much or more equity in his or her home than you do in yours and the bank may be willing to substitute that home as security in place of yours, if the buyer consents.

Closing Down. So much for selling your financially troubled business. If you can't sell it, consider closing it down. Even if you can't pay all your debts immediately, this option at least allows you to avoid running up more. In addition, you'll normally want to negotiate with your creditors to pay them off for less than the full amount the business owes. Why should creditors accept this? It's often a better choice than either of their other options: suing you and chasing down your assets to collect every last dollar or taking what's available in a bankruptcy liquidation. Trying this approach can be particularly sensible, too, if you have a corporation or LLC and have personally guaranteed some business debts. If you can reach a negotiated settlement, you'll not only avoid a business bankruptcy but also you won't have to go through personal bankruptcy to get out from under the debts you've guaranteed.

If you haven't personally guaranteed any debts of the corporation or LLC, one option is to simply close the business and pay the debts on a pro rata basis to the extent the business has funds. Then, let the corporation or LLC die on its own. Since any remaining debts aren't your personal responsibility, this should, in theory at least, end matters. Sometimes, however, you may want to consider having the business file for bankruptcy in this situation. If the corporation or LLC hasn't gone through bankruptcy, some creditors may go ahead and sue the business and get judgments against it. If that happens, you may be subpoenaed and have to go to court to explain that the business used up all its assets. That can be a nuisance. So if you have a number of creditors who are likely to pursue you to the bitter end, putting the business through bankruptcy may make sense since it will save you from having to testify in multiple lawsuits. Creditors, of course, lose their right to sue once the corporation or LLC is bankrupt.

⚠️ **Watch out for preferential treatment.** *If at first you decide simply to close down your business but later decide to file for bankruptcy, you may have backed into trouble. If your business eventually has to file for bankruptcy, giving preferential treatment to some creditors in the months before you file by paying off all or part of their bills can create a problem. Creditors who didn't receive preferential treatment may complain, in which case the favored creditors will have to return the money or property they received so it can part of an asset pool available for equitable distribution among all creditors. (See Section B4, above.) So even if you hope not to file for bankruptcy, try to work out similar deals with all creditors.*

F. Understanding Bankruptcy

If your business is in serious financial trouble, you'll want to consider the possibility that you'll eventually need to file for bankruptcy if the other strategies mentioned in this chapter won't work for you. Fortunately, thoroughly understanding how bankruptcy works and how you can best cope with it if it becomes inevitable can result in major savings later on.

1. Different Types of Bankruptcy

Bankruptcy is a legal proceeding handled in the federal court system. It's based on the federal Bankruptcy Code, which is divided into different chapters, each covering a different type of bankruptcy as

described below. Bankruptcy is usually voluntary, but be aware that one or more creditors may force you into bankruptcy by filing an involuntary bankruptcy petition against you. Because lawyers and others with bankruptcy knowledge refer to the various types of bankruptcy protection by their chapter numbers, you too will need to learn this jargon, which I explain below.

⚠️ **As it has been for years, Congress is still considering major changes to the bankruptcy law.** *For the latest information, check the Legal Updates section of Nolo's website (www.nolo.com). Another good site is www.bankruptcyreformnews.com.*

💼 **Legal advice may be essential.** *If you're a sole proprietor and have a relatively small amount of business debt, you may be able to handle a bankruptcy yourself or with a limited amount of professional help. But be forewarned: a number of issues (property exempt from being taken to pay debts, for one example) can be complicated when business and personal affairs are intertwined. For sole proprietors with significant debt and for partnerships, corporations, and LLCs, it generally makes sense to seek advice from a lawyer who specializes in small business bankruptcy. Professional help is essential for corporations and LLCs because you can't represent these entities in a bankruptcy proceeding unless you're a lawyer. Seek out an experienced bankruptcy lawyer who will take the time to explain all your options—both bankruptcy and nonbankruptcy—before he or she files papers for you. Be wary of any lawyer who instantly assumes that you should proceed with a Chapter 7 liquidation, which in many cases, will prove to be a poor choice.*

2. Liquidating the Business Under Chapter 7

A Chapter 7 filing is sometimes called a "straight bankruptcy." It's available to businesses organized in all the usual ways—sole proprietorship, partnership, corporation, and LLC. Under Chapter 7, your business property is sold and the proceeds are used to pay off debts to the extent funds are available.

If your business is a partnership, each partner is personally liable for all partnership debts. Putting the partnership through Chapter 7 won't do away with your personal liability for these debts. To accomplish that, you'd need to file for personal bankruptcy.

If your business is a corporation or LLC, you're generally not personally liable for debts of the business, unless you've personally guaranteed a business debt, in which case you're liable for repaying it. And if you've put up any property as collateral, that property can be taken unless you pay the creditor—known as a "secured creditor"—the value of the property or agree to have the debt survive the bankruptcy. To escape from personal liability for business debts, you'll have to file for personal bankruptcy after the corporate or LLC bankruptcy is wound up.

A personal filing under Chapter 7 will free you from personal liability for most business debts—but it bears some potential disadvantages. The fact that you've filed for personal bankruptcy remains on your credit record for ten years. This can cause trouble when you apply for a mortgage, a bank loan, a charge account, or a credit card. What's more, employers sometimes use credit information to screen job applicants, as do some landlords in checking out potential tenants.

⚠ Cosigners and guarantors are still on the hook. *If a friend or family member has cosigned for a business loan or guaranteed payment of a business debt, putting the business or yourself through Chapter 7 bankruptcy won't relieve the cosigner or guarantor from personal liability for the debt. This can be an added reason to try to resolve your debt problems through a workout or other non-bankruptcy alternative. (See Section D.)*

 For in-depth guidance, including forms and instructions for filing, *see* How to File for Chapter 7 Bankruptcy, *by Stephen Elias, Robin Leonard, Kathleen Michon, and Albin Renauer (Nolo).*

Two Kinds of Creditors

Bankruptcy law distinguishes broadly between two types of creditors: secured and unsecured.

A secured creditor is either one to whom you or your business has pledged collateral in exchange for a loan or line of credit (voluntary secured creditor) or one who has filed a lien (tax, judgment, or mechanic's) against your property (involuntary secured creditor). Pledged collateral to a voluntary secured creditor may consist of business property such as inventory and equipment or your own property such as your house, car, or boat. Either way, the creditor ends up with a lien on the property. This means that if you or the business can't pay back the debt, the creditor can take the property to satisfy the debt.

An unsecured creditor is either one to whom no collateral has been pledged or one who hasn't filed a lien. Typically, these debts will include amounts your business owes for inventory, office supplies, minor equipment and furnishings, rent and advertising, as well as what's owed for services such as maintenance contracts, equipment repair, and professional advice. Credit card charges, too, are unsecured.

In bankruptcy, the secured creditor is in a much more favorable legal position than one who is unsecured. If the bankrupt business has little or no money, the unsecured creditor is likely to wind up with little or nothing, whereas the secured creditor walks away with whatever the collateral is worth. A Chapter 7 bankruptcy gets rid of the debt but not the security interest.

3. Reorganizing Your Business Debts

As an alternative to liquidation under Chapter 7, you may prefer to reorganize your debts under Chapters 11, 12, or 13 so that you can continue to operate your business while the bankruptcy court protects you from the demands of creditors. In a reorganization, you can often reduce the amounts you must pay back to unsecured creditors. In addition, under a court-approved repayment plan, you can spread your payments over a number of years.

Among the situations in which Chapters 11, 12, and 13 are worth considering are these:

- You want to retain all your assets and keep the business going.
- You want to partially liquidate your assets and then keep the business alive on a scaled-down basis.
- You want to totally liquidate the business by selling it either as a going concern or by selling any remaining assets.
- You want to buy time to put the business in decent shape so that it's more attractive to potential purchasers.
- You want to pay your taxes in installments to stave off the IRS or state or local tax collectors who are poised to seize your assets, which would put you out of business.

In each case, a Chapter 11, 12, or 13 proceeding may offer the possibility of helping you achieve your objectives.

a. Chapter 11

A Chapter 11 reorganization allows your sole proprietorship, partnership, corporation, or LLC to continue doing business while often reducing or even eliminating the amounts you must pay back to unsecured creditors. Under a court-approved repayment plan, you can spread your payments over a number of years. Five years is typical.

If you file for a Chapter 11 reorganization, you'll immediately receive the protection of the bankruptcy court. All lawsuits and other collection actions against your business will come to a screeching halt. You'll then have 90 days in which to submit a plan—called a reorganization plan—showing how you propose to pay past-due debts while keeping up to date on current ones. If your business debts don't exceed $2 million, you can use a new, fast-track version of Chapter 11 that simplifies procedures and gives the creditors less control than they have in a regular Chapter 11 reorganization.

Your plan will have to meet a few legal guidelines; for example, it must show that back taxes will be fully paid within five years. And secured creditors—those to whom your business has pledged collateral—must receive the collateral or the current value of the collateral or the current value of the debt. Your plan doesn't have to include payment to unsecured creditors unless those creditors would receive some payment if your business were to file for liquidation under Chapter 7.

After you file the plan, creditors vote on it. Secured and unsecured vote separately. To be adopted, the plan must be approved by 51% of the creditors in each class. If your plan is carefully crafted, the creditors will likely accept it. But if the creditors reject the reorganization plan, all may not be lost. A solution may be found in the "cram down"—a phrase used to describe the last-resort powers of the bankruptcy court. If your plan is basically fair and equitable, the judge can cram it down the throats of all the creditors.

To help your business stay alive, the judge can terminate burdensome or unprofitable leases or contracts. If, for example, your business is occupying expensive space under a lease that runs for seven years, your business is contractually obligated to keep paying rent throughout those seven years. But in Chapter 11, the judge can allow your business to move to a less costly location, with no further obligation to your current landlord.

With these many benefits, Chapter 11 sounds like a good deal for a financially troubled business, but the grim truth is that it rarely succeeds. It's usually an overwhelming task for a typical business owner to keep up with current bills while simultaneously chopping away at large past-due debts and paying chunky administrative and legal fees. The result is that more than 90% of businesses that file under Chapter 11 eventually switch to Chapter 7 and liquidate their assets—although the new, fast-track procedures may lead to a higher success rate.

Compare the payoffs to creditors.
Basically, if you're convinced that you can get more money for the creditors by reorganizing under Chapters 11, 12, or 13 than by filing for a straight liquidation under Chapter 7, then reorganize. Otherwise, don't waste your time, energy, and money. Proceed directly with a Chapter 7 filing. Why worry about how much the creditors get? Because the more they get, the less you may be personally liable for.

b.   Chapter 12

A Chapter 12 bankruptcy is available to family-owned farming businesses. As in a Chapter 11 proceeding, the total amount of debt owed to unsecured creditors may be reduced in the Chapter 12 plan. In addition, the financially ailing farm operation is allowed to continue doing business under a court-approved plan for repaying its remaining debts over a number of years. A court-appointed trustee serves as the intermediary between the farm and its creditors. Because this book is primarily for nonfarm businesses, Chapter 12 won't be treated further.

c.   Chapter 13

Businesses, per se, are not permitted to file for Chapter 13 bankruptcy. A sole proprietor, however, may file as an individual and include the business debts for which he or she is personally liable. There are financial limits, which are adjusted annually based on a cost-of-living index. You can file for Chapter 13 bankruptcy if you have no more than $922,975 in secured debts and no more than $307,675 in unsecured debts. (These limits are adjusted periodically to reflect changes in the Consumer Price Index.) Contingent or unliquidated claims—such as a sexual harassment claim against you that's not yet resolved—don't count against these limits. As in a Chapter 11 reorganization, the amount you must pay back to unsecured creditors is reduced (sometimes to as little as zero) and, under a court-approved plan, you continue to run the business while paying off debts over a period that can last up to five years. A court-appointed trustee —whose fees you pay—makes payments to creditors under the pay-back plan.

As noted in the next section, there can be advantages to filing under Chapter 13 rather than Chapter 11 if your business qualifies. Prospects for keeping your business afloat over the long term are better with a Chapter 13.

See *Chapter 13 Bankruptcy: Repay Your Debts,* *by Robin Leonard (Nolo), for a clear and in-depth look at how to get a court-approved repayment plan—either with or without a lawyer.*

d.   Choosing Between Chapter 11 and Chapter 13

All types of business entities—sole proprietorships, partnerships, corporations, and limited liability companies—can choose to file under Chapter 7 for a straight liquidation bankruptcy or under Chapter 11 for a reorganization of their business debts. Since Chapter 11 and Chapter 13 both allow a business to remain in operation under a court-approved plan, a sole proprietor who qualifies for both may face the dilemma of choosing between the two. Generally, it's more advantageous to choose Chapter 13, for a number of reasons:

- A Chapter 13 reorganization plan is usually approved by the court in less time than a Chapter 11 plan.

- You don't have to deal with a creditors' committee—a committee that's appointed in a Chapter 11 filing to represent the interests of the unsecured creditors. This means you'll expend a lot less time and energy on paperwork, meetings, and possibly attorney fees. Creditors may object separately to your Chapter 13 plan, but they don't carry the same weight as a committee would in a Chapter 11.

- You'll be able to pay less than 100 cents on the dollar for unsecured debts. The bankruptcy judge in a Chapter 13 can approve a plan which provides for partial debt repayment.

- If you meet the terms of the court-approved payment plan, virtually all remaining, unpaid debts will be wiped away even if some of them were obtained under circumstances the law might consider fraudulent. For example, if you obtain credit by misrepresenting your credit history, the debt probably won't be discharged under either Chapter 7 or 11 and the creditor will be able to sue you personally—but under Chapter 13, if you make all payments as called for by the plan, the creditor can't sue you for that debt.

- A Chapter 13 filing will stop collection action against a cosigner or guarantor if the Chapter 13 plan treats creditors fairly. In short, this option can help you protect friends and relatives who have obligated themselves to pay your debts.

- Going the Chapter 13 route is usually less expensive than the Chapter 11 alternative. That's because the filing fees are lower and, if you hire a lawyer to help you, the legal fees will be lower too,

There is, however, one area in which Chapter 11 may be a better choice. In a Chapter 13 reorganization, you generally can't modify the terms of a mortgage loan or other credit agreement that is secured by your home. This means that even if your house is worth less than what you owe, you must still pay the balance. There are a few technical exceptions to this rule, but they're of little practical value to most people. A different rule applies to Chapter 11 filings, creating the possibility of reducing the loan if the value of your home has dropped. So if you have a huge mortgage on your home and the value of the property has dropped, then Chapter 11 is probably better for you than Chapter 13.

4. Who's Who in Bankruptcy

In addition to understanding the various types of bankruptcy, you'll quickly need to understand who the major players are and at least some of the jargon involved in a bankruptcy proceeding. Here's a brief overview.

- *Debtor.* The debtor is the person or business entity that owes the money. This can be you or your business or both. If your business isn't a sole proprietorship, you and your business each need to file separate sets of bankruptcy papers. Generally, it's the debtor that files for bankruptcy, although creditors can sometimes start the ball rolling, in which case it's called an involuntary bankruptcy.

- *Creditor.* This can be any person, business, or governmental agency that has or may have a claim against you or your business. A secured creditor is one that has a lien (claim) against specific property—usually either in the form of a real estate mortgage or a security interest in a vehicle or other equipment. A secured creditor is usually in a better legal position than an unsecured creditor, because if money isn't available to pay the debt, the secured creditor is entitled to grab the assets pledged as security.

- *Trustee.* A bankruptcy trustee takes possession of the debtor's business assets in a Chapter 7 proceeding and liquidates them to pay creditors. In a Chapter 7 personal bankruptcy, the trustee gathers the debtor's nonexempt property (a second home, for example), liquidates it, and distributes the proceeds to the unsecured creditors. In a Chapter 11 proceeding, the debtor usually retains control over the business assets while the business continues to operate. But, especially if the business owner has committed fraud or seriously mismanaged the business, the court may appoint a trustee to take over in a Chapter 11 proceeding so that the creditors' interests are better protected. In a Chapter 12 or 13 bankruptcy, the debtor remains in possession of the property; the trustee collects monthly payments and distributes them to creditors. Trustees are appointed by the bankruptcy judge unless the district has a U.S. Trustee—a full-time federal employee with a staff of assistant trustees who serve as trustees in Chapter 11 cases and appoint and supervise outside trustees in Chapter 7, 12, and 13 cases.

- *Judge.* A bankruptcy judge is part of the federal district court and has broad control over bankruptcy proceedings, including authority to resolve all disputes between the business and its creditors, as well as any issues involving the business's property. Despite this broad authority, the judge may abstain from trying issues that can be litigated in a state court—for example, actions to foreclose on real estate or to gain possession of cars and equipment, and cases involving environmental cleanups. Bankruptcies are supervised, for the most part, by the trustee where one's been appointed—but debtors and creditors who disagree with a trustee's decision can seek a ruling from the bankruptcy judge who can overrule the trustee.

- *Creditors' committee.* In a Chapter 11 proceeding, an unsecured creditors' committee may be appointed to represent the interests of all the unsecured creditors. If the proceeding is complicated, there may be additional creditors' committees representing special interests—for example, pension and profit-sharing recipients, undersecured creditors, and secured creditors. A creditor's committee may object that a proposed plan writes off too much of the debt owed to its members or that it gives the debtor too much time to pay.

5. Key Bankruptcy Concepts

Unfortunately, your mini-education in how bankruptcy works isn't quite complete. Since bankruptcy law is unique, with its own concepts, procedures, and jargon, it's crucially important to understand the legal basics.

a. Bankruptcy Estate

Once you or your business file for bankruptcy, the property—called the bankruptcy estate—is controlled by the bankruptcy proceedings. Creditors can't get their hands on it without the court's permission. Property subject to court control includes not only the property your business owned when you filed the bankruptcy papers, but also money your business earned but hadn't collected before you filed for bankruptcy. Also, in a Chapter 11, 12, or 13 proceeding, if your business acquires property after your case is filed, that property becomes part of the bankruptcy estate. However, if your business holds money in trust for third parties—such as withholding taxes that are to be paid to the IRS—that money isn't part of the bankruptcy estate.

You may need a separate bank account. *If you don't pay the employment taxes immediately, keep them in a separate bank account designated as a trust account so that it's clear that these funds are separate from other funds of the business. Then you'll be able to use these funds to pay the taxes and avoid personal liability and penalties. In a Chapter 11 filing, you'll probably need to* *set up several separate accounts—for example, accounts for payroll and general operations, in addition to the one for employment taxes.*

b. The Automatic Stay

As soon as your business has filed a bankruptcy petition, creditors are stayed (stopped) from continuing their collection efforts against the business. In addition, creditors can no longer seize any property owned or leased by the business that secures its debts, such as a car, building, or equipment. Further, it's illegal for creditors to contact you to push for payment, start a lawsuit against you, or pursue any other collection action without permission of the bankruptcy court. Utilities such as the power, phone, and water company must continue to serve your business as long as you can guarantee payment for future services—for example, by posting a deposit.

Be aware that the IRS can continue an audit, issue a tax deficiency notice, demand a tax return, issue a tax assessment, and demand payment, but can't record a lien or seize your property.

c. The Bankruptcy Filing

To start a bankruptcy case, your business must file a form called a Petition for Relief with the clerk of the federal bankruptcy court. To learn the location of the bankruptcy court, call the clerk of the U.S. District Court that's nearest your business.

A list of creditors (everyone your business owes money to) and their addresses should accompany your Petition, using a special format so that copies of your creditor list can be used as a mailing list.

Within 15 days, you must also file lists of debts, assets, and a history of your business. In bankruptcy jargon, these lists are called bankruptcy schedules and Statement of Financial Affairs. You'll want to include all debts your business may owe and any claims that creditors may have against your business—even those you have some doubts about or you dispute.

d. Claims

Once notified of your bankruptcy, creditors may file claims for payment of their debts with the bankruptcy court. Your business—and, in a Chapter 7 or Chapter 13 filing, the bankruptcy trustee—can challenge a claim that seems to be improper. The judge will decide whether the claim is valid.

In a liquidation of a business, since there's almost never enough money to pay all allowed claims, the law establishes priorities. Your bankruptcy estate (any money or property salvaged from your business) is used to pay the highest priority claims first, then the next highest priority, and so on as long as the money lasts. Creditors in the lowest category, to actually receive any money, will typically have to take much less than the amount they're owed, since by definition there isn't enough money to go around. In fact, it's not uncommon for unsecured creditors to receive nothing.

Some creditors can obtain a super-priority status. In a Chapter 11, 12, or 13 bankruptcy where the trustee or debtor must borrow new money to keep the business running, the lender of these funds would obtain a super-priority claim and be first in line when assets are distributed. Next come the secured creditors who have liens on specific real estate, vehicles, equipment, or other property. After that come such claims as the expenses of administering the bankruptcy, wages and commissions earned during the 90 days before the bankruptcy started, money owed to an employee benefit plan, deposits made on consumer goods, and most taxes.

At the bottom of the heap are general, unsecured claimants who, if they're lucky, receive a pittance. Often, unsecured claimants get a few cents for each dollar they were owed or come away entirely empty-handed. In a Chapter 13, secured creditors with liens and priority debts could be paid simultaneously through the Chapter 13 plan.

e. The Effect of Bankruptcy on Secured Debts

If you go through a Chapter 7 personal bankruptcy, the creditor will lose the right to get a personal judgment against you requiring you to pay the debt that's owed. But even though the creditor can no longer demand that you repay the debt, if you've pledged property as collateral, the creditor will still have a lien on that specific property. Because the creditor will be able to enforce the lien and take or sell the property, you need to be aware of the three options available to you—which can be summarized as The Three Rs:

- *Relinquishment.* You can simply give up the house, car, or other property on which the creditor has a lien.
- *Redemption.* You may buy it by paying the creditor, usually in a lump sum, the value of the property. If there's a dispute about how much the property is worth, the bankruptcy judge will determine the value.
- *Reaffirmation.* You may reaffirm your obligation to pay the debt secured by your property before the debt is discharged in bankruptcy. Then, you continue to make payments as you had agreed before the bankruptcy. Of course, the lien will remain on the property and, if you later miss payments, the creditor will be able to enforce the lien by taking back property to pay for the balance of the reaffirmed debt.

f. Exempt Property

If you go through a Chapter 7 personal bankruptcy where your assets are liquidated to pay your debts, you don't have to give up all of your personal property to pay back creditors. The law allows you to keep some items (called exempt property) to help you get a fresh start. Exempt property is listed in the federal bankruptcy code, but states also have laws listing exemptions. Generally, you'll rely on your state law exemptions—either because the state law exemptions are more advantageous or because, as is the case in most states, the state law gives you no choice. If you do have a choice, check the homestead allowance carefully, as it's usually more generous under state law.

Most state exemptions allow you to keep property in these broad categories:

- motor vehicles, to a certain modest value
- clothing other than furs
- household furnishings and goods
- household appliances
- jewelry such as a wedding or engagement ring and a watch
- personal effects—personal possessions that don't fall into the categories of clothing and jewelry
- life insurance (cash or loan value, or proceeds) to a certain value
- pensions for public employees or pensions that qualify under ERISA
- part of the equity in your home
- tools of your trade or profession, to a certain value
- portion of unpaid but earned wages, and
- public benefits (welfare, Social Security, unemployment compensation) accumulated in a bank account.

 For detailed state-by-state lists of exemptions: *See* Solve Your Money Troubles, *or* Bankruptcy: Is It the Right Solution to Your Debt Problems?, *both by Robin Leonard (Nolo).*

LAW IN THE REAL WORLD
Carl and Phyllis Save Their Home

Carl starts a neighborhood restaurant, organizing his business as a one-person corporation. To raise capital, Carl and his wife Phyllis borrow $50,000 from a bank on their signature and additionally secure the loan by giving the bank a second mortgage on their home.

In its first year, the business runs up a pile of debts. With prospects of becoming profitable looking bleak, Carl decides to close down. Carl considers putting the corporation through bankruptcy to make a clean break with creditors. Unfortunately, this won't help with the bank loan since Carl and Phyllis are personally liable for that debt and their home is at risk if they can't pay it. Since this is a secured debt, even if they go through personal bankruptcy they'll lose their home.

So Carl and Phyllis reduce the bank loan with $10,000 of personal savings that Phyllis had set aside from her salary as a school teacher. They then refinance their home by getting a new first mortgage that pays off both the old mortgages. (Fortunately, Carl is able to get his old job back, so he and Phyllis have income to qualify for the new mortgage.) Carl and Phyllis now have 30 years to pay off the new mortgage in monthly installment payments.

Carl closes the business, sells the corporation's few remaining assets, and before dissolving the corporation, distributes the proceeds pro rata to the business's unsecured creditors.

The business failed but with this small-scale workout, Carl and Phyllis saved their home.

Resolving Legal Disputes

Legal disputes—actual and potential—come in all shapes and sizes when you run a small business. Consider these examples:

- The phone company puts your Yellow Pages ad in the wrong classification and refuses to do anything about it.
- A former employee claims that you wrongfully fired him or her.
- Your landlord puts off repairing a leaky roof. As a result, valuable merchandise is ruined in a rainstorm.
- Your insurance company offers a ridiculously low settlement when one of your trucks is totalled.
- You refuse to accept a dozen custom-built display cases because they don't meet your specifications. The shop that constructed them threatens to sue.
- You want to stop a former employee from opening a competing business two blocks away and soliciting customers using a copy of your customer list.
- Just when your business begins to do well, your partners claim that you're not doing everything you promised to do in the partnership agreement. They want to terminate the agreement and continue the business without you.

How you handle such disputes can have a profound effect on your bottom line, not to mention your mental health and the morale of your employees. Fortunately, you usually have a number of options available, giving you some control over the time, energy, and money that you spend on resolving legal problems.

We live in a litigious society. Often, the first reaction to a business dispute is, "I'll see you in court!" But rarely is litigation the only method for resolving a dispute. Litigation is enormously expensive and almost always results in hard feelings that prevent the contending parties from ever doing business with one another again, so it's always smart to think about alternatives. Commonly available options include negotiation, mediation, and

arbitration. These noncourtroom approaches to handling legal disputes are often referred to as Alternative Dispute Resolution or ADR. This chapter explores the various types of dispute resolution so that, whether or not you work with a lawyer, you'll be better able to take charge of tactical and settlement decisions.

A. Negotiating a Settlement

In most situations, a negotiated solution is far better and cheaper than one imposed by an arbitrator or a judge. A settlement often can be reached speedily and at minimum expense. Litigation (and, to some extent, arbitration) can not only empty your wallet—they can also eat up an amazing amount of your time and that of your employees.

Always seek a negotiated settlement before you sue, even if you're so angry you don't want to speak to the other party. Try to evaluate the legal and financial realities objectively. Your goal should be to achieve the best result at the lowest cost. If instead you act on the conviction (whether it's right or wrong) that you're being victimized by the other side, chances are you'll end up fighting for the last dollar because of the principle involved. A business person who is controlled by this sort of emotional reaction is almost sure to get ensnared in a lawsuit that will take too long and cost too much.

Here are some helpful pointers for negotiations:

- *Listen closely to what your opponent says.* Acknowledge that you hear the points your opponent is making even if you disagree with them.
- *Avoid personal attacks.* This only raises the level of hostility and makes settlement more difficult. Equally important, don't react impulsively to the emotional outbursts of your opponent.
- *Try to structure the negotiation as a mutual attempt to solve a problem.* Jointly seek solutions that recognize the interests of both parties.
- *Learn your opponent's priorities.* Maybe dollars are less important than a formula for future business relations. You may not be as far apart as you think.
- *Put yourself in your opponent's shoes.* What can you offer to make the settlement more palatable? The best settlements are those in which both sides feel they've won (or at least not given up anything fundamental).
- *When you propose a specific settlement, make it clear that you're attempting to compromise.* Offers of settlement (clearly labeled as such) can't be introduced against you if you ever go to trial.
- *If a settlement is reached, promptly write it down and have all parties sign it.* You or your lawyer should volunteer to prepare the first draft. That way, you can include protective language that, once included, your opponent may see as too minor to quibble about.
- *Money is a powerful incentive to settlement.* If your business is going to have to pay something eventually, come to the negotiating table with your checkbook or a wad of $100 bills. The other side may settle at a surprisingly low figure if they can walk away from the bargaining table with payment in hand. Of course, if you pay with cash, be sure to get a receipt.

 Want to learn more about negotiation?
See: Getting to Yes, *by Roger Fisher and William Ury (Penguin Books).*
Getting Past No: Negotiating With Difficult People, *by William Ury (Bantam Books).*

B. Understanding Mediation

Many people confuse mediation with arbitration (discussed in Section C). While both are nonjudicial ways to resolve disputes, there's a huge difference: arbitration is binding; mediation isn't. The mediator simply helps the parties work out a solution to their dispute. Neither side is committed in advance to accept the mediator's advice.

Where to Find a Mediator

You and the other party can choose anyone you both respect to act as mediator. Local small business or community groups may provide trained mediators, as do the arbitration services listed in Section C.

"Turbo-charged negotiation" is how one lawyer describes mediation. In mediation, you ask the mediator, as a neutral expert, to help both sides negotiate. If you follow the classic model—used by big business for, say, a labor-management dispute—the mediator typically meets separately with each side. Everything said in those meetings is confidential. The mediator helps each party analyze its needs. When both sides get close to a settlement, everyone meets together to work out the details.

Mediators in small business disputes often prefer a much less formal approach. More likely than not, the mediator will have everyone sit down together from the very beginning and allow both parties to express all their issues—even emotional ones. Often this works because the people are mad at each other for reasons that go well beyond the legal issues that are supposed to define the dispute. Once everything is on the table, a good mediator helps the parties find a mutually acceptable solution.

LAW IN THE REAL WORLD
Getting at the Real Problems

Doug rents a storefront from Tom for five years. Although they occasionally have their differences over Tom's duty to keep the building in good repair and Doug's to maintain the grounds, they get along reasonably well. Then Doug has a bad financial month and is late with the rent. Tom, who has given Doug an extension several times in the past, threatens to begin eviction proceedings immediately. Doug responds by pointing out that Tom failed to fix a roof leak that damaged some of his inventory. Clearly, the stage is set for a nasty court fight. To head this off, a neighboring business owner suggests that Tom and Doug mediate their dispute under a program cosponsored by the Chamber of Commerce.

At the mediation, Doug wants to know why Tom is being so unreasonable. The answer, it turns out, is simple. Doug has repeatedly left the gate open in the yard behind the building letting Tom's beloved dog run into the street. Tom finds it hard to forgive such carelessness and is ready to punish Doug by using whatever legal leverage is available. When Doug and Tom work out the dog problem (Tom will put in a better gate, Doug absolutely guarantees to keep it closed), the rest of the issues are quickly resolved, and a lawsuit is avoided.

But does mediation work? Perhaps surprisingly, given the fact there's no one to impose a solution, the answer is yes, in as many as 80% of mediations.

One reason is apparently that by agreeing to mediate a dispute in the first place, you and the other side must cooperate to establish the rules which, in turn, sets the stage for cooperating to find a solution to the dispute.

Sample mediation clauses that you can include in your business contracts are shown below.

Sample Mediation Clause 1

If a dispute arises relating to this agreement, the parties will follow this procedure before pursuing any other remedy:

1. The parties will promptly meet to attempt in good faith to negotiate a resolution of the dispute.

2. If, within 30 days after that meeting, the parties have not resolved the dispute, they will submit the dispute to good faith mediation in accordance with the rules of the [*name of organization such as American Arbitration Association*] and to bear equally the costs of the mediation.

3. After a mediator is appointed, the parties will participate in good faith in the mediation. If the dispute is not resolved within 30 days, it will be settled by arbitration in accordance with the rules of [*name of organization*], and judgment upon the award rendered by the arbitrator may be entered in any court having jurisdiction.

Sample Mediation Clause 2

If a dispute arises between the parties to this contract, the parties agree to participate in at least four hours of mediation in accordance with the mediation procedures of United States Arbitration & Mediation, Inc. The parties agree to split equally the costs of mediation. The mediation will be administered by [*designate either the specific USA&M office or a local USA&M office designated by the USA&M National Headquarters*].

If your original contract is silent on the subject of mediation or arbitration, you and the other party still can agree to use either or both of these methods to resolve a dispute. Chances are good that your adversary (if a businessperson) will be as receptive as you are to some method of avoiding the expense and delay of litigation. Even if a negotiating impasse has led to a lawsuit, you can change horses in midstream; you can agree to mediation or arbitration, and cancel the lawsuit when you reach a settlement.

 For in-depth guidance: *read* How to Mediate Your Dispute, *by Peter Lovenheim (Nolo).*

C. Arbitration

With arbitration, you get a relatively quick, relatively inexpensive solution to a business dispute without going to court. Like a judge, the arbitrator—or arbitration panel—has power to hear the dispute and make a final, binding decision. Where does this power come from? From you and the other party. You agree to submit to arbitration and to be bound by the arbitrator's decision.

Almost any commercial dispute that can be litigated can be arbitrated. Disputes with employees can be arbitrated, as can disagreements with a landlord, supplier, business partner, franchisor, architect, builder, customer, or equipment rental company.

Arbitration clauses are becoming a part of most commercial contracts. Insurance contracts, for example, frequently provide that any dispute over the amount of benefits to be paid by the insurance

company will be decided by arbitration rather than litigation. The same goes for construction contracts: There's often a clause that requires arbitration for any contractual disputes. Through such clauses, you can provide in advance for arbitration to be used. You and the other party can also decide to use arbitration after a dispute arises.

If the losing party doesn't pay the money required by an arbitration award, the winner can easily convert the award to a court judgment, which can be enforced like any other court judgment. Unlike a judgment based on litigation, however, you generally can't take an appeal from an arbitration-based judgment. (An exception is when there was some element of fraud in the procedures leading to the arbitration award.)

Here are the chief advantages of arbitration:

- Arbitration is usually much less expensive than litigation. The American Arbitration Association, for example, charges on a sliding scale, based on the amount of the claim:

Amount of Claim	Filing Fee	Case Service Fee
Up to $10,000	$500	$200
$10,001 to $75,000	$750	$300
$75,001 to $150,000	$1,500	$750
$150,001 to $300,000	$2,750	$1,250
$300,001 to $500,000	$4,250	$1,750
$500,001 to $1,000,000	$6,000	$2,500
$1,000,001 to $7,000,000	$8,000	$3,250
$7,000,001 to $10,000,000	$10,000	$4,000
Above $10,000,000	Contact Regional Office	

- You're likely to receive an arbitrator's decision within six months after the demand for arbitration is submitted. And, under certain circumstances, the American Arbitration Association has expedited procedures leading to a quicker decision. Lawsuits, on the other hand, usually aren't decided for a year or often much more—and an appeal may add several more years of delay.

- Unlike a trial, arbitration proceedings are private. There's no need for your competitors or the general public to know your business.
- The rules of evidence are relaxed in an arbitration proceeding. This makes it easier to get to the heart of the matter. Courtroom trials often get bogged down in evidentiary arguments that obscure rather than clarify the facts.
- Arbitration often avoids the bitter acrimony that can affect the parties in a lawsuit. It's not unusual for parties to resume their normal business relationship after their dispute has been arbitrated.

How Arbitration Works: An Example

Smooth Shift Transmission hires Better Builders to add two service bays to its transmission shop for a total of $60,000. The contract calls for a $30,000 down payment. The balance is due when the job is completed. However, after the work is done, Smooth Shift isn't satisfied with the job. There are several large cracks in the concrete floor installed by Better Builders. On the advice of its architect, Smooth Shift delays making the final payment.

A few weeks later the floor begins to settle, creating several gaps where it meets an outside wall. Better Builders claims that these problems are minor and threatens to sue Smooth Shift for the final payment of $30,000. But Smooth Shift points to a clause in the construction contract: "All disputes concerning this project will be submitted to arbitration."

Better Builders sends a "demand for arbitration" to the American Arbitration Association (AAA), a nationwide organization that administers many of the arbitration proceedings in this country. In response, the AAA sends a list of five proposed arbitrators to each side. The parties agree on one of the listed people to serve as their arbitrator. (If parties can't agree, the AAA makes the selection.) A hearing is scheduled a month later.

During the hearing, which takes only three hours, each side makes a brief opening statement describing the controversy. Smooth Shift's owner then shows the arbitrator the construction contract, the plans and specs for the job, and photographs of the floor. The architect hired by Smooth Shift testifies that the floor problems are serious, and that the floor must be replaced.

Now it's Better Builders' turn. The president of Better Builders testifies that the floor problems are minor and can be fixed with $1,000 worth of patching material. A week later, the arbitrator sends the parties his findings and his decision: The floor needs to be replaced at a cost of $18,000. That amount is to be deducted from the $30,000 final payment owed to Better Builders, meaning Smooth Shift owes Better Builders only $12,000. End of case.

How to Find an Arbitrator

- *The American Arbitration Association.* The oldest and largest organization of its kind, with regional offices in 38 U.S. cities. The main office is in New York City. Contact at www.adr.org or 212-716-5800.
- *Judicial Arbitration and Mediation Services, Inc./Endispute.* This is the largest private dispute resolution company with offices nationwide; mediates and arbitrates a wide range of commercial disputes. Contact at www.jamsadr.com.
- *U.S. Arbitration and Mediation.* A network of nationwide offices provides general arbitration and mediation of commercial disputes. Contact at www.usam.com or 800-318-2700.

Keep in mind that you are not required to use an organization for arbitration. You and the other party are free to choose your own arbitrator or arbitration panel, and to set your own procedural rules. Just remember that for arbitration to be binding and legally enforceable, you need to follow the simple guidelines set down in your state's arbitration statute. You can usually find the statute by looking in the statutory index under "arbitration" or checking the table of contents for the civil procedure sections.

Here's a sample clause you can use in a contract to provide for the arbitration of disputes:

Sample Arbitration Clause 1

Any controversy or claim rising out of or relating to this contract, or the breach of this contract, shall be settled by arbitration in accordance with the rules of the American Arbitration Association. A judgment of a court having jurisdiction may be entered upon the arbitrator's award.

Here's an example of an agreement you and the other party should sign if you want to go to arbitration with a dispute that has already arisen and that isn't covered by an arbitration agreement in an existing contract:

Sample Arbitration Clause 2

We agree to submit the following controversy to arbitration under the rules of the American Arbitration Association: [*describe the controversy*]

We further agree that a judgment of a court having jurisdiction may be entered upon the arbitrator's award.

If you and the other party want to choose an arbitrator on your own to act outside the administrative framework of an organization, use a clause like this one:

Sample Arbitration Clause 3

We agree to submit the following controversy to arbitration by [*name of arbitrator*]: [*describe the controversy*]

We further agree that the arbitration procedures shall be as prescribed by the arbitrator and the costs of arbitration shall be as apportioned by the arbitrator.

Consider using arbitration for employment disputes. *Lawsuits by former employees claiming wrongful discharge or illegal discrimination can be costly and extremely contentious. By planning ahead, you should be able to avoid these lawsuits and use arbitration instead. The key is to have employees agree in writing that all disputes will be submitted to arbitration. True, some courts have rejected these agreements, believing that the agreements weren't really voluntary or else were calculated to help the employer avoid the full impact of civil rights laws. Still, if you draft the arbitration* *agreement carefully and the employee signs it before being hired, it will probably be enforceable. The agreement should use plain language to tell what disputes are covered and what rights (such as the right to a jury trial) the employee is giving up. Give employees a few days to review the agreement before they have to sign. Try for a balanced agreement that benefits both you and the employee. If it's tipped too far in your favor, a court may rule that it's unconscionable and refuse to enforce it.*

D. Going to Court

If your attempts at settling a dispute fail and you end up in a lawsuit, you'll need more help than this book can offer. Unless you go to small claims court, in fact, you'll probably need to hire a lawyer to represent you.

Despite its ample drawbacks, litigation may offer advantages in some situations. For example, you may decide you want a jury trial if you're the underdog. If you're a small franchisee going toe to toe with a multinational corporation, and the factual questions are pretty evenly balanced, the jury's sympathy may tip the scales of justice in your direction.

Another reason for considering litigation is that various procedural safeguards can help ensure that only trustworthy evidence is presented. The judge will consider only evidence that has been submitted according to a strict set of rules. In addition, using various methods of pretrial discovery, such as depositions, you can force the other side to disclose the evidence it plans to offer at trial and can also uncover evidence helpful to you. Of course, discovery is a two-way street. The other side can force you to disclose information you'd rather keep to yourself.

1. The Federal and State Court Systems

In the United States, two court systems operate side by side: the federal and state courts. Most business lawsuits (in fact, most lawsuits of every kind) are handled in state courts.

Broadly, federal courts have jurisdiction over only two types of cases. The first type involves what lawyers call federal questions: cases based on provisions in the U.S. Constitution, treaties, and federal laws. This includes such things as discrimination cases arising under federal civil rights laws, and bankruptcy, patent, copyright, and trademark cases arising under specific federal statutes.

The second type of case heard by federal district courts involves controversies between citizens of two different states; in these cases, the amount in controversy must exceed $50,000 before a federal court can get involved. This authority of the federal courts is called diversity jurisdiction because the litigants come from different (diverse) states. When a federal court exercises diversity jurisdiction, it's not necessary for a federal question to be involved. The court applies the law of the state in which the case arose.

EXAMPLE: A truck owned by an Arizona corporation is in an accident on a California freeway with a truck owned by a California corporation. Valuable computer equipment in the Arizona company's truck is ruined. If the ruined equipment was worth more than $50,000, the

Arizona corporation can sue the California corporation in either the California state courts or in a federal district court located in California. If the Arizona company sues in federal court, the judge will apply California law relating to vehicle accidents.

In handling cases based on diversity of citizenship, a corporation—a fictional legal person—is treated as a "citizen" of the state where it's incorporated.

As a practical matter, it often doesn't make much difference whether a business case proceeds in federal court or state court. When there's a choice between going to state or federal court, the decision is usually a tactical one based on comparisons between the caliber and philosophy of the state and federal judges, as well as comparisons between the likely composition of the juries in the two courts. Delay may also be a consideration; sometimes one court may have less of a backlog than another.

2. The Litigation Process

In a typical commercial case, the plaintiff (the person or company who sues) asks the judge to issue a judgment against the defendant (the person or company being sued). In many business cases, the plaintiff wants a money judgment—or, in legal parlance, "damages."

But judges have power to grant many other kinds of relief to the plaintiff. For example, in a civil (that is, noncriminal) case, a judge may:

- Order a building official to issue a permit allowing the plaintiff company to expand its office building.
- Issue an injunction (order) prohibiting a former corporate officer from improperly disclosing or benefiting from trade secrets.
- Require a seller to transfer legal title to real estate in accordance with a purchase agreement.
- Have the sheriff remove a tenant from business premises and restore possession to the landlord.

- Place business assets in the hands of a receiver for short-term management.
- Order a business to stop infringing on a patent owned by another business.
- Require a partner to make an accounting to other partners.
- Order a state administrative board to issue a license.
- Interpret the meaning of a contract or declare a contract void.
- Force a corporation to open its books and records to all shareholders.

This is just a partial list; the point is that judges have broad powers. The powers of a small claims court (and some other local courts) are more limited. For example, in small claims court, you're generally limited to seeking a judgment for money damages—although the judge may have some additional limited authority such as requiring one of the parties to return goods to the other party as a condition of receiving payment. (For more on small claims court, see Chapter 23.)

It may surprise you to learn that most commercial lawsuits never go to trial. Frequently, a business starts a lawsuit mainly to get the attention of an adversary after attempts at a negotiated settlement have broken down. The message is, "We're serious. This thing can't drag on forever. We've got to resolve it on realistic terms." As costs mount and both parties gain a clearer picture of what they'll be able—or unable—to prove in court, and judges make rulings in preliminary courtroom skirmishes (known as "motions"), the parties often decide to compromise and settle the case.

Never lose sight of the fact that you can reach a negotiated settlement at any time. Any experienced lawyer can recite examples of cases settled "on the courthouse steps" just before the trial was to begin. And many cases have been settled after the evidence was presented and the jurors were in the jury room discussing what the verdict should be.

The High Cost of Justice

We all know lawsuits are expensive. But did you know just how expensive? The business lawyer's meter typically runs at $150 to $250 an hour for a long list of legal chores, including:

- conferences and telephone calls with you, witnesses, and other lawyers
- legal research
- drafting documents such as a complaint, answer, countercomplaint, motions, requests for production of documents, briefs, and jury instructions
- taking the depositions of witnesses or potential witnesses
- arguing motions in court (including many that affect only the litigation process and not the merits of the case)
- attending conferences in the judge's chambers
- driving to the courthouse and waiting for his or her turn to argue pretrial motions
- conducting the trial.

Other costs include paying the public stenographer to take down depositions and type up the transcripts, jury fees, investigator costs, and expert witness fees.

In most situations, each party pays its own attorney fees, although you can provide in a contract (such as a lease) that if a contract-related dispute goes to court, the losing party pays the fees of the winner's lawyer. If you don't have such a clause, the cost of winning may be so high that it's a hollow victory.

3. Getting Speedy Relief Through an Injunction

With clogged dockets and rules that allow extensive pretrial discovery (depositions, interrogatories, and other devices aimed at learning the facts of the other party's case), it's not always easy to get a speedy hearing in a commercial case. A case may be tied up in court for months or even years before it's decided. These built-in delays generally work to the advantage of the defendant and the disadvantage of the plaintiff. (It's the plaintiff who's taken the case to court and wants some action.)

In some instances, however, a plaintiff can go to court and get prompt attention. Two key elements must be present:

- The defendant must be causing irreparable harm to plaintiff's business—harm that can't be rectified by monetary damages; and
- There must be a need for immediate relief.

EXAMPLE: The grand opening of Trudy's new store in a neighborhood shopping plaza is scheduled for Saturday. Trudy's lease gives her the right to use the adjoining parking lot for customer parking. On the Monday before the grand opening, Trudy is stunned to see that a contractor, who is about to build an addition to the plaza, has occupied 16 of the plaza's 20 parking spaces with trucks and a large construction shed. Unable to convince her landlord or the contractor to move the equipment, Trudy goes to court for an injunction.

The judge orders a quick hearing (scheduled for the following day) to hear arguments on whether a preliminary injunction should be issued immediately to prevent harm to Trudy's business, pending a full-scale hearing.

In a case that involves an urgent threat to health or safety, or imminent damage to property, a judge also has the power to issue a temporary restraining order (TRO) to keep any harm from occurring or continuing until a hearing on a preliminary injunction can be scheduled. Because a TRO is issued at a hearing at which only one side is heard (ex parte), it's a radical remedy. So, before issuing a TRO, the judge has to be convinced that the circumstances are extreme; even then, the restraining order will be in effect only for a day or two—just long enough to make arrangements to bring both sides to court.

To go back to Trudy's situation, if earth movers were about to dig up the pavement of the parking spaces, a judge might issue a TRO for a day based mostly on Trudy's sworn statement (affidavit) that she was about to suffer irreparable harm (once the pavement was gone, it would be difficult to use the parking spaces). The TRO would last until a hearing was held, at which point the court would decide whether or not to issue an injunction.

4. Testifying in Court

Especially if you're not paying the bill, a lawsuit can be a fascinating experience. Our system of trying cases has evolved and been tested for many hundreds of years. And, although some of the conventions of a trial can seem quaint, litigation remains a largely effective (although not necessarily cost-effective) way to ferret out the truth and reach a just result.

Even if you hire a lawyer to handle your lawsuit, you still need to understand some of the nuts and bolts of the system to make it work for you. You may well be called on to testify in a legal proceeding—either as a plaintiff, a defendant, or a witness. Here are some suggestions to help you do it effectively.

- Treat pretrial discovery—especially depositions—seriously. At a deposition, a party or witness is put under oath and cross-examined by the opponent's lawyer in the presence of a public stenographer. A transcript is typed up. Cases are frequently settled on the basis of deposition testimony. The other lawyer will not only be listening carefully to your testi-

mony but will be sizing you up as a witness. What will the jury think about you? Will you get flustered easily? Can you be baited into an argument? Do you project confidence or fear? In addition, if the case does go to trial, you'll have a lot of explaining to do if your testimony at trial differs from what you said at your deposition. Be accurate.

- Watch what you wear. Your clothing at a deposition or in court should indicate that you treat the case seriously. It should be conservative—not sporty, flashy, or obviously expensive.

- In court, you're always "on stage"—not just when you're on the witness stand. If there's a jury, you'll be studied continually, at the counsel table or relaxing in the corridor. So maintain a serious demeanor, and be careful about conversations that the judge or jury may overhear.

- Before testifying, carefully review the typed transcript of your deposition as well as any written statements you've given about your case. You'll be embarrassed on cross-examination if you say something on the witness stand that differs from your earlier statements.

- If your business is incorporated, go to extra lengths to let the jury know that you're a small business—not General Motors. This is particularly important if your opposition is not a corporation. You don't want the jury to think of this as a battle between David and Goliath, with you cast as Goliath.

- On the witness stand, give the lawyer time to complete the question before you attempt to answer. If you're unsure or didn't hear the question, ask the lawyer to repeat it. If you still don't understand what he or she is seeking, ask for clarification.

- Keep your emotions under control during cross-examination. If you get angry, lose your temper, or try to meet a lawyer's sarcasm with sarcasm of your own, you'll hurt your case. Be courteous even if the lawyer isn't.

- If possible, answer with a simple yes or no. This is particularly important on cross-examination. If more than a yes or no answer is needed, give only the requested facts. Then stop. Be careful about volunteering information just because you think it will be helpful. Such information may suggest whole new areas of questioning to the cross-examiner.

- Conversely, if the lawyer cross-examining tries to limit you to answering yes or no to a question that you feel you can't properly answer in a single word, say that you're unable to give a yes or no answer. The judge probably will let you explain.

- Unless you're testifying as an expert witness (someone with specialized knowledge who can give opinions in court), limit your testimony to facts—things you've personally seen or heard or done or said. Your opinions and conclusions usually aren't admissible.

- A definite answer is desirable. For example, "It was 10 p.m." is better than "I think it was about 10 p.m." But if you can't speak with such assurance, it's perfectly acceptable—and

advisable—to qualify your answer. And there will be times when the only honest answer is "I don't know," or "I don't remember."

- Watch out for words like "always" and "never." Sometimes in cross-examination a lawyer will try to get you to agree with an overly broad statement. For example: "Is it your testimony that your company never extends credit to first-time customers?" "Are you saying that you always send confirming letters?" Chances are the lawyer is setting the stage for further questions that will require you to back off from such an absolute statement. This can undermine your testimony. So your answer might be: "Our general policy is to not extend credit to first-time customers, but we have made some exceptions." Or, "We almost always send confirming letters but I can remember a few times when we did not."

Want to learn more about handling a trial? *See:* Represent Yourself in Court: How to Prepare & Try a Winning Case, *by Paul Bergman and Sara J. Berman-Barrett (Nolo). Explains how to handle a civil trial yourself, without a lawyer, from start to finish.* ■

Representing Yourself in Small Claims Court

Y ou might think that paying a lawyer is unavoidable when you file a lawsuit. But that's not necessarily so. There are many times when you, as a business owner, can represent yourself in court. Of course, you wouldn't want to be your own lawyer in defending a $100,000 contract case or a $1 million personal injury suit. But how about suing customers for unpaid bills or a supplier for $5,000 for a breach of contract?

In cases like those, consider using a court designed for nonlawyers: small claims court. In a few states, other names are used, but the purpose is the same: to provide a speedy, inexpensive resolution of disputes that involve relatively small amounts of money. The jurisdictional limits (the amount for which you can sue) in these courts are rising fairly quickly. You may be surprised to learn that in a number of states you can sue for $5,000 or more. (A chart listing each state's small claims court limit is in Section C.)

A businessperson can use small claims court to collect bills, to obtain a judgment for breach of contract, or to seek money for minor property damage claims—for example, suing someone who broke a sign in your parking lot. Small claims court offers a great opportunity to collect money that would otherwise be lost because it would be too expensive to sue in regular court. True, for very small cases, it's not always cost-effective, and occasionally you'll have problems collecting your judgment. But small claims should still be part of the collection strategies of many businesses.

Before you start a lawsuit in small claims court, investigate alternatives. If your case involves a written contract, check to see whether the contract requires mediation or arbitration of disputes. (See Chapter 22, Sections B and C.) If so, this may limit or cut off your right to go to any court, including small claims court. Second, consider other cost-effective options such as free or low-cost publicly operated mediation programs. If you're in a dispute with a customer, or perhaps another business, and you still have hopes of preserving some aspect of the relationship, mediation—even if not provided

for in a contract—is often a better alternative than small claims court. Any litigation tends to harden peoples' feelings.

Everybody's Guide to Small Claims Court, *by Ralph Warner (Nolo), goes into great depth on all of the topics covered in this chapter. It will be especially valuable in helping you prepare evidence and present your case to the judge.*

A. Deciding Whether to Represent Yourself

Most people who go to small claims court handle their own cases. In fact, in some states, lawyers aren't allowed to represent clients in small claims court. In any case, representing yourself is almost always the best choice—after all, the main reason to use the small claims court is because the size of the case doesn't justify the cost of hiring a lawyer. (The second benefit of using small claims court may be to satisfy any courtroom fantasies inspired by shows such as "L.A. Law"—although this one wears out pretty quickly.)

If you're doing business as a corporation and wish to proceed on your own, check the law in your state. In a few states, even if you're the president and sole shareholder of your corporation, you aren't allowed to represent the corporation. The reasoning is that the corporation legally is a separate entity and, therefore, appearing in court for a corporation amounts to practicing law without a license. Most states, however, allow a corporation to designate an officer or employee to appear for the corporation in small claims court. Even better, in some states, you can send your bookkeeper to testify in a small claims matter involving unpaid debts—the most common type of case. The clerk of the court can tell you what the rules are in your state.

Viewed strictly in terms of dollars and cents, if you can spare time away from your business, it's almost always better to represent yourself in small claims court than to hire a lawyer. To see just how great the savings can be, let's value your time at $30 an hour and assume that a typical small claims case takes 15 hours from filing to collection.

Lawyer's Time at $150 an hour
x 15 hours = $2,250
Lawyer's Time at $250 an hour
x 15 hours = $3,750
Your Time at $30 an hour
x 15 hours = $450

Clearly, we're looking at more than pennies here. And several studies show that people who represent themselves in small claims court do just as well as those represented by a lawyer. So it's hardly surprising that many businesspeople who regularly use small claims court swear by it.

On the other hand, if your business is keeping you so busy that you can't easily afford the time to deal with a small claims case (chances are you'll still have to show up in court), you may have no choice but to hire a lawyer. In some states, this can be done in small claims court; in others, such as California, Idaho, Michigan, and Nebraska, lawyers can't appear in small claims. The case will have to go to formal court, where chances are that more complicated procedures will add considerably to the time it takes. In that situation, you might want to seek a lawyer willing to take the case on a contingent fee basis. This means the lawyer gets a percentage of your recovery if you win and nothing if you lose. A lawyer who takes a $5,000 case on a contingent basis calling for a legal fee of one third will receive $1,667 if there's a verdict for the full amount of the claim and if (sometimes a big if) the full amount is actually collected. This is substantially less than the $2,250 or $3,750 you'd be obligated to pay the lawyer—win or lose—under a straight hourly arrangement.

Another alternative is a partial contingent fee arrangement. Following this approach, you might find a lawyer who would charge you $100 an hour plus 15% or 20% of the amount actually recovered. Under such an arrangement, you spread between yourself and the lawyer some of the risks of not recovering the full amount of your claim. (For more on lawyers and fee arrangements, see Chapter 24, Section B.)

A far less costly approach is to represent yourself but have a lawyer occasionally give advice on legal points or help with strategy.

LAW IN THE REAL WORLD
Using a Lawyer Wisely

George is a skillful, honest, and hard-working real estate appraiser. While most of his customers pay their bills promptly, each year a dozen or so drag their feet. It drives George up the wall to think that people are ripping him off by not paying their bills. Several years ago, he decided to pursue every nonpaying customer if the amount involved was significant and there was a reasonable chance of collection.

Initially, he spent some time with his lawyer to become familiar with court procedures and to discuss precourt strategies such as sending an effective collection letter. He also spent $15 for a complete copy of the court rules that apply in all courts of the state. (George is more ambitious than most businesspeople and sometimes ventures into the regular courts, where legal matters can get a bit more complicated.)

Over the years, George has done very well in collecting unpaid accounts. Occasionally, if matters get complicated, he calls or visits his lawyer. Phone calls rarely last longer than 15 minutes, and visits rarely last longer than a half-hour. Wisely, George groups together several problems so he can discuss them at the same time. Occasionally, George has his lawyer draft a legal pleading or a notice or letter.

(See Chapter 24 for more on effective ways to work with a lawyer.)

B. Learning the Rules

Small claims court procedures are simple and easy to master. Basically, you pay a small fee, file your lawsuit with the court clerk, see to it that the papers are served on your opponent, show up on the appointed day, and tell your story. Check with the court clerk for the specifics. The court rules are usually published in a booklet or information sheet.

In addition, clerks in small claims court are expected to explain procedures to you. They may even help you fill out the necessary forms, which are quite simple anyhow. If necessary, be persistent. If you ask enough questions, you'll get the answers you need to handle your own case comfortably. Also, in some states such as California, you can consult a small claims court advisor for free.

C. Meeting the Jurisdictional Limits

How much can you sue for in small claims court? The maximum amount varies from state to state. Generally, the limit is between $3,000 and $15,000. Check your state's limit on the chart below, but also ask the court clerk to see if the limit has been increased since the chart was prepared; state legislatures regularly increase these limits.

Don't assume that your case can't be brought in small claims court if it's for slightly more than the limit. You may want to ask for the jurisdictional limit and forget about the rest. For example, suppose you're in the wholesale lighting fixture business, and a local retailer owes you $3,650 for some lamps. If the jurisdictional limit in your state's small claims court is $3,000, in the long run, it may be less expensive for you to forget about the $650 excess. Hiring a lawyer and going to regular court would be even more expensive.

SMALL CLAIMS COURT LIMITS

State	Amount	State	Amount
Alabama	$3,000	Montana	$3,000
Alaska	$7,500	Nebraska	$2,400
Arizona	$2,500	Nevada	$5,000
Arkansas	$5,000	New Hampshire	$5,000
California	$5,000	New Jersey	$3,000
Colorado	$7,500	New Mexico	$10,000
Connecticut	$3,500	New York	$5,000
Delaware	$15,000	North Carolina	$5,000
District of Columbia	$5,000	North Dakota	$5,000
Florida	$5,000	Ohio	$3,000
Georgia	$15,000	Oklahoma	$6,000
Hawaii	$3,500	Oregon	$5,000
Idaho	$4,000	Pennsylvania	$8,000
Illinois	$5,000	Rhode Island	$2,500
Indiana	$3,000*	South Carolina	$7,500
Iowa	$5,000	South Dakota	$8,000
Kansas	$4,000	Tennessee	$15,000**
Kentucky	$3,000	Texas	$5,000
Louisiana	$3,000	Utah	$7,500
Maine	$4,500	Vermont	$3,500
Maryland	$5,000	Virginia	$2,000
Massachusetts	$2,000	Washington	$4,000
Michigan	$3,000	West Virginia	$5,000
Minnesota	$7,500	Wisconsin	$5,000
Mississippi	$2,500	Wyoming	$3,000
Missouri	$3,000		

* $6,000 in Marion County and Allen County
** $25,000 in Shelby County and Anderson County
Source: *Everybody's Guide to Small Claims Court*, by Ralph Warner (Nolo).

D. Before You File Your Lawsuit

Before you start your lawsuit by filing papers in small claims court, ask yourself some questions to figure out whether a small claims court suit is right for you.

1. Do You Have a Good Case?

First, you want to be relatively sure of your legal position. You must have a valid legal basis for a lawsuit. Do you have a decent chance of proving in court that the defendant refused to pay a fair and just bill, broke a contract, or negligently damaged your property? If not, any talk about going to small claims court is just an idle threat that will hurt your credibility. *Everybody's Guide to Small Claims Court*, by Ralph Warner (Nolo), has a good chapter on how to analyze common types of cases, including breach of contract, personal injury, property damage, and breach of warranty.

2. Can You Sue the Defendant in Your State?

If you conclude that your case is legally sound, next determine whether or not you can sue the defendant in your state. In legal terms, you must find out whether or not your state courts have jurisdiction over the defendant. Generally, you can sue in your state if the defendant resides there or regularly does business there.

If all your contacts with an out-of-state defendant have been by mail and telephone, and the defendant doesn't have an office, warehouse, or sales staff in your state, you may not be able to sue that defendant in your local courts. You could sue in the defendant's home state, but unless it's right next door, it's probably more trouble than a small claims case is worth.

3. Can You Settle Out of Court?

Your next step is to call the other side to see if the matter can be settled without going to court. Mention that you're planning to go to court if the matter can't be resolved. The other side may decide to pay the claim or suggest terms for a fair settlement.

If the response to your call is negative, follow up with a demand letter in which you state your claim, demand payment by a certain date, and again inform the other side that you'll go to court if the matter isn't promptly settled.

In your letter, restate the facts in the dispute even though the other side knows them. That way, if you do go to court later, you can use the demand letter to show the judge that you made every reasonable effort to collect the bill. In some states, a demand letter is required before you can sue. In any state, it's a good idea. A sample letter is shown below.

SAMPLE DEMAND LETTER

December 12, 20___

Sonya Renaud
Chez Posh
54 Lakeshore Ave.
Seattle, WA

Dear Sonya:

It's been three months since I finished installing the sound system at your new restaurant, Chez Posh. As you know, our deal was that you'd pay me $1,000 before I started work, with the balance ($3,500) to be paid when the job was done. All I've received so far is the down payment.

You've told me several times that the sound system works perfectly. But when I press you for payment, you keep putting me off. As the owner of a small business, I need a steady flow of cash to keep going. I'm making this final request for payment before I take this matter to small claims court. Please bring me your check for $3,500 by Thursday. If I don't receive it by then, I will file a lawsuit.

I think it's in your best interest to pay voluntarily. If I have to sue, I'm sure the judge will order you to pay my court costs, as well as interest. Also, a lawsuit may hurt your credit—something a new business can't afford. So please bring your check to me by Thursday.

Sincerely,

Bill Presley
Owner, King Sound Company

4. Could You Collect If You Win?

Before you actually file your papers, determine whether you're likely to collect if you win. If you won't be able to collect, there's no point in throwing good money after bad in a small claims court lawsuit. If you think the defendant might not pay a small claims court judgment voluntarily, ask yourself these questions:

- Is the defendant employed? If so, usually it is fairly easy to collect from (garnish) the defendant's paycheck unless he or she has a very low income job or lots of other judgment creditors are already in line. However, you can't collect from a welfare, Social Security, unemployment, pension, or disability check.

- Does he or she have a bank account? Do you know where? And are you confident that it will stay open? If so, you'll be able to collect the judgment from funds in the account.

- Does the defendant own a home or other real estate? If so, you can place a lien (legal claim) on the property. The lien must be paid off when the property is sold. And if you want to go to a lot of trouble, you can force the sale of the property to pay the judgment if the defendant's equity exceeds prior debts (such as mortgages) and protected amounts called "statutory exemptions."

- Is the defendant a solvent business, or at least one with a positive cash flow? If so, you can probably collect a judgment.

If the defendant is unlikely to pay a judgment voluntarily and lacks a job, a bank account, or other assets that you can go after to satisfy the judgment, you should probably forget about suing—unless you're reasonably sure the defendant will be solvent soon, as might be the case with a college student or someone who stands to inherit money. Although judgments can usually be collected for five to ten years, depending on the state (and can sometimes be renewed), a significant number of small claims judgments are never collected.

E. Figuring Out Whom to Sue

Normally, it makes sense to sue all defendants who are reasonably likely to be legally liable to you. This increases the chances of getting a collectible judgment from at least one person or business. For example, if a husband and wife purchased some merchandise for their house and owe you money, sue both of them—that is, name both of them as defendants in your lawsuit. Similarly, if an employee of a computer repair company damaged your equipment while repairing it, sue both the employee and the company.

When suing a business, check to see whether it's a sole proprietorship, a partnership, a corporation, or an LLC.

- If it's a sole proprietorship, the defendant would be "John Smith doing business as Smith Furniture Company."
- In a partnership, name all of the individual partners and also give the name of the part-

nership. For example: "Smith-Jones Software Specialists, an Indiana partnership, John Smith and Ida Jones, jointly and severally."

- In the case of a corporation, name the corporation as the defendant: "Rackafrax Inc., a California corporation." The lawsuit papers can be served on the resident agent—the person designated by the corporation as the official recipient of lawsuit papers—or on one of several officers of the corporation.
- If it's a limited liability company, name the LLC, for example, Garth's Film Scores, LLC. As with a corporation, you can serve papers on the resident agent or LLC officer.

You may need to do a little research to find out who owns a business or what its correct legal name is. Check the county office that accepts filings of assumed or fictitious names. They'll tell you the owner or owners of a sole proprietorship. Corporate names and corporate assumed names are usually on file with the a state office such as the secretary of state's office.

Don't worry if you're not 100% accurate when you name a business or the owners in a lawsuit. In most states if you name a business defendant incorrectly (you sue Joe's Bar, which is owned by Abdul Irani), you can correct it in court. And in some states, such as Michigan, you can sue a business in small claims court in any name used in an advertisement, sign, invoice, sales slip, register tape, business card, contract, or other communication or document used by the business.

F. Handling Your Small Claims Court Lawsuit

Small claims court is designed to be used without lawyers—that's one of its best features. You shouldn't have any trouble going it alone.

1. File Your Complaint

The first formal step in starting your small claims case is to fill out a form known as a "complaint" or "statement of claim" or "affidavit and claim." These forms are available from the court clerk. You'll write a brief statement (perhaps one or two sentences) describing your claim and why the defendant is liable. You'll also state how much money you're asking for. If you're suing on a written contract—as would be common if the defendant failed to pay a bill—you may be asked to attach a photocopy of the contract to the court papers. The court clerk will issue a document called a "summons," which informs the defendant that the suit has been filed and where and when to appear for the hearing.

2. Serve Your Papers

Every state has rules on how the defendant must be notified of a lawsuit. If you don't follow the rules carefully, the court cannot rule against the defendant. In many states, papers can be served on (delivered to) the defendant by registered or certified mail. Also in many states, the clerk's office takes care of sending the papers to the defendant, often by certified mail with a return receipt requested. If state law requires that the papers be given to the defendant in person (or if he or she refuses to accept certified mail), this can be done at modest cost by a private process server or by a public officer, such as a sheriff or marshal. Depending on the law in your state, you may be able to recover the costs of doing this only if you first try to serve the papers by mail.

About half of defendants refuse to accept registered or certified mail, so you'll probably have to turn to personal service a good deal of the time.

3. Prepare for Court

Many small claims cases involve only an unpaid bill, and there's no dispute about the amount owed. You may win such a case by default because the defendant doesn't bother to show up for the hearing. In more complicated cases, your success in court may turn on how well you prepare. You need to think carefully about how you're going to convince that judge that you're right.

Since there's lots of truth to the old saying that a picture is worth at least 1,000 words, bring pictures to court whenever possible.

> **EXAMPLE:** Rosalie, suing ABC Contractors for damage they did to her roof, brings photos showing the condition of her building before and after ABC workers damaged it.

You may be able to make a point effectively by preparing a drawing or chart. For a few dollars, you can pick up a huge piece of poster board on which you can create a chart or diagram with a felt tip pen. You can use a drawing to show how a room is laid out or how a complicated piece of machinery works. Judges, like everybody else, focus their attention on pictures, graphs, and charts.

Incidentally, if your business provides custom goods or services, consider routinely taking pictures of your completed jobs and products. If you later must sue for an unpaid bill, this will make it more difficult for the customer to concoct a bogus claim that he or she failed to pay because the job was badly done. Another good technique is to include a request on every invoice that the customer notify you immediately if there is any problem with the goods or services. Then, if you have to sue to collect on an unpaid bill and the defendant shows up and says that there were problems with the goods or services, you can argue convincingly that the customer never complained before you pressed for payment.

It's almost always helpful to have an eyewitness testify on your behalf. In an undisputed case involving the collection of a bill, you or your bookkeeper can testify about past billings and how much the customer or supplier still owes. Be sure to have copies of the bills. In a contested case, you may want to line up appropriate witnesses. For example, if the unpaid bill is for your company's installation of a telephone system, you might arrange for the person who actually installed the system to come to court.

You're entitled to subpoena witnesses, but usually you won't want to use that power to compel a reluctant witness to appear. A person who is hostile can do you more harm than good. A subpoena is useful, however, so that a friendly witness can show it to his or her employer and not have any problems getting off work to come to court.

You may want to present an expert opinion, such as an appraisal of a car repair. As long as it can easily be presented in written form, many states allow this type of evidence in the form of a letter, even though technically it's hearsay—a type of evidence that's not admissible in most other courts. This special treatment recognizes that it's not economical to have expert witnesses standing by in small claims court. If you're in doubt as to the rules in your state ask the court clerk.

> **EXAMPLE:** Cyril pays $3,000 to have Roxanne build some laminated countertops for his kitchenware shop. He later has to pay someone else $2,000 to repair the job because Roxanne botched it. Cyril sues Roxanne in small claims court to recover the extra $2,000 he had to pay. He contacts another countertop contractor to testify, as an expert witness, that the original job was well below usual standards.

Business records (including letters you sent the defendant) can be very useful at the hearing. Be prepared with all contracts and other records and papers that relate to the transaction involved in the lawsuit. It's better to come with too many papers than too few.

4. Present Your Case at the Court Hearing

Many small claims court defendants simply fail to show up for the trial. Normally, that means the plaintiff can probably get a judgment (by default) after briefly stating his or her case. A default judgment that grants you the relief you want is as valid as any other. But if the properly served defendant comes into court a few days later with a good reason for not showing up (illness, emergency business trip, transportation problems), the judge may be willing to set aside the default judgment and hold a new hearing. However, if the defendant waits more than a month to ask for relief, the judge probably won't grant the request.

In small claims court, the rules of evidence and procedure are informal. Especially if no lawyer is involved, each side simply stands and tells the judge its story and presents its witnesses and other evidence.

Begin your presentation by telling the judge in a sentence or two what the case is about, for example: "My company sells and installs telephone systems. We installed a system for Dr. Jones, a veterinarian. He owes us $2,800 and refuses to pay." Or: "We have a video rental store. Superior Decorating Service signed a contract to paint our store for $2,500. They didn't show up and we had to hire somebody else. It cost us $4,000 to complete the job."

After the short summary of the case, be prepared to lay out the important facts in chronological order. This will be much more helpful than a long rambling presentation that skips back and forth. During the hearing, you can present your photographs and drawings. Usually you do this by showing them to the other party and then handing them to the court clerk or bailiff to give to the judge. Most courts have blackboards if you need to improvise during the hearing.

Be sure to bring to court a copy of the demand letter you sent to the defendant and present it to the judge. This not only shows that you made a reasonable effort to resolve the dispute without a hearing in court, but is another way to present the facts as you see them.

Address your testimony to the judge, not to the other side. Avoid arguing with the other side. Often small claims judges interrupt and ask questions. Always respond directly to the point the judge is inquiring about; then go back to making your points. If the judge keeps interrupting and throws you off balance, politely ask for a moment to review your notes to be sure you've covered all key points. At the end of the case, it's appropriate to point out inconsistencies or fallacies in your opponent's testimony. But stick to the facts and never put your argument on a personal basis.

As you conclude your presentation, ask the judge to award you the amount you're suing for plus court costs. If you win, you're normally entitled to have the other side pay your filing fee, any fees for service of papers, and any fees that you paid to witnesses you had to subpoena.

Judges sometimes give their decisions at the end of the hearing. It's also common for the judge to mail out a written decision a few days after the case has been heard. If the case goes against you, check out your appeal rights. (See Section H, below.)

G. Representing Yourself If You're the Defendant

If you receive small claims papers naming you as the defendant, read the papers carefully. In most states, a written answer is not required. You just show up in court and tell your story. When in doubt, call the court clerk or check the local rules. Also, based on your time and energy constraints, decide whether you want to hire a lawyer (lawyers are prohibited in a few states) or perhaps exercise your option to transfer the case to regular court where formal rules of evidence and procedure apply and you always have the right to be represented by a lawyer.

Consider calling the plaintiff with an offer to settle. Often the person suing will accept far less than the amount claimed in the complaint. If you do arrange for a compromise, be sure to get the lawsuit formally dismissed and get a written release from any further liability. Local practice varies, but a common phrase is that the lawsuit is "dismissed with prejudice." This means that the plaintiff can't sue you again over the same transaction.

If the case can't be compromised, think about filing a counterclaim. Suppose the Acme Rug Cleaning Company sues you for $500 for failing to pay them for cleaning the carpets in your office. Let's assume you had two reasons for not paying their bill. First, they did a terrible job of cleaning the rug, and, in your judgment, aren't entitled to any payment. Second, they destroyed an antique chair valued at $1,000. In addition to denying liability for the $500 cleaning bill, you may want to file a counterclaim for $1,000 for the ruined chair. If your counterclaim is over the limits of the small claims court, the case will be transferred from small claims to the regular court.

Even if you don't have much of a defense, it may pay you to show up in court if you wish to pay a judgment in installments. In a number of states, a judge can order a small claims judgment to be paid over time if you so request.

If you don't show up for a hearing, the plaintiff can get a default judgment. And if you, as a defendant, show up at a hearing but the plaintiff doesn't, you're entitled to have the case dismissed. If this happens, ask the judge to dismiss the case "with prejudice." As noted above, this means that the plaintiff can't start up the case against you later on. However, if the plaintiff had a good reason for not showing up in court, the judge may set a new hearing date and keep the case alive.

H. Appealing Small Claims Decisions

In a few states, one price you pay for going to small claims court is the loss of your right to appeal. In most, though, you can appeal a decision of a small claims court to a higher court. In some states, such as California and Massachusetts, only the defendant is permitted to appeal. Where an appeal is allowed, check with the court rules to see whether you're entitled to a complete new trial on the facts of what happened or whether the higher court simply reviews the small claims judgment to see whether the judge applied the correct legal rules.

As a practical matter, the right to take an appeal may not be all that important. Especially in smaller cases, spending time on an appeal is usually not cost-effective.

I. Collecting Your Judgment

Winning a judgment in small claims court will make you feel good. But you haven't really won your case until the other side pays up. Fortunately, many individuals and most reputable businesses pay voluntarily after a judge renders a decision. People recognize that they've had their day in court and that an outsider (the judge) has determined they truly owe the money.

When the losing party does pay you, you must give that person a "satisfaction of judgment" form. This form is usually available from the court clerk and simply acknowledges that you've been paid. It helps the losing party maintain good credit. One word of caution: Don't sign a satisfaction of judgment form until you're sure you've been paid in full. Because the person who pays you may be tempted to stop payment on a personal check, wait until the check clears or insist on cash, a certified or cashier's check, or a money order.

Unfortunately, a significant number of debtors refuse to pay even after a court enters a judgment against them. There are many ways that debtors can protect themselves and, in effect, become "judgment-proof." Many people who are not completely without assets are still beyond the reach of your efforts to collect from them. For example, a creditor can't legally take the food from a debtor's table, or the TV from his living room, or even (in many cases) the car from his driveway.

If the defendant (now called a "judgment debtor") has a job and a bank account, garnishment may be the answer if the defendant refuses to pay you. By filing certain forms with the court where you obtained your judgment, you can require the debtor's employer to pay the judgment out of wages, or the debtor's bank to pay it out of a bank account. If you garnish wages, you'll be able to obtain only a portion of the person's paycheck. You may have to go through repeated garnishments.

Judgments can also be collected from other sources. For example, you may be able to use the debtor's motor vehicles and real estate as a collection source. The procedure is called "attachment." But many types of property are exempt from attachment. For example, in many states a portion, or all, of the equity in a debtor's home is exempt under a "homestead" exemption.

If the judgment debtor is a going business, you may be able to impose a "till tap"—that is, a right to collect a certain part of the daily receipts of the business. You'll have to check the procedures in your state.

If you don't know where a judgment debtor works or has assets, you can file forms requiring the person to come back into court and disclose these things to you. After being put under oath, the judgment debtor will have to reveal information that may lead to collection of the judgment, including:

- where he or she works and the amount of wages he or she receives
- the location and extent of bank accounts
- any personal property, such as stocks and bonds or cars
- real estate holdings, and
- business assets.

Then, through garnishment and other proceedings, you may be able to obtain enough money to satisfy your judgment. Most of the time, however, if you have to force the judgment debtor into court to disclose assets, you'll find yourself wasting a lot of valuable time with very little likelihood of ever getting full payment.

For more on debt collection, see Chapter 19.

LAW IN THE REAL WORLD
Big Payoff From Small Claims

Tim operates Tree Craft, a tree planting and trimming business. At the end of each year he writes off about $10,000 in bad debts—accounts that customers haven't paid after receiving numerous invoices and at least one phone contact. Since this is only 3% of Tim's total annual billings, he doesn't worry about it.

Jennifer, Tim's wife, who handles the books, decides she isn't going to put up with it any more. "The money for the winter vacation to Hawaii that we have never had is sitting in those deadbeats' pockets, and I'm going to do something about it," she declares.

She writes each debtor saying that small claims actions will be filed pronto if the check isn't in the mail PDQ. Much to Tim's surprise, 10% of the deadbeats pay. But he's really flabbergasted when, after the small claims cases are actually filed and papers served, another 20% pay. Even better, a further 10% pay at (or just before) the small claims hearing—some of them because Tim and Jennifer agree to reduce the bill slightly after listening to a hard luck story.

Although 20% of the defendants have moved and can't be reached and a few have gone bankrupt, wiping out their debt, Tim and Jennifer get judgments against the rest—many of whom don't show up in court. (Those that do they confront with photos showing Tim's good work.) Since most have real estate and don't want judgment liens filed, all but a few judgment-proof debtors pay up. The final tally is that Tree Craft collects all or part of the fee from over 60% of the nonpayers.

And later, when Jennifer sees Tim eyeing new pickup trucks, she laughs and says, "Forget it. You and I and the kids are spending two weeks in Hawaii—and we'll toast the deadbeats who made it all possible."

Lawyers and Legal Research

When you own or run a small business, you need lots of legal information. Lawyers, of course, are prime sources of this information, but if you bought all the needed information at their rates—$150 to $250 an hour—you'd quickly empty your bank account. Fortunately, as an intelligent businessperson, there are a number of efficient ways you can acquire on your own a good working knowledge of the legal principles and procedures necessary to start and run a small business.

But can you run your business without ever consulting a lawyer? Probably not. Lawyers do more than dispense legal information. They also offer strategic advice and apply sophisticated technical skills. How frequently you'll need professional help is hard to say. It depends on the nature of your business, the number of employees you hire, how many locations you have, and the kinds of problems you run into with customers, suppliers, landlords, contractors, the government, the media, insurance companies, and a host of other people and entities. Your challenge isn't to avoid lawyers altogether but rather to use them on a cost-effective basis.

Ideally, you should find a lawyer who's willing to serve as a legal coach and help you educate yourself. Then you can often negotiate legal transactions on your own and prepare preliminary drafts of documents, turning to your lawyer from time to time for advice, review, and fine-tuning.

In working with a lawyer, remember that you're the boss. A lawyer, of course, has specialized training, knowledge, skill, and experience in dealing with legal matters. But that's no reason for you to abdicate control over legal decision making and how much time and money should be spent on a particular legal problem. Because you almost surely can't afford all the legal services that you'd benefit from, you need to set priorities. When thinking about a legal problem, ask yourself: "Can I do this myself?" "Can I do this myself with some help from a lawyer?" "Should I simply put this in my lawyer's hands?"

How a Business Lawyer Can Help You

Here's a brief checklist of ways that a lawyer can help you:

- Assist with the startup of your business (review a partnership agreement or incorporation documents, for example).
- Look over a proposed lease.
- Analyze land use regulations in zoning ordinances and private title documents.
- Review employment agreements and sensitive employee terminations.
- Represent you before governmental bodies and help to cut through bureaucratic red tape.
- Assist you with "intellectual property" issues—patents, copyrights, trademarks, trade secrets, and business names.
- Coach or represent you in lawsuits or arbitrations where the stakes are high or the legal issues particularly complex.
- Review or draft documents for the purchase or sale of a business or real estate.
- Check or draft estate planning documents—wills, trusts, and powers of attorney.
- Advise on public offerings of corporate stock (compliance with Blue Sky laws).

A. How to Find the Right Lawyer

Locating a good lawyer for your small business may not be as easy as you think. The fact is that most lawyers lack in-depth experience in working for small businesses. Of about 900,000 lawyers in America today, probably fewer than 50,000 possess sufficient training and experience in small business law to be of real help to you.

1. Compile a List of Prospects

Don't expect to locate a good business lawyer by simply looking in the phone book, consulting a law directory, or reading an advertisement. There's not enough information in these sources to help you make a valid judgment. Almost as useless are lawyer referral services operated by bar associations. Generally, these services make little attempt to evaluate a lawyer's skill and experience. They simply supply the names of lawyers who have listed with the service, often accepting the lawyer's own word for what types of skills he or she has.

A better approach is to talk to people in your community who own or operate truly excellent businesses. These people obviously understand quality in other ways, so why not in lawyers? Ask them who their lawyer is and what they think of that person. Ask them about other lawyers they've used and what led them to make a change. If you talk to half a dozen businesspeople, chances are you'll come away with several good leads.

Other people who provide services to the business community can also help you identify lawyers you should consider. For example, speak to your banker, accountant, insurance agent, and real estate broker. These people come into frequent contact with lawyers who represent business clients and are in a position to make informed judgments. Friends, relatives, and business associates within your own company can also provide names of possible lawyers. But ask them specifically about lawyers who have had experience working for business clients and consider carefully whether they really know enough about business and human nature to know what they're talking about.

In some types of specialized businesses—software design, restaurants, plant nurseries—it can pay to work with a lawyer who already knows the field. That way you can take advantage of the fact that the lawyer is already fairly far up the learning curve. Besides having knowledge about a certain type of business, a specialist may have experience with specific types of legal problems; for example, a lawyer may have special expertise in zoning law, liquor licenses, or intellectual property matters. Sometimes specialists charge a little more, but if their specialized information is truly valuable, it can be money well spent. Trade associations are often a good place to get referrals to specialists.

Here are a few other sources you can turn to for possible candidates in your search for a lawyer:

- The director of your state or local chamber of commerce may know of several business lawyers who have the kind of experience that you're looking for.
- A law librarian can help identify authors in your state who have written books or articles on business law.

- The director of your state's continuing legal education (CLE) program—usually run by a bar association, a law school, or both—can identify lawyers who have lectured or written on business law for other lawyers. Someone who's a "lawyer's lawyer" presumably has the extra depth of knowledge and experience to do a superior job for you—but may charge more.

- The chairperson of a state or county bar committee for business lawyers may be able to point out some well-qualified practitioners in your vicinity.

Once you have the names of several lawyers, a good source of more information about them is the *Martindale-Hubbell Law Directory*, available at most law libraries and some local public libraries. This resource contains biographical sketches of most practicing lawyers and information about their experience, specialties, education, and the professional organizations they belong to. Many firms also list their major clients in the directory—an excellent indication of the types of practice the firm is engaged in. In addition, almost every lawyer listed in the directory, whether or not he or she purchased space for a biographical sketch, is rated "AV," "BV," or "CV." These ratings come from confidential opinions that *Martindale-Hubbell* solicits from lawyers and judges. The first letter is for "Legal Ability," which is rated as follows:

"A"—Very High to Preeminent

"B"—High to Very High

"C"—Fair to High.

The "V" part stands for "Very High General Recommendation," meaning that the rated lawyer adheres to professional standards of conduct and ethics. But it's practically meaningless because lawyers who don't qualify for it aren't rated at all.

(*Martindale-Hubbell* prudently cautions that the absence of a rating shouldn't be construed as a reflection on the lawyer; some lawyers ask that their rating not be published, and there may be other reasons for the absence of a rating.)

I believe that the rating system works remarkably well. Don't make it your sole criterion for deciding on a potential lawyer for your business, but be reasonably confident that a lawyer who gets high marks from other business clients and an "AV" rating from *Martindale-Hubbell* knows what he or she is doing.

You can reach *Martindale-Hubbell* online at www.martindale.com. Another excellent source of information about lawyers is West's Legal Directory at www.lawoffice.com.

2. Shop Around

After you get the names of several good prospects, shop around. If you announce your intentions in advance, most lawyers will be willing to speak to you for a half hour or so at no charge so that you can size them up and make an informed decision. Look for experience, personal rapport, and accessibility. Some of these characteristics will be apparent almost immediately. Others may take longer to discover. So even after you've hired a lawyer who seems right for you, keep open the possibility that you may have to make a change later.

Pay particular attention to the rapport between you and your lawyer. No matter how experienced and well recommended a lawyer is, if you feel uncomfortable with that person during your first meeting or two, you may never achieve an ideal lawyer-client relationship. Trust your instincts and seek a lawyer whose personality is compatible with your own.

Your lawyer should be accessible when you need legal services. Unfortunately, the complaint logs of all law regulatory groups indicate that many lawyers are not. If every time you have a problem there's a delay of several days before you can talk to your lawyer on the phone or get an appointment, you'll lose precious time, not to mention sleep. And almost nothing is more aggravating to a client than to leave a legal project in a lawyer's hands and then have weeks or even months go by without anything happening. You want a lawyer who will work hard on your behalf and follow through promptly on all assignments.

Try to find a lawyer who seems interested in your business and either already knows a lot about your field or who seems genuinely eager to learn more about it. Avoid the lawyer who's aloof and doesn't want to get involved in learning the nitty-gritty details of what you do.

Some lawyers are nitpickers who get unnecessarily bogged down in legal technicalities. They point out a million reasons why something can't be done. Meanwhile, a valuable business opportunity slips away. You want a lawyer who blends legal technicalities with a practical approach—someone who figures out a way to do something, not one who offers reasons why it can't be done.

B. Fees and Bills

When you hire a lawyer, have a clear understanding about how fees will be computed. And as new jobs are brought to the lawyer, ask specifically about charges for each. Many lawyers initiate fee discussions, but others forget or are shy about doing so. Bring up the subject yourself. Insist that the ground rules be clearly established. In California, all fee agreements between lawyers and clients must be in writing if the expected fee is $1,000 or more, or is contingent on the outcome of a lawsuit. Perhaps this will be common everywhere soon.

1. How Lawyers Charge

There are four basic ways that lawyers charge. The first is by the hour. In most parts of the United States, you can get competent services for your small business for $150 to $250 an hour.

Sometimes a lawyer quotes a flat fee for a specific job. For example, the lawyer may offer to draw up a real estate purchase agreement for $300. Or to represent you before a state licensing board for

$3,000. You pay the same amount regardless of how much time the lawyer spends.

In some cases, a lawyer may charge a contingent fee. This is a percentage (such as 33⅓%) of the amount the lawyer obtains for you in a negotiated settlement or through a trial. If the lawyer recovers nothing for you, there's no fee. However, the lawyer does generally expect reimbursement for out-of-pocket expenses, such as filing fees, long distance phone calls, and transcripts of testimony. Contingent fees are common in personal injury lawsuits but relatively unusual in small business cases.

Finally, you may be able to hire a lawyer for a flat annual fee (retainer) to handle all of your routine legal business. You'll usually pay in equal monthly installments and, normally, the lawyer will bill you an additional amount for extraordinary services—such as representing you in a major lawsuit. Obviously, the key to making this arrangement work is to have a written agreement clearly defining what's routine and what's extraordinary.

Comparison shopping among lawyers will help you avoid overpaying. But the cheapest hourly rate isn't necessarily the best. A novice who charges only $80 an hour may take three hours to review a consultant's work-for-hire contract. A more experienced lawyer who charges $200 an hour may do the same job in half an hour and make better suggestions. Take into account the lawyer's knowledge in your field, his or her reputation, and personal rapport.

2. Ways to Save on Legal Fees

There are many ways to hold down the cost of legal services. Here's a summary.

- *Group together your legal affairs.* You'll save money if you consult with your lawyer on several matters at one time. For example, in a one-hour conference, you may be able to review the annual updating of your corporate record book, the renewal of your lease, and a noncompetition agreement you've drafted for new employees to sign.

- *Help out.* You or your employees can do a lot of work yourselves. Help gather documents needed for a real estate transaction. Line up witnesses for a trial. Write the first couple of drafts of a contract; give your lawyer the relatively inexpensive task of reviewing and polishing the document.

- *Ask the lawyer to be your coach.* Make it clear that you're eager to do as much work as possible yourself with the lawyer coaching you from the sidelines. Many lawyers find it gratifying to impart their knowledge and experience to others, but they're used to clients who simply drop their problems on the lawyer's desk to solve. Unless you specifically ask for coaching, you may never tap into your lawyer's ability to help you in that way.

- *Read trade journals in your field.* They'll help you keep up with specific legal developments that your lawyer may have missed. Send pertinent clippings to your lawyer—this can dramatically reduce legal research time—and encourage your lawyer to do the same for you.

- *Show that you're an important client.* The single most important thing you can do to tell your lawyer how much you value the relationship is to pay your bills on time. Also, let your lawyer know about plans for expansion and your company's possible future legal needs. And if your business wins an award or otherwise is recognized as being a leader in its field, let your lawyer know about it—everyone feels good when an enterprise they're associated with prospers. Also, let your lawyer know when you recommend him or her to your business colleagues.

- *Use nonlawyer professionals.* Often, nonlawyer professionals perform some tasks better and at less cost than lawyers. For example, look to management consultants for strategic business planning; real estate brokers or appraisers for valuation of properties; accoun-

tants for preparation of financial proposals; insurance agents for advice on insurance protection; and CPAs for the preparation of tax returns. Each of these concerns is likely to have a legal aspect, and you may eventually want to consult your lawyer, but normally you won't need to until you've gathered information on your own.

A tax tip. *If you visit your lawyer on a personal legal matter (such as reviewing a contract for the purchase of a house) and you also discuss a business problem (such as a commercial lawsuit you've been threatened with), ask your lawyer to allocate the time spent and send you separate bills. At tax time, you can easily list the business portion as a tax-deductible business expense.*

C. Problems With Your Lawyer

Relations between lawyers and clients are not always perfect. If you see a problem emerging, nip it in the bud. Don't just sit back and fume; call, visit, or write to your lawyer. The problem won't get resolved if your lawyer doesn't even know there's a problem. Sure, it's hard to confront someone whom you may need to rely on for future help and advice—but an open exchange is essential for a healthy lawyer-client relationship.

Whatever it is that rankles, have an honest discussion about your feelings. Maybe you're upset because your lawyer hasn't kept you informed about what's going on in your case or has failed to meet a promised deadline. Or maybe last month's bill was shockingly high or lacked any breakdown of how your lawyer's time was spent.

One good test of whether a lawyer-client relationship is a good one is to ask yourself if you feel able to talk freely with your lawyer about your degree of participation in any legal matter and your control over how the lawyer carries out a legal assignment.

If you can't frankly discuss these sometimes sensitive matters with your lawyer, get another lawyer. Otherwise, you'll surely waste money on unnecessary legal fees and risk having legal matters turn out badly. Remember that you're always free to change lawyers and to get all important documents back from a lawyer you no longer employ.

Your Rights As a Client

As a client, it's reasonable to expect that you'll:

- be treated courteously by your lawyer and the members of his or her staff
- receive an itemized statement of services rendered and a full explanation of billing practices
- be charged reasonable fees
- receive a prompt response to phone calls and letters
- have confidential legal conferences, free from unwarranted interruptions
- be kept informed of the status of your case
- have your legal matters handled diligently and competently, and
- receive clear answers to all relevant questions.

If any of these expectations aren't met, consider going elsewhere for legal services.

D. Do-It-Yourself Legal Research

Law libraries are chock full of valuable information—information that you can easily ferret out on your own. All you need is a rudimentary knowledge of how the information is organized.

1. Finding a Law Library

Your first step is to find a law library that's open to the public. You may find such a library in your county courthouse or at your state capitol. Public law schools generally permit the public to use their libraries, and some private law schools grant access to their libraries—sometimes for a modest user fee. The reference department of a major public library may have a fairly decent legal research collection. If you're lucky enough to have access to several law libraries, select one that has a reference librarian to assist you.

Finally, don't overlook the law library in your own lawyer's office. Most lawyers, on request, will gladly share their books with their clients.

Want more in-depth information on legal research? *See:* Legal Research: How to Find & Understand the Law, *by Stephen Elias and Susan Levinkind (Nolo). A nontechnical book written for the average person and covering basic legal materials. Among other things, it explains how to use all major legal research tools and helps you frame your research questions.*

2. Federal and State Law

Every business is governed by both federal law and state law. If yours is a typical small business, you'll be concerned primarily with state law. For example, the law dealing with how you form a sole proprietorship, partnership, or corporation is almost entirely based on state sources, as is the law controlling buying a business, leasing space, hiring employees, forming contracts, and resolving disputes through arbitration or small claims court. Federal law deals with federal taxes, trademarks, consumer protection, and equal opportunity standards. In some areas of business (such as consumer protection and equal opportunity legislation) federal and state laws may overlap.

3. Primary and Secondary Sources

In doing legal research, you'll refer to both primary and secondary sources. Primary sources are statements of the law itself, including:

- *Constitutions* (federal and state)
- *Legislation* (laws—also called statutes or ordinances—passed by Congress, your state legislature, and local governments)
- *Administrative rules and regulations* (issued by federal and state administrative agencies charged with implementing statutes)
- *Case law* (decisions of federal and state courts interpreting statutes—and sometimes making law, known as "common law," if the subject isn't covered by a statute).

A small business rarely gets involved in questions of constitutional law. You're far more likely to be concerned with law created by a federal or state statute, or by an administrative rule or regulation. At the federal level, that includes the Internal Revenue Code and regulations adopted by the Internal Revenue Service; regulations dealing with advertising, warranties and other consumer matters adopted by the Federal Trade Commission; and equal opportunity statutes such as Title VII of the Civil Rights Act administered by the Justice Department and Equal Employment Opportunities Commission.

At the state level, you'll likely be interested in statutes dealing with licensing, partnership law, corporate law, commercial transactions (your state's version of the Uniform Commercial Code), employment matters, and court procedures. You may also need to get into local laws dealing with zoning, health, and building and safety regulations.

Depending on the type of business you have, you may also want to research statutes and regulations dealing with other legal topics such as the environment, labor relations, product liability, real estate, copyrights, and so on.

4. How to Begin

Obviously, primary sources—statements of the "raw law"—are important. But most legal research begins with secondary sources—books that comment on, organize, or describe primary materials.

It often makes sense to start with one of the two national encyclopedias, *American Jurisprudence 2d* (cited as *AmJur2d*) or *Corpus Juris Secundum* (cited as *CJS*). If your state has its own encyclopedia, check that too. These encyclopedias organize the case law and some statutes into narrative statements organized alphabetically by subject. Through citations in footnotes, you can locate the cases and statutes themselves.

It's also helpful if you can find a treatise on the subject you're researching. A treatise is simply a book (or series of books) that covers a specific area of law. I've always been impressed by the Nutshell Series published by West Publishing Co. You may want to look at *Contracts in a Nutshell,* by Claude D. Rohwer and Gordon D. Schaber, and *The Law of Corporations in a Nutshell,* by Robert W. Hamilton.

Law reviews published by law schools and other legal periodicals may also contain useful summaries of the law. The *American Bar Association Journal* as well as the journal published by your state bar association should be available in the law library that you use. In these journals, you'll often find well-written and timely articles on legal issues that affect small businesses. You can locate law review and bar journal articles through *The Index to Legal Periodicals.* Be warned, however, that law school reviews contain articles by law professors and students, and are of more academic than practical interest.

I highly recommend *The Practical Lawyer,* published by the Joint Committee on Continuing Legal Education of the American Law Institute and American Bar Association (ALI-ABA). Each edition contains half a dozen clear and practical articles—many of which address topics of interest to small businesses. The checklists and forms are superb. This resource is virtually unknown outside the legal profession. If you get hooked on the law, consider subscribing.

Finally, practically every state has an organization that provides continuing legal education to practicing lawyers. Especially in the more populous states, these organizations publish excellent books on business law subjects which, unlike nationally published treatises, focus on the law in your state and contain state-specific forms and checklists. You can also find a wealth of relevant information in the course materials prepared for continuing legal education seminars.

5. Online Research

For the computer savvy, online research can be speedy and inexpensive.

Be sure to stop at Nolo's own site, www.nolo.com, where you'll discover valuable online information, including loads of material on small business law and legal research links.

Lawyers who do computer research rely primarily on two systems—Westlaw and Lexis. A small but growing number of public law libraries offer these services. Those that do offer them usually require a sizable advance or a credit card; you pay as you go. Ask a law librarian for details, but be prepared for sticker shock. You can end up paying as much as $300 an hour.

It's more practical to use other online sources that cost you nothing other than the usual charges for online access time. For an introduction to the vast amount of cyber-info that's out there, you might sample these sites:

- Lawyers Weekly at www.lawyersweeklyusa.com. Here you'll find up-to-date news on a wide range of legal topics.

- Martindale-Hubbell at www.lawyers.com. As with the martindale.com site described in Section A, this site will help you locate a lawyer, but it contains other very helpful features as well. For example, by clicking on "Ask a Lawyer," you can pose a question of general interest and receive an online answer from a practitioner on Martindale-Hubbell's panel. Or you can browse fascinating articles on current legal topics.

- FindLaw, at www.findlaw.com. Their business section has a number of interesting articles and guides, as well as useful forms and checklists for business use.

- The Thomas Legislative Information site at http://thomas.loc.gov. Named for Thomas Jefferson, this site contains a wealth of information on bills pending in Congress and laws recently adopted.

- Lectric Law Library at www.lectlaw.com. This is a good place to explore a wide range of business law issues. Many business law topics are covered in reasonable depth.

- The Internal Revenue Service at www.irs.gov. You can download tax forms, instructions, and a wide range of IRS publications.

- National Federation of Independent Business at www.nfibonline.com. If you want to check on small business news and get practical tips, try this site.

- U.S. Small Business Administration at www.sbaonline.sba.gov. Here you'll find information on starting and financing your small business.

Tips for Researching Business Law

- When looking up statutes, use an annotated version. It comes in a multivolume set and contains the laws themselves plus references to court and administrative decisions interpreting the statutes and often to treatises and articles that discuss the law.

- Statutes are frequently amended. Always check the pocket-part supplement at the back of statute (code) books to make sure you have the latest edition.

- When you look up a state court decision (case), use the regional reporter published by West Publishing Co. if it's available. Before the text of the case begins, an ingenious system of notes (called the "key number" system) helps you tap into other similar cases. Ask the reference librarian to explain, or consult one of the books on legal research referred to earlier.

- Use the Shepard Citation system to see if and where the court case you're looking at has been relied on, discounted, or overruled by a later court. *Legal Research: How to Find & Understand the Law,* by Stephen Elias and Susan Levinkind (Nolo), has a good, easy-to-follow explanation of how to use the Shepard's system.

- A relatively unknown resource for quickly locating state business laws is the United States Law Digest volume of the *Martindale-Hubbell Law Directory*. There's a handy summary of laws, including statutory citations, for each state. Dozens of business law topics are covered, including Commercial Code, Consumer Protection, Corporations, Employer and Employee, Insurance, Landlord and Tenant, Leases, Partnership, Principal and Agent, Real Property, Statute of Frauds, and Trademarks, Trade Names, and Service Marks. But you may need a magnifying glass: the print is minuscule.

- The Gigalaw site at www.gigalaw.com specializes in Internet law issues—perfect if you're considering taking your business online.

- Findlaw at www.findlaw.com is well named. Here you'll find a rich collection of forms, articles, and links to statutes and court decisions. Be sure to visit the business section.

Appendix A

STATE OFFICES THAT PROVIDE SMALL BUSINESS START-UP HELP

Alabama
Department of Revenue
www.ador.state.al.us/licenses/index.html

Alaska
Small Business Development Center
www.aksbdc.org

Arizona
Department of Commerce
www.azcommerce.com/smallbus

Arkansas
Department of Economic Development
www.1800arkansas.com

California
Secretary of State
www.ss.ca.gov/business/resources.htm

Colorado
Office of Economic Development &
International Trade
www.state.co.us/oed/index.cfm

Connecticut
Connecticut Licensing Information Center
www.ct-clic.com/business/business.htm

Delaware
Department of Finance
www.state.de.us/revenue/services/
BusServices.shtml

District of Columbia
Department of Consumer and Regulatory
Affairs
http://dcra.dc.gov

Florida
Enterprise Florida
www.eflorida.com

Georgia
Secretary of State
First Stop Business Information Center
www.sos.state.ga.us/FirstStop

Hawaii
Department of Commerce and
Consumer Affairs
Business Registration Division
www.businessregistrations.com

Idaho
Department of Commerce and Labor
http://cl.idaho.gov/portal

Illinois
Department of Commerce and
Economic Opportunity
www.illinoisbiz.biz

Indiana
State Information Center
www.state.in.us/sic/owners/ia.html

Iowa
Department of Business and Economic
Development
www.iowa.gov/state/main/business.html

Kansas
Kansas Business Center
www.accesskansas.org

Kentucky
Cabinet for Economic Development Business
www.thinkkentucky.com

Louisiana
Department of Economic Development
www.lded.state.la.us

Maine
Department of Economic and Community
Development
www.econdevmaine.com

Maryland
Department of Business and Economic
Development
www.choosemaryland.org

Massachusetts
Department of Business and Technology
www.mass.gov/portal/
index.jsp?pageID=agca&agid=ded&agca=
businessassistance

Michigan
Economic Development Corp.
www.michigan.gov/businessstartup

Minnesota
Department of Employment and Economic
Development
www.deed.state.mn.us/bizdev/
smallbus_assist.htm

Mississippi
Development Authority
www.mississippi.org

Missouri
Department of Economic Development
www.ded.mo.gov/business/startabusiness

Montana
Department of Commerce
http://commerce.state.mt.us/indexBRD.asp

Nebraska
Department of Economic Development
www.neded.org

Nevada
Small Business Development Center
www.nsbdc.org

New Hampshire
Small Business Development Center
www.nhsbdc.org

New Jersey
State of New Jersey
www.state.nj.us/Business.shtml

New Mexico
Economic Development Department
www.edd.state.nm.us/index3.html

New York
Governor's Office of Regulatory Reform
www.gorr.state.ny.us/gorr/startbus

North Carolina
Department of Commerce Business
ServiCenter
www.nccommerce.com/servicenter/blio

North Dakota
Department of Business and Finance
www.discovernd.net/business

Ohio
Small Business Development Center
www.odod.state.oh.us/edd/osb/sbdc

Oklahoma
Tax Commission
www.oktax.state.ok.us

Oregon
Oregon Small Business Development Centers
www.bizcenter.org

Pennsylvania
Pennsylvania Small Business Development
Centers
www.pasbdc.org

Puerto Rico
Commonwealth Department of Commerce
www.puertorico.com

Rhode Island
Economic Development Corp.
www.riedc.com/riedc/business_services

South Carolina
Small Business Development Center
http://scsbdc.moore.sc.edu

South Dakota
Governor's Office
of Economic Development
www.sdgreatprofits.com

Tennessee
Department of Economic and Community
Development
www.state.tn.us/ecd/res_guide.htm

Texas
Department of Economic Development
www.tded.state.tx.us

Utah
Department of Community and Economic
Development
http://dced.utah.gov/business/business.html

Vermont
Department of Economic Development
www.thinkvermont.com/start/index.cfm

Virginia
Department of Business Assistance
www.dba.state.va.us

Washington
Department of Licensing
www.dol.wa.gov/businesses.htm

West Virginia
Secretary of State
www.wvsos.com/common/startbusiness.htm

Wisconsin
Department of Commerce
www.commerce.state.wi.us

Wyoming
Small Business Development Center
http://uwadmnweb.uwyo.edu/SBDC/
starting.html

Appendix B

FEDERAL TRADE COMMISSION OFFICES

Headquarters
Federal Trade Commission
6th and Pennsylvania Avenue, NW
Washington, DC 20580
202-326-3175
www.ftc.gov

Regional Offices

Western Region
10877 Wilshire Boulevard, Suite 700
Los Angeles, CA 90024

Western Region
901 Market Street, Suite 570
San Francisco, CA 94103

Southeast Region
225 Peachtree Street, NE
Suite 1500
Atlanta, GA 30303

Midwest Region
55 East Monroe Street, Suite 1860
Chicago IL 60603

Northeast Region
1 Bowling Green
New York, NY 10004

East Central Region
1111 Superior Avenue, Suite 200
Cleveland, OH 44114

Southwest Region
1999 Bryan St., Suite 2150
Dallas, TX 75201

Northwest Region
2896 Federal Building
915 Second Avenue
Seattle, WA 98174

Index

Little publishers have big ears.
We really listen to you.

Your comments make a big difference in the development and revision of Nolo books and software. Please take a few minutes and register your Nolo product—and your comments—with us. Not only will your input make a difference, you'll receive special offers available only to registered owners of Nolo products on our newest books and software. Register now by:

PHONE	**FAX**	**EMAIL**	or **MAIL** us
1-800-728-3555	1-800-645-0895	cs@nolo.com	this registration card

fold here

Registration Card

NAME _____ DATE _____

ADDRESS _____

_____

CITY _____ STATE _____ ZIP _____

PHONE _____ E-MAIL _____

WHERE DID YOU HEAR ABOUT THIS PRODUCT? _____

WHERE DID YOU PURCHASE THIS PRODUCT? _____

DID YOU CONSULT A LAWYER? (PLEASE CIRCLE ONE)   YES   NO   NOT APPLICABLE

DID YOU FIND THIS BOOK HELPFUL?   (VERY)   5   4   3   2   1   (NOT AT ALL)

COMMENTS _____

_____

_____

WAS IT EASY TO USE?   (VERY EASY)   5   4   3   2   1   (VERY DIFFICULT)

We occasionally make our mailing list available to carefully selected companies whose products may be of interest to you.

❑   If you do not wish to receive mailings from these companies, please check this box.

❑   You can quote me in future Nolo promotional materials.
Daytime phone number _____.

RUNS 8.0

Nolo in the NEWS

"Nolo helps lay people perform legal tasks without the aid—or fees—of lawyers."

—USA TODAY

Nolo books are ..."written in plain language, free of legal mumbo jumbo, and spiced with witty personal observations."*

—ASSOCIATED PRESS

"...Nolo publications...guide people simply through the how, when, where and why of law."

—WASHINGTON POST

"Increasingly, people who are not lawyers are performing tasks usually regarded as legal work... And consumers, using books like Nolo's, do routine legal work themselves."

—NEW YORK TIMES

"...All of [Nolo's] books are easy-to-understand, are updated regularly, provide pull-out forms...and are often quite moving in their sense of compassion for the struggles of the lay reader."

—SAN FRANCISCO CHRONICLE

fold here

Place
stamp here

Nolo
**950 Parker Street
Berkeley, CA 94710-9867**

Attn: RUNS 8.0